ENVIRONMENTAL POLICY

Ninth Edition

To Carol and Sandy,
For their love and support

ENVIRONMENTAL POLICY

New Directions for the Twenty-First Century

Ninth Edition

Edited by

Norman J. Vig
Carleton College

Michael E. Kraft
University of Wisconsin–Green Bay

Los Angeles | London | New Delhi
Singapore | Washington DC | Boston

Los Angeles | London | New Delhi
Singapore | Washington DC | Boston

FOR INFORMATION:

CQ Press

An Imprint of SAGE Publications, Inc.

2455 Teller Road

Thousand Oaks, California 91320

E-mail: order@sagepub.com

SAGE Publications Ltd.

1 Oliver's Yard

55 City Road

London EC1Y 1SP

United Kingdom

SAGE Publications India Pvt. Ltd.

B 1/I 1 Mohan Cooperative Industrial Area

Mathura Road, New Delhi 110 044

India

SAGE Publications Asia-Pacific Pte. Ltd.

3 Church Street

#10-04 Samsung Hub

Singapore 049483

Printed in the United States of America

Cataloging-in-publication data is available from the Library of Congress.

ISBN 978-1-4833-5258-9

This book is printed on acid-free paper.

Acquisitions Editor: Sarah Calabi

Editorial Assistant: Raquel Christie

Production Editor: Olivia Weber-Stenis

Copy Editor: Melinda Masson

Typesetter: C&M Digitals (P) Ltd.

Proofreader: Sally Jaskold

Indexer: Molly Hall

Cover Designer: Scott Van Atta

Marketing Manager: Amy Whitaker

SUSTAINABLE FORESTRY INITIATIVE

Certified Chain of Custody
Promoting Sustainable Forestry
www.sfiprogram.org
SFI-01268

SFI label applies to text stock

15 16 17 18 19 10 9 8 7 6 5 4 3 2 1

Contents

Tables, Figures, and Boxes

Preface

In the second decade of the twenty-first century, environmental policy is being challenged as never before. New demands worldwide for dealing with the risks of climate change, threats to biological diversity, and meeting the rising aspirations of the planet's seven billion people will force governments everywhere to rethink policy strategies and find effective ways to reconcile environmental and economic goals. In the United States, the early part of this new decade saw a stagnant economy and persistently high unemployment, which encouraged policymakers and the business community to blame environmental policies and regulations for hindering economic growth and job creation, even where the evidence of such an impact was weak or nonexistent. The economy improved considerably by 2014, but the dialogue over environmental policy remained much the same.

Many of these criticisms deeply divide members of the major parties as Republicans, particularly in the House of Representatives, have called for repealing, reducing, and reining in environmental policies and regulations in the face of strong Democratic defense of the same policies and actions. The result has been continuing partisan debate on Capitol Hill and at the state and local levels where many of the same conflicts have been evident, particularly in states with new Republican leadership. Yet environmentalists have blamed Democrats as well for what they see as their often timid defense of environmental policy or for the way they seek to balance competing economic and environmental goals. For example, they harshly criticized the Obama White House for deferring action on new (and costly) ozone standards recommended by the U.S. Environmental Protection Agency (EPA) and for its indecision on the Keystone XL oil pipeline that is to carry Canadian tar sands oil from Alberta to refineries in Texas.

The election of President Barack Obama in November 2008 brought a dramatic change in policy positions and priorities after eight years of the George W. Bush administration. Yet by late 2014, President Obama had, at best, a mixed record on energy and environmental actions. To be sure, he departed significantly from the actions of the Bush administration in many policy areas, for example in pushing for strong investment in renewable energy resources and "green jobs" over excessive reliance on fossil fuels. Obama was widely praised for setting strikingly higher auto fuel efficiency standards, his announcement in 2013 of a new Climate Action Plan in the face of congressional inaction, and the EPA's proposal in mid-2014 of a Clean Power Plan designed to greatly reduce greenhouse gas emissions from coal-fired power plants. Yet while the energy department invested tens of billions of dollars in renewable energy technologies, it also supported other actions in defense of fossil fuels and nuclear power, including increased oil and natural gas drilling, both before and after the catastrophic Deepwater Horizon oil spill in the Gulf of Mexico. Some of these actions were said to have been taken to attract Republican support for the congressional climate change and energy policy proposals, although the administration's efforts did not appear to improve prospects for those bills, at least in the short term. The House, for instance, enacted a far-reaching climate change policy in June 2009, but the Senate failed to take up the companion bill, in part because the Obama White House exerted too little leadership to advance it.

When Obama's appointments to key environmental and energy positions were announced in late 2008, environmentalists applauded the selections, particularly Lisa P. Jackson as administrator of the EPA, Steven Chu as secretary of energy, John Holdren as the White House science adviser, and Carol Browner, President Clinton's EPA administrator, as the White House coordinator of energy and climate policy. Yet in early 2011, Browner announced that she was leaving the administration, and by late 2011, Jackson found the White House unwilling to back the EPA on critical regulatory decisions, such as the newly proposed ozone standards. Jackson herself was replaced at the EPA by Gina McCarthy, who secured Senate confirmation in July 2013 only after a record 136-day confirmation battle. Other changes in the top environmental and energy positions were made in Obama's second term, including the appointment of Ernest Moniz at the Department of Energy to replace Steven Chu and Sally Jewell at the Department of the Interior to replace Ken Salazar. By any measure, the environmental and energy personnel in place during Obama's second term remained strong and distinctively different from the Bush administration staff in their approach to policy issues. Our contributors address many of those differences throughout the book.

One consequence of the ongoing debate over the direction of environmental policy is that too little consensus has existed in Congress to revise the nation's major environmental laws, which most scholars and specialists in the field believe must be changed to address contemporary challenges. Even with the Democratic majorities that President Obama had in the 111th Congress (2009–2011), little was done to deal with the problem. As noted, after the 2010 elections, this task became all but impossible as the 112th Congress (2011–2013) and the 113th Congress (2013–2015) were deeply divided over environmental and energy policies, with Republicans solidly in control in the House and with only a slim Democratic majority in the Senate. Yet one conclusion is clear enough. As much as the debate over the environment shifted in important ways during the 1990s and early 2000s, there is no doubt that government and politics will continue to play a central role in shaping our environmental future.

When the first environmental decade was launched in the early 1970s, protecting our air, water, and other natural resources seemed a relatively simple proposition. The polluters and exploiters of nature would be brought to heel by tough laws requiring them to clean up or get out of business within five or ten years. But preserving the life support systems of the planet now appears a far more daunting task than anyone imagined back then. Not only are problems such as global climate change more complex than controlling earlier sources of pollution, but also the success of U.S. policies is tied, now more than ever, to the actions of other nations.

This book seeks to explain the most important developments in environmental policy and politics since the 1960s and to analyze the central issues that face us today. Like the previous editions, it focuses on the underlying trends, institutional strengths and shortcomings, and policy dilemmas that all policy actors face in attempting to resolve environmental controversies. Chapters have been thoroughly revised and updated, and five are new to this edition. We have also attempted to place both the George W. Bush and Barack Obama administrations, and actions in Congress, in the context of the ongoing debate over the cost and effectiveness of past environmental policies, as well as the search for ways to reconcile and integrate economic, environmental, and social goals through sustainable development. As such, the book has broad relevance for the environmental community and for all concerned with the difficulties and complexities of finding solutions to environmental problems in this second decade of the twenty-first century.

Part I provides a retrospective view of policy development as well as a framework for analyzing policy change in the United States. Chapter 1 serves as an introduction to the book by outlining the basic issues in U.S. environmental policy since the late 1960s, the development of institutional capabilities for addressing them, and the successes and failures in implementing policies and achieving results. In Chapter 2, Barry G. Rabe considers the evolving role of the states in environmental policy at a time when the recent devolution of responsibilities may face scrutiny from new federal leaders. He focuses on innovative policy approaches used by the states and the promise of—as well as the constraints on—state action on the environment. Part I ends with a chapter by Matthew C. Nisbet that analyzes changes in environmental advocacy strategies in recent years and addresses a fundamental question about the capacity of environmentalists to make their case to the American public and policymakers at a time when conventional movement strategies have not been very successful and when opposition from industry and political conservatives is on the rise.

Part II analyzes the role of federal institutions in environmental policymaking. Chapter 4, by Norman J. Vig, discusses the role of recent presidents as environmental actors, evaluating their leadership on the basis of several common criteria. In Chapter 5, Michael E. Kraft examines the role of Congress in environmental policy, with special attention to partisan conflicts over the environment and policy gridlock. The chapter focuses on recent debates and actions on national energy policy and climate change, over which Congress has struggled for much of the past decade. Chapter 6 presents Rosemary O'Leary's use of several in-depth case studies of judicial action to explore how the courts shape environmental policy. In Chapter 7, Richard N. L. Andrews examines the EPA and the way it uses the policy tools granted to it by Congress, especially its regulatory authority, to address environmental challenges. Because regulations inherently place restrictions and burdens on businesses and state and local governments, Andrews uses three major case studies to illuminate how the agency implements environmental policy while addressing the concerns of these constituencies and others, such as the president, members of Congress, the news media, and the courts, about varied environmental risks and the costs and benefits of acting on them.

Some of the broader dilemmas in environmental policy formulation and implementation are examined in Part III. Chapter 8, by Edward P. Weber, David Bernell, and Hilary S. Boudet, examines comparable tensions and actions in the natural resource agencies, primarily within the Department of Energy and the Department of the Interior. They focus on energy policy, particularly controversies surrounding hydraulic fracturing or fracking, development of renewable energy on public lands, and the Keystone XL pipeline. In Chapter 9, Christopher J. Bosso and Nicole E. Tichenor examine the fascinating relationships between food and the environment, specifically the environmental impacts of the dominant food system on which the United States and other developed nations rely, the federal environmental laws that affect the production and sale of food, and the growing criticism about and ideas for change in the food system that are intended to reduce its ecological footprint while also ensuring that the nation and planet can continue to feed a growing number of people. In Chapter 10, Sheila M. Olmstead introduces economic perspectives on environmental policy, including the use of benefit-cost analysis, and she assesses the potential of market forces as an alternative or supplement to conventional regulation. She sees great potential in the use of market-based environmental and resource policies. Chapter 11 moves the spotlight to evolving business practices. Daniel Press and Daniel A. Mazmanian examine the "greening of industry" or sustainable production, particularly the increasing use of market-based initiatives such as voluntary pollution prevention, information disclosure, and environmental management systems. They find that a creative combination of voluntary actions and government regulation offers the best promise of success. Finally, in Chapter 12, Kent E. Portney examines the intriguing efforts by communities throughout the nation to integrate environmental sustainability into policy decisions in areas as diverse as energy use, housing, transportation, land use, and urban social life—considerations made even more important today in an era of higher energy costs. He also assesses the dilemmas that local policymakers face in trying to move toward more sustainable communities, and the reasons why some cities have made more progress toward these goals than have others.

Part IV shifts attention to selected global issues and controversies. In Chapter 13, Henrik Selin and Stacy D. VanDeveer survey the key scientific evidence and major disputes over climate change, as well as the evolution of the issue since the late 1980s. They also assess government responses to the problem of climate change and the outlook for public policy actions. Chapter 14 examines the plight of developing nations that are struggling with a formidable array of threats brought about by rapid population growth and resource exploitation. Richard J. Tobin surveys the pertinent evidence, recounts cases of policy success and failure, and outlines the remaining barriers (including insufficient commitment by rich countries) to achieving sustainable development in these nations. In Chapter 15, Kelly Sims Gallagher and Joanna I. Lewis analyze the fascinating case of environmental policy in China, as that nation struggles to address its long history of neglecting severe environmental pollution while it rapidly develops a range of new technologies—cleaner coal plants, wind and solar power, high-speed rail—that suggest a brighter environmental and economic outlook for the future. The Chinese case speaks to both the risks and the promises of globalization as developing nations seek rapid economic growth, often without much realization of the ecological and public health consequences or an ability to control them. In the final chapter, we review the agenda of environmental challenges that continue to face the nation and the world and discuss innovative policy instruments that might help us to better address these issues in the future.

We thank the contributing authors for their generosity, cooperative spirit, and patience in response to our seemingly endless editorial requests. It is a pleasure to work with such a conscientious and punctual group of scholars. Special thanks are also due to the staff of CQ Press/SAGE, including Charisse Kiino, Suzanne Flinchbaugh, Davia Grant, Catherine Forrest, Amy Whitaker, Olivia Weber-Stenis, and copy editor Melinda Masson, for their customarily splendid editorial work. To our reviewers, William G. Holt, Birmingham-Southern College; Daniel Fiorino, American University; Jeff W. Justice, Tarleton State University; Jack Rasmus, St. Mary's College; Ninian Stein, Smith College; Gerald A. Emison, Mississippi State University; Rebecca Bromley-Trujillo, University of Kentucky; Sarah Anderson, University of California, Santa Barbara; and Irasema Coronado, University of Texas at El Paso, thank you for your suggestions and insight. We also gratefully acknowledge support from the Department of Public and Environmental Affairs at the University of Wisconsin–Green Bay. Finally, we thank our students at Carleton College and UW–Green Bay for forcing us to rethink our assumptions about what really matters. As always, any remaining errors and omissions are our own responsibility.

Norman J. Vig
Michael E. Kraft

About the Editors

Norman J. Vig is the Winifred and Atherton Bean Professor of Science, Technology and Society emeritus at Carleton College. He has written extensively on environmental policy, science and technology policy, and comparative politics and is coeditor, with Michael G. Faure, of *Green Giants? Environmental Policies of the United States and the European Union* (2004), and coeditor with Regina S. Axelrod and David Leonard Downie of *The Global Environment: Institutions, Law, and Policy*, 2nd ed. (2005).

Michael E. Kraft is a professor of political science and the Herbert Fisk Johnson Professor of Environmental Studies emeritus at the University of Wisconsin–Green Bay. He is the author of *Environmental Policy and Politics*, 6th ed. (2015), and coauthor of *Coming Clean: Information Disclosure and Environmental Performance* (2011, winner of the Lynton K. Caldwell award for best book in environmental politics and policy) and *Public Policy: Politics, Analysis, and Alternatives*, 5th ed. (2015). In addition, he is coeditor of the *Oxford Handbook of Environmental* Policy (2013) and *Business and Environmental Policy* (2007) with Sheldon Kamieniecki; and *Toward Sustainable Communities: Transition and Transformations in Environmental Policy*, 2nd ed. (2009), with Daniel A. Mazmanian.

About the Contributors

Richard N. L. Andrews is a professor of public policy and environmental sciences and engineering at the University of North Carolina at Chapel Hill. A primary focus of his research and writing is the history of U.S. environmental policy. He is the author of *Managing the Environment, Managing Ourselves: A History of American Environmental Policy*, 2nd ed. (2006); "The EPA at 40: An Historical Perspective" (*Duke Environmental Law and Policy Forum*, 2011); "Reform or Reaction: EPA at a Crossroads" (*Environmental Sciences & Technology*, 1995); and many other articles on related topics.

David Bernell is an assistant professor of political science in the School of Public Policy at Oregon State University, and the coordinator of the energy policy concentration in the master's and PhD programs in public policy. His research and teaching focus on U.S. energy policy, energy security, and international relations. He is the author of *Constructing U.S. Foreign Policy: The Curious Case of Cuba* (2011), and the coauthor with Christopher Simon of the forthcoming book *The Energy Security Dilemma: U.S. Policy and Practice*. He formerly served with the U.S. Office of Management and Budget in the natural resources, energy, science, and water divisions, and with the U.S. Department of the Interior as an adviser on trade and the environment.

Christopher J. Bosso is a professor of public policy at Northeastern University. His areas of interest include food and environmental policy, science and technology policy, and the governance of emerging technologies. He is editor of *Governing Uncertainty: Environmental Regulation in the Age of Nanotechnology* (2010). His 2005 book, *Environment, Inc.: From Grassroots to Beltway*, is cowinner of the American Political Science Association's Lynton K. Caldwell award for best book in environmental politics and policy.

Hilary S. Boudet is an assistant professor of climate change and energy in the School of Public Policy at Oregon State University. Her research interests include environmental and energy policy, social movements, and public participation in energy and environmental decision making. She coauthored, with Doug McAdam, *Putting Social Movements in Their Place: Explaining Opposition to Energy Projects in the United States, 2000–2005* (2012). Her recent work focuses on public acceptance of hydraulic fracturing and community-based interventions designed to encourage sustainable behavior.

Kelly Sims Gallagher is an associate professor of energy and environmental policy at The Fletcher School, Tufts University, where she directs the Energy, Climate, and Innovation (ECI) research program in the Center for International Environment and Resource Policy. She also is a senior associate and a member of the Board of Directors of the Belfer Center for Science and International Affairs at Harvard University. Broadly, she focuses on energy and climate policy in both the United States and China. She is the author of *The Globalization of Clean Energy Technology: Lessons from China* (The MIT Press, 2014) and *China Shifts Gears: Automakers, Oil, Pollution, and Development* (The MIT Press, 2006).

Joanna I. Lewis is an associate professor of Science, Technology, and International Affairs (STIA) at Georgetown University's Edmund A. Walsh School of Foreign Service. Her research focuses on energy, environment, and innovation in China, including renewable energy industry development and climate change policy. Her recent book, *Green Innovation in China: China's Wind Power Industry and the Global Transition to a Low-Carbon Economy*, was awarded the 2014 Harold and Margaret Sprout Award by the International Studies Association for best book of the year in environmental studies. Dr. Lewis is a Lead Author of the Intergovernmental Panel on Climate Change's Fifth Assessment Report and a visiting faculty affiliate with Lawrence Berkeley National Laboratory's China Energy Group.

Daniel A. Mazmanian is a professor of public policy and academic director of the USC Schwarzenegger Institute for State and Global Policy, in the Sol Price School of Public Policy, at the University of Southern California. From 2000 to 2005, he served as the C. Erwin and Ione Piper Dean and Professor of the School of Policy, Planning, and Development (today, the Price School), and prior to that, he was Dean of the School of Natural Resources and Environment at the University of Michigan. Among his several books are *Can Organizations Change? Environmental Protection, Citizen Participation, and the Corps of Engineers* (1979), *Implementation and Public Policy* (1989), *Beyond Superfailure: America's Toxics Policy for the 1990s* (1992), *Toward Sustainable Communities*, 2nd ed. (2009), and *Elgar Companion to Sustainable Cities* (2014).

Matthew C. Nisbet is an associate professor of communication studies, public policy, and urban affairs at Northeastern University. The author of more than seventy peer-reviewed studies, book chapters, and reports, Nisbet focuses on the role of communication and the media in environmental advocacy and politics. Among awards and recognition, he has served as a Shorenstein Fellow at Harvard University's Kennedy School of Government, a Health Policy Investigator with the Robert Wood Johnson Foundation, and a member of the National Academies Roundtable on Public Interfaces of the Life Sciences. The editors at the journal *Nature* have recommended his research as "essential reading for anyone with a passing interest in the climate change debate," and the *New Republic* magazine has highlighted his work as a "fascinating dissection of the failures of climate activism." More information on his research and writing can be found at www.climateshiftproject.org.

Rosemary O'Leary is an environmental lawyer, Stene Chair, and a distinguished professor of public administration at the School of Public Affairs at the University of Kansas. She has written extensively on the courts and environmental policy. She is the winner of eleven national research awards, including two "best book" awards for *Managing for the Environment*, written with Robert Durant, Daniel Fiorino, and Paul Weiland (1999). Her book *The Promise and Performance of Environmental Conflict Resolution*, coedited with Lisa Bingham, won the 2005 award for "Best Book in Environmental and Natural Resources Administration," given by the American Society for Public Administration. She is also coeditor, with Robert Durant and Daniel Fiorino, of *Environmental Governance Reconsidered: Challenges, Choices, and Opportunities* (2004). She has served as a consultant to federal and state environmental agencies and spent 2014 as an Ian Axford Fellow in New Zealand researching collaborative governance.

Sheila M. Olmstead is an associate professor of public affairs at the Lyndon B. Johnson School of Public Affairs at the University of Texas at Austin and a Visiting Fellow at Resources for the Future (RFF) in Washington, DC. She was previously a Fellow and Senior Fellow at RFF (2010–2013), and an associate professor (2007–2010) and assistant professor (2002–2007) of environmental economics at the Yale School of Forestry and Environmental Studies. Her research has been published in leading journals such as the *Journal of Economic Perspectives*, *Proceedings of the National Academy of Sciences*, *Journal of Environmental Economics and Management*, and *Journal of Urban Economics*. With Nathaniel Keohane, she is the author of the 2007 book *Markets and the Environment*.

Kent E. Portney is a professor of political science and public affairs at the Bush School of Government and Public Service at Texas A&M University. Previously he taught for many years at Tufts University. He is the author of *Taking Sustainable Cities Seriously: Economic Development, the Environment, and Quality of Life in American Cities*, 2nd ed. (2013), *Approaching Public Policy Analysis* (1986), *Siting Hazardous Waste Treatment Facilities: The NIMBY Syndrome* (1991), and *Controversial Issues in Environmental Policy* (1992). He is also the coauthor of *Acting Civically* (2007) and *The Rebirth of Urban Democracy* (1993), which won the American Political Science Association's 1994 Gladys M. Kammerer award for best book in American politics and the American Political Science Association Organized Section on Urban Politics' 1994 award for best book in urban politics.

Daniel Press is the Olga T. Griswold Professor of Environmental Studies at the University of California, Santa Cruz, where he teaches environmental politics and policy. He is the author of *Democratic Dilemmas in the Age of Ecology* (1994) and *Saving Open Space: The Politics of Local Preservation in California* (2002). His book, *American Environmental Policy: The Failures of Compliance, Abatement, and Mitigation*, is forthcoming with Edward Elgar.

California governors Gray Davis and Arnold Schwarzenegger appointed him to the Central Coast Regional Water Quality Control Board, a state agency charged with enforcing state and federal water quality laws and regulations. He served from 2001 to 2008. He currently serves as the executive director of the UC Santa Cruz Center for Agroecology and Sustainable Food Systems, the country's foremost university-based organic agriculture teaching and training farm.

Barry G. Rabe is the J. Ira and Nicki Harris Family Professor of Public Policy and the Arthur F. Thurnau Professor of Environmental Policy at the Gerald R. Ford School of Public Policy at the University of Michigan. He also serves as a nonresident senior fellow at the Brookings Institution and is a fellow of the National Academy of Public Administration. In 2012, he became the director of the Center for Local, State, and Urban Policy (CLOSUP) at the Ford School, where he codirects the National Surveys on Energy and Environment. Rabe is the editor of *Greenhouse Governance: Addressing Climate Change in America* (2010) and author of *Statehouse and Greenhouse: The Emerging Politics of American Climate Change Policy* (2004), both with Brookings Institution Press. He is currently examining energy taxation policy and the conditions under which federal and subfederal governments impose some form of carbon pricing.

Henrik Selin is an associate professor in the Frederick S. Pardee School of Global Studies at Boston University where he conducts research and teaches classes on global and regional politics and policymaking on environment and sustainable development. He is the author of *Global Governance of Hazardous Chemicals: Challenges of Multilevel Management* (MIT Press, 2010), coauthor of *The European Union and Environmental Governance* (Routledge, 2015), and coeditor of *Changing Climates in North American Politics: Institutions, Policymaking and Multilevel Governance* (MIT Press, 2009) and *Transatlantic Environment and Energy Politics: Comparative and International Perspectives* (Ashgate, 2009). In addition, he has authored and coauthored more than four dozen reviewed journal articles and book chapters, as well as numerous reports, reviews, and commentaries.

Nicole E. Tichenor is a PhD candidate in the agriculture, food, and environment program at the Friedman School of Nutrition Science and Policy, Tufts University. She has experience in domestic food and agricultural policy spanning the local to national levels. Her dissertation analyzes the environmental impacts of U.S. beef production and the potential for alternative, regional systems to viably reduce burdens. She is a Friedman Nutrition and Citizenship Fellow and was recently named a Switzer Environmental Fellow (Robert and Patricia Switzer Foundation), Tufts Institute of the Environment Fellow, and Dennis R. Washington Achievement Scholar (The Horatio Alger Association of Distinguished Americans).

Richard J. Tobin has spent most of his professional career working on international development. After retiring from the World Bank, he has served as a consultant to UNICEF, the United Nations Development Programme, the United Nations Population Fund, the African Development Bank, the Asian Development Bank, the Arab Administrative Development Organization, and the Organization for Security and Co-operation in Europe. He continues to serve as consultant to the World Bank and has also worked on projects funded by the U.S. Agency for International Development, the United Kingdom's Department for International Development, and the Bill and Melinda Gates Foundation.

Stacy D. VanDeveer is a professor and department chair in political science at the University of New Hampshire. His research and teaching interests include global politics of resource overconsumption, international environmental policymaking and institutions, connections between environmental and security issues, and comparative and EU environmental politics. In addition to authoring and coauthoring over ninety articles, book chapters, working papers, and reports, he is the coeditor or coauthor of nine books, including *EU Enlargement and the Environment* (2005), *Changing Climates in North American Politics* (2009), *Transatlantic Environment and Energy Politics* (2009), *Comparative Environmental Politics* (2012), *Transnational Climate Change Governance* (2014), *The Global Environment*, 4th ed. (2015), *The European Union and Environmental Governance* (2015), and *Want, Waste or War?* (2015). He also coedits the journal *Global Environmental Governance*.

Edward P. Weber is the Ulysses G. Dubach Professor of Political Science in the School of Public Policy at Oregon State University. His research focuses on natural resource/environmental policymaking, policy implementation, democratic accountability, sustainability, and the design and operation of alternative decision making/governance institutions, particularly collaborative governance arrangements. He is the author of *Bringing Society Back In: Grassroots Ecosystem Management, Accountability, and Sustainable Communities* and over forty articles and book chapters. He also is the former leader of the Thomas Foley Public Policy Institute at Washington State University (2001–2008).

Part I

Environmental Policy
and Politics in Transition

1

U.S. Environmental Policy
Achievements and New Directions
Michael E. Kraft and Norman J. Vig

Environmental issues soared to a prominent place on the political agenda in the United States and other industrial nations in the early 1970s. The new visibility was accompanied by abundant evidence, domestically and internationally, of heightened public concern over environmental threats.[1] By the 1990s, policymakers around the world had pledged to deal with a range of important environmental challenges, from protection of biological diversity to air and water pollution control. Such commitments were particularly manifest at the 1992 United Nations Conference on Environment and Development (the Earth Summit) held in Rio de Janeiro, Brazil, where an ambitious agenda for redirecting the world's economies toward sustainable development was approved, and at the December 1997 Conference of the Parties in Kyoto, Japan, where delegates agreed to a landmark treaty on global warming. Although it received far less media coverage, the World Summit on Sustainable Development, held in September 2002 in Johannesburg, South Africa, reaffirmed the commitments made a decade earlier at the Earth Summit, with particular attention to the challenge of alleviating global poverty. The far-reaching goals of the Earth Summit and the 2002 Johannesburg meeting were revisited at the 2012 Rio+20 United Nations Conference on Sustainable Development held once again in Brazil.

Despite the notable pledges and actions taken at these and many other meetings, rising criticism of environmental programs also was evident throughout the 1990s and in the first two decades of the twenty-first century, both domestically and internationally. So too were a multiplicity of efforts to chart new policy directions. For example, intense opposition to environmental and natural resource policies arose in the 104th Congress (1995–1997), when the Republican Party took control of both the House and Senate for the first time in forty years. Ultimately, much like the earlier efforts in Ronald Reagan's administration, that antiregulatory campaign on Capitol Hill failed to gain much public support.[2] Nonetheless, pitched battles over environmental and energy policy continued in every Congress through the 113th (2011–2015), and they were equally evident in the executive branch, particularly during the Bush administration as it sought to rewrite environmental rules and regulations to favor industry and to increase development of U.S. oil and natural gas supplies on public lands (see Chapter 4).[3] Yet growing dissatisfaction with the effectiveness, efficiency, and equity of environmental policies was by no means confined to congressional conservatives and the Bush administration. It could be found among a broad array of interests, including the business community, environmental policy analysts, environmental justice groups, and state and local government officials.[4]

Since 1992, governments at all levels have struggled to redesign environmental policy for the twenty-first century. Under Presidents Bill Clinton and George W. Bush, the U.S. Environmental Protection Agency (EPA) tried to "reinvent" environmental regulation through the use of collaborative decision making involving multiple stakeholders, public-private partnerships, market-based incentives, information disclosure, and enhanced flexibility in rulemaking and enforcement (see Chapters 7, 10, and 11).[5] Particularly during the Clinton administration, new emphases within the EPA and other federal agencies and departments on ecosystem management and sustainable development sought to foster comprehensive, integrated, and long-term strategies for environmental protection and natural resource management.[6] Many state and local governments have pursued similar goals with adoption of innovative policies that promise to address some of the most important criticisms directed at contemporary environmental policy (see Chapters 2 and 12). The election of President Barack Obama in 2008 brought additional attention to new policy ideas, although with less commitment than many of Obama's supporters had anticipated (see Chapter 4). Taken together, however, over the past two decades, we have seen a new sense of urgency emerge about climate change and other third-generation environmental challenges and, at least in some quarters, a determination to address those problems despite weak economic conditions.

The precise way in which Congress, the states, and local governments—and other nations—will change environmental policies in the years to come remains unclear. The prevailing partisan gridlock of recent years may give way to greater consensus on the need to act; yet policy change rarely comes easily in the U.S. political system. Its success likely depends on several key conditions: the saliency of the issues and the degree of public support for action on them, the way various policy actors stake out and defend their positions on the issues, media coverage of the problems as well as the political disputes over them, the relative influence of opposing interests, and the state of the economy. Political leadership, as always, will play a critical role, especially in articulating the problems and potential solutions, mobilizing the public and policy actors, and trying to reconcile the deep partisan divisions that exist today on environmental protection and natural resource issues. Political conflict over the environment is not going to vanish anytime soon. Indeed, it may well increase as the United States and other nations struggle to define how they will respond to the latest generation of environmental problems.

In this chapter, we examine the continuities and changes in environmental politics and policy since the late 1960s and discuss their implications for the early twenty-first century. We review the policymaking process in the United States, and we assess the performance of government institutions and political leadership. We give special attention to the major federal programs adopted in the 1970s, their achievements to date, and the need for policy redesign and priority setting for the years ahead. The chapters that follow address in greater detail many of the questions explored in this introduction, and those in Part IV of the book examine global issues and controversies.

The Role of Government and Politics

The high level of political conflict over environmental protection efforts in the past several decades underscores the important role government plays in devising solutions to the nation's and the world's mounting environmental ills. Global climate change, population growth, the spread of toxic and hazardous chemicals, loss of biological diversity, and air and water pollution require various actions by individuals and institutions at all levels of society and in both the public and private sectors. These actions range from scientific research and technological innovation to improved environmental education and significant changes in corporate and individual behavior. As political scientists, we believe government has an indispensable role to play in environmental protection and improvement even as we acknowledge the importance of corporate and individual choices. Because of this conviction, we have commissioned chapters for this volume that focus on environmental policies and the government institutions and political processes that affect them. Our goal is to illuminate that role and to suggest needed changes and strategies.

Government plays a preeminent role in this policy arena primarily because environmental threats, such as urban air pollution and climate change, pose risks to the public's health and well-being that cannot be resolved satisfactorily through private actions alone. That said, there is no question that individuals and nongovernmental organizations, such as environmental groups and research institutes, can do much to protect environmental quality and promote public health. There is also no doubt that business and industry can do much to promote environmental quality and foster pursuit of national energy goals, such as improved energy efficiency and increased reliance on renewable energy sources. We see evidence of extensive and often creative individual, nonprofit, and corporate actions of this kind regularly, for example, in sustainable community efforts and sustainable business practices, as discussed in Chapters 11 and 12.

Yet such actions often fall short of national needs without the backing of public policy, for example, laws mandating control of toxic chemicals that are supported by the authority of government or standards for drinking water quality and urban air quality that are developed and enforced by the EPA, the states, and local governments. The justification for government intervention lies partly in the inherent limitations of the free market system and the nature of human behavior. Self-interested individuals and a relatively unfettered economic marketplace guided mainly by a concern for short-term profits tend to create spillover effects, or externalities; pollution and other kinds of environmental degradation are examples. As economists have long recognized, collective action is needed to correct such market failures (see Chapter 10). In addition, the scope and urgency of environmental problems typically exceed the capacity of private markets and individual efforts to deal with them quickly and effectively. For these reasons, among others, the United States and other nations have relied on government policies—at local, state, national, and international levels—to address environmental and resource challenges.

Adopting public policies does not imply, of course, that voluntary and cooperative actions by citizens in their communities or various environmental initiatives by businesses cannot be the primary vehicle of change in many instances. Nor does it suggest that governments should not consider a full range of policy approaches—including market-based incentives, new forms of collaborative decision making, and information provision strategies—to supplement conventional regulatory policies where needed. Public policy intervention should be guided by the simple idea that we ought to use those policy approaches that offer the greatest promise of working to resolve the problem at hand. Sometimes that will mean government setting and enforcement of public health or environmental standards (regulation), and sometimes it will mean relying on market incentives or information disclosure. More often than not, today, governmental agencies will employ a combination of policy tools to reach agreed-upon objectives: improving environmental quality, minimizing health and ecological risks, and helping to integrate and balance environmental and economic goals.

Political Institutions and Public Policy

Public policy is a course of government action or inaction in response to social problems. It is expressed in goals articulated by political leaders; in formal statutes, rules, and regulations; and in the practices of administrative agencies and courts charged with implementing or overseeing programs. Policy states the intent to achieve certain goals and objectives through a conscious choice of means, usually within a specified period of time. In a constitutional democracy like the United States, policymaking is distinctive in several respects: It must take place through constitutional processes, it requires the sanction of law, and it is binding on all members of society.

The constitutional requirements for policymaking were established well over two hundred years ago, and they remain much the same today. The U.S. political system is based on a division of authority among three branches of government and between the federal government and the states. Originally intended to limit government power and to protect individual liberty, today this division of power translates into a requirement that one build an often elusive political consensus among members of Congress, the president, and key interest groups for any significant national policymaking to take place. That is, fragmented authority may impede the ability of government to adopt timely and coherent environmental policy, as has been evident for some of the most challenging of modern environmental problems. Weak national climate change policy is something of a poster child for such governmental gridlock, or an inability to act on the problems because of divided authority and prevailing political conflict.

Dedication to principles of federalism means that environmental policy responsibilities are distributed among the federal government, the fifty states, and thousands of local governments. Here, too, strong adherence to those principles may result in no agreement on national policy action. Yet a federal structure also means that states often are free to adopt environmental and energy policies as they see fit, as has been the case for natural gas "fracking" where no national policies have been in force. At least some of the states have a track record of favoring strong environmental policies that go well beyond what is possible politically in Washington, DC. California's adoption of a strong climate change policy and Minnesota's successful encouragement of renewable energy sources are two notable illustrations of the considerable power that states have in the U.S. political system (see Chapter 2).[7] The flip side of that coin is that some states will choose to do far less than others in the absence of national requirements.

Responsibility for the environment is divided within the branches of the federal government as well, most notably in the U.S. Congress, with power shared between the House and Senate, and jurisdiction over environmental policies scattered among dozens of committees and subcommittees (Table 1-1). For example, approximately twenty Senate and twenty-eight House committees have some jurisdiction over EPA activities.[8] The executive branch is also institutionally fragmented, with at least some responsibility for the environment and natural resources located in twelve cabinet departments and in the EPA, the Nuclear Regulatory Commission, and other agencies (Figure 1-1). Most environmental policies are concentrated in the EPA and in the Interior and Agriculture Departments; yet the Departments of Energy, Defense, Transportation, and State are increasingly important actors as well. Finally, the more than one hundred federal trial and appellate courts play key roles in interpreting environmental legislation and adjudicating disputes over administrative and regulatory actions (see Chapter 6).

Table 1-1   Major Congressional Committees with Environmental Responsibilities[a]

Committee	Environmental Policy Jurisdiction
HOUSE	
Agriculture	Agriculture generally; forestry in general and private forest reserves; agricultural and industrial chemistry; pesticides; soil conservation; food safety and human nutrition; rural development; water conservation related to activities of the Department of Agriculture
Appropriations[b]	Appropriations for all programs
Energy and Commerce	Measures related to the exploration, production, storage, marketing, pricing, and regulation of energy sources, including all fossil fuels, solar, and renewable energy; energy conservation and information;

Committee	Environmental Policy Jurisdiction
	measures related to general management of the Department of Energy and the Federal Energy Regulatory Commission; regulation of the domestic nuclear energy industry; research and development of nuclear power and nuclear waste; air pollution; safe drinking water; pesticide control; Superfund and hazardous waste disposal; toxic substances control; health and the environment
Natural Resources	Public lands and natural resources in general; irrigation and reclamation; water and power; mineral resources on public lands and mining; grazing; national parks, forests, and wilderness areas; fisheries and wildlife, including research, restoration, refuges, and conservation; oceanography, international fishing agreements, and coastal zone management; Geological Survey
Science, Space, and Technology	Environmental research and development; marine research; energy research and development in all federally owned nonmilitary energy laboratories; research in national laboratories; NASA, National Weather Service, and National Science Foundation
Transportation and Infrastructure	Transportation, including civil aviation, railroads, water transportation, and transportation infrastructure; Coast Guard and marine transportation; federal management of emergencies and natural disasters; flood control and improvement of waterways; water resources and the environment; pollution of navigable waters; bridges and dams
SENATE	
Agriculture, Nutrition, and Forestry	Agriculture in general; food from fresh waters; soil conservation and groundwater; forestry in general; human nutrition; rural development and watersheds; pests and pesticides; food inspection and safety
Appropriations[b]	Appropriations for all programs
Commerce, Science, and Transportation	Interstate commerce and transportation generally; coastal zone management; inland waterways; marine fisheries; oceans, weather, and atmospheric activities; transportation and commerce aspects of outer continental shelf lands; science, engineering, and technology research and development; surface transportation
Energy and Natural Resources	Energy policy, regulation, conservation, research and development; coal; oil and gas production and distribution; civilian nuclear energy; solar energy systems; mines, mining, and minerals; irrigation and reclamation; water and power; national parks and recreation areas; wilderness areas; wild and scenic rivers; public lands and forests; historic sites

(Continued)

Table 1-1   (Continued)

Committee	Environmental Policy Jurisdiction
Environment and Public Works	Environmental policy, research, and development; air, water, and noise pollution; climate change; construction and maintenance of highways; safe drinking water; environmental aspects of outer continental shelf lands and ocean dumping; environmental effects of toxic substances other than pesticides; fisheries and wildlife; Superfund and hazardous wastes; solid waste disposal and recycling; nonmilitary environmental regulation and control of nuclear energy; water resources, flood control, and improvements of rivers and harbors; public works, bridges, and dams

Sources: Compiled from descriptions of committee jurisdictions reported in Rebecca Kimitch, "CQ Guide to the Committees: Democrats Opt to Spread the Power," *CQ Weekly Online* (April 16, 2007): 1080–83, http://library.cqpress.com/cqweekly/weeklyreport110-000002489956, and from House and Senate committee websites.

a. In addition to the standing committees listed here, select or special committees may be created for a limited time. Each committee also operates with subcommittees (generally five or six) to permit further specialization. Committee webpages offer extensive information about jurisdiction, issues, membership, and pending actions, and include both majority and minority views on the issues. See www.house.gov/committees/ and www.senate.gov/pagelayout/committees/d_three_sections_with_teasers/committees_home.htm.

b. Both the House and Senate appropriations committees have interior and environment subcommittees that handle all Interior Department agencies as well as the Forest Service and the EPA. The Energy Department, Army Corps of Engineers, and Nuclear Regulatory Commission fall under the jurisdiction of the subcommittees on energy and water development. Tax policy affects many environmental, energy, and natural resource policies and is governed by the Senate Finance Committee and the House Ways and Means Committee.

The implications of this constitutional arrangement for policymaking were evident in the early 1980s as Congress and the courts checked and balanced the Reagan administration's efforts to reverse environmental policies of the previous decade. They were equally clear during the 1990s when the Clinton administration vigorously opposed actions in Congress to weaken environmental programs. They could be seen again in the presidency of George W. Bush, when Congress challenged the president's proposed national energy policy and many other environmental initiatives, particularly when the Democrats regained both houses of Congress following the 2006 election. They were just as evident in Barack Obama's presidency when the Republican House of Representatives frequently took strong exception to the president's budget recommendations and proposals for new rules and regulations in the agencies, especially the EPA's efforts to reduce toxic pollution from coal-fired power plants and to restrict release of greenhouse gases linked to climate change.

During the last two decades, the conflict between the two major parties on environmental issues had one striking effect. It shifted attention to the role of the states in environmental policy. As Barry G. Rabe discusses in Chapter 2, the

Figure 1-1 Executive Branch Agencies with Environmental Responsibilities

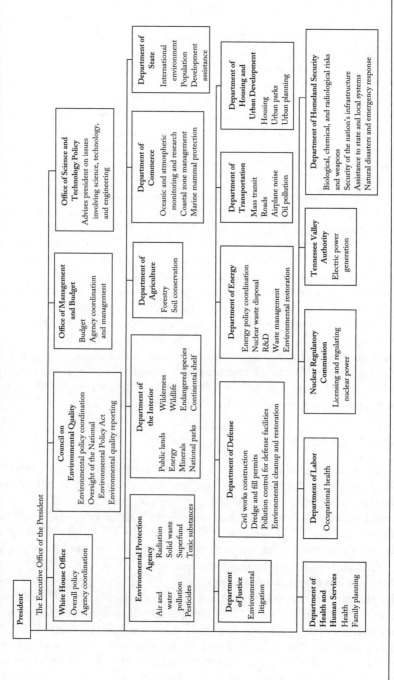

Sources: Council on Environmental Quality, *Environmental Quality: Sixteenth Annual Report of the Council on Environmental Quality* (Washington, DC: Government Printing Office, 1987); United States Government Manual 2013, available at www.usgovernmentmanual.gov/.

states often have been at the center of the most innovative actions on environmental and energy policy, including climate change, when the federal government remained mired in partisan disputes. By 2014, for example, over half of the states had adopted some form of climate change policy, particularly to favor use of renewable energy sources, when Congress and the White House could reach no agreement on what to do.[9]

Generally, after broad consultation and agreement among diverse interests, both within and outside of government, divided authority typically produces slow and incremental alterations in public policy. Such political interaction and accommodation of interests enhance the overall legitimacy of the resulting public policies. Over time, however, the cumulative effect often results in disjointed policies that fall short of the ecological or holistic principles of policy design so often touted by environmental scientists, planners, and activists.

Nonetheless, when issues are highly visible or salient, the public is supportive, and political leaders act cohesively, the U.S. political system has proved flexible enough to permit substantial policy advancement.[10] As we shall see, this was the case in the early to mid-1970s, when Congress enacted major changes in U.S. environmental policy, and in the mid-1980s, when Congress overrode objections of the Reagan administration and greatly strengthened policies on hazardous waste and water quality, among others. Passage of the monumental Clean Air Act Amendments of 1990 is an example of the same alignment of forces. With bipartisan support, Congress adopted the act by a margin of 401 to 25 in the House and 89 to 10 in the Senate. Comparable bipartisanship during the mid-1990s produced major changes in the Safe Drinking Water Act and in regulation of pesticide residues in food, and in 2005 and 2007, it led Congress to approve new national energy policies and significantly expand protection of wilderness areas (see Chapter 5).

Policy Processes: Agendas, Streams, and Cycles

Students of public policy have proposed several models for analyzing how issues get on the political agenda, how they are defined or framed, and how they move through the policy processes of government. These theoretical frameworks help us to understand both long-term policy trends and short-term cycles of progressive action and political reaction. One set of essential questions concerns *agenda setting*: How do new problems emerge as political issues that demand the government's attention, if they do achieve such recognition, and how are they defined in the public mind? For example, why did the federal government initiate controls on industrial pollution in the 1960s and early 1970s but do little about national energy issues until well into the 1970s, and even then only to a limited extent? Why was it so difficult for climate change to gain the attention of policymakers over the years, and why did various policy actors frame the issue in such different ways and interpret climate science in such disparate ways? Climate change's rise on the political agenda was quite slow, and then it became a significant issue by the 2008 presidential election campaign, only to fade again in prominence as the nation's attention was fixed on the economy and persistently high unemployment (see Chapter 3).

As the case of climate change illustrates, hurdles almost always must be overcome for an issue to rise to prominence. The issue must first gain societal recognition as a problem, often in response to demographic, technological, or other social changes. It must be defined or framed as a particular kind of problem, which in turn affects the way possible solutions are developed and appraised.[11] Then it must get on the docket of government institutions, usually through the exercise of organized interest group pressure. Finally, it must receive enough attention by government policymakers to reach the stage of decisional or policy action. An issue is not likely to reach this latter stage unless conditions are ripe—for example, a triggering event that focuses public opinion sharply, as occurred with the Exxon Valdez oil spill in 1989 and again with the Deepwater Horizon oil spill in the Gulf of Mexico in 2010.[12] One model by political scientist John Kingdon analyzes agenda setting according to the convergence of three streams that can be said to flow through the political system at any time: (1) evidence of the existence of problems, (2) available policies to deal with them, and (3) the political climate or willingness to act. Although largely independent of one another, these problem, policy, and political streams can be brought together at critical times when policy entrepreneurs (key activists and policymakers) are able to take advantage of the moment and make the case for policy action.[13]

Once an issue is on the agenda, it must pass through several more stages in the policy process. These stages are often referred to as the *policy cycle*. Although terminology varies, most students of public policy delineate at least five stages of policy development beyond agenda setting. These are (1) *policy formulation* (designing and drafting policy goals and strategies for achieving them, which may involve extensive use of environmental science, economics, and policy analysis), (2) *policy legitimation* (mobilizing political support and formal enactment by law or other means), (3) *policy implementation* (putting programs into effect through provision of institutional resources and administrative decisions), (4) *policy evaluation* (measuring results in relation to goals and costs), and (5) *policy change* (modifying goals or means, including termination of programs).[14]

The policy cycle model is useful because it emphasizes all phases of policymaking. For example, how well a law is implemented is as important as the goals and motivations of those who designed and enacted the legislation. The model also suggests the continuous nature of the policy process. No policy decision or solution is final because changing conditions, new information, and shifting opinions will require policy reevaluation and revision. Other short-term forces and events, such as presidential or congressional elections or environmental accidents, can profoundly affect the course of policy over its life cycle. Thus policy at any given time is shaped by the interaction of long-term social, economic, technological, and political forces and short-term fluctuations in the political climate. All of these factors are manifest in the development of environmental policy.

The Development of Environmental
Policy from the 1970s to the Twenty-First Century

As implied in the policy cycle model, the history of environmental policy in the United States is not one of steady improvement in human relations with the natural environment. Rather, it has been highly uneven, with significant discontinuities, particularly since the late 1960s. The pace and nature of policy change, as is true for most areas of public policy, reflect the dominant social values at any given time, the saliency of the issues, and the prevailing economic and political conditions.

Sometimes, as was the case in the 1970s, the combination facilitates major advances in environmental policy, and at other times, such as the early 1980s and 2000s, we have periods of reaction and retrenchment. A third possibility, evident in the 2010s during President Obama's second term, is that no political consensus exists on what to do and consequently no major legislative actions take place. Yet, even in times like this, we see governments responding to changing environmental challenges through executive authority, rulemaking in administrative agencies, and court decisions. That is, policy change need not come only through adoption of new legislation.[15] Despite these variations in political conditions and policy responses, it is fair to say that since the late 1960s, we have seen substantial public support for environmental protection and expanding government authority to act.[16] We focus here on the major changes from that time through the middle of the second decade of the twenty-first century, and we discuss the future challenges for environmental politics and policy in the concluding chapter of the book.

Policy Actions Prior to 1970

Until about 1970, the federal government played a sharply limited role in environmental policymaking—public land management being a major exception to this pattern. For nearly a century, Congress had set aside portions of the public domain for preservation as national parks, forests, grazing lands, recreation areas, and wildlife refuges. The multiple use and sustained yield doctrines that grew out of the conservation movement at the beginning of the twentieth century, strongly supported by President Theodore Roosevelt, ensured that this national trust would contribute to economic growth under the stewardship of the Interior and Agriculture Departments.

Steady progress was also made, however, in managing the lands in the public interest and protecting them from development.[17] After several years of debate, Congress passed the Wilderness Act of 1964 to preserve some of the remaining forestlands in pristine condition, "untrammeled by man's presence." At the same time, it approved the Land and Water Conservation Fund Act of 1964 to fund federal purchases of land for conservation purposes, and the Wild and Scenic Rivers Act of 1968 to protect selected rivers with "outstandingly remarkable features," including biological, scenic, and cultural value.[18]

During the mid-1960s, the United States also began a major effort to reduce world population growth in developing nations through financial aid for foreign population programs, chiefly voluntary family planning and population research. President Lyndon B. Johnson and congressional sponsors of the programs tied them explicitly to a concern for "growing scarcity in world resources."[19]

Despite this longtime concern for resource conservation and land management, and the new interest in population and development issues, federal environmental policy was only slowly extended to control of industrial pollution and human waste. Air and water pollution were long considered to be strictly local or state matters, and they were not high on the national agenda until around 1970. In a very early federal action, the Refuse Act of 1899 required individuals who wanted to dump refuse into navigable waters to obtain a permit from the Army Corps of Engineers; however, the agency largely ignored the pollution aspects of the act.[20] After World War II, policies to control the most obvious forms of pollution were gradually developed at the local, state, and federal levels, although some of the earliest local actions to control urban air pollution date back to the 1880s and the first limited state actions to the 1890s.

By the late 1940s and 1950s, we see the forerunners of contemporary air and water pollution laws. For example, the federal government began assisting local authorities in building sewage treatment plants and initiated a limited program for air pollution research. Following the Clean Air Act of 1963 and amendments to the Water Pollution Control Act of 1948, Washington began prodding the states to set pollution abatement standards and to formulate implementation plans based on federal guidelines.[21]

Agenda Setting for the 1970s

The first Earth Day was April 22, 1970. Nationwide "teach-ins" about environmental problems demonstrated the environment's new place on the nation's social and political agendas. With an increasingly affluent and well-educated society placing new emphasis on the quality of life, concern for environmental protection grew apace and was evident across the population, if not necessarily to the same degree among all groups.[22] The effect was a broadly based public demand for more vigorous and comprehensive federal action to prevent environmental degradation. In an almost unprecedented fashion, a new environmental policy agenda rapidly emerged. Policymakers viewed the newly salient environmental issues as politically attractive, and they eagerly supported tough new measures, even when the full impacts and costs were unknown. As a result, laws were quickly enacted and implemented throughout the 1970s but with a growing concern over their costs and effects on the economy and an increasing realization that administrative agencies at all levels of government often lacked the capacity to assume their new responsibilities.

Congress set the stage for the spurt in policy innovation at the end of 1969 when it passed the National Environmental Policy Act (NEPA). The act declared that

> it is the continuing policy of the Federal Government, in cooperation with State and local governments, and other concerned public and private organizations, to use all practicable means and measures, including financial and technical assistance, in a manner calculated to foster and promote the general welfare, to create and maintain conditions under which man and nature can exist in productive harmony, and fulfill the social, economic, and other requirements of present and future generations of Americans.[23]

The law required detailed environmental impact statements for nearly all major federal actions and established the Council on Environmental Quality to advise the president and Congress on environmental issues. President Richard Nixon then seized the initiative by signing NEPA as his first official act of 1970 and proclaiming the 1970s as the "environmental decade." In February 1970, he sent a special message to Congress calling for a new law to control air pollution. The race was on as the White House and congressional leaders vied for environmentalists' support.

Policy Escalation in the 1970s

By the spring of 1970, rising public concern about the environment galvanized the Ninety-First Congress to action. Sen. Edmund Muskie, D-Maine, then the leading Democratic hopeful for the presidential nomination in 1972, emerged as the dominant policy entrepreneur for environmental protection issues. As chair of what is now called the Senate Environment and Public Works Committee, he formulated proposals that went well beyond those favored by the president. Following a process of policy escalation, both houses of Congress approved the stronger measures and set the tone for environmental policymaking for much of the 1970s. Congress had frequently played a more dominant role than the president in initiating environmental policies, and that pattern continued in the 1970s. This was particularly so when the Democratic Party controlled Congress during the Nixon and Ford presidencies. Although support for environmental protection was bipartisan during this era, Democrats provided more leadership on the issue in Congress and were more likely to vote for strong environmental policy provisions than were Republicans.[24]

The increase in new federal legislation in the next decade was truly remarkable, especially since, as we noted earlier, policymaking in U.S. politics usually takes place through incremental change. Appendix 1 lists the major environmental protection and natural resource policies enacted from 1969 to 2014. They are arranged by presidential administration primarily to show a pattern of significant policy development throughout the period, not to attribute chief responsibility for the various laws to the particular presidents.

These landmark measures covered air and water pollution control (the latter enacted in 1972 over a presidential veto), pesticide regulation, endangered species protection, control of hazardous and toxic chemicals, ocean and coastline protection, improved stewardship of public lands, requirements for restoration of strip-mined lands, the setting aside of more than one hundred million acres of Alaskan wilderness for varying degrees of protection, and the creation of a "Superfund" (in the Comprehensive Environmental Response, Compensation, and Liability Act, or CERCLA) for cleaning up toxic waste sites. Nearly all of these policies reflected a conviction that the federal government must have sufficient authority to compel polluters and resource users to adhere to demanding national pollution control standards and new decision-making procedures that ensure responsible use of natural resources.

There were other signs of commitment to environmental policy goals as Congress and a succession of presidential administrations (through Jimmy Carter's term) cooperated on conservation issues. For example, the area designated as national wilderness (excluding Alaska) more than doubled, from 10 million acres in 1970 to more than 23 million acres in 1980. Seventy-five units, totaling some 2.5 million acres, were added to the national park system in the same period. The national wildlife refuge system grew similarly. Throughout the 1970s, the Land and Water Conservation Fund, financed primarily through royalties from offshore oil and gas leasing, was used to purchase additional private land for park development, wildlife refuges, and national forests.

The government's enthusiasm for environmental and conservation policy did not extend to all issues on the environmentalists' agenda. Two noteworthy cases are population policy and energy policy. The Commission on Population Growth and the American Future recommended in 1972 that the nation should "welcome and plan for a stabilized population," but its advice was ignored. Birthrates in the United States were declining, and population issues were politically controversial. Despite occasional reports that highlighted the effect of population growth on the environment, such as the *Global 2000 Report to the President* in 1980, the issue remained largely dormant over the next four decades even as world population soared by 2014 to 7.24 billion and the U.S. population reached 318 million.[25]

For energy issues, we also see a pattern of inattention or neglect. Public concern over energy has tended to follow its price. When prices are low, we see little public or policymaker interest in the issues, but when they rise, people express great concern, for example, over the cost of gasoline. In addition to the historical neglect of energy issues, we have seen a pattern of policy gridlock. Here the connection to environmental policy was clearer to policymakers than it had been on population growth. Indeed, opposition to pollution control programs as well as land preservation came primarily from conflicting demands for energy production in the aftermath of the Arab oil embargo in 1973. The Nixon, Ford, and Carter administrations all attempted to formulate national policies for achieving energy independence by increasing energy supplies, with Carter's efforts by far the most sustained and comprehensive. Carter also emphasized conservation and environmental safeguards. However, for the most part, these efforts were unsuccessful. No consensus on national energy policy emerged among the public or in Congress, and presidential leadership was insufficient to overcome these political constraints until major energy policies were adopted in 1992 and again in 2005.[26]

Congress maintained its strong commitment to environmental policy throughout the 1970s, even as the salience of these issues for the public seemed to wane. For example, it revised the Clean Air Act of 1970 and the Clean Water Act of 1972 through amendments approved in 1977. Yet, by the end of the Carter administration, concerns over the impact of environmental regulation on the economy and specific objections to implementation of the new laws, particularly the Clean Air Act, began creating a backlash.

Political Reaction in the 1980s

The Reagan presidency brought to the federal government a markedly different environmental policy agenda (see Chapter 4). Virtually all environmental protection and resource policies enacted during the 1970s were reevaluated in light of the president's desire to reduce the scope of government regulation, shift responsibilities to the states, and depend more on the private sector. Whatever the merits of Reagan's new policy agenda, it was put into effect through a risky strategy that relied on ideologically committed presidential appointees to the EPA and the Agriculture, Interior, and Energy Departments and on sharp cutbacks in budgets for environmental programs.[27]

Congress initially cooperated with Reagan, particularly in approving budget cuts, but it soon reverted to its accustomed defense of existing environmental policy, frequently criticizing the president's management of the EPA and the Interior Department under Anne Gorsuch (later Burford) and James Watt, respectively; both Burford and Watt were forced to resign by the end of 1983. Among Congress's most notable achievements of the 1980s were its strengthening of the Resource Conservation and Recovery Act (Hazardous and Solid Waste Amendments, 1984), enactment of the Superfund Amendments and Reauthorization Act (1986)—which toughened the act and also established the federal Toxics Release Inventory—, and amendments to the Safe Drinking Water Act (1986) and the Clean Water Act (1987) (see Appendix 1).

As we discuss later in this chapter, budget cuts and the loss of capacity in environmental institutions took a serious toll during the 1980s. Yet even the determined efforts of a popular president could not halt the advance of environmental policy. Public support for environmental improvement, the driving force for policy development in the 1970s, increased markedly during Reagan's presidency and represented the public's stunning rejection of the president's agenda.[28]

Paradoxically, Reagan actually strengthened environmental forces in the nation. Through his lax enforcement of pollution laws and prodevelopment resource policies, he created political issues around which national and grass-roots environmental groups could organize. These groups appealed success-fully to a public that was increasingly disturbed by the health and environmental risks of industrial society and by threats to ecological stability. As a result, membership in national environmental groups soared, and new grassroots organizations developed, creating further political incentives for environmental activism at all levels of government.[29]

By the fall of 1989, there was little mistaking congressional receptivity to continuing the advance of environmental policy into the 1990s. Especially in his first two years as president, George H. W. Bush was eager to adopt a more positive environmental policy agenda than his predecessor, particularly evi-dent in his support for the demanding Clean Air Act Amendments of 1990. Bush's White House, however, was deeply divided on environmental issues for both ideological and economic reasons.

Seeking New Policy Directions: From the 1990s to the Twenty-First Century

Environmental issues received considerable attention during the 1992 presidential election campaign. Bush, running for reelection, criticized envi-ronmentalists as extremists who were putting Americans out of work. The Democratic candidate, Bill Clinton, took a far more supportive stance on the environment, symbolized by his selection of Sen. Al Gore, D-Tenn., as his running mate. Gore was the author of a best-selling book, *Earth in the Bal-ance*, and had one of the strongest environmental records in Congress.

Much to the disappointment of environmentalists, Clinton exerted only sporadic leadership on the environment throughout his two terms in office. However, he and Gore quietly pushed an extensive agenda of environmental policy reform as part of their broader effort to "reinvent government," making it more efficient and responsive to public concerns. Clinton was also generally praised for his environmental appointments and for his administration's sup-port for initiatives such as restoration of the Florida Everglades and other actions based on new approaches to ecosystem management. Clinton reversed many of the Reagan- and Bush-era executive actions that were widely criti-cized by environmentalists, and he favored increased spending on environ-mental programs, alternative energy and conservation research, and international population policy.

Clinton also earned praise from environmental groups when he began speaking out forcefully against anti-environmental policy decisions of Repub-lican Congresses (see Chapters 4 and 5), for his efforts through the Presi-dent's Council on Sustainable Development to encourage new ways to reconcile environmental protection and economic development, and for his "lands legacy" initiatives.[30] Still, Clinton displeased environmentalists as often as he gratified them.

The environmental policy agenda of George W. Bush's presidency is addressed in Chapter 4 and throughout the rest of the book, as are actions taken during Barack Obama's presidency from January 2009 through 2014. As widely expected from statements Bush made on the campaign trail and from his record as governor of Texas, he and his cabinet departed significantly from the positions of the Clinton administration. The economic impact of environmental policy emerged as a major concern, and the president gave far more emphasis to economic development than he did to environmental protection or resource conservation.

Like his father, Bush recognized the political reality of popular support for environmental protection and resource conservation. Yet as a conservative Republican, he was also inclined to represent the views of the party's core constituencies, particularly industrial corporations and timber, mining, agriculture, and oil interests. He drew heavily from those constituencies, as well as conservative ideological groups, to staff the EPA and the Interior, Agriculture, and Energy Departments, filling positions with what the press termed industry insiders.[31] In addition, he sought to further reduce the burden of environmental protection through the use of voluntary, flexible, and cooperative programs and to transfer to the states more responsibility for enforcement of federal laws.

Perhaps the most remarkable decision was the administration's unilateral withdrawal of the United States from the Kyoto Protocol on global climate change, ostensibly out of concern for its adverse economic impact on the nation and its failure to compel significant reduction in greenhouse gas emissions from India and China. The withdrawal from the Kyoto agreement, however, significantly weakened U.S. leadership on global environmental issues. The administration's tendency to minimize environmental concerns was equally clear in its 2001 proposal for a national energy policy (which concentrated on increased production of fossil fuels) and, throughout Bush's two terms, in many decisions on clean air rules, water quality standards, mining regulations, and protection of national forests and parks that were widely denounced by environmentalists.[32] Many of these decisions received considerably less media coverage than might have been expected. In part, this appeared to reflect the administration's strategy of keeping a low profile on potentially unpopular environmental policy actions. But the president benefited further from the sharply altered political agenda after the terrorist attacks of September 11, 2001, as well as the decision in 2003 to invade Iraq.[33]

Barack Obama's environmental policy priorities and actions are described in some detail in Chapter 4 and in many of the chapters that follow. Hence we leave much of that appraisal until later in the volume. However, we address budgetary and administrative changes during the Obama presidency in the next section.

Budgets and Policy Implementation

In this review of environmental policy development since 1970, we have highlighted the adoption of landmark policies and the political conflicts that shaped them. Another part of this story is the changes over time in budgetary support for the agencies responsible for implementing the policies.

Agency budgets are an important part of institutional capacity, which in turn affects the degree to which public policies might help to improve environmental quality. Although spending more money hardly guarantees policy success, substantial budget cuts can significantly undermine established programs and hinder achievement of policy goals. For example, the massive reductions in environmental funding during the 1980s had long-term adverse effects on the government's ability to implement environmental policies. Equally sharp budget cuts proposed by Congress in the mid- to late 1990s, by the Bush administration in the 2000s, and by the Republican House between 2011 and 2015 raised the same prospect, although some of the proposed cuts failed to win approval. Changes since the 1980s in budgetary support for environmental protection merit brief comment here. More detail is provided in the appendixes.

In constant dollars (that is, adjusting for inflation), the total spending authorized by the federal government for all natural resource and environmental programs was only slightly higher in 2015 than it was in 1980 (see Appendix 4). However, in some program areas reflecting the core functions of the EPA, such as pollution control and abatement, spending declined substantially (about 34 percent) from 1980 to 2015, in constant dollars. In contrast, spending on conservation and land management rose appreciably between 1980 and 2015, more than tripling, again in constant dollars. For most budget categories, spending decreased during the 1980s before recovering under the administrations of George H. W. Bush and Bill Clinton, and to some extent under George W. Bush and Barack Obama. A notable exception, other than the case of pollution control, is spending on water resources, where the phaseout of federal grant programs resulted in a steady decline in expenditures between 1980 and 2015, eventually dropping by about 50 percent.

Even when the budget picture was improving, most agencies faced important fiscal challenges. Agency responsibilities rose under environmental policies approved between the 1970s and the 2010s, and the agency staffs often found themselves with insufficient resources to implement those new policies fully and to achieve the environmental quality goals they embodied.

These constraints can be seen in the budgets and staffs of selected environmental and natural resource agencies. For example, in constant dollars, the EPA's operating budget as we calculate it (the EPA determines it somewhat differently) was only a little higher in 2015 than it was in 1980, despite the many new duties Congress gave the agency during this period (see Appendix 2). The agency's budget authority rose from 2000 to 2010, enjoying a big boost in Obama's first year in office (to $10.3 billion). It then declined in 2011, rose to $10.8 billion in 2012, but declined again to $8.4 billion in 2013. By 2014, it stood at $8.2 billion, and the recommended budget authority in Obama's fiscal 2015 budget reflected additional cuts, down to $7.8 billion.

The EPA's staff grew by a greater percentage than its budget, rising from slightly fewer than 13,000 in 1980, the last year of the Carter administration, to around 17,200 by 2011; however, the agency saw its staff decline substantially after 2011; by 2014, it stood at less than 15,500.[34] Most other agencies saw a decrease in staff from 1980 through 2010, some remained at about the same level, and a few enjoyed an increase in staff size (see Appendix 3).

For the near term, the reality is that budgets are likely to be sharply constrained, as will staffing levels, and they will be an important factor in the performance of environmental and resource agencies. Even before the economic downturn of 2008, the fiscal 2009 budget projections of the Bush administration showed steady or decreasing funding for environmental programs estimated to 2013. Under President Obama's fiscal year 2015 budget proposal, which may well be reduced by Congress, the projections are similar, with decreases in spending for 2015 and 2016 and flat to slightly increased spending through 2019.[35] The federal fiscal picture worsened considerably in recent years because of the lagging U.S. economy, leading to often highly contentious debates over the rising deficit (excess of spending over revenue) and accumulated national debt, and how best to deal with both of them. Many Republicans favored sharp reductions in federal spending, including environmental program spending, while Democrats sought a balance of spending cuts and increases in tax revenues. No matter which side wins in this ongoing contest, it is hard to imagine that environmental budgets will enjoy any real improvements in the near term.

Improvements in Environmental Quality

It is difficult, both conceptually and empirically, to measure the success or failure of environmental policies.[36] Yet one of the most important tests of any public policy is whether it achieves its stated objectives. For environmental policies, we should ask if air and water quality are improving, hazardous waste sites are being cleaned up, and biological diversity is protected adequately. Almost always, we also want to know what these improvements cost, not just to government but for society as a whole. There is no simple way to answer those questions, and it is important to understand why that is the case, even if some limited responses are possible.[37]

Measuring Environmental Conditions and Trends

Environmental policies entail long-term commitments to broad social values and goals that are not easily quantified. Short-term and highly visible costs are easier to measure than long-term, diffuse, and intangible benefits, and these differences often lead to intense debates over the value of environmental programs. For example, should the EPA toughen air quality standards to reduce adverse health effects or hold off out of concern for the economic impacts? The answer often seems to depend on which president sits in the White House and how sensitive the EPA is to public concerns over the relative benefits and costs.

Variable and often unreliable monitoring of environmental conditions and inconsistent collection of data over time also make it difficult to assess environmental trends. The time period selected for a given analysis can affect the results, and many scholars discount some data collected prior to the mid-1970s as unreliable. One thing is certain, however. Evaluation of environmental policies depends on significant improvements in monitoring and data collection at both state and federal levels. With better and more appropriate data, we should be able to speak more confidently in the future of policy successes and failures.

In the meantime, scientists and pundits continue to debate whether particular environmental conditions are deteriorating or improving, and for what reasons. Many state-of-the-environment reports that address such conditions and trends are issued by government agencies and environmental research institutes.[38] For the United States, EPA and other agency reports, discussed below, are available online and offer authoritative data.[39] Not surprisingly, interpretations of the data may differ. For instance, critics of environmental policy tend to cite statistics that show rather benign conditions and trends (and therefore little reason to favor public policies directed at them), whereas most environmentalists focus on what they believe to be indicators of serious environmental decline and thus a justification for government intervention. The differences sometimes become the object of extensive media coverage and public debate.

Despite the many limitations on measuring environmental conditions and trends accurately, it is nevertheless useful to examine selected indicators of environmental quality. They tell us at least something about what we have achieved or failed to achieve after nearly four decades of national environmental protection policy. We focus here on a brief overview of trends in air quality, greenhouse gas emissions, water quality, toxic chemicals and hazardous wastes, and natural resources.[40]

Air Quality. Perhaps the best data on changes in the environment can be found for air quality, even if disagreement exists over which measures and time periods are most appropriate. The EPA estimates that, between 1980 and 2012, aggregate emissions of the six principal, or criteria, air pollutants decreased by 67 percent even while the nation's gross domestic product (GDP) grew by 133 percent, its population grew by 38 percent, vehicle miles traveled increased by 92 percent, and energy consumption grew by 27 percent, all of which would likely have increased air pollution without federal laws and regulations.[41]

Progress generally continues, for example between 2000 and 2012, when monitored levels of the six criteria pollutants (that is, ambient air concentrations) showed improvement, with all declining during this period by between 9 and 57 percent. Ozone concentrations (using the eight-hour standard) declined by 9 percent, particulate matter by 27 percent and fine particulates (which pose a greater health risk) by 37 percent, lead by 52 percent, nitrogen dioxide by 38 percent, carbon monoxide by 57 percent, and sulfur dioxide by

54 percent. In addition, between 1990 and 2008, the release of toxic chemicals to the air declined by about 62 percent, largely as a result of new regulation of stationary sources such as power plants as well as mobile sources such as cars and trucks. The EPA celebrates these achievements, saying that the "air quality benefits will lead to improved health, longevity, and quality of life for all Americans."[42]

Despite these impressive gains in air quality, as of 2012, over 142 million people (about 45 percent of the U.S. population) lived in counties with pollution levels above the standards set for at least one of these criteria pollutants, particularly ozone and fine particulates. These figures vary substantially from year to year, reflecting changing economic activity and weather patterns. The 2012 levels were much higher than those reported during the recent recession. As one indicator of continuing problems, in 2012, many urban areas experienced a substantial number of "unhealthy" air days (when the air quality index exceeds 100), including Los Angeles (74), Pittsburgh (58), New York (37), Baltimore (33), Houston (33), Philadelphia (32), Washington, DC (30), Atlanta (27), Sacramento (23), Cleveland (22), and St. Louis (21).[43]

One of most significant remaining problems is toxic or hazardous air pollutants, which have been associated with cancer, respiratory diseases, and other chronic and acute illnesses. The EPA was extremely slow to regulate these pollutants and had established federal standards for only seven of them by mid-1989. Public and congressional concern over toxic emissions led Congress to mandate more aggressive action in the 1986 Superfund amendments as well as in the 1990 Clean Air Act Amendments. The former required manufacturers of more than 300 different chemicals (later increased by the EPA to over 650) to report annually to the agency and to the states in which they operate the amounts of those substances released to the air, water, or land. The EPA's Toxics Release Inventory (TRI) indicates that for the core chemicals from industry that have been reported in a consistent manner over time, total releases on- and off-site decreased by over 60 percent between 1988 and 2012.

At the same time, the annual TRI reports also tell us that industries continue to release very large quantities of toxic chemicals to the environment—3.63 billion pounds a year from about twenty-one thousand facilities across the nation, based on the latest report. About 760 million pounds of the chemicals are released into the air, and those may pose a significant risk to public health.[44] It should be noted, however, that the TRI and related numbers on toxics do not present a full picture of public health risks. For instance, many chemicals and industries were added to TRI reporting requirements during the 1990s and 2000s, complicating the determination of change over time. Using the original or core list of chemicals obviously doesn't account for those put on the list more recently. In addition to the TRI, under the 1990 Clean Air Act Amendments, the EPA regulates 188 listed air toxics, but nationwide monitoring of emissions is not standard.

Greenhouse Gas Emissions. The United States is making only slow progress in addressing the worsening problem of climate change. The nation withdrew from the Kyoto Protocol during the George W. Bush administration, and it remains a significant outlier on international response to climate change despite adoption of climate change and renewable energy policies by over half of the states. Congress remains unlikely to approve a national climate change policy. However, in 2013, the Obama administration adopted a Climate Action Plan to build on its previous initiatives. The plan's numerous executive actions could lead to important gains over the next decade if implemented as designed.[45]

According to the EPA's inventory of greenhouse gases, U.S. emissions in 2012 totaled 6,526 million metric tons of CO_2 equivalent, a common way of accounting for emissions of all forms of greenhouse gases. Total U.S. emissions of greenhouse gases from 1990 to 2012 increased by 4.7 percent; yet, they have been declining in recent years from a peak in 2007. They dropped by 3.4 percent from 2011 to 2012.[46] Projections for the next several years are mixed, and much depends on the pace of the nation's movement away from extensive reliance on coal for generating electricity, and its shift to cleaner-burning natural gas, or renewable forms of energy such as wind and solar power. Still, according to the U.S. Department of Energy, global release of greenhouse gases continues to increase, surpassing even the "worst case" scenario outlined in the 2007 report of the Intergovernmental Panel on Climate Change. In this context, it is worth adding that the United States remains by far the world's leading emitter of greenhouse gases on a per capita basis, and recent reports thoroughly document the risks to both the nation and the world (see Chapter 13).[47]

Water Quality. The nation's water quality has improved since passage of the Clean Water Act of 1972, although more slowly and more unevenly than has air quality. Monitoring data are less adequate for water quality than for air quality. For example, the best evidence for the state of water quality can be found in the EPA's consolidation of biennial state reports (mandated by the Clean Water Act), which are accessible at the agency website. For the most recent reporting period, the states collectively assessed only 29 percent of the entire nation's rivers and streams; 43 percent of lakes, ponds, and reservoirs; 38 percent of estuaries and bays; and a mere 14 percent of coastal shorelines and 3 percent of oceans and near coastal areas.

Based on these inventories, 48 percent of the surveyed river and stream miles were considered to be of good quality and 51 percent impaired. Some 67 percent of lakes, ponds, and reservoirs also were found to be impaired. A classification of impaired means that water bodies are not meeting or fully meeting the national minimum water quality criteria for "designated beneficial uses" such as swimming, fishing, drinking-water supply, and support of aquatic life. These numbers indicate some improvement over time, yet they also tell us that many problems remain. The same survey found that 72 percent of the nation's estuaries and bays were impaired, as were 86 percent of assessed coastal shorelines and 63 percent of assessed oceans and near coastal waters.[48] In the face of a growing population and strong economic growth, prevention of further degradation of water quality could be considered an important achievement. At the same time, water quality clearly falls short of the goals of federal clean water acts.

The causes of impaired waters today are fairly well understood. The EPA reports that the leading sources of impairment are agriculture, atmospheric deposition of chemicals, human modification of waterways, urban and storm-water runoff, and municipal discharges (in that order). That is, the causes no longer are point sources of pollution, such as industrial discharges, which have been well controlled with regulation under the Clean Water Act. Rather, they are nonpoint sources that are much more difficult to control and will take longer to affect.

To date, little progress has been made in halting groundwater contamination despite passage of the Safe Drinking Water Act of 1974, the Resource Conservation and Recovery Act of 1976, and their later amendments. In its 2000 National Water Quality Inventory, the EPA reported that groundwater quality can be adversely affected by human actions that introduce contaminants and that "problems caused by elevated levels of petroleum hydrocarbon compounds, volatile organic compounds, nitrate, pesticides, and metals have been detected in ground water across the nation." The agency also noted that measuring groundwater quality is a complex task and data collection "is still too immature to provide comprehensive national assessments." Heading the list of contaminant sources are leaking underground storage tanks, septic systems, landfills, spills, fertilizer applications, large industrial facilities, hazardous waste sites, and animal feedlots.

With some 46 percent of the nation's urban population relying on groundwater for drinking water (99 percent in rural areas), far more remains to be done.[49] For that reason, public concern has risen over possible contamination of groundwater as a result of the surge in natural gas drilling around the nation through hydraulic fracturing or fracking, where massive amounts of water mixed with sand and various chemicals are injected under high pressure to release natural gas from shale formations. Thousands of such wells have been drilled, and many more are under development.[50]

Toxic and Hazardous Wastes. Progress in dealing with hazardous wastes and other toxic chemicals has been the least satisfactory of all pollution control programs. Implementation of the major laws has been extraordinarily slow due to the extent and complexity of the problems, scientific uncertainty, litigation by industry, public fear of siting treatment and storage facilities nearby, budgetary limitations, and poor management and lax enforcement by the EPA. As a result, gains have been modest when judged by the most common measures.

Much the same could be said about the nation's lack of progress in addressing the challenge posed by high-level radioactive wastes from civilian nuclear power plants. Despite legislation in 1982 and again in 1987 to create a national nuclear waste repository to bury the waste, public and state opposition as well as technical uncertainties have left the country without a permanent solution to the problem. Power plant wastes continue to be stored at some seventy reactor sites across the nation with no agreement to date on a national storage site or geological repository. The Department of Energy now anticipates that it might not be able to operate such a repository until 2048. However, in 2014, the U.S. Nuclear Regulatory Commission ruled that the waste can be stored indefinitely in steel and concrete containers at reactor sites and other locations.[51]

One of the most carefully watched measures of government actions to reduce the risk of toxic and hazardous chemicals pertains to the federal Superfund program. For years, it made painfully slow progress in cleaning up the nation's worst hazardous waste sites. By the late 1990s, however, the pace of action improved. The EPA reported that at the end of fiscal year 2013, 1,701 sites were included on the National Priorities List (NPL), and of those, the agency had completed construction of the final cleanup remedy at 1,156, or 68 percent of the sites. At the remaining sites, it said that designs for cleanup were being prepared, assessments were ongoing, or construction was under way. Yet it also has noted in prior reports that "Superfund cleanup work EPA is doing today generally is more difficult, is more technically demanding, and consumes considerable resources at fewer sites than in the past." That is, the challenge is greater today, and site cleanup is also more costly and more contentious, which often translates into slower remediation of the sites.[52]

Historically, the EPA has set a sluggish pace in the related area of testing toxic chemicals, including pesticides. For example, under a 1972 law mandating control of pesticides and herbicides, only a handful of chemicals used to manufacture the fifty thousand pesticides in use in the United States had been fully tested or retested. The Food Quality Protection Act of 1996 required the EPA to undertake extensive assessment of the risks posed by new and existing pesticides. Following a lawsuit, the EPA apparently is moving more quickly toward meeting the act's goal of protecting human health and the environment from these risks. The agency said in 2006 that it had begun a new program to reevaluate all pesticides in use on a regular basis, at least once every fifteen years.[53]

Natural Resources. Comparable indicators of environmental progress can be cited for natural resource use. As is the case with pollution control, however, interpretation of the data is problematic. We have few good measures of ecosystem health or ways to value ecosystem services, and much of the usual information in government reports concerns land set aside for recreational and aesthetic purposes rather than for protection of ecosystem functions.[54] Nonetheless, the trends in land conservation and wilderness protection suggest important progress over more than three decades of modern environmental and natural resource policies.

For example, the national park system grew from about 26 million acres in 1960 to over 84 million acres by 2014, and the number of units (that is, parks) in the system doubled. Since adoption of the 1964 Wilderness Act, Congress has set aside more than 109 million acres of wilderness through the national wilderness preservation system. Since 1968, it has designated parts of over 200 rivers in 38 states as wild and scenic, with nearly 12,600 river miles protected by 2014. The Fish and Wildlife Service manages more than 150 million acres in more than 560 units of the national wildlife refuge system in all fifty states, far in excess of the total acreage in the system in 1970; about 93 million acres of this total are set aside as wildlife habitat.[55]

Protection of biological diversity through the Endangered Species Act has produced some success as well, although far less than its supporters believe essential. By 2014, forty-one years after passage of the 1973 act, more than 1,470 U.S. plant and animal species had been listed as either endangered or threatened. Over 600 critical habitats have been designated, more than 1,000 habitat conservation plans have been approved, and more than 1,100 recovery plans have been put into effect. Yet only a few endangered species have recovered fully. The Fish and Wildlife Service reported in 2008 that 41 percent of those listed were considered to be stable or improving, but that 34 percent were considered to be declining in status, and that for 23 percent their status was unknown. About 2 percent were presumed to be extinct.[56]

Assessing Environmental Progress

As the data reviewed in the preceding sections suggest, the nation made impressive gains between 1970 and 2014 in controlling many conventional pollutants and in expanding parks, wilderness areas, and other protected public lands. Despite some setbacks, progress on environmental quality continues, even if it is highly uneven from one period to the next. In the future, however, further advances will be more difficult, costly, and controversial. This is largely because the easy problems have already been addressed. At this point, marginal gains—for example, in air and water quality—will cost more per unit of improvement than in the past. Moreover, second-generation environmental threats such as toxic chemicals, hazardous wastes, and nuclear wastes are proving even more difficult to regulate than the "bulk" air and water pollutants that were the main targets in the 1970s. In these cases, substantial progress may not be evident for years to come, and it will be expensive.

The same is true for the third generation of environmental problems, such as global climate change and protection of biodiversity. Solutions require an unprecedented degree of cooperation among nations and substantial improvement in institutional capacity for research, data collection, and analysis as well as policy development and implementation. Hence, success is likely to come slowly as national and international commitments to environmental protection grow and capabilities improve.

Some long-standing problems, such as population growth, will continue to be addressed primarily within nation-states, even though the staggering effects on natural resources and environmental quality are felt worldwide. By 2014, the Earth's population of 7.24 billion people was increasing at an estimated 1.2 percent (or about 86 million people) each year, with a middle-range projection for the year 2050 at about 9.7 billion. The U.S. population was growing at less than 1 percent a year, and middle-range projections by the Population Reference Bureau put it at about 395 million by 2050 (see Chapter 14).[57]

Conclusion

Since the 1970s, public concern and support for environmental protection have risen significantly, spurring the development of an expansive array of policies that substantially increased the government's responsibilities for the environment and natural resources, both domestically and internationally. The implementation of these policies, however, has been far more difficult and controversial than their supporters ever imagined. Moreover, the policies have not been entirely successful, particularly when measured by tangible improvements in environmental quality. Further progress will likely require the United States to search for more efficient and effective ways to achieve these goals, including the use of alternatives to conventional command-and-control regulation, such as use of flexible regulation, market incentives, and information disclosure or public education.[58] Despite these qualifications, the record since the 1970s demonstrates convincingly that the U.S. government is able to produce significant environmental gains through public policies. Unquestionably, the environment would be worse today if the policies enacted during the 1970s and 1980s, and since then, had not been in place.

Emerging environmental threats on the national and international agenda are even more formidable than the first generation of problems addressed by government in the 1970s and the second generation that dominated political debate in the 1980s. Responding to these threats will require creative new efforts to improve the performance of government and other social institutions, and effective leadership to design appropriate strategies to combat these threats, both within government and in society itself, such as sustainable community initiatives and corporate social responsibility actions. This new policy agenda is addressed in Part IV of the book and in the concluding chapter.

Government obviously is an important player in the environmental arena, and the federal government will continue to have unique responsibilities, as will the fifty states and the eighty thousand local governments across the nation. President Obama assembled an experienced and talented environmental policy team to address these challenges and, at the launch of his administration, vowed to make energy and environmental issues "a leading priority" of his presidency and a "defining test of our time." He said that we "cannot accept complacency nor accept any more broken promises."[59] Readers can judge for themselves how well the president and his appointees have lived up to those promises as they peruse the chapters in this volume. It is equally clear, however, and evident since President Obama took office in January 2009, that government rarely can pursue forceful initiatives without broad public support. Ultimately, society's values and priorities will shape the government's response to a rapidly changing world environment that, in all probability, will involve major economic and social dislocations over the coming decades.

Notes

1. See survey data reviewed in Chapter 3; Riley E. Dunlap, "Public Opinion and Environmental Policy," in *Environmental Politics and Policy: Theories and Evidence*, 2nd ed., ed. James P. Lester (Durham, NC: Duke University Press, 1995); Riley E. Dunlap, George H. Gallup Jr., and Alec M. Gallup, "Of Global Concern: Results of the Health of the Planet Survey," *Environment* 35, no. 9 (1993): 7–15, 33–40; and David P. Daniels et al., "Public Opinion on Environmental Policy in the United States," in *The Oxford Handbook of U.S. Environmental Policy*, ed. Sheldon Kamieniecki and Michael E. Kraft (New York: Oxford University Press, 2013).

2. Norman J. Vig and Michael E. Kraft, eds., *Environmental Policy in the 1980s: Reagan's New Agenda* (Washington, DC: CQ Press, 1984).

3. See, for example, Natural Resources Defense Council, *Rewriting the Rules (2005 Special Edition): The Bush Administration's First Term Environmental Record*, January 19, 2005, www.nrdc.org/legislation/rollbacks/rollbacksinx.asp. The effort continued to the end of the Bush presidency. See, for example, R. Jeffrey Smith, "Unfinished Business: The White House Is Rushing to Weaken Rules That Protect the Environment and Consumers," *Washington Post National Weekly Edition*, November 10–16, 2008, 33.

4. Robert Durant, Rosemary O'Leary, and Daniel Fiorino, eds., *Environmental Governance Reconsidered: Challenges, Choices, and Opportunities* (Cambridge, MA: MIT Press, 2004); Daniel Fiorino, *The New Environmental Regulation* (Cambridge, MA: MIT Press, 2006); Marc Allen Eisner, *Governing the Environment: The Transformation of Environmental Regulation* (Boulder, CO: Lynne Rienner, 2007); Christopher McGrory Klyza and David Sousa, *American Environmental Policy: Beyond Gridlock*, updated and expanded edition (Cambridge, MA: MIT Press, 2013); and Judith A. Layzer, *Open for Business: Conservatives' Opposition to Environmental Regulation* (Cambridge, MA: MIT Press).

5. Daniel A. Mazmanian and Michael E. Kraft, eds., *Toward Sustainable Communities: Transition and Transformations in Environmental Policy*, 2nd ed. (Cambridge, MA: MIT Press, 2009); Durant, O'Leary, and Fiorino, *Environmental Governance Reconsidered*; Klyza and Sousa, *American Environmental Policy*; and Michael E. Kraft, Mark Stephan, and Troy D. Abel, *Coming Clean: Information Disclosure and Environmental Performance* (Cambridge, MA: MIT Press, 2011).

6. Judith A. Layzer, *Natural Experiments: Ecosystem-Based Management and the Environment* (Cambridge, MA: MIT Press, 2008); Hanna J. Cortner and Margaret A. Moote, *The Politics of Ecosystem Management* (Washington, DC: Island Press, 1998); Marian R. Chertow and Daniel C. Esty, eds., *Thinking Ecologically: The Next Generation of Environmental Policy* (New Haven, CT: Yale University Press, 1997); President's Council on Sustainable Development, *Sustainable America: A New Consensus for Prosperity, Opportunity, and a Healthy Environment* (Washington, DC: President's Council on Sustainable Development, 1996).

7. The California policy is discussed in Chapter 2. On Minnesota's multifaceted and very successful energy policy, see Michel Wines, "Without Much Straining, Minnesota Reins in Its Utilities' Carbon Emissions," *New York Times*, July 17, 2014. Nine northeastern states similarly have demonstrated that it is possible to reduce carbon dioxide emissions while fostering economic growth. See Hannah Fairfield, "The Best of Both Worlds in Cutting Emissions?" *New York Times*, June 8, 2014.

8. See Walter A. Rosenbaum, "Science, Policy, and Politics at the EPA," in *Environmental Policy*, 8th ed., ed. Norman J. Vig and Michael E. Kraft. See also National Academy

of Public Administration (NAPA), *Setting Priorities, Getting Results: A New Direction for EPA* (Washington, DC: NAPA, 1995), 124–25.

9. See also Klyza and Sousa, *American Environmental Policy*, Chapter 7.

10. John W. Kingdon, *Agendas, Alternatives, and Public Policies*, 2nd ed. (New York: Harper-Collins, 1995); Frank R. Baumgartner and Bryan D. Jones, *Agendas and Instability in American Politics* (Chicago: University of Chicago Press, 1993).

11. For a review of how this process works, see Deborah Lynn Guber and Christopher J. Bosso, "Issue Framing, Agenda Setting, and Environmental Discourse," in *The Oxford Handbook of U.S. Environmental Policy*, ed. Sheldon Kamieniecki and Michael E. Kraft (New York: Oxford University Press, 2013).

12. Roger W. Cobb and Charles D. Elder, *Participation in American Politics: The Dynamics of Agenda-Building* (Boston: Allyn & Bacon, 1972). See also Thomas A. Birkland, *After Disaster: Agenda Setting, Public Policy, and Focusing Events* (Washington, DC: Georgetown University Press, 1997).

13. Kingdon, *Agendas*.

14. For a more thorough discussion of how the policy cycle model applies to environmental issues, see Michael E. Kraft, *Environmental Policy and Politics*, 6th ed. (New York: Pearson, 2015), Chapter 3. The general model is discussed at length in James E. Anderson, *Public Policymaking: An Introduction*, 8th ed. (Boston: Houghton Mifflin, 2014), and in Thomas A. Birkland, *An Introduction to the Policy Process: Theories, Concepts, and Models of Public Policy Making*, 3rd ed. (Armonk, NY: M. E. Sharpe, 2011).

15. Klyza and Sousa, *American Environmental Policy*.

16. Dunlap, "Public Opinion and Environmental Policy"; and Deborah Lynn Guber, *The Grassroots of a Green Revolution: Polling America on the Environment* (Cambridge, MA: MIT Press, 2003).

17. Paul J. Culhane, *Public Lands Politics: Interest Group Influence on the Forest Service and the Bureau of Land Management* (Baltimore: Johns Hopkins University Press, 1981), esp. Chapter 1. See also Richard N. L. Andrews, *Managing the Environment, Managing Ourselves: A History of American Environmental Policy*, 2nd ed. (New Haven, CT: Yale University Press, 2006); and Sally K. Fairfax, Lauren Gwin, Mary Ann King, Leigh Raymond, and Laura A. Watt, *Buying Nature: The Limits of Land Acquisition as a Conservation Strategy: 1780–2004* (Cambridge, MA: MIT Press, 2005).

18. Andrews, *Managing the Environment*; Kraft, *Environmental Policy and Politics*, Chapter 4.

19. Michael E. Kraft, "Population Policy," in *Encyclopedia of Policy Studies*, 2nd ed., ed. Stuart S. Nagel (New York: Marcel Dekker, 1994).

20. J. Clarence Davies III and Barbara S. Davies, *The Politics of Pollution*, 2nd ed. (Indianapolis, IN: Bobbs-Merrill, 1975).

21. Evan J. Ringquist, *Environmental Protection at the State Level: Politics and Progress in Controlling Pollution* (Armonk, NY: M. E. Sharpe, 1993), Chapter 2; Davies and Davies, *The Politics of Pollution*, Chapter 2. A much fuller history of the origins and development of modern environmental policy than is provided here can be found in Andrews, *Managing the Environment*, and Michael J. Lacey, ed., *Government and Environmental Politics: Essays on Historical Developments since World War Two* (Baltimore: Johns Hopkins University Press, 1989).

22. Samuel P. Hays and Barbara D. Hays, *Beauty, Health, and Permanence: Environmental Politics in the United States, 1955–1985* (Cambridge, UK: Cambridge University Press, 1987). See also Dunlap, "Public Opinion and Environmental Policy," and Robert Cameron Mitchell, "Public Opinion and Environmental Politics in the 1970s and 1980s," in *Environmental Policy in the 1980s*, ed. Norman J. Vig and Michael E. Kraft (Washington, DC: CQ Press, 1984).

23. Public Law 91-90 (42 USC 4321–4347), Sec. 101. See Lynton Keith Caldwell, *The National Environmental Policy Act: An Agenda for the Future* (Bloomington: Indiana University Press, 1998).

24. Michael E. Kraft, "Congress and Environmental Policy," in *The Oxford Handbook of U.S. Environmental Policy*, ed. Sheldon Kamieniecki and Michael E. Kraft (New York: Oxford University Press, 2013); Amy Below, "Parties, Campaigns, and Elections," in *The Oxford Handbook of U.S. Environmental Policy*, ed. Sheldon Kamieniecki and Michael E. Kraft (New York: Oxford University Press, 2013); Charles R. Shipan and William R. Lowry, "Environmental Policy and Party Divergence in Congress," *Political Research Quarterly* 54 (June 2001): 245–63.

25. Kraft, "Population Policy"; Council on Environmental Quality and Department of State, *The Global 2000 Report to the President* (Washington, DC: Government Printing Office, 1980).

26. James Everett Katz, *Congress and National Energy Policy* (New Brunswick, NJ: Transaction, 1984).

27. Vig and Kraft, *Environmental Policy in the 1980s*.

28. See Riley E. Dunlap, "Public Opinion on the Environment in the Reagan Era," *Environment* 29 (July–August 1987): 6–11, 32–37; Mitchell, "Public Opinion and Environmental Politics."

29. The changing membership numbers can be found in Kraft, *Environmental Policy and Politics*, Chapter 4. See also Christopher J. Bosso, *Environment, Inc.: From Grassroots to Beltway* (Lawrence: University Press of Kansas, 2005).

30. President's Council on Sustainable Development, *Sustainable America*.

31. Katharine Q. Seelye, "Bush Picks Industry Insiders to Fill Environmental Posts," *New York Times*, May 12, 2001.

32. See Natural Resources Defense Council, "Rewriting the Rules"; Bruce Barcott, "Changing All the Rules," *New York Times Magazine*, April 4, 2004; and Margaret Kriz, "Vanishing Act," *National Journal*, April 12, 2008, 18–23.

33. Eric Pianin, "War Is Hell: The Environmental Agenda Takes a Back Seat to Fighting Terrorism," *Washington Post National Weekly Edition*, October 29–November 4, 2001, 12–13. See also Barcott, "Changing All the Rules"; and Joel Brinkley, "Out of the Spotlight, Bush Overhauls U.S. Regulations," *New York Times*, August 14, 2004.

34. On the staff numbers, see "FY 2015: EPA Budget in Brief" (EPA, Office of the Chief Financial Officer, March 2014), available at http://www2.epa.gov/sites/production/files/2014-03/documents/fy15_bib.pdf. The overall EPA budget numbers come from the Obama administration's fiscal year 2015 budget. Annual budget numbers in EPA's "FY 2015" document cited here differ somewhat from the budget authority figures in the historical tables of the fiscal year 2015 budget. For consistency, we use the latter for comparisons over time.

35. These projections are taken from President Obama's fiscal year 2015 budget proposal, available at the Office of Management and Budget (www.omb.gov). Budget numbers and projections are available by federal agency as well as for government "functions," such as spending on natural resources and the environment. The historical tables provide the best view of budget changes over time, including projections through 2019.

36. Robert V. Bartlett, "Evaluating Environmental Policy," in *Environmental Policy in the 1990s*, 2nd ed., ed. Norman J. Vig and Michael E. Kraft (Washington, DC: CQ Press, 1994); Evan J. Ringquist, "Evaluating Environmental Policy Outcomes," in *Environmental Politics and Policy*, ed. James P. Lester (Durham, NC: Duke University Press, 1995); Gerrit J. Knaap and Tschangho John Kim, eds., *Environmental Program Evaluation: A Primer* (Champaign: University of Illinois Press, 1998).

37. One of the most thorough evaluations of environmental protection policies of this kind can be found in J. Clarence Davies and Jan Mazurek, *Pollution Control in the United States: Evaluating the System* (Washington, DC: NAPA, 1995).

38. See, for example, UN Development Programme, UN Environment Programme, World Bank, and World Resources Institute, *World Resources 2010–11: Decision Making in a Changing Climate* (Washington, DC: World Resources Institute, 2011), available at www.wri.org.

39. The EPA's National Center for Environmental Assessment offers a diversity of reports on the state of the environment in addition to the specific agency analyses cited in this section of the chapter. They are available at www.epa.gov/ncea/.

40. For a fuller account, see Kraft, *Environmental Policy and Politics*, Chapter 2.

41. U.S. Environmental Protection Agency (EPA), "Air Quality Trends: Comparison of Growth Areas and Emissions, 1980–2012," available at www.epa.gov/airtrends/aqtrends.html#airquality.

42. Ibid.

43. See U.S. EPA, "Our Nation's Air: Status and Trends through 2010" (Washington, DC: February 2012), available at www.epa.gov/airtrends/2011/report/fullreport.pdf. A map of the United States covering air quality over time in major cities can be found on p. 8.

44. U.S. EPA, "2012 Toxics Release Inventory: National Analysis Overview" (Washington, DC: U.S. EPA, February 2014), available at http://www2.epa.gov/sites/production/files/2014-01/documents/complete_2012_tri_na_overview_document.pdf. The volume of releases refers only to TRI facilities that reported to the EPA that year. Facilities falling below a threshold level are not required to report, nor are many smaller facilities. To see TRI data for anywhere in the United States via an interactive map, see http://toxictrends.org/.

45. See Andrew C. Revkin, "Obama's Ambitious Global Warming Action Plan," *New York Times*, June 25, 2013.

46. See U.S. EPA, "Inventory of U.S. Greenhouse Gas Emissions and Sinks: 1990–2012" (Washington, DC: U.S. EPA, April 2014), available at http://epa.gov/climatechange/emissions/usinventoryreport.html.

47. Associated Press, "World Emissions of Carbon Dioxide Soar Higher Than Experts' Worst Case Scenario," *Washington Post*, November 3, 2011; and Justin Gillis, "Climate Panel Says Upper Limit on Emissions Is Nearing," *New York Times*, September 27, 2013. A National Climate Assessment released by the Obama administration in mid-2014 illustrated the many risks associated with the nation's greenhouse gas emissions. See Justin Gillis, "Climate Change Study Finds U.S. Is Already Widely Affected," *New York Times*, May 5, 2014; and the authoritative reports from the IPCC released in 2013 and 2014, which can be located at the organization's website: www.ipcc.ch/.

48. U.S. EPA, "Watershed Assessment, Tracking, and Environmental Reports: National Summary of State Information," available at http://ofmpub.epa.gov/waters10/attains_nation_cy.control. The same page allows review of reports on each of the fifty states.

49. *National Water Quality Inventory: 2000 Report to Congress* (Washington, DC: Office of Water, U.S. EPA). The EPA no longer includes an assessment of groundwater in these reports. The U.S. Geological Survey has an extensive program of monitoring and assessing groundwater. See its website (www.usgs.gov). See also the EPA's page on groundwater: http://water.epa.gov/drink/.

50. Ian Urbina, "A Tainted Water Well, and Concern There May Be More," *New York Times*, August 3, 2011. The EPA is studying the risk of water contamination from this kind of drilling. See its webpage on the subject: http://www2.epa.gov/hfstudy.

51. For a recent review of the history of policy efforts on nuclear waste, see Michael E. Kraft, "Nuclear Power and the Challenge of High-Level Waste Disposal in the United States," *Polity* 45, no. 2 (April 2013): 265–80. See also Matthew L. Wald, "A Texas County Sees Opportunity in Toxic Waste," *New York Times*, August 7, 2014; and Matthew L. Wald, "Nuclear Waste Is Allowed above Ground Indefinitely," *New York Times*, August 29, 2014. The Obama administration created a Blue Ribbon Commission on America's Nuclear Future to examine the challenge, but its final report led to no action as of 2014. The commission's report is available at www.energy.gov/ne/downloads/blue-ribbon -commission-americas-nuclear-future-report-secretary-energy.

52. U.S. EPA, "Superfund National Accomplishments Summary Fiscal Year 2013," available at www.epa.gov/superfund/accomplishments.htm.

53. The pertinent documents can be found at the EPA's website for pesticide programs: www.epa.gov/pesticides/.

54. Hallett J. Harris and Denise Scheberle, "Ode to the Miner's Canary: The Search for Environmental Indicators," in *Environmental Program Evaluation: A Primer*, ed. Gerrit J. Knaap and Tschangho John Kim (Champaign: University of Illinois Press, 1998). See also Gretchen C. Daily, ed., *Nature's Services: Societal Dependence on Natural Ecosystems* (Washington, DC: Island Press, 1997); and Water Science and Technology Board, *Valuing Ecosystem Services: Toward Better Environmental Decision-Making* (Washington, DC: National Academies Press, 2004).

55. The numbers come from the various agency websites and from Kraft, *Environmental Policy and Politics*, Chapters 6 and 7.

56. The Fish and Wildlife Service website (www.fws.gov) provides extensive data on threatened and endangered species and habitat recovery plans. The figures on improving and declining species come from the U.S. Fish and Wildlife Service, "Report to Congress on the Recovery of Threatened and Endangered Species: Fiscal Years 2009–2010" (Washington, DC: Fish and Wildlife Service, January 2012), available at www.fws.gov/endangered/esa-library/pdf/Recovery_Report_2010.pdf.

57. Population Reference Bureau, "2014 World Population Data Sheet," available at www .prb.org.

58. See Mazmanian and Kraft, *Toward Sustainable Communities*; Fiorino, *The New Environmental Regulation*; Eisner, *Governing the Environment*; and Kraft, Stephan, and Abel, *Coming Clean*. A number of the chapters in Sheldon Kamieniecki and Michael E. Kraft, eds., *The Oxford Handbook of U.S. Environmental Policy* (New York: Oxford University Press, 2013), also analyze the promise of new policy approaches.

59. The quotation is from John M. Broder and Andrew C. Revkin, "Hard Task for New Team on Energy and Climate," *New York Times*, December 16, 2008. See also David A. Fahrenthold, "Ready for Challenges: Obama's Environmental Team: No Radicals," *Washington Post National Weekly Edition*, December 22, 2008–January 4, 2009, 34.

2

Racing to the Top, the Bottom, or the Middle of the Pack?
The Evolving State Government Role in Environmental Protection

Barry G. Rabe

The problem which all federalized nations have to solve is how to secure an efficient central government and preserve national unity, while allowing free scope for the diversities, and free play to the . . . members of the federation. It is . . . to keep the centrifugal and centripetal forces in equilibrium, so that neither the planet States shall fly off into space, nor the sun of the Central government draw them into its consuming fires.

Lord James Bryce,
The American Commonwealth, 1888

Before the 1970s, the conventional wisdom on federalism viewed "the planet States" as sufficiently lethargic to require a powerful "Central government" in many areas of environmental policy. States were widely derided as mired in corruption, hostile to innovation, and unable to take a serious role in environmental policy out of fear of alienating key economic constituencies. If anything, they were seen as "racing to the bottom" among their neighbors, attempting to impose as few regulatory burdens as possible. In more recent times, the tables have turned—so much so that current conventional wisdom now berates an overheated federal government that squelches state creativity and capability to tailor environmental policies to local realities. The decentralization mantra of recent decades has endorsed an extended transfer of environmental policy resources and regulatory authority from Washington, DC, to states and localities. Governors-turned-presidents, such as Ronald Reagan, Bill Clinton, and George W. Bush, extolled the wisdom of such a strategy, at least in their rhetoric. Many recent heads of the U.S. Environmental Protection Agency (EPA), including Gina McCarthy in the Obama administration, took federal office after extended state government experience and frequently endorsed the idea of shifting more authority back to statehouses. Of course, such a transfer would pose a potentially formidable test of the thesis that more localized units know best and has faced major political hurdles.

What accounts for this sea change in our understanding of the role of states in environmental policy? How have states evolved in recent decades, and what types of functions do they assume most comfortably and effectively? Despite state resurgence, are there areas in which states fall short? Looking ahead, should regulatory authority devolve to the states, or are there better ways to sort out federal and state responsibilities?

This chapter addresses these questions, examining evidence of state performance in environmental policy. It provides both an overview of state evolution and a set of brief case studies that explore state strengths and limitations. These state-specific accounts are interwoven with assessments of the federal government's role, for good or ill, in the development of state environmental policy.

The States as "New Heroes" of American Federalism

Policy analysts are generally most adept at analyzing institutional foibles and policy failures. Indeed, much of the literature on environmental policy follows this pattern, with criticism particularly voluminous and potent when directed toward federal efforts in this area. By contrast, states have received much more favorable treatment. Many influential books and reports on state government and federalism portray states as highly dynamic and effective. Environmental policy is often depicted as a prime example of this general pattern of state effectiveness. Some analysts routinely characterize states as the "new heroes" of American federalism, having long since eclipsed a doddering federal government. According to this line of argument, states are consistently at the cutting edge of policy innovation, eager to find creative solutions to environmental problems, and "racing to the top" with a goal of national preeminence in the field. When the states fall short, an overzealous federal partner is often said to be at fault.

Such assertions have considerable empirical support. The vast majority of state governments have undergone fundamental changes since the first Earth Day in 1970. Many states have drafted new constitutions and gained access to unprecedented revenues through expanded taxing powers. In turn, many state bureaucracies have grown and become more professionalized, as have staffs serving governors and legislatures. Expanded policy engagement has been further stimulated by increasingly competitive two-party systems in many regions through at least 2010, intensifying pressure on elected officials to deliver desired services. Heightened use of direct democracy provisions, such as the initiative and referendum, and increasing activism by state courts and elected state attorneys general create alternative routes for policy adoption. On the whole in recent decades, public opinion data have consistently found that citizens have a considerably higher degree of "trust and confidence" in the package of public services and regulations dispensed from their state capitals than those generated from Washington.[1] These factors have converged to expand state capacity and commitment to environmental protection.

This transformed state role is evident in virtually every area of environmental policy. States directly regulate approximately 20 percent of the total U.S. economy, including many areas in which environmental concerns come into play.[2] The Environmental Council of the States has estimated that states operate 96 percent of all federal environmental programs that can be delegated to them.[3] Collectively, they approach that high level of engagement in issuance of all environmental permits and implementation of all environmental enforcement actions. Despite this expanded role, federal financial support to states in the form of grants to support environmental protection efforts has generally declined since the early 1980s, forcing states to find ways to fund most of their operations.

Many areas of environmental policy are clearly dominated by states, including most aspects of waste management, groundwater protection, land use management, transportation, and electricity regulation. This state-centric role is also reflected in rapidly emerging areas such as protection of air, land, and water quality related to the dramatic expansion in the exploration of shale gas and oil via hydraulic fracturing (or "fracking") techniques. In many instances, this represents "compensatory federalism," whereby Washington proves "hesitant, uncertain, distracted, and in disagreement about what to do," with states responding with a "step into the breach."[4] Even in policy areas with an established federal imprint, such as air and water pollution control, states often have considerable opportunity to oversee implementation and move beyond federal standards if they so choose. In air quality alone, more than a dozen states routinely adopt policies to either exceed federal standards or fill federal regulatory gaps, often setting models for national consideration. Political scientists Christopher McGrory Klyza and David Sousa confirm that "the greater flexibility of state government can yield policy innovation, opening the way to the next generation of environmental policy."[5]

That flexibility and commitment is further reflected in the institutional arrangements established by states to address environmental problems. Many states have long since moved beyond their historical placement of environmental programs in public health or natural resource departments in favor of comprehensive agencies that gather most environmental responsibilities under a single organizational umbrella. These agencies have sweeping, cross-programmatic responsibilities and have grown steadily in staff and complexity in recent decades. Ironically, many of these agencies mirror the organizational framework of the much maligned EPA, dividing regulatory activity by environmental media of air, land, and water and thereby increasing the likelihood of shifting environmental contamination back and forth across medium boundaries. Despite this fragmentation, such institutions provide states with a firm institutional foundation for addressing a variety of environmental concerns. In turn, many states have continued to experiment with new organizational arrangements to meet evolving challenges, including the use of informal networks, special task forces, and interstate compacts to facilitate cooperation among various departments and agencies.[6]

This expanded state commitment to environmental policy may be accelerated, not only by the broader factors introduced above, but also by features somewhat unique to this policy area. First, a growing number of scholars contend that broad public support for environmental protection provides considerable impetus for more decentralized policy development. Such "civic environmentalism" stimulates numerous state and local stakeholders to take creative collective action independent of federal intervention. As opposed to top-down controls, game-theoretic analyses of efforts to protect so-called common-pool resources such as river basins and forests side decisively with local or regional approaches to resource protection. Much of the leading scholarly work of the late Elinor Ostrom, who in 2009 became the first political scientist to win the Nobel Prize in economics, actively embraced "bottom-up" environmental governance.[7]

Second, the proliferation of environmental policy professionals in state agencies and legislative staff roles has created a sizable base of talent and ideas for state-level policy innovation. Contrary to conventional depictions of agency officials as shackled by elected "principals," an alternative view finds considerable policy innovation or "entrepreneurship" in state policymaking circles. This pattern is especially evident in environmental policy, where numerous areas of specialization place a premium on expert ideas and allow for considerable innovation within agencies.[8] Recent scholarly work on the performance of state environmental agencies gives generally high marks to officials for professionalism, constructive problem solving, and increasing emphasis on improving environmental outcomes, albeit with considerable state-to-state variation.[9] Networks of state professionals, working in similar capacities but across jurisdictional boundaries, have become increasingly influential in recent decades. These networks facilitate information exchange, foster the diffusion of innovation, and pool resources to pursue joint initiatives. Such multistate groups as the Environmental Council of the States, the National Association of Clean Air Agencies, and the National Association of State Energy Officials also band together to influence the design of subsequent federal policies, seeking either latitude for expanded state experimentation or federal adoption of state "best practices." Other entities, such as the Northeast States for Coordinated Air Use Management, the Great Lakes Commission, and the Pacific Coast Collaborative represent state interests in certain regions.

Third, environmental policy in many states is stimulated by direct democracy, which is not allowed at the federal level, through initiatives, referendums, and the recall of elected officials. In every state except Delaware, state constitutional amendments must be approved by voters via referendum. Thirty-one states and Washington, DC, also have some form of direct democracy for approving legislation, representing well over half the U.S. population. Use of this policy tool has grown at an exponential rate to consider a wide array of state environmental policy options, including nuclear plant closure, mandatory disclosure of commercial product toxicity, and public land acquisition. In November 2013, Washington voters narrowly rejected required labeling of any food that was genetically engineered whereas they joined voters in Colorado and Missouri in previous years in enacting ballot propositions requiring a steady increase in the amount of electricity derived from renewable sources. Western states have generally made the greatest use of these provisions on environmental issues, particularly Oregon, California, and Colorado. In November 2010, California decisively rejected a proposal that would have brought far-reaching climate legislation enacted four years earlier to a virtual halt, demonstrating that ballot propositions can be used to either initiate or curtail environmental policies.

The Cutting Edge of Policy: Cases of State Innovation

The convergence of these various political forces has unleashed substantial new environmental policy at the state level. A variety of scholars have attempted to analyze some of this activity through ranking schemes that determine which states are most active and innovative. They consistently conclude that certain states tend to take the lead in most areas of policy innovation, followed by an often uneven pattern of innovation diffusion across state and regional boundaries.[10] For example, data collected in 2015 by the Center for Local, State, and Urban Policy examine state willingness to adopt a wide range of possible environmental policy innovations weighted on a ten-point scale. The fifty states are ranked in Table 2-1 according to the total number of these policies that they have adopted, ranging from water conservation and efficiency programs to air toxics programs for utilities. This ranking suggests considerable variation among states, with the highest scores generally among states in the Northeast and with larger populations, and is broadly consistent with earlier analyses of this type.

Additional analyses have attempted to examine which economic and political factors are most likely to influence the rigor of state policy or the level of resources devoted to it.[11] An important but less examined question concerns whether recent developments in state environmental policy have actually served to demonstrably improve environmental quality. Emerging research evidence suggests that a number of state innovations offer promising alternatives to prevailing approaches, often representing a direct response to local environmental crises and revelation of shortcomings in existing policy design. Brief case studies that follow indicate the breadth and potential effectiveness of state innovation.

Anticipating Environmental Challenges

One of the greatest challenges facing U.S. environmental policy is the need to shift from a pollution control mode that reacts after damage has occurred to one that anticipates potential problems and attempts to prevent them. Growing evidence suggests that some states have launched serious planning processes and are attempting to pursue preventative strategies in an increasingly systematic and effective way. All fifty states have adopted at least one pollution prevention

Table 2-1   Receptiveness of States to Environmental Policies

State	Total Points Received	States	Total Points Received
California	10	West Virginia	6
Colorado	10	Arkansas	5
Connecticut	10	Florida	5
Delaware	10	Kansas	5
Illinois	10	Michigan	5
Minnesota	10	Nevada	5
Maine	9	Utah	5
New York	9	Virginia	5
Rhode Island	9	Arizona	4.5
Texas	8.5	Georgia	4
Iowa	8	Mississippi	4
Maryland	8	Nebraska	4
Massachusetts	8	New Hampshire	4
New Jersey	8	Oklahoma	4
Oregon	8	South Carolina	4
Washington	8	South Dakota	4
Wisconsin	8	Tennessee	4
Ohio	7.5	Alabama	3
Vermont	7.5	Missouri	3
New Mexico	7	North Dakota	3
Hawaii	6.5	Wyoming	3
North Carolina	6.5	Alaska	2
Pennsylvania	6.5	Idaho	2
Indiana	6	Kentucky	2
Montana	6	Louisiana	2

Source: Compiled by the author from data collected in 2015 by the Center for Local, State, and Urban Policy.

program. The oldest and most common of these involve technical assistance to industries and networking services that link potential collaborators. But some states have increasingly redefined pollution prevention in bolder terms, cutting across conventional programmatic boundaries with a series of mandates and incentives to pursue prevention opportunities. Thirty-four states have adopted laws that move beyond federal standards in preventing risks from chemical exposure, such as bans of specific chemicals thought to pose health risks or comprehensive chemical management systems.[12]

Among the more active states, Minnesota has one of the most far-reaching programs. A series of state laws requires hundreds of Minnesota firms to submit annual toxic pollution prevention plans and give priority treatment to "chemicals of concern."[13] These plans must outline each firm's current use and release of a long list of toxic pollutants and establish formal goals for their reduction or elimination over a specified period of time. Firms have considerable latitude in determining how to attain these goals, contrary to the technology-forcing character of much federal regulation. But they must meet state-established reduction timetables and pay fees on releases. The state was also one of the first two states to ban bisphenol A, a controversial chemical used in plastics.[14]

From these earlier efforts, Minnesota and other states have established multidisciplinary teams that attempt to forecast emerging environmental threats and respond before problems arise. This has included pioneering efforts in recent years to review potential environmental risks from nanotechnology and its generation of staggeringly small particles that may improve product design but also harbor environmental risks.[15] Minnesota has also taken a lead role in pricing the environmental impacts of carbon dioxide emissions in long-term planning for electricity generation. This latter practice contributed to the 2007 enactment of the Next Generation Energy Act that requires new coal-burning power plants to fully offset their greenhouse gas emissions, although this was challenged in court by coal interests based in North Dakota. In 2013, the state adopted model standards that developed unusually strong safeguards to regulate silica sand mining, a substance in increasing demand for use in oil and gas drilling.

Illinois has taken a "race-to-the-top" approach to policy designed to anticipate and thereby minimize environmental risks from hydraulic fracturing practices. After a two-year review of potential "fracking" risks and policy options by a diverse committee of stakeholders, the Illinois legislature in 2013 overwhelmingly adopted comprehensive shale drilling legislation on a bipartisan basis that had a strong risk reduction emphasis. This legislation requires water quality testing by an independent third party both before any drilling and in a series of subsequent intervals, a seismic "traffic-light" warning system to slow or halt drilling if earthquakes increase or expand in intensity, and an expansive state-operated disclosure system on the chemicals used in the drilling process.[16]

Economic Incentives

Economists have long lamented the penchant for command-and-control rules and regulations in U.S. environmental policy. Most would prefer to see a more economically sensitive set of policies, such as taxes on emissions to capture social costs or "negative externalities" and provide monetary incentives for good environmental performance. The politics of imposing such costs has proven contentious at all governmental levels, although a growing number of states have begun to pursue some form of this approach in recent years. In all, the states have enacted hundreds of measures that can be characterized as "green taxes," including environmentally related "surcharges" and "fees" that avoid the explicit use of the label "tax."[17] States use related revenues to cover approximately 60 percent of their total environmental agency expenses and, in some cases, the full costs of some popular programs such as recycling and energy efficiency.[18]

A growing number of states have begun to revisit their general tax policies with an eye toward environmental purposes. For example, Iowa exempts from taxation all pollution control equipment purchased for use in the state, whereas Maryland and other states offer major tax incentives to purchasers of hybrid and electric vehicles. Numerous states provide a series of tax credits or low-interest loans for the purchase of recycling or renewable energy equipment or capital investments necessary to develop environmentally friendly technologies. Many states and localities have also developed some form of tax on solid waste, usually involving a direct fee for garbage pickup while offering free collection of recyclables.

One of the earliest and most visible economic incentive programs involves refundable taxes on beverage containers. Ten states—covering 30 percent of the population—have such programs in place. Deposit collections flow through a system that includes consumers, container redemption facilities such as grocery stores, and firms that reuse or recycle the containers. Michigan's program is widely regarded as among the most successful of these state efforts and, similar to a number of others, is a product of direct democracy. Michigan's program places a dime deposit on containers—double the more conventional nickel—which may contribute to its unusually high redemption rate of 97 percent. This type of policy has diffused to other products, including scrap tires, used motor oil, pesticide containers, appliances with ozone-depleting substances, and electronic waste materials such as used computers.

States also have constitutional authority to tax all forms of energy, including transportation fuel and electricity. Many policy analysts across ideological divides have long argued that such taxation would be one of the most effective ways to deter environmental degradation, as use of conventional energy sources contributes to many environmental problems. Many states have been reluctant to move beyond their traditional levels of taxation for fuels such as gasoline. These averaged 31.46 cents per gallon among the fifty states in 2014, ranging from a low of 8 cents per gallon in Alaska to a high of 46.5 cents per gallon in California. This began to change in 2013–2014, as nearly half of the states adopted either an increase in their excise tax or some alternative form of tax designed to produce greater revenue for related transportation costs. One possible model in this area involves so-called public benefit funds or social benefit charges, an electricity tax used in eighteen states that generates funds for energy efficiency and renewable energy programs.[19] Yet another area for state innovation based on economic incentives may be the application of severance tax revenues from oil and gas drilling operations to help alleviate related environmental impacts. Nearly all states that allow drilling have such taxes, with rates generally highest in more conservative states. Funds generated from these taxes have soared in many states with the onset of expanded drilling through fracking techniques. In North Dakota, for example, nearly half of total state revenue for fiscal 2013 was generated by this tax; the state has established a Legacy Fund that sets aside 30 percent of proceeds for longer-term use and has also designated increasing portions to address "oil and gas drilling impacts" and related environmental concerns.

Filling the Federal Void: Reducing Greenhouse Gases

Global climate change and the challenge of reducing the release of greenhouse gases such as carbon dioxide and methane have been character-ized almost exclusively as the responsibility of national governments and international regimes. The United States has commonly been perceived as disengaged regarding climate policy. This is reflected in the country's 2001 withdrawal from the Kyoto Protocol, the failure during the Clinton and Bush administrations to enact policies to reduce these emissions, and Obama-era difficulties in reaching consensus on federal climate legislation. Throughout this period, states have steadily begun to fill the "policy gap" created by federal inaction. This has produced an increasingly diverse set of policies that address every sector of activity that generates greenhouse gases and collectively would reduce national emission levels if fully implemented.[20]

Many states are responsible for substantial amounts of greenhouse gas emissions, even by global standards. If all states were to secede and become independent nations, eighteen of them would rank among the top fifty nations in the world in terms of releases. In response, many states have adopted policies that promise to reduce their greenhouse gas releases, although they tend to also pursue these policies for other environmental rea-sons. Twenty-nine states and Washington, DC, have enacted "renewable portfolio standards (RPS)," mandating that a certain level of state electricity must come from such renewable sources as wind, geothermal, and solar. These policies generally follow a similar structure, although they vary in terms of the definition of eligible sources and the overall targets and timetables for expanding capacity.[21] For example, Hawaii has set a target of 40 percent renewables by 2030 whereas Kansas is aiming for a 20 percent level by 2020. Five states (Illinois, Minnesota, Nevada, Oregon, and West Virginia) have adopted 25-by-25 programs, reaching for 25 percent renewable capacity by 2025. In turn, twenty-six states have adopted an energy-efficiency equivalent of an RPS, mandating a steady increase in overall energy efficiency that in some cases is integrated with renewable energy mandates.[22]

California has been among the world's most active governments in addressing climate change. Along with renewable energy and energy-efficiency mandates, California pioneered legislation in 2002 that estab-lished the world's first carbon dioxide emissions standards for motor vehicles. This ultimately prodded federal government acceptance in 2009 of an ambitious national fuel economy standard and subsequent expansion in 2013. California also forged ahead with additional legislation, including the 2006 Global Warming Solutions Act. AB 32 imposes a statutory target to reduce statewide emissions to 1990 levels by 2020 and steadily reduce them 80 percent below 1990 levels by 2050. It proposes to attain those goals through an all-out policy assault on virtually every sector that generates greenhouse gases, including industry, electricity, transportation, agriculture, and residential activity. The state launched an ambitious cap-and-trade program in 2013 and added the Canadian province of Quebec as a formal partner the following year. California lost six potential state (Arizona, Montana, New Mexico, Oregon, Utah, and Washington) and three Canadian provincial (British Columbia, Manitoba, and Ontario) partners in political shifts in those jurisdictions after 2010 but revisited possible emissions trading alliances with some western states and subfederal jurisdictions in Canada, Mexico, and China in 2013–2014. On the East Coast, nine states launched a Regional Greenhouse Gas Initiative in 2009, featuring a cap-and-trade mechanism that also sought additional state and Canadian partners and tightened its emissions cap by more than 30 percent in 2013.

Taking It to the Federal Government

At the same time that states have eclipsed the federal government through new policies, they have also made increasingly aggressive use of litigation to attempt to force the federal government to take new steps or reconsider previous ones. In the George W. Bush administration, some states pursued litigation to attempt to push the federal government into taking bolder environmental steps; under Barack Obama, some states have turned to litigation to compel added federal efforts whereas others have sought to thwart new steps by federal environmental agencies. In both cases, state responses have been guided by an increasingly active set of state attorneys general who have begun to develop multistate litigation strategies to influence federal policy. Unlike their federal counterpart, most state attorneys general are elected officials, and their powers have expanded significantly since the mid-1970s. They frequently represent a political party different from that of the sitting governor and often use their powers as a base from which to seek higher office, most commonly governorships.

Collectively, these officials have increasingly become a force to be reckoned with, not only in their home states but also as they expand their engagement through challenges brought into the federal courts. In a 2014 Supreme Court case reviewing federal authority to establish greenhouse gas emission limits for power plants, fifteen states, including California and New York, implored the court to sustain federal regulatory authority. In turn, twelve states, including Texas and Michigan, filed a court brief that decried the federal plan as "one of the most brazen power grabs ever attempted by an administrative agency." No state has been as aggressive in combating federal environmental authority as Texas, where Attorney General Greg Abbott filed more than twenty suits attempting to block environmental actions by the

Obama administration. "I go to the office in the morning," quipped Abbott in 2014, "I sue the federal government, and I go home."

State Limits

Such a diverse set of policy initiatives would seem to augur well for the states' involvement in environmental policy. Any such enthusiasm must be tempered, however, by a continuing concern over how evenly that innovative vigor extends over the entire nation. One enduring rationale for giving the federal government so much authority in environmental policy is that states appear to face inherent limitations. Rather than a consistent, across-the-board pattern of dynamism, we see a more uneven pattern of performance than conventional wisdom might anticipate. Just as some states consistently strive for national leadership, others appear to seek the middle or bottom of the pack, seemingly doing as little as possible and rarely taking innovative steps. This imbalance becomes particularly evident when environmental problems are not confined to a specific state's boundaries. Many environmental issues are by definition transboundary, raising important questions of interstate and interregional equity in allocating responsibility for environmental protection.

Uneven State Performance

Many efforts to rank states according to their environmental regulatory rigor, institutional capacity, or general innovativeness find the same subset of states at the top of the list year after year. By contrast, a significant number of states consistently tend to fall much farther down the list, somewhat consistent with their placement in Table 2-1, raising questions as to their overall policy capacity and commitment. As political scientist William R. Lowry notes, "Not all states are responding appropriately to policy needs within their borders . . . If matching between need and response were always high and weak programs existed only where pollution was low, this would not be a problem. However, this is not the case."[23] Given all the hoopla surrounding the newfound dynamism of states racing to the top in environmental policy, there has been remarkably little analysis of the performance of states that not only fail to crack top-ten rankings but may view racing to the bottom as an economic development strategy. Such a downward race may be particularly attractive during recessions, reflected in recent efforts in states such as West Virginia, Michigan, and Wisconsin to weaken dramatically the implementation of existing policies with the express goal of promoting economic growth by creating an environment friendlier to industry.[24]

What we know more generally about state policy commitment should surely give one pause over any claims that state dynamism is truly national in scope. Despite considerable economic growth in formerly poor regions, such as the Southeast, substantial variation endures among state governments in their rates of public expenditure, including their total and per capita expenditures on environmental protection.[25] Such disparities are consistent with studies of state political culture and social capital, which indicate vast differences in probable state receptivity to governmental efforts to foster environmental improvement.

Although many states have unveiled exciting new programs, EPA Inspector General reports and other external reviews generate serious questions about how effectively states handle core functions either delegated to them under federal programs or left exclusively to their oversight. Studies of water quality program implementation have found that states use highly variable water quality standards in areas such as sewage contamination, groundwater protection, nonpoint water pollution from diffuse sources, wetland preservation, fish advisories, and beach closures. Inconsistencies abound in reporting accuracy, suggesting that national assessments of water quality trends that rely on data from state reports may be highly suspect.[26] More than half of the states lack comprehensive water management and drought response plans, and several with such plans have not revised them in many years.[27]

Even in many high-saliency cases, such as Everglades protection, states have sought a federal rescue rather than taking serious unilateral action. As political scientist Sheldon Kamieniecki notes, Florida's "state government, which has been continuously pressured from all sides, has waffled in its intentions to improve the wetlands ecosystem in South Florida."[28] Agricultural interests, particularly those promoting sugar production in this region, have proven formidable opponents of major restoration that would restrict their access to massive volumes of water.[29] Similar issues have arisen as states have struggled in recent years to formulate policies to reduce potential risks to groundwater supplies from shale gas and oil development, with some states such as Pennsylvania racing in the opposite direction as Illinois, downplaying environmental concerns and local government reservations in order to maximize immediate development.[30]

Comparable problems have emerged in state enforcement of air quality and waste management programs. Despite efforts in some states to integrate and streamline permitting, many states have extensive backlogs in the permit programs they operate and lack any real indication of facility compliance with various regulatory standards. Measurement of the impact of state programs on environmental outcomes remains imprecise in many areas. Existing indicators confirm enormous variation among states, although we likely know less about such variation than in the 1990s, given that the EPA lacks funding and staff to continue collecting state-by-state data in many areas of environmental policy. State governments—alongside their local counterparts—have understandably claimed much of the credit for increasing solid waste recycling rates from a national average of 6.6 percent in 1970 to 16 percent in 1990 to 33.8 percent in 2009. At the same time, state recycling policy and performance varies markedly, and the EPA last updated its estimate of national trends in 2009. Growing gaps in state and federal data gathering and dissemination capacity raise sobering questions about the transparency of environmental policy and any ability to assess important indicators of performance.

There was also growing indication in some states during the first years of the 2010s that environmental policy faced major challenges in cases where power shifted rapidly toward exclusive Republican control. North Carolina was an increasingly prominent example of this pattern after Republicans won both legislative chambers after the 2010 election for the first time since the 1870s and Republican Pat McCrory was elected governor two years later. This shift produced a Regulatory Reform Act that emphasized "customer service" for regulated parties and reversed numerous established provisions for air and water quality. The state's new leadership also embraced formal efforts to thwart new federal climate policies and banned state agency use of climate change science to shape coastal protection policy. Controversy surrounding these changes reached new heights in early 2014 when a pipe ruptured at a Duke Energy power plant and led to the release of thirty thousand tons of coal ash into the Dan River. In this case, political conflict only escalated given Governor McCrory's long-standing prior employment with Duke Energy and failure to disclose his considerable stock holdings in the utility before the incident. Conflict extended to other areas when new shale development legislation enacted in June 2014 bore considerable resemblance to the controversial form developed two years earlier in Pennsylvania. Critics of Governor McCrory and Republican legislative leaders decried a policymaking process that largely excluded environmental group views and those of Democratic legislators.[31]

Enduring Federal Dependency

More sweeping assertions of state resurgence are undermined further by the penchant of many states to cling to organizational designs and program priorities set in Washington, DC. Some states have demonstrated that far-reaching agency reorganization and other integrative policies can be pursued without significant opposition—or grant reduction—from the federal government, but the vast majority of states continue to adhere to a medium-based pollution control framework for agency organization that contributes to enduring programmatic fragmentation. Although a growing number of state officials speak favorably about shifting toward integrative approaches, many remain hard pressed to demonstrate how their states have begun to move in that direction. Many Clinton-era federal initiatives to give states more freedom to innovate were used to streamline operations rather than foster prevention or integration. The Bush administration weakened many of these initiatives and, more generally, proved extremely reluctant to give states expanded authority or encouragement to innovate. The Obama administration was not initially seen as fostering state innovation and capacity, although it pumped considerable short-term environmental funding into states through economic stimulus support in 2009–2011 and began to outline in 2013–2014 a climate policy that could create considerable incentive for creative state approaches.

Indeed, a good deal of the most innovative state-level activity has been at least partially underwritten through federal grants, which serve to stimulate additional state environmental spending.[32] In contrast, in Canada, where central government grant assistance—and regulatory presence—is extremely limited, provinces have proven somewhat less innovative than their American state counterparts. Although a number of states have developed fee systems to cover the majority of their operational costs, many continue to rely heavily on federal grants to fund some core environmental protection activities. States have continued to receive other important types of federal support, including grants and technical assistance to complete "state-of-the-state" environment reports, undertake comparative risk assessment projects, launch inventories and action plans for greenhouse gas reductions, and implement some voluntary federal programs. On the whole, states have annually received between one-quarter and one-third of their total environmental and natural resource program funding from federal grants in recent years, although a few states (such as Colorado, Hawaii, Idaho, North Dakota, West Virginia, and Utah) relied on the federal government for between 40 and 70 percent of their total funding in 2012–2013. The overall level of federal support dropped to 23 percent in 2008, increased to 30 percent three years later due to temporary injections of federal stimulus dollars, but declined to 25 percent in 2013. It appeared likely to drop further due to anticipated federal budget cuts.[33]

Furthermore, for all the opprobrium heaped on the federal government in environmental policy, it has provided states with at least four other forms of valuable assistance, some of which has contributed directly to the resurgence and innovation of state environmental policy. First, federal development in 1986 of the Toxics Release Inventory, modeled after programs initially attempted in Maryland and New Jersey, has emerged as an important component of many of the most promising state policy initiatives. This program has generated considerable data concerning toxic releases and provided states with a vital data source for exploring alternative regulatory approaches.[34] Many state pollution prevention programs would be unthinkable without such an annual information source. This program has also provided lessons for states to develop supplemental disclosure registries for greenhouse gases and may also do so for chemical use disclosure related to hydraulic fracturing.[35]

Second, states remain almost totally dependent on the federal government for essential insights gained through research and development. Each year, the federal government outspends the states in environmental research and development by substantial amounts, and states have shown little inclination to assume this burden by funding research programs tailored to their particular technological and informational needs.

Third, many successful efforts to coordinate environmental protection on a multistate, regional basis have received substantial federal input and support. A series of initiatives in the Chesapeake Bay, the Great Lakes Basin, and New England have received considerable acclaim for tackling difficult issues and forging regional partnerships; federal collaboration—via grants, technical assistance, coordination, and efforts to unify regional standards—with states has proven useful in these cases.[36] By contrast, other major bioregions, including Puget Sound, the Gulf of Mexico, the Columbia River system, and the

Mississippi River Basin, have lacked comparable federal participation and have generally not experienced creative interstate partnerships. Their experience contradicts the popular thesis that regional coordination is most likely in the absence of federal engagement, and two of the three recent regional initiatives to reduce greenhouse gases have struggled to endure in the absence of federal engagement or support.

Fourth, the EPA's ham-handedness is legendary, but its role in overseeing state-level program implementation looks far more constructive when examining the role played by the agency's ten regional offices. Most state-level interaction with the EPA involves such regional offices, which employ approximately two-thirds of the total EPA workforce. Relations between state and regional officials are generally more cordial and constructive than those between state and central EPA officials, and such relations may even be, in some instances, characterized by high levels of mutual involvement and trust.[37] Surveys of state environmental officials confirm that they have a more positive relationship with regional rather than central agency staff.[38] Regional offices have played a central role in many of the most promising state-level innovations, including those in Minnesota and New Jersey. Their involvement may include formal advocacy on behalf of the state with central headquarters, direct collaboration on meshing state initiatives with federal requirements, and special grant support or technical assistance. This appears to be particularly common when regional office heads have prior state experience, as demonstrated in a number of instances in the Clinton, Bush, and Obama administrations.

The Interstate Environmental Balance of Trade

States may be structurally ill equipped to handle a large range of environmental concerns. In particular, they may be reluctant to invest significant energies to tackle problems that might literally migrate to another state or nation in the absence of intervention. The days of state agencies being captured securely in the hip pockets of major industries are probably long gone, reflecting fundamental changes in state government.[39] Nonetheless, state regulatory dynamism may diminish when cross-boundary transfer is likely.

The state imperative of economic development clearly contributes to this phenomenon. As states increasingly devise economic development strategies that resemble the industrial policies of European Union nations, a range of scholars have concluded they are far more deeply committed to strategies that promote investment or development than to those that involve social service provision or public health promotion.[40] A number of states offer incentives in excess of $50,000 per new job to prospective developers and have intensified efforts to retain jobs in the struggling manufacturing sector. Environmental protection can be eminently compatible with economic development goals, promoting overall quality of life and general environmental attractiveness that entices private investment. In many states, the tourism industry has played an active role in seeking strong environmental programs designed to maintain natural assets. In some instances, states may be keen to take action that may produce internal environmental benefits while not having much localized economic impact. California and other states that have formally endorsed setting strict carbon emissions standards from vehicles, for example, have very few jobs to lose in the vehicle manufacturing sector while also seeing potential economic advantages if they can take a lead role nationally in developing alternative transportation technologies.

But much of what a state might undertake in environmental policy may largely benefit other states or regions, thereby reducing an individual state's incentive to take meaningful action. In fact, in many instances, states continue to pursue a "we make it, you take it" strategy. As political scientist William T. Gormley Jr. notes, sometimes "states can readily export their problems to other states," resulting in potentially serious environmental "balance of trade" problems.[41] In such situations, states may be inclined to export environmental contaminants to other states while enjoying any economic benefits to be derived from the activity that generated the contamination. One careful study of state air quality enforcement found no evidence of reduced effort along state borders but a measurable decline in effort along state borders with Mexican states or Canadian provinces.[42]

Such cross-boundary transfers take many forms and may be particularly prevalent in environmental policy areas in which long-distance migration of pollutants is most likely. Air quality policy has long fit this pattern. States such as Ohio and Pennsylvania, for example, have depended heavily on burning massive quantities of coal to meet energy demands. Prevailing winds invariably transfer pollutants from this activity to other regions, particularly New England, leading to serious concern about acid deposition and related contamination threats. At times, states throughout the nation have utilized so-called dispersion enhancement as one approach to improve local air quality. Average industrial stack height in the United States soared from 243 feet in 1960 to 730 feet in 1980.[43] Although this increase resulted in significant air quality improvement in many areas near elevated stacks, it generally served to disperse air pollution problems elsewhere. It also contributed to the growing problem of airborne toxics that ultimately pollute water or land in other regions. Between 80 and 90 percent of many of the most dangerous toxic substances found in Lake Superior, for example, stem from air deposition, much of which is generated outside of the Great Lakes Basin.

Interstate conflicts, often becoming protracted battles in the federal courts, have endured in recent decades as states allege they are recipients of such unwanted "imports." In April 2014, the Supreme Court voted decisively to reinstate the EPA's Cross-State Air Pollution Rule, the agency's "good neighbor" provision that restricts cross-border exports of nitrogen oxides and sulfur dioxide emissions from twenty-eight midwestern and southern states into the Northeast. No region of the nation or environmental media appears immune from this kind of conflict. Prolonged battles between Alabama, Florida, and Georgia over access to waters from Lake Lanier and six rivers that cross their borders, for example, reached new intensity in recent years, resulting in extended mediation, litigation, and uncertainty about long-term approaches. Growing water scarcity linked to increased demand for water and extended drought in many regions has only exacerbated these conflicts.

Perhaps nowhere is the problem of interstate transfer more evident than in the disposal of solid, hazardous, and nuclear wastes. States have generally retained enormous latitude to devise their own systems of waste management and facility siting, working either independently or in concert with neighbors. Many states, including a number of those usually deemed among the most innovative and committed environmentally, continue to generate substantial quantities of waste and have struggled to establish comprehensive treatment, storage, and disposal capacity. Instead, out-of-state (and -region) export has been an increasingly common pattern, with a system that often resembles a shell game in which waste is ultimately deposited in the least resistant state or facility at any given moment. This pattern is repeated in emerging areas, such as disposal of wastes generated by hydraulic fracturing procedures, perhaps best illustrated in the migration of wastes generated in western Pennsylvania to deep-injection wells in eastern Ohio. This has triggered considerable controversy in Ohio, especially following a significant expansion of earthquake activity in areas near wells that accept large amounts of out-of-state fracking wastes.

No area of waste management, however, is as contentious as nuclear waste. In the case of so-called high-level wastes, intensely contaminated materials from nuclear power plants which require between ten thousand and a hundred thousand years of isolation, the federal government and the vast majority of states have supported a thirty-year effort to transfer all of these wastes to a geological repository in Nevada. Ferocious resistance by Nevada and concerns among states who would host transfer shipments have continued to scuttle this approach, leaving each of the hundred nuclear reactors spread across thirty-one states a *de facto* storage site. In the case of "low level" wastes, greater in volume but posing a less severe threat, states received considerable latitude from Washington in the early 1980s to develop a strategy for creating a series of regional sites, as well as access to funds to develop facilities. But subsequent siting efforts were riddled with conflict, and the growing reality is that increasing amounts of such waste must be stored near its point of generation.[44] One facility in western Texas has emerged as a potential "host" for such waste, though it is remote, actually closest to settled communities across the New Mexico border and thousands of miles away from the bulk of generated waste.

Rethinking Environmental Federalism

Federalism scholars and some political officials have explored models for constructive sharing of authority in the American federal system, many of which attempt to build on the respective strengths of varied governmental levels and create a more functional intergovernmental partnership.[45] But it has generally proven difficult to translate these ideas into actual policy, particularly in the area of environmental policy. Perhaps the most ambitious effort to reallocate intergovernmental functions in environmental protection took place in the 1990s during the Clinton administration, under the National Environmental Performance Partnership System (NEPPS). This effort was linked to Clinton's attempts to "reinvent government," heralded by proponents as a way to give states substantially greater administrative flexibility over many federal environmental programs if they could demonstrate innovation and actual performance that improved environmental outcomes. NEPPS also offered Performance Partnership Grants that would allow participating states to concentrate resources on innovative projects that promised environmental performance improvements.

More than forty states elected to participate in the NEPPS program, which required extensive negotiations between state and federal agency counterparts. Although a few promising examples of innovation can be noted, this initiative failed to approach its ambitious goals, and in the words of two recent analysts, "there have been few real gains."[46] NEPPS stemmed from an administrative action by a single president and thereby lacked the clout of legislation or resilient political support. In response, federal authorities often resisted altering established practices and failed to assume the innovative role anticipated by NEPPS proponents. In turn, states proved considerably less amenable to innovation than expected. They tended to balk at any possibility that the federal government might establish—and publicize—serious performance measures that would evaluate their effectiveness and environmental outcomes.

Ultimately many NEPPS agreements were signed, especially in the waning years of the Clinton administration, and these generally remain in place. But the Bush administration never pursued NEPPS with enthusiasm, and the Obama administration has made little effort to revitalize this program. It thereby remains a very modest test of the viability of accountable decentralization, whereby state autonomy is increased formally in exchange for demonstrable performance. As we shall see, however, one Obama-era initiative may provide a new test of the possibility for a more flexible and functional environmental federalism.

Challenges to State Routines

The future role of states in environmental policy may be further shaped by four additional developments. First, given the impact of the Great Recession, it remains increasingly unclear whether states will have sufficient fiscal resources to maintain core environmental protection functions and continue to consider new initiatives. Most states enjoyed generally robust fiscal health during the middle years of the 2000s, with growing tax revenues producing healthy budgets that helped facilitate a period of considerable state environmental policy innovation. However, state fiscal conditions turned increasingly gloomy in subsequent years, as the precipitous economic decline and twin crises in the housing and banking sectors served to shrink state coffers and prompt consideration of substantial program cuts in many statehouses. Federal stimulus funds provided some stabilization in 2009–2011, but significant budget reductions followed in many states, leading to an overall reduction in state government employment outside the education sector of 6.8 percent between 2008 and 2012.[47] In turn, pressures for expanded spending in certain domains, such as medical care and unemployment insurance, further threatened any restoration of state fiscal support for environmental protection as the economic recovery accelerated.

Second, the 2010, 2012, and 2014 elections reversed a long-standing pattern of divided, joint-party control of most state governments in favor of sweeping control by one party, with particularly strong gains among Republicans. As of 2015, Republicans controlled both legislative chambers and the governorship in 23 states. Of the remaining states, only seven featured exclusive Democratic control of the legislative and executive branches, 18 had divided partisan control, and the remaining two included either an independent governor or nonpartisan legislature. This represented the largest Republican domination over state government in generations and also the most unified period in which one party controlled all state functions in many decades. This raised the possibility of major shifts in environmental priorities in various states such as North Carolina and expanding heterogeneity in the kinds of state policies produced given such partisan divides.

Third, one early testing ground for potential environmental policy shifts was reflected in a flurry of new legislative proposals in 2013–2014 to either downsize or repeal many of the twenty-nine operational state renewable portfolio standards. More than 120 reform bills were introduced in 2013 alone, and while many of these involved relatively minor modifications, an "all-out attack" was launched in twenty states, facilitated by a standardized "Electricity Freedom Act" template produced by the Republican-leaning American Legislative Exchange Council. However, none of these repeal efforts passed, even in a bitterly contentious battle in Kansas, and the only eight RPS bills that were enacted in 2013 involved expansion or technical modification of existing policies.[48]

Fourth, states began to adjust by mid-decade from somewhat earlier expectations that major new federal environmental legislation or changes in established federal statutes might be politically feasible. The years 2009 and 2010 marked a period in which states faced not only economic decline but enormous uncertainty over whether many of their homegrown environmental policy initiatives would be eliminated by far-reaching federal legislative action. This form of "contested federalism" had a somewhat chilling effect on new initiatives, compounded further by the realization of likely state budget cuts and possible challenge from incoming state government leaders.[49] More recent years suggest not only a likelihood of declining federal financial support for state environmental operations but also a marked reduction in the prospects for any new or revised federal environmental legislation. Indeed, the one exception to this pattern was unilateral action by the executive branch, as will be discussed below.

Looking Ahead

Amid the continued squabbling over the proper role of the federal government vis-à-vis the states in environmental policy, remarkably little effort has been made to sort out which functions might best be concentrated in Washington and which ones ought to be transferred to state capitals. Some former governors and federal legislators of both parties offered useful proposals during the 1990s that might allocate such responsibilities more constructively than at present. These proposals have been supplemented by thoughtful scholarly works by think tanks, political scientists, economists, and other policy analysts. Interestingly, many of these experts concur that environmental protection policy defies easy designation as warranting extreme centralization or decentralization. Instead, many observers endorse a process of selective decentralization, one leading to an appropriately balanced set of responsibilities across governmental levels. It might be particularly useful to revisit these options before taking major new environmental policy steps, including any far-reaching effort to retract state policy commitments.

In moving toward a more functional environmental federalism, certain broad design principles might be useful to consider. The Clinton-era experiment with NEPPS was billed as a major attempt at such reallocation, but a more substantial effort would require establishment of state environmental performance measures that were publicized and utilized to determine a more appropriate allocation of functions. One such opportunity to move in this direction could emerge through ongoing negotiations between the EPA and the fifty states over federal efforts to establish a national permitting system for greenhouse gases. Given the collapse of serious congressional deliberations over climate policy in 2010, the Obama administration moved ahead with a process to cap emissions from new power plants, and initial permitting began in 2013.

The administration's selection of Section 111(d) of the 1990 Clean Air Act Amendments as its climate compliance tool meant that states must develop plans for emissions reductions from each new plant through existing state air quality "implementation plans." Failure to do so would lead to federal imposition of reduction requirements and a possible federal takeover of permitting operations. Sixteen states joined an effort by Nebraska Attorney General Jon Bruning in late 2013 arguing that they should have complete latitude to determine what would be acceptable ways to respond to this federal requirement. EPA Administrator Gina McCarthy repeatedly responded by lauding those states that have taken early steps to reduce greenhouse gas emissions but noting that ultimate responsibility for approval of state plans rests with the federal government. "The states have been leaders, I don't need EPA to tell them what to do," she said in a December 2013 speech. That said, McCarthy also noted that "it is not the intent of the federal government to take over their duties, but if they don't perform as the Clean Air Act requires them to, we will be forced to do that."

In 2014, McCarthy returned to these themes in introducing the next installment of this climate approach, unveiling a "Clean Power Plan" that would set different state emission reduction targets that would collectively produce a national reduction of 30 percent in greenhouse gas emissions from 2005 levels in the power sector by 2030. These reductions would be phased in over time, and states were given many options for achieving them, including cap and trade, carbon taxes and fees, and energy efficiency and renewable energy requirements. Initial state plans were required to be submitted to the EPA by 2016, beginning a process of intergovernmental negotiation.[50] The agency also encouraged multiple states to work collaboratively, noting the possibility that existing regional programs could expand to include other states.

While some states quickly adopted statutes and resolutions challenging a strong federal role and others such as Texas lobbed multiple litigation and administrative hurdles in front of the advancing federal effort, other states moved in a very different direction. Those states with an established track record of climate policy development, including commitment to a cap-and-trade program, have advanced the case for "equivalency." Under this approach, they assembled empirical evidence that they already operate programs designed to accomplish all (or at least some) of the EPA's goals and argued that they should be rewarded for that early engagement with maximum flexibility while the federal agency could then focus on laggard states. This would be a model of decentralization linked to measurable performance, perhaps consistent with larger goals of federalism reform. Some midwestern states began in 2014 to explore how best to follow this model, including a possible "carbon fee" under the auspices of the Midwestern Power Sector Collaborative, whereas both California and Regional Greenhouse Gas Initiative states began to openly court other states to join as cap-and-trade partners. According to Mary D. Nichols, director of the California Air Resources Board and one of the leading advocates for this form of selective decentralization, "When you step back from the fray, the seemingly disjointed pieces of climate policy are actually coming together—perhaps not quite seamlessly or uniformly—but in a pattern. And you can see that we have been creating a very lovely and effective patchwork quilt."[51] However, not all states were so sanguine about this emerging national tapestry or the potential changes they might have to make under emerging federal regulations.

Beyond this initiative, a more discerning environmental federalism might also begin by concentrating federal regulatory energies on problems that are clearly national in character. Many air and water pollution problems, for example, are by definition cross-boundary concerns unlikely to be resolved by a series of unilateral state actions. In contrast, problems such as protecting indoor air quality and cleanup of abandoned hazardous waste dumps may present more geographically confinable challenges; they are perhaps best handled through substantial delegation of authority to states. As policy analyst John D. Donahue notes, "Most waste sites are situated within a single state, and stay there," yet are governed by highly centralized Superfund legislation, in direct contrast to more decentralized programs in environmental areas in which cross-boundary transfers are prevalent.[52] Under a more rational system, the federal regulatory presence might intensify as the likelihood of cross-boundary contaminant transfer escalates. Emerging issues such as environmental protection of expanded shale gas and oil drilling present an opportunity to test this approach, combining a highly decentralized system of relatively small and localized drilling operations with considerable cross-border movement of wastes and chemicals as well as transport of natural gas and oil via rail and pipelines. Such an initial attempt to sort out functions might be reinforced by federal policy efforts to encourage states or regions to take responsibility for internally generated environmental problems rather than tacitly allow exportation to occur. In the area of waste management, for example, federal per-mile fees on waste shipments would provide a disincentive for long-distance transfer, instead encouraging states, regions, and waste generators to either develop their own capacity or pursue waste reduction options more aggressively.

In many areas, shared federal and state roles likely remain appropriate, reflecting the inherent complexity of many environmental problems. Effective intergovernmental partnerships are already well established in certain areas. But even if essentially sound, these partnerships could clearly benefit from further maturation and development. Alongside the sorting-out activities discussed earlier in this section, both federal and state governments could do much more to promote creative sharing of policy ideas and environmental data, ultimately developing a system informed by "best practices." Such information has received remarkably limited dissemination across state and regional boundaries, and potentially considerable advantage is to be gained from an active process of intergovernmental policy learning. More broadly, the federal government might explore other ways to encourage states to work cooperatively, especially on common boundary problems. As we have discussed, state capacity to find creative solutions to pressing environmental problems has been on the ascendance. However, as Lord Bryce concluded many decades ago, cooperation among states does not arise automatically, although at times it can, in the words of Mary D. Nichols, "produce a very lovely and effective patchwork quilt."[53]

Suggested Websites

Environmental Council of the States (www.ecos.org) The Environmental Council of the States represents the lead environmental protection agencies of all fifty states. The site contains access to state environmental data and periodic "Green Reports" on major issues.

Center for Local, State, and Urban Policy (www.closup.umich.edu) The Center for Local, State, and Urban Policy's Energy and Environmental Policy Initiative places a strong emphasis on state and local policy issues. It also features public opinion surveys that emphasize state and intergovernmental questions in collaboration with the Muhlenberg Institute of Public Opinion.

National Conference of State Legislatures (www.ncsl.org) The National Conference of State Legislatures conducts extensive research on a wide range of environmental, energy, and natural resource issues for its primary constituency and state legislators, as well as the general citizenry. The organization offers an extensive set of publications, including specialized reports.

National Governors Association (www.nga.org) The National Governors Association maintains an active research program concerning state environmental protection, natural resource, and energy concerns. It has placed special emphasis on maintaining a database on state "best practices," which it uses to promote diffusion of promising innovations and to demonstrate state government capacity in federal policy deliberations.

Stateline (www.stateline.org) The Pew Charitable Trusts sponsors this site, which provides a number of useful vantage points for examining state politics and policy, including special sections for environmental and energy policy. This site is particularly strong in providing information on state election results and offering links to articles about state issues published in periodicals across the nation.

Notes

1. John Kincaid and Richard L. Cole, "Citizen Attitudes toward Issues of Federalism in Canada, Mexico and the United States," *Publius: The Journal of Federalism* 41 (Winter 2011): 53–75.
2. Paul Teske, *Regulation in the States* (Washington, DC: Brookings Institution Press, 2004), 9.
3. R. Steven Brown, *State Environmental Expenditures* (Washington, DC: Environmental Council of the States, 2008).
4. Martha Derthick, "Compensatory Federalism," in *Greenhouse Governance*, ed. Barry Rabe (Washington, DC: Brookings Institution Press, 2010), 66.
5. Christopher McGrory Klyza and David Sousa, *American Environmental Policy: Beyond Gridlock*, updated and expanded edition (Cambridge, MA: MIT Press, 2013), 247.
6. Stephen Goldsmith and Donald F. Kettl, eds., *Unlocking the Power of Networks* (Washington, DC: Brookings Institution Press, 2009).
7. Elinor Ostrom, *Governing the Commons: The Evolution of Institutions for Collective Action* (New York: Cambridge University Press, 1990); Ostrom, *A Polycentric Approach to Climate Change* (Washington, DC: World Bank, 2009).
8. Barry G. Rabe, *Statehouse and Greenhouse: The Emerging Politics of American Climate Change Policy* (Washington, DC: Brookings Institution Press, 2004).
9. Michelle Pautz and Sara Rinfret, *The Lilliputians of Environmental Regulation: The Perspective of State Regulators* (New York: Routledge, 2013).
10. Andrew Karch, *Democratic Laboratories: Policy Diffusion among the American States* (Ann Arbor: University of Michigan Press, 2007).
11. Evan J. Ringquist, *Environmental Protection at the State Level: Politics and Progress in Controlling Pollution* (Armonk, NY: M. E. Sharpe, 1993).
12. Kathy Kinsey, "Neither of These Bills Address the Law's Failings," *Environmental Forum* 31 (May–June 2014): 48.
13. Linda Breggin, "Broad State Efforts on Toxic Controls," *Environmental Forum* 28 (March–April 2011): 10.

14. Andy Kim, "Time to Ban BPA?" *Governing* (March 2011): 13.
15. Christopher Bosso, ed., *Governing Uncertainty: Environmental Regulation in the Age of Nanotechnology* (Washington, DC: Resources for the Future, 2010), 105–30.
16. Barry G. Rabe, "Shale Play Politics: The Intergovernmental Odyssey of American Shale Governance," *Environmental Science & Technology* 48 (August 2014): 8369–75.
17. Barry G. Rabe and Christopher Borick, "Carbon Taxation and Policy Labeling: Experience from American States and Canadian Provinces," *Review of Policy Research* 29 (May 2012): 358–82.
18. R. Steven Brown, *Status of State Environmental Agency Budgets: 2011–2013* (Washington, DC: Environmental Council of the States, 2012).
19. Sanya Carley, "The Era of State Energy Policy Innovation: A Review of Policy Instruments," *Review of Policy Research* 28 (May 2011): 265–94.
20. Neil Craik, Isabel Studer, and Debora Van Nijnatten, *Climate Change Policy in North America* (Toronto, ON: University of Toronto Press, 2013).
21. Linda Breggin, "Portfolio Standards Entrench across US," *Environmental Forum* (January–February 2014): 10.
22. Annie Downs and Celia Cui, *Energy Efficiency Resource Standards: A New Progress Report on State Experience* (Washington, DC: American Council for an Energy-Efficient Economy, 2014).
23. William R. Lowry, *The Dimensions of Federalism: State Governments and Pollution Control Policies*, rev. ed. (Durham, NC: Duke University Press, 1997), 125.
24. Evan Osnos, "Chemical Valley," *New Yorker* (April 7, 2014): 38–49; Keith Matheny, "Did State Agency Lobby to Bend Rules on Pollutants at Steel Mill?" *Detroit Free Press*, May 5, 2014; Trip Gabriel, "Ash Spill Shows How Watchdog Was Defanged," *New York Times*, February 28, 2014.
25. Brown, *Status of State Environmental Agency Budgets*.
26. John A. Hoornbeek, "The Promise and Pitfalls of Devolution: Water Pollution Policies in the American States," *Publius: The Journal of Federalism* 35 (Winter 2005): 87–114.
27. Shama Ghamkar and J. Mitchell Pickerill, "The State of American Federalism 2011–2012," *Publius: The Journal of Federalism* 42 (Summer 2012): 357–86.
28. Sheldon Kamieniecki, *Corporate America and Environmental Policy* (Palo Alto, CA: Stanford University Press, 2006), 253.
29. William Lowry, *Repairing Paradise: The Restoration of Nature in America's National Parks* (Washington, DC: Brookings Institution Press, 2010), Chapter 4.
30. Barry G. Rabe and Christopher Borick, "Conventional Politics for Unconventional Drilling?" *Review of Policy Research* 30 (May 2013): 321–40.
31. Chris Kardish, "A Hard Right," *Governing* (July 2014): 32–39; Daniel Bush and Josh Kurtz, "Wrenching Political Change Comes to N.C., and Energy Is Part of the Struggle," *E&E News*, May 22, 2014.
32. Benjamin Y. Clark and Andrew B. Whitford, "Does More Federal Environmental Funding Increase or Decrease States' Efforts?" *Journal of Policy Analysis and Management* 30 (Winter 2010): 136–52.
33. Brown, *Status of State Environmental Agency Budgets*.
34. Michael E. Kraft, Mark Stephan, and Troy D. Abel, *Coming Clean: Information Disclosure and Environmental Performance* (Cambridge, MA: MIT Press, 2011).
35. Matthew J. Hoffmann, *Climate Governance at the Crossroads* (New York: Oxford University Press, 2011); Michael E. Kraft, "Using Information Disclosure to Achieve Policy Goals: How Experience with the Toxics Release Inventory Can Inform Action on Natural Gas Fracturing," *Issues in Energy and Environmental Policy* 6 (March 2014).

36. Paul Posner, "Networks in the Shadow of Government: The Chesapeake Bay Program," in *Unlocking the Power of Networks*, ed. Stephen Goldsmith and Donald F. Kettl (Washington, DC: Brookings Institution Press, 2009), Chapter 4; Barry G. Rabe and Marc Gaden, "Sustainability in a Regional Context: The Case of the Great Lakes Basin," in *Toward Sustainable Communities: Transition and Transformations in Environmental Policy*, ed. Daniel A. Mazmanian and Michael E. Kraft, 2nd ed. (Cambridge, MA: MIT Press, 2009), 266–69.

37. Denise Scheberle, *Federalism and Environmental Policy: Trust and the Politics of Implementation*, rev. ed. (Washington, DC: Georgetown University Press, 2004), Chapter 7.

38. Michelle Pautz and Sarah Rinfret, *The Lilliputians of Environmental Regulations*, 50–51.

39. Paul Teske, *Regulation in the States*; Pautz and Rinfret, *The Lilliputians of Environmental Regulation*.

40. John D. Donahue, *Disunited States: What's at Stake as Washington Fades and the States Take the Lead* (New York: Basic Books, 1997); Paul E. Peterson, *The Price of Federalism* (Washington, DC: Brookings Institution Press, 1995), Chapter 4.

41. William T. Gormley Jr., "Intergovernmental Conflict on Environmental Policy: The Attitudinal Connection," *Western Political Quarterly* 40 (1987): 298–99.

42. David M. Konisky and Neal D. Woods, "Exporting Air Pollution? Regulatory Enforcement and Environmental Free Riding in the United States," *Political Research Quarterly* 63 (2010): 771–82.

43. Lowry, *The Dimensions of Federalism*, 45.

44. Daniel J. Sherman, *Not Here, Not There, Not Anywhere* (Washington, DC: Resources for the Future, 2011).

45. Alice Rivlin, "Rethinking Federalism for More Effective Governance," *Publius: The Journal of Federalism* 42 (Summer 2012): 357–86; Jenna Bednar, *The Robust Federation* (New York: Cambridge University Press, 2008); R. Daniel Keleman, *The Rules of Federalism* (Cambridge, MA: Harvard University Press, 2004).

46. Klyza and Sousa, *American Environmental Policy, 1990–2006*, 253.

47. Lucy Dadayan and Donald Boyd, *The Depth and Length of Cuts in State-Local Government Employment Is Unprecedented* (Albany, NY: Rockefeller Institute of Government, 2013).

48. Jonathan Walters, "A Second Wind," *Governing* (April 2014); Breggin, "Portfolio Standards Entrench across US."

49. Barry G. Rabe, "Contested Federalism and American Climate Policy," *Publius: The Journal of Federalism* 40 (Summer 2011): 1–28.

50. Paul Hibbard, Andrea Okie, and Susan Tierney, *EPA's Clean Power Plan: States' Tools for Reducing Costs and Increasing Benefits to Consumers* (Boston: Analysis Group, 2014).

51. Mary D. Nichols, "Policymaking Is a Patchwork Quilt," Presentation at the CAPCOA Climate Change Forum, San Francisco (August 30, 2010).

52. Donahue, *Disunited States*, 65.

53. Nichols, "Policymaking Is a Patchwork Quilt."

3

Environmental Advocacy in the Obama Years
Assessing New Strategies for Political Change
Matthew C. Nisbet

O n a cold day in February 2013, on the National Mall in Washington, DC, an estimated thirty thousand people gathered to protest the Keystone XL pipeline, the controversial project intended to link the Alberta oil sands in Canada with Gulf of Mexico refineries and distribution centers in the United States. "All I ever wanted to see was a movement of people to stop climate change," declared writer turned 350.org activist group leader Bill McKibben, addressing the crowd from a stage. "And now," he told them, "I've seen it."[1] Minor political players just three years earlier as the major environmental groups failed to pass congressional cap-and-trade legislation, McKibben and 350.org have in the years since redefined the way environmental groups practice politics, generating levels of grassroots activism not seen since the first Earth Day four decades ago. To do so, McKibben has melded his storytelling ability as a popular writer with 350.org's innovative methods of Internet-enabled political organizing.

These grassroots strategies have been joined by a new approach to electoral politics, bankrolled by California billionaire Tom Steyer. Adopting campaign-financing methods first employed by his billionaire counterparts on the right, Steyer in 2013 launched the super PAC NextGen Climate. Promising to spend upwards of $100 million in the 2014 Senate and governor's races, Steyer's goal is to make denial of climate change by Republican candidates politically unacceptable and action on the issue a priority among Democrats, all the while setting the stage for climate change to be a dominant point of contention during the 2016 presidential election.

These complementary outside-the-Beltway strategies address a long-standing weakness on the part of the national environmental movement and the major DC-based groups that, despite immense budgets, hundreds of highly credentialed staff, and millions of members, have struggled to shape public opinion or to generate grassroots pressure on elected officials. Instead, these national groups have specialized in insider coalition building, think tank–style analysis, and lobbying. Yet, the defeat in 2010 of cap-and-trade legislation, after years of planning and the expenditure of vast financial resources, forced many environmental leaders and their funders to refocus attention on the need for an "outside" game and a new approach to environmental advocacy.

In the latter years of Barack Obama's presidency, the effort to mobilize public opinion and grassroots activism on climate change has led to a broader shift in environmental politics, as environmental organizations and their allies devote ever greater resources to shaping the outcome of elections, framing debates in stark moral terms, and melding innovative Internet-based strategies with traditional face-to-face field organizing. Yet as I review in this chapter, on the road to meaningfully dealing with climate change and other environmental problems, this new brand of pressure politics as practiced by 350.org, NextGen Climate, and their allies among national environmental groups is not without its potential trade-offs, flaws, and weaknesses.

Most notably, critics charge that although blocking the Keystone XL pipeline and divesting from fossil fuel companies make for potent symbolic goals, they detract from more important goals such as the passage of new federal rules limiting emissions from coal-fired power plants, and promoting government investment in a broad range of cleaner, more efficient energy technologies. Evidence also suggests that the strategies that environmental groups and climate advocates have used to mobilize a progressive base of voters and donors may in fact be only strengthening political polarization, turning off core constituencies, dividing moderate and liberal Democrats, and promoting broader public disgust with "Washington" and government.

Lessons Learned from the Cap-and-Trade Fight

Scholars, journalists, and commentators have focused on a range of factors that contributed in 2010 to the demise in the Senate of a cap-and-trade bill (for review, see Chapter 5). To be sure, no single factor can be considered primarily responsible. The economic recession, the heavy focus on the health care debate, a perceived lack of leadership by the White House, the country's intense political polarization, the rise of the Tea Party movement, the difficulty in passing legislation that strongly challenged the political status quo, and miscalculations by key leaders in the Senate all contributed to the bill's demise.[2]

Most notably, several analysts have emphasized the intense lobbying against the bill by the fossil fuel industry and the political spending by an aligned network of industry associations, conservative groups, and think tanks. In this regard, the billionaire brothers Charles and David Koch, along with a handful of other ultrawealthy donors, have funded conservative groups opposed to most forms of environmental regulation,[3] with these groups efficiently folding opposition to the cap-and-trade bill into a broader narrative about the need to protect free markets and personal freedom from Obama-style "socialism," whether in relation to health care or the environment.[4]

In all, the precise role of political spending in the defeat of the climate bill— as political scientists have shown is the case across issues[5]—is extremely difficult to determine. Despite the belief that environmental groups and their allies were massively outspent in the debate, a more accurate assessment is that environmentalists, industry, and conservatives each brought considerable resources and key advantages to the fight.[6]

Relevant to understanding the nature of environmental advocacy today, following their defeat, environmentalists and their funders debated how to move forward and more effectively apply their considerable financial and organizational resources to future political debates. In this regard, several analysts focused on the need to invest more significantly in building a grassroots movement in support of comprehensive policy action, an emphasis that has guided the strategies of many environmental groups and climate advocates in the years since.

In the cap-and-trade fight, environmental leaders acknowledged that they had lacked the capacity for grassroots mobilization in key House districts and in states where Senate seats were at stake. Among critiques, the campaign to pass cap-and-trade legislation had focused too much on a "big fix," communicating about the technical details of the policy rather than showing the public how climate change action might personally benefit people and their communities. Environmental groups had conducted a "policy" campaign rather than a "cultural" campaign, and lacked the ability to punish or reward members of Congress.[7] In a much debated assessment of the bill's failure, Harvard University political scientist Theda Skocpol argued that groups like the Environmental Defense Fund (EDF) and the Natural Resources Defense Council (NRDC) had relied too heavily on traditional inside-the-Beltway strategies of coalition building and lobbying, and had not done enough to rally grassroots support for cap-and-trade legislation. The design of the policy itself, argued Skocpol, was confusing to the public, focusing too heavily on providing giveaways to corporations rather than direct benefits to the public. The bill also generated skepticism from more activist-minded environmental groups and progressive leaders who either threw their support behind the bill reluctantly or remained quietly on the sidelines.[8]

General public apathy about the bill was deemed reflective of a fatal communication mistake on the part of major environmental groups and their allies, a mistake that they have sought to correct in the years since. The issue could have been identified in stark moral terms, which might have led to greater public backing. But environmentalists instead focused on trying to generate public support for cap-and-trade legislation, which tended to push the public to see the issue through the technical lens of science and economics. If the public did perceive a moral dimension to climate change, it was as a duty to care for the environment, a moral intuition that is easily overlooked in the context of economic concerns, and that engages only a small segment of Americans.[9]

In making their case, appeals to the public offered the promise of economic benefits, but did not build a case for why Americans should become involved politically and why elected officials had a moral obligation to vote for the cap-and-trade bill. The emphasis on economic benefits in the context of the recession also turned the debate into "some economic benefits" as claimed by backers of the bill versus "dramatic economic costs" as claimed by conservatives and the U.S. Chamber of Commerce, a balance that given the economic context favored the opposition.[10]

For many Republican-leaning Americans, skepticism of climate science became a stand-in for opposition to a climate bill that was framed for them as deeply damaging to the economy, as violating strongly held moral beliefs relative to free markets and personal freedom, and as favoring President Obama's political goals.[11] Conservative media—led by Fox News—likely helped drive strong opposition among the Republican base, an influence that continues today. According to one study, at Fox News, close to two-thirds of all network segments mentioning climate change rejected the need to take action. Predictably, Republicans who were heavier viewers of Fox News were more dismissive in their views of climate change than their lighter-viewing counterparts.[12]

New Movements and Strategies

After the demise of cap-and-trade legislation, the coordinated alliance among the EDF, the NRDC, and other big-budget environmental groups lobbying on behalf of congressional action split apart. With Republicans winning control of the House in 2010, there was little chance of a major climate bill passing, leaving this coalition without a defining goal to align around. Instead, the NRDC focused on passing a federal clean energy standard, increasing fuel efficiency for cars, and promoting new rules by the Environmental Protection Agency (EPA) to limit greenhouse gas emissions from power plants. At the state and local levels, other groups led by the Sierra Club and the League of Conservation Voters took legal action against coal-fired power plants, waged grassroots pressure to shut them down, and funded electoral campaigns to elect Democrats supportive of action on climate change. "The national environmental groups said, 'We need to do more in-your-face activism,'" Gene Karpinski, president of the League of Conservation Voters, told the *New York Times*. "You can't just lobby members of Congress with a poll that says people support you."[13]

The campaign effort against coal-fired power plants was greatly aided by the expansion in shale gas drilling or "fracking," which dramatically lowered the cost of natural gas energy production, and made older coal power plants increasingly costly for companies to keep in operation. Although the NRDC, the Sierra Club, and other groups also led opposition efforts against natural gas drilling, the EDF, recognizing the potential of the energy source as a bridge fuel away from coal reliance, worked with industry to assess risks and methane leakages, and to promote stronger regulation.[14]

Most significantly, the period 2011–2014 is notable for the rise to prominence of a new form of environmental advocacy group, much smaller in size and budget and focused specifically on climate change. Groups like 350 .org specialize in a sophisticated form of Internet-enabled grassroots activism designed to pressure political leaders, institutions, and industry members by rallying a liberal base of activists around symbolic issues like the Keystone XL pipeline and divestment from fossil fuel industries.

Of similar importance, in the wake of the 2010 *Citizens United* ruling by the U.S. Supreme Court, which eliminated major restrictions on election spending by corporations, individuals, and labor unions, the influx of funding from the billionaire Koch brothers and other ultrawealthy conservative donors triggered intense alarm among environmentalists and their liberal donor base. Yet by 2013, environmental groups had their own free-spending super PAC billionaire in Tom Steyer, who was pouring tens of millions of dollars into campaigns to morally stigmatize Republican elected officials and candidates who denied climate change and opposed policy action.

Mobilizing the Progressive Choir on Climate Change

The Republican victory in the 2010 midterm elections and the rise of the Tea Party not only led to a rethink of strategy on the part of environmentalists, but also helped catalyze a reinvigorated U.S. progressive movement. At the center of this movement was an emerging new paradigm for thinking about the economy and social justice, a paradigm that not only resonated strongly with the long-standing vision of prominent environmental leaders arguing for action on climate change, but also was reflected in the consumer choices and behaviors of younger (mostly white) Americans and wealthy urban liberals.

These trends included strong interest in localized economies and "buy local" efforts; a preference for organic farming, urban gardens, and farmers' markets over industrial agriculture; and intense opposition to natural gas drilling and genetically modified food, sentiments that reflected an idealized preference for "natural" food and energy sources like solar or wind. These trends were popularized not only by advocates and social entrepreneurs, but also by way of the dramatic growth online in liberal media outlets such as *Mother Jones*, Grist.org, *The Nation*, and documentary film campaigns such as *Food, Inc.* and *GasLand*, with articles or video excerpts widely spread and shared by way of social media.

Though relatively new in their broader popularity and visibility, each of these arguments and trends had long been fused together and articulated by way of the writing, advocacy, and warnings of Bill McKibben. Yet it took the failure of the national environmental organizations to pass cap and trade, the search among funders and advocates for new grassroots strategies and leaders, and the cultural, media, and economic factors that converged in the wake of the 2010 elections to help push McKibben and the activist group he cofounded into national prominence.[15]

In 1989, McKibben published *The End of Nature*, recognized as the first popular book about climate change. In this book and in many subsequent works, he warned that humans had become the "most powerful source for change on the planet," a potentially catastrophic achievement that marked an end to our traditional understanding of nature. Deeply skeptical of technological approaches to climate change such as genetic engineering or nuclear energy, McKibben controversially argued that the only possible path to survival was through a fundamental reconsideration of our worldviews, aspirations, and life goals.

The creation of this new consciousness, he argued, would dramatically reorganize society, ending our addiction to fossil fuels, economic growth, and consumerism. As he wrote at the time and elaborated on in more recent books, in this pastoral, idealized future free of consumerism or material ambition, Americans would rarely travel, experiencing the world instead via the Internet; grow much of their own food; power their communities through solar and wind; and divert their wealth to developing countries. Only under these transformational conditions, argued McKibben, would we be able to set a moral example for countries like China to change course, all in the hope that these countries will accept a "grand bargain" toward a cleaner energy path.[16]

In February 2005, as a scholar in residence at Middlebury College, McKibben began meeting informally with students to discuss strategies for mobilizing political action on climate change, which led in 2006 to a thousand-person, five-day hike to call attention to climate change. The perceived success of the event prompted McKibben and his collaborators in 2007 to organize national "Step It Up" days of action, which they coordinated by way of the Step It Up website. To share insight about their new model for organizing, McKibben and his five co-organizers published in 2007 *Fight Global Warming Now: The Handbook for Taking Action in Your Community*.[17]

In 2008, McKibben and his collaborators from Middlebury College launched 350.org. The name of the organization was derived from climate scientist James Hansen's declaration that 350 parts per million was the "safe" level for the stabilization of atmospheric carbon dioxide levels, a goal required to avoid the worst effects of climate change. In comparison to the EDF or NRDC, each of which boasts a budget greater than $100 million and hundreds of highly credentialed staff,[18] as of 2012, 350.org employed just twenty-six staff in the United States and eleven abroad, and that year, 350.org spent $2.5 million on campaign work and grassroots field organizing.[19]

The main goal of 350.org was to use Internet-enabled organizing strategies to increase the intensity of political activity among those members of the public already alarmed about climate change. In targeting this segment, McKibben was appealing directly to the base of readers and fans he had built up over the past twenty years as a best-selling author. Yet despite an avid interest in climate change and a shared worldview, activism among this segment of the public historically has been relatively low, as was evident in the cap-and-trade debate. As May Boeve, executive director of 350.org, said in a 2011 interview, "Our most consistent audience is the community of people who care about climate change and see it as a problem and are committed to do something about it. The metaphor we like to use is, yes, there's an issue of preaching to the choir, but imagine if you could have the choir all singing from the same song sheet."[20]

Sparking a National Pipeline Controversy

Following the demise of cap-and-trade legislation and with international negotiations stalled, McKibben and 350.org began the search for a new political target to mobilize a movement around. In early 2011, McKibben learned of the proposed Keystone XL pipeline and the pending approval by the U.S. State Department. Most experts had predicted that the Obama administration would approve the Keystone XL pipeline. Yet, McKibben and 350.org have played a central role in delaying its approval by morally dramatizing the stakes involved and rallying a small, yet intense, base of opposition.

To be approved, the pipeline had to be judged in the "national interest" by the Obama administration and U.S. State Department. McKibben realized that the pipeline was not only a potent symbol to rally activists against, but also an action that Obama could demonstrate his commitment to climate change, bypassing a gridlocked Congress. Turning again to James Hansen to muster rhetorical authority, McKibben cited Hansen's (contested) conclusion that by speeding up the development of the oil sands, approval of the pipeline would mean "Essentially, it's game over for the planet."[21]

Using Hansen's dramatic assessment as a rallying cry, in August 2011, 350.org and its allies mobilized thousands to protest in front of the White House, with more than twelve hundred participants arrested. They followed in November by turning out an estimated fifteen thousand activists who encircled the White House in a last push to convince President Obama to reject the pipeline. Later, in February 2012, after Obama had delayed the decision on the pipeline until 2013, the Senate took up legislation revisiting the pipeline. In response, McKibben and 350.org joined with other environmental groups to generate more than eight hundred thousand messages to senators, an effort that aided the defeat of the bill. In February 2013, an estimated thirty thousand gathered on the National Mall to once again pressure the president as they waited on a decision.[22]

The staged protests, arrests, and related strategies were the first in an ongoing series that for a second time pressured the Obama administration into delaying a decision on the Keystone pipeline until at least 2015. Protests have not only occurred in Washington, DC, but have been coordinated across other cities and states. In Nebraska, environmentalists have joined with ranchers, farmers, and Native Americans to oppose the pipeline. This self-described "Cowboy Indian Alliance" has cited risks from pipeline spills to local groundwater and public safety. Activists have also challenged the Nebraska governor's authority to approve the construction of the pipeline within the state, taking the case to the state supreme court. Local spin-offs of the national 350.org effort such as 350 Maine and 350 Massachusetts have applied similar protest strategies in opposing regional oil pipeline projects, coal power plants, and natural gas development.[23]

Major environmental groups joining with 350.org in opposing the Keystone pipeline include the NRDC, the League of Conservation Voters, Friends of the Earth, and the Sierra Club. Along with supporting protest actions, the Sierra Club and Friends of the Earth have also used freedom of information requests to call attention to what they allege are corrupting ties between the State Department, the consulting firm hired to assess environmental impacts, and related industry members.[24]

In delaying a decision on the Keystone pipeline, Obama and his advisers feared that a decision to reject the pipeline might hurt the 2014 electoral chances of Democrats in swing states and districts, giving Republicans a ready-made issue to intensify support and turnout among their own grass-roots base. Alternatively, if Obama were to approve the pipeline, the decision would risk provoking a rebellion among a network of major liberal donors and/or depress electoral support among progressive activists and voters.[25]

At his influential Dot Earth blog at the *New York Times*, environmental writer Andrew Revkin has been critical of McKibben's effort at the Keystone XL pipeline, arguing that the controversy was a "distraction from core issues and opportunities on energy and largely insignificant if your concern is averting a disruptive buildup of carbon dioxide in the atmosphere."[26] The Editorial Board at the *Washington Post*[27] and the editors of the journal *Nature* have offered similar lines of criticism. As the *Nature* editors wrote, "The pipeline is not going to determine whether the Canadian tar sands are developed or not. Only a broader—and much more important—shift in energy policy will do that." A more comprehensive action, according to the *Nature* editors, would be the implementation of pending EPA regulations for power plants that would "send a message to the coal industry: clean up or fade away."[28]

Not only does the Keystone pipeline divide commentators and analysts, but the issue also reactivates long-standing fault lines between environmentalists and labor groups. In this regard, during the cap-and-trade battle, environmentalists had forged important alliances with organized labor to lobby for the bill. But in the case of the Keystone XL pipeline debate, several labor groups representing construction workers have broken ranks, criticizing environmentalists for distorting the significance of the pipeline to the livelihoods of their members. These groups have formally withdrawn from the BlueGreen Alliance, a long-standing coalition of labor and environmental groups.[29]

In terms of broader public opinion, even after three years of campaigning against the pipeline, by 2014, nationally representative surveys showed that although the efforts had predictably helped trigger opposition among liberal Democrats, majorities of moderate Democrats and Independents favored construction of the project. In other words, instead of forging a coalition of moderates and liberals opposed to the project, the anti-pipeline campaign had instead served to divide the opinions of liberal and centrist Democrats.[30]

This division is even more strongly reflected in Congress, where moderate Democrats from fossil fuel–producing states have openly distanced themselves from President Obama's delay in approving the project, been outspoken in their support for the pipeline, and been harshly critical of environmentalists.[31] Following the 2014 elections, as Democratic senator Mary Landrieu of Louisiana faced a runoff election against her Republican candidate, she pushed her caucus leadership to hold a vote to approve the pipeline. Fourteen Democrats joined Republicans in supporting the bill, which failed by one vote to pass.[32]

Morally Stigmatizing the Fossil Fuel Industry

Along with opposition to the Keystone XL pipeline, McKibben and 350.org in 2012 also turned their focus to pressuring universities and other institutions to divest their financial holdings from fossil fuel companies, a campaign that draws direct parallels to the 1980s antiapartheid movement. In this case again, McKibben used his influence as a writer and storyteller to catalyze a new campaign aimed directly at recruiting college students, contributing a six-thousand-word article to the August 2012 issue of *Rolling Stone* magazine that warned of "Global Warming's Terrifying New Math."[33]

As he explained, fossil fuel companies and many countries were committed to extracting as much of their oil, gas, and coal holdings as possible, a morally irresponsible commitment that would exceed what scientists had determined was the world's safe level of carbon extraction. "Given this hard math, we need to view the fossil-fuel industry in a new light," McKibben argued. "It has become a rogue industry, reckless like no other force on Earth. It is Public Enemy Number One to the survival of our planetary civilization." Drawing comparisons to the antiapartheid effort, McKibben urged a mass movement pressuring universities, colleges, churches, and local governments to divest their holdings in fossil fuel companies.

The divestment movement's controversial goal—as McKibben outlined at *Rolling Stone*—is to morally stigmatize the fossil fuel industry, much like the antiapartheid movement helped frame in stark moral terms the policies of the white supremacist South African government. The call is for universities and other institutions to "immediately freeze any new investment in fossil fuel companies, and divest from direct ownership and any commingled funds that include fossil fuel public equities and corporate bonds within 5 years." The pressuring of university boards of trustees—many of whom are affiliated with major corporations and investment banks—is also intended to force these individuals to "to choose which side of the issue they are on."[34]

Yet paired with this moral call to action is a secondary frame focused on financial prudence. In this regard, divestment advocates argue the risk of a "carbon bubble," specifically the overvaluation by way of the stock market of the estimated $670 billion invested in fossil fuel industries. Once society shifts to regulate and sufficiently price carbon energy sources, the value of these companies is likely to "crash," according to the carbon bubble thesis. Therefore, universities and other institutions would be wise to eliminate these industries from their investment portfolio while their value remains high, advocates argue.[35]

As of 2014, according to 350.org, students at more than two hundred campuses across the country had pressured their institutions to divest from fossil fuel industries, with the most intense efforts occurring at smaller northeastern colleges. In response, ten small liberal arts colleges took action to divest all or part of their endowments. Most notably, Stanford University announced it would divest its financial holdings from approximately one hundred coal companies, and Yale University directed its money managers to consider how its investments could affect climate change. Several cities and college towns with a strong base of liberal voters also took divestment actions including Seattle, San Francisco, Cambridge, Berkeley, Ithaca, Ann Arbor, and Boulder.[36]

At Harvard University—a lead target of the divestment campaign given the size of its endowment and national profile—the administration initially strongly resisted calls for divestment, arguing that the university's most effective response to climate change would be to maximize investments in research, teaching, and students. In December 2012, the university announced that it was setting up a "social choice fund," separate from its endowment, where donations to the fund would be invested "in one or more external mutual funds that take special account of social responsibility considerations." Facing additional pressure from students, faculty, alumni, and liberal bloggers, the university in 2014 announced that it would raise $20 million to invest in clean energy research, refocus its goals to decrease campus-related greenhouse gas emissions, and participate in two voluntary initiatives to invest in social responsibly funds and pressure companies to disclose their greenhouse gas emissions.[37]

The divestment movement has provided students and their allies a personally relevant focus on their local institutions, and the hope that their actions can make at least a limited political difference. The campaign has also created important opportunities for students to learn about coalition building, negotiation, and compromise, with campus forums and events sparking critical self-reflection on what climate change means for society and institutions and how everyday citizens, especially young people, can become involved.

Yet critics of the divestment movement argue correctly that there are only a few socially responsible mutual funds fully divested from fossil fuel companies. Moreover, these fossil fuel–free funds offer lower returns on investment than traditional investment options. Such funds might become more competitive if governments start to take action to regulate emissions from fossil fuel sources, but until then, universities and municipalities will have to accept greater risks and lower returns. Critics also argue that the focus on campus divestment might have little impact on the behavior of oil companies—much less oil-producing countries—since most of the stock in companies is controlled by pension and hedge funds and individuals with large net worth. Previous research evaluating the impact of the antiapartheid movement, for example, concludes that divestment strategies had no discernible financial effect on the South African economy, or its companies, currency, or major industries.[38]

Unlike apartheid, considering fossil fuel divestment from a moral standpoint makes it far more difficult to choose which side you stand on, given what is for all of us a heavy dependence on fossil fuels. Reliable energy alternatives like hydropower and nuclear energy each also have their own moral trade-offs and risks. Critics argue that a more effective strategy might be for universities to buy up, rather than divest, their shares in energy companies, thereby gaining more influence on industry practices. A similar strategy would be to maximize university finances to leverage research and deployment of cleaner energy technologies.[39]

Beyond the focus of the divestment movement, there are signs that McKibben and 350.org's efforts to build a broader social justice movement in support of action on climate change is gaining momentum. In October 2014, legions of demonstrators totaling more than three hundred thousand marched in New York City to pressure world leaders gathered at the United Nations to discuss an international climate accord.[40] The same month, writer and 350 .org board member Naomi Klein published her best-selling book *This Changes Everything: Capitalism Versus the Climate*,[41] which appeared for several weeks on the best-seller list, generating considerable media attention. "Only mass movements can save us now," Klein says. She argues that "profound and radical economic transformation" is needed to avoid certain catastrophe.[42]

Super PACs and Election Campaigns

As McKibben and 350.org have focused on building a new progressive grassroots movement pressuring President Obama and universities, California billionaire Tom Steyer and his political advisers have sought to spend his vast wealth to influence key U.S. Senate and governor's races. This strategy is intended to lay the groundwork for climate change to be a dominant issue during the 2016 presidential election, while positioning Steyer as a candidate for future electoral office.

The San Francisco–based billionaire first began to gain political attention by bankrolling a series of California ballot initiative campaigns that boosted state energy efficiency actions, promoted land conservation, and defended the state's cap-and-trade law against industry rollback. In recent years, he has devoted much of his wealth and time into supporting climate and energy initiatives at Yale University and Stanford University (where as a trustee he played a key role in pushing through coal divestment), managing clean energy investment funds, and cofounding a climate risk assessment initiative with former New York mayor Michael Bloomberg and U.S. Treasury Secretary Henry Paulson. Along the way, he has hosted major political fund-raisers for Democratic congressional leaders and President Obama, lobbying for stronger action on climate change, including rejecting the Keystone XL pipeline.[43]

Most notably, however, in 2013 he launched NextGen Climate, a super PAC that has run a national ad campaign opposing the Keystone XL pipeline while investing heavily in several key electoral races. In Democratic-leaning Massachusetts, Steyer's NextGen super PAC joined with activists in spring 2013 to elect Rep. Edward Markey to the U.S. Senate, campaigning against fellow Congressman Stephen Lynch in the primary race. At issue was Lynch's support for the Keystone XL pipeline. The Steyer-backed attack on Lynch demanded the candidate "act like a real Democrat and oppose Keystone's dirty energy," framing him otherwise as working for Big Oil.[44] In all, Steyer spent $1.8 million on the Senate race. "Once politicians start to become aware that this issue can either help them or hurt them, you begin to change the conduct and behavior of those who are in elected office," chief campaign adviser Chris Lehane said of their electoral strategy.[45]

In fall 2013, Steyer's super PAC played an influential role in electing Democrat Terry McAuliffe as Virginia governor, spending an estimated $8 million to frame his Republican opponent Ken Cuccinelli as an elected official who "denies basic science" and who as state attorney general "wasted taxpayer money" by investigating the research activities of climate scientists. The main goal was to mobilize Virginians who had voted in the 2012 presidential election but who were otherwise unlikely to vote in the 2013 governor's race.[46]

NextGen commissioned pollsters who recommended that successful messaging would link climate change to daily concerns such as asthma rates or the price of food. Instead of referring to Cuccinelli as a "climate denier," a term favored by activists, the recommendation was to say he "denies basic science." Their strategy also explicitly recognized latent ambivalence about climate change among voters: "I'm no environmentalist . . . ," began one digital ad, "but droughts are ruining my farm."[47]

Their primary objective was to portray Cuccinelli as a "wild man." Direct mail fliers told voters that not only did Cuccinelli dismiss climate science, but he also wanted "to eliminate all forms of birth control" and "let criminals, even those convicted of sexually abusing children, buy guns at gun shows." By the end of the campaign, Steyer's super PAC had spent an estimated $4.3 million on TV and digital ads, $1.3 million on phone calls and canvassers, and $1.1 million on direct mail.[48]

With the Virginia race serving as a model to build on, in May 2014, Steyer's super PAC announced plans to spend at least $50 million of his own money, plus another $50 million in matching funds from other donors, to support Democratic candidates in seven competitive Senate and governor's races. These included the Senate races in New Hampshire, Michigan, Iowa, and Colorado and the governor's races in Florida, Pennsylvania, and Maine. The goal was to demonstrate that climate change could be used as a wedge issue to elect Democratic candidates, testing the premise in advance of the 2016 presidential and congressional elections.[49]

The strategy is to drive a "wedge" between conservative candidates and moderate voters, framing conservatives as standing on the morally wrong side of the climate change issue, as they have been portrayed in the same-sex marriage and civil rights debates.[50] In this regard, the NextGen campaign applies a master narrative that is adapted to each state emphasizing that climate change poses a serious threat to the economy, public health, and children and that if candidates don't believe in climate change, they can't be trusted. Among those targeted are young, female, and minority voters who are otherwise less likely to turn out in midterm elections.[51]

Yet by the end of the 2014 elections, specific to fund-raising and targeted races, Steyer and NextGen had fallen well short of their goals. NextGen raised $67.7 million with $57.6 million contributed by Steyer himself, a total considerably less than the $100 million target.[52] Of the seven Senate and gubernatorial races that NextGen targeted, the Democratic candidates backed by NextGen won in just three.[53] Overall, Republicans won control of the Senate holding fifty-four out of one hundred seats, strengthened their majority in the House, and increased the number of state legislatures and governorships that they control.

Steyer, however, claimed many positives from NextGen's efforts. With an eye toward the 2016 election, positives included raising the overall profile of climate change as an election issue, building up a relevant network of voters and volunteers in key battleground states, and pressuring candidates to shift their position. "In every state we were active, Democrats and Republicans had to deal with this issue," said Steyer. "Not only do Democrats have to be good on it to turn out votes, but the Republicans really had to move away from denial."[54]

Escalating Polarization and a Spiral of Disengagement

Looking ahead to the next several years and beyond, by framing climate change in stark moral terms and by emphasizing Republicans' "denial" of the problem, environmentalists and Democratic strategists believe that they have identified a successful strategy that will result in policy victories and electoral advantage. Polling suggests that a carefully tailored "wedge strategy" as pursued by Steyer's super PAC might be able to isolate Tea Party–identifying Republicans from their more moderate-leaning GOP counterparts. This latter group, though supporting the Keystone XL pipeline, also accepts the reality of climate change and supports specific actions such as EPA limits on coal power plants.[55] According to the *New York Times*, Democratic strategists believe that Republicans who oppose the EPA rules or deny climate change are likely to be viewed by most voters as "ideologically rigid and unwilling to accept scientists' conclusions," a perception that will damage Republicans' efforts to expand their support among young people and women.[56]

In response to this strategy, Republicans joined by political reform advocates criticize Democratic leaders for opposing super PAC spending by conservative billionaires like the Koch brothers yet readily endorsing Steyer's efforts.[57] In this case, conservatives argue that Democratic leaders are catering to the interests of their liberal activist and donor base rather than looking out for the interests of working-class Americans.[58] Front-page stories at the *New York Times* and the *Washington Post* have also highlighted Steyer's past investments in the fossil fuel industry and the profits accrued by the hedge fund he founded, noting the apparent inconsistency with his political advocacy.[59] McKibben, who helped inspire Steyer's opposition to the Keystone pipeline and who consults with the billionaire activist, offers an opposing perspective: "After years of watching rich people manipulate and wreck our political system for selfish personal interests, it's great to watch a rich person use his money and his talents in the public interest."[60] Yet to be sure, Steyer's advisers have been open about his own personal ambitions, as he promotes his national profile and climate advocacy work leading up to a possible future electoral candidacy as governor of California.[61]

Perhaps the most notable criticism of Steyer's super PAC efforts and the allied strategies of environmentalists and Democrats is that they likely portend further ideological escalation by both sides in the climate debate, with ever more financial and political resources spent on demonizing opponents. Indeed, liberals, environmentalists, and conservatives speculate endlessly as to the fund-raising prowess of the other side, each warning of dramatic disparities as a way to mobilize its respective donors and activists. Across election cycles and legislative battles, as one side gains a perceived advantage, the other side predictably attempts to catch up in terms of spending, ever more advanced campaign strategies, and polarizing rhetoric.[62] In months leading up to the 2014 midterm elections, liberals led by Steyer gave more to super PACs than conservatives, a reversal from the 2012 election cycle.[63] The surge in spending by either side resulted in a record amount of TV advertising focused on energy, climate change, and the environment, with more than 125,000 mostly negative attack ads running specific to Senate races alone.[64]

Yet by defining almost everything about the climate change debate as "us versus the radical fringe," environmentalists and liberals continue to reinforce a bunker mentality that rewards groupthink and substantially reduces opportunities for developing innovative ideas and approaches to climate change that broker support among moderates and conservatives. Those experts, advocates, or political leaders who break with conventional perspectives or attempt to cross the fault lines that polarization over climate change has etched into our political culture are too often "debunked" as contrarians, or dismissed as compromise-seeking centrists.[65]

Extreme polarization on issues like climate change has also led to public disgust with politics, government, and "Washington." The resulting damage to our civic culture disproportionately harms environmentalists and liberals, whose core objectives to combat climate change and seek greater social and economic justice almost always entail government services, investments, and interventions in private markets. Democrats have also increasingly come to depend upon young people, women, and minorities, who make up a growing proportion of eligible voters. But among these potential supporters, intense negativity and extreme polarization on issues like climate risk reinforce feelings of cynicism and inefficacy while likely adding to the propensity to tune out the debate. Indeed, in order to mobilize these voter groups in midterm elections, Steyer's Super PAC, environmental groups, and allied Democratic campaigns are forced to spend ever greater resources each election cycle on canvassing, texting, social media, and narrowly targeted appeals.[66]

Conclusion: Balancing Activism and Pragmatism

In the wake of the failure of cap and trade, as reviewed in this chapter, McKibben's 350.org and Steyer's NextGen super PAC have helped address a long-standing weakness among major environmental organizations, providing a potent grassroots base of activism and a sophisticated, well-financed electoral strategy. Yet, these strategies, as discussed, are not without their unintended negative consequences or potential pitfalls.

Yet, as much attention as these "outside" mobilizing strategies have received, in the final years of the Obama presidency, the most significant progress on climate change has occurred not by way of these advocacy efforts, but through a traditional insider legal strategy with roots dating to the 1970 Clean Air Act. In this case, going to work behind the scenes after Obama's 2012 reelection, the NRDC through its legal and economic specialization has strongly shaped the EPA's proposed rules to regulate greenhouse emissions from existing coal-fired power plants. The rules, many experts predict, can have a substantial impact on U.S. greenhouse gas emissions and provide more persuasive leverage in negotiations with other countries to agree to international emissions targets (see Chapter 13).[67] The landmark agreement between the United States and China in which each pledged to substantially reduce their emissions by 2025 and 2030, respectively, is a leading example.[68]

The proposed EPA rules, however, will undergo a lengthy comment period, with environmental and industry groups mobilizing key constituencies to weigh in. The rules will also face major legal challenges from companies and states that are the most heavily affected. In this regard, the major environmental groups led by the Sierra Club, the League of Conversation Voters, and the NRDC plan well-financed TV advertising campaigns and grassroots mobilization to defend the rules. The EPA rules, along with the U.S.-China climate deal and other international agreements to limit emissions, are also likely to be the focus of heavy campaigning and debate leading up to the 2016 elections.[69]

For several years to come, rather than grassroots activism and electoral campaigning, the EPA rules, along with similar executive actions, may be environmental advocates' best bet to meaningfully reduce U.S. greenhouse gas emissions and achieve progress on other environmental problems. Looking ahead to after the 2016 election, even assuming that an experienced Democrat like Hillary Clinton is elected president, there are likely to be strong barriers to passing major climate legislation such as a carbon tax, given that Republicans are likely to control at least half of Congress. Moreover, just as was the case with cap-and-trade legislation, other issues, including immigration, gun control, income inequality, banking regulation, and revisions to the health care bill, may take top legislative priority over climate change.

All of this suggests that in combination with new approaches to grassroots advocacy and election campaigns, a complementary paradigm for climate advocacy may be needed with a shift in focus from national legislation to a broader portfolio of smaller-scale policy actions and to the promotion of a more diverse array of technological options. Indeed, to the extent that the Obama administration has been able to make substantive progress on climate change, it has been through a combination of smaller-scale, less politically visible approaches like fuel efficiency standards or EPA rules rather than pushing for society transforming solutions like an economy-wide price on carbon (see Chapter 4).[70]

In the post-2016 political world, Obama's policy strategy may be the new blueprint for achieving progress on climate change. Success, however, will ultimately depend on environmental advocates joining with moderates and right-of-center interest groups in pushing for a range of smaller-scale policy actions across levels of government. But in the process, for a number of reasons, they will also need to keep a diversity of technological solutions—including nuclear power, carbon capture and storage, and natural gas fracking—on the table as part of the discussion.

In his 2010 book *The Climate Fix*, political scientist Roger Pielke Jr. notes that polls show the public for several years has favored action on climate change but at low levels of intensity, suggesting that it is not a lack of public support limiting policy action. "The challenge facing climate policy is to design policies that are consonant with public opinion, and are effective, rather than try to shape public opinion around particular policies," he argues. In this regard, "A broad portfolio of technologies and practices should be supported . . . despite the fact that no one energy technology will be universally popular." Examples include combining a focus on wind, solar, and energy efficiency with a similar focus on developing nuclear energy and carbon capture and storage technology. Drawing on case studies of past environmental policy debates such as those over acid rain and ozone depletion, Pielke argues that once next-generation technologies are available that make meaningful action on climate change lower in cost, then much of the argument politically over scientific uncertainty is likely to diminish.[71]

In their research on cultural identity and risk perceptions, the findings of Yale University's Dan M. Kahan and colleagues similarly suggest that risk perceptions of climate change are policy and technology dependent and that political agreement is more likely to occur under conditions of a diverse rather than narrow set of proposed solutions. In these studies, when conservative-leaning Americans read that the solution to climate change is investment in nuclear power or geoengineering, their skepticism of expert statements relative to climate change decreased, and their support for policy responses increased. The reason, argue Kahan and colleagues, is that these technologies affirm rather than challenge their worldviews relative to the need to maintain economic growth and the ability of human ingenuity to solve environmental problems. In contrast, when the solution to climate change was framed as stricter pollution controls, conservative-leaning Americans' acceptance of expert statements on climate change decreased, since these measures conflict with their belief in free markets and individual freedom.[72]

If we apply Pielke and Kahan's reasoning to the climate debate, it follows that building political consensus on climate change will depend heavily on advocates for action calling attention to a broad portfolio of policy actions and technological solutions, with some actions such as tax incentives for nuclear energy, government support for clean energy research, or proposals to invest in resilience and adaptation (thereby protecting local communities against climate change impacts) more likely to gain support from both Democrats and Republicans. Under these conditions, in regions, states, and cities, not only will it be easier to gain public support from across the political and cultural spectrum, but it will also give members of Congress and future presidents, when they are ready to return to the business of governing, more options by which to reach agreement and compromise.[73]

In the post-Obama era of environmental advocacy, grassroots mobilization and electoral pressure can provide added incentive for members of Congress and future presidents to cooperate on actions to address climate change and other environmental problems. But the opportunities for such cooperation along with the effectiveness of any implemented actions will depend heavily on environmentalists, experts, and other political entrepreneurs promoting a broader range of policy options and technological solutions that can be adopted across levels of government.

Suggested Websites

350.org (www.350.org) An advocacy group specializing in grassroots mobilization and industry pressure campaigns, 350.org was cofounded by environmental writer Bill McKibben. The site features multimedia campaign updates, backgrounders, blogs, and video.

Ensia (www.ensia.com) Web magazine *Ensia* features news and commentary about environmental science and policy with a focus on identifying new ideas, voices, and opportunities for collaboration in support of policy solutions and actions.

The Breakthrough Institute (www.thebreakthrough.org) The Breakthrough Institute is a San Francisco–based progressive think tank focused on an "eco-modernist," pragmatic approach to environmental problems and advocacy. The website features commentary, articles, analysis, and reports from experts and journalists analyzing trends and directions related to climate change and energy policy.

The Climate Shift Project (www.climateshiftproject.org) The Climate Shift Project provides discussion, commentary, and analysis by Northeastern University professor Matthew C. Nisbet of new studies, reports, books, and public opinion survey trends related to environmental politics and climate change. The site includes access to related courses, workshops, podcasts, and other resources including "The Age of Us: Communication, Culture & Politics in the Anthropocene," a column he writes at *The Conversation* (https://theconversation.com/columns/matthew-nisbet-114648).

Inside Climate News (insideclimatenews.org) Pulitzer Prize–winning advocacy news site Inside Climate News features coverage and analysis of the debate over the Keystone XL pipeline, the fossil fuel divestment movement, and climate change–related electoral politics.

The *New York Times'* Dot Earth blog (www.nytimes.com/dotearth) Dot Earth features commentary and analysis of trends in climate science, politics, and policy ideas by veteran environmental writer Andrew Revkin.

Notes

1. Talia Buford, "Thousands Rally in Washington to Protest Keystone Pipeline," *Politico*, February 2, 2013.
2. Theda Skocpol, *Naming the Problem: What It Will Take to Counter Extremism and Engage Americans in the Fight against Global Warming* (Cambridge, MA: Scholars Strategy Network, 2013), www.scholarsstrategynetwork.org/sites/default/files/ skocpol_captrade_report_january_2013y.pdf; and Petra Bartosiewicz and Miley Marissa, *The Too Polite Revolution: Why the Recent Campaign to Pass Comprehensive Climate Legislation in the United States Failed* (Cambridge, MA: Scholars Strategy Network, 2013), www.scholarsstrategynetwork.org/sites/default/files/rff_final_ report_bartosiewicz_miley.pdf.
3. Robert Brulle, "Institutionalizing Delay: Foundation Funding and the Creation of U.S. Climate Change Counter-Movement Organizations," *Climatic Change* 122, no. 4 (2014): 681–94.
4. Matthew C. Nisbet, *Climate Shift: Clear Vision for the Next Decade of Public Debate* (Washington, DC: American University, 2011), http://climateshiftproject.org/wp -content/uploads/2011/08/ClimateShift_report_June2011.pdf.
5. Frank Baumgartner, Jeffrey M. Berry, Marie Hojnacki, David C. Kimball, and Beth L. Leech, *Lobbying and Policy Change: Who Wins, Who Loses, and Why* (Chicago: University of Chicago Press, 2009).
6. Nisbet, *Climate Shift*.
7. EcoAmerica, *America the Best: Social Solutions for Climate* (Washington, DC: EcoAmerica, 2010), http://ecoamerica.org/wp-content/uploads/2013/02/America_ The_Best.pdf.
8. Theda Skocpol, "You Can't Change the Climate from Inside Washington," *Foreign Policy*, January 24, 2013.
9. Matthew C. Nisbet, Ezra Markowitz, and John Kotcher, "Winning the Conversation: Framing and Moral Messaging in Environmental Campaigns," in *Talking Green: Exploring Current Issues in Environmental Communication*, ed. Lee Ahern and Denise Bortree (New York: Peter Lang, 2013).
10. Nisbet, Markowitz, and Kotcher, "Winning the Conversation."
11. Nisbet, *Climate Shift*.
12. Lauren Feldman, Edward W. Maibach, Connie Roser-Renouf, and Anthony Leiserowitz, "Climate on Cable: The Nature and Impact of Global Warming Coverage on Fox News, CNN, and MSNBC," *International Journal of Press/Politics* 17, no. 1 (2012): 3–31.
13. Michael Wines, "Environmental Groups Focus on Change by Strengthening Their Political Operations," *New York Times*, May 31, 2014.
14. Joe Nocera, "How to Extract Gas Responsibly," *New York Times*, February 27, 2012.
15. Matthew C. Nisbet, *Nature's Prophet: Bill McKibben as Journalist, Public Intellectual, and Advocate*, Discussion Paper Series, D-78 March (Cambridge, MA: Kennedy School of Government, Harvard University, 2012), http://shorensteincenter.org/ natures-prophet-bill-mckibben-as-journalist-public-intellectual-and-activist/.
16. Nisbet, *Nature's Prophet*.
17. Bill McKibben, *Fight Global Warming Now: The Handbook for Taking Action in Your Community* (New York: St. Martin's Griffin, 2007).
18. Nisbet, *Climate Shift*.
19. Nisbet, *Nature's Prophet*.

20. Luis Hestres, "Preaching to the Choir: Internet-Mediated Advocacy, Issue Public Mobilization, and Climate Change," *New Media & Society* 16, no. 2 (2014): 323–39.
21. Hestres, "Preaching to the Choir."
22. Matthew C. Nisbet, "The Opponent: How Bill McKibben Took On the Oil Patch and Changed Environmental Politics," *Policy Options* (May 2013), http://policyoptions .irpp.org/issues/arctic-visions/nisbet/.
23. Saul Elbein, "Jan Kleeb vs. the Keystone Pipeline," *New York Times Magazine*, May 16, 2014.
24. Lauren Barron-Lopez, "Greens Demand State Hand over Keystone Docs," *The Hill*, August 14, 2014.
25. Andrew Restuccia and Darren Goode, "Keystone Decision Delayed Yet Again," *Politico*, April 14, 2014.
26. Andrew Revkin, "Can Obama Escape the Alberta Tar Pit?" *New York Times*, September 5, 2011.
27. "Keystone XL Is Coming Back," *Washington Post*, January 23, 2013.
28. "Change for Good: The US Must Boost Its Spending on Clean Energy to Make Its Mark on the Climate Debate," *Nature*, January 29, 2013.
29. Darren Goode, "Keystone Pipeline Sparks Labor Civil War," *Politico*, January 20, 2012.
30. Bruce Drake, "Democrats Find Themselves Divided on the Keystone Pipeline" (Washington, DC: Pew Research Center, May 6, 2014), www.pewresearch.org/fact -tank/2014/05/06/democrats-find-themselves-divided-on-keystone-pipeline/; "Little Enthusiasm, Familiar Divisions after the GOP's Big Midterm Victory" (Washington, DC: Pew Research Center for the People and the Press, November 12, 2014), www .people-press.org/2014/11/12/little-enthusiasm-familiar-divisions-after-the-gops -big-midterm-victory/.
31. Andrew Restuccia and Darren Goode, "Keystone Decision Delayed Yet Again," *Politico*, April 14, 2014.
32. Ashley Parker and Coral Davenport, "Senate Defeats Bill on Keystone XL Pipeline in Narrow Vote," *New York Times*, November 18, 2014.
33. Bill McKibben, "Global Warming's Terrifying New Math," *Rolling Stone*, July 19, 2012.
34. "FAQ: Fossil Free Campaign," http://gofossilfree.org/faq/.
35. Thomas Watson, "Oil Giants Could Feel Major Pain Should World Get Serious about Reducing Global Temperatures," *The Financial Post*, June 21, 2013.
36. "Divestment Commitments," http://gofossilfree.org/commitments/.
37. Office of the President, "Fossil Fuel Divestment Statement," Harvard University, October 3, 2013, www.harvard.edu/president/fossil-fuels.
38. Cary Krosinsky, "Why the 'Do the Math' Tour Doesn't Add Up," *GreenBiz*, November 27, 2012, www.greenbiz.com/blog/2012/11/19/do-math-tour-doesnt-add-up; and Ivo Welch, "Why Divestment Fails," *New York Times*, May 9, 2014.
39. Welch, "Why Divestment Fails."
40. Lisa W. Foderarosept, "Taking a Call for Climate Change to the Streets," *New York Times*, September 21, 2014.
41. Naomi Klein, *This Changes Everything: Capitalism Versus the Climate* (New York: Simon & Schuster, 2014).
42. Matthew C. Nisbet, "Naomi Klein or Al Gore? Making Sense of Contrasting Views on Climate Change," *The Conversation*, October 5, 2014.

43. Ryan Lizza, "The President and the Pipeline," *The New Yorker*, September 16, 2013; and Edward Robinson, "Climate Change Rescue in U.S. Makes Steyer Converge with Paulson," *Bloomberg*, October 1, 2013.

44. Maggie Haberman, "Enviros Threaten Stephen Lynch on Keystone Pipeline," *Politico*, March 18, 2013.

45. Lizza, "The President and the Pipeline."

46. Alexander Burns and Andrew Restuccia, "Inside a Green Billionaire's Virginia Crusade," *Politico*, November 11, 2013.

47. Burns and Restuccia, "Inside a Green Billionaire's Virginia Crusade."

48. Ibid.

49. Coral Davenport, "Pushing Climate Change as an Issue This Year but with an Eye Towards 2016," *New York Times*, May 22, 2014; Kate Sheppard, "Tom Steyer Claims Success in Very Expensive Effort to Make Climate Change a 'Wedge Issue,'" *Huffington Post*, November 5, 2014.

50. Lizza, "The President and the Pipeline."

51. Davenport, "Pushing Climate Change as an Issue This Year but with an Eye Towards 2016."

52. Timothy Cama, "Steyer Group Raises $68M," *The Hill*, December 5, 2014.

53. Sheppard, "Tom Steyer Claims Success in Very Expensive Effort to Make Climate Change a 'Wedge Issue.'"

54. Ibid.

55. "GOP Deeply Divided over Climate Change" (Washington, DC: Pew Research Center, November 1, 2013), www.people-press.org/2013/11/01/gop-deeply-divided-over-climate-change/.

56. Carl Huse and Michael D. Shear, "Democrats See Winning Issue in Carbon Plan," *New York Times*, June 9, 2014.

57. Michael Levenson, "Outside Money Attacking Stephen Lynch in Senate Race," *Boston Globe*, April 8, 2013.

58. Clare Foran, "Why Democrats Are Afraid of the Man Who Is Giving Them Millions," *National Journal*, May 12, 2014.

59. Michael Barbaro and Carol Davenport, "Aims of Donor Are Shadowed by Past in Coal," *New York Times*, July 4, 2014.

60. Lizza, "The President and the Pipeline."

61. Ibid.

62. Matthew C. Nisbet and Dietram A. Scheufele, "The Polarization Paradox: Why Hyperpartisanship Promotes Conservatism and Undermines Liberalism," *The Breakthrough Journal* 3 (2012): 55–69, http://thebreakthrough.org/index.php/journal/past-issues/issue-3/the-polarization-paradox.

63. Scott Bland and Adam Wollner, "Soros, Steyer Spend Big in Bid to Rescue Democrats' Majority," *National Journal*, August 22, 2014.

64. Coral Davenport and Ashley Parkeroct, "Environment Is Grabbing Big Role in Ads for Campaigns," *New York Times*, October 21, 2014.

65. Nisbet and Scheufele, "The Polarization Paradox."

66. Ibid.

67. Coral Davenport, "Taking Oil Industry Cue, Environmentalists Drew Emissions Blueprint," *New York Times*, July 6, 2014.

68. Coral Davenport, "In Climate Deal with China, Obama May Set 2016 Theme," *New York Times*, November 12, 2014.

69. Davenport, "In Climate Deal with China, Obama May Set 2016 Theme."

70. Jonathan Chait, "Obama Might Actually Be the Environmental President," *New York Magazine*, May 5, 2013.
71. Roger Pielke Jr., *The Climate Fix: What Scientists and Politicians Won't Tell You About Climate Change* (New York: Basic Books, 2010), 43.
72. Dan M. Kahan, Ellen Peters, Maggie Wittlin, Paul Slovic, Lisa Larrimore Ouellette, Donald Braman, and Gregory Mandel, "The Polarizing Impact of Science Literacy and Numeracy on Perceived Climate Change Risks," *Nature Climate Change* 2 (2012): 732–35.
73. Matthew C. Nisbet, "A New Model for Climate Advocacy," *Ensia*, November 26, 2013, http://ensia.com/voices/a-new-model-for-climate-advocacy/.

Part II

Federal Institutions and Policy Change

4

Presidential Powers and Environmental Policy

Norman J. Vig

We will respond to the threat of climate change, knowing that the failure to do so would betray our children and future generations. Some may deny the overwhelming judgment of science, but none can avoid the devastating impact of raging fires, and crippling drought, and more powerful storms.

President Barack Obama,
Second Inaugural Address, 2013

I do not believe that human activity is causing these dramatic changes to our climate the way these scientists are projecting it.

Senator Marco Rubio, May 11, 2014

President Barack Obama entered office in 2009 with strong support from environmentalists. He had promised to address a broad array of environmental problems neglected by the George W. Bush administration, including air quality and climate change. During his first term, he had some success in fulfilling these promises, especially by greatly increasing federal support for renewable energy technologies and by sharply raising fuel efficiency standards for automobiles in the future. Yet his landmark climate change legislation died in the Senate in 2010, and public support for other parts of his environmental agenda weakened as public concern shifted toward measures to overcome the great economic recession.[1]

The rise of the Tea Party and conservative reactions to Obama's economic policies and health care reform enabled the Republicans to win a large majority in the House of Representatives in November 2010. It quickly became apparent that Congress would oppose any new environmental regulations as potential "job killers" (see Chapter 5). Partly in response to this opposition, and partly due to concerns over the fragile economic recovery and his own reelection prospects, Obama delayed a number of key environmental decisions in 2011–2012. Environmentalists were dismayed in September 2011 when he rejected a long-awaited proposal from the Environmental Protection Agency (EPA) for reducing allowable levels of smog-causing ozone.[2] And more than 1,200 of them were arrested in front of the White House for demonstrating against possible approval of the Keystone XL pipeline that would carry oil from tar sands in Canada to refineries in Texas (Chapter 3). President Obama postponed a decision on that issue as well, but it appeared that his environmental agenda had stalled.

Although environmental issues were little discussed during the 2012 presidential election, Obama took a more proactive approach to environmental policy in his second term. His inaugural address in January 2013 devoted more space to climate change than to any other topic, signaling that it would now be a top priority.[3] Obama also stated that if Congress continued to block his programs he would utilize his presidential powers to the fullest extent possible to achieve his goals. In June 2013, he announced a comprehensive Climate Action Plan, and the administration issued a series of regulations to control greenhouse gas emissions from power plants. Then in November 2014 the president announced a major new agreement with China to further limit carbon emissions between 2025 and 2030. In response to these and other executive actions, Republicans accused Obama of creating an "imperial presidency" and threatened to sue him for abuse of powers.[4] And virtually all Republican leaders and potential candidates for the presidency—such as Sen. Marco Rubio—continued to question climate science and to oppose government actions to address global warming.[5]

Obama's policies thus raised the question of how much a president can accomplish without the support of Congress or a clear public mandate. Presidents of both parties have utilized executive powers to shape environmental and natural resource policies throughout our history, with varying degrees of success.[6] In periods of divided government or congressional deadlock, unilateral presidential action arguably becomes even more important.[7] However, presidents also operate within a system of constitutional, legal, and political constraints that limit their authority. I will examine Obama's environmental record and those of other recent presidents later in this chapter, but first it is important to take a closer look at the powers of the presidency itself.[8]

Presidential Powers and Constraints

The formal roles of the president have been summarized as commander-in-chief of the armed forces, chief diplomat, chief executive, legislative leader, and opinion/party leader.[9] If we look only at environmental policy, the president's role as chief executive has probably been most important.[10] But some presidents, including Theodore Roosevelt, Franklin Roosevelt, and Richard Nixon, have played a leading role in enacting environmental legislation and in using the "bully pulpit" to rally public opinion behind new environmental policies. The role of chief diplomat has also become more important as many environmental problems have required international solutions; for example, Ronald Reagan supported and signed the landmark Montreal Protocol on Substances That Deplete the Ozone Layer in 1987. And as commander-in-chief of the armed forces, presidents also deal with a growing range of environmental threats.[11]

Some of the president's powers are "contextual"; that is, they shape the general context of policymaking and the broad directions of the administration. Presidents can draw attention to issues and frame the political agenda through speeches, press conferences, and other media events; they can propose legislation and budgets; they nominate and appoint cabinet members and other key officials; and they can reorganize their staffs and departments to better implement their policies. Other powers of the president are more "unilateral" and allow the president to directly influence policy decisions. These include the power to veto legislation; to issue executive orders, directives, and proclamations; to make executive agreements; and to monitor and control regulatory processes.[12]

Article II of the Constitution directs the president to "faithfully execute the laws." Most legislation passed by Congress is quite broad, however, and leaves much to the discretion of the president and the implementing agencies. The EPA, for example, is charged by the Clean Air Act to formulate and issue detailed standards, rules, and regulations to control emission of pollutants necessary to ensure healthy air quality (see Chapter 7). These rules and regulations are adopted through lengthy administrative proceedings, and once finalized they have the full force of law. Presidents therefore try to centralize and control rulemaking to ensure that it reflects their policy agenda. All presidents since Nixon have required that important regulations be cleared by the Office of Management and Budget (OMB) before they are proposed by the EPA and other regulatory agencies. Presidents can thus have a major impact on policy decisions through control of the bureaucracy rather than through passage of new legislation.[13]

Ultimately, however, presidents cannot govern alone; they are part of a government of "separated powers."[14] Their policies must be grounded in statutes passed by Congress, and Congress also determines the budgets and spending limits of all executive agencies. The Senate can refuse to confirm the president's nominees for office and deny ratification of treaties. Executive-legislative relations have become increasingly strained in recent years due to greater ideological polarization and frequent use of Senate filibuster. Even with a majority in both houses, the president may not be able to get sufficient support to pass new legislation (as in the case of climate change legislation in 2010). Without such legislation, executive actions may be difficult to carry out. Most major rules and regulations are challenged in the courts by affected parties, often tying up policies in litigation for years (see Chapter 6). And finally, in our federal system, most environmental laws depend heavily on the states for implementation (see Chapters 2 and 7).

Classifying Environmental Presidencies

A president's influence on environmental policy can be evaluated by examining a few basic indicators: (1) the president's environmental *agenda* as expressed in campaign statements, policy documents, and major speeches such as inaugural and State of the Union addresses; (2) presidential *appointments* to key positions in government departments and agencies and to the White House staff; (3) the relative priority given to environmental programs in the president's proposed *budgets*; (4) presidential *legislative initiatives* or *vetoes*; (5) *executive orders and other unilateral actions* by the president; and (6) presidential support for or opposition to *international environmental agreements*. By these criteria, some presidents can be seen as a great deal more pro-environmental than others.

Measuring actual performance outcomes is more difficult. For example, President Bill Clinton achieved few of the policy changes he espoused during his 1992 campaign, yet he ended his presidency with a strong contribution to public lands conservation. Incumbents should be judged in terms of not only how much of their initial agenda they achieved but also how successful they were relative to the circumstances and constraints they faced. Ultimately, of course, the success of policy changes should be gauged in terms of their effects on the environment. But given the multitude of factors that affect the environment and the difficulties of monitoring and measuring environmental quality, it is rarely possible to make definitive statements about specific policy outcomes (see Chapter 1).

We can, however, generally classify presidents in terms of their attitudes toward the seriousness of environmental problems, the relative priority they give to environmental protection compared with other policy problems, and whether they attempt to strengthen or weaken existing environmental policies and institutions. In this broad perspective, recent presidents seem to fall into three main categories: opportunistic leaders, frustrated reformers, and roll-back advocates.[15]

Opportunistic Leaders

Two presidents, Richard Nixon and George H. W. Bush, held office at the peak of public opinion surges demanding action to strengthen environmental protection. Although both had served as vice president in conservative Republican administrations, and neither had a strong record on environmental policy, both adopted the conservationist mantle of Theodore Roosevelt and supported major advances in national environmental protection early in their presidencies. President Nixon proclaimed the 1970s the "environmental decade"; signed the National Environmental Policy Act, the Clean Air Act, the Endangered Species Act, and other foundational environmental legislation (see Appendix 1); and created the EPA by executive action after gaining approval of his reorganization plan by Congress.[16] George H. W. Bush campaigned for and signed the 1990 Clean Air Act Amendments, which greatly strengthened controls over urban air pollution and acid rain. However, as opposition to further policy changes mounted from traditional Republican constituencies, both Reagan and Bush reverted to more conservative policies later in their terms. Nixon, for example, vetoed the Federal Water Pollution Control Act Amendments of 1972 (which passed over his veto), and Bush declared a moratorium on all new environmental regulation and refused to endorse binding international agreements to deal with climate change and biodiversity at the 1992 Earth Summit in Rio de Janeiro, Brazil.

Frustrated Reformers

Two Democratic presidents, Jimmy Carter and Bill Clinton, came to office with large environmental agendas and strong support from environmental constituencies, but accomplished less than expected. Carter failed to gain congressional support for his policies to address the energy crisis of the late 1970s, whereas Clinton had only minor legislative achievements in the field of environmental policy. Both presidents were forced by competing priorities and lack of public and congressional support to compromise their environmental agendas. Nevertheless, both achieved belated success in protecting public lands and tightening environmental regulations before leaving office. After losing the 1980 election, Carter preserved millions of acres of Alaskan wilderness and helped pass the Superfund bill to clean up toxic waste sites, and during his waning days in office, Clinton issued executive orders creating or enlarging twenty-two national monuments and protecting millions of acres of forestlands.

Rollback Advocates

Two presidents have entered office with negative environmental agendas: Ronald Reagan and George W. Bush. Both represented antiregulatory forces in the Republican Party that sought to roll back or weaken existing environmental legislation. Reagan launched a crusade against what he considered unnecessary social regulation that he believed impeded economic growth. His stance on the environment aroused enormous controversy, and by 1983, he was forced to moderate his policies. Bush also stressed the importance of economic growth over environmental protection. He launched a wide range of initiatives to soften environmental regulation during his first term but ultimately failed to alter basic environmental legislation.

In the following sections, I first review the presidencies of Ronald Reagan, George H. W. Bush, and Bill Clinton as examples of these three categories. In each case, I briefly examine their use of presidential powers and evaluate their presidencies using the criteria mentioned in this introduction. I then compare the use of executive powers by George W. Bush and Barack Obama in more detail and offer a preliminary assessment of Obama's record.

The Reagan Revolution: Environmental Backlash

The "environmental decade" of the 1970s came to an abrupt halt with Reagan's victory in 1980. Although the environment was not a major issue in the election, Reagan was the first president to come to office with an avowedly anti-environmental agenda. Reflecting the Sagebrush Rebellion—an attempt by several western states to claim ownership of federal lands—as well as long years of public relations work for corporate and conservative causes, Reagan viewed environmental conservation as fundamentally at odds with economic growth and prosperity. He saw environmental regulation as a barrier to "supply side" economics and sought to reverse or weaken many of the policies of the previous decade.[17] Although only partially successful, Reagan's agenda laid the groundwork for renewed attacks on environmental policy in later decades.

After a period of economic decline, Reagan's landslide victory appeared to reflect a strong mandate for policy change. And with a new Republican majority in the Senate, he was able to gain congressional support for the Economic Recovery Tax Act of 1981, which embodied much of his program. He reduced income taxes by nearly 25 percent and deeply cut spending for environmental and social programs. Despite this initial victory, however, Reagan faced a Congress that was divided on most issues and did not support his broader environmental goals. On the contrary, the bipartisan majority that had enacted most of the environmental legislation of the 1970s remained largely intact.

Faced with this situation, Reagan turned to what has been termed an "administrative presidency."[18] Essentially, this involved an attempt to change federal policies by maximizing control of policy implementation within the executive branch. The administrative strategy initially had four major components: (1) careful screening of all appointees to environmental and other agencies to ensure compliance with Reagan's ideological goals; (2) tight policy coordination through cabinet councils and White House staff; (3) deep cuts in the budgets of environmental agencies and programs; and (4) an enhanced form of regulatory oversight to eliminate or revise regulations considered burdensome by industry.

Reagan's appointment of officials who were overtly hostile to the mission of their agencies aroused strong opposition from the environmental community. In particular, his selection of Anne Gorsuch (later Burford) to head the EPA and James Watt as secretary of the interior provoked controversy from the beginning because both were attorneys who had spent long years litigating against environmental regulation. Both made it clear that they intended to rewrite the rules and procedures of their agencies to accommodate industries such as mining, logging, and oil and gas. Watt was also designated head of the new cabinet council to coordinate policies in all of the environmental and natural resource agencies in line with the president's agenda.

In the White House, Reagan lost no time in changing the policy machinery to accomplish the same goal. He all but eliminated his environmental advisers and instead appointed Vice President George H. W. Bush to head a new Task Force on Regulatory Relief, to identify and modify or rescind regulations targeted by business and industry. More importantly, in February 1981 Reagan issued Executive Order 12291, which carried White House control of the regulatory process to a new level. All major regulations (costing over $100 million) were now to undergo prepublication review by the Office of Information and Regulatory Affairs (OIRA) in the Office of Management and Budget. They were to be accompanied by rigorous benefit-cost analyses demonstrating that benefits exceeded costs, and to include evaluation of alternatives to ensure that net social benefits were maximized. OIRA consequently held up, reviewed, and revised hundreds of EPA and other regulations to reduce their effect on industry. The number of new environmental rules thus declined sharply in the Reagan years.[19]

At the same time, Reagan's budget cuts had major effects on the capacity of environmental agencies to implement their growing policy mandates. The EPA lost approximately one-third of its operating budget and one-fifth of its personnel in the early 1980s. The White House Council on Environmental Quality (CEQ) lost most of its staff and barely continued to function. In the Interior Department and elsewhere, funds were shifted from environmental to development programs.[20]

Not surprisingly, Congress responded by investigating OIRA procedures and other activities of Reagan appointees, especially Burford and Watt. Burford came under heavy attack for confidential dealings with business and political interests that allegedly led to sweetheart deals on matters such as Superfund cleanups. After refusing to disclose documents, she was found in contempt of Congress and forced to resign (along with twenty other high-level EPA officials) in March 1983. Watt was pilloried in Congress for his efforts to open virtually all public lands (including wilderness areas) and offshore coastal areas to mining and oil and gas development, and left office later in 1983.[21]

Because of these embarrassments and widespread public and congressional opposition to weakening environmental protection, Reagan's deregulatory campaign was largely spent by the end of his first term. Recognizing that his policies had backfired, the president took few new initiatives during his second term. His appointees to the EPA and Interior diffused some of the political conflict generated by Watt and Burford. But Congress passed a series of amendments (over his objections) to existing laws such as Superfund (specifically, the Superfund Amendments and Reauthorization Act of 1986), the Safe Drinking Water Act, and the Clean Water Act (see Appendix 1). These laws mandated stricter regulatory timetables and enforcement and were intended to reduce the discretionary authority of the EPA and other executive agencies.

On the positive side, Reagan deserves credit for supporting and signing the Montreal Protocol on Substances That Deplete the Ozone Layer in 1987. This treaty, which banned the use of chlorofluorocarbons (CFCs) and other chemicals that were destroying the atmospheric ozone layer, has proven to be one of the most effective international environmental agreements.[22] However, Reagan continued to oppose actions on other air pollution issues such as acid rain.

President George H. W. Bush: Clean Air Legislation

George H. W. Bush's presidency returned to a more moderate tradition of Republican leadership, particularly in the first two years. While promising to "stay the course" on Reagan's economic policies, Bush also pledged a "kinder and gentler" America. Although his domestic policy agenda was the most limited of any recent president, it included action on the environment. Indeed, during the campaign, Bush declared himself a "conservationist" in the tradition of Teddy Roosevelt and promised to be an "environmental president."

If Bush surprised almost everyone by seizing the initiative on what most assumed was a strong issue for the Democrats, he impressed environmentalists even more by soliciting their advice and by appointing a number of environmental leaders to his administration. William Reilly, the highly respected president of the World Wildlife Fund and the Conservation Foundation, became EPA administrator; and Michael Deland, formerly New England director of the EPA, became chairman of the CEQ. Bush promised to restore the CEQ to an influential role and made it clear that he intended to work closely with the Democratic Congress to strengthen the Clean Air Act early in his administration.

Yet Bush's nominees to head the public lands and natural resource agencies were not much different from those of the Reagan administration. In particular, his choice of Manuel Lujan Jr., a ten-term retired representative from New Mexico, to serve as secretary of the interior indicated that no major departures would be made in western land policies. The president's top White House advisers were also much more conservative on environmental matters than were Reilly and Deland. This was especially true of his chief of staff, John Sununu.

Bush pursued a bipartisan strategy in passing the Clean Air Act Amendments of 1990, arguably the single most important legislative achievement of his presidency. His draft bill, sent to Congress on July 21, 1989, had three major goals: to control acid rain by reducing by nearly half sulfur dioxide emissions from coal-burning power plants by 2000, to reduce air pollution in eighty urban areas that still had not met 1977 air quality standards, and to lower emissions of nearly two hundred airborne toxic chemicals by 75 to 90 percent by 2000. To reach the acid precipitation goals—to which the White House devoted most of its attention—Bush proposed a cap-and-trade system rather than command-and-control regulation to achieve emissions reductions more efficiently (see Chapter 10).[23] The act also prohibited the use of CFCs and other ozone-depleting chemicals by 2000.

But it was probably Bush's role as chief diplomat that most defined his environmental image. The president threatened to boycott the UN Conference on Environment and Development (the Earth Summit) in June 1992 until he had ensured that the climate change convention to be signed would contain no binding targets for carbon dioxide reduction. He further alienated the environmental community by refusing to sign the Convention on Biological Diversity despite efforts by his delegation chief, William Reilly, to seek a last-minute compromise.[24] Thus, despite Bush's other accomplishments in foreign policy, the United States failed to lead in environmental diplomacy.

The Clinton Presidency: Frustrated Ambitions

President Bill Clinton entered office in 1993 with high expectations from environmentalists. His campaign promises included many environmental pledges: to raise the Corporate Average Fuel Economy (CAFE) standard for automobiles, encourage mass transit programs, support renewable energy research and development, limit U.S. carbon dioxide emissions to 1990 levels by 2000, create a new solid waste reduction program and provide other incentives for recycling, pass a new Clean Water Act with standards for nonpoint sources, reform the Superfund program and tighten enforcement of toxic waste laws, protect ancient forests and wetlands, preserve the Arctic National Wildlife Refuge, sign the biodiversity convention, and restore funding to UN population programs.[25]

Clinton's early actions indicated that he intended to deliver on his environmental agenda. The environmental community largely applauded his appointments to key environmental positions. Perhaps most important, Vice President Al Gore was given the lead responsibility for formulating and coordinating environmental policy in the White House. Several of his former Senate aides were also appointed to high positions, including EPA administrator Carol Browner. Other appointments to the cabinet and executive office staffs were largely pro-environmental. The most notable environmental leader was Bruce Babbitt, a former Arizona governor and president of the League of Conservation Voters, who became secretary of the interior. In contrast to his predecessors in the Reagan and Bush administrations, Babbitt came to office with a strong reform agenda for western public lands management.[26]

Although Clinton entered office with an expansive agenda and Democratic majorities in both houses of Congress, his environmental agenda quickly got bogged down. Two events early in the term gave the administration an appearance of environmental policy failure. Babbitt promptly launched a campaign to "revolutionize" western land use policies, including a proposal in Clinton's first budget to raise grazing fees on public lands closer to private market levels (something natural resource economists had advocated for many years). The predictable result was a furious outcry from cattle ranchers and their representatives in Congress. After meeting with several western Democratic senators, Clinton backed down and removed the proposal from the bill. Much the same thing happened on the so-called BTU tax. This was a proposal to levy a broad-based tax on the energy content of fuels as a means of promoting energy conservation and addressing climate change. Originally included in the president's budget package at Gore's request, it was eventually dropped in favor of a much smaller gasoline tax (4.3 cents per gallon) in the face of fierce opposition from members of both parties in Congress.

These and other failures (including Clinton's proposed health care reform) contributed to a Republican takeover of Congress after the 1994 elections. Claiming a mandate for the "Contract with America," the new House Speaker, Newt Gingrich, R-Ga., vowed "to begin decisively changing the shape of the government." With the help of industry lobbyists, the new congressional leaders unleashed a massive effort to rewrite the environmental legislation of the past quarter-century.[27] Although Clinton derailed most of these initiatives, he followed a more centrist course thereafter. He was able to get bipartisan support for passage of two relatively uncontroversial bills in 1996, the Food Quality Protection Act and the Safe Drinking Water Act Amendments (discussed in Chapter 7).

Clinton also relied heavily on his executive powers to pursue his environmental agenda. A "reinventing environmental regulation" initiative launched in 1995 created some fifty new EPA programs to encourage voluntary pollution reduction and to reward states and companies that exceeded regulatory requirements.[28] EPA administrator Browner also strengthened existing regulations and enforcement. For example, in 1997, she issued tighter ambient air quality standards for ozone and small particulate matter. In the final year of the Clinton administration, the EPA proposed a series of new regulations tightening standards on other forms of pollution, including diesel emissions from trucks and buses and arsenic in drinking water.

In addition to strengthening the EPA, the Clinton administration took numerous executive actions to protect public lands and endangered species. For example, it helped to broker agreements to protect old-growth forests in the Pacific Northwest, the Florida Everglades, and Yellowstone National Park. The White House actively promoted voluntary agreements to establish habitat conservation plans to protect wildlife throughout the country.[29] Clinton also used his authority under the Antiquities Act to establish or enlarge twenty-two national monuments covering more than six million acres.[30] Finally, in January 2001, Clinton issued a long-awaited executive order protecting nearly sixty million acres of "roadless" areas in national forests from future road construction and hence from logging and development. He could thus claim to have preserved more public land in the contiguous United States than any president since Theodore Roosevelt.[31]

However, the Clinton administration largely failed to develop an effective response to perhaps the greatest challenge of the new century: climate change. After defeat of the BTU tax in 1993, Clinton's climate change proposals called for only voluntary actions; and the administration refused to commit the United States to binding reductions prior to the Kyoto treaty negotiations in December 1997. By then, the president was severely constrained by congressional opposition to any agreement limiting U.S. emissions.[32] Ultimately, Clinton authorized Vice President Gore to break the deadlock at Kyoto with an offer to reduce U.S. emissions to 7 percent below 1990 levels by 2008–2012, and the United States signed the treaty in 1998. However, Congress made it clear that it would not ratify the agreement and prohibited all efforts to implement it.

President George W. Bush: Regulatory Retreat

George W. Bush took office in 2001 with a weak mandate to govern. He had lost the popular vote to Al Gore and had been declared the Electoral College winner only after several weeks of wrangling over contested Florida ballots, culminating with intervention by the Supreme Court. However, in the wake of the September 11, 2001, terrorist attacks on New York City and Washington, DC, his powers were greatly enlarged. Like Reagan, Bush used the executive powers of the presidency to advance an antiregulatory, pro-business agenda, though not to the same degree. He exercised the powers of appointment, budget, regulatory oversight, and rulemaking to weaken environmental policies.[33] Vice President Dick Cheney played a leading role in selecting cabinet appointees and, like previous vice presidents, in shaping energy and environmental policies.[34]

Appointments With the exception of Christine Todd Whitman, the former governor of New Jersey who was picked to head the EPA, Bush's initial appointments to environmental and natural resource agencies were largely drawn from business corporations or from conservative interest groups, law firms, and think tanks. Among the more controversial of these appointees were Secretary of Interior Gale Norton, a protégée of James Watt and a strong advocate of resource development; J. Steven Griles, her deputy secretary and a long-time coal and oil industry lobbyist; Julie MacDonald, deputy assistant secretary of interior for fish and wildlife (responsible for the Endangered Species Act); and Mark Rey, a timber industry lobbyist, as undersecretary of agriculture for natural resources and environment (including the U.S. Forest Service). All of these officials left office under a cloud of investigation after ignoring numerous environmental roadblocks to resource exploitation.

Bush's White House and Executive Office staffs were also filled with conservatives, including chief of staff Andrew H. Card Jr., CEQ chairman James Connaughton, and OIRA director John D. Graham.[35] Some of Bush's other environmental appointees were less controversial, if not less partisan. When Whitman resigned in 2003 after being undercut on climate change and clean air standards by the vice president and other cabinet members, Bush appointed Michael Leavitt, the conservative governor of Utah, as EPA administrator. Leavitt moved on to become secretary of health and human services in 2005, and Stephen L. Johnson was named EPA administrator. Although a career scientist at the EPA, Johnson had little influence in the White House and failed to restore the reputation of the agency.[36] The former governor and senator from Idaho, Dirk Kempthorne, succeeded Norton as secretary of interior in 2006 and largely continued her policies.

Budget Priorities President Bush's first budget proposal, for fiscal year 2002, called for a modest 4 percent increase in overall domestic discretionary spending, but an 8 percent reduction in funding for natural resource and environmental programs (the largest cut for any sector). The EPA's budget was to be slashed by nearly $500 million, or 6.4 percent, and the Interior Department budget was slated for a 3.5 percent cut.[37] Congress, however, did not approve these budget cuts; in fact, the EPA's budget was increased to $7.9 billion, $600 million more than the president had requested. EPA spending remained at near $8 billion through 2008, but federal outlays for the Departments of Energy and Interior increased significantly. Although Bush continued to call for reductions, overall spending for natural resources and the environment rose by about 25 percent between 2001 and 2008.[38] Thus, environmental agencies did not suffer budget cuts as they did during the Reagan administration.

Regulatory Oversight After suspending or rejecting many of Clinton's last-minute regulations, the Bush White House reestablished the Reagan-era rules for regulatory review. OIRA carried out extensive analysis of proposed regulations, demanding that agencies justify all new rules on the basis of strict benefit-cost analysis. At the behest of business groups, existing rules were also reviewed in order to reduce the burden of regulation wherever possible.[39] Going one better than Reagan, in January 2007, the president issued a new executive order (13422) requiring that each agency must have a regulatory policy office run by a political appointee to manage the regulatory review process.[40] The order also granted OIRA new authority to review and edit "agency guidance documents," including scientific reports and memoranda, and to hold up proposed regulations indefinitely. In addition to these formal procedures, which had the effect of delaying or weakening regulations, the vice president and White House staff often intervened directly in the details of agency decision making.

The result was a highly politicized form of administration in which the political interests of the president and his supporters frequently overrode scientific and technical considerations in the bureaucracy. Indeed, the Bush-Cheney administration was repeatedly accused of having ignored the advice of scientific experts or distorting scientific information to justify policy decisions. A report by the Union of Concerned Scientists released in April 2008 found that 889 of nearly 1,600 staff scientists at the EPA reported that they had experienced political interference in their work in the previous five years.[41] And in December 2008, the inspector general of the Interior Department issued a report finding that Julie MacDonald and other department officials had altered scientific evidence regarding protection of endangered species in at least fifteen cases.[42]

Administrative Policymaking President Bush's energy and environmental agenda was quickly shaped after he took office. During spring 2001, a national energy plan was drafted in secrecy by a task force appointed by Vice President Cheney.[43] By all accounts, virtually all of the outside experts consulted were from energy producers and related industries, and many of the report's 106 recommendations directly reflected these interests.[44] The plan called for major increases in future energy supplies, including domestic oil, gas, nuclear, and "clean coal" development, and for streamlining environmental regulations to accelerate new energy production. A bill incorporating these and other aspects of the Bush-Cheney plan, together with additional tax breaks for the energy industries, quickly passed the House of Representatives in 2001, but later stalled in the Senate when authorization to drill in the Arctic National Wildlife Refuge was defeated. Eventually, an energy bill passed in 2005 providing large subsidies, loan guarantees, and other incentives to conventional energy producers (see Appendix 1), but by then, many of the original plan's recommendations had already been implemented by administrative actions. For example, coal, oil, and gas leasing had already been greatly expanded in the West. President Bush also set aside or rewrote many of the Clinton administration's last-minute resource conservation rules, including the Roadless Area Conservation Rule.[45]

The administration's "Clear Skies" bill, introduced in Congress in 2002, incorporated many of industries' suggestions for scaling back pollution control requirements of the Clean Air Act. When this legislation went nowhere, Bush proceeded to issue executive orders that, in effect, implemented similar rules. For example, one of the more controversial rules relaxed requirements for installation of new pollution equipment when power plants and oil refineries expanded or increased production (see Chapter 7). A broader Clean Air Interstate Rule issued in 2005 set standards for conventional air pollutants such as sulfur dioxide and ozone in twenty-eight eastern states, while another rule regulated mercury emissions from coal-fired power plants. These rules raised current standards but were less rigorous than those recommended by EPA scientists, and in most cases were overturned by the courts (Chapter 6).[46]

Perhaps President Bush's most significant executive action was his rejection of the Kyoto Protocol on climate change in 2001. Calling the treaty "fatally flawed," the president officially withdrew United States participation in the international regime for regulating greenhouse gases. This was part of a larger shift away from international treaty obligations in the Bush administration, but it presaged an eight-year effort to block any mandatory requirements for controlling greenhouse gases (despite Bush's campaign promises to regulate carbon dioxide). During his first term, Bush refused to acknowledge the growing scientific consensus on global warming and opposed all efforts to limit greenhouse gas emissions. Instead, he supported continuing research programs on climate science and technological development, including new efforts to develop hydrogen energy and other alternative fuels. However, as dependence on foreign oil and rising fuel prices became a more important national security issue, Bush began to revise his stance. In his 2006 State of the Union address, he decried the United States' "addiction to oil" and called for a 75 percent reduction of oil imports by 2025. In part, this was to be achieved by massive expansion in production of ethanol and other biofuels.[47] The Energy Independence and Security Act of 2007 incorporated many of these proposals and also modestly raised fuel efficiency standards for the first time in twenty years.[48] But despite a landmark U.S. Supreme Court decision in April 2007 holding that the EPA could regulate greenhouse gases under the Clean Air Act, the White House refused to allow the agency to develop a regulatory strategy for climate change or to grant California a waiver to regulate carbon dioxide emissions from vehicles (see Chapter 7).

On the more positive side, President Bush used his executive authority to create four national monuments in the Pacific Ocean. In 2006, he established the world's largest marine reserve covering 140,000 square miles in the Northwestern Hawaiian Islands. Then, just before leaving office in January 2009, he designated three more monuments over large tracts of ocean in the western Pacific near American Samoa. These sparsely inhabited areas of reefs, atolls, and undersea mountains will be protected from commercial fishing, drilling, and mineral extraction, thereby preserving their unique ecological features. Thus, although he did not create new national monuments within the continental United States, Bush began a process of protecting threatened areas of the ocean.[49]

President Barack Obama: Climate Breakthrough?

Barack Obama took office in January 2009 with what appeared to be a strong electoral mandate. Although he inherited the multiple economic and foreign policy crises left by the Bush administration, his campaign based on messages of "hope" and "change we can believe in" seemed to provide an opening for far-reaching reforms. Obama had also endorsed a strong environmental agenda. Among other things, he promised to create a cap-and-trade program for reducing U.S. greenhouse gas emissions; to make massive investments in renewable energy to create millions of new jobs; to double auto fuel economy standards by 2025; to tighten air pollution standards for mercury and other pollutants from power plants; to make major improvements in energy efficiency standards for buildings and in the national electricity grid; and to reverse Bush administration policies on mining and protection of roadless areas.[50] The Democratic Party also gained the largest majorities in Congress in decades, making a legislative strategy appear feasible.

However, as noted in the introduction to this chapter, the climate change bill failed in the Senate, and after the Republicans regained a majority in the House of Representatives in 2010, it became impossible to enact any environmental legislation (Chapter 5). Thus, like his predecessors Ronald Reagan, Bill Clinton, and George W. Bush, Obama turned increasingly to an administrative strategy to carry out his agenda. Although he had criticized Bush during the 2008 campaign for misusing his executive powers, by 2012 Obama saw no alternative other than to utilize these same powers—but to strengthen rather than weaken environmental protection.[51] After his reelection, the president made it clear that he would act with or without the support of Congress.[52]

Appointments President Obama's choices for cabinet and top White House staff positions were well regarded by environmentalists. His first-term "green team" included Carol Browner, EPA head in the Clinton administration, as White House coordinator of energy and climate policy (a new position); Lisa Jackson, a chemical engineer who had served in the EPA and as commissioner of the New Jersey Department of Environmental Protection, as EPA administrator; Steven Chu, a Nobel Prize–winning physicist who directed the Lawrence Berkeley National Laboratory, as energy secretary; and Sen. Ken Salazar, D-Colo., as interior secretary.[53] Obama also appointed a number of other top scientists to the administration. In addition to Chu, he chose John Holdren as White House science adviser, director of the Office of Science and Technology Policy, and chair of the President's Council of Advisors on Science and Technology. Holdren, a physics professor at Harvard, is a leading expert on energy and an advocate for action on climate change.[54]

Obama's second-term appointments were considered strong environmentalists but pragmatic administrators as well. Gina McCarthy, the assistant administrator in charge of air and radiation at the Environmental Protection Agency, became the new EPA head; Ernest J. Moniz, a distinguished physicist from the Massachusetts Institute of Technology, replaced Steven Chu at the energy department; and Sally Jewell, an oil geologist, banker, and president of the REI outdoor equipment company, became secretary of the interior. Finally, in December 2013, President Obama made a dramatic move to strengthen White House capabilities by bringing John Podesta, former chief of staff in the Clinton administration and founder of the Center for American Progress, in as special adviser. Podesta was given management and oversight responsibilities for implementing EPA's new power plant regulations and played a key role in negotiating an agreement with China to limit future carbon emissions (see below).[55]

Budget Priorities Despite taking office amidst the worst recession since the 1930s and strong opposition from Republicans to raising the national debt, President Obama presided over a significant increase in federal spending on energy, natural resources, and the environment. Many of his goals for developing new energy technologies were incorporated into his emergency "stimulus bill" (the American Recovery and Reinvestment Act of 2009), which included some $80 billion in new spending, tax incentives, and loan guarantees to promote energy efficiency, renewable energy sources, fuel-efficient cars, mass transit, and cleaner fuel technologies. He also called for large increases in the budget of the EPA and other environmental agencies. His first budget (for fiscal year 2010) requested $10.5 billion for the EPA (48 percent more than requested by President Bush in his final budget), and Congress approved $10.2 billion. Actual EPA spending rose from $8 billion in 2009 to over $12.7 billion in 2012, then fell back to an estimated $8.1 billion in 2014 (about the same as in the Bush administration). Energy Department spending rose from $23.7 billion in 2009 to a peak of $32.4 billion in 2012 before retreating to $27.8 billion in 2014. And overall spending for natural resources and the environment increased from $35.5 billion in 2009 to a peak of $45.9 billion in 2011 before settling back to an estimated $39.1 billion in 2014.[56] Some of the later reductions were the result of across-the-board budget cuts (the "sequester") that the administration was forced to accept after threats by Republicans to default on the national debt in 2011 and a partial shutdown of the government in 2013. There have also been some reductions in EPA personnel, and budgets are projected to hold steady or decline in future years (see Chapter 1).

Executive Actions Given his experience as a senator, criticism of George W. Bush's style of leadership, and preference for legislative solutions, it is not surprising that President Obama was slower to develop an administrative presidency. Nevertheless, he utilized some executive powers from the beginning. Upon taking office, he suspended or revoked a number of Bush's executive orders and regulations, including those on California's request for a waiver to regulate greenhouse gas emissions from automobiles, oil and gas leasing in potential wilderness areas, and political direction of regulatory review. In March 2009, he issued a "Presidential Memorandum on Scientific Integrity" to heads of agencies and departments to prevent political misuse of scientific research and information such as was alleged to have occurred during his predecessor's tenure.[57]

In general, however, Obama took a relatively cautious approach to the use of unilateral powers during his first term. He issued a total of 147 executive orders (compared to 173 by Bush in his first term), but only 7 of these dealt with environmental or energy policy.[58] Several provided for the establishment of national commissions to investigate the Deepwater Horizon oil spill of 2010 and restoration of Gulf Coast ecosystems, preservation of the Chesapeake Bay, and protection of the oceans and Great Lakes. Perhaps the most significant, on "Federal Leadership in Environmental, Energy, and Economic Performance," required all federal agencies to develop strategic sustainability plans to sharply increase energy efficiency, reduce greenhouse gas emissions, and improve all other aspects of environmental management.[59] But these orders were balanced by others that were designed to reassure business that the administration would not impede the economic recovery.[60] Obama's first OIRA director, Cass Sunstein, also required extremely rigorous economic analysis of all proposed rules and regulations; indeed, by some counts, fewer new regulations were issued during his tenure than in a comparable period under Bush.[61] Some major regulations, such as the EPA's initial proposal to lower allowable levels of ambient ozone, were rejected on grounds that the benefits did not clearly outweigh the costs, while others were apparently held up by the White House to avoid political repercussions.[62]

Nevertheless, among others, the EPA issued new regulations to control mercury and other toxic emissions from industrial boilers, incinerators, and power plants; to tighten standards for emission of sulfur dioxide, nitrogen oxides, and particulates that drift downwind from twenty-eight eastern states and the District of Columbia (the Cross-State Air Pollution Rule); and to limit some carbon emissions from large industries. More significantly, in 2010, President Obama raised the CAFE standards for automobile fuel efficiency to 35.5 miles per gallon in 2016 (roughly equal to the California standard the Bush administration had rejected) and, in August 2012, following negotiations with the auto industry, environmentalists, and energy experts, to 54.5 miles per gallon by 2025.[63] In October 2010, the government also proposed mileage standards for heavy trucks and buses for the first time.[64] These and other measures laid the basis for a more comprehensive attack on climate change in Obama's second term.

Administrative Policies At the Copenhagen climate change conference in December 2009, President Obama pledged to reduce U.S. greenhouse gas emissions by 17 percent over 2005 levels by 2020, roughly the reduction expected from passage of the climate change bill then pending in Congress. Despite the failure of the bill, Obama has continued to espouse this goal and in his second term has made its achievement a top priority. Indeed, action on climate change has been called "the defining domestic initiative of Mr. Obama's second term" and his "legacy" issue.[65]

Obama outlined his strategy for climate change in a speech at George-town University in June 2013.[66] The plan, which contained some seventy-five specific proposals, relied heavily on executive action and existing law. It included regulation of carbon dioxide emissions from new and existing power plants and a continuing shift to cleaner fuels such as natural gas; a redoubling of wind and solar energy production (which had doubled in the previous four years) and opening public lands and military bases to renewable energy con-struction; a new goal for the federal government to consume 20 percent of its electricity from renewable sources by 2020; increased preparedness for the impacts of climate change through support of infrastructure improvements such as seawalls and hardened power, water, and fuel supply systems; and reas-sertion of American international leadership on climate change including cooperative agreements with rapidly developing countries such as China, end-ing U.S. aid and support for construction of coal-fired power plants abroad, and seeking a new global treaty to cut carbon pollution (see Chapter 13).[67]

The first of these policies—especially regulation of carbon emissions from nearly six hundred coal-fired power plants—has been the most impor-tant departure from past policies since these plants are the largest single source of greenhouse gases in the nation. Here the president has relied heav-ily on the statutory authority conferred on the EPA by the Clean Air Act, as affirmed by the U.S. Supreme Court's *Massachusetts v. EPA* decision in 2007 (see Chapter 6). Whereas the Bush administration had refused to act on the basis of the court decision, Obama saw it as an opportunity to carry out much of his climate change agenda through the executive branch (see Chapter 7). His administration first issued mobile source regulations for automobiles and trucks, as mentioned above, and then extended greenhouse gas regulation to power plants and other large stationary sources for the first time. In Septem-ber 2013, the EPA proposed a carbon emission standard for all *new* electric power plants that would make future construction of coal-fired plants pro-hibitively expensive; and in June 2014, it issued a draft rule that would require *existing* coal plants to reduce their carbon emissions by approximately 30 percent from 2005 levels by 2030.[68] After a year of public comment and nego-tiation, a final rule was expected to be issued in June 2015. If upheld by the courts and implemented by the states, this policy could force the closure of most of the oldest and dirtiest coal plants in the nation (see Chapter 7 for a detailed discussion).[69] The proposed regulation would give considerable flex-ibility to the states in designing their implementation plans, but it was never-theless denounced by the Republican Party—and some Democrats—as a "war on coal" during the 2014 congressional elections.

Despite losses in the elections, President Obama followed through on his promise to pursue a new international climate change agreement. Although no binding climate treaty is likely to be ratified by the Senate in the foreseeable future, Obama announced a landmark executive agreement with China a week after the elections. Under the agreement, China made a com-mitment to limit its use of fossil fuels for the first time by pledging that its carbon emissions will peak no later than 2030, and also agreed to produce 20 percent of its total energy consumption from clean sources by the same year. On its side, the United States pledged to reduce its carbon emissions by 26–28 percent by 2025, compared to 2005.[70] This joint leadership by the United States and China raised hopes that a broader set of international agreements could be reached at the United Nations climate change meeting in Paris in December 2015 (see Chapter 13).[71]

In late November 2014, the EPA also issued its long-delayed national ozone standard. Ground-level ozone, or smog, is produced by factories, power plants, and vehicles, and is the most pervasive urban air pollutant linked to asthma, heart disease, and premature death. The new rules would lower threshold levels of ambient ozone to 65–70 parts per billion (compared to the current standard of 75 parts per billion) and put dozens, if not hundreds, of cities and counties out of compliance with the Clean Air Act. Although possibly less restrictive than originally proposed in 2011, the rules could require $15 billion or more in additional pollution control expenditure by the time they are fully implemented in 2025. Nevertheless, the benefits are estimated to greatly outweigh the costs.[72]

Senator Mitch McConnell, the incoming majority leader, denounced the new ozone rules and vowed to block them as well as the rules limiting emissions from coal-fired power plants when the Republicans took control of the Senate in 2015. Since the new rules and regulations are based on existing authority under the Clean Air Act, it is unlikely that Congress will be able to repeal them.[73] However, the Republican majority is expected to attempt to prevent their implementation through the appropriations process or other means. The courts will also have to rule on their legality. The success of Mr. Obama's climate initiatives and other environmental policies thus remains uncertain, and they are likely to remain controversial for some time.

Conclusion

The records of recent presidents demonstrate that the White House has had a significant but hardly singular or consistent role in shaping national environmental policy. Presidents Richard Nixon and George H. W. Bush had their greatest successes in supporting environmental legislation. Facing more hostile Congresses, Presidents Ronald Reagan, Bill Clinton, and George W. Bush had the most influence (for better or worse) as chief executives who used administrative strategies to shape the direction of environmental policies. Nixon and George H. W. Bush responded to public pressures to become opportunistic, but largely constructive, environmental presidents. Carter and Clinton had positive environmental agendas when they entered office but had more modest success in achieving reforms. Reagan and George W. Bush attempted to rescind or weaken environmental protections as part of their deregulation policy but failed to permanently alter the structure of environmental legislation adopted in the 1970s.

President Obama has faced exceptional opposition in Congress and, like Reagan, Clinton, and George W. Bush, has had his greatest influence on environmental policy as chief executive. Although he failed to achieve comprehensive climate legislation, Obama is the first president to have seriously addressed climate change and to have carried out virtually all of his environmental agenda through executive actions. Indeed, he has put in place the most far-reaching environmental policy changes since Richard Nixon. He can thus be considered an opportunistic leader who has fully used the powers of the presidency to advance environmental causes despite lack of congressional support. The ultimate success of his initiatives remains to be seen, but it appears that he has made a critical start in facing the challenges of the future (Chapter 16). In any case, presidents will remain central to the development of environmental policy.

Suggested Websites

Council on Environmental Quality (www.whitehouse.gov/ceq) Provides analysis of environmental conditions and links to other useful sources throughout the federal government.

Department of the Interior (www.interior.gov) Official website for the department and bureaus within it.

Environmental Protection Agency (www.epa.gov) Official website for the EPA.

The Heritage Foundation (www.heritage.org) Offers research and analysis on energy and environmental issues from a conservative perspective.

Natural Resources Defense Council (www.nrdc.org) Provides analysis and criticism by a leading environmental organization.

Center for Effective Government (www.foreffectivegov.org/) Follows budgets and regulatory policies.

Center for Climate and Energy Solutions (www.C2ES.org) Provides information from a leading think tank on climate change issues.

The White House (www.whitehouse.gov) President's official website.

Notes

1. Deborah Lynn Guber and Christopher J. Bosso, "'High Hopes and Bitter Disappointment': Public Discourse and the Limits of the Environmental Movement in Climate Change Politics," in *Environmental Policy*, 8th ed., ed. Norman J. Vig and Michael E. Kraft (Thousand Oaks, CA: Sage/CQ Press, 2013), 54–82.
2. The administration did not propose a new ozone regulation until November 2014; see Coral Davenport, "E.P.A. Ozone Rules Divide Industry and Environmentalists," *New York Times*, November 26, 2014.
3. Richard W. Stevenson and John M. Broder, "Climate Change Given Prominence in Obama's Address," *New York Times*, January 21, 2013; and Broder, "A New Path on Emissions," *New York Times*, February 6, 2013.
4. Ashley Parker, "'Imperial Presidency' Becomes a Rallying Cry for Republicans," *New York Times*, April 1, 2014; Parker, "Boehner to Seek Bill to Sue Obama over Executive Actions," *New York Times*, June 25, 2014; and Parker, "House Republicans Sue Obama Administration over Health Law," *New York Times*, November 21, 2014. The House

of Representatives voted along party lines to sue the president over implementation of the Affordable Care Act.

5. Brian Bennett, "Marco Rubio Says Human Activity Isn't Causing Climate Change," *Los Angeles Times*, May 11, 2014. For dissenting views, see Jon M. Huntsman Jr., "The GOP Can't Ignore Climate Change," *New York Times*, May 7, 2014; and Henry B. Paulson, Jr., "The Coming Climate Crash," *New York Times*, June 22, 2014.

6. For a ranking of the last twelve presidents, see Byron W. Daynes and Glen Sussman, *White House Politics and the Environment: Franklin D. Roosevelt to George W. Bush* (College Station: Texas A&M University Press, 2010).

7. See Christopher McGrory Klyza and David Sousa, *American Environmental Policy: Beyond Gridlock*, updated and expanded ed. (Cambridge, MA: MIT Press, 2013).

8. For a more detailed discussion, see Norman J. Vig, "The American Presidency and Environmental Policy," in *The Oxford Handbook of U.S. Environmental Policy*, ed. Sheldon Kamieniecki and Michael E. Kraft (Oxford: Oxford University Press, 2013), 306–328.

9. Dennis L. Soden, ed., *The Environmental Presidency* (Albany: State University of New York Press, 1999), 3.

10. Ibid., 346.

11. See, for example, Coral Davenport, "Climate Change Deemed Growing Security Threat by Military Researchers," *New York Times*, May 14, 2014; and Davenport, "Pentagon Signals Security Risks of Climate Change," *New York Times*, October 14, 2014.

12. Kenneth R. Mayer, "Going Alone: The Presidential Power of Unilateral Action," in *The Oxford Handbook of the American Presidency*, ed. George C. Edwards III and William G. Howell (Oxford: Oxford University Press, 2009), 427–54.

13. Robert F. Durant and William G. Resh, "Presidential Agendas, Administrative Strategies, and the Bureaucracy," in *The Oxford Handbook of the American Presidency*, ed. George C. Edwards III and William G. Howell (Oxford: Oxford University Press, 2009), 577–600; and David E. Lewis and Terry M. Moe, "The Presidency and the Bureaucracy: The Levers of Presidential Control," in *The Presidency and the Political System*, 9th ed., ed. Michael Nelson (Washington, DC: CQ Press, 2010), 367–400.

14. Charles O. Jones, *The Presidency in a Separated System* (Washington, DC: Brookings Institution Press, 1994); and Jones, *Separate but Equal Branches: Congress and the Presidency* (Chatham, NJ: Chatham House, 1995).

15. The presidency of Gerald R. Ford is not considered here because he essentially continued Richard Nixon's policies and did not leave a distinctive environmental legacy.

16. Russell E. Train, "The Environmental Record of the Nixon Administration," *Presidential Studies Quarterly* 26 (1996): 185–96.

17. For a more detailed analysis of Reagan's environmental record, see Michael E. Kraft and Norman J. Vig, "Environmental Policy in the Reagan Presidency," *Political Science Quarterly* 99 (Fall 1984): 414–39; Norman J. Vig and Michael E. Kraft, eds., *Environmental Policy in the 1980s: Reagan's New Agenda* (Washington, DC: CQ Press, 1984).

18. Richard P. Nathan, *The Administrative Presidency* (New York: Wiley, 1983).

19. Lewis and Moe, "The Presidency and the Bureaucracy," 390; and Marc Allen Eisner, *Governing the Environment: The Transformation of Environmental Regulation* (Boulder, CO: Lynne Rienner, 2007), 80–85.

20. On the impact of the Reagan budget cuts, see especially Robert V. Bartlett, "The Budgetary Process and Environmental Policy," and J. Clarence Davies, "Environmental Institutions and the Reagan Administration," in *Environmental Policy in the 1980s: Reagan's New Agenda*, ed. Norman J. Vig and Michael E. Kraft (Washington, DC: CQ Press, 1984).

21. For a detailed summary of Watt's policies, see Paul J. Culhane, "Sagebrush Rebels in Office: Jim Watt's Land and Water Policies," in *Environmental Policy in the 1980s: Reagan's New Agenda*, ed. Norman J. Vig and Michael E. Kraft (Washington, DC: CQ Press, 1984).

22. Cass R. Sunstein, "Climate Change: Lessons from Ronald Reagan," *New York Times*, November 11, 2012; and Justin Gillis, "The Little Treaty That Could," *New York Times*, December 10, 2013.

23. See Gary C. Bryner, *Blue Skies, Green Politics: The Clean Air Act of 1990 and Its Implementation*, 2nd ed. (Washington, DC: CQ Press, 1995).

24. Keith Schneider, "White House Snubs U.S. Envoy's Plea to Sign Rio Treaty," *New York Times*, June 5, 1992.

25. Bill Clinton and Al Gore, *Putting People First* (New York: Times Books, 1992), 89–99.

26. Timothy Egan, "Sweeping Reversal of U.S. Land Policy Sought by Clinton," *New York Times*, February 24, 1993.

27. For a summary of the Republican agenda and responses to it, see "GOP Sets the 104th Congress on New Regulatory Course," *Congressional Quarterly Weekly Report*, June 17, 1995, 1693–1701.

28. On the "reinvention" effort, see Daniel J. Fiorino, *The New Environmental Regulation* (Cambridge, MA: MIT Press, 2006), Chapter 5.

29. As an alternative way of implementing the Endangered Species Act, the Clinton administration supported completion of more than 250 habitat conservation plans protecting some 170 endangered plant and animal species while allowing controlled development on twenty million acres of private land. William Booth, "A Slow Start Built to an Environmental End-run," *Washington Post*, January 13, 2001.

30. For a description of these monuments, see Reed McManus, "Six Million Sweet Acres," *Sierra*, September–October 2001, 40–53.

31. Bill Clinton, *My Life* (New York: Knopf, 2004), 948.

32. In particular, the Byrd-Hagel resolution (passed 95–0 on June 12, 1997) opposed any agreement that would harm the U.S. economy or that did not require control of greenhouse gas emissions by developing countries.

33. Douglas Jehl, "On Rules for Environment, Bush Sees a Balance, Critics a Threat," *New York Times*, February 23, 2003; Jonathan Weisman, "In 2003, It's Reagan Revolution Redux," *Washington Post*, February 4, 2003; Bill Keller, "Reagan's Son," *New York Times Magazine*, January 26, 2003.

34. On Cheney's role, see Jo Becker and Barton Gellman, "Leaving No Tracks," *Washington Post*, June 27, 2007; and Barton Gellman, *Angler: The Cheney Vice Presidency* (New York: Penguin, 2008).

35. On Graham's role, see "New Regulatory Czar Takes Charge," *Science*, October 5, 2001, 32–33; and Rebecca Adams, "Regulating the Rule-Makers: John Graham at OIRA," *CQ Weekly*, February 23, 2002, 520–26.

36. See Margaret Kriz, "Vanishing Act," *National Journal*, April 12, 2008. On Christine Whitman's resignation, see Whitman, *It's My Party, Too* (New York: Penguin, 2005).

37. "Bush's Budget: The Losers," *Washington Post*, April 10, 2001; "Who Gets What Slice of the President's First Federal Budget Pie," *New York Times*, April 10, 2001.

38. Budgets for the EPA and other agencies since 1976 can be found at www.whitehouse.gov/omb/budget/Historicals.

39. Joel Brinkley, "Out of Spotlight, Bush Overhauls U.S. Regulations," *New York Times*, August 16, 2004; Bruce Barcott, "Changing All the Rules," *New York Times Magazine*, April 4, 2004; and Christopher Klyza and David Sousa, *American Environmental Policy, 1990–2006* (Cambridge, MA: MIT Press, 2008), 135–52.

40. Robert Pear, "Bush Directive Increases Sway on Regulation," *New York Times*, January 30, 2007; and C. W. Copeland, "The Law: Executive Order 13422: An Expansion of Presidential Influence in the Rulemaking Process," *Presidential Studies Quarterly* 37 (2007): 531–44.

41. Union of Concerned Scientists, "Hundreds of EPA Scientists Report Political Interference Over Last Five Years," April 23, 2008. See www.ucsusa.org.

42. Charlie Savage, "Report Finds Manipulation of Interior Dept. Actions," *New York Times*, December 16, 2008.

43. See also David E. Sanger and Joseph Kahn, "Bush, Pushing Energy Plan, Offers Scores of Proposals to Find New Power Sources," *New York Times*, May 18, 2001; "Energy Report Highlights," *Washington Post*, May 18, 2001.

44. Neela Banerjee, "Documents Show Energy Official Met Only with Industry Leaders," *New York Times*, March 26, 2002.

45. Klyza and Sousa, *American Environmental Policy: Beyond Gridlock*, 112–23.

46. For details on these actions and their outcomes, see Klyza and Sousa, ibid., Chapters 4 and 9.

47. In his 2007 State of the Union address, Bush called for mandatory standards requiring that thirty-five million gallons of renewable and alternative fuels be produced by 2017, nearly a fivefold increase.

48. See John M. Broder, "Bush Signs Broad Energy Bill," *New York Times*, December 19, 2007.

49. John M. Broder, "Bush to Protect Vast New Pacific Tracts," *New York Times*, January 6, 2009; and Editorial, "Mr. Bush's Monument," *New York Times*, January 7, 2009.

50. "Barack Obama and Joe Biden: Promoting a Healthy Environment," and "Barack Obama and Joe Biden: New Energy for America," www.barackobama.com (campaign website).

51. Charlie Savage, "Shift on Executive Power Lets Obama Bypass Rivals," *New York Times*, April 22, 2012.

52. Emmarie Huetteman, "Aides Say Obama Is Willing to Work with or without Congress to Meet Goals," *New York Times*, January 26, 2014; Charles M. Blow, "A Pen, a Phone and a Meme," *New York Times*, February 7, 2014.

53. John M. Broder, "Obama Team Set on Environment," *New York Times*, December 11, 2008; "Title, but Unclear Power, for a New Climate Czar," *New York Times*, December 12, 2008; "Praise and Criticism for Proposed Interior Secretary," *New York Times*, December 18, 2008.

54. Gardiner Harris, "4 Top Science Advisers Are Named by Obama," *New York Times*, December 21, 2008; and Editorial, "A New Respect for Science," *New York Times*, December 22, 2008.

55. John M. Broder and Matthew L. Wald, "Cabinet Picks Could Take on Climate Policy," *New York Times*, March 4, 2013; Editorial, "Two Enlistees in the Climate Wars," *New York Times*, March 6, 2013; Bruce Barcott, "Sizing Up Sally Jewell," *Outside*, November 12, 2013; Robert B. Semple, Jr., "The Return of John Podesta," *New York Times*, December 14, 2013; Darren Goode, "John Podesta Will Dig into Energy and Climate Policy," *Politico*, December 12, 2013; and Mark Landler, "U.S. and China Reach Deal on Climate Change in Secret Talks," *New York Times*, November 11, 2014.

56. See Note 38. These numbers refer to budget outlays rather than budget authority.

57. "Presidential Memorandum on Scientific Integrity" (March 9, 2009).

58. Presidential executive orders are available online at www.federalregister.gov/executive -orders/.

59. Executive Order 13514 (October 5, 2009).

60. See Executive Orders 13563, "Improving Regulation and Regulatory Review" (January 18, 2011); 13579, "Regulation and Independent Regulatory Agencies" (July 11, 2011); and 13610, "Identifying and Reducing Regulatory Burdens" (May 14, 2012).

61. Sunstein left the administration in mid-2012; see John M. Broder, "Powerful Shaper of U.S. Rules Quits, Leaving Critics in Wake," *New York Times*, August 4, 2012.

62. John M. Broder, "Obama Abandons a Stricter Limit on Air Pollution," *New York Times*, September 3, 2011; Editorial, "Rules Delayed, Governing Denied," *New York Times*, August 12, 2012; Broder, "Environmental Rules Delayed as White House Slows Reviews," *New York Times*, June 12, 2013.

63. John M. Broder, "Obama Seeking a Steep Increase in Auto Mileage," *New York Times*, July 4, 2011. These rules were also converted to greenhouse gas emission limits; see Bill Vlasic, "U.S. Sets High Long-Term Fuel Efficiency Goals for Automakers," *New York Times*, August 29, 2012.

64. Matthew L. Wald, "Heavy Trucks to Be Subject to New Rules for Mileage," *New York Times*, August 10, 2011; Peter Baker and Coral Davenport, "Obama Orders New Efficiency for Big Trucks," *New York Times*, February 19, 2014.

65. Peter Baker and Coral Davenport, "Using Executive Powers, Obama Begins His Last Big Push on Climate Policy," *New York Times*, June 1, 2014; and Editorial, "Nearing a Climate Legacy," *New York Times*, June 3, 2014.

66. "Remarks by the President on Climate Change," June 25, 2013, www.whitehouse.gov/the-press-office/2013/06/25/remarks-president-climate-change; and Editorial, "At Last, an Action Plan on Climate," *New York Times*, June 26, 2013.

67. See Center for Climate and Energy Solutions, "President Obama's Climate Action Plan: One Year Later" (June 2014), for a list of proposals and actions taken.

68. Michael D. Shear, "Administration Presses Ahead with Limits on Emissions from Power Plants," *New York Times*, September 20, 2013; Coral Davenport, "E.P.A. Staff Struggling to Create Pollution Rule," *New York Times*, February 5, 2014; Davenport, "E.P.A. to Seek 30 Percent Cut in Carbon Emissions," *New York Times*, June 2, 2014; and Davenport and Peter Baker, "Taking Page from Health Care Act, Obama Climate Plan Relies on States," *New York Times*, June 3, 2014.

69. The Supreme Court upheld the EPA's statutory authority to regulate greenhouse gas emissions from stationary sources, with some limitations, in an important decision in June 2014; see Adam Liptak, "Justices Uphold Emission Limits on Big Industry," *New York Times*, June 24, 2014.

70. Landler, "U.S. and China Reach Deal on Climate Change in Secret Talks"; Editorial, "Climate Change Breakthrough in Beijing," *New York Times*, November 12, 2014; Henry Fountain and John Schwartz, "Climate Accord Relies on Environmental Policies Now in Place," *New York Times*, November 12, 2014; and Edward Wong, "In Step to Lower Carbon Emissions, China Will Place a Limit on Coal Use in 2020," *New York Times*, November 20, 2014.

71. Coral Davenport, "Deal on Carbon Emissions by Obama and Xi Jinping Raises Hopes for Upcoming Paris Climate Talks," *New York Times*, November 12, 2014.

72. Davenport, "E.P.A. Ozone Rules Divide Industry and Environmentalists" (Note 2). The draft rules are expected to be finalized in late 2015.

73. Coral Davenport, "Obama Builds Environmental Legacy with 1970 Law," *New York Times*, November 26, 2014.

5

Environmental Policy in Congress
Michael E. Kraft

This legislation contains important provisions to rein in the harmful regulatory overreach of federal bureaucracies that will unnecessarily cause job loss and that will weaken our recovering economy.

Rep. Hal Rogers, R-Ky., Chairman of the House
Appropriations Committee, July 2014[1]

[This bill is] an ideological dumping ground of short-sighted environmental policies.

Rep. Debbie Wasserman Schultz, D-Fla., July 2014

In July 2014, the U.S. House Appropriations Committee voted largely on party lines to approve a spending bill that would sharply reduce funding for the Environmental Protection Agency (EPA) and also block the agency's efforts to limit emissions of greenhouse gases from coal-fired power plants. The Republican majority's position, captured in Rep. Rodgers's comment above, prevailed while the Democratic minority, whose views are represented by Rep. Wasserman Schultz's criticism, lost. The committee voted to cut the EPA's budget by over $700 million on top of other reductions made over the past few years (see Chapter 1). The EPA had announced its proposed rule for existing coal-fired power plants on June 2, 2014, and it was a key component of President Barack Obama's 2013 Climate Action Plan. Both that plan and the EPA draft rule reflected the administration's belief that Congress was so unlikely to act on climate change legislation that progress in addressing the problem could come only through executive action, such as EPA rulemaking.[2] House Republicans had long challenged the president on such rulemaking, and the Appropriations Committee vote spoke to what had become a deep partisan divide on climate change, energy use, and environmental policy issues since Republicans won control of the House in the 2010 elections, with strong Tea Party backing.[3]

As was often the case in recent years, however, the committee vote had little practical consequence since the Democratic-controlled Senate was unlikely to go along, and the White House already had threatened to veto the appropriations measure.[4] Sen. Mitch McConnell, R.-Ky., the Senate's minority leader, backed a similar amendment in that body's Appropriations Committee, but here too action was largely symbolic as the full Senate would not block such a major White House policy initiative. Nonetheless, Republicans, as well as some Democrats from coal-mining states or those heavily dependent on the use of coal for generating electricity, were eager to demonstrate their opposition to the EPA power-plant rule, which they had characterized as a "war on coal," by voting for such an amendment.

The bitter partisan battles over the president's climate change policies, as shown in these committee debates and votes, had some real consequences. These were evident in the fate of a bipartisan bill that sought to encourage energy efficiency in buildings when it failed on a procedural vote in the Senate in May 2014. The bill, cosponsored by Senators Rob Portman, R.-Ohio, and Jeanne Shaheen, D-N.H., had widespread support among senators from both parties and in both chambers of Congress, a rarity in the 2010s. Congressional staff members had worked on the bill for over a year to find language acceptable to leaders and members of both parties. The modest legislation was designed to cut homeowners' energy use and utilities bills by allowing them to buy so-called smart metered water heaters and also reducing the cost of manufacturing energy-efficient cooling and heating systems. However, when the bill reached the Senate floor for debate, Republican members pressed for amendments to approve the controversial Keystone XL pipeline and also to block the EPA's power-plant rules if adopted without congressional action; such congressional action was, of course, highly unlikely given the adamant opposition of House Republicans. The Senate's majority leader, Harry Reid, D-Nev., would not allow these amendments to come up for a vote, and neither side in the dispute would back down. The bipartisan energy efficiency bill died on a procedural motion, 55 to 36, five votes short of the sixty needed to move the measure to a final vote.[5]

In a telling commentary on the state of congressional policymaking on the environment today, Robert Dillon, a spokesperson for Sen. Lisa Murkowski, the ranking Republican on the Senate's Energy and Natural Resources Committee and a cosponsor of the bipartisan energy bill, said: "It's embarrassing that even an energy-efficiency bill can't get past the floor." The Senate today, Dillon noted, faced political gridlock on these kinds of issues. "We used to have hundreds of votes on amendments. Now it's all politics all the time. It's all rhetoric," he said. "It's frustrating to Republicans, and it's frustrating to Democrats. There's a lot of pent-up demand to have a real debate on energy."[6]

That outcome in 2014 had many precedents in congressional actions after Republicans gained the majority in the House in 2011. By October of that year, congressional Democrats tallied the number of times House Republicans had voted to block various environmental policy actions. They counted 168 such votes, and Rep. Henry Waxman, D-Calif., the ranking Democrat on the Energy and Commerce Committee, asserted that, taken together, those votes made the 112th Congress (2011–2013) "the most anti-environmental Congress in history."[7] Republicans countered that they were not anti-environmental at all, but rather were advancing a "jobs agenda." Republican successes in the 2014 midterm elections, when the party strengthened its majority in the House and captured the Senate, suggest that these patterns of partisan disagreement on environmental policy will continue in the near term.

Environmental Challenges and Political Constraints

The battles over environmental budgets and regulations in 2013 and 2014, as well as over the past two decades, say much about the way Congress deals with environmental, energy, and natural resource issues today, and the many obstacles it will face in trying to chart new policy directions to better address twenty-first-century challenges.[8] The capacity of the 113th Congress (2013–2015) to act, like many Congresses before it, was deeply affected by what analysts have called an "era of partisan warfare" on Capitol Hill. Increasingly, each party had appealed to its core constituency through a continuous political campaign that emphasized an ideological "message politics" that was more about taking positions on the issues than crafting good policies. In this context, policy compromise between the parties was never easy, as each often sought to deny the other any semblance of victory, even at the cost of stalemate in dealing with pressing national problems such as energy use and climate change.[9]

Whichever party dominates Congress in the years ahead, it will not be easy to regain the broad bipartisan support for environmental policies that prevailed during the 1970s and even through the 1980s. This is particularly the case for major policy actions, such as rewriting the core environmental laws, most of which were adopted more than forty years ago. It was not always so. For nearly three decades, from the late 1960s to the mid-1990s, Congress enacted—and over time strengthened—an extraordinary range of environmental policies, typified by the 1970 Clean Air Act, the 1972 Clean Water Act, the 1973 Endangered Species Act, and the 1976 Resource Conservation and Recovery Act (see Chapter 1 and Appendix 1). In doing so, members within both political parties recognized and responded to rising public concern about environmental degradation. For the same reasons, they stoutly defended and even expanded those policies during the 1980s when they were assailed by Ronald Reagan's White House.[10]

This pattern of bipartisan cooperation and compromise changed dramatically with the election of the 104th Congress in 1994, as the new Republican majority brought to the Hill a very different position on the environment. It was far more critical of regulatory bureaucracies, such as the EPA, and the policies they are charged with implementing.[11] On energy and natural resource issues, such as drilling for oil in the Arctic National Wildlife Refuge (ANWR) or on offshore public lands, and more recently with the Keystone XL pipeline, Republicans have tended to lean heavily toward increasing resource use and economic development rather than conservation or environmental protection.

As party leaders pursued these goals from 1995 through 2014, they invariably faced intense opposition from Democrats who were just as determined to block what they characterized as ill-advised attempts to roll back years of progress in protecting public health and the environment.[12] The 2006 election put Democrats in control of Congress once again, giving them substantial opportunities to challenge President George W. Bush on environmental and energy issues, and they did so frequently. But the short-term effect of political conflict over many of President Bush's proposals, from drilling for oil in ANWR to his Clear Skies initiative, was partisan polarization and policy stalemate. As noted at the chapter's opening, when Republicans regained control of the House and narrowed the Democratic majority in the Senate following the 2010 midterm elections, building consensus on environmental issues, with very few exceptions, proved to be exceptionally difficult. As a result, Congress has been unable to approve either the sweeping changes sought by Republicans or the moderate policy reforms preferred by most Democrats. Thus existing policies—with their many acknowledged flaws—have largely continued in force even as state and local governments have sought to develop innovative policy strategies and some progress has been evident in administrative proceedings and through judicial action.[13]

Whatever the future holds, it is clear that Congress is the only national political institution that can redesign environmental policy for the twenty-first century. For that reason, it is important to understand how it makes decisions on environmental issues and why members adopt the positions and take the actions they do. In the sections below, I examine efforts at policy change on Capitol Hill and compare them with the way Congress dealt previously with environmental issues. This assessment highlights the many distinctive roles that Congress has played historically in the policymaking process, and the way it responds to these issues today. I give special consideration to the phenomenon of policy stalemate or gridlock, which at times, including the 2010s, has been a defining characteristic of congressional involvement with environmental policy.

Congressional Authority and Environmental Policy

Under the Constitution, Congress shares authority with the president for federal policymaking on the environment. In most years, members of Congress make critical decisions on hundreds of measures that affect environmental policy broadly defined. These range from funding the operations of the EPA and other agencies to supporting highways, mass transit, forestry, farming, oil and gas exploration, energy research and development, protection of wilderness areas, and international population and development assistance programs. These actions are rarely front-page news, and the public may hear little about them.[14]

As discussed in Chapter 1, we can distinguish congressional actions in several different stages of the policy process: agenda setting, formulation and adoption of policies, and implementation of them in executive agencies.

Presidents have greater opportunities than does Congress to set the political agenda, that is, to call attention to specific problems and define or frame the terms of debate. Yet, members of Congress can have a major impact on the agenda through legislative and oversight hearings as well as through the abundant opportunities they have for introducing legislation, requesting and publicizing studies and reports, making speeches, taking positions, voting, and campaigning for reelection.

All of these actions can assist them in framing issues in a way that promotes their preferred solutions, as was evident in the House climate change debate in June 2014, and especially in Republican arguments against EPA rulemaking. Similarly, in March 2014, some thirty Democrats staged what the press called a fifteen-hour, all-night "talkathon," the purpose of which was to raise the agenda status of climate change.[15] In June 2014, Senate Democrats also invited former EPA heads under Republican presidents Richard Nixon, Ronald Reagan, George H. W. Bush, and George W. Bush to testify at a well-publicized committee hearing. They sought to demonstrate bipartisan support for climate change policy despite the prevailing skepticism toward climate science among Republican members of Congress.[16]

Because of their extensive executive powers, presidents also can dominate the process of policy implementation in the agencies (see Chapter 4). Here too, however, Congress can significantly affect agency actions, particularly through its budgetary decisions, as noted earlier. These powers translate into an influential and continuing role of overseeing, and often criticizing, actions in executive agencies such as the EPA, Department of Energy, U.S. Geological Survey, Fish and Wildlife Service, Bureau of Land Management, and Forest Service. For example, when Republicans assumed control of the House following the 2010 elections, they launched repeated oversight investigations into the operations of the EPA and the Department of Energy, among other agencies.[17] In one highly visible case, Republican members of a House Energy and Commerce subcommittee frequently criticized the Obama administration's decision to offer loan guarantees to solar industry manufacturers after one of the firms that received a large loan, Solyndra, declared bankruptcy. Supporters of the program countered that most DOE loan guarantees of this kind were successful and returned billions of dollars to the federal treasury.[18]

Moreover, through its constitutional power to advise and consent on presidential nominations to the agencies and the courts, the Senate has a key role in choosing who is selected to fill critical positions. The Senate almost always approves presidential nominees when the same party controls both institutions, but when a president faces a Congress controlled by the other party, approval is far less certain.

Even if it cannot compete on an equal footing with the president in some of these policymaking activities, historically, Congress has been more influential than the White House in the formulation and adoption of environmental policies.[19] Yet the way in which Congress exercises its formidable policymaking powers is shaped by several key variables, such as public opinion on the environment, whether the president's party also controls Congress—and by what margins—and members' willingness to defer to the president's recommendations.

Congress's actions on the environment also invariably reflect its dual mission to be deeply engaged with both lawmaking and representation. In addition to serving as a national legislative body, the House and Senate are assemblies of elected officials who represent politically disparate districts and states. It is hardly surprising that members are politically motivated to try to represent local, state, and regional concerns and interests, which can put them at odds with the president or their own party leaders. Indeed, powerful electoral incentives continually induce members of Congress to think at least as much about local and regional impacts of environmental policies as they do about the larger national interest.[20] Such political pressures led members in the early 2000s, for example, to drive up the cost of President Bush's energy proposals with what one journalist called an "abundance of pet projects, subsidies and tax breaks" to specific industries in their districts and states.[21]

Another distinctive institutional characteristic is the system of House and Senate standing committees, where most significant policy decisions take place. Dozens of committees and subcommittees have jurisdiction over environmental policy (see Table 1-1 in Chapter 1), which tends to fragment decisions and erect barriers to integrated or holistic approaches to energy, the environment, and sustainable development. Such a committee structure also means that the outcomes of specific legislative battles often turn on which members sit on and control those committees. For example, when Republicans gained the majority in the House in 2011, Rep. Fred Upton, R-Mich., became chair of the Energy and Commerce Committee. He used that position to hold hearings on climate change, thereby providing an invaluable opportunity for the committee's Republican majority to question the science of climate change.[22]

Taken together, these congressional characteristics have important implications for environmental policy. First, building policy consensus in Congress is rarely easy because of the diversity of members and interests whose concerns need to be met and the conflicts that can arise among committees and leaders. Second, policy compromises invariably reflect members' preoccupation with local and regional impacts of environmental decisions, for example, how climate change policy will affect industries and homeowners in coal-producing states and those heavily dependent on coal-fired power plants, such as West Virginia, Kentucky, Ohio, and Indiana. Third, the White House matters a great deal in how the issues are defined and whether policy decisions can be made acceptable to all concerned, but the president's influence is nevertheless limited by independent political calculations made on Capitol Hill. President Obama's relatively low standing in the polls in 2014 doubtless played a role in congressional opposition to his climate change actions.

Given these constraints, Congress frequently finds itself unable to make crucial decisions on environmental policy. The U.S. public may see a "do-nothing Congress," or as one pundit put it describing the paucity of legislation enacted in 2013 and 2014, a "do-even-less Congress." [23] Yet the reality is that all too often members can find no way to reconcile the conflicting views of multiple interests and constituencies. It remains to be seen if this pattern will change in 2015 and beyond.

There are, however, some striking exceptions to this common pattern of policy stalemate. A brief examination of the way Congress has dealt with environmental issues since the early 1970s helps to explain this seeming anomaly. Such a review also provides a useful context in which to examine and assess the actions of recent Congresses and the outlook for environmental policymaking for the early twenty-first century.

Causes and Consequences of Environmental Gridlock

Policy gridlock refers to an inability to resolve conflicts in a policymaking body such as Congress, which results in government inaction in the face of important public problems. There is no consensus on *what* to do, and therefore no movement occurs in any direction. Present policies, or slight revisions of them, continue until agreement is reached on the direction and magnitude of change. Sometimes environmental or other programs officially expire but continue to be funded by Congress through a waiver of the rules governing the annual appropriations process. The failure to renew the programs, however, contributes to administrative and public policy drift, ineffectual congressional oversight, and a propensity for members to use the appropriations process to achieve what cannot be gained through statutory change.[24] It should be said, however, that policy gridlock in Congress also has had some positive effects. It often has stimulated innovative environmental policy change at the state and local levels, in executive agencies, and in the courts.[25]

So why does policy gridlock occur so frequently in Congress? There is no one answer that fits every situation, but among the major reasons are the sharply divergent policy views of Democrats and Republicans, the influence of organized interest groups in both elections and policymaking, and the inherent complexity of environmental problems. The lack of public consensus on the issues or unclear public preferences, the constitutionally mandated structure of U.S. government (especially the separation of powers between the presidency and Congress), and weak or ineffectual political leadership also make a difference.[26]

Most of these factors are easy to understand. For example, Republicans and Democrats bring very different political philosophies and beliefs to the table, and those views are reinforced by the nature of congressional elections today. Most members come from safe districts or states that lean strongly toward one party or the other; only about two to three dozen House seats out of 435 are competitive between the major parties. One result is that the electoral system gives exceptional clout to the majority party's base or core voters, particularly in low-turnout, off-year elections. Members are forced to appeal more to these voters (such as the Tea Party forces within the Republican Party) than to those in the political center or in the other party. That in turn tends to promote ideological rigidity among members and also to discourage the kind of compromise and consensus building in policymaking that long prevailed in Congress until recent years.

It is also understandable that when a given issue sparks involvement by diverse and opposing interests (such as oil and gas companies, renewable energy companies, electric utilities, the coal industry, the automobile industry, labor unions, and environmentalists), finding politically acceptable solutions may be difficult. Similarly, public opinion polls may show a strong public preference for certain actions on the environment, energy, or climate change, but the public tends not to be well informed on the issues, which often are low in salience for most people. These conditions significantly diminish the public's political influence. Absent a clear and forceful public voice, members of Congress look elsewhere when deciding how to vote on measures before them, and most people are not likely to notice how their representatives are voting.[27] It is for that reason that some groups, such as the Citizens' Climate Lobby, try to change the political calculus. They organize grassroots campaigns on climate change in congressional districts nationwide that are designed to convince members of Congress that their constituents do desire strong policies and that they are watching the votes.[28]

The notable differences in policy preferences between Republicans and Democrats on environmental and energy issues today reflect a striking trend toward ideological polarization that has developed over the past several decades. The shift has been well documented by scholars, and it is evident in recent public opinion surveys as well as rankings of members' voting on environmental issues.[29] For example, based on rankings by the League of Conservation Voters (LCV), the parties showed increasing divergence from the early 1970s through the early 2000s. On average, they have differed by nearly 25 points on a 100-point scale, and those differences grew wider during the last two decades.[30] The gap is exceptionally large today. In recent years, Senate Democrats averaged about 85 percent support for the positions endorsed by the LCV and the environmental community. Senate Republicans averaged about 8 percent. In the House, Democrats averaged about 86 percent and Republicans 10 percent.[31] For reasons that are not entirely clear, environmental policies have become at least as polarizing as any other issue in the 2010s, a dramatic shift from the public consensus and bipartisanship that prevailed in the 1970s.[32]

From Consensus in the Environmental Decade to Deadlock in the 1990s

As Chapter 1 makes clear, the legislative record for the environmental decade of the 1970s is remarkable. The National Environmental Policy Act, Clean Air Act, Clean Water Act, Endangered Species Act, and Resource Conservation and Recovery Act, among others, were all signed into law in that decade, and most of them were enacted in a six-year period: 1970 to 1976. We can debate the merits of these early statutes with the clarity of hindsight and in light of contemporary criticism of them. Yet their adoption demonstrates vividly that the U.S. political system is capable of developing major environmental policies in fairly short order under the right conditions. Consensus on environmental policy could prevail in the 1970s, in part, because the issues were new and politically popular, and attention was focused on broadly supported program goals such as cleaning up the nation's air and water rather than on the means used (command-and-control regulation) or the costs to achieve them. At that time, there was also little overt and sustained opposition to these measures.

Environmental Gridlock Emerges

The pattern of the 1970s did not last. Congress's enthusiasm for environmental policy gradually gave way to apprehension about its impacts on the economy, and policy stalemate became the norm in the early 1980s. Ronald Reagan's election as president in 1980 also altered the political climate and threw Congress into a defensive posture. It was forced to react to the Reagan administration's aggressive policy actions. Rather than proposing new programs or expanding old ones, Congress focused its resources on oversight and criticism of the administration's policies, and bipartisan agreement became more difficult. Members were increasingly cross-pressured by environmental and industry groups, partisanship on these issues increased, and Congress and President Reagan battled repeatedly over budget and program priorities.[33] The cumulative effect of these developments in the early 1980s was that Congress was unable to agree on new environmental policy directions.

Gridlock Eases: 1984–1990

The legislative logjam began breaking up in late 1983, as the U.S. public and Congress repudiated Reagan's anti-environmental agenda (see Chapter 4). The new pattern was evident by 1984 when, after several years of deliberation, Congress approved major amendments to the 1976 Resource Conservation and Recovery Act that strengthened the program and set tight new deadlines for EPA rulemaking on control of hazardous chemical wastes. The 99th Congress (1985–1987) compiled a record dramatically at odds with the deferral politics of the 97th and 98th Congresses (1981–1985). In 1986, the Safe Drinking Water Act was strengthened and expanded, and Congress approved the Superfund Amendments and Reauthorization Act, adding a separate Title III, the Emergency Planning and Community Right-to-Know Act (EPCRA), which created the Toxics Release Inventory. Democrats regained control of the Senate following the 1986 election, and Congress reauthorized the Clean Water Act over a presidential veto. Still, Congress was unable to renew the Clean Air Act and the Federal Insecticide, Fungicide, and Rodenticide Act— the nation's key pesticide control act—as well as to pass new legislation to control acid rain.

However, with the election of George H. W. Bush in 1988, Congress and the White House were able to agree on enactment of the innovative and stringent Clean Air Act Amendments of 1990 and the Energy Policy Act of 1992. The latter was an important, if modest, advancement in promoting energy conservation and a restructuring of the electric utility industry to promote greater competition and efficiency. Success on the Clean Air Act was particularly important because for years it was a stark symbol of Congress's inability to reauthorize controversial environmental programs. Passage was possible in 1990 because of improved scientific research that clarified the risks of dirty air and reports of worsening ozone in urban areas, and President Bush's leadership. He had vowed to "break the gridlock" and support renewal of the Clean Air Act, and Sen. George Mitchell, D-Maine, newly elected as Senate majority leader, was equally determined to enact a bill.[34]

Policy Stalemate Returns

Unfortunately, approval of the 1990 Clean Air Act Amendments was no signal that a new era of cooperative and bipartisan policymaking on the environment was about to begin. Nor was the election of Bill Clinton and Al Gore in 1992, even as Democrats regained control of both houses of Congress. Most of the major environmental laws were once again up for renewal. Yet despite an emerging consensus on many of the laws, in the end, the 103rd Congress (1993–1995) remained far too divided to act. Coalitions of environmental groups and business interests clashed regularly on all of these initiatives, and congressional leaders and the Clinton White House were unsuccessful in resolving the disputes.

The 104th Congress: Revolutionary Fervor Meets Political Reality

Few analysts had predicted the astonishing outcomes of the 1994 midterm elections, even after one of the most expensive, negative, and anti-Washington campaigns in modern times. Republicans captured both houses of Congress, picking up an additional fifty-two seats in the House and eight in the Senate. They also did well in other elections throughout the country, contributing to their belief that voters had endorsed the Contract with America, which symbolized the new Republican agenda.[35] The contract had promised a rolling back of government regulations and a shrinking of the federal government's role. There was no specific mention of environmental policy, however, and the document's language was carefully constructed for broad appeal to a disgruntled electorate. It drew heavily from the work of conservative and pro-business think tanks that for years had waged a multifaceted campaign to discredit environmentalist thinking and policies. Those efforts merged with a carefully developed GOP plan to gain control of Congress to further a conservative political agenda.[36]

The preponderance of evidence suggests that the Republican victory in November conveyed no public mandate to roll back environmental protection.[37] Yet the political result was clear enough. It put Republicans in charge of the House for the first time in four decades and initiated an extraordinary period of legislative action on environmental policy characterized by bitter relations between the two parties, setting the stage for a similar confrontation that emerged following the 2010 elections.

The environmental policy deadlock in the mid-1990s should have come as no surprise. With several notable exceptions, consensus on the issues simply could not be built, and the Republican revolution under Speaker Newt Gingrich failed for the most part. The lesson seemed to be that a direct attack on popular environmental programs could not work because it would provoke a political backlash. Those who supported a new conservative policy agenda turned instead to a strategy of evolutionary or incremental environmental policy change through a more subtle and less visible exercise of Congress's appropriations and oversight powers. Here they were more successful.[38] The George W. Bush administration relied on a similar strategy of quiet pursuit of a deregulatory agenda from 2001 to early 2009.

Environmental Policy Actions in Recent Congresses

As discussed earlier, Congress influences nearly every environmental and resource policy through exercise of its powers to legislate, oversee executive agencies, advise and consent on nominations, and appropriate funds. Sometimes these activities take place largely within the specialized committees and subcommittees, and sometimes they reach the floor of the House and Senate, where they may attract greater media attention. Some of the decisions are made routinely and are relatively free of controversy (for example, appropriations for the national parks) whereas others stimulate more political conflict, as was the case with George W. Bush's Clear Skies bill, the long-running dispute over drilling for oil in ANWR, and debates over the Keystone XL pipeline, energy legislation, and climate change. In this section, I briefly review some of the most notable congressional actions from 1995 to 2014 within three broad categories: regulatory reform initiatives (directed at the way agencies make decisions), appropriations (funding levels and use of budgetary riders), and proposals for changing the substance of environmental policy.

Regulatory Reform: Changing Agency Procedures

Regulatory reform has long been of concern in U.S. environmental policy (see Chapters 1 and 4). There is no real dispute about the need to reform agency rulemaking that has been widely faulted for being too inflexible, intrusive, cumbersome, and adversarial and sometimes based on insufficient consideration of science and economics.[39] However, considerable disagreement exists over precisely what elements of the regulatory process need to be reformed and how best to ensure that the changes are both fair and effective.

Beginning in 1995 and continuing for several Congresses, the Republican Party and conservative Democrats favored omnibus regulatory reform legislation that would affect all environmental policies by imposing broad and stringent mandates on executive agencies, particularly the EPA. Those mandates were especially directed at the use of benefit-cost analysis and risk assessment in proposing new regulations. Proponents of such legislation also sought to open agency technical studies and rulemaking to additional legal challenges to help protect the business community against what they viewed as unjustifiable regulatory action. Opponents of both kinds of measures argued that such impositions and opportunities for lawsuits were not reform in any meaningful sense and they would wreak havoc within agencies that already faced daunting procedural hurdles and frequent legal disputes as they developed regulations.[40]

Ultimately, Congress did approve several bills in 1995 and 1996 that Republicans characterized as regulatory reform, including the Unfunded Mandates Reform Act (1995) and the Small Business Regulatory Enforcement Fairness Act (1996). As part of the latter, the separately named Congressional Review Act, Congress may reject an agency rule if a majority in each house approves a "resolution of disapproval" that is also signed by the president.

With the election of George W. Bush in 2000, the regulatory reform agenda shifted from imposing these kinds of congressional mandates on Clinton administration agencies to direct intervention by the White House. Bush appointed conservative and pro-business officials to nearly all environmental and natural resource agencies, and rulemaking shifted decisively toward the interests of the business community (see Chapter 4).[41]

Barack Obama's election coincided with another shift in regulatory philosophy. In light of the financial meltdown on Wall Street in 2008 and reports of ineffective federal regulation of banking institutions and of food, drugs, consumer products, and the environment, public sentiment at least temporarily shifted back in favor of strong, or at least "smart," regulation that achieves its purposes without imposing unreasonable burdens.[42] However, following the 2010 elections, Republicans once again controlled the House, and anti-regulatory sentiment returned as members sought to reduce perceived burdens on the business community in a slowly recovering economy and to limit or repeal regulations that they believed were hindering job creation.

Appropriations Politics: Budgets and Riders

The implementation of environmental policies depends heavily on the funds that Congress appropriates each year. Thus, if certain policy goals cannot be achieved through changing the governing statutes, or altering the rulemaking process through regulatory reform, attention may turn instead to the appropriations process. This was the case during the Reagan administration in the 1980s, which severely cut environmental budgets, and it was a major element of the Republican strategy in Congress from 1995 to 2006, as well as in the George W. Bush administration.

The importance of budgetary politics depends in part on which party controls Congress and the White House. Democrats tend to favor increased spending on the environment, and Republicans generally favor decreased spending. The 112th and 113th Congresses produced a mixed picture, with the Republican House eager to cut environmental spending sharply, but with the Senate and the Obama White House not prepared to go along. However, with the United States facing large budget deficits and both parties pledged to reduce government expenditures, spending decisions will become increasingly linked to such overall fiscal constraints (see Chapter 1).

Regardless of which party controls Congress, the appropriations process has been used in two distinct ways to achieve policy change. One is through the use of riders, loosely related legislative stipulations attached to appropriations bills; they ride along with the bill, and hence the name. The other is through changes in the level of funding, either a cut in spending for programs that are not favored or an increase for those that are endorsed.

Appropriations Riders Use of appropriations riders became a common strategy following the 1994 election. For example, in the 104th Congress, more than fifty anti-environmental riders were included in seven different budget bills, largely with the purpose of slowing or halting enforcement of laws by the EPA, the Interior Department, and other agencies until Congress could revise them.[43]

The use of riders has continued in subsequent years, as has opposition to the strategy by environmental groups. In late 2004, for example, as Congress rolled a number of budget measures together in an omnibus package in a final effort to complete work on the fiscal year 2005 budget, a number of environmental riders were attached. These included exclusion of grazing permit renewals from environmental review and limitations on judicial review and public participation in logging projects in the Tongass National Forest. In 2011, a rider attached to the fiscal year 2012 spending bill would have kept the Obama administration EPA from issuing any proposed regulations on emissions of greenhouse gases from power plants or industrial facilities. Another would have prevented the Interior Department from using any federal funds to limit oil, gas, or other commercial development on public lands that might qualify in the future for wilderness designation.[44]

Why use budgetary riders to achieve policy change rather than to introduce freestanding legislation to pursue the same goals? Such a budgetary strategy is attractive to its proponents because appropriations bills, unlike authorizing legislation, typically move quickly, and Congress must enact them each year to keep the government operating. Many Republicans and business lobbyists also argue that use of riders is one of the few ways they have to rope in a bureaucracy that they believe needs additional constraints. They feel they are unable to address their concerns through changing the authorizing statutes themselves, a far more controversial and uncertain path to follow.[45] Even if members fail, their efforts on such riders help to assure critical constituency groups of their determination to change the law.

Critics of the process, however, say that relying on riders is an inappropriate way to institute policy change because the process provides little opportunity to debate the issues openly, and there are no public hearings or public votes. For example, provisions of the Data Quality Act of 2000, a rider designed to ensure the accuracy of data on which agencies base their rulemaking, were written largely by an industry lobbyist and were enacted quietly as twenty-seven lines of text buried in a massive budget bill that President Clinton had to sign.[46] In a retrospective review in 2001, the Natural Resources Defense Council (NRDC) counted hundreds of anti-environmental riders attached to appropriations bills since 1995. Clinton blocked more than seventy-five of them, but many became law, including the Data Quality Act.[47]

Cutting Environmental Budgets The history of congressional funding for environmental programs was discussed in Chapter 1, and it is set out in Appendix 2 for selected agencies and in Appendix 4 for overall federal spending on natural resources and the environment. These budgets have been the focus of continuing conflict within Congress since the 1980s. For example, in the 104th Congress, GOP leaders enacted deep cuts in environmental spending only to face President Clinton's veto of the budget bill. Those conflicts led eventually to a temporary shutdown of the federal government, with the Republicans receiving the brunt of the public's wrath for the budget wars. Most of the environmental cuts were reversed. Disagreements over program priorities have continued since that time.[48]

George W. Bush regularly sought to cut the EPA's budget but was rebuffed by Congress until 2004, after which it tended to go along with the president. Since then, overall appropriations for the environment and natural resources have increased, although only slightly in real terms, while spending on pollution control (by the EPA, for example) has declined markedly after adjusting for inflation.

The most recent pattern has been an increase in spending on the environment and natural resources in the first years of the Obama administration (fiscal years 2009 and 2010), and a reduction after that time. As noted in the chapter opening, the House Appropriations Committee in 2014 approved a massive reduction in the EPA's budget, but generally, congressionally approved spending has been stable in recent years. In 2014, the long-term estimates from the Office of Management and Budget projected a leveling off of spending on the environment through 2019. Given the overall fiscal picture for the federal government, public disillusionment with governmental programs, and a Congress that is increasingly critical of environmental policies, environmental agencies seem unlikely to do much better over the next four to five years.[49] Indeed, following the 2014 elections, Republicans vowed to further cut EPA and other agency spending in an effort to limit regulatory actions, particularly on power plant emissions and climate change.[50]

Legislating Policy Change

As noted earlier, in most years, Congress makes decisions that affect nearly all environmental or resource programs. In this section, I highlight selective actions in recent Congresses that demonstrate both the ability of members to reach across party lines to find common ground and the continuing ideological and partisan fights that often prevent legislative action.

Pesticides, Drinking Water, and Transportation Among the most notable achievements of the otherwise anti-environmental 104th and 105th Congresses are three conspicuous success stories involving control of pesticides and other agricultural chemicals, drinking water, and transportation. Especially for the first two of these actions, years of legislative gridlock were overcome as Republicans and Democrats uncharacteristically reached agreement on new policy directions.

The Food Quality Protection Act of 1996 was a major revision of the nation's pesticide law, long a prime example of policy gridlock as environmentalists battled with the agricultural, chemical, and food industries. The act required the EPA to use a new, uniform, reasonable-risk approach to regulating pesticides used on food, fiber, and other crops, and it required that special attention be given to the diverse ways in which both children and adults are exposed to such chemicals. The act sped through Congress in record time without a single dissenting vote because the food industry was desperate to get the new law enacted after court rulings that would have adversely affected it without the legislation. In addition, after the bruising battles of 1995, GOP lawmakers were eager to adopt an election year environmental measure.[51]

The 1996 rewrite and reauthorization of the Safe Drinking Water Act sought to address many long-standing problems with the nation's drinking water program. It dealt more realistically with regulating contaminants based on their risk to public health and authorized $7 billion for state-administered loan and grant funds to help localities with compliance costs. It also created a new right-to-know provision that requires large water systems to provide their customers with annual reports on the safety of local water supplies. Bipartisan cooperation on the bill was made easier because it aided financially pressed state and local governments and, like the pesticide bill, allowed Republicans to score some election year points with environmentalists.[52]

Another important legislative enactment took place in the 105th Congress. After prolonged debate over renewal of the nation's major highway act, in 1998, the House and Senate overwhelmingly approved the Transportation Equity Act for the 21st Century. It was a sweeping six-year, $218 billion measure that provided a 40 percent increase in spending to improve the nation's aging highways and included $5.4 billion for mass transit systems.[53] For reasons discussed early in the chapter, members of Congress find it easier to reach agreement when federal dollars are distributed among the states and congressional districts, as is the case with transportation funding.

Brownfields, Healthy Forests, Agriculture, and Wilderness Congress also completed action on a number of somewhat less visible issues that demonstrated its potential to fashion bipartisan compromises. In 2001, President Bush gained congressional approval of important legislation to reclaim so-called urban brownfields. The measure represented an unusual compromise between House Republicans who sought to reduce liability for small businesses under the Superfund program and Democrats who wanted to see contaminated and abandoned industrial sites in urban areas cleaned up.[54]

In a somewhat similar action, in 2003 the 108th Congress approved one of the Bush administration's environmental priorities, the Healthy Forests Initiative. The measure was designed to permit increased logging in national forests to lessen the risk of wildfires. It reduced the number of environmental reviews that would be required for such logging projects and sped up judicial reviews of legal challenges to these projects. Environmental groups opposed the legislation, but bipartisan concern over communities at risk from wildfires was sufficient for enactment. Wildfires struck Southern California only days before the Senate voted 80–14 to approve the bill.[55]

The nation's farm bills always have important environmental components. In 2007, Congress approved a new farm bill that authorized nearly $8 billion over ten years for environmental protection, such as soil conservation and incentives to grow grasses that can be converted into cellulosic ethanol rather than to rely on corn-based ethanol. However, the measure also left largely intact much criticized agricultural subsidies. Battles over those farm subsidies continued in later years.

Finally, throughout 2007 and 2008, Congress considered a dozen proposals for setting aside large parcels of federal land for wilderness protection, totaling about two million acres in eight states, largely without much media coverage. The measures were broadly supported within both parties, in part because environmentalists helped to build public support by working with opposing interests at the local level. Progress like this was also possible because of Democratic victories in the 2006 election that switched control of the House Natural Resources Committee from Republican Richard Pombo of California to Democrat Nick J. Rahall of West Virginia. Pombo was a fierce opponent of such wilderness protection, and Rahall strongly favored it. Congress couldn't approve the wilderness bills in 2008, but by March 2009, in a more favorable political climate, they were approved as part of an Omnibus Public Land Management Act.[56]

National Energy Policy In 2005, Congress finally enacted one of the Bush administration's priorities that the president had sought since 2001: the Energy Policy Act of 2005. It was the first major overhaul of U.S. energy policy since 1992. The original Bush energy plan, formulated in 2001 by a task force headed by Vice President Dick Cheney, called for an increase in the production and use of fossil fuels and nuclear energy, gave modest attention to the role of energy conservation, and sparked intense debate on Capitol Hill with its emphasis on oil and gas drilling in ANWR. The Republican House quickly approved the measure in 2001, after what the press called "aggressive lobbying by the Bush administration, labor unions and the oil, gas, and coal industries."[57] The vote largely followed party lines. The bill provided generous tax and research benefits to the oil, natural gas, coal, and nuclear power industries; and it rejected provisions that would have forced the auto industry to improve fuel efficiency for sport utility vehicles. The Senate was far more skeptical about the legislation and remained so over the next four years.

Competing energy bills were debated on the Hill through mid-2005 without resolution and served as another prominent example of legislative gridlock. Senate Democrats favored measures that balanced energy production and environmental concerns, including increases in auto and truck fuel-efficiency standards; they drew strong support from environmentalists and denunciation by industry officials and Republicans. Neither side was prepared to compromise as lobbying by car manufacturers, labor unions, the oil and gas industry, and environmentalists continued. As one writer put it in 2002, the "debate between energy and the environment is important to core constituencies of both parties, the kind of loyal followers vital in a congressional election year."[58]

Finally, the House and Senate reached agreement on an energy package, and the president signed the 1,700-page bill on August 8, 2005.[59] In the end, the ANWR provisions were dropped from the bill, as were stipulations for improved fuel-efficiency standards. The bill included no mandate for reduction in greenhouse gas emissions, and it imposed no requirement that utilities rely on renewable power sources. The thrust of the legislation remained largely what Bush and Cheney sought in 2001, with substantial federal subsidies for expanding supplies of energy, particularly fossil fuels and nuclear power. However, the final measure included significant funding for energy research and development (including work on renewable energy sources), some new energy efficiency standards for federal office buildings, and short-term tax credits for purchase of hybrid vehicles and renewable power systems for homes—and similar provisions for commercial buildings.[60]

One other important change in energy policy took place in 2007, when Congress finally agreed to the first significant change in the Corporate Average Fuel Economy (CAFE) standards since 1975. The Energy Independence and Security Act of 2007 set a national automobile fuel economy standard of 35 miles per gallon by 2020. The act also sought to increase the supply of alternative fuel sources, particularly biofuels other than corn-based ethanol. In one of his first actions in office, President Obama in January 2009 ordered the Department of Transportation to move ahead on issuing regulations to put the new fuel economy standards into effect for cars sold in 2011. Those requirements were soon replaced by two new agreements that Obama reached with automobile companies, the last of which set requirements of 54.5 miles per gallon by 2025.[61]

Beyond these issues, other energy policy goals were advanced by President Obama's economic stimulus measure, which Congress approved in February 2009. The bill contained about $80 billion in spending, tax incentives, and loan guarantees, including funds for energy efficiency, renewable energy sources, mass transit, and technologies for capture and storage of greenhouse gases produced by coal-fired power plants. Had the energy components been a stand-alone measure, the *New York Times* observed, they would have amounted to "the biggest energy bill in history." Yet bipartisan cooperation was largely absent. In the end, only three Republicans in Congress, all in the Senate, voted for the bill.[62]

Continuing Partisan Conflict and Stalemate The examples discussed here and many more that could be cited, such as approval of an historic Great

Lakes Compact in 2008 to prevent water diversion from the lakes, and a new Higher Education Sustainability Act in 2008, show that over the past decade Congress has been able to move ahead on a wide range of environmental and natural resource policies.[63] Yet continuing partisan conflict has blocked action on key federal laws such as the Superfund program, the Endangered Species Act, the Clean Water Act (for example, the Clean Water Restoration Act to reaffirm broad federal protection undercut by Supreme Court decisions), the Clean Air Act, climate change, and reform of the notorious General Mining Law of 1872, emblematic of what some have called legislative lost causes.[64]

The Superfund program, for example, has not been reauthorized for over two decades, and except for the brownfields measure discussed earlier, congressional agreement has not been forthcoming. In 1995, Congress let the special industry tax that funds the program expire, which shifted the program from one for which "polluters pay" to one for which general tax revenues must be used instead. One result is that the program's fund is no longer adequate for cleanup of contaminated sites across the nation.[65]

The Endangered Species Act presents a similar level of conflict and lack of resolution. In 2001, then House Resources Committee chair James V. Hansen, R-Utah, captured the dilemma well: "We haven't reauthorized it because no one could agree on how to reform and modernize the law. Everyone agrees there are problems with the Act, but no one can agree on how to fix them."[66] By late 2004, most Republican-backed proposals sought to require greater consideration of the rights of property owners and to force the Fish and Wildlife Service to rely more on peer-reviewed science in its species decisions. Opponents have argued that such bills would gut the act to appease small landowners and corporate developers, and prevent the service from acting.[67]

Climate change policy, of course, is something of a poster child for legislative gridlock. In 2009, the House approved a cap-and-trade bill, the American Clean Energy and Security Act of 2009 (also known as Waxman-Markey for its chief sponsors, Rep. Henry A. Waxman, D-Calif., and Rep. Edward J. Markey, D-Mass.), after extensive and prolonged negotiations and major concessions for the various industries likely to be affected by it. These included automakers, steel companies, natural gas drillers, oil refiners, utilities, and farmers, among others. The final vote was 219 to 212, with all but eight Republicans voting in opposition, along with forty-four Democrats. The bill sought to reduce carbon dioxide emissions by 17 percent below 2005 levels by 2020 and 83 percent by 2050, to set a national renewable energy (and gain in efficiency) target of 20 percent by 2020, and to allocate billions of dollars for energy research and development. President Obama hailed its passage as a "bold and necessary step" that, pending Senate action, would signal the nation's willingness to tackle its energy use and minimize adverse impacts on the world's climate future.[68]

That Senate action was not to be. Republicans quickly branded the measure as a "cap and tax" bill because it would increase the cost of carbon-based fuels. They argued instead for an energy bill that would favor nuclear power and create new incentives for oil and gas production on public lands and offshore.

A number of key senators (particularly John Kerry, D-Mass.; Lindsey Graham, R-S.C.; and Joseph Lieberman, I-Conn.) tried repeatedly over the next year to formulate climate change legislation that might appeal enough to a coalition of environmentalists and industries to secure Senate passage, but in the end, they were unable to gain sufficient support from the White House and their Senate colleagues to succeed in building the necessary bipartisan coalition. Despite that outcome, members of the House and Senate continue to introduce climate change legislation to help lay the groundwork for a time when political conditions change.[69] As discussed in Chapter 4, by late 2014, President Obama vowed to advance climate change policy through executive orders and agency regulations in the face of continued congressional inaction.

Conclusions

The political struggles on Capitol Hill over the last twenty years reveal sharply contrasting visions for environmental policy. The revolutionary rhetoric of the 104th Congress had dissipated by the 2000s, but it was replaced in the 2010s by similar views held by Tea Party Republicans, especially in the House. During this two-decade period, Congress was able to revise several major statutes in an uncommon display of bipartisan cooperation. Nonetheless, for many other environmental programs, policy gridlock continued to frustrate all participants, and deep partisan differences prevented emerging issues such as climate change from being addressed seriously.

The election of President Obama did little to alter legislative prospects on the Hill, particularly after Republican gains in the 2010 and 2012 elections. The electoral success of Tea Party activists within the Republican Party led to heightened levels of ideological polarization and political conflict between the White House and Congress on both economic and environmental issues. Under these conditions, it is no surprise that by 2014 public ratings of Congress fell to historic lows, with strong public disapproval of both parties.[70]

The constitutional divisions between the House and Senate, and between Congress and the White House, guarantee that newly emergent forces, whether on the left or the right of the political spectrum, cannot easily push a particular legislative agenda. The 2014 elections did not change this outlook, and it is likely that the 2016 elections will not do so either. Nor will it be easy for the next several Congresses to address the remaining environmental and energy challenges facing the nation and world, especially climate change and the imperative of fostering sustainable development (see Chapter 16).

Yet the environmental policy battles of the past decade remind us that in the U.S. political system, effective policymaking will always require cooperation between the two branches and leadership within both to advance sensible policies and secure public approval for them. The public also has a role to play in these deliberations, and the history of congressional policymaking on the environment strongly suggests the power of public beliefs and action. Public disillusionment with government and politics today creates significant barriers to policy change that would serve the public's interest. However, at the same time, it facilitates the power of special interests to secure the changes that they desire, which may differ greatly from public preferences. Ultimately, the solution can only be found in a heightened awareness of the problems and active participation by the American public in the political process.

Suggested Websites

Environmental Protection Agency (www.epa.gov/epahome/rules.html) The EPA site for laws, rules, and regulations includes the full text of the dozen key laws administered by the EPA. It also has a link to current legislation before Congress.

League of Conservation Voters (www.lcv.org) The LCV compiles environmental voting records for all members of Congress.

Congress.gov (www.congress.gov) This site is one of the most comprehensive public sites available for legislative searches. See also www.house.gov and www.senate.gov for portals to the House and Senate, and the committee and individual member websites.

National Association of Manufacturers (www.nam.org) This leading business organization offers policy news, studies, and position statements on environmental issues, as well as extensive resources for public action on the issues.

Natural Resources Defense Council (www.nrdc.org) Perhaps the most active and influential of national environmental groups that lobby Congress, the NRDC also provides detailed news coverage of congressional legislative developments in its *Legislative Watch* newsletter.

Sierra Club (www.sierraclub.org) The Sierra Club is one of the leading national environmental groups that track congressional legislative battles.

U.S. Chamber of Commerce (www.uschamber.com) The U.S. Chamber of Commerce is one of the nation's leading business organizations, and frequently challenges legislative proposals that it believes may harm business interests.

Notes

1. Chairman Rodgers is quoted in Keith Goldberg, "House Panel Advances Funding Bill Blocking EPA GHG Rules," reported on the website www.law360.com. Wasserman Schultz is quoted in Andrew Taylor, "House GOP Slashes IRS Tax Enforcement Budget," Associated Press, July 15, 2014.

2. Andrew C. Revkin, "Obama's Ambitious Global Warming Action Plan," *New York Times*, June 25, 2013; and Coral Davenport, "Unveiling New Carbon Plan, E.P.A. Focuses on Flexibility," *New York Times*, June 2, 2014. For the same reasons, the president chose to bypass the Senate in developing a policy strategy for international climate change action. A formal treaty would require Senate approval, which he could not get. The White House chose to sidestep the Senate by seeking what the press called a "politically binding" climate change "agreement" rather than a treaty. See Davenport, "Obama Pursuing Climate Accord in Lieu of Treaty," *New York Times*, August 26, 2014; Davenport, "In Climate Deal with China, Obama May Set 2016

Theme," *New York Times*, November 12, 2014; and Davenport, "Obama to Announce $3 Billion U.S. Contribution to Climate Change Fund," *New York Times*, November 14, 2014.

3. See, for example, Leslie Kaufman, "Republicans Seek Big Cuts in Environmental Rules," *New York Times*, July 27, 2011; Robert B. Semple Jr., "Concealed Weapons against the Environment," *New York Times*, July 31, 2011; and Paul Kane, "House GOP Revs Up a Repeal, Reduce and Rein-in Agenda for the Fall," *Washington Post*, August 28, 2011.

4. Goldberg, "House Panel Advances Funding Bill Blocking EPA GHG Rules."

5. Coral Davenport, "Amid Pipeline and Climate Debate, Energy-Efficiency Bill Is Derailed," *New York Times*, May 12, 2014. For a tabulation of votes by party and by state on the motion, see "Inside Congress: Senate Vote 142 - Blocks Energy Efficiency Bill," *New York Times*, August 16, 2014, available at http://politics.nytimes.com/congress/votes/113/senate/2/142. Only three Republicans voted for the motion.

6. The quotations are from Davenport, "Amid Pipeline and Climate Debate, Energy-Efficiency Bill Is Derailed."

7. Quoted in an editorial, "G.O.P. vs. the Environment," *New York Times*, October 14, 2011. Waxman's staff compiled the tally of anti-environmental House votes.

8. See Daniel J. Fiorino, *The New Environmental Regulation* (Cambridge, MA: MIT Press, 2006); Marc Allen Eisner, *Governing the Environment: The Transformation of Environmental Regulation* (Boulder, CO: Lynne Rienner, 2007); and Daniel A. Mazmanian and Michael E. Kraft, eds., *Toward Sustainable Communities: Transition and Transformation in Environmental Policy*, 2nd ed. (Cambridge, MA: MIT Press, 2009).

9. See Eric Schickler and Kathryn Pearson, "The House Leadership in an Era of Partisan Warfare," in *Congress Reconsidered*, 8th ed., ed. Lawrence C. Dodd and Bruce I. Oppenheimer (Washington, DC: CQ Press, 2005). See also Thomas E. Mann and Norman J. Ornstein, *The Broken Branch: How Congress Is Failing America and How to Get It Back on Track* (New York: Oxford University Press, 2006).

10. See Chapter 1 in this volume, and Michael E. Kraft, "Congress and Environmental Policy," in *The Oxford Handbook of U.S. Environmental Policy*, ed. Sheldon Kamieniecki and Michael E. Kraft (New York: Oxford, 2013).

11. Ed Gillespie and Bob Schellhas, eds., *Contract with America* (New York: Times Books/Random House, 1994); Bob Benenson, "GOP Sets the 104th Congress on New Regulatory Course," *Congressional Quarterly Weekly Report*, June 17, 1995, 1693–705.

12. For a general review of much of this period, see Lawrence C. Dodd and Bruce I. Oppenheimer, "A Decade of Republican Control: The House of Representatives, 1995–2005," in *Congress Reconsidered*, 8th ed., ed. Lawrence C. Dodd and Bruce I. Oppenheimer (Washington, DC: CQ Press, 2005).

13. See Mazmanian and Kraft, *Toward Sustainable Communities*; Eisner, *Governing the Environment*; and Christopher McGrory Klyza and David Sousa, *American Environmental Policy: Beyond Gridlock*, updated and expanded edition (Cambridge, MA: MIT Press, 2013).

14. For a general analysis of roles that Congress plays in the U.S. political system, see Roger H. Davidson, Walter J. Oleszek, Frances E. Lee, and Eric Schickler, *Congress and Its Members*, 14th ed. (Washington, DC: CQ Press, 2014).

15. Coral Davenport, "'Senate Democrats' All-Nighter Flags Climate Change," *New York Times*, March 10, 2014.

16. "Republican EPA Chiefs to Congress: Act on Climate," Associated Press, June 18, 2014. See also William D. Ruckelshaus, Lee M. Thomas, William K. Reilly, and Christine Todd Whitman, "A Republican Case for Climate Action," *New York Times*, August 1, 2013.

17. Kaufman, "Republicans Seek Big Cuts in Environmental Rules."
18. Matthew L. Wald, "Republicans Suggest White House Rushed Solar Company's Loans," *New York Times*, September 14, 2011. The committee later subpoenaed the White House to force release of thousands of pages of documents, including internal memos and e-mails, in an effort to demonstrate White House pressure on the Department of Energy to grant the loan to Solyndra. By 2014, assessments of the DOE loan program found it to be highly profitable for the federal government despite several failed projects such as the Solyndra loan. See Justin Doom, "U.S. Expects $5 Billion from Program That Funded Solyndra," Bloomberg News Service, November 12, 2014.
19. Kraft, "Congress and Environmental Policy."
20. Davidson, Oleszek, Lee, and Schickler, *Congress and Its Members*. See also Gary C. Jacobson, *The Politics of Congressional Elections*, 8th ed. (New York: Pearson, 2013).
21. Carl Hulse, "Consensus on Energy Bill Arose One Project at a Time," *New York Times*, November 19, 2003. The energy bill, which ultimately was approved as the Energy Policy Act of 2005, is summarized in Michael E. Kraft, *Environmental Policy and Politics*, 6th ed. (New York: Pearson, 2015), 195.
22. See John M. Broder, "At House E.P.A. Hearing, Both Sides Claim Science," *New York Times*, March 8, 2011.
23. Charles M. Blow, "The Do-Even-Less Congress," *New York Times*, August 3, 2014.
24. On the general idea of policy drift and failure to reform key public policies, see Jacob S. Hacker and Paul Pierson, *Winner-Take-All Politics: How Washington Made the Rich Richer—and Turned Its Back on the Middle Class* (New York: Simon and Schuster, 2010).
25. See Barry Rabe's chapter in this volume on state and local actions (Chapter 2); and Klyza and Sousa, *American Environmental Policy*.
26. One of the few scholarly analyses of the subject is Sarah A. Binder, *Stalemate: Causes and Consequences of Legislative Gridlock* (Washington, DC: Brookings Institution Press, 2003). Aside from what the chapter covers, other factors also affect legislative gridlock today. Among them are the constitutional specification that the Senate be composed of two senators for each state (thus giving small and often conservative states an oversized representation in that body), the effects of legislative redistricting or gerrymandering that can distort the public's partisan preferences, and the weak national laws on campaign financing in the wake of the Supreme Court's *Citizens United* decision. Even the filibuster in the Senate plays a role; it prevents the majority party from taking action without the sixty votes needed to overcome frequent filibusters by the minority party.
27. Studies show that members of Congress generally do vote in a way that is consistent with their campaign promises on environmental issues, but that Republicans are "far more likely to break their campaign promises," and that pro-environmental campaign promises are more likely to be broken than are others. See Evan J. Ringquist and Carl Dasse, "Lies, Damned Lies, and Campaign Promises? Environmental Legislation in the 105th Congress," *Social Science Quarterly* 85 (June 2004): 400–419. The quotation is from p. 417. See also Evan J. Ringquist, Milena I. Neshkova, and Joseph Aamidor, "Campaign Promises, Democratic Governance, and Environmental Policy in the U.S. Congress," *Policy Studies Journal* 41, no. 2 (2013): 365–87.
28. Recent polls document the continued low saliency of environmental issues, including climate change, even though the public favors a wide range of policy actions on climate change, and has for several years according to the Yale Project on Climate Change Communication (survey results available at http://environment.yale.edu/climate-communication/) and other surveys. For example, a *Wall Street Journal*/NBC poll released in June 2014 found that more than two-thirds of the American public

supported the new EPA power-plant rule even though public hearings around the nation in August 2014 drew opponents, many of them organized to turn out by the fossil fuel industry. On the continued low saliency of these issues, see the Gallup poll's "most important problem" reports, available at www.gallup.com. The low salience of environmental issues in election campaigns may be changing. Studies showed that these issues were significant in selected Senate campaigns in 2014. See Coral Davenport and Ashley Parker, "Environmental Issues Become a Force in Political Advertising," *New York Times*, October 21, 2014.

29. See, for example, "Political Polarization in the American Public: How Increasing Ideological Uniformity and Partisan Antipathy Affect Politics, Compromise and Everyday Life" (Pew Research Center for the People and the Press, June 2014), available at www.people-press.org/2014/06/12/political-polarization-in-the-american-public. For an overview of the evidence and academic scholarship on the subject, see Thomas E. Mann, "Admit It, Political Scientists: Politics Really Is More Broken Than Ever," *The Atlantic*, May 26, 2014. The historical trends in party polarization in Congress are reported in Nolan McCarty, Keith Poole, and Howard Rosenthal, *Polarized America: The Dance of Ideology and Unequal Riches* (Cambridge, MA: MIT Press, 2008).

30. See Charles R. Shipan and William R. Lowry, "Environmental Policy and Party Divergence in Congress," *Political Research Quarterly* 54 (June 2001): 245–63. See also Amy Below, "Parties, Campaigns, and Elections," in *The Oxford Handbook of U.S. Environmental Policy*, ed. Sheldon Kamieniecki and Michael E. Kraft (New York: Oxford, 2013).

31. League of Conservation Voters (LCV), "National Environmental Scorecard" (Washington, DC: LCV, November 2004, and later years). The scorecards are available at the league's website (www.lcv.org).

32. See Aaron M. McCright, Chenyang Xiao, and Riley E. Dunlap, "Political Polarization on Support for Government Spending on Environmental Protection in the USA, 1974–2012," *Social Science Research* 48 (2014): 251–60.

33. Mary Etta Cook and Roger H. Davidson, "Deferral Politics: Congressional Decision Making on Environmental Issues in the 1980s," in *Public Policy and the Natural Environment*, ed. Helen M. Ingram and R. Kenneth Godwin (Greenwich, CT: JAI, 1985). See also Norman J. Vig and Michael E. Kraft, eds., *Environmental Policy in the 1980s: Reagan's New Agenda* (Washington, DC: CQ Press, 1984).

34. For a fuller discussion of the gridlock over clean air legislation, see Gary C. Bryner, *Blue Skies, Green Politics: The Clean Air Act of 1990 and Its Implementation* (Washington, DC: CQ Press, 1995).

35. Rhodes Cook, "Rare Combination of Forces May Make History of '94," *Congressional Quarterly Weekly Report*, April 15, 1995, 1076–81.

36. Katharine Q. Seelye, "Files Show How Gingrich Laid a Grand G.O.P. Plan," *New York Times*, December 3, 1995. See also John B. Bader, "The Contract with America: Origins and Assessments," in *Congress Reconsidered*, 6th ed., ed. Lawrence C. Dodd and Bruce I. Oppenheimer (Washington, DC: CQ Press, 1997). On the broader history of conservative and business campaigns against environmental policy, see Judith A. Layzer, *Open for Business: Conservatives' Opposition to Environmental Regulation* (Cambridge, MA: MIT Press, 2012).

37. Everett Carll Ladd, "The 1994 Congressional Elections: The Postindustrial Realignment Continues," *Political Science Quarterly* 110 (Spring 1995): 1–23; Alfred J. Tuchfarber et al., "The Republican Tidal Wave of 1994: Testing Hypotheses about Realignment, Restructuring, and Rebellion," *PS: Political Science and Politics* 28 (December 1995): 689–96.

38. Allan Freedman, "GOP's Secret Weapon against Regulations: Finesse," *CQ Weekly*, September 5, 1998, 2314–20; and Charles Pope, "Environmental Bills Hitch a Ride through the Legislative Gantlet," *CQ Weekly*, April 4, 1998, 872–75.

39. See Fiorino, *The New Environmental Regulation*; and Eisner, *Governing the Environment*.

40. See Sara R. Rinfret and Scott R. Furlong, "Defining Environmental Rulemaking," in *The Oxford Handbook of Environmental Policy*, ed. Sheldon Kamieniecki and Michael E. Kraft (New York: Oxford, 2013).

41. See Kraft and Kamieniecki, *Business and Environmental Policy*.

42. See Jackie Calmes, "Both Sides of the Aisle Say More Regulation, and Not Just of Banks," *New York Times*, October 14, 2008.

43. John H. Cushman Jr., "G.O.P.'s Plan for Environment Is Facing a Big Test in Congress," *New York Times*, July 17, 1995.

44. Semple, "Concealed Weapons against the Environment."

45. Pope, "Environmental Bills Hitch a Ride."

46. Andrew Revkin, "Law Revises Standards for Scientific Study," *New York Times*, March 21, 2002. See also Rick Weiss, "'Data Quality' Law Is Nemesis of Regulation," *Washington Post*, August 16, 2004; and Paul Raeburn, "A Regulation on Regulations," *Scientific American*, July 2006, 18–19. Raeburn reported that by 2006, perhaps one hundred Data Quality Act petitions had been filed with dozens of different government agencies, most of them by industry groups. In a comparable action late in 2014, the House passed two bills that critics said were likely to undermine the EPA's capacity to use scientific studies in support of its policy decisions. The 114th Congress that takes office in 2015 may well pursue similar legislation in an effort to rein in the EPA and other regulatory agencies. See Ronald White, "Congress's Latest Stealth Attack on EPA Standards—Restrict Expert Scientific Advice" (Washington, DC: Center for Effective Government, November 24, 2014), available at www.foreffectivegov.org.

47. Susan Zakin, "Riders from Hell," *Amicus Journal* (Spring 2001): 20–22.

48. Carroll J. Doherty and the staff of *CQ Weekly*, "Congress Compiles a Modest Record in a Session Sidetracked by Scandal: Appropriations," *CQ Weekly*, November 14, 1998, 3086–87 and 3090–91.

49. The projections to 2019 are taken from the president's fiscal year 2015 budget's historical tables, particularly Budget Authority by Function and Subfunction: 1976–2019.

50. Coral Davenport, "Republicans Vow to Fight E.P.A. and Approve Keystone Pipeline," *New York Times*, November 10, 2014.

51. David Hosansky, "Rewrite of Laws on Pesticides on Way to President's Desk," *Congressional Quarterly Weekly Report*, July 27, 1996, 2101–03; Hosansky, "Provisions: Pesticide, Food Safety Law," *Congressional Quarterly Weekly Report*, September 7, 1996, 2546–50.

52. David Hosansky, "Drinking Water Bill Clears; Clinton Expected to Sign," *Congressional Quarterly Weekly Report*, August 3, 1996, 2179–80; Allan Freedman, "Provisions: Safe Drinking Water Act Amendments," *Congressional Quarterly Weekly Report*, September 14, 1996, 2622–27.

53. Alan K. Ota, "What the Highway Bill Does," *CQ Weekly*, July 11, 1998, 1892–98.

54. Rebecca Adams, "Pressure from White House and Hastert Pries Brownfields Bill from Committee," *CQ Weekly*, September 8, 2001, 2065–66.

55. Mary Clare Jalonick, "Healthy Forests Initiative Provisions," *CQ Weekly*, January 24, 2004, 246–47.

56. Juliet Eilperin, "Keeping the Wilderness Untamed: Bills in Congress Could Add as Much as Two Million Acres of Unspoiled Land to Federal Control," *Washington Post*

National Edition, June 23–July 6, 2008, 35; and Avery Palmer, "Long-Stalled Lands Bill Gets Nod from Senate," *CQ Weekly*, January 19, 2009, 128.

57. Chuck McCutcheon, "House Passage of Bush Energy Plan Sets Up Clash with Senate," *CQ Weekly*, August 4, 2001, 1915–17.

58. Rebecca Adams, "Politics Stokes Energy Debate," *CQ Weekly*, January 12, 2002, 108.

59. Carl Hulse, "House Votes to Approve Broad Energy Legislation," *New York Times*, April 22, 2005.

60. See Ben Evans and Joseph J. Schatz, "Details of Energy Policy Law," *CQ Weekly*, September 5, 2005, 2337–45.

61. John M. Broder, "Obama to Toughen Rules on Emissions and Mileage," *New York Times*, May 18, 2009; and Bill Vlasic, "Carmakers Back Strict New Rules for Gas Mileage," *New York Times*, July 28, 2011.

62. Editorial, "An $80 Billion Start," *New York Times*, February 18, 2009.

63. The education act was part of the Higher Education Opportunity Act of 2008. It authorized competitive grants to institutions and associations in higher education to promote development of sustainability curricula, programs, and practices. It was the first new federal environmental education program in eighteen years.

64. The House has favored reform of the mining law, but the Senate has not. In 2007, the House voted 244–166 for an act that for the first time set a royalty payment to the government for mining on public lands and established a clear and enforceable set of environmental protections for mining. The Senate has not gone along so far, and one of the key opponents has been Senate majority leader Harry Reid, who represents a state heavily dependent on mining.

65. Michael Janofsky, "Changes May Be Needed in Superfund, Chief Says," *New York Times*, December 5, 2004. On the drop in program revenues, see Jennifer 8. Lee, "Drop in Budget Slows Superfund Program," *New York Times*, March 9, 2004.

66. Cited in *Science and Environmental Policy Update*, the Ecological Society of America online newsletter, April 20, 2001.

67. Mary Clare Jalonick, "Environmental Panels' Chairmen Chip Away at Endangered Species Act, Refocusing Resources and Definitions," *CQ Weekly*, March 27, 2004, 756; Jalonick, "House Panel OKs Softening of Species Act," *CQ Weekly*, July 24, 2004, 1811.

68. Carl Hulse, "In Climate Change Bill, a Political Message," *New York Times*, June 28, 2009; John M. Broder, "House Backs Bill, 219–212, to Curb Global Warming," *New York Times*, June 27, 2009; and Coral Davenport and Avery Palmer, "A Landmark Climate Bill Passes," *CQ Weekly*, June 29, 2009, 1516.

69. The Senate negotiations and White House action on the bill are recounted in detail in Ryan Lizza, "As the World Burns," *The New Yorker*, October 11, 2010. As an example of new legislative proposals, Rep. Chris Van Hollen, D.-Md., authored a so-called "cap and dividend" bill in 2014 to require coal, oil, and natural gas companies to purchase a permit for each ton of carbon they sell, the permits to be auctioned, and the proceeds to be returned directly to the American public. See James K. Boyce, "The Carbon Dividend," *New York Times*, July 29, 2014.

70. The Gallup poll reports regularly on the public's trust and confidence in government and in the Congress. See, for example, "Congressional Approval Rating Languishes at Low Level," *Gallup Politics*, July 15, 2014, available at www.gallup.com.

6

Environmental Policy in the Courts

Rosemary O'Leary

In 1966, on one of her frequent trips to a family cabin in rural upstate New York, Carol Yannacone was shocked to find hundreds of dead fish floating on the surface of Yaphank Lake, where she had spent her summers as a child. After discovering that the county had sprayed the foliage surrounding the lake with DDT to kill mosquitoes immediately prior to the fish kill, Yannacone persuaded her lawyer husband to file suit on her behalf against the county mosquito control commission. The suit requested an injunction to halt the spraying of pesticides containing DDT around the lake.

Although Carol Yannacone and her husband initially were able to win only a one-year injunction, they set into motion a chain of events that would permanently change environmental policy in the courts. It was through this lawsuit that a group of environmentalists and scientists formed the Environmental Defense Fund (EDF), a nonprofit group dedicated to promoting change in environmental policy through legal action. After eight years of protracted litigation, the EDF won a court battle against the U.S. Environmental Protection Agency (EPA) that Judge David Bazelon heralded as the beginning of "a new era in the ... long and fruitful collaboration of administrative agencies and reviewing courts."[1] That judicial decision triggered a permanent suspension of the registration of pesticides containing DDT in the United States.

Now fast forward to 2008. By the end of his second term as president, George W. Bush was fully immersed in the concept of environmental policymaking in the courts. Environmental advocates were waging an all-out attack in the courts in an effort to challenge the president's attempted change of environmental policies. In February 2008, for example, a three-judge federal court of appeals panel in Washington, DC, issued a blow to President Bush when it unanimously struck down one of the administration's most significant attempts to change environmental policy in the form of EPA limits on mercury emissions from coal-fired power plants. The court said that the Bush administration had substituted weaker regulations for the "plain text" of the Clean Air Act without following the process set out in the law. The appellate court called this "the logic of the Queen of Hearts," referring to the character from Lewis Carroll's book *Alice's Adventures in Wonderland*. In the book, the foul-tempered queen has only one way of settling all difficulties, great or small, by yelling "Off with his head!" and severing the heads of anyone who dared to disagree with her. This was merely one of over a thousand lawsuits filed against the EPA while George W. Bush was president.[2]

The Obama administration also has had its fair share of lawsuits brought against it on environmental issues. One of the most controversial 2014 cases concerned cross-state air pollution rules. These rules, promulgated by the EPA under the Clean Air Act, seek to hold states responsible for air pollution that drifts across their borders and causes harm in downwind states. Calling this a "complex challenge"[3] and a "tough" "hard" problem,[4] the Supreme Court clarified five years of contradictory lower court decisions that struck down the agency's approach. In a 6-2 decision, the Supreme Court ended up supporting the EPA's approach, writing that "EPA's cost-effective allocation of emission reductions among upwind States . . . is a permissible, workable, and equitable interpretation of the Good Neighbor Provision" [of the Clean Air Act]."[5] Environmental advocates said the case was "5 years late"[6] and lamented that the EPA's efforts had been bogged down in the courts for over a decade.

Both in legal analyses and in "dicta" (remarks or observations made by a judge in a decision), courts are an integral part of environmental policymaking. An important aspect of environmental conflicts, however, is that multiple forums exist for decision making. Litigation is by no means the only way to resolve environmental disputes. Most environmental conflicts never reach a court, and an estimated 50 to 90 percent of those that do are settled out of court. Discussion and debate are informal ways of resolving environmental conflict. Enacting legislation is another way to deal with such conflict. Environmental conflict resolution approaches, ranging from collaborative problem solving to mediation, are becoming more common in environmental policy.

The focus of this chapter, however, is environmental policy in the courts. First, a profile of the U.S. court system and a primer on judicial review of agency actions are offered. Next, the focus changes to how courts shape environmental policy, with several in-depth case analyses provided. The chapter concludes with a view to the future.

The Organization and Operation of the U.S. Court System

To understand environmental policy in the courts, a brief profile of the U.S. court system is essential. The United States has a dual court system, with different cases starting either in federal court or in state or county court. Keeping in mind that most legal disputes never go to court (they are resolved through one of the informal methods mentioned in the introduction to this chapter), this section describes the organization of the U.S. court system (Figure 6-1).

When legal disputes do go to court, most are resolved in state courts. Many of these disputes are criminal or domestic controversies. They usually start in trial courts and are heard by a judge and sometimes a jury. If the case is lost at the trial court level, appeal to an intermediate court of appeals is possible. At this level, the appeals court usually reviews only questions of law, not fact. If a party to a case is not satisfied with the outcome at the intermediate level, then the party may appeal to the state supreme court. In cases involving federal questions, final appeal to the U.S. Supreme Court is possible, but the court has wide discretion as to which cases it will review.

Figure 6-1   The Dual Court System

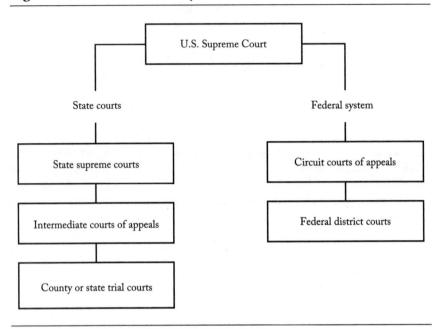

Most of the environmental cases discussed in this chapter began in the federal court system because they concerned interpretations of federal statutes or the Constitution. Cases that begin in the federal court system usually begin in the federal district courts. There are ninety-four federal district courts staffed by approximately 678 active judges. (There are also so-called specialty courts such as the U.S. bankruptcy courts, the U.S. Court of Appeals for the Armed Forces, and the U.S. Court of Federal Claims. There are also tribal courts.)

Some statutes, however, provide for appeal of decisions of federal regulatory agencies directly to the federal courts of appeals rather than through district courts. These cases, coupled with appeals from federal district courts, make for a full docket for the federal courts of appeals. There are thirteen federal circuit courts of appeals with about 179 active judges in total. Here, judges sit in groups of three when deciding cases. When there are conflicting opinions among the lower federal district courts within a circuit, all the judges of the circuit will sit together and hear a case. An unsatisfactory outcome in a circuit court can be appealed to the U.S. Supreme Court. Less than 10 percent of the requests for Supreme Court review usually are granted.

Sources of Law

The decisions of appellate courts are considered precedent. Precedent is judge-made law that guides and informs subsequent court decisions involving similar or analogous situations. But precedent is only one of several sources of environmental law. The major sources of environmental law are as follows:

- Constitutions (federal and state)
- Statutes (federal, state, and local)
- Administrative regulations (promulgated by administrative agencies)
- Treaties (signed by the president and ratified by the Senate)
- Executive orders (proclamations issued by presidents or governors)
- Appellate court decisions

Judicial Review of Agency Actions

One of the pivotal issues in environmental law today is the scope of judicial review of an agency's action. The purpose of judicial review of administrative decision making generally is to ensure at least minimum levels of fairness. It has been said that the scope of review for a specific administrative decision may range from 0 to 100 percent, meaning that depending on the issue in question, a reviewing court may have broad or narrow powers to decide a case—or somewhere in between.

When an agency makes a decision, it usually does three things. First, it interprets the law in question. Second, it collects facts concerning a particular situation. Third, it uses its discretionary power to apply the law to the facts. A court's review of an agency's actions in each of these three steps is very different. (At the same time, it must be acknowledged that separating an agency's actions into three categories can be difficult, as in instances when there are mixed questions of law and fact.)

An agency's *interpretation of the law* usually demands a strong examination by a reviewing court. When constitutional issues are of concern, judges will rarely defer to administrative interpretations. However, when an agency's interpretation of its own regulation is at issue, it is said that deference is "even more clearly in order."[7] The general practice is that a court will give less deference to an agency's legal conclusions than to its factual or discretionary decisions.

At the same time, courts have shown deference to administrative interpretations of the law. The signature case that illustrates this point is *Chevron U.S.A., Inc. v. Natural Resources Defense Council*,[8] which concerned the EPA's "bubble concept" pursuant to the Clean Air Act. Under the bubble concept, the EPA allows states to adopt a plant-wide definition of the term *stationary source*. Under this definition, an existing plant that contained several pollution-emitting devices could install or modify one piece of equipment without meeting the permit conditions, if the alteration did not increase the total emissions from the plant. This allowed a state to treat all of the pollution-emitting sources within the same industrial group as if they were encased in a single bubble. Environmentalists sued the EPA, asserting that this definition of a stationary source violated the Clean Air Act. In a unanimous decision, the Supreme Court held that the EPA's plant-wide definition was permissible. The Supreme Court's opinion is now referred to as the *Chevron* doctrine. It holds that when Congress has spoken clearly to the precise question at issue, the rule of law demands agency adherence to its intent. However, if Congress has not addressed the matter precisely, then an agency may adopt any reasonable interpretation—regardless of whether a reviewing court may consider some other interpretation more reasonable or sensible. As such, the *Chevron* doctrine is often thought of as making it more difficult for courts to overrule agency interpretations.

An agency's *fact finding* usually demands less scrutiny by reviewing courts than do legal issues. Although an agency's decision may be reversed if it is unwarranted by the facts, courts generally acknowledge that agencies are in a better position to ascertain facts than is a reviewing court.

Judicial review of an agency's *discretionary powers* is usually deferential to a point, while maintaining an important oversight role for the courts. A court usually will make sure the agency has done a careful job of collecting and analyzing information, taking a hard look at the important issues and facts.

Even if a reviewing court decides that the agency correctly understood the law involved and concludes that the agency's view of the facts was reasonable, it may still negate the decision if the agency's activity is found to be "arbitrary, capricious, an abuse of discretion, or otherwise not in accordance with the law."[9] This can involve legal, factual, or discretionary issues. This type of review has been called several things: a rational basis review, an arbitrariness review, and an abuse of discretion review.

How Courts Shape Environmental Policy

As they decide environmental cases to ensure minimum levels of fairness, courts shape environmental policy in many ways. First, the courts determine who does or does not have standing, or the right, to sue. Although many environmental statutes give citizens, broadly defined, the right to sue polluters or regulators,[10] procedural hurdles must still be cleared in order to gain access to the courts. Plaintiffs usually must demonstrate injury in fact, which is often not clear-cut and is subject to interpretation by judges. By controlling who may sue, courts affect the environmental policy agenda.

Second, and related to the first power, courts shape environmental policy by deciding which cases are ripe, or ready for review. For a case to be justiciable, an actual controversy must exist. The alleged wrong must be more than merely anticipated. To decide whether an issue is ripe for judicial review, courts will examine both the fitness of the issue for judicial decision and the hardship on the parties if a court withholds consideration. Deciding which cases are ripe and which are not makes the courts powerful gatekeepers.

A third way in which courts shape environmental policy is by their choice of standard of review. Will the court, for example, take a hard look at the actions of public environmental officials in this particular case, or will it defer to the administrative expertise of the agency? Under what conditions will government environmental experts be deemed to have exceeded their legislative or constitutional authority? To what standards will polluters be held?

A fourth way in which courts shape environmental policy is by interpreting environmental laws. Courts interpret statutes, administrative rules and regulations, executive orders, treaties, constitutions, and prior court decisions. Often these laws are ambiguous and vague. Situations may arise that the laws' drafters did not anticipate. Hence, judicial interpretation becomes of paramount importance. And given the precedent-setting nature of court orders, a judicial interpretation made today may determine not only current environmental policy, but also that of the future.

A final major way in which courts shape environmental policy is through the remedies they choose. Will the court, for example, order a punitive fine for polluters, or probation? Judges generally have great discretion in their choice of remedy, thus affecting environmental policy.

The Supreme Court, the final arbiter of many precedent-setting environmental cases, shapes environmental policy primarily through the selection of cases it chooses to hear, the limits it places on other branches of government, and the limits it places on the states. Justices' values, ideological backgrounds, and policy preferences at times influence the outcome of environmental court decisions. Thus the implications of courts shaping environmental policy are formidable, and one may easily see why environmental advocates, concerned citizens, and big businesses often use lawsuits as tools to force policy changes in public environment and natural resource agencies. The cases discussed in the sections that follow paint a vivid portrait of environmental policymaking in the courts.

Standing to Sue: The Case of Global Warming

On October 12, 2007, Al Gore was awarded the Nobel Peace Prize for his campaign to curb global climate change. Gore shared the prize with the UN Intergovernmental Panel on Climate Change, whose head, Rajendra Pachauri, told leaders at a climate conference in Indonesia that a well-documented rise in global temperatures has coincided with a significant increase in the concentration of carbon dioxide in the atmosphere. "Heed the wisdom of science," Pachauri told conference participants on behalf of the UN, as scientists believe the two trends are related. When carbon dioxide is released into the atmosphere, it acts like the ceiling of a greenhouse, trapping solar energy and retarding the escape of reflected heat.

In 1999, eight years before Gore received the Nobel Peace Prize, the International Center for Technology Assessment joined other parties in petitioning the EPA to set standards for four greenhouse gases emitted by new motor vehicles: carbon dioxide, methane, nitrous oxide, and hydrofluorocarbons. The petition argued that these greenhouse gases are air pollutants and that scientists had concluded that global warming will endanger public health and the environment. Hence, the petition argued, the EPA is obligated to regulate greenhouse gas emissions from new mobile sources.

The EPA refused to regulate greenhouse gases, citing several reasons: First, the EPA said that the Clean Air Act "does not authorize regulation to address global climate change."[11] Tied in with this, the agency maintained that air pollutants associated with climate change "are not air pollutants under the [act's] regulatory provisions."[12] Moreover, the EPA stated that it disagreed with the regulatory approach urged by the petitioners and that it would not be "effective or appropriate for EPA to establish [greenhouse gas] standards for motor vehicles" at this time.[13] Instead, the EPA chose to encourage voluntary actions to curb emissions through incentives for more technological development.

The agency noted that "the science of climate change is extraordinarily complex and still evolving."[14] The agency also said that since many sources of air pollutants were associated with global climate change, to regulate only pollutants emitted by new motor vehicles would "result in an inefficient, piecemeal approach to addressing the climate change issue."[15] The agency concluded that it is the president's prerogative to address global climate change as an important foreign policy issue.

The petitioners appealed the EPA's decision to the U.S. Court of Appeals for the District of Columbia Circuit. That court split three different ways, with the majority ruling in favor of the EPA.[16] In 2006, the Supreme Court agreed to review the case, *Massachusetts v. Environmental Protection Agency*,[17] focusing on whether the EPA had authority to regulate greenhouse gases under the Clean Air Act and whether it could decline to exercise that authority based on policy considerations not mentioned in the statute.[18] One of the pivotal issues the Supreme Court had to grapple with in the case was whether the plaintiffs—the state of Massachusetts as well as other states, local governments, and nonprofit environmental advocacy groups—had standing to sue. The Supreme Court has ruled consistently that, to have standing to sue, a party must demonstrate injury—in fact, "a concrete and particularized, actual or imminent invasion of a legally protected interest."[19] In federal cases, this requirement arises out of the U.S. Constitution's "case or controversy" requirement.[20] In response, the EPA, supported by another group of states paired with six trade associations, countered that the plaintiffs did not have standing to sue. The EPA and its supporters maintained that because greenhouse gas emissions inflict widespread harm, the doctrine of standing presents an insurmountable obstacle. They argued that those who filed the lawsuit did not have a personal stake in the outcome of the controversy; specifically, they could not demonstrate a particularized injury, actual or imminent, traceable to the defendant, as precedent requires. They also argued that the EPA's decision not to regulate greenhouse gas emissions from new motor vehicles contributed so insignificantly to any alleged injuries that the agency could not be made to answer for them.

On April 2, 2007, the Supreme Court disagreed with the EPA, siding with the state of Massachusetts, its partner states and local governments, and environmental advocates. Only one plaintiff needs to show standing, the court said, and the state of Massachusetts clearly demonstrated a stake in the outcome of the controversy, given the projected rise in sea levels predicted to come from global warming. Calling the harms associated with climate change serious and well recognized, the court found the risk of catastrophic harm, though remote, to be real. That risk would be reduced to some extent if the plaintiffs received the relief they requested in their lawsuit. Therefore, the court found that the plaintiffs had standing to challenge the EPA.

After affirming the standing of the plaintiffs, the Supreme Court went on to issue a remarkable decision in which five of the nine justices chastised the Bush administration for its inaction on global warming. The court declared that carbon dioxide and other greenhouse gases are air pollutants and must be regulated by the EPA under the Clean Air Act. The court rebuked the administration's argument that, even if it did have authority to act, it would be unwise to regulate those pollutants at the current time. Rejecting rulemaking based on these impermissible considerations was arbitrary, capricious, and otherwise not in accordance with law, the court said. The court ordered the EPA to decide, pursuant to the mandates of the Clean Air Act, whether greenhouse gases may reasonably be anticipated to endanger public health or welfare.

This landmark case illustrates how courts shape environmental policy by determining who has standing. Without a finding by the Supreme Court that the state of Massachusetts had standing, it would not have had the legal authority to sue. Without the legal authority to sue, this case never would have come to court. Calling the decision "a watershed moment in the fight against global warming," a spokesperson for the Sierra Club environmental group said, "This is a total repudiation of the refusal of the Bush administration to use the authority he has to meet the challenge of global warming."[21] Legal scholars pointed out that the EPA will no longer have any excuse to refuse to regulate pollutants from other sources, such as power plants, that are governed by the same Clean Air Act sections.

In June 2011, the Supreme Court added another interesting twist to the issue of regulating carbon emissions. In *American Electric Power Company, Inc. et al. v. Connecticut et al.*,[22] the court considered whether the lower courts could still hear cases against four private power companies and the federal Tennessee Valley Authority by several states, the city of New York, and three private land trusts, as they were initiated prior to *Massachusetts v. EPA*. The plaintiffs were asking for judicial decrees setting carbon dioxide emissions for each defendant pursuant to the federal common law of interstate nuisance, as well as state tort law. Reversing a lower court decision, the Supreme Court held that Congress clearly delegated to the EPA the decision as to whether and how to regulate carbon dioxide emissions from power plants. That delegation, the court said, displaces federal common law, even if the EPA's regulations were still being developed. In addition, Congress's scheme outlined in the Clean Air Act prescribes a specific order of decision making that must be followed, first by the experts at the EPA, and then by federal judges. In response to this Supreme Court case, there have been attempts in Congress (unsuccessful to date) to repeal the EPA's authority to regulate carbon emissions.

A more recent decision, the 2014 Supreme Court case *Utility Air Group v. EPA*,[23] examined whether the EPA permissibly determined that its regulation of greenhouse gas emissions from new motor vehicles under the

Clean Air Act also triggered permit requirements for stationary sources of greenhouse gas emissions. In a complex decision that split the court, the justices voted 5-4 to reject the EPA's broadest view of its power over greenhouse gas emissions, but also voted 7-2 to allow the EPA to impose its air pollution control strategy on 83 percent of the power plants and other fixed sources of greenhouse gases in the United States.

On the one hand, the court chastised the agency for exceeding its statutory mandates by attempting to regulate all forms of greenhouse gas emissions as well as changing the limits enacted by Congress in order to make the implementation of the law more manageable, saying that "an agency may not rewrite clear statutory terms to suit its own sense of how the statute should operate. We are not willing to stand on the dock and wave goodbye as EPA embarks on a multiyear voyage of discovery" about how it wants to regulate greenhouse gases. On the other hand, the court held that the EPA does have the power, if it is already regulating a specific source because it emits other kinds of air pollution, to require that source to use the best available technology also to control greenhouse gases. Overall, the case was heralded as a victory for environmentalists. "E.P.A. is getting almost everything it wanted in this case," Justice Antonin Scalia wrote. This will surely remain an area of contention in Congress over the next few years.

Ripeness and Standard of Review: The Case of Timber Cutting

The U.S. National Forest System is vast. It includes 155 national forests, twenty national grasslands, eight land utilization projects, and other lands that together occupy nearly three hundred thousand square miles of land located in forty-four states, Puerto Rico, and the Virgin Islands. To manage those lands, the U.S. Forest Service, housed in the U.S. Department of Agriculture, develops land and resource management plans, as mandated by the National Forest Management Act of 1976. In developing the plans, the Forest Service must take into account both environmental and commercial goals.

In the late 1980s, the Forest Service developed a plan for the Wayne National Forest located in southern Ohio. When the plan was proposed, several environmental groups, including the Sierra Club and the Citizens Council on Conservation and Environmental Control, protested in administrative hearings that the plan was unlawful in part because it allowed below-cost timber sales and so encouraged clear-cutting. Opposing the environmental groups was the Ohio Forestry Association.

When the plan was not changed, the Sierra Club brought suit in federal court against the Forest Service and the secretary of agriculture. Among its requests to the district court, the Sierra Club asked for a declaration that the plan was unlawful because it authorized below-cost timber cutting. The Sierra Club also asked for an injunction to halt below-cost timber harvesting.

In a case full of twists and turns,[24] the Supreme Court eventually ruled in favor of the Ohio Forestry Association in the 1998 case *Ohio Forestry*

Association, Inc. v. Sierra Club.[25] Among the many arguments cited in its rationale, the court said that the case was not ripe for review because it concerned abstract disagreements over administrative policies. The court said that immediate judicial intervention would require the court to second-guess thousands of technical decisions made by scientists and other forestry experts and might hinder the Forest Service's efforts to refine its policies. Further, delayed judicial review would not cause significant hardship for the parties. (The forest plan for the Wayne National Forest, at issue in *Ohio Forestry*, was again challenged unsuccessfully by environmental advocates in 2005, in *Buckeye Forest Council v. U.S. Forest Service,*[26] which concerned the Endangered Species Act.)

The *Ohio Forestry* case is still good law today and is an example of how courts shape environmental policy by applying the concepts of standard of review and ripeness. Notable is the court's reluctance to second-guess the judgments of government scientists and other technical analysts. In a case in which there is no showing of arbitrary or capricious government action, the court will give great deference to experts in its review. Also notable is the court's reluctance to review a plan that had not yet been implemented. Because no clear-cutting or timber sales had occurred, there was not yet a case or controversy, and so the case was not ripe for review. Regrettably, however, the interpretation is that concrete damage to the environment is needed before the court will act.

Though wise from a legal perspective, this approach is shortsighted from an environmental perspective. Two legal scholars called for Congress to respond to this case by changing the law.[27] The scholars concluded that the case, coupled with other cases, created significant roadblocks in the path of those wishing to challenge federal government planning decisions. In addition, these cases have encouraged land management agencies to change their uses of land management plans to "paperwork that makes no commitments about land suitability and sets few, if any, standards for governing future activities."[28]

Standard of Review: The Case of Air Quality

The Clean Air Act mandates that the EPA administrator promulgate National Ambient Air Quality Standards for each air pollutant for which air quality criteria have been issued. Once a standard has been promulgated, the administrator must review the standard and the criteria on which it is based every five years and revise the standard if necessary. On July 18, 1997, the EPA administrator revised the standards for particulate matter and ozone. Because ozone and particulate matter are both nonthreshold pollutants—that is, any amount harms the public health—the EPA set stringent standards that would cost hundreds of millions of dollars to implement nationwide.

The American Trucking Associations, as well as other business groups and the states of Michigan, Ohio, and West Virginia, challenged the new standards in the U.S. Court of Appeals for the District of Columbia Circuit and then in the U.S. Supreme Court. Among other things, the plaintiffs argued that the statute that delegated the authority to the EPA to set the standards was unconstitutionally vague. They also argued that the EPA, in order to keep costs in check, should perform a benefit-cost analysis when setting national air quality standards.

In a unanimous decision in 2001, in the case of *Whitman v. American Trucking Associations*,[29] the Supreme Court mostly upheld the EPA and its new regulations. The court wrote that the statute, while ambiguous, was not overly vague and reversed the court of appeals. Furthermore, no benefit-cost analysis was needed. The EPA, based on the information about health effects contained in the technical documents it compiled, is to identify the maximum airborne concentration of a pollutant that the public health can tolerate, decrease the concentration to provide an adequate margin of safety, and set the standard at that level. Nowhere are the costs of achieving such a standard made part of that initial calculation, according to the court.

Concerning the appropriate standard of review, the court invoked the rule that if a statute is silent or ambiguous with respect to an issue, then a court must defer to a reasonable interpretation made by the agency administrator. The key words for understanding the concept of standard of review are *ambiguous, reasonable*, and *defer*. The statute must be silent or ambiguous, the agency's actions must be judged by the court to be reasonable, and the court will then defer to the agency.

The key word for understanding the essence of this specific case is *reasonable*, for in one ambiguous instance in this case the court found the EPA's actions reasonable, whereas in another ambiguous instance in the same case, the court found the EPA's actions unreasonable. Specifically, the EPA's actions concerning benefit-cost analysis were found to be reasonable. Contrasted to this, the EPA's interpretation concerning the implementation of the act in another ambiguous section was found to be unreasonable. In the second instance, the EPA read the statute in a way that completely nullified text meant to limit the agency's discretion. This, the court said, was unlawful.

Once again, we have a case that is a clear example of how courts shape environmental policy—here by choosing and applying a standard of review. An appropriate standard of review can, and should, change from case to case. In addition, reasonable judges can differ on what constitutes an appropriate standard of review. Further, once a standard of review is selected, the application of that standard becomes important. Crucial in this case were judgments concerning whether the EPA administrator acted reasonably. Hence, when judges are selected, an examination of their judicial philosophies and predispositions becomes important.

Interpretation of Environmental Laws

Judges shape environmental policy in how they interpret laws. Environmental laws are often broad and vague. Circumstances arise that the drafters of the laws did not foresee. Environmental statutes sometimes conflict with each other. Different stakeholders interpret mandates contrarily. The cases analyzed in this section exemplify how courts shape environmental policy through judicial interpretation of laws.

Interpreting Statutes: Two Cases
Concerning the Endangered Species Act

The Endangered Species Act of 1973 contains a variety of protections designed to save from extinction selected species that the secretary of the interior designates as endangered or threatened.[30] Section 9 of the act makes it unlawful for any person to "take" any endangered or threatened species. *Taking* is defined by the law as "harassing, harming, pursuing, hunting, shooting, wounding, killing, trapping, capturing or collecting any of the protected wildlife."[31] In the early 1990s, the secretary promulgated a regulation that defined the statute's prohibition on takings to include "significant habitat modification or degradation where it actually kills or injures wildlife."[32] A group calling itself the Sweet Home Chapter of Communities for a Great Oregon filed suit alleging that the secretary of the interior exceeded his authority under the Endangered Species Act by promulgating that regulation. The plaintiff group comprised small landowners, logging companies, and families dependent on the forest products industries of the Pacific Northwest. They argued that the legislative history of the act demonstrated that Congress considered, and rejected, such a broad definition. Further, they argued that the regulation as applied to the habitat of the northern spotted owl and the red-cockaded woodpecker had injured them economically, because there were now vast areas of land that could not be logged. If the secretary wanted to protect the habitat of these endangered species, they maintained, the secretary would have to buy their land.

The district court entered summary judgment for the secretary of the interior, finding that the regulation was a reasonable interpretation of congressional intent.[33] In the U.S. Court of Appeals for the District of Columbia, a divided panel first affirmed the judgment of the lower court. After granting a rehearing, however, the panel reversed the lower court's ruling. The confusion, and final decision, centered on how to interpret the word *harm* in the Endangered Species Act, looking at the totality of the act.

The secretary of the interior appealed to the U.S. Supreme Court. In a 6-3 decision, in the case of *Babbitt v. Sweet Home Chapter of Communities for a Great Oregon* (1995),[34] the Supreme Court reversed the decision of the court of appeals and upheld the Department of the Interior's regulation. Examining the legislative history of the Endangered Species Act, and applying rules of statutory construction, the majority of the court concluded that the secretary's definition of *harm* was reasonable. Further, the court concluded that the writing of this technical and science-based regulation involved a complex policy choice. Congress entrusted the secretary with broad discretion in these matters, and the court expressed a reluctance to substitute its views of wise policy for those of the secretary.

This pathbreaking endangered species case demonstrates how courts shape environmental policy by the way they interpret statutes. Different judges at different stages of review in this case interpreted the statutory word *harm* differently. The protection of endangered species hinged on these interpretations. Tied in with this is the important notion of which rules of statutory construction courts choose to apply and how they apply them. Further, this case is another example of how courts are hesitant to substitute their view for the views of experts in scientific and technical matters, absent a showing of arbitrary or capricious action, or obvious error. The final Supreme Court decision set a precedent that strengthened endangered species policy throughout the United States.

Twelve years later, in 2007, the Supreme Court decided a case that concerned "dueling statutes," resulting in a *weakening* of the Endangered Species Act. In its interesting rationale, the court juxtaposed the reasoning of the *Babbitt* decision with the reasoning of the *Chevron* decision.

Under the Clean Water Act (CWA), the EPA initially administers each state's National Pollutant Discharge Elimination System (NPDES) permitting program. Once a state meets nine criteria, the EPA must transfer authority for the NPDES program to the state.

At the same time, the Endangered Species Act requires federal agencies to consult with agencies designated by the secretaries of commerce and the interior to ensure that a proposed agency action is unlikely to jeopardize an endangered or a threatened species. The Fish and Wildlife Service and the National Marine Fisheries Service administer the Endangered Species Act. Once a consultation process is complete, a written biological opinion is issued, which may suggest alternative actions to protect a jeopardized species or its critical habitat.

When Arizona officials sought EPA authorization to administer the state's NPDES program, the EPA initiated consultation with the Fish and Wildlife Service to determine whether the transfer would adversely affect any listed species. The Fish and Wildlife Service regional office wanted potential impacts taken into account, but the EPA disagreed, finding that the Clean Water Act's mandatory language stripped the EPA of authority to disapprove a transfer based on any other considerations. The dispute was referred to the agencies' national offices for resolution.

The Fish and Wildlife Service's biological opinion concluded that the requested transfer would not jeopardize listed species. The EPA concluded that Arizona had met each of the Clean Water Act's nine criteria and approved the transfer, noting that the biological opinion had fulfilled the Endangered Species Act consultation mandate.

Defenders of Wildlife, an environmental advocacy group, filed a lawsuit against the EPA in the Ninth Circuit Court of Appeals. The National Association of Home Builders intervened to support the EPA. The Court of Appeals held in favor of Defenders of Wildlife, stating that the EPA's transfer to the state of Arizona of the authority to run its own NPDES program was arbitrary and capricious. It did not dispute that Arizona had met the Clean

Water Act's nine criteria, but instead concluded that the Endangered Species Act required the EPA to determine whether its transfer decision would jeopardize listed endangered species.

The National Association of Home Builders appealed the court of appeals decision to the U.S. Supreme Court. On June 25, 2007, in a 5-4 decision, *National Association of Home Builders v. Defenders of Wildlife*,[35] the Supreme Court reversed the decision of the court of appeals, noting that this case entailed a conflict of statutes.

Among its conclusions, the Supreme Court found that the Ninth Circuit's determination that the EPA's action was arbitrary and capricious was not supported by the record. The EPA is mandated by the Clean Water Act to turn over the operation of an NPDES program to a state if that state meets all nine criteria enumerated in the statute. The state of Arizona met all nine criteria; therefore, the EPA had no choice but to turn over the program to the state, the majority of the court said.

As to the Endangered Species Act, the court said that the statute's mandate applies only to discretionary agency actions. It does not apply to actions like the NPDES permitting transfer authorization that an agency is *required* by statute to undertake once certain specified triggering events have occurred. To decide otherwise would be to add a tenth criterion to the Clean Water Act.

The court emphasized that while a later-enacted statute such as the Endangered Species Act can sometimes operate to amend or even repeal an earlier statutory provision such as that of the Clean Water Act, Congress did not expressly override the Clean Water Act in this case. The Supreme Court acknowledged that it owes "some degree of deference" to the secretary of the interior's reasonable interpretation of the Endangered Species Act under the *Babbitt* decision. At the same time, the Supreme Court, citing the *Chevron* case, said that deference is not due if Congress has made its intent clear in a statute, but "if the statute is silent or ambiguous . . . the question . . . is whether the agency's answer is based on a permissible construction of the statute."[36] In this case, the EPA's interpretation was a reasonable construction of the Clean Water Act, and so the EPA was entitled to "*Chevron* deference."

Justice John Paul Stevens, joined by Justices David Hackett Souter, Ruth Bader Ginsburg, and Stephen Breyer, wrote a twenty-seven-page dissenting opinion, in which they argued that when faced with competing statutory mandates, the U.S. Supreme Court should balance both laws instead of choosing one over the other. In the dissenting justices' view, the EPA acted arbitrarily and capriciously by choosing the Clean Water Act over the Endangered Species Act. Citing the famous 1978 snail darter case, in which the discovery of the endangered snail darter halted the construction of a dam, the justices proclaimed that Congress had already given endangered species priority over the primary missions of federal agencies.

This fascinating case, which is still good law, demonstrates how courts shape environmental policy by the way judges interpret "dueling" statutes and "dueling" precedents governing "dueling" federal agencies. The majority of justices chose the rationale of *Chevron* over the rationale of *Babbitt*. In addition, different judges interpreted the mandate of the Endangered Species Act differently, with the result being a general weakening of the act.

Interpreting Statutes and the
Constitution: Regulatory Takings and Land Use

In 1986, David H. Lucas purchased two vacant oceanfront lots on the Isle of Palms in Charleston County, South Carolina, for $975,000. He intended to build single-family residences on the lots, but in 1988, the South Carolina Legislature enacted the Beachfront Management Act.[37] In Lucas's case, this act prohibited him from constructing any permanent structure (including a dwelling) except for a small deck or walkway on the property. Lucas filed suit in the court of common pleas, asserting that the restrictions on the use of his lots amounted to the government taking his property without justly compensating him, a so-called *regulatory taking*. The lower court agreed with Lucas, maintaining that the act rendered the land valueless, and awarded him over $1.2 million for the regulatory taking. Upon appeal, the Supreme Court of South Carolina reversed the lower court's decision. The judges maintained that the regulation under attack prevented a use seriously harming the public. Consequently, they argued, no regulatory taking occurred.[38]

On June 29, 1992, however, the U.S. Supreme Court, in a 6-3 decision, reversed the holding of the highest court in South Carolina and remanded the case to it for further action.[39] In its decision, the court articulated several pivotal principles that constitute a test for regulatory takings. First, the justices emphasized that regulations denying a property owner all "economically viable use of his land" require compensation, regardless of the public interest advanced in support of the restraint. As such, even when a regulation addresses or prevents a "harmful or noxious use," government must compensate owners when their property is rendered economically useless to them.

At the same time, however, the court threw back to the South Carolina courts the issue of whether a taking occurred in Lucas's case. The lower courts had to examine the context of the state's power over the "bundle of rights" Lucas acquired when he took title to his property. Put differently, the pivotal question for all state regulators today is this: Do state environmental regulations merely make explicit what already was implicit in any property title (that is, the right to regulate its use), or are they decisions that come after a person acquires a title that were not originally implied? In the latter case, they are takings that governments must compensate.

Equally important in *Lucas* was what the court did *not* discuss in its narrowly worded opinion. First, the court did not say that Lucas was entitled to compensation. Rather, it implied that the South Carolina Supreme Court was hasty in concluding that Lucas was not entitled to recompense. Second, the court did not address the issue of property that is merely diminished in value—a far more common occurrence. Instead, it addressed only the issue of property that was rendered totally valueless. Finally, in pushing the regulatory takings issue back onto the state, the court did not say that state laws may never change. Indeed, the majority held that "changed circumstances or new knowledge may make what was previously permissible no longer so." Hence, the court left the door open for some regulation of newly discovered environmental harms after title to a property changes hands. Still, Lucas did prevail. Upon remand, the South Carolina Supreme Court reversed its earlier decision and awarded Lucas over $1.5 million.

A few years later, the Supreme Court continued to develop the area of regulatory takings in a local government planning and zoning case that also is having profound effects on environmental policy. In *Dolan v. Tigard* (1994),[40] the owner of a plumbing and electrical supply store applied to the City of Tigard, Oregon, for a permit to redevelop a site. The plaintiff wanted to expand the size of her store and to pave the parking lot.

The city, pursuant to a state-required land use program, had adopted a comprehensive plan, a plan for pedestrian-and-bicycle pathways, and a master drainage plan. As such, the city's planning commission conditioned Dolan's permit on her doing two things. First, she had to dedicate (that is, convey title) to the city the portion of her property lying within a hundred-year floodplain so that the city could improve a storm drainage system for the area. Second, she had to dedicate an additional fifteen-foot strip of land adjacent to the floodplain as a pedestrian-and-bicycle pathway. The planning commission argued that its conditions regarding the floodplain were "reasonably related" to the owner's request to intensify use of the site, given its impervious surface. Likewise, the commission claimed that creating the pedestrian-and-bicycle pathway system could lessen or offset the increased traffic congestion that the permit would cause.

In a previous case, *Nollan v. California Coastal Commission* (1987),[41] the court had ruled that an agency needs to show that an "essential nexus" exists between the "end advanced" (that is, the enunciated purpose of the regulation) and the "condition imposed" by applying the regulation. The "essential nexus" requirement is still good law today. The *Nollan* court also held that a government must be prepared to prove in court that a "legitimate state interest" is "substantially advanced" by any regulation affecting property rights. In 2005, the Supreme Court removed the "substantially advanced" requirement as improper in a nonenvironmental case, *Lingle v. Chevron*,[42] because it did not address the effect of a regulation on property but rather was concerned solely with whether the underlying regulation itself was valid.

After reviewing various doctrines that state courts had used to guide such analyses, the court in *Dolan* enunciated its own test of "rough proportionality" that is still valid today. It stated that "no precise mathematical calculation is required, but the city must make some sort of individualized determination that the required dedication is related both in nature and extent to the impact of the proposed development." If there is rough proportionality, then there is no taking. In this instance, the court decided that the city had not made any such determination and concluded that the city's findings did not show a relationship between the floodplain easement and the owner's proposed new building. Furthermore, the city had failed to quantify precisely how much the pedestrian-and-bicycle pathway would proportionately offset some of the demand generated.

The implications of the court's doctrine in this case are profound. The facts are hardly unique and represent the types of zoning decisions that local governments make daily. What is more, its logic potentially extends to all local government regulatory activities. Finally, the decision means that the courts can become even more involved than they had been in reviewing and judging the adequacy—the dissent in *Dolan* called this "micromanaging"—of local regulatory decisions.

These and other cases together indicate that with the burden of proof in takings cases falling on the government, considerable litigation is inevitable. As such, local governments will have to do more individualized analysis of the expected impacts of land use changes and the conditions they impose on them. Not only will this be more costly, but it will likely have a chilling effect on regulatory activity at that level. Finally, because no clear guidance exists concerning how to operationalize concepts such as *rough proportionality*, local regulators should expect continuing litigation in different regulatory contexts. Lower and appellate courts have been busy trying to clarify this test for them.

There have been hundreds of takings cases in the courts since *Dolan* and *Nollan*. One of the most important current decisions is *Koontz v. St. Johns River Water Management District*.[43] Coy Koontz Sr. sought permits to develop a section of his property from the St. Johns River Water Management District (District), which, consistent with Florida law, requires permit applicants wishing to build on wetlands to offset the resulting environmental damage. Koontz offered to mitigate the environmental effects of his development proposal by deeding to the District a conservation easement on nearly three-quarters of his property. The District rejected Koontz's proposal and informed him that it would approve construction only if he either reduced the size of his development and, among other things, deeded to the District a conservation easement on the resulting larger remainder of his property, or hired contractors to make improvements to District-owned wetlands several miles away. Believing the District's demands to be excessive in light of the environmental effects his proposal would have caused, Koontz filed suit under a state law that provides money damages for agency action that is an "unreasonable exercise of the state's police power constituting a taking without just compensation."

In a case with many twists and turns, Koontz won at the trial level, won again at the district court of appeals level, but lost at the state supreme court level. In a 5-4 decision, the U.S. Supreme Court reversed the Florida Supreme Court and ruled in favor of Koontz, writing that when a government engages in land use regulation, including by denying a permit or demanding payment as a condition for a permit, the government must show that there is a nexus and rough proportionality between its demand on the landowner and the effects of the proposed land use, and that was not done here. In essence, the Supreme Court clarified that the *Nollan/Dolan* nexus and proportionality requirements apply in the context of permit denials, not just approvals. It also held that these requirements apply to demands for money (or actions that cost money), not just demands for an interest in land. The case is likely to trigger even more takings lawsuits.

Environmental advocates charge that if takings suits are successful, the trend will destroy years of hard-fought incremental progress in protecting the environment. Government regulators agree, adding that the trend could devastate already ailing government budgets. This will be true especially if proposed federal legislation is enacted that would take compensation payments from the coffers of the agency that issued such regulations. These are excellent examples of how courts help shape environmental policy.

Choice of Remedy

A final way in which courts affect environmental policy is through their choice of remedies. When a recalcitrant polluter is taken to court, the two most common actions ordered by a court are mandatory compliance with environmental law and punitive monetary penalties to deter future violations. For example, in a Clean Water Act case, *Friends of the Earth, Inc. v. Laidlaw Environmental Services*,[44] which concerned a company that repeatedly violated the conditions of its permit, discharging pollutants such as mercury numerous times into a river, the settlement decree ordered Laidlaw to comply with the Clean Water Act, and the district court assessed punitive monetary penalties. In a case involving criminal violations of environmental law, the penalty might involve jail time or probation. In each of these scenarios, considerable judicial discretion is involved.

The Clean Air Act, the Clean Water Act, the Resource Conservation and Recovery Act, and the Emergency Planning and Community Right-to-Know Act also allow those who win citizen suits to seek monetary penalties, which go to the U.S. Treasury rather than to the plaintiff. In these circumstances, again, a judge has immense discretion. Most often, the only curbs on judges in these circumstances are statutorily set maximum amounts, as well as lists of factors that judges must weigh.

A relatively new remedy being used more often in both judicial decrees and administrative orders is a supplemental environmental project (SEP). SEPs are alternative payments in the form of projects or activities. Examples include environmental restoration, environmental education, and the establishment of green space such as parks. The Clean Air Act, for example, contains the following language concerning SEPs:

> The court in any action under this subsection . . . shall have discretion to order that such civil penalties, in lieu of being deposited in the [U.S. Treasury Fund], be used in beneficial mitigation projects which are consistent with this chapter and enhance the public health or the environment.[45]

To award SEPs, judges must have the statutory authority to do so or at least be assured that the statute does not forbid them to do so. Although the EPA has included SEPs in its orders in various forms and under various names since the late 1970s, they became more widely accepted in the 1990s. In February 1994, President Clinton issued Executive Order 12898, which directed federal agencies to integrate environmental justice issues into agency policy. The EPA seized this opportunity by incorporating SEPs into many consent decrees that address environmental challenges in minority and low-income neighborhoods. The EPA's policy on SEPs was finalized in 1998.

An example of an early SEP is the case in which the EPA's Region 1 received an anonymous tip to check out properties of the Massachusetts Highway Department (MHD). There they found nearly two hundred barrels of illegally stored hazardous wastes in 149 MHD facilities. The resulting settlement, negotiated in less than a year and approved by a court, included over $20 million in cleanup costs and $5 million in SEPs.[46] A relatively small penalty of $100,000 also was ordered to be paid to federal government coffers. The SEPs undertaken by the MHD made a concrete difference in a way that traditional penalties often do not. They ranged from the development of an environmental education program for MHD personnel and the public, to the cleanup of environmentally contaminated minority neighborhoods throughout Massachusetts.

Recent SEPs have branched into other areas. In 2014, the DeKalb County, Georgia, Department of Watershed Management's Capital Improvement Projects Division announced a one-time SEP involving the removal of trash and debris from the banks and streambeds of South River, South Fork Peachtree Creek, and Snapfinger Creek as part of a Clean Water Act settlement with the EPA. Also in 2014, the Town of Canaan, Vermont, agreed to fund a diversified agriculture vocational program at Canaan High School that included many units of study that involve water quality, as part of a settlement involving multiple violations of a Clean Water Act discharge permit. In 2011, the San Diego, California, Regional Water Quality Control Board approved an SEP with the Santa Margarita Water District that involved the design and realignment of a portion of the Plano force main on the east side of Tijeras Creek, to avoid the direct discharge of sewage to the creek in the event of a force main failure. (Force mains move wastewater under pressure by using pumps or compressors located in lift stations.)

These are just a few examples from the hundreds of SEPs ordered annually. Although mandatory compliance with environmental laws and monetary penalties remain the most often court-ordered remedies, one legal scholar sees real promise in the future use of SEPs.[47] The EPA has a special website on SEPs[48] as does the State of Colorado.[49] The choice of remedy is yet another way in which courts shape environmental policy.

Conclusion: A View to the Future

Judge Bazelon was right: Since 1971, administrative agencies and reviewing courts have collaborated fruitfully, especially in the area of environmental policy. A study examining the impact of over two thousand federal court decisions on the EPA's policies and administration in its first two decades found that from an agency-wide perspective, compliance with court orders has become one of the EPA's top priorities, at times overtaking congressional mandates.[50] A more recent study predicts that the courts will become an increasingly important pathway for revising policies since Congress has been legislatively gridlocked since 1990.[51]

The courts in the United States have become permanent players in environmental policymaking. Supporting this conclusion are dozens of websites concerning environmental policy in the courts. The most useful of these sites are listed at the end of this chapter. Although the extent of judicial involvement in environmental cases will ebb and flow over the years, the courts will always be involved in environmental policy to some degree.

As this chapter has demonstrated, courts have a major influence in how environmental laws work in practice. Courts shape environmental policy in many ways. The most significant ways are by determining who has standing to sue, by deciding which cases are ripe for review, by the court's choice of standard of review, by interpreting statutes and the Constitution, by the remedies judges choose, and simply by resolving environmental conflicts.

Environmental court decisions are influenced by the state of the law, such as precedent and rules for interpreting statutes. They are also influenced by the courts' environment, such as mass public opinion, litigants and interest groups, congressional expansion or perhaps narrowing of jurisdiction, and presidential appointments. Environmental court decisions are influenced as well by justices' values: liberal, moderate, conservative, or somewhere in between. In addition, environmental court decisions are affected by group interaction on the bench, with individual justices at times influencing others.

The importance of judicial appointments cannot be overemphasized. Federal judges are appointed for life, barring illegal or unethical behavior. As of the writing of this chapter, President Obama had appointed more than half of the federal judges, who were deemed "liberal, but not that liberal."[52] In early 2014, the Senate held up more judicial appointments than in the past, resulting in a high vacancy rate. In response, a divided Senate voted to ease the confirmation process for most presidential nominees by changing the Senate rules to allow most executive branch and judicial nominations to be approved with a simple majority—fifty-one votes rather than the sixty votes required previously. This "nuclear option" limited the ability of Republicans to block Obama's choices for most judicial posts. By the fall of 2014, Democratic appointees held a majority of seats on nine of the thirteen courts of appeals.

When President Obama took office, only one of those courts had more full-time judges nominated by a Democrat. It remains to be seen how President Obama's judicial appointments will affect environmental policy and the role of the courts in making it.

In addition to this phenomenon, two other trends seem to be emerging. One trend concerns the added obstacles that environmental justice attorneys face in getting into court. At the state level, standing requirements have tightened. At the federal level, enforcement of federal laws and regulations that do not come with their own citizen suit provisions has become increasingly difficult. Courts have rejected implied private rights of action and tightened access under the Civil Rights Act. As of the writing of this chapter, there is no evidence of these requirements easing.

Another trend concerns the increased use of environmental conflict resolution and collaboration, which is effectively group problem solving. Advocates of this approach produce two primary criticisms of litigation as a dispute resolution process for environmental conflicts. First, litigation does not allow for adequate public participation in important environmental decisions. Second, litigation is ineffective for resolving the basic issues in dispute between the parties.[53] Many of the underlying controversies remain unresolved; hence, more lawsuits often emerge in the future.

Despite these criticisms, the environmental policies that are developed, expanded, narrowed, and clarified in our courts will continue to affect the air we breathe, the water we drink, and the food we eat. The United States is the most litigious country in the world. Clearly, environmental policy in the courts—at least in the United States—is here to stay.

Suggested Websites

Council on Environmental Quality (www.whitehouse.gov/ceq) Provides links to important environmental and natural resource agencies, as well as to reports. Especially helpful is the CEQ National Environmental Policy Act (NEPA) link (www.nepa.gov).

Environmental Law Institute (www.eli.org) Provides objective, nonpartisan analysis of current environmental law issues.

Lexis and Westlaw (www.lexis.com; www.westlaw.com) Excellent commercial websites for basic materials concerning domestic environmental law.

Natural Resources Defense Council (www.nrdc.org) Provides expert analyses of issues and reports that are relevant to ongoing legal decisions.

U.S. Department of the Interior (www.doi.gov) Lists laws and regulations for the major agencies within the department.

U.S. Environmental Protection Agency (www.epa.gov/epahome/lawregs .htm) Offers links to laws, regulations, the U.S. Code, and pending legislation in Congress concerning the EPA.

U.S. Forest Service (www.fs.fed.us/publications) Gives access to laws, regulations, and publications concerning federal forests.

U.S. Institute for Environmental Conflict Resolution (www.ecr.gov)
Provides a primer on environmental conflict resolution with an emphasis on
evaluating its effectiveness.

Notes

1. *Environmental Defense Fund v. Ruckelshaus*, 439 F. 2d 584 (1971).
2. United States Government Accountability Office, "Environmental Litigation: Cases
   against EPA and Associated Costs over Time," GAO-11-650, August 2011. See also
   www.nrdc.org/bushrecord/default.asp.
3. *EPA v. EME Homer City Generation*, 572 U.S. ___ (2014).
4. Adam Liptak, "Justices Hear Case on Cross-State Pollution Rules," *New York Times*,
   December 10, 2013
5. Slip Opinion at 32.
6. William Yeatman, www.globalwarming.org, April 30, 2013.
7. *Udall v. Tallman*, 380 U.S. 1 (1965).
8. *Chevron U.S.A., Inc. v. Natural Resources Defense Council*, 467 U.S. 837 (1984).
9. Administrative Procedure Act, Section 706[2][A].
10. Six of the EPA's seven major environmental statutes have citizen suit provisions.
11. "Control of Emissions from New Highway Vehicles and Engines," 68 Fed. Reg. at
    52,930 (September 8, 2003).
12. Ibid. at 52,928.
13. Ibid. at 52,929.
14. Ibid. at 52,930.
15. Ibid. at 52,931.
16. *Massachusetts v. Environmental Protection Agency*, 415 F. 3d 50 (DC Cir. 2005).
17. *Massachusetts v. Environmental Protection Agency*, 127 S. Ct. 1438 (2007).
18. *Massachusetts v. Environmental Protection Agency*, 126 S. Ct. 2960 (2006).
19. For a good discussion of this requirement, see *Lujan, Secretary of the Interior v. Defenders
    of Wildlife et al.*, 504 U.S. 555 (1992).
20. See U.S. Constitution, Article III, Section 2.
21. Fanny Carrier, "Environmentalists Hail 'Watershed' US Supreme Court Ruling,"
    Agence France Presse, April 3, 2007.
22. *American Electric Power Company, Inc. et al. v. Connecticut et al.*, 131 S. Ct. 2527 (2011).
23. 573 U.S. ___ (2014).
24. *Sierra Club v. Thomas*, 105 F. 3d 248 (1997).
25. *Ohio Forestry Association, Inc. v. Sierra Club*, 523 U.S. 726 (1998).
26. *Buckeye Forest Council v. U.S. Forest Service*, 378 F. Supp. 2d 835 (2005).
27. Michael C. Blumm and Sherry L. Bosse, "*Norton v. SUWA* and the Unraveling of
    Federal Public Land Planning," *Duke Environmental Law and Policy Forum* 18 (Fall
    2007): 105–61.
28. Ibid., 111.
29. *Whitman v. American Trucking Associations*, 531 U.S. 457 (2001).
30. Endangered Species Act, 16 U.S.C. Section 1531 et seq.
31. 16 U.S.C. Section 1538 (a)(1).
32. 50 C.F.R. Section 17.3 (1994).
33. *Sweet Home Chapter of Communities for a Great Oregon v. Lujan*, 806 F. Supp. 279
    (1992); 1 F. 3d 1 (1993); 17 F. 3d 1463 (1994).
34. *Babbitt v. Sweet Home Chapter of Communities for a Great Oregon*, 515 U.S. 687 (1995).

35. *National Association of Home Builders v. Defenders of Wildlife*, 551 U.S. 644 (2007).
36. *Chevron U.S.A. Inc. v. Natural Resources Defense Council, Inc.*, 467 U.S. 837 (1984).
37. S.C. Code Ann. (1989) Sections 48-39-10 et seq.
38. *Lucas v. South Carolina Coastal Council*, 304 S. C. 376 (1991).
39. *Lucas v. South Carolina Coastal Council*, 505 U.S. 1003 (1992).
40. *Dolan v. Tigard*, 512 U.S. 374 (1994); *Dura Pharmaceuticals, Inc. v. Broudo*, 544 U.S. 2974 (2005).
41. *Nollan v. California Coastal Commission*, 483 U.S. 825 (1987).
42. *Lingle v. Chevron*, 544 U.S. 528 (2005).
43. 133 S. Ct 2586 (2013).
44. *Friends of the Earth, Inc. v. Laidlaw Environmental Services*, 528 U.S. 167 (2000).
45. Clean Air Act, 42 U.S.C. 7604 (g)(2).
46. In the Matter of: The Commonwealth of Massachusetts, Massachusetts Highway Department, EPA Docket No. RCRA-I-94-1071, Consent Agreement and Order, October 3, 1994.
47. Kenneth T. Kristl, "Making a Good Idea Even Better: Rethinking the Limits on Supplemental Environmental Projects," *Vermont Law Review* 31 (Winter 2007): 217.
48. U.S. EPA, "Supplemental Environmental Projects" (Washington, DC: U.S. EPA), available at www2.epa.gov/enforcement/supplemental-environmental-projects-seps.
49. State of Colorado, "Supplemental Environmental Projects" (Department of Public Health and Environment), available at www.colorado.gov/pacific/cdphe/supplemental -environmental-projects.
50. Rosemary O'Leary, *Environmental Change: Federal Courts and the EPA* (Philadelphia, PA: Temple University Press, 1993).
51. Christopher McGrory Klyza and David Sousa, *American Environmental Policy: Beyond Gridlock*, updated and expanded edition (Cambridge, MA: MIT Press, 2013), Chapter 5.
52. John Sides, "Obama's Judicial Appointments: Liberal, but Not That Liberal," *Washington Post*, April 14, 2014, available at www.washingtonpost.com/blogs/monkey-cage/wp/2014/04/14/obamas-judicial-appointments-liberal-but-not-that-liberal/.
53. See Rosemary O'Leary and Lisa Bingham, eds., *The Promise and Performance of Environmental Conflict Resolution* (Washington, DC: Resources for the Future, 2003).

7

The Environmental Protection Agency

Richard N. L. Andrews

The Environmental Protection Agency (EPA) is the lead U.S. agency responsible for protecting the environment from air and water pollution, and for protecting people from health hazards of pollution and toxic chemicals in the environment. Created in 1970, just a few months after the first Earth Day and before most of today's major pollution control laws were enacted, it regulates air pollution from cars and smokestacks, water pollution from urban sewers and industrial outfalls, hazardous wastes and municipal landfills, drinking water contaminants, and pesticides and toxic chemicals; and it has recently begun to impose regulations to reduce carbon emissions from motor vehicles as well as power plants and other industries that contribute to global warming. Environmental and public health advocates see it as the government's champion for those widely shared values. Some critics, however, accuse it of imposing excessive red tape and unjustified costs on businesses, property owners, and state and local governments; and others accuse it of at least not using the most economically efficient and effective policy tools to achieve its goals.

The EPA has itself pioneered the development of innovative new policy tools beyond traditional regulations, to try to reduce environmental risks in the most cost-effective ways. Examples include "market-oriented" incentives such as tradable emission allowances, information disclosure requirements such as the Toxics Release Inventory and radon disclosure requirements, and elaborate procedures for risk assessment. Much of its day-to-day work also includes technical assistance and enforcement cooperation to support state environmental protection programs (see also Chapter 2 on state environmental policymaking). The EPA also provides subsidized loans for drinking water and wastewater treatment facilities, and conducts research to reduce pollution.

A constant challenge for the EPA is that the primary tools it has been given by Congress are regulations, and regulations inherently place new restrictions and costs on influential businesses and state and local governments. This chapter discusses how the EPA makes decisions in the face of constant pressures, not only from advocates of environmental protection and the news media but also from businesses, the president, members of Congress, state and local officials, and the courts.

Background[1]

The EPA was created in 1970 by President Richard Nixon, in the midst of a widespread public outcry for the federal government to "do something" about pollution.[2] The EPA was created not by an act of Congress, but through a presidential reorganization plan that pulled together a number of separate programs into a single new agency. Air pollution and waste management programs were transferred from the Department of Health, Education, and Welfare, water pollution programs from the Department of the Interior, pesticide programs from the Department of Agriculture, and some radiation protection programs from the Atomic Energy Commission.

Since its overall mission and authority derive only from a presidential reorganization plan rather than an act of Congress, the EPA even today functions largely as an umbrella organization administering fragmented programs that operate under separate laws and budgets. Its basic organizational units include separate programs for air and radiation, water, solid wastes, and chemical safety, plus crosscutting units for enforcement, legal counsel, research and development, and more recently information and financial management. Its administrator has only limited authority to integrate, coordinate, or set priorities among its separate program units except through its annual budget requests. And Congress often does not grant its requests: in recent years, a gridlocked Congress has often passed only continuing resolutions to maintain specified levels of its existing funding, not new budget bills, let alone new environmental laws. Much of the EPA's work also consists of technical and compliance assistance to state governments, through ten regional offices: it thus relies heavily on environmental federalism, discussed in Chapter 2.[3]

Beginning in 1970, Congress passed a series of far-reaching new laws to address pollution and other environmental health hazards, and assigned them to the EPA to carry out. These included the Clean Air Act, the Federal Water Pollution Control Act, the Safe Drinking Water Act, and laws regulating pesticides, toxic substances, and solid and hazardous wastes (see Chapter 1 and Appendix 1). In these laws, Congress gave the EPA a number of tools to use to achieve the laws' purposes, but most of them relied mainly on regulation.

To reduce air pollution, for instance, Congress directed the EPA to set National Ambient Air Quality Standards (NAAQS) specifying how clean the air around us must be in order to protect public health, and to require states to produce state implementation plans (SIPs) for achieving them. The law also required all new sources of air pollution to have EPA permits, and to use the "best available control technology" to minimize their emissions. Important amendments in 1990 set an overall cap on total emissions of sulfur and nitrogen emissions from all large power plants, and allowed polluters to buy and sell their shares of that total—their "emission allowances"—so that companies that do better than the requirements could sell their allowances to companies that found it cheaper to buy more allowances and keep polluting. Finally, the law ordered the EPA to set tailpipe emission standards for cars and trucks that all manufacturers must meet on average across the "fleet" of new vehicles they sell each year.

For water pollution, *all* "point" sources (such as factory outfalls and municipal wastewater treatment plants) must get a permit from the EPA (not just new sources, unlike air polluters), and must use the "best available technology." However, the EPA was not authorized to regulate pollution from "nonpoint" sources such as farm runoff, due to the influence of the farm lobby when the law was passed. All treatment, storage, and disposal facilities for hazardous wastes must also have EPA permits, as must municipal landfills and incinerators; and all shipments of hazardous wastes must be documented, from the factory where they were generated as waste to their ultimate disposal in a permitted facility.

Each of these statutes addressed a particular environmental problem, but many of them affected the same industries, often with conflicting consequences. Many electric companies complied with air pollution regulations in the 1970s, for instance, by building taller smokestacks, to disperse and dilute their pollutants so that they would reduce health effects immediately downwind; but this simply caused the pollutants to rain out further downwind as acid rain, damaging forests and lake fisheries.[4] More recently, the EPA tightened regulations on sulfur dioxide and mercury emissions to protect public health, and to comply, electric utilities put expensive "wet scrubbers" on their stacks to capture these pollutants before they were released into the air; but these materials then were piped into coal ash ponds, some of which later leaked and caused serious water pollution.[5] Similarly, sewage treatment improves water quality by removing contaminants from wastewater, but these materials must then themselves be managed, often by landfilling, incineration, or spraying them on farmlands where they may cause new hazards.

In an ideal world, the EPA would design an integrated set of policy incentives to promote pollution *prevention*, minimizing the use of polluting materials and energy all the way from the initial extraction of resources through production, consumer use, reuse and recycling, and eventual disposal. In practice, however, the EPA must use limited tools aimed at separate problems—such as technology-based standards for air and water pollution—to try to solve complex environmental problems whose outcomes are often environmentally interconnected as well as expensive. More recently, Congress has sometimes allowed the EPA to adopt more flexible tools, such as cap-and-trade systems, to reduce pollutants such as sulfur, nitrogen, and greenhouse gas (GHG) emissions from power plants, but these options are available only for a few specific uses approved by Congress.

The EPA also regulates individual substances that have environmental health risks, such as pesticides, drinking water contaminants, and toxic chemicals used in manufacturing. Before doing so, however, it must undertake an elaborate process of "risk assessment" to determine how serious a hazard it is and how many people might be exposed to it, and then balance that risk against the economic benefits and costs of restricting it.

Consider, therefore, three examples of EPA regulations and how they were developed. How can the EPA reduce air pollution from coal-fired power plants? How can it reduce human exposure to toxic chemicals such as arsenic? And how can it reduce emissions of GHGs such as carbon dioxide, which contribute to global warming but were not considered when Congress passed the Clean Air Act?

Air Pollution from Electric Power Plants

Coal-fired power plants are one of the most significant sources of air pollution, including particularly sulfur dioxide (SO_2), nitrogen oxides (NO_x), particulates, and mercury (as well as GHGs, discussed later). Most of them were built more than forty years ago, before the landmark Clean Air Act requirements of the 1970s. As of 2008, 844 of the 1,140 coal-fired power plants in the United States—representing 63 percent of their total capacity—dated from 1977 or earlier.[6]

When Congress passed the Clean Air Act in 1970, it directed the EPA to set air pollution emission standards for all *new* facilities. Each of these must meet "new source performance standards," based on "the best emission reduction technology that had been adequately demonstrated, taking into account its cost." However, it exempted *existing* power plants so long as they were not modified. Retrofitting existing plants would have been far more expensive, and some state economies were heavily dependent on coal mining and use (including such politically important "swing-vote" states as Ohio and Illinois), so Congress preferred to assume that these old sources would gradually be phased out anyway. If an existing facility underwent "any" physical change or change in method of operation that would increase emissions, however, it would become subject to the new source standards as well.[7] The 1977 amendments to the Clean Air Act added a specific permit requirement, New Source Review (NSR), before construction of any new or modified facility that might increase air pollution.[8]

The EPA faced the question, therefore, of how to interpret this mandate. Did Congress really intend it to require costly new pollution controls for literally "any" physical or operational change in an existing facility? Or did Congress really mean to leave existing facilities alone so long as changes to them did not cause significant increases in air pollution? The EPA's initial regulations tried to strike this balance by setting a threshold: "any," it said, meant only a modification that would increase emissions by more than fifty tons of emissions per year. But it was immediately sued, both by environmental groups and by electric utility companies, and the court rejected this interpretation, holding that the "plain language" of the law meant "any" modification that results in more than a minimal increase in emissions.[9]

The EPA then revised its regulations to exempt "routine maintenance, repair, and replacements," as well as modifications that added only minimal amounts of pollutants. But once new power plants were more strictly controlled than existing ones, the utilities had greater incentive to keep the old plants operating longer, and also to upgrade them as much as they could without triggering the NSR process. They did this by "spreading out" upgrades to the facilities over multiple years, and integrating them into their operating and maintenance schedules, then arguing that this was all part of "routine" maintenance for plant "rehabilitation"—even though the intended effect was to keep these old facilities operating longer, and sometimes at higher levels of emissions.[10]

These practices were tolerated by the EPA under Presidents Ronald Reagan and George H. W. Bush through the 1980s, but President Bush also introduced an innovative new solution by creating a "cap-and-trade" system, capping total emissions of sulfur and nitrogen from all large power plants and allowing the utilities to trade emission allowances among both existing and new plants to stay within the cap. While this allowance market was highly effective in reducing total emissions, however, it did not protect downwind communities from the emissions of particular facilities that bought the allowances and kept on polluting. President Bill Clinton's EPA administrator, Carol Browner, therefore began an aggressive investigation into evasion of the NSR requirements by old coal-fired power plants, and filed suit against thirteen electric utilities for violations at fifty-one plants in thirteen states.[11] The utilities fought back, arguing that the EPA was now trying to enforce a more restrictive definition of "routine maintenance" than in the past; and they also spent heavily to support George W. Bush's successful presidential campaign over Clinton's vice president, Al Gore.

Once Bush was elected, the utilities lobbied vigorously to loosen the NSR rules, working through Vice President Dick Cheney and Energy Secretary Spencer Abraham to pressure Bush's EPA administrator Christine Todd Whitman.[12] Whitman and the EPA's chief of enforcement subsequently resigned, and in 2003 her successor proposed a new NSR rule that redefined "routine maintenance" as any upgrades that did not cost more than 20 percent of the plant's value—a huge loophole—and announced a weaker enforcement policy, dropping some seventy-five NSR enforcement investigations.[13] Environmental and public health groups objected strenuously to the rule changes, and fourteen states sued to block them. In 2003, a court ruled that one of the utilities had indeed violated the NSR rules eleven times at one of its plants; and in 2005 and 2006, the Court of Appeals rejected the Bush EPA's changes to the rules, holding that when Congress had originally applied NSR to "any" physical or operational changes that would increase pollution, it did indeed mean "any," not just those costing more than 20 percent of the facility's value.[14]

In the closing months of the Bush administration, his EPA officials adopted a new rule that would substitute broader, more discretionary, and thus less enforceable criteria on when facility modifications must be considered together, rather than separately as more minor or routine changes. Once the Obama administration took office, however, an environmental advocacy group immediately petitioned its new EPA administrator to reverse this change, which she did.

As recently as 2008, in short, most of the old coal-fired units were still operating.[15] But the newly elected Obama administration once again reaffirmed a policy of reducing air pollution from coal-fired power plants, including strict NSR rules as well as stricter regulation of nitrogen oxides, mercury, and interstate emissions affecting downwind states, and even new restrictions on carbon dioxide emissions.

What lessons does this case offer about how the EPA makes decisions? First, the issues involved are rarely simple and straightforward. While the Clinton and Obama administrations as well as the courts have generally supported the "plain language" of the NSR requirement, some independent critics—not just the utilities—have argued that the NSR requirement itself perpetuates the problem, by perpetuating the difference in cost that motivates power companies to keep using old coal-fired power plants rather than new ones with expensive end-of-pipe controls.[16] In these critics' view, a strict cap on overall emissions of both new and old power plants, combined with tradable permits, would achieve far greater pollution reduction. Others would support a trading program, but with safeguards to prevent regional "hot spots" of continued pollution downwind of the plants that choose to buy permits and keep polluting. Still others have argued that the EPA should simply phase out the "routine repair and maintenance" exemption over time.[17]

Second, the EPA itself is rarely the final decision maker. Almost any significant EPA decision will be challenged in lawsuits, either by regulated businesses or by environmental advocacy groups or both. The courts thus play an essential role in EPA decision making, often supporting protective interpretations of the environmental laws, but not always (see also Chapter 6 on environmental policy in the courts).

Finally, the EPA's decisions rarely remain settled. Its decisions change economic outcomes for businesses that are regulated, and thus create ongoing incentives for companies to challenge them rather than comply. These challenges include not only petitions and lawsuits, but also attempts to reverse its policies by congressional legislation or budget provisions and by electing presidents with different philosophies.

Toxic Chemicals: Arsenic in Drinking Water

In addition to pollutant emissions and other wastes, the EPA is responsible for protecting public health from toxic chemicals in drinking water, pesticides, and other products. These include thousands of substances, far too many to address individually in laws. Many have not been well studied, and many are not wastes but have profitable economic uses. How should the EPA decide which ones even to study, let alone to regulate, and how tightly should it regulate them? And to what extent should those decisions be based on public health risks, on the economic costs and anticipated benefits of restricting them, and on scientific uncertainty about their risks and benefits?

To control toxic chemicals, Congress enacted "risk-based" and "risk-balancing" statutes. These required the EPA to assess the risks of each substance it proposed to regulate, and then either to protect the public with "adequate margins of safety" against "unreasonable risks," or to balance those risks against economic benefits. The air and water emission standards had required the EPA only to show that the "best available technology" they required was already being used by the best firms in each industry. In contrast, for risk-based regulation, the EPA must present "substantial evidence" to prove that a chemical poses an "unreasonable risk" to public health, and that that risk outweighs the economic costs of restricting it.[18] And the agency must continually update all the scientific and economic evidence for each chemical if it is challenged. This places a heavy burden of proof on the agency, especially with a limited budget and staff and the fact that scientific knowledge about many chemicals is limited, uncertain, contested, and constantly changing.

An example is the risk of arsenic contamination in drinking water.[19] Arsenic can cause nausea, diarrhea, numbness, blindness, paralysis, and even death, and has been linked with several lethal kinds of cancer. As one member of Congress commented, "Anyone who has read an Agatha Christie novel knows that arsenic is a poison."[20] Yet it can be found in many Americans' drinking water, sometimes due to industrial wastes or agricultural use, but often also as a natural contaminant. How then should the EPA decide how much to protect people from a health risk, when that decision also imposes costs on them to do so?

Under the Safe Drinking Water Act of 1974 (SDWA), the EPA became responsible for setting maximum contaminant levels (MCLs) for contaminants in public water supplies. These water supplies included not only large cities and towns, but also rural communities serving as few as fifteen households or twenty-five people, for which even testing regularly for contaminants would be a major expense, let alone removing them. In the 1970s, the federal government provided generous grants to help small communities meet the standards, but beginning in the 1980s, the Reagan administration and Congress converted this to a low-interest loan program, leaving a significant expense for small communities whose costs were spread over fewer households. In 1996, Congress amended the SDWA, requiring the EPA to determine that the health benefits of its proposed MCLs exceeded their economic costs; if they did not, the EPA was to impose an MCL that "maximizes the benefits of health risk reduction only to the extent that the cost is justified by the benefits." For small water systems, the EPA administrator also was allowed to require a technology that did not fully meet the MCL but was considered affordable and provided some public health benefits.

The EPA adopted an initial MCL for arsenic in 1975, set at fifty micrograms per liter (equivalent to parts per billion, or ppb), based on a standard set by the Public Health Service—based on limited scientific knowledge—in 1942. From the outset, however, many EPA scientists as well as public health and environmental advocacy groups questioned whether that level adequately protected public health. As early as 1962, the Public Health Service had recommended that "the concentration of arsenic in drinking water should not exceed 0.01 mg/l and concentrations in excess of 0.05 mg/l are grounds for rejection of the supply" (that is, 10 and 50 ppb, respectively).[21]

In 1988, an EPA risk assessment concluded that based on three recent epidemiological studies conducted in other countries, arsenic in drinking water should be considered a potential carcinogen as well as a poison. In 1993, the World Health Organization adopted the 10 ppb limit, as did the European Union. Local U.S. water suppliers, however, continued to resist requirements that they provide costly water treatment, and there was still enough controversy over scientific uncertainties that the EPA did not tighten the standard. For instance, how similar were U.S. populations to those exposed to arsenic in other countries, how accurately could the EPA measure arsenic at levels of 3 ppb, and how much was it really worth to require very small water systems to pay to prevent small numbers of statistical cancer risks? A citizen group sued the EPA to require it to tighten its regulations, however, and the EPA signed a consent decree promising to do so, but then continued to request extensions to the court's deadlines. Finally, in 1996, Congress passed amendments to the SDWA that ordered the EPA to issue a revised draft MCL for arsenic by 2000 and a final rule by 2001. The EPA's appropriations bill in 2000 further ordered it to issue a final arsenic standard no later than June 22, 2001.

Beginning in 1996, the EPA responded by commissioning an independent scientific review by the National Research Council (NRC), and also conducted extensive meetings over several years with state, local, and tribal governments; water supply utilities; and other stakeholder groups. In 1999, the NRC concluded that based on both the earlier studies and more recent scientific information, arsenic should be considered a serious carcinogen. It also concluded that arsenic could cause non-cancer health effects at as little as 1 ppb exposure, and that it could be reliably measured down to a level of at least 4 ppb. It recommended therefore that the 50 ppb standard should be significantly tightened.[22]

On the basis of these studies, the EPA set an MCL goal of zero, and considered setting an actual MCL of 3 ppb. Recognizing the cost burden this might impose on small water systems, however, as well as the measurement challenges at such low levels, in June 2000 it proposed an MCL of 5 ppb as the level that "maximizes health risk reduction at a level where costs and benefits are balanced." It also conducted a "regulatory impact assessment"—a benefit-cost analysis—which concluded that if one based a decision solely on the costs and benefits of reducing bladder cancer, an MCL of 3, 5, 10, or even 20 ppb would have economic costs greater than its benefits; but that reducing arsenic exposure would also provide many other health benefits, although data did not exist to quantify them.[23]

The EPA then requested comment on the draft regulation from the public and from its Science Advisory Board, and was also sued by an environmental group pressing for the 3 ppb standard. In January 2001, it finally issued a regulation reducing the arsenic MCL from 50 to 10 (rather than 5) ppb.

In short, it took nearly forty years from the Public Health Service's recommendation of 10 ppb in 1962, and twenty-seven years from the time the
EPA was given responsibility to regulate drinking water contaminants under
the SDWA, before the EPA finally limited arsenic in drinking water to 10
ppb. Despite all the scientific reviews and risk assessments, the EPA's decision
ultimately was still a discretionary administrative judgment, based on assumptions about the effects of arsenic on cancer and other health risks, the economic benefits of preventing these effects, the practical costs of doing so, the
relevance and persuasiveness of the scientific studies available, and other factors. EPA data also suggest that another reason for choosing 10 ppb may have
been simply the number of water utilities that would have to comply: in the
twenty-five states for which data were then available, fewer than 1,300 water
systems would have to reduce their arsenic to reach 10 ppb, but more than
twice as many would require action to reach 5 ppb and nearly 2,000 more to
reach 3 ppb.[24]

This "final" rule was not the end of the story, however. In late January
2001, the Clinton administration departed, and in March President Bush's
new EPA administrator suspended the rule for further review, claiming that
she wanted to "replace sound-bite rule making with sound-science rule making" and to be "sure that the conclusions about arsenic in the rule are supported by the best available science." The implied message was that despite
nearly forty years of study since the Public Health Service's recommendation
in 1962, and nine years since the World Health Organization had adopted the
same recommendation, the Clinton administration had somehow rushed the
rule to completion before its term ended based on poor science.

Whitman's decision was applauded by westerners concerned about the
rule's cost for communities with naturally occurring arsenic in their water, by
the industries that produced and used arsenic, by antiregulatory conservatives
more generally, and by some economists who argued that the EPA's benefit
estimates were overstated. However, a firestorm of public opposition and
media criticism followed. The decision to suspend the arsenic rule came just
a week after Bush had reversed his commitment to reduce greenhouse gas
emissions and withdrawn U.S. participation in the Kyoto Protocol on global
climate change: suspension of the arsenic rule as well seemed to prove the
Bush administration's hostility to environmental regulation. An environmental group sued the EPA again, demanding that it implement the regulation.
Even the House of Representatives, with significant Republican support,
proposed legislation to require a standard no higher than 10 ppb. Whitman
commissioned several reviews of the rule, both within the EPA and by the
NRC; the NRC reconfirmed its 1999 findings, and added that new information might justify an even stronger standard.[25] In October, Whitman finally
reconfirmed the new rule at the 10 ppb level, acknowledging that whatever
the scientific and economic uncertainties, her suspension of the rule had been
a political and public relations disaster.[26]

The arsenic MCL was thus finally confirmed at 10 ppb, and the EPA
then had to implement it. According to the EPA, only 4,100 of the nation's

74,000 water systems would have to reduce arsenic contamination to comply with the rule, but the vast majority of these were very small systems: 73 percent served less than one thousand people, and 30 percent served less than one hundred. For many of these, the arsenic rule required the first water treatment of any kind that they had had to provide.[27] Many of these systems might thus need exceptions or waivers, which in turn would reduce the rule's effectiveness in protecting public health.

What lessons does this case teach? First, substance-by-substance regulation of contaminants is a far slower and more difficult process than technology-based or cap-and-trade regulation of air or water pollution. Despite decades of precedents by the Public Health Service and the World Health Organization, sustained lobbying and lawsuits by public health and environmental advocacy organizations, and even congressional mandates and deadlines, in the face of resistance from water utilities and their public officials, it required an outgoing presidential administration that was determined to leave a strong environmental legacy and had relatively few political debts to most of the states most affected, and a major public outcry in the media, to force the EPA finally to issue the regulation in 2001.

Second, a key reason for the EPA's slow regulatory process is that risk-based, substance-by-substance regulation imposes a heavy burden of proof on the agency. The EPA relies heavily on independent external scientific organizations, such as its Science Advisory Board and the NRC, to validate its justifications; but despite the best science and economics available, significant uncertainties remain, as well as budget and staff constraints.[28] The agency's decisions therefore remain discretionary administrative judgments, relying on assumptions about the remaining uncertainties, and knowing that these assumptions will always be attacked by opposing interests in the courts and the Congress. One could even argue that the EPA regulates most effectively when it has *least* discretion: when Congress sets a specific criterion by statute, for instance, as it did for motor vehicle emissions (95 percent reduction of average new car emissions by 1975) or new air pollution sources (requiring best available technology for new or modified emissions sources).

Finally, the EPA's decisions are deeply influenced by their anticipated impacts on small businesses and local governments, and these impacts pose significant challenges for the EPA in designing effective policies. As of 2012, an estimated six hundred water systems were still out of compliance with the 10 ppb standard. One could argue therefore that a 10 ppb national standard was too stringent to be achieved by the very small systems, yet not as stringent as would be justifiable for larger ones.[29] Some economists argued that since drinking water quality was an inherently local issue, the EPA should simply require disclosure of contaminant levels and their associated risks and leave regulation to local choice.[30] However, this approach would run contrary to the EPA's mandate to protect all Americans, and to a substantial literature showing that people often make bad choices in such situations and that the resulting burdens of ill health often fall on others (such as children, and extra health care costs paid by taxpayers).[31]

Greenhouse Gas Emissions and Climate Change

A final case raises the question, how does the EPA deal with a newly identified environmental problem that was not anticipated when its regulatory statutes were enacted?

Climate change has been an important public policy issue since the late 1980s, when scientists proposed that global warming was increasing beyond its historic range due to carbon dioxide emissions from human activities: in particular, fossil fuel combustion in power plants, other industries, and motor vehicles. In 1987, Congress directed the EPA to develop a coordinated national policy on climate change, but most early policymaking focused on crafting an international agreement—the 1992 Framework Convention on Climate Change, which the United States adopted, and the 1997 Kyoto Protocol, which it did not—rather than on policies to control domestic emissions.

The Kyoto Protocol included binding targets for GHG emission reductions, which President Clinton agreed to but the U.S. Senate in 1997 voted overwhelmingly to reject unless industrializing countries such as China were also held to them. With the Clinton administration's support, therefore, the EPA began to assert a more active policy role in 1998, when its legal office issued an opinion that the EPA had the authority to regulate GHG emissions under the Clean Air Act even though it had not previously done so. In 1999, a group of environmental organizations and renewable energy businesses, citing this opinion, petitioned the EPA to regulate GHG emissions from new motor vehicles under the Clean Air Act; and in January 2001, just as the Clinton administration left office, the EPA invited public comments on this petition, which produced nearly fifty thousand responses during the first five months of the incoming Bush administration.

While Bush was campaigning for the presidency against Al Gore in September 2000, he pledged in one of his speeches that "[w]e will require all power plants to meet clean-air standards in order to reduce emissions of carbon dioxide within a reasonable period of time."[32] Once he took office, his EPA administrator, Whitman, took this as a commitment and began acting on it. Within two months, however, Bush reversed his support for GHG regulations, and also ended U.S. participation in the Kyoto Protocol negotiations. Whitman resigned in May 2003, and in August the EPA's new legal counsel issued a decision arguing that contrary to its predecessor's opinion, the EPA did *not* have authority to regulate GHGs as air pollutants under the Clean Air Act. Bush's EPA officials also rejected the petition that had called on the EPA to regulate GHG emissions from motor vehicles. Unlike other regulated air pollutants, they argued, GHGs were only significant at a global scale, and therefore were not amenable to the national- and state-level regulations provided by the Clean Air Act. Moreover, they argued that in the 1990 Clean Air Act amendments, Congress itself had only directed the EPA to pursue research and nonregulatory solutions for GHG emissions: such a far-reaching new regulatory initiative should only be undertaken with explicit direction by Congress and after more extensive research.[33]

Led by the state of Massachusetts, however, a group of states, cities, and environmental groups challenged this reinterpretation, and asked the courts to require the EPA to regulate GHG emissions from motor vehicles. In 2005, the initial court upheld the Bush EPA's interpretation, but in 2007, the Supreme Court ruled that GHGs *did* fall within the Clean Air Act's definition of air pollutants, and that the EPA therefore did have authority to regulate them. Given that authority, the court said, the EPA also had a legal *responsibility* to determine whether they "cause, or contribute to, air pollution which may reasonably be anticipated to endanger public health or welfare" (an "endangerment finding").[34] An affirmative endangerment finding, in turn, would automatically trigger an obligation for the EPA to set emission standards.

The EPA's response, during the final year of the Bush administration, was to issue only an "advance notice of proposed rulemaking," in which it restated once again all the reasons why it objected to regulating global warming under the Clean Air Act. Documents later made public showed that after the *Massachusetts* decision, EPA Administrator Stephen Johnson and his staff had in fact prepared plans to issue an endangerment finding, and had even thought they had the administration's approval to do so, but that they had been overruled by President Bush after counterarguments by Vice President Cheney, some other agencies, and Exxon Mobil.[35]

Beginning in 2009, however, with the support of newly elected president Barack Obama and the Supreme Court's *Massachusetts* decision as a mandate—and with the failure of Congress to pass new legislation on climate change—the EPA became the primary locus for decision making on GHG emissions. The EPA issued an endangerment finding in 2009, concluding that GHGs did indeed contribute to risks to public health and welfare and that emissions from new cars and trucks contributed to these effects. It also announced a major joint initiative to regulate GHG emissions and fuel efficiency of motor vehicles, and several of the major car manufacturers—and several other major corporations—announced their support. The motor vehicle standards (the "Tailpipe Rule") were finalized in 2010, and tightened further in 2012.[36]

An additional consequence of the endangerment finding for motor vehicle emissions was that once an emission was regulated as an air pollutant under *any* part of the Clean Air Act, all major *stationary* sources—coal-fired power plants and other industrial facilities, for instance—automatically became subject to regulation as well.[37] In 2008, the EPA's Environmental Appeals Board, the agency's final decision maker on administrative appeals to its regulations, ruled that the Bush administration's narrow interpretation of the EPA's regulatory authority did not justify the EPA's decision not to require the best available control technology for GHG emissions on a new coal-fired power plant, and it ordered the agency to reconsider this option.[38]

While only large industrial facilities and power plants counted as "major" sources for traditional air pollutants, however—the trigger was one hundred tons of emissions per year—thousands more facilities might emit that amount of carbon dioxide: for instance, many hospitals, schools, restaurants, office buildings, farm buildings, and others. The number of sources required to have permits could potentially increase from fewer than fifteen thousand to over six million, even though most of them were relatively small contributors to total GHG emissions; annual administrative costs would increase from $62 million to $21 billion, and the newly regulated sources would face estimated permitting costs of $147 billion.[39] In 2010, the EPA therefore issued a rule requiring permits for new or modified GHG sources, but "tailoring" these regulations to focus only on the largest sources—the power plants and other industrial facilities that emitted more than one hundred *thousand* tons of GHGs per year—while excluding the many smaller and nonindustrial facilities.[40] In 2012, the EPA also proposed performance standards for all new or modified power plants emitting more than a threshold level of GHGs, requiring that they use the "best system of emission reduction" (BSER), and in 2013, it issued a revised version of this standard.[41]

These standards relied on a crucial assumption: that the EPA had the authority to determine that carbon capture and storage (CCS) technologies had been "adequately demonstrated" as a BSER for new coal-fired power plants, even though only a handful of CCS facilities were actually operating so far, or that other options such as energy efficiency improvements could be used to achieve the reductions. The EPA's rationale was that few new coal-fired power plants were planned before 2020, and that new plants after that were already being designed to include CCS technology. Businesses and states opposed to the rule argued, however, that these technologies had not yet been adequately demonstrated at a commercial scale.

Two further complications also followed. First, issuing a performance standard for *new* power plants also triggered a requirement for the EPA to develop guidelines that *states* must use to reduce emissions from *existing* facilities, as part of their required "state implementation plans" for complying with the Clean Air Act. In June 2014, the EPA issued the Obama administration's "Clean Power Plan," a set of proposed rules that set state-specific goals based on each state's power-plant GHG emission rates, and also included flexible guidelines for state plans to achieve the goals.[42] The overall intent of the rules was to reduce overall power-plant GHG emissions by 30 percent from 2005 levels, while allowing each state to adopt strategies best suited to its circumstances. If a state does not submit a plan that satisfies the EPA's guidelines, however, the EPA can write a plan for the state itself. A final rule was to be adopted by June 2015, and state plans were to be completed by June 2016.

The second complication, however, was that since only a small percentage of the necessary emission reductions would likely be achieved by the existing power plants, the states would have to use additional measures to achieve the goals, such as increasing the substitution of natural gas and renewable energy for coal, avoiding retirement of existing nuclear plants, increasing energy efficiency, adopting market-based incentives, and perhaps joining multistate cap-and-trade programs. The EPA's proposal was thus based on a legal theory that had never been tested in court, and the outcome—which would not be known for several years, until after the rule was finalized in 2015 and tested in court—may depend on which judges hear the case.

In the meantime, in 2013, a group of utilities, other carbon-intensive industries, and some states and public officials petitioned the Supreme Court to overrule the EPA's GHG rules for stationary sources, arguing that CCS technology had not yet been adequately demonstrated, and that trying to regulate GHG emissions from stationary sources would expand EPA regulation far beyond what Congress had intended in the Clean Air Act (the *Massachusetts* decision had only addressed motor vehicle emissions, not the effects of this decision in triggering regulation of other sources as well).

In June 2014, the Supreme Court ruled that the EPA did have the authority to regulate GHG emissions from sources that also emitted other pollutants specifically covered by the Clean Air Act, but not to "tailor" its rule so as to regulate only the largest GHG emitters, nor to regulate other sources that emitted only GHGs. In effect, it said, the EPA already had the authority to require the best available control technology for most of the big GHG emission sources, and the flexibility it offered to achieve reductions through CCS, energy efficiency improvements, and other possible options made this a reasonable rule. However, it said, the EPA could not begin regulating whole new types of sources for GHGs alone without congressional approval, nor could it use administrative flexibility to change ("tailor") the specific tonnage triggers in the law (from one hundred to one hundred thousand tons per year) to solve the awkwardness of trying to apply these provisions to GHGs.

In effect, as even conservative Justice Antonin Scalia said in the decision, under this decision the EPA got most of what it wanted—authority to regulate sources of 83 percent of the GHG emissions, rather than 86 percent—but the court justified this by a different rationale. In the process, it also clarified and simplified somewhat the awkwardness of the EPA's effort to apply the Clean Air Act to GHG emissions, reiterated the principle that the EPA is limited by the "plain language" of its laws, and also protected a wide range of businesses from becoming newly subject to EPA regulation without congressional action.[43] Importantly, the court's ruling also did not affect the new rules for coal-fired power plants announced by the EPA earlier in June 2014.

Opponents of the rules continued to threaten to block them by legislation, but while the House of Representatives might do so, it was unlikely that the current Senate would, and President Obama would likely veto such legislation as well. A further major test would be whether President Obama's successor in 2017 would continue to support them or not.

This case thus offers several further lessons. First, as in both the previous cases, the EPA's decisions are driven by both internal and external forces, including its own staff, environmental and business advocacy groups, presidential policy preferences, and court decisions. Key decision points in this case included a memo from the EPA's legal staff under a supportive Clinton administration; a petition by environmental groups, based on this memo, asking the EPA to regulate carbon emissions from motor vehicles; a contrary memo by President Bush's EPA officials, disavowing that interpretation and rejecting the petition; a Supreme Court decision reaffirming the previous interpretation; a series of subsequent EPA rules under the Obama administration implementing that interpretation; and finally another Supreme Court decision affirming the EPA's authority to regulate, but specifying more clearly the rationale and limits of that authority.

Second, as in the previous two cases, the EPA's policies clearly are influenced by presidential politics. Its first administrator, William Ruckelshaus, sought vigorously to establish its independence as a regulatory agency responsible first and foremost to faithfully execute the laws, based on the best science and economics available. Beginning with the Reagan administration in the 1980s, however, its policies became much more subject to change based on presidential politics, though those changes remain constrained by judicial oversight. The EPA's position on regulating GHG emissions changed significantly from the Clinton to the Bush administration and again under Obama; a critical question for the future will be the policy commitment of the next president.

Third, what may appear to be relatively straightforward choices, such as whether the EPA should protect the environment by regulating GHG emissions from cars and trucks, can trigger far more complex consequences. In this case, it triggered automatic regulatory consequences for thousands of stationary sources as well, and for state governments that must develop state implementation plans to meet the EPA's compliance targets. The Clean Air Act is thus a legally available tool for reducing U.S. GHG emissions, but it can be an awkward and potentially burdensome one. Most observers would agree that a broad-based carbon tax or cap-and-trade system would be both more effective and more workable, whether or not they support that goal; but either of those tools would require new legislation, which Congress has so far been unable to pass. State cap-and-trade programs may be another option, but a more effective national solution would require congressional action (see also Chapter 2 on state environmental policymaking).

Achievements and Limitations

In short, using the regulatory tools it has been given, the EPA has accomplished a great deal in making the environment cleaner (see Chapter 1). Air pollution has been dramatically reduced, and regulations for cars and trucks have produced major improvements in motor vehicle design to reduce air pollution and increase fuel efficiency. The EPA's permit requirements also have greatly reduced water pollution from wastewater treatment plants and industrial discharges, although runoff from farms, construction sites, and other nonpoint sources continues to cause serious problems. Solid and hazardous wastes are now managed far more safely: the EPA's regulations closed more than five thousand open-burning dumps in the 1970s, and municipal and commercial landfills are now far more safely managed by professionals under permit standards set by the EPA.[44] The EPA itself has pioneered some of the most important innovations in environmental policy, such as emissions trading and information disclosure requirements.

The EPA's risk-based, substance-by-substance regulations of hazardous chemicals have had far more limited success. They have banned or restricted a few highly visible and controversial toxic chemicals, but due to scientific uncertainties, limited staff and resources, political and legal resistance, and the heavy burden of proof it must sustain, overall the EPA has actually studied and regulated very few.

Both business advocates and policy scholars have sometimes criticized the EPA's regulations. Businesses often criticize them because of the additional costs of compliance, sometimes disregarding the "external" costs of the health effects and other economic damage that their own pollution imposes on others. Policy scholars often criticize them as economically inefficient, and for discouraging innovation: technology-based permit requirements, they argue, sometimes impose extra costs on firms that could reduce pollution more cheaply in other ways, and "best available technology" requirements tend to "lock in" the best existing technology rather than encouraging the discovery of more innovative solutions. Policy scholars have repeatedly recommended the use of markets, environmental taxes, information disclosure, and other innovative policy tools to achieve environmental protection more efficiently and effectively (see Chapter 9).[45]

In reality, however, the EPA can use only the tools that Congress has authorized, which often do not yet include innovative solutions that have been proposed.[46] It therefore has tried to use the regulatory powers it does have to address new problems, such as allowing trading of emission allowances, redefining animal feedlots as point sources, regulating genetically modified organisms as pesticides, and regulating greenhouse gases as dangers to public health and welfare. These are sometimes awkward substitutes, however, for designing more effective policies by statute.

Rays of Hope

Despite attacks by some businesses and other opponents, the basic frameworks and scientific foundations of the EPA's decisions remain largely intact. Even during less supportive presidencies, the courts have frequently upheld the EPA's statutory responsibilities to protect the environment and overruled attempts to reinterpret them in less protective ways. Both environmental advocacy groups and some state governments—and even some supportive businesses—have played key roles in bringing such lawsuits.

There is additional hope in the recent proliferation of state-level policy innovations (see Chapter 2). California and New Jersey led in developing hazardous chemical "right-to-know" laws in the 1980s, which led to the EPA's nationwide Toxics Release Inventory. More recently, California has led in regulating GHG emissions and in promoting energy efficiency and renewable energy. More than half the states have passed renewable energy mandates, and twenty-four have passed tax credits for renewable energy. North Carolina passed a Clean Smokestacks Act in 2001, a state-level cap-and-trade requirement that forced its electric utilities to clean up or close down old coal-fired power plants that had been "grandfathered" under federal law, reducing sulfur emissions by more than 80 percent.[47] The proposed new GHG rule gives states many further options to innovate. At the same time, however, polluting industries and wealthy individuals opposed to regulation have begun pouring money into state election campaigns as well as national ones, and proposing "model" state legislation that would block such initiatives at the state level as well.

There is also hope in coalitions between some environmental advocates and businesses that would prosper in a greener economy. Some leading businesses have identified ways in which good environmental management can be good business, and in cooperation with some environmental organizations are positioning themselves to prosper in a more environmentally sustainable economy. But the EPA's regulations remain an important element of that motivation. And many other businesses are still polluting, either because they lack the means or the will to modernize old facilities or because it is inherently more expensive for them to control pollution than to pay for lawyers, lobbyists, and politicians to resist regulation.

The EPA thus remains an essential institution, and a relatively effective one within the limits of its authority and resources. The limits and imperfections of its policy tools are real, but more often than not, they result more from the inability of Congress to authorize better tools—due to the partisan and ideological gridlock that has characterized recent U.S. politics, as well as the influence of regulated businesses—than from any unwillingness by the EPA itself to consider them. Any hope of truly fundamental policy improvement must lie with broader political reforms, and broader coalitions of environmental and public health advocates with those businesses and state governments that are supportive of environmental protection.

Suggested Websites

U.S. Environmental Protection Agency (www.epa.gov) There are numerous links on this site that provide access to all major activities and issues of concern at the EPA, including environmental laws and regulations.

U.S. Environmental Protection Agency History (www2.epa.gov/aboutepa/epa-history) A useful site for exploring the agency's history and significant changes over time in environmental laws and regulations.

U.S. Environmental Protection Agency New Source Review (www.epa.gov/nsr) The EPA site dedicated to New Source Review provisions under the Clean Air Act.

U.S. Environmental Protection Agency Arsenic Rule (http://water.epa.gov/lawsregs/rulesregs/sdwa/arsenic/regulations.cfm) The EPA site for arsenic regulations under the Safe Drinking Water Act.

U.S. Environmental Protection Agency Carbon Pollution Standards and Greenhouse Gases (www2.epa.gov/carbon-pollution-standards) A major source of information about federal regulation of GHGs.

U.S. Environmental Protection Agency Clean Power Plan (www2.epa .gov/carbon-pollution-standards/clean-power-plan-proposed-rule) The major agency website for developments under the president's Clean Power Plan, including proposed regulation of coal-fired power plants.

Notes

1. For a more detailed history of the EPA, see Richard Andrews, "The EPA at 40: An Historical Perspective," *Duke Environmental Law and Policy Forum* 21 (2011): 223–58.
2. Russell Train, "The Environmental Record of the Nixon Administration," *Presidential Studies Quarterly* 26 (1996): 185–96.
3. For more detail on EPA budgets and staffing, see Chapter 1 and Appendixes 2 and 3.
4. Philip Shabecoff, "E.P.A. Aims to Curb Tall Smokestacks," *New York Times*, June 28, 1985, www.nytimes.com/1985/06/28/us/epa-aims-to-curb-tall-smokestacks.html.
5. See, for instance, Trip Gabriel, "Utility Cited for Violating Pollution Law in North Carolina," *New York Times*, March 3, 2014, www.nytimes.com/2014/03/04/us/utility -cited-for-violating-pollution-law-in-north-carolina.html?_r=0.
6. U.S. Energy Information Administration, Annual Electric Generator Report 2008, available at www.eia.gov/cneaf/electricity/page/capacity/existingunitsbs2008.xls.
7. Clean Air Act of 1970, Public Law 91-604, Section 111.
8. U.S. Environmental Protection Agency, *New Source Review*, www.epa.gov/nsr.
9. *Alabama Power Co. v. Costle*, 636 F.2d 323, 400 (D.C. Cir. 1979).
10. Larry Parker, *Clean Air: New Source Review Policies and Proposals*, Congressional Research Service Report RL31757 (2003); and *Clean Air and New Source Review: Defining Routine Maintenance*, Congressional Research Service Report RS21608 (2005).
11. James E. McCarthy, "Clean Air Act: A Summary of the Act and Its Major Require- ments," Chapter 1 in *Clean Air Act: Interpretation and Analysis*, ed. James P. Lipton (New York: Nova Science, 2006), 41–43.
12. Christopher Drew and Richard Oppel Jr., "Air War—Remaking Energy Policy: How Power Lobby Won the Battle of Pollution Control at E.P.A.," *New York Times Maga- zine*, March 6, 2004; Jo Becker and Martin Gellman, "Leaving No Tracks," *Washington Post*, June 27, 2007.
13. John Shiffman and John Sullivan, "EPA's Court Follies Sow Doubt, Delay," *Philadelphia Inquirer*, December 8, 2008.
14. *New York v. EPA*, 413 F. 3d 3 (D.C. Cir. 2005); *New York v. EPA*, 443 F. 3d 880 (D.C. Cir. 2006).
15. Id.
16. Howard Gruenspecht and Robert Stavins, "New Source Review under the Clean Air Act: Ripe for Reform," *Resources* 147 (2002): 19–23.
17. Victor Flatt and Kim Diana Connolly, "'Grandfathered' Air Pollution Sources and Pollution Control: New Source Review under the Clean Air Act," Center for Progres- sive Regulation White Paper (2005), www.progressivereform.org/articles/NSR_504 .pdf.
18. John Applegate, "The Perils of Unreasonable Risk," *Columbia Law Review* 91 (1991): 261–333, www.repository.law.indiana.edu/cgi/viewcontent.cgi?article=1715&context =facpub.
19. U.S. EPA, "Arsenic in Drinking Water," last updated September 17, 2013, http:// water.epa.gov/lawsregs/rulesregs/sdwa/arsenic/index.cfm.

20. Rep. Anna Eshoo, *Cong. Rec.* H4751 (July 27, 2001).
21. U.S. Public Health Service, *Public Health Service Drinking Water Standards* (1962), p. 26, https://archive.org/stream/gov.law.usphs.956.1962/usphs.956.1962#page/n5/mode/2up.
22. National Research Council, *Arsenic in Drinking Water* (1999).
23. U.S. EPA, *Proposed Arsenic in Drinking Water Rule: Regulatory Impact Analysis*, EPA 815-R-00-013 (2000), p. 113.
24. Natural Resources Defense Council, *Arsenic and Old Laws* (2000), www.nrdc.org/water/drinking/arsenic/aolinx.asp, Table 1.
25. Katherine Seelye, "EPA to Adopt Clinton Arsenic Rule," *New York Times*, November 1, 2001.
26. Greg Easterbrook, "Hostile Environment," *New York Times Magazine*, August 19, 2001.
27. U.S. EPA, *Arsenic Rule: Small Systems Implementation Strategy & Exemptions* (2002), www.epa.gov/safewater/arsenic/pdfs/arsenic_training_2002/train3-implementation.pdf.
28. Cass Sunstein, "The Arithmetic of Arsenic," *Georgetown Law Journal* 90 (2001–2002): 2255–309.
29. U.S. EPA, Arsenic Small Systems Working Group, *Synthesis of Individual Participant Input* (2012), www.ruralwater.org/arsenicreportdraft.pdf.
30. Wallace Oates, "The Arsenic Rule: A Case for Decentralized Standard Setting?" *Resources* 147 (2002): 16–18.
31. Tom Gorman, "Nevada Town's Residents Unperturbed about Arsenic in Its Drinking Water," *Los Angeles Times*, April 9, 2001.
32. Seth Borenstein, "Bush Changes Pledge on Emissions," *Philadelphia Inquirer*, March 14, 2001.
33. Robert Fabricant (EPA General Counsel), "EPA's Authority to Impose Mandatory Controls to Address Global Climate Change under the Clean Air Act" (August 28, 2003), http://yosemite.epa.gov/OA/EAB_WEB_Docket.nsf/Attachments%20By%20ParentFilingId/BC82F18BAC5D89FF852574170066B7BD/$File/UARG%20Attchmnt%20G...43.pdf; see also *Federal Register* 68(173): 52922–32.
34. *Massachusetts v. EPA*, 549 U.S. 497 (2007).
35. Letter from Stephen Johnson to President Bush, January 31, 2008, www.motherjones.com/files/enclosureletter_presdidentfromstephenjohnson_2.8.2011_2.pdf; Darren Samuelson, "Bush EPA Chief Prepped Climate Plan," *Politico*, February 8, 2011.
36. James McCarthy, *Cars, Trucks, and Climate: EPA Regulation of Greenhouse Gases from Mobile Sources*, Congressional Research Service Report R40506 (2014).
37. The "timing rule" (also known as the "PSD Triggering Rule") was issued in 1980, and made any source emitting more than one hundred tons of any regulated air pollutant subject to requirements for an EPA permit for "prevention of significant deterioration" of air quality (PSD).
38. Bryan Walsh, "Environmentalists Win Big EPA Ruling," *Time*, November 13, 2008.
39. See Note 43 below.
40. *Federal Register* 75: 31514, June 3, 2010; Robin Bravender, "EPA Issues Final 'Tailoring' Rule for Greenhouse Gas Emissions," *New York Times*, May 13, 2010.
41. *Federal Register* 77 (2012): 22392; James McCarthy, *EPA Standards for Greenhouse Gas Emissions from Power Plants: Many Questions, Some Answers*, Congressional Research Service Report R43127 (2013).
42. Environmental Protection Agency, *Carbon Pollution Emission Guidelines for Existing Stationary Sources: Electric Utility Generating Units*, 40 *CFR* Part 60, *Fed. Reg.* 79:34830 (2014).

43. *Utility Air Regulatory Group v. EPA*, 573 U.S. ____ (June 23, 2014).
44. Richard Andrews, *Managing the Environment, Managing Ourselves: A History of American Environmental Policy* (New Haven, CT: Yale, 2006), pp. 245–49.
45. At least one scholar, however, has argued that this conventional wisdom is overstated and often wrong, and that "there are solid reasons to suspect that an emissions trading program does a poorer job of stimulating innovation than a comparably designed traditional regulation." See David Driesen, "Does Emissions Trading Encourage Innovation?" *Environmental Law Reporter* 33 (2003): 10094–108.
46. Andrews, "The EPA at 40," pp. 229–34.
47. Richard Andrews, "State Environmental Policy Innovations: North Carolina's Clean Smokestacks Act," *Environmental Law* 43 (2013): 881–940.

Part III

Public Policy Dilemmas

8

Energy Policy
Fracking, Renewables, and the Keystone XL Pipeline
Edward P. Weber, David Bernell, and Hilary S. Boudet

Energy is a core component of modern economies. A functioning economy requires not only labor and capital, but also energy, for manufacturing processes, transportation, communication, agriculture, and more. Access to energy is also critical for basic social needs, such as lighting, heating, cooking, and health care. As a result, the price of energy has a direct effect on jobs, economic productivity and business competitiveness, and the cost of goods and services. For example, sustained increases in the price of oil were a key contributor to the economic recessions of 1974, 1979, and the early 1990s. On the other hand, recent declines in the price of natural gas in the United States have led to lower operating costs at manufacturing facilities, spurring new facilities and jobs, while lowering home heating and cooling costs, which leaves more money in consumers' pockets.

Providing the energy needed for economic growth is rife with challenges. Heavy reliance on fossil fuel, or carbon-based, energy sources—oil, coal, and natural gas—is responsible for releasing massive amounts of greenhouse gases (GHGs), particularly carbon dioxide, into the atmosphere and contributing significantly to global warming and climate change (see Chapter 13). The production and transportation of oil and gas through pipelines and oceangoing tankers risks disastrous spills, as highlighted by the 2010 Deepwater Horizon accident in the Gulf of Mexico. Coal extraction poses its own set of risks, including serious health problems from coal dust, safety issues associated with underground working conditions, and pollution from mining wastes. As well, the human health and ecological risks associated with nuclear energy are illustrated by accidents at Three Mile Island (U.S., 1979), Chernobyl (Ukraine, 1986), and Fukushima (Japan, 2011). Even wind and solar energy, often cited as a panacea to our energy challenges, present environmental risks to endangered species, habitat degradation, and water resources in arid areas.

The many technical, economic, and environmental challenges associated with energy resources inevitably means that controversy and conflict are all too common in the U.S. energy policy arena. The classic NIMBY, or Not in My Backyard, resistance applies to energy development, whether it is fossil fuels or renewables. There are serious internal disagreements within the broader environmental movement as some groups, for example, promote "green" priorities such as endangered species protection, water conservation in arid areas, and forest and grassland protection that directly

interfere with renewable energy siting and development. There are organized and massive protests against major fossil fuel projects such as the
Keystone XL pipeline from Canada and in support of policies to combat
climate change (Chapter 3). There are legislative- and voter-approved bans
or restrictions on hydraulic fracturing (fracking) in states as varied as
Colorado, Pennsylvania, California, and New York. And there is stiff resistance from political conservatives to government policies subsidizing and
otherwise facilitating renewable energy development.

The conflict often translates into a partisan divide, with each presidential
administration bringing different sets of values and priorities for how to
address these challenges (see Chapter 4). With Republican president George
W. Bush, oil, gas, and nuclear energy all received strong rhetorical and policy
support, including a push for additional oil and gas drilling on public lands
and in offshore (near ocean) zones, or through large government subsidies for
new nuclear plants. However, as this chapter shows, President Barack Obama,
a Democrat, has charted a different direction. The Department of the Interior
(DOI) has reduced new oil and gas leases for federal public lands and offshore
areas, while also aggressively promoting the development of renewable energy.
Moreover, the Obama administration has used the 2007 Supreme Court ruling allowing the Environmental Protection Agency (EPA) to regulate greenhouse gases as the rationale for the EPA's new, stricter regulations on
power-plant pollution that many believe signals the "end of coal" in the U.S.
power industry (see Chapter 7).

These partisan differences between presidents, and between Democrats
and Republicans, have become ever more important given congressional gridlock on environmental and energy issues, and the increasing willingness of
presidents to use their executive powers to pursue policy goals unilaterally.
Such developments place even greater pressure on each government agency
involved in energy issues, from the EPA to the Department of Energy
(DOE) and DOI agencies, as they struggle to balance competing needs and
priorities in the face of intensive lobbying by energy interests. They also place
greater pressure on state legislatures, governors, and energy-policy-oriented
regulatory officials at that level given the lack of an overall national energy
policy and the fact that they make many of the nation's critical energy development decisions.

It is these issues—the technical, economic, and environmental challenges
of energy; the contemporary conflict and controversies; and the partisan
divide over energy—that frame the analysis in this chapter. To bring these
issues to light, we use three case studies important to contemporary energy
politics and policy in the United States:

- The emergence and growth of hydraulic fracturing to exploit previ-
  ously inaccessible shale gas and "tight" oil
- Renewable energy development on federal public lands
- The fight over the Keystone XL pipeline from Canada to the southern
  United States

Prior to these cases, the chapter dissects the dynamic underlying the politics of energy.

U.S. Energy Policy and Politics Today

Currently, the major issues in U.S. energy policy revolve around the rapidly growing production of domestic and other North American energy resources. Technological advances in hydraulic fracturing and horizontal drilling have allowed access to oil and natural gas in shale rock formations. The high price of oil and vast Canadian tar sands have converged into the proposed Keystone XL pipeline to carry this oil to the United States. At the same time, the development of renewable, or "green," energies such as solar, wind, biomass, and geothermal has greatly expanded due to new policies and growing concern over climate change. In fact, in 2013, wind power accounted for 4 percent of U.S. electricity generation, up from less than 1 percent fifteen years earlier.[1] The explosion in U.S. supplies of natural gas due to hydraulic fracturing since 2000, and consequent low prices, has increased natural gas's share of the national energy portfolio from 16 percent of all electricity generated in 2000 to 27 percent in 2013. By contrast, coal use has dropped from 51 percent to 39 percent.[2] Taken together, these developments suggest that the United States could soon achieve energy independence.

However, the U.S. drive toward energy independence and less reliance on oil and coal is fraught with partisan conflict because these issues revolve around how best to balance competing values, such as environmental protection and economic growth, or to balance the demands from organized interests, such as those of the fossil fuel industry and newer renewable energy businesses. Just as importantly, many of these disputes directly involve the executive branch agencies responsible for writing regulations.

In order to better understand U.S. energy politics and policy today, we first describe the technical, economic, and environmental elements of energy policy using a four-part lens—supply expansion, demand management and reduction, cost analysis, and reliability of supply. The analysis then turns to the contours of contemporary U.S. energy politics.

Supply Expansion

This approach seeks to determine the extent to which policy measures impact the expansion of different forms of energy supplies. Analyzing policy through this lens tends to be based upon an understanding that the ever-growing demands for energy need to be met. Energy shortages are not the problem—there are a wide variety of resources available—but converting these resources into usable energy is. The focus thus is on the barriers that exist to such a goal, be they technical, policy (statutory or regulatory), economic, environmental, geographical, or political, and how to overcome them through policy solutions (financing, tax incentives, direct appropriations, demonstration projects, regulatory mandates). And the key to determining the value of a policy is its ability to expand energy supplies.

Demand Management and Reduction

This approach takes the opposite tack, determining the extent to which policy measures reduce energy demand—in other words, how well policy promotes and achieves efficiency and conservation. Analyzing policy through this lens acknowledges that energy needs are growing and that new supplies are necessary but suggests that new supplies are not sufficient. Because so much energy is wasted through overconsumption and inefficiency, one of the best ways to become more energy secure is to reduce demand. The policy focus here has been on incentives (tax credits and rebates for energy-efficient equipment), consumer education (energy rating information on appliances), technological development, mandates (Corporate Average Fuel Economy [CAFE] standards, building codes), and reducing barriers to lifestyle changes that would result in reduced energy usage (city planning that would encourage walking and biking over driving). This type of analysis seeks to determine the value of policy by measuring its ability to reduce energy demand.

Cost Analysis

A cost analysis approach seeks to capture the expected and unintended costs of energy resources and associated policies. This approach reflects an understanding that the best energy resources (and this includes efficiency and conservation) are those that minimize the costs associated with their production and use. Costs can be defined narrowly—in terms of the financial costs to consumers (the price of a kilowatt-hour of electricity or a gallon of gasoline) or taxpayers (government appropriations and tax expenditures) or, broadly, in terms of environmental, national security, and social costs. Broadly defined costs can include the health and environmental impacts of coal (mining, transportation, pollution from combustion, and disposal of hazardous wastes) or the cost of military operations incurred in securing access to oil (for example, efforts in Iraq and the larger Persian Gulf region).

Reliability of Supply

Another key consideration for energy policy is reliability of supply. Every energy source has inherent limitations on its reliability. When supply falls short of demand, fuel prices are likely to rise steeply and cause economic disruptions, particularly in countries dependent on a single fuel type and/or supplier. Historically, the reliability problem for oil and natural gas stems from a mismatch between the locations of major supplies and the locations of major demand centers—a problem that becomes more acute when supplies are located in politically volatile regions of the world like the Middle East and Russia.

Reliability of supply is also critically important to electricity production and delivery. A key reason why electric systems rely heavily on coal, oil, natural gas, and nuclear power is that they can be managed to generate electrical outputs that match widely varying demands, including peaks in energy demand by households and industry. The push to produce more electricity from solar and wind power has brought the reliability question into sharper relief because solar and wind are intermittent sources of energy: they produce electricity only when the sun shines or the wind blows. Intermittent renewable energy sources thus require backup sources of generation to produce a more predictable flow of electricity to match demand. As a result, these renewable systems are often paired with traditional energy sources, such as coal, gas, nuclear, or hydropower.

Politics and Energy

Understanding U.S. energy policy also requires analysis of politics and the conflict behind policy choices, particularly the changing values of the American public, the emergence of climate change on the policy agenda, and partisan battles over whether and how much government intervention is warranted in support of a particular type of energy. Other fault lines include the level of government in charge of energy development and the value-based disagreements over the costs and benefits associated with different energy types.

The first piece in the energy politics puzzle involves the level of public support for different energy types and the issues associated with energy development and use. For example, prior to the emergence of the contemporary environmental movement in the 1960s, policies promoting the aggressive exploitation of fossil fuels were not controversial, but widely supported as engines for economic growth. Key to this support were the narrow and largely invisible policy subgovernments of congressional committees, federal agencies, and organized industry interests surrounding oil and gas leasing on public lands, nuclear power, and coal development. However, as more citizens came to understand the social costs of pollution, including concerns over climate change, public opinion has shifted to be less supportive of fossil fuels and more supportive of green energy sources.

A second component of energy politics involves the conflict over whether and how much government intervention is warranted in support of a particular type of energy. For example, considerable disagreement exists over the role government should play in the transition toward a green energy economy, with conservatives and Republicans in staunch opposition to both the premise that green energy is necessary and that government has a major role to play in promoting the development of green energy sources. Despite the resistance, the trend is toward more government promotion of renewable energies, which finds strong support among Democrats, their "green energy" industry allies, and environmentalists. The Obama administration, in particular, has pushed forward with many "green energy" initiatives, especially when compared to the Bush administration. These federal and state policies have taken four general forms:

Corporate subsidies for energy development and new energy technologies. More than a dozen states refund up to half of wind energy development costs, with Oregon willing to pay up to $10 million per site. The U.S. Energy

Policy Act of 2005 offered grants, loans, and tax credits to firms developing renewable energy and "green" technologies such as solar panels, zero emission vehicles, and hybrid cars. In addition, the Energy Policy Act of 1992 provided a tax credit of 2.3 cents per kilowatt-hour to renewable energy generators in order to make renewables more competitive with natural gas and coal. The Obama administration dramatically expanded government subsidies for renewable energy development in 2009, when under the auspices of the American Recovery and Reinvestment Act they created the Section 1603 U.S. Treasury grant program. Over three years, the Treasury awarded $9 billion in "1603" grants to small and startup green energy companies, which accounted for 50 percent of the total nonhydropower renewables capacity added between 2009 and 2011.[3]

Regulatory incentives to lower carbon emissions. These policies are designed to either raise the costs of nonrenewables, thus discouraging their use, or lower the costs of preferred green energy and related technologies. The three primary types are carbon taxes, emissions trading (for carbon), and tax credits for individual consumers (e.g., for rooftop solar panels or hybrid vehicles). President Obama and congressional Democrats made clear in 2009, in their unsuccessful push for national climate change legislation, that a carbon emissions trading, or cap-and-trade, program was their preferred approach. At the state level, emissions trading programs have also found political support. Major efforts have included the Regional Greenhouse Gas Initiative (RGGI) to cap and reduce carbon dioxide emissions from the power sector in nine Northeast and Atlantic region states, and in California, where Democratic governor Jerry Brown implemented a statewide cap-and-trade program for GHGs in 2012 (see Chapter 2).

Leniency in regulatory and permitting processes for green energy. A growing number of state and federal agencies such as the Bureau of Land Management (BLM) now practice streamlining, or "fast-track" permitting, for green energy development projects. At the same time, shortly after President Obama took office, the DOI relaxed the long-standing "strict liability" approach to the Migratory Bird Treaty Act (MBTA) of 1918 as one way of protecting wind energy projects from legal liability. The MBTA prohibited the taking or killing of migratory birds, including eagles, even if preventative measures were taken and even if the activity was not directed against wildlife. In 2010, the DOI's Fish and Wildlife Service designed a specific program—the Bird and Bat Conservation Strategy (BBCS)—for wind energy installations that allows for takes of migratory birds.[4] Critics such as the National Audubon Society called the rule "a blank check" for the wind power industry.[5]

Renewable portfolio standards (RPS). Employed by thirty states, RPS set a minimum standard, or share of electricity, to be provided from renewable resources, including wind, solar, geothermal, biomass, landfill gas, and solid waste. A leading example is California, where electric utilities must derive 25 percent of their retail sales from renewables by the end of 2016 and 33 percent by 2020 (see Chapter 2).

There also is political conflict over which level of government should be in charge. Currently, a large number of agencies have energy policy responsibilities at the federal level, including but not limited to the DOE, Federal Energy Regulatory Commission (FERC), Nuclear Regulatory Commission (NRC), and EPA. Moreover, with federally controlled offshore zones and public lands in the western United States amenable to all types of energy development, federal agencies such as the Bureau of Ocean Energy Management (BOEM) and BLM will likely continue to play an important, and perhaps decisive, role in many projects. And it is often in these federal bureaucracies where the differences in partisan preferences for different types of energy, approaches to regulation, and values are on full display. A key example, which is developed in the "World of Fracking" and "Renewable Energy Development on Federal Lands" sections below, involves the dramatic differences in how the DOI approached oil, gas, and coal leasing and the advancement of renewable energy projects under two different presidents—Bush and Obama. Another important example involves the significant differences in the EPA's approach to power industry regulation under Presidents Bush and Obama. Despite some momentum for reducing carbon dioxide emissions from power plants at the end of the Clinton administration, the Bush administration decided against EPA rules for capping carbon dioxide emissions and actively sought to delay their implementation despite a 2007 Supreme Court ruling (*Massachusetts v. EPA*) that carbon dioxide was a covered pollutant under the Clean Air Act (CAA). Bush also promoted his 2002 Clear Skies Initiative calling for a market-based approach to CAA goals, which necessarily would weaken the requirement that coal-fired plants reduce mercury emissions. President Obama, on the other hand, took a top-down, command-and-control approach to air pollution and viewed the EPA as one of his most powerful tools for fighting climate change. His administration took the 2007 *Massachusetts v. EPA* ruling and retailored the CAA "major source" rule to cover over 86 percent of industrial GHG emissions (see Chapter 7). Likewise, in June 2014, the frustration with congressional inaction on climate change led Obama's EPA to issue notice it would unilaterally oversee a 30 percent reduction in coal-fired power-plant carbon emissions by the year 2030.

At the same time, federal policy gridlock over climate change and the lack of an overall strategic national energy policy has created opportunities for states to take the lead in battling climate change and forging the transition to new types of energy.[6] Complicating the issue further are the strong private property and mineral rights in the United States that give individual citizens significant control over whether energy development will take place in a specific area. In fact, the United States is the only country in which surface property rights also include the rights to subsurface mineral deposits, including hydrocarbons. Taken together with the fact that energy development of any type is disruptive, visible, and high impact, with benefits and externalities directly affecting the local "place" of development, local governments have a genuine stake in energy policy, too.

A full understanding of the politics of energy also requires attention to costs and benefits. Political opposition to new alternative energy forms often focuses on its higher *economic* cost relative to fossil fuels such as coal or natural gas. Chief opponents include economic conservatives and Republicans, energy-intensive heavy industries, and labor unions involved in energy infrastructure and energy-intensive manufacturing enterprises. Such differences at present are significant if the focus is on kilowatt-hour costs of electricity. For example, the average per-kilowatt-hour cost of electricity in Germany, a world leader in installing solar and wind capacity, was 36.2 cents in 2012 compared to the U.S. average of 11.88 cents. Another comparative measure is the levelized cost of electricity, which represents the per-kilowatt-hour cost of building and operating a generating plant over the full life of the facility. This measure shows that renewables, with one exception, are significantly more expensive than conventional fuel sources. The one exception is onshore wind energy at 8 cents per kilowatt-hour, which is competitive with advanced nuclear energy and 20 percent less expensive than coal, but 25 percent more expensive than natural gas. By comparison, photovoltaic solar costs 11.9 cents.[7]

Proponents of green energy, on the other hand, typically include environmental and climate change advocates, industries with low energy needs, public sector unions, political liberals and Democrats. Their focus is on the negative "social," or health and environmental, costs of fossil fuels (which are largely externalized), the long-term benefits from weaning society off carbon-based fuels, and the expectation that green energy costs will eventually become competitively priced, particularly as technological innovation continues apace and once the true social costs of carbon are factored into the equation. In fact, the cost of onshore wind energy declined 43 percent between 2009 and 2013, while the price of solar panels has dropped 99 percent since the 1970s.[8] Moreover, according to three prominent economists, the "social" cost of six major air pollutants emitted by coal power plants add 2.8 cents per kilowatt-hour to coal's cost, while a relatively conservative estimate of $27 per ton for the social cost of carbon adds another 0.8 cent per kilowatt-hour. With this adjustment, the levelized cost of conventional coal increases to roughly 13 percent more than photovoltaic solar energy.[9]

Yet, in many cases, it can be the geographical distribution of costs and benefits that determines where the political battle lines will be drawn around a specific energy facility proposal. While specific local economies do benefit from more jobs and tax revenues from energy development, many of the negative costs are also direct and localized. In contrast, actual energy usage and many, if not most, of the economic benefits of a particular facility are dispersed to users and corporations in other places. This geographic mismatch of costs and benefits can explain, for example, why many stakeholders in rural areas may be against a particular renewable energy project that creates localized costs in terms of blighted landscapes, but benefits neighboring states and faraway cities in terms of a green energy supply. It can also explain why coal-producing and heavy coal-use states like West Virginia, Ohio, and Indiana tend to oppose climate change regulations that negatively affect the price and demand for coal.

Three Cases of Conflict over Values and Priorities

The technical, economic, and environmental challenges of energy have translated into conflict over values and priorities, which is often expressed as a political divide over energy types, development, and use. Three cases—fracking, renewables on public lands, and the Keystone XL pipeline—illustrate the challenges and political landscape associated with contemporary U.S. energy policy.

The World of Fracking: New Technologies for Old Fuels

Hydraulic fracturing (or "fracking") is a technique for tapping unconventional oil and natural gas reserves that are otherwise inaccessible. In the late 1990s and early 2000s, energy companies began combining horizontal (or directional) drilling with hydraulic fracking to tap these reserves. The process involves drilling horizontally through a rock layer and injecting a pressurized mixture of water, sand, and other chemicals that fractures the rock and facilitates the flow of oil and gas. These combined methods have allowed for expanded development in shale and other formations in the United States, Europe, Asia, Australia, and elsewhere. The rapid expansion of fracking is projected to make the United States a net exporter of natural gas in the coming years and potentially the world's largest oil producer by 2017.[10] Shale gas, which currently accounts for 23 percent of the nation's natural gas production, is projected to increase to 49 percent by 2035.[11]

Hydraulic fracking is just one part of the unconventional oil/gas development process, which also includes clearing land for well pads, construction of access roads and associated infrastructure (e.g., pipelines, compressor stations), transporting and processing extracted fossil fuels, transporting millions of gallons of water and wastewater for treatment/disposal, and bringing large (and often transient) populations to a community. These activities involve potential economic, environmental, social, and health impacts.

At the local level, potential economic benefits include job creation, increased income and wealth for individuals who sign gas leases on private lands, expanded local business opportunities for those who directly (i.e., construction) and indirectly service the energy industry (i.e., hotels and restaurants), and rising tax revenue for communities.[12] At a national level, the potential for U.S. energy self-sufficiency created by the fracking boom may decrease national security concerns associated with securing and protecting energy supplies overseas and could lead to a resurgence of U.S. manufacturing industries dependent on natural gas as a fuel stock.[13] If the natural gas produced from hydraulic fracking replaces more carbon-intensive fuels like coal, it would lower GHG emissions.[14] Yet if, as some research suggests and as many environmentalists have argued, the emissions from methane leakage negate other GHG reductions from a transition to natural gas, such a transition might essentially serve as a "bridge to nowhere" as opposed to a "bridge to renewable energy."[15]

A major environmental impact of hydraulic fracking relates to water availability and quality. Hydraulic fracking requires two to ten million gallons of water per well per fracture,[16] which raises concerns about depletion of water resources. Also, contamination of subterranean and surface water can occur because of the release into rivers and streams of inadequately treated drilling wastewater with potentially toxic materials, surface spills of chemicals, and methane migration from gas wells into aquifers.[17] Social impacts are a third area of concern and relate to a community's ability to accommodate the frenzied activity associated with an energy development boom.[18] And, more recently, concerns have arisen about the potential link between fracking and increased seismic, or earthquake, activity, particularly resulting from the pressure created by injection wells used to dispose of wastewater, but also from the fracking process itself.[19]

For all of the controversy and hype, recent national surveys have found Americans to be relatively uninformed about fracking.[20] Among those who have made a decision, Americans are equally divided in their support and opposition. Like other emerging technologies, women, individuals with egalitarian worldviews, and those who associated fracking with environmental issues were more likely to oppose fracking. Older, more conservative individuals, and those who associated fracking with economic issues, were more likely to support it.[21] Moreover, as for many energy issues, public support and opposition largely fall along party lines, with Republicans in support and Democrats in opposition.[22] Yet President Obama has done little to limit fracking's expansion—which was also supported strongly by the Bush administration. In fact, the Obama administration has made the case for increased domestic oil and gas production as part of its "All-of-the-Above Energy Strategy" whose objectives are "to support economic growth and job creation, to enhance energy security, and to deploy low-carbon energy technologies and lay the foundation for a clean energy future."[23] At the same time, however, federal agencies under Obama are making moves to regulate the more controversial aspects of the process, as described below.

As with many emerging energy technologies, regulation of fracking and its impacts in the United States has been a fragmented process, likely resulting from its numerous technical, economic, and environmental challenges that feed into conflict over values and priorities. The Safe Drinking Water Act (SDWA) of 1974 required the EPA to regulate underground fluid injection and banned the injection of hazardous materials, but exempted hydraulic fracking. In 1997, after a fracking operation in Alabama contaminated drinking water supplies, the Legal Environmental Assistance Foundation sued to regulate fracking under the SDWA and won.[24] After a three-year investigation, however, the EPA determined that fracking posed no serious threat to drinking water supplies and needed no further regulation under the SDWA.[25] The Energy Policy Act of 2005 sealed this exemption into law via the "Halliburton loophole"—so named because Halliburton engineers invented the fracking process.[26]

Surface water discharge, a common practice in fracking operations, is also regulated under the 1972 Clean Water Act, while the 1970 National Environmental Policy Act requires the preparation of environmental impact assessments prior to drilling on federal lands. Hazardous chemicals are regulated under the Comprehensive Environmental Response, Compensation, and Liability Act of 1980 ("Superfund"); and the EPA is currently in the process of mandating the reporting of fracking fluids under the Toxic Substances Control Act of 1976. More recently, the EPA has begun to develop a comprehensive strategy to cut methane emissions from fracking and new effluent guidelines under the Clean Water Act for shale oil and gas production, while the BLM has begun to develop rules for fracking on public lands.

As with much oil and gas development, regulation has largely been left to the states, resulting in significant heterogeneity.[27] One recent study of fracking in the twenty-seven states with significant shale gas development found considerable variation in the use of twenty different regulatory elements related to site selection and preparation, well drilling, hydraulic fracking, wastewater storage and disposal, excess gas disposal, and plugging and abandonment.[28] In general, they found that states tend to prefer command-and-control regulations (e.g., requiring wells to be cased and cemented to a specific depth below the water table), as opposed to performance standards (e.g., requiring wells to be cased and cemented to a level sufficient to protect all "freshwater bearing zones").

Some states have taken a leadership role in regulating fracking. For example, since 2008, New York has had a moratorium pending health and safety studies. In 2010, Wyoming became the first state to require disclosure of fracking chemicals.[29] In 2014, Ohio released new permitting conditions to regulate fracking near known active faults,[30] while Colorado became the first state to regulate methane emissions. Some of these policy efforts have created strange bedfellows. For example, Colorado's regulations were developed using collaboration between the Environmental Defense Fund and three oil and gas companies under the watch of Democratic governor John Hickenlooper.[31]

Further, an increasing number of local governments have sought to ban fracking. In Pennsylvania, the State Supreme Court recently ruled that a state law restricting the ability of local governments to control drilling in their area was unconstitutional.[32] In New York, the town of Dryden created zoning laws to ban fracking—laws that were upheld in state court.[33] Dozens of other counties in the state of New York, several communities in Colorado, and the City of Los Angeles have imposed similar bans.

Local regulation can also be found in the leases that private landowners sign with oil and gas companies. These leases establish not only financial terms, but also other conditions that may impact drilling operations. These leases provide a critical piece of the policy puzzle because in the absence of comprehensive state or federal policies, leases offer immediate protection to landowners seeking to control what happens on their property.

Renewable Energy Development on Federal Lands

To help meet the goal of diversifying energy supplies, the U.S. government has recently given higher priority to the growth of renewable energy resources such as wind, solar, geothermal, and ocean power. While tax incentives—the Investment Tax Credit and the Production Tax Credit—have been critical to the growing adoption of wind and solar power, the federal government has also recently begun to make public lands available for renewable energy development.

The United States owns 640 million acres of land (about 28 percent of all U.S. territory), most of it in the West and Alaska, and manages millions of acres offshore. These lands and offshore areas are used for military bases, national parks and forests, wildlife reserves, energy production, and water management. They are also leased to the private sector for commercial uses such as timber harvesting, grazing, mining, and energy production.

The BLM has a leading role in the development of energy resources on federal lands, while the recently established the Bureau of Ocean Energy Management (BOEM), which replaced the Minerals Management Service, is responsible for offshore energy production. Energy development on federal lands has traditionally involved the extraction of coal, oil, and natural gas, although President Obama has placed a high priority on rapid expansion of renewable energy development, while diminishing the focus on fossil fuels. For example, in President Bush's second term, the BLM issued 13,175 oil and gas leases on federal public lands. By contrast, in President Obama's first term, the BLM issued 7,297 oil and gas leases, a decrease of 45 percent.[34]

With respect to renewables, prior to 2009, the BLM had approved no solar projects, 566 megawatts (MW) of wind power, and 942 MW of geothermal power. After this time, the pace quickened, and from 2009 through 2013, the BLM authorized fifty-one projects to provide over 13,000 MW of power.[35] As of 2014, the total capacity of all approved renewable energy projects on public lands included twenty-eight solar facilities (8,586 MW), eleven wind farms (5,557 MW), and twelve geothermal plants (1,500 MW).[36] No offshore wind farms or ocean energy projects currently operate in the United States, though technology testing and application for permits have occurred for several projects.

The benefits of generating renewable energy on public lands are significant. Approved solar power projects on BLM lands provide enough electricity to power roughly 2.6 million homes, while wind and geothermal projects can each supply 1.5 million homes,[37] thus avoiding millions of tons of carbon emissions every year. With dozens more renewable energy projects on public lands pending, the environmental and energy benefits will increase considerably in the coming years.

In addition, the growing use of renewable energy is having an impact on the U.S. workforce. One study found that every megawatt of solar photovoltaic (PV) power installed can create up to thirty "job years" (the equivalent of thirty people working for one year). The Solar Foundation found that the solar industry employed more than 142,000 people in 2013, up from 93,000 in 2010.[38] With respect to both wind and geothermal energy, organizations supportive of these industries estimate that every megawatt installed results in four new jobs.[39]

Despite these benefits, and even though solar, wind, and geothermal technologies emit no air pollution or carbon dioxide, the placement of renewable energy on public lands has not been without conflict. Some of the most significant disputes involve environmental impacts on land and water usage, along with disruption of habitat for native species. This has put supporters of renewable energy projects at odds with interest groups committed to environmental preservation. As Defenders of Wildlife stated, "We must accelerate the transition to clean energy in America . . . [but] unless renewable energy generation and transmission projects are carefully planned and their environmental impacts thoroughly evaluated, wildlife, habitat, key corridors, and unique wild lands and natural resources can be substantially altered, impacted, or destroyed."[40]

Solar. Siting solar power on public lands has rapidly increased, but project authorization can be time-consuming and costly. Projects require the approval of right-of-way applications, special use requests, and environmental impact statements. These allow the BLM to evaluate whether a project meets regulatory requirements, and to ensure that the environmental impacts are understood.[41] As part of the Obama administration's emphasis on accelerating the development of renewable energy, the DOI has sought to speed up this process, and in 2012, it released a "Programmatic Environmental Impact Statement" that identified seventeen solar energy zones on federal lands in Arizona, California, Colorado, Nevada, New Mexico, and Utah. It also placed millions of acres off limits due to potential environmental impacts, along with areas of historic or cultural value.[42]

Moreover, the development of large solar farms on public lands continues to be controversial. While solar power is considered a clean energy source, it can prove taxing on natural resources. Solar PV requires six to eight acres for every megawatt of power. Concentrating solar power (CSP), which uses mirrors to focus solar energy onto a boiler that heats water and spins a turbine, requires even more space. For example, the Ivanpah CSP project in the Mojave Desert uses almost 3,500 acres of land (5.5 square miles) to produce 370 MW of power. (In contrast, a coal plant requires less than one acre for each megawatt of power, not counting the land used for coal mining.) Most BLM projects approved to date involve tens of thousands of acres in the desert lands of California, Nevada, and Arizona.[43]

Solar can also have an effect on wildlife habitat and water usage. Projects require land to be cleared and leveled (and sometimes fenced) for both generation facilities and transmission lines. In the Mojave and Sonoran deserts, this can result in habitat loss or habitat fragmentation for endangered or threatened species such as the desert tortoise, the golden eagle, and the Mojave ground squirrel. The Ivanpah project has faced scrutiny and opposition for destroying or altering wildlife habitat, clearing away native plants, and even killing or wounding birds (usually a criticism of wind turbines, not solar power) that fly into the path of the concentrated solar rays and get burned. It has also demonstrated the drawbacks of CSP technology in dry climates. Unlike solar PV, which uses no water to generate electricity, CSP typically requires 600–650 gallons of water to generate steam for every megawatt-hour produced.[44]

An unexpected impact of the push to expand solar power on public lands has been the political divide among different interest groups on the political left. While the Bush administration faced criticism from environmentalists and Democrats for making insufficient use of public lands to develop renewable energy resources, the Obama administration has faced criticism from some of the same organizations for insufficient regard to the negative environmental impacts of solar energy. Environmental advocates have been divided on this issue, depending upon whether a group's primary focus is carbon emissions and climate change or wildlife and habitat protection.

Wind. The development of wind energy on public lands is similar to that for solar power. Permits are required for rights of way and special uses, and environmental impacts have to be assessed. The BLM completed a Programmatic Environmental Impact Statement in 2005 to identify suitable areas for wind turbines and speed up the approval process. However, wind energy development has proceeded more slowly on public lands than solar energy.

Similar to solar power, wind energy has generated conflict regarding environmental impacts, most notably the threat to birds and bats from spinning turbines. Colliding with wind turbines, which extend up to four hundred feet tall, can prove fatal to birds, and many endangered species and migratory birds such as eagles, cranes, hawks, raptors, and falcons have suffered fatalities from wind turbines. It is estimated that 140,000 to 328,000 birds are killed by U.S. wind turbines each year, though the American Bird Conservancy estimates the loss at 573,000 deaths per year.[45]

Wind power has also faced opposition from communities located near wind farms. In addition to the potential effect on birds, large wind turbines are charged with harming the pristine nature of certain locations. The Cape Wind project, a planned offshore wind farm in Nantucket Sound, was granted a lease by the BOEM, but the project prompted several lawsuits, as leading environmentalists such as Robert F. Kennedy Jr. fought for years alongside their conservative opposition, David Koch, of Koch Industries, in association with tourist and commercial fishing interests to stop the farm. Opponents of wind power also cite concerns with public health, arguing that turbines produce sounds and vibrations that can cause headaches, nausea, dizziness, insomnia, and blurred vision. And despite the fact that a significant body of research has shown that "wind turbine syndrome" is not real, these criticisms continue to energize wind power opponents.[46]

Geothermal. Geothermal power has also seen growth on public lands in recent years. The BLM currently manages fifty-nine geothermal leases with a capacity of 1,500 MW. Unlike wind and solar, but like oil and gas deposits, geothermal power on federal land is administered by issuing leases obtained through competitive bidding. This process has netted the BLM over $76 million since 2007.[47] The primary concerns associated with geothermal power are potential water contamination and gas leaks, but there is also evidence to indicate that geothermal energy can cause increased seismic activity. Concerns over earthquakes have led Hawaiians to call for a hold on geothermal development until stricter regulations are put in place.[48]

The Keystone XL Pipeline

In Alberta, Canada, there is an immense deposit of oil sands—a mixture of oil, sand, and water. Requiring a price of $50 per barrel to be considered economically recoverable, the estimated 170 billion–barrel reserve is second in size only to Saudi Arabia. With the expected doubling of the production level by 2020 to over three million barrels per day, the oil sands would produce more than Venezuela, Nigeria, or Iraq, and supply the equivalent of nearly 20 percent of U.S. oil consumption. The expansion plans are the reason behind TransCanada's proposed seventeen-hundred-mile, 800,000-barrel-per-day, highly contested Keystone XL pipeline to the United States, which, together with expanded development, raises concerns about environmental damage.

The battle over Keystone XL is occurring despite the fact that "[t]he American public is firmly behind the pipeline," with majorities in favor ranging from 57 to 65 percent.[49] The support for building Keystone XL reaches across the partisan divide with majority support among Democrats (51 percent), Republicans (82 percent), and Independents (64 percent). It also reaches across age groups, with 55 percent support from those under age thirty and 67 percent from those over thirty. As well, the more information individuals have about Keystone XL, the more likely they are to support it (70 percent).[50] The political realities behind the decision to build or not to build Keystone XL, of course, are more complicated than this and are grounded in passionate support for different sets of values and priorities by influential actors in the American political system. Understanding the underlying politics, all too often grounded in the strategic symbolic importance of Keystone to partisans on both sides of the "carbon (fossil fuels)–climate change" divide, helps to explain why the Obama administration long delayed its decision on whether to approve the pipeline.

Understanding two different sides of the same coin. Proponents of Keystone XL are concerned primarily with expanding supply and energy reliability. Believing that a growing U.S. economy requires significantly more oil, even with expected efficiency gains from new technologies and stricter CAFE fuel standards for vehicles, the pipeline is viewed as important for securing more oil. Further, it reduces U.S. reliance on less reliable sources like the Middle East and Venezuela in favor of Canada, with its stable democracy and shared interests. This perspective coincides with the belief, shared by 65 percent of the U.S. public, that renewables will be unable to fill the need for more energy.[51] Polling also indicates that while Americans and Canadians "believe that reducing greenhouse gases is important, energy security is driving views ... [and] trumps reducing greenhouse gases as a policy priority."[52]

Nor do proponents think that the environmental costs of building Keystone XL will be significant. The cornerstone of this argument is their firm belief that the strategic and economic value of the Alberta oil sands to Canada are such that Canada will exploit the energy anyway, whether by the alternative Northern Gateway pipeline to the Pacific Ocean to serve Asian markets or the expansion of rail shipping capacity.

These expectations are supported by the final U.S. State Department environmental review released in January 2014, which concluded that Keystone XL would not significantly exacerbate climate change for these same reasons, finding instead that carbon emissions are more likely to increase given the added energy and emissions "costs" emanating from "substitute" rail transportation. Proponents also note that the risks, and environmental costs, from pipeline leaks are far less than carrying oil by rail.[53]

Finally, the economics of building Keystone XL are critical for its supporters. With a total estimated construction cost of $5.4 billion, they claim that project spending would support anywhere from 30,000 to 90,000 jobs (direct, indirect, and induced) and approximately $2 billion in earnings throughout the United States. Of these jobs, approximately 3,900 would be direct construction jobs.[54] In addition, long-term benefits are expected through lower energy costs, as well as added jobs at refineries and shipping companies in Texas and at U.S. oil companies, more generally.

Opponents, on the other hand, are concerned far more with how supply expansion from the oil sands will contribute to environmental degradation, including climate change. From this perspective, the environmental costs are simply too great to ignore, whether it is from pipeline spills or the severe degradation to the boreal forests, wetlands, and wildlife given the "strip mining" character of most oil recovery. In areas with deeper oil, steam must be injected into the ground in order to melt the oil tar prior to extracting it. Both processes are heavily energy intensive, requiring the energy equivalent of one barrel of oil for every four to eight barrels recovered. In addition, environmentalists are concerned about the impacts of the pipeline itself, forcing TransCanada to reroute around the Nebraska Sandhills, a unique ecosystem of grassland directly over the Ogallala Aquifer, the main source of groundwater for many Midwesterners.

Opponents also point to estimates that Canada's oil sands crude emits more GHGs on a life cycle basis than other oils. When compared to "average" *imported* U.S. crude oil, Alberta's crude emits 17 percent more GHGs.[55] When compared to *all* crude oil refined in the United States, the EPA found that "[l]ifecycle emissions from oil sands crude could be 81 percent greater."[56]

Other than the short-term boost in construction hiring, opponents also discount the economic benefits, arguing that lower gasoline prices are unlikely.[57] Many expect the majority of Keystone's oil to be exported outside the United States given that they will be free to sell the Canadian tar sands oil at the highest price they can find globally, while the pipeline's capacity constitutes only 4.2 percent of the 18.87 million daily U.S. demand (year 2013).[58]

Given this, environmentalists argue that a smarter way forward would entail policies either reducing the demand for oil and gasoline, or expanding supply using wind, solar, geothermal, and biomass sources. And while the employment gains for renewable energy development are not expected to be as much as Keystone XL, they have the added benefit of reducing carbon emissions.

Those against Keystone XL are likewise convinced that stopping the pipeline will also stop the expansion of oil development, pointing to a Canadian pro-oil think tank, which found that "investment and expansion will grind to a halt" without the pipeline.[59] Opponents also point to EPA analyses suggesting that the considerable legal and logistical hurdles associated with increasing railroad traffic will also hamper future development.[60]

Politics and the decision to build ... or delay? All of these considerations, and the partisan battling among competing interests, would pose a political dilemma for any president with responsibility for making a decision on the Keystone XL pipeline. Bill McKibben of 350.org and other environmentalists think it's an easy call for President Obama given that climate change and environmental costs should trump other priorities (see Chapter 3). Yet, the Obama administration's decision has been made more difficult by the realities of American politics that help to explain why he long delayed the final decision.[61]

First, Keystone presented Obama with an intraparty dilemma. Stopping the pipeline would uphold the longstanding Democratic Party commitment to its climate change agenda, thus satisfying environmentalists—a core constituency. But it also would be counter to the preferences of most private sector unions, another major constituency and a source of hundreds of millions in campaign funding.

Second, President Obama received pressure to build Keystone XL from both Democratic and Republican politicians from Montana, South Dakota, Nebraska, Kansas, Oklahoma, and Texas. These are the states most directly affected by the pipeline and poised to see more jobs and tax revenue, which has contributed to strong public support. Despite this, there are grassroots groups in some of these states that oppose the pipeline. For example, many ranchers in Nebraska, a traditional Republican constituency, oppose Keystone for fear of potential pipeline leaks onto their land and into the Ogallala Aquifer, their main water source, and the fact that it is an "export pipeline not in the national interest."[62]

Third, the experts in two major executive branch agencies—the EPA and State Department—have given the president conflicting advice on the pipeline's environmental and economic "facts." Which set of experts should he rely on?

Fourth, united opposition by the GOP and American business has been a double-edged sword. The president scored political points for delay from environmentalists and liberals, but in preventing construction during a period of weak economic growth and with an average gasoline price increase of over

50 percent since taking office, he risked seeming insensitive to the plight of consumers and the unemployed. The dramatic, and expected-to-be-prolonged, drop in the international price of oil in late 2014 from over $100 to under $65 a barrel, however, will make the GOP's case for building Keystone harder.

Finally, the heated battle over Keystone points to the importance of symbolism. The oil pipeline debate has been less about technical and economic "facts," and more about the strategic importance of Keystone as a symbol of American values and priorities in the larger battle over climate change. Many opponents view Keystone as an assault on, and rejection of, the proposition that climate change is occurring, while also distracting from the urgent need to develop renewable energy sources. Thus, if built, it would signal a major defeat in their push to wean the United States and the world off their dependence on fossil fuels.[63] For business and GOP conservatives, on the other hand, Keystone symbolizes the value of free markets, economic growth (and jobs), and technological progress. Building Keystone thus would represent a victory for a more conservative political agenda.[64]

Conclusion

The cases of hydraulic fracturing, renewable energy on public lands, and the Keystone XL pipeline show that the quest for the energy required to power modern economies and meet basic social needs is a critical public policy issue beset with major challenges as well as sharp political and partisan conflicts. These challenges have been made more explicit by the U.S. drive to seek greater energy independence using an amalgamation of policies and new technologies that not only support oil and natural gas development, but also renewable energy development and conservation through energy efficiency measures. Complicating the picture is the specter of climate change, with consequent pressure to lessen carbon emissions.

Taken together, these developments make it clear that modern societies, the U.S. included, want energy to do more things than ever before: support and grow the economy while minimizing or eliminating environmental and national security impacts. Put differently, we want energy that is abundant, reliable, affordable, clean, and diversified (in terms of both fuel sources and the countries that supply it). Yet, precisely because no single energy source gives us all of these things, we inevitably end up with policies that support some of these goals at the cost of others.

Another key lesson is the fragmented nature of U.S. energy policy and the seeming lack of national priorities, which in turn reflects the sharp partisan divisions over energy policy. There is no agreement in Congress on what to do, and different presidents can, and do, have dramatically different energy priorities. The climate change debate—and gridlock in Congress—as much as anything, illustrates the disagreement over contemporary and future energy policy (see Chapter 5). Each side of the debate claims to be fighting for the public interest, but neither side appears willing to explore the "radical middle" upon which a national climate change policy, much less a national energy policy, is likely to be built. This fragmentation also results from shared policy control by multiple federal and state authorities, and democratic processes that allow vocal and well-funded interest groups to influence policy choices. In addition, the United States' distinctive property (mineral) rights system grants significant power to individual landowners. Seen from this perspective, and as evidenced in the three cases outlined above, the conflict and cacophony that define contemporary U.S. energy politics seems unlikely to change anytime soon. This is likely to remain the case in spite of Republicans retaking control of the U.S. Senate and adding to their majority in the U.S. House in the 2014 elections.

Suggested Websites

U.S. Energy Information Administration (EIA) *Total Energy* website (www.eia.gov/totalenergy) Contains independent energy statistics and analysis across energy types, trends, and more. A great basic source of information.

The State Energy Data System (www.eia.gov/state/seds/?src=email& src=Total-f4) The source of the EIA's comprehensive state energy statistics. The EIA's goal in maintaining the system is to create historical time series of energy production, consumption, prices, and expenditures by state that are defined as consistently as possible over time and across sectors for analysis and forecasting purposes.

Global Statistical Energy Yearbook 2013 (http://yearbook.enerdata.net) A comprehensive database on energy supply, demand, prices, and GHG emissions for 186 countries.

Database of State Incentives (and Policies) for Renewables and Efficiency (www.dsireusa.org/incentives/index.cfm?state=us) U.S. Department of Energy.

Notes

1. Energy Information Administration, *Annual Energy Outlook 2014*, Early Release, December 2013; "Pricing Sunshine," *The Economist*, December 28, 2012.
2. Energy Information Administration, *Monthly Energy Review*, April 2014.
3. Daniel Steinberg, Gian Porro, and Marshall Goldberg, *Preliminary Analysis of the Jobs and Economic Impacts of the Renewable Energy Projects Supported by the 1603 Treasury Grant Program* (Golden, CO: National Renewable Energy Laboratory, NREL/TP-6A20-52739, April 2012).
4. Brian Ferrasci-O'Malley, "Recent Developments Regarding Avian Take at Wind Farms," January 27, 2014, available at www.martenlaw.com/newsletter/20140127 -avian-take-wind-farms#_edn37.
5. National Audubon Society, "Interior Dept. Rule Greenlights Eagle Slaughter at Wind Farms, Says Audubon CEO," December 5, 2013, available at www.audubon.org/ newsroom/press-releases/2013/interior-dept-rule-greenlights-eagle-slaughter-wind -farms-says-audubon.
6. Barry Rabe, *Statehouse and Greenhouse: The Emerging Politics of American Climate Change Policy* (Washington, DC: Brookings, 2004).

7. For plants coming online in year 2019. Energy Information Administration, *Levelized Costs: Annual Energy Outlook* (Washington, DC: U.S. Department of Energy, April 17, 2014), available at www.eia.gov/forecasts/aeo/electricity_generation.cfm.

8. Energy Information Administration, *Levelized Costs*.

9. Nicholas Z. Muller, Robert Mendelsohn, and William Nordhaus, "Environmental Accounting for Pollution in the United States Economy," *American Economic Review* 101, no. 5 (2011): 1649–75.

10. International Energy Agency, *World Energy Outlook 2012* (Paris, France: International Energy Agency, 2012).

11. U.S. Department of Energy, *Annual Energy Outlook, 2012* (Washington, DC: U.S. Department of Energy, 2012).

12. David Kay, "The Economic Impact of Marcellus Shale Gas Drilling: What Have We Learned? What Are the Limitations?" Working paper series: *A Comprehensive Economic Impact Analysis of Natural Gas Extraction in the Marcellus Shale* (Ithaca, NY: Cornell University, 2011).

13. Elizabeth Rosenberg, *Energy Rush: Shale Production and U.S. National Security* (Washington, DC: Center for New American Security, Report of the Unconventional Energy and U.S. National Security Task Force, 2014).

14. U.S. Department of Energy, *Annual Energy Outlook 2013 Early Release Overview* (Washington, DC: U.S. Department of Energy, 2013).

15. Robert W. Howarth, "A Bridge to Nowhere: Methane Emissions and the Greenhouse Gas Footprint of Natural Gas," *Energy Science & Engineering* 2, no. 2 (2014): 47–60, doi: 10.1002/ese3.35. See also Adam R. Brandt et al., "Methane Leaks from North American Natural Gas Systems," *Science* 343, no. 6172 (2014): 733–35.

16. Daniel J. Soeder and William M. Kappel, *Water Resources and Natural Gas Production from the Marcellus Shale* (Washington, DC: U.S. Geological Survey, Department of the Interior, 2009).

17. David M. Kargbo, Ron G. Wilhelm, and David J. Campbell, "Natural Gas Plays in the Marcellus Shale: Challenges and Potential Opportunities," *Environmental Science & Technology* 44, no. 15 (2010): 5679–84.

18. Jeffrey Jacquet, "Energy Boomtowns and Natural Gas: Implications for Marcellus Shale Local Governments and Rural Communities," *NERCRD Rural Development* (2009).

19. Katie M. Keranen et al., "Sharp Increase in Central Oklahoma Seismicity Since 2008 Induced by Massive Wastewater Injection," *Science* 345, no. 6195 (2014): 448–51. doi: 10.1126/science.1255802.

20. Hilary Boudet et al., "Fracking Controversy and Communication: Using National Survey Data to Understand Public Perceptions of Hydraulic Fracturing," *Energy Policy* 65 (2013): 57–67.

21. Ibid.

22. Ibid.

23. Executive Office of the President of the United States, "The All-of-the-Above Energy Strategy as a Path to Sustainable Economic Growth" (Washington, DC: White House, May 2014), available at www.whitehouse.gov/sites/default/files/docs/aota_energy_strategy_as_a_path_to_sustainable_economic_growth.pdf, p. 5.

24. Lisa Sumi, "Our Drinking Water at Risk: What EPA and the Oil and Gas Industry Don't Want Us to Know about Hydraulic Fracturing," *Oil and Gas Accountability Project* (2005).

25. U.S. Environmental Protection Agency, "Evaluation of Impacts to Underground Sources of Drinking Water by Hydraulic Fracturing of Coalbed Methane Reservoirs," 816-R-01-003 (Washington, DC: Environmental Protection Agency, 2004).

26. Dianne Rahm, "Regulating Hydraulic Fracturing in Shale Gas Plays: The Case of Texas," *Energy Policy* 39, no. 5 (2011): 2974–81.
27. Nathan Richardson, Madeline Gottlieb, Alan Krupnick, and Hannah Wiseman, *The State of State Shale Gas Regulation* (Washington, DC: Resources for the Future, 2013).
28. Ibid.
29. Mead Gruver, "Wyoming High Court Remands Fracking Secrets Case," *Associated Press*, May 12, 2014, available at http://bigstory.ap.org/article/wyoming-high-court -remands-fracking-secrets-case.
30. Julie C. Smyth, "Ohio Geologists Link Small Quakes to Fracking," *Associated Press*, April 11, 2014.
31. Stephanie Paige Ogburn and ClimateWire, "Colorado First State to Limit Methane Pollution from Oil and Gas Wells," *Scientific American*, February 25, 2014.
32. Associated Press, "Pennsylvania Supreme Court Strikes Part of Industry-Friendly Fracking Law," December 20, 2013.
33. Mireya Navarro, "New York Judge Rules Town Can Ban Gas Hydrofracking," *New York Times*, February 21, 2012.
34. Bureau of Land Management, "Summary of Onshore Oil and Gas Statistics" (Washington, DC: U.S. Department of the Interior, 2013), available at www.blm .gov/wo/st/en/prog/energy/oil_and_gas/statistics.html.
35. Bureau of Land Management, "Renewable Energy Projects Approved Since the Beginning of Calendar Year 2009" (Washington, DC: U.S. Department of the Interior, 2014), available at www.blm.gov/wo/st/en/prog/energy/renewable_energy/Renewable_ Energy_Projects_Approved_to_Date.html.
36. Bureau of Land Management, "New Energy for America" (Washington, DC: U.S. Department of the Interior, 2014), available at www.blm.gov/wo/st/en/prog/energy/ renewable_energy.html.
37. Ibid.
38. Daniel M. Kammen, Kamal Kapadia, and Mattias Fripp, "Putting Renewables to Work: How Many Jobs Can the Clean Energy Industry Generate?" Report of the Renewable and Appropriate Energy Laboratory (Berkeley: University of California, April 2004); Solar Foundation, *National Solar Jobs Census 2013* (Washington, DC: Solar Foundation, January 2014). These studies use different approaches to measuring employment impacts.
39. Natural Resources Defense Council, *American Wind Farms: Breaking Down the Benefits from Planning to Production* (Washington, DC: Natural Resources Defense Council, September 2012); Geothermal Energy Association, "Geothermal Basics—Employment" (Washington, DC: Geothermal Energy Association, 2014), available at www.geo-energy .org/geo_basics_employement.aspx.
40. Defenders of Wildlife, *Making Renewable Energy Wildlife Friendly* (Washington, DC: Defenders of Wildlife, 2014), available at www.defenders.org/sites/default/files/ publications/making_renewable_energy_wildlife_friendly.pdf.
41. Timothy Duane and Siobhan McIntyre, "Water, Work, Wildlife, and Wilderness: The Collaborative Federal Public Lands Planning Framework for Utility-Scale Solar Energy Development in the Desert Southwest," *Environmental Law* 41 (Fall 2011): 1093–102.
42. Bureau of Land Management, "Solar Energy Program" (Washington, DC: U.S. Department of the Interior, 2014), available at http://blmsolar.anl.gov/.
43. National Renewable Energy Laboratory, *Land-Use Requirements for Solar Power Plants in the United States* (Technical Report NREL/TP-6A20-56290) (Golden, CO: National Renewable Energy Laboratory, June 2013), available at www.nrel.gov/docs/ fy13osti/56290.pdf; Bureau of Land Management, *Renewable Energy Projects Approved Since the Beginning of Calendar Year 2009.*

44. Union of Concerned Scientists, *Environmental Impacts of Solar Power* (Cambridge, MA: Union of Concerned Scientists, 2014), available at www.ucsusa.org/clean_energy/our-energy-choices/renewable-energy/environmental-impacts-solar-power.html.

45. Scott R. Loss, Tom Will, and Peter P. Marra, "Estimates of Bird Collision Mortality at Wind Facilities in the Contiguous United States," *Biological Conservation* 168 (December 2013): 202–07, available at 10.1016/j.biocon.2013.10.007.

46. For example, see Fiona Crichton et al., "Can Expectations Produce Symptoms from Infrasound Associated with Wind Turbines?" *Health Psychology* 33, no. 4 (March 11, 2013): 360–64.

47. Bureau of Land Management, "Geothermal Energy" (Washington, DC: U.S. Department of the Interior, 2014), available at www.blm.gov/wo/st/en/prog/energy/geothermal.html.

48. John Burnett, "Hundreds Protest against Geothermal Development," *Hawaii Tribune-Herald*, August 20, 2013.

49. Steven Mufson, "Continued Support for Keystone XL Pipeline," *Washington Post*, September 26, 2012. Polls include 2012–2014 polls from Gallup, *New York Times, Washington Post*, the Pew Center, Rasmussen, and *Wall Street Journal*.

50. Mufson, "Continued Support for Keystone XL Pipeline."

51. Rasmussen Reports, "65% Don't Think U.S. Does Enough to Develop Its Energy Resources" (2013), available at www.rasmussenreports.com/public_content/archive/environment_energy_update_archive/65_don_t_think_u_s_does_enough_to_develop_its_energy_resources.

52. Theophilos Argitis, "Poll Finds More U.S. Support for Keystone Than Canadian," *Bloomberg Sustainability*, April 22, 2013, available at www.bloomberg.com/news/2013-04-22/americans-support-keystone-more-than-canadians-poll-says.html.

53. U.S. Department of State, *Keystone Pipeline Project, Final Supplemental Environmental Impact Statement (SEIS)* (January 2014), available at http://keystonepipeline-xl.state.gov/finalseis/.

54. Ibid.

55. Richard K. Lattanzio, "Canadian Oil Sands: Life-Cycle Assessments of Greenhouse Gas Emissions" (Washington, DC: Congressional Research Service, March 2014), available at www.fas.org/sgp/crs/misc/R42537.pdf.

56. David Biello, "EPA on Keystone XL: Significant Climate Impacts from Tar Sands Pipeline" (Washington, DC: Environmental Protection Agency, April 2013).

57. Mark Clayton, "Inside the Keystone Pipeline: How Much Would It Really Help US Consumers?" *Christian Science Monitor*, March 9, 2012.

58. Jeremiah Goulka, "Pipeline or Pipe Bomb?" *American Prospect*, February 6, 2014, available at http://prospect.org/article/pipeline-or-pipe-bomb.

59. As quoted in Goulka (2014). The report is "Pipe or Perish: Saving an Oil Industry at Risk," Canada West Foundation, February 7, 2013, available at http://cwf.ca/publications-1/pipe-or-perish.

60. Biello, "EPA on Keystone XL."

61. Even though the U.S. State Department has jurisdiction, the final decision is left to the discretion of the president.

62. Dan Frosch, "Keystone Pipeline Foes Vent in Nebraska," *New York Times*, April 18, 2013.

63. See 350.org and the Sierra Club website at http://content.sierraclub.org/beyondoil/.

64. Good examples here come from the Heritage Foundation's webpage and journal—*The Daily Signal*.

9

Eating and the Environment
Ecological Impacts of Food Production
Christopher J. Bosso and Nicole E. Tichenor

Eating is an agricultural act.

—Wendell Berry[1]

In 1971, President Richard Nixon nominated Purdue University agricultural economist Earl Butz to lead the U.S. Department of Agriculture (USDA). Butz, who served as assistant secretary of agriculture in the Dwight D. Eisenhower administration, faced questioning from farm state senators during his confirmation hearing over whether his links to agribusiness firms would bias his views on farm policy. In response, Butz averred that companies like Ralston Purina were essential because they converted raw commodities into food products. Otherwise, "the bushel of wheat in Kansas has no value until it becomes bread for Mrs. Housewife." Even so, Butz promised, he would be a "vigorous spokesman" for all farmers.[2]

Butz gained confirmation, and in his five years in office shaped a U.S. agricultural policy that would encourage, if not compel, unlimited production of commodities like corn, soybeans, cattle, and pigs. "Get big or get out," Butz was known to say about (if not to) farmers. Under Butz, and to this day, U.S. agricultural policy would be guided by one goal: plentiful, inexpensive food for all Americans.

That policy, enshrined in successive "farm bills," achieved its objectives. Over the next four decades, even as fewer Americans farmed the land, U.S. agricultural output skyrocketed. Farms grew larger and became more productive as farmers tapped new seed and animal varieties, more sophisticated farm machinery, chemical inputs ranging from herbicides to animal antibiotics, and technologies like genetically modified (GM) seeds. Butz always defended the system he shaped, noting in 1998: "We feed ourselves in this country now with about 11% of our take-home pay, which means we feed ourselves with about 6% of our gross domestic product. That includes all the built in service you get at the store now. Imagine: 11% of take home pay, leaves 89% for everything that makes life so wonderful in America."[3] Today, the average American spends 10 percent of net income on food, whether eaten at home or outside of it, the lowest level per capita in the world.[4]

Also in 1971, a 26-year-old activist named Frances Moore Lappé penned *Diet for a Small Planet*, which went on to sell over 3 million copies.

While Lappé's intent was to pose a vegetarian alternative to a "wasteful" meat-based diet and shift use of grain to address global food scarcity, she also took aim at the very logic of the food system that Butz promoted. Large-scale beef production in particular, Lappé argued, not only diverted grain from other uses; it also depended on massive inputs of energy, water, and synthetic chemicals (in the form of fertilizers and pesticides), and produced externalities like water pollution from animal manure.[5]

Earl Butz built and exemplified the dominant food system; Frances Moore Lappé became his, and his system's, antithesis. As such, the two stand as compelling bookends for examining the environmental impacts of food production. Butz and his successors promoted a food system defined by economies of scale, norms of specialization, mechanization, efficiency, and high reliance on capital, energy, and technology.[6] Lappé and a growing community of activists like her, speaking from diverse ideological perspectives, serve as critics and reformers, shining harsh lights on a food system that, for all of its productivity, comes at real human and ecological costs.[7]

This chapter examines the ecological impacts of the food system, the U.S. environmental laws relevant to (if not always addressing) those impacts, and ideas for reducing the food system's negative externalities even as it continues to focus on feeding the greatest number at the lowest possible monetary cost. That inherent tension pervades our discussion.

The Food System

It bears reminding: Americans are accustomed to food that is plentiful, diverse, convenient, and inexpensive. Or, to put it plainly, for most Americans, the food system gives us what we want, when we want it, at a price we're willing to pay. This is no trivial achievement. While the United States started out with advantages in arable land and conducive growing conditions, much of today's abundance is due to key characteristics of the food system Earl Butz promoted.

Industrial Scale

A sector once marked by millions of small farms gave way over time to far fewer and larger operations. Farm consolidation was already a fact when Butz took office, the total number having plummeted from 6.5 million in 1935 to 2.7 million in 1975, and average size growing from 155 to 391 acres. Despite a modest uptick in the number of smaller farms (fewer than 10 acres) due to rising demand for local food, the overall number continues to fall, to about 2.1 million in 2012, with average size now 434 acres.[8] More telling, by 2012, 3.8 percent of farms accounted for 66 percent of the market value of all agricultural products.[9] In this instance, scale matters. While 1,000 acres devoted to strawberries would be a large and profitable operation, a 1,000-acre corn farm is considered small or mid-scale, and economically marginal.[10] As one USDA study put it, "An economically viable crop/livestock operation in the Corn Belt would have between 2,000 and 3,000 acres of row crops and between 500 and 600 sows."[11]

Emphasis on Efficiency

The system is efficient in classical industrial terms. For example, in 1970, approximately 67 million acres were dedicated to field corn (versus sweet corn, which is less than 1 percent of all corn produced), with each acre yielding 72 bushels on average. By 2013, due partly to federal farm policies stressing production and mandates supporting corn ethanol (see Box 9-1), land devoted to corn had gone up to 95 million acres. More important, production per acre *doubled*, to 160 bushels—about 14 billion bushels overall. Put in perspective, the United States produces 2 bushels (or 120 pounds) of field corn for each of the 7 billion persons now alive. About 40 percent of that output goes to ethanol, another 40 percent into animal feed.[12] What Michael Pollan vividly describes as a "river of corn"[13] thus enables the United States to produce around 43 billion pounds of poultry, 26 billion pounds of beef, and 23 billion pounds of pork each year—290 pounds per American.[14]

Box 9-1   Debating Corn Ethanol

By law, gasoline in the United States must contain at least 10 percent ethanol, an oxygenated "biofuel" derived from various feedstocks, including sugarcane, certain grasses, and field corn. Most ethanol in the United States is derived from corn, with annual production escalating from 175 million barrels in the early 1980s to 13 billion barrels in 2013.[1]

The merits of corn ethanol are contested. To supporters, which include Midwest corn growers, ethanol producers, and Corn Belt members of Congress, governors, state legislatures, and affected communities, it is renewable, lessens U.S. dependence on imported oil, reduces greenhouse gas emissions, and supports American farmers.[2] To critics, which include national environmental groups, alternative energy advocates, and free market economists, it depends on billions in government subsidies and encourages overproduction of corn, with attendant commodity market distortions and ecological harms. Moreover, fermenting corn into ethanol requires massive amounts of water and energy—more net energy than ethanol generates—via a process that itself emits greenhouse gases.[3] Despite severe criticism, corn ethanol survives, nurtured by its political support in the nation's Corn Belt.

---

1. Darrel Good, *Corn Used in Ethanol Production*, University of Illinois at Urbana-Champaign, 2013, farmdocdaily.illinois.edu/2013/11/corn-used-ethanol-production.html.
2. Renewable Fuels Association, *Ethanol Facts*, www.ethanolrfa.org/pages/ethanol-facts-environment.
3. Gary Libecap, "Agricultural Programs with Dubious Environmental Benefits: The Political Economy of Ethanol," in *Agricultural Policy and the Environment*, ed. Roger Meiners and Bruce Yandle (Lanham, MD: Rowman and Littlefield, 2003), 89–106.

Or take dairy. From 1970 to 2012, the number of dairy cows in the United States dropped from 12 million to just over 9 million, and the number of dairy operations from 650,000 to about 90,000, due in part to federal policies favoring larger and more efficient operations. At the same time, average herd sizes went from 20 to 100 cows and per-cow milk output from 9,700 to 21,700 pounds per year. The result was a near *doubling* of dairy production from 117 billion pounds in 1970 to over 200 billion pounds in 2012.[15] Fewer farms, fewer cows—more milk than ever.

Specialized

Imperatives of scale and efficiency drive specialization. Where American farmers once practiced some version of *polyculture*—such as rotating two or three row crops annually while also raising some cattle and hogs—today's "factory in the field" stresses *monoculture*—devoting all acreage to one crop, such as corn or soybeans. While farmers may alternate years of corn with soy depending on market demand, it is typically *all* corn or *all* soy. Specialization extends to animals, notably in Concentrated Animal Feeding Operations (CAFOs) in which thousands of cattle or hogs, and tens of thousands of chickens or turkeys, are fattened for market in controlled environments on calibrated and nutritionally augmented corn- or soy-based feed.[16] In Iowa, for example, the percentage of farmers raising hogs fell from 70 percent in 1964 to 11 percent by 2000, yet *total* hog production stayed stable.[17] Nationally, the number of farms raising hogs dropped from 700,000 in 1980 to 68,300 in 2012, and facilities of more than 5,000 head now produce 62 percent of all hogs.[18] Similar trends are seen for beef and poultry.

Technologized

Agriculture is a temple to technology, from large global positioning system–guided seeders (to ensure straight rows) and harvesters to computer-calibrated application of fertilizers, animal and seed hybrids (GM and otherwise), animal growth hormones and antibiotics, and synthetic chemical herbicides, pesticides, and fungicides. Such capital-intensive technologies have replaced people in the fields, enabling the few who farm to obtain greater yields on more land with less labor. In 1940, nearly 31 million Americans, 25 percent of the population, worked the farm. In 2012, it was 3.1 million—a farming 1 percent feeding everyone else.[19]

Energy-Dependent

Industrial-scale, mechanized, technologized agriculture runs on energy— a lot of it. Not including the largely carbon-based fuels that power the nation's electrical grid and move food from processing facilities to consumers, contemporary agriculture depends on natural gas to produce the ammonium nitrate that is the building block of synthetic nitrogen fertilizers, petroleum to catalyze

a wide range of chemical pesticides, and gasoline and diesel fuel to power trac-
tors, combines, trucks, irrigation pumps, and on-site processing facilities. Total
energy use in agriculture comes to about 1.6 trillion British thermal units
(BTU) per year, compared to 8 trillion BTUs used annually by all U.S. households.[20] While agriculture has made efficiency gains in terms of gallons of oil
per bushel of crops produced, the economic health of this sector, as with the
nation, is affected by the availability and cost of oil and natural gas.[21]

Globalized

Finally, the food system is inextricably global. U.S. farmers produce far
more food than Americans can possibly eat, and agricultural exports come to
more than $140 billion a year, about 10 percent of total U.S. exports by
value.[22] Yet Americans also import 40 percent of fresh fruits and vegetables
and 85 percent of seafood.[23] If you live in Green Bay and want fresh raspber-
ries in February, you can get them, shipped in by air from South America.
What you want, when you want it, at a price you're willing to pay.

Ecological Impacts of Food Production

It also bears reminding that agriculture, *however* practiced, has ecological impacts. As plant geneticist Nina Fedoroff put it, with perhaps a little
hyperbole, "agriculture is more devastating ecologically than anything else we
could do except pouring concrete on the land."[24] In the United States,
despite a lingering agrarian ideal of small scale, self-sufficient farms, the reality of contemporary conventional food production is industrial, in all the
term's connotations and ecological impacts.

Land and Water Use

The United States devotes approximately 45 percent of its total land to
agriculture, as compared to 84 percent for Nigeria, for example.[25] However,
unlike Nigeria, that 45 percent is typically farmed in highly intensive ways. The
shift to large-scale, mechanized monoculture, combined with a global commodity market that places a premium on volume and price, has resulted in the literal
application of Earl Butz's oft-cited exhortation to plant "fencepost to fencepost." Those growing crops like corn and soy have every incentive to maximize
production, leaving little land to lie fallow and refresh the soil, or set aside for
woodlands. The result, critics argue, is a tragic loss of topsoil to degraded fertility through overuse or to erosion from wind and water. In the Midwest grain
belt, for example, topsoil loss from erosion is estimated to be 343 million tons
per year, much of it eventually washing down the Mississippi River into the
Gulf of Mexico.[26] While erosion can be lessened through "no till" methods that
disturb the soil as little as possible, doing so may require greater use of herbicides to combat weeds and maintain production levels, a telling example of the
trade-offs in the nexus between agriculture and the environment.[27]

Intensive agricultural land use by itself harms wildlife. For example, farmers working under the aegis of federal "swamp reclamation" programs have drained millions of acres of wetlands to expand tillable acreage. This practice so diminished wildlife habitats by the 1920s that concerned anglers and hunters established groups like the Izaak Walton League (1922), National Wildlife Federation (1935), and Ducks Unlimited (1937) to preserve what wetlands remained.[28] Intensive cultivation has also reduced the number and diversity of native honeybees essential to producing foods such as almonds, apples, and peaches. Large-scale farms now depend on commercial bee operations that transport hives from field to field to pollinate crops, but the survival of these managed bee colonies is threatened by pesticides and disease, calling into question the future viability of this system.[29]

Contemporary agriculture also depends on sufficient and predictable supplies of water, especially in regions where rainfall is irregular. For example, crop production in much of the lower Great Plains relies on water pumped up from the Ogallala Aquifer, an ancient water table running from South Dakota to Texas that also provides drinking water to the region's cities. Heavy reliance on the Ogallala in recent decades, combined with low natural recharge rates, has severely degraded the water table and forced many to return to dry land farming, with consequent impacts on crop yields, and inspired (so far unfulfilled) proposals to pipe in water from the Great Lakes.[30] The picture is starker in Arizona and in California's Imperial Valley, key fruit- and vegetable-producing areas whose existence depends on water supplied from sources hundreds of miles away and according to complex permitting rights set decades ago, under far different demand and climactic conditions.[31] The reservoirs on which the West depends are also controversial for their impacts on fish populations, in particular migratory species like salmon whose spawning grounds were cut off by dams built for water and hydropower.

Chemical Inputs

Conventional agriculture depends on chemicals derived from petroleum or natural gas. The list starts with inorganic fertilizers, which with hybrid seeds and synthetic pesticides were key to the "Green Revolution" of the 1960s that enabled countries like India to become more food self-sufficient.[32] However, overuse of fertilizer adds significant and harmful amounts of nitrogen and phosphorus to terrestrial and aquatic ecosystems. In the United States, 97 percent of acres devoted to corn are treated with synthetic nitrogen fertilizer, the application-per-acre rate of which has gone from 112 pounds in 1970 to 140 in 2010. Such increases helped to boost corn production, but are subject to the law of diminishing returns: as yields increase, each additional bushel produced requires even more fertilizer than the one before. Indeed, top corn states like Indiana apply nitrogen at much higher rates—178 pounds per acre—than the national average.[33]

Next come a broad array of compounds used to decrease crop loss at various stages of production, processing, or shipment, which include insecticides, herbicides, fungicides, fumigants, nematicides (for soil-borne nematodes, microscopic plant parasites), and rodenticides. Agriculture accounts for about 80 percent of all U.S. pesticide use, with 877 million pounds of pesticide active ingredients applied in 2007 alone (the most recently available data), nearly two-thirds of which went to five crops: corn, cotton, potatoes, soybeans, and wheat.[34] Leading the way is glyphosate, a broad-spectrum herbicide (i.e., effective on many types of plants) that is the most widely applied pesticide in the United States, with about 170 million pounds applied annually on average to the top five pesticide-receiving crops.[35] Its popularity is due to wide adoption of Monsanto's Roundup Ready seeds, which allow farmers to spray the herbicide over entire fields, wiping out weeds while sparing their genetically modified corn, soy, cotton, alfalfa, canola, or sugar beet plants. This technological breakthrough, brought to market in 1996, was heralded as an economic and ecological achievement. Not only would farmers save time and effort in herbicide application; it was projected that herbicide use and toxicity would decrease as farmers would only need to spray Roundup (or its generic equivalents), a chemical with lower toxicity and residence time in the environment than older formulations (e.g., atrazine), to kill weeds. Such hopes were important given the known and potential negative health effects of heavy pesticide use on non–target species, including humans.[36]

While use of Roundup Ready variants did lead to lower herbicide use early on, the logic of monoculture soon imposed itself. That is, applying the same chemical repeatedly on the same land over time breeds resistance. Weeds evolve and adapt. Agrichemical firms responded to new "superweeds" by "stacking" multiple resistance traits in seeds' genetic code, which over time made the plant resistant to applications of multiple types of pesticides.[37] The trade-off, then, for producing a simplified but technology-dependent pest management system means that farmers came to apply greater quantities and more toxic formulations. Indeed, it is estimated that reliance on herbicide-resistant packages such as Roundup Ready led to a 527 million–pound *increase* in U.S. herbicide application between 1996 and 2011.[38]

Waste

Industrial-scale agriculture produces a lot of waste. About 60 percent of the nitrogen fertilizer used ends up in surface and ground waters, contributing to eutrophication (excessive plant growth) and compromised drinking water supplies.[39] Fertilizer is a significant contributor to stream loads of nitrogen and phosphorus throughout the central United States.[40] As noted, diminishing yield gains that occur with each incremental increase in fertilizer result in its overapplication to maintain production. Farmers often also overapply because of their uncertainty about existing nutrients in the soil and desire to mitigate potential economic losses from suboptimal production. Additionally, much of the Corn Belt uses tile drainage to remove excess water from the soil and foster crop growth. These subsurface tubes (which are "nonpoint" sources under the Clean Water Act and thus not regulated by the federal government) sluice water, often highly polluted with nitrate, directly into surface water bodies and other catchments. Many of these waters ultimately drain into the Gulf of Mexico, where algae feed on the nutrients and create an oxygen-poor "dead zone" the size of Connecticut. Similar conditions occur off the delta of the San Joaquin and Sacramento Rivers, which drains California's fertile Central Valley.[41] In addition to killing fish and producing foul odors, such dead zones can emit nitrous oxide, a greenhouse gas 300 times more powerful than carbon dioxide.[42]

Animal Waste. Almost 10 billion animals are raised and slaughtered for food in the United States each year. While the increasing specialization and concentration of meat production in large-scale CAFOs made economic sense, the shift called into question the capacity of surrounding environments to assimilate excess nutrients from animals' liquid and solid manure. Despite decreases in nitrogen and phosphorus excretion per unit of meat, increased production and low nutrient recovery in crop and livestock systems rapidly concentrated nutrients in excess of the capacity of the soil to absorb and filter them.[43] Manure that enters local soil or escapes from CAFO containment lagoons adds to the eutrophication problem in even far-off waters.

Chemical Runoff. A significant but as of yet undetermined portion of the hundreds of millions of pounds of pesticides used annually in agriculture also ends up in water—as does a significant but undetermined amount applied to residential lawns, golf courses, and other nonagricultural spaces.[44] Atrazine, the second most widely applied pesticide in the United States, has been detected in surface and drinking waters throughout the Midwest. While the herbicide has documented carcinogenic and endocrine-disrupting activities in animals, and concerns about its ubiquity in groundwater led to its ban in the European Union in 2003, to date the Environmental Protection Agency (EPA) has found no definitive evidence of atrazine's impacts on human health.

Antibiotics. Almost 80 percent of all antibiotics sold in the United States are used in livestock and poultry production, an unknown amount of which also ends up in water.[45] Farmers can purchase these drugs without veterinary oversight, and use them for animal growth promotion, disease prevention, and treatment. Prophylactic use of antibiotics is central to the CAFO system, where large numbers of animals are packed into confined spaces that are ideal conditions for the spread of disease. They also facilitate antibiotic resistance, with potential human health effects. Bacteria have the ability to share genes, so once a resistance gene evolves in one bacterium, it binds to another. Then, when producers use an antibiotic, all nonresistant bacteria are exterminated, leaving the resistance gene to spread to other bacteria. Resistant pathogens, such as *E. coli*, thus can be spread on the landscape in manure, can be transported to communities via workers and equipment, and can eventually make their way into the supermarket meat case.[46]

Greenhouse Gas Emissions

Industrial-scale agriculture generates significant greenhouse gas emissions, calculated at approximately 7 percent of the nation's total by economic sector.[47] For the average American household, about 83 percent of its food consumption carbon footprint stems from agricultural production.[48] A large portion of its impact—not including land use change—is due to large-scale animal production, particularly of ruminants (e.g., beef cattle), which emit greenhouse gases like methane.[49] Red meat is the most greenhouse gas–intensive part of the American diet, leading some to argue that the average American family could reduce its carbon footprint more by going without red meat once a week than by obtaining all food from local sources.[50]

Genetically Modified Variants

Beyond intensifying use of chemical inputs (e.g., via use of Roundup Ready seed), GM crops also raise concerns about impacts on organic agriculture (see Box 9-2) and about the acceleration of overall reliance on a few variants. In this regard, the proliferation of GM technology in commodity crop production has dramatically shaped the landscape and business of farming. One company, Monsanto, owns or has legally enforceable control of over 87 percent of GM seed planted worldwide.[51] In the United States, about 90 percent of corn, soybean, and cotton acres are planted with GM seed to resist pests or herbicides.[52] As a result, in some areas, there are few non-GM seed choices for farmers, thereby reducing the biodiversity of planted acreage and farmers' options to opt out of using GM technology if they continue to farm conventionally.

Box 9-2   GM and Organic: The Case of Bt

Regulations based on the Organic Foods Production Act of 1990 define genetically modified (GM) variants as "synthetic," and not legal in organic production.[1] Yet, questions arise over what is "natural," and whether genetic modification can contribute to reducing the harmful impacts of synthetic pesticides in agriculture.

Take *Bacillus thuringiensis* (Bt), in its "natural" state a soil bacterium with insecticidal properties widely used in organic agriculture. As with *any* pesticide, the more Bt is used, the more resistance to it pests develop. To compensate, firms developed GM variants expressing Bt genes. By one study, use of Bt corn and cotton reduced synthetic insecticide use by 123 million pounds between 1996 and 2011.[2]

Proponents see no genetic difference between "natural" and GM Bt. Critics retort that Bt sprayed *on* plants can be washed off but toxins *in* GM variants remain, with uncertain effects. To genetic modification's

---

proponents, the legal definition of "organic" rests on a mistaken notion of "natural." To critics, genetic modification is an agribusiness assault on organic agriculture. As the Bt case suggests, this debate is not easily resolved.

1. Miles McEvoy, *Can GMOs Be Used in Organic Production?* USDA, May 17, 2013, blogs.usda.gov/2013/05/17/organic-101-can-gmos-be-used-in-organic-products/.
2. Charles Benbrook, "Impacts of Genetically Engineered Crops on Pesticide Use in the U.S.: The First Sixteen Years," *Environmental Sciences Europe* 24 (2012), www.enveurope.com/content/24/1/24.

Agriculture and U.S. Environmental Law

Despite the externalities of industrial-scale agriculture, U.S. environmental laws typically do not apply to or carve out exemptions for farm and ranch operations. In part, such differential treatment reflects the iconography of the small family farm in American culture. In part, it reflects the still potent (if waning) political clout of the farm sector in Congress. At minimum, as Megan Stubbs observes, "environmental policies have focused on large industrial sources such as factories and power plants, because attempting to regulate numerous individual crop and livestock operations can be a challenge for government regulators. Therefore, the current federal farm policy addressing environmental concerns is in large part voluntary; that is, it seeks to encourage agricultural producers to adopt conservation practices through economic incentives."[53]

While incentives have always been part of the EPA's tool kit, in this instance, its reliance on them reflects *realpolitik* by a perpetually beleaguered regulatory agency facing strong congressional support for farmers as local small businesses, regardless (or because) of their actual size and economic clout. Take, for example, the EPA's consideration of having large CAFOs voluntarily report methane emissions, based on legislative directives in its fiscal year 2008 appropriations requiring "mandatory reporting of greenhouse gas (GHG) emissions above appropriate thresholds in all sectors of the economy of the United States." Two years later, Congress explicitly *barred* the EPA from using its budget to apply GHG reporting rules to CAFOs, even on a voluntary basis.[54] This rider has been extended in subsequent appropriations, reflecting an overall pattern of congressional intervention in federal environmental policy as it applies to agriculture.

Table 9-1 lays out elements of major U.S. environmental laws that can apply to agriculture. Most were enacted in the 1970s, the "golden age" of environmental policy formation in the United States; few have been formally updated.[55] These laws typically set threshold limits that exempt small farm operations (variously defined) and, in many instances, as with the Clean Air Act, leave implementation to the states, raising concerns about variability in monitoring and enforcement.

Table 9-1   U.S. Environmental Laws Affecting Agriculture

	Applies to	*Requirements*
Endangered Species Act		
Pesticide use (via FIFRA)	All operations	Possible limits on pesticide use
Forests and other habitats	All operations	Restrict activities that could adversely affect habitat of listed species
Clean Water Act		
National Pollutant Discharge Elimination System (NPDES)	Concentrated Animal Feeding Operation	Federal permit if discharging into waterways
	Pesticide application on or near irrigation ditches, other water bodies	No federal permit required
	Application of biosolids to land	No federal permit required, but farms must meet regulatory requirements
Wetlands	Discharges of dredged or fill material into "waters of the United States"	Federal permit for nonexempt activities
Clean Air Act		
Particulates	Some operations in specified areas	Varies based on state implementation plans
Ozone (nitrogen oxides, volatile organic compounds)	Some operations in specified areas	
Federal Insecticide, Fungicide, and Rodenticide Act		
	All practices that involve pest control	Follow label instructions
	Restricted use applicators	Certain training requirements
Resource Conservation and Recovery Act		
Waste pesticides	All operations	Proper disposal of unused pesticides
Underground storage tanks	Farms with fuel storage tanks > 1,100 gallons	Meet design and tech requirements
Emergency Planning and Right to Know Act		
Hazardous chemicals	Operations storing above-threshold amounts ("routine agricultural operations") excluded	Report inventory to state and local authorities

Source: Adapted from *Major Existing EPA Laws and Programs That Could Affect Agricultural Producers,* EPA, 2007, http://www.epa.gov/oecaagct/agmatrix.pdf.

Endangered Species

Agriculture's impact on the land includes effects on wildlife, whether as a result of "swamp" clearance, woodlands loss, or the externalities of practices ranging from extensive fertilizer and chemical use to the size and density of CAFOs.[56] While land use issues are for the most part state and local matters, the Endangered Species Act (ESA) comes into play when agriculture threatens a listed species. The law's "incidental takings" provision protects farmers and ranchers in instances where "routine" activities (e.g., proper use of authorized rodenticides) lead inadvertently to deaths of otherwise protected species. Even so, complaints about the ESA's purported negative impacts on farming and ranching are a perennial feature of congressional attacks on the law, which in many instances hearkens back to decades-old battles over Interior Department "predator control" efforts. For example, Western grazing interests, backed by conservative activists seeking local control over federal rangelands, have pushed the U.S. Fish and Wildlife Service to "delist" the gray wolf and leave its management to the states, a move opposed by wildlife groups.[57] Conflicts over the ESA also reflect broader tensions over the Fifth Amendment's "takings" clause in balancing private property rights with the needs of the common, including nonhuman species, embodied in any environmental policy.[58]

Air Pollution

The Clean Air Act authorizes the EPA to set National Ambient Air Quality Standards (NAAQS) for pollutants that "may reasonably be anticipated to endanger public health or welfare," and then assigns to the states a significant duty to implement those standards.[59] The act applies to agricultural activities as they generate specific pollutants, such as particulates from CAFOs (e.g., feedlot dust), nitrogen oxides from fertilizers, and various GHG emissions. To date, the EPA has been reluctant to treat large-scale agriculture in the same manner as other industries, and instead grants states flexibility in doing so within their respective state implementation plans (SIPs). For their part, states with large farm sectors tend to treat food production and processing activities with care, leaving critics to argue that industrial farming gets off too easily.

The EPA also has authority to regulate "hazardous" air pollutants (HAPs), those known or reasonably anticipated to pose serious health risks, including cancer, neurological disorders, and reproductive dysfunction. While the agency has promulgated standards on manufacturers of agriculture-related products such as pesticides, it has been reluctant to extend oversight directly to agricultural activities. For example, CAFOs can emit significant amounts of hydrogen sulfide, which at low doses is a respiratory irritant and at high doses can be fatal. The substance was "inadvertently" included on the list of HAPs to be regulated under the 1990 amendments to the Clean Air Act, but was removed from it a year later by a joint resolution of Congress, signed by President George H. W. Bush, at the behest of farming interests.[60] Despite intensified lobbying by environmental and public health advocates, spurred on by new releases of hydrogen sulfide in hydraulic fracturing processes, the EPA to date has declined to add the substance to the HAP list.[61]

Water Pollution

The Clean Water Act's differential treatment of *point* and *nonpoint* sources exempts most agricultural practices from direct EPA oversight. CAFOs that discharge animal waste directly into waterways may be required to obtain a National Pollutant Discharge Elimination System (NPDES) permit, so most store it in large manure lagoons, which are considered nonpoint. That distinction is controversial given the size of many such containment structures and the chance of accidental spills. In 2001, the EPA proposed to require that large CAFOs obtain permits unless they demonstrated that they had no potential to discharge waste. The proposed rule provoked considerable criticism, with livestock producers opposing it as too stringent and environmental groups as too lenient. The controversy went to federal court, and in *Waterkeeper Alliance v. EPA* (2005), the Second Circuit Court of Appeals ruled that the EPA could only regulate *actual* discharge, and thus exceeded its statutory authority in requiring mandatory permitting of all CAFOs.[62] The EPA issued a new rule in 2008, requiring a NPDES permit only if facilities discharge or propose to discharge into local waters; it does not cover application of manure onto fields that may leach into those waters. Today, of 4,917 CAFOs defined by the Clean Water Act in Iowa, Kansas, Missouri, and Nebraska *alone*, only 978 are permitted operations.[63]

Chemicals

Given the centrality of synthetic pesticides to conventional agriculture, it is no surprise that the Federal Insecticide, Fungicide, and Rodenticide Act (FIFRA) is at the center of some of the nation's most charged environmental battles, including over Rachel Carson's *Silent Spring* in 1962, the EPA's suspension of the growth regulator Alar on apples in 1989, and use of atrazine today.[64] In each, the conflict is between those defending chemicals as key to food production and those for whom chemical use, or overuse, poses unacceptable ecological and human health risks. This said, most of FIFRA's focus is on chemical manufacturers and their products, not on applicators, and farmers who apply pesticides as directed are generally exempt from oversight. Controversies over pesticides tend to focus on chemical efficacy, toxicity, and chronic effects, and in such instances farmers fearful about losing any tool in their fight against crop loss tend to side with chemical makers against regulators and non–farm interests when environmental and health concerns are raised. In the case of atrazine, for example, Midwest corn growers have opposed tighter restrictions on the herbicide even after it was found in the region's public drinking water supplies.[65]

Making Agriculture More Ecologically Sustainable

The food system's central players—including the USDA and state departments of agriculture, agribusinesses, agricultural research centers at land grant universities, and members of Congress concerned about farming's future—have not remained complacent as these externalities accrued and, in many instances, threaten the system's capacity to maintain production. They also have been pushed by critics, ranging from environmental and animal rights activists to nutritionists and proponents of "alternative" agriculture, to make the food system more sustainable (however defined), more transparent, and more connected to the citizen/consumer it serves. In the middle is the farmer, caught between immediate economic incentives to maximize production and an array of long-term societal imperatives, including agriculture's contributions to climate change.

Improving Conventional Production

Such innovations begin with new, or reintroduced, methods of planting. Conservation tillage (reduced or no till) reduces soil exposure to wind or water erosion.[66] Cover cropping, or planting a crop such as alfalfa or rye in the off-season, can add fertility, reduce soil erosion, and suppress pests.[67] Using legumes as a cover crop in a rotation with other crops fixes nitrogen in soils, thereby reducing the need for synthetic fertilizer and resultant nutrient loss.[68] In some cases, integrated use of conservation practices in conventional farming can be as effective as organic approaches in reducing negative impacts.[69] Despite their potential, such practices are not the norm, particularly among growers of major commodity crops pushed by economic imperatives to maximize production.[70] While the USDA offers support to farmers who adopt conservation practices, less than 12 percent of corn- and soybean-planted acres are enrolled in such programs, in part due to limits on funding.[71]

Expanding Organic

Organic production is seen as an ecologically preferable alternative to conventional systems, and done well results in increased soil organic matter and biodiversity, less energy use, and lower nutrient loss across the landscape.[72] At the same time, going organic requires more land—84 percent more, in one analysis—to produce the same amount of a crop or livestock product as a conventional system due to 25 percent lower average yield per acre, lower animal productivity, and more land in rotation for soil fertility.[73] The implications of higher land needs are important in debates over addressing imbalances in federal supports for conventional versus organic farming. Moreover, those concerned about global food security see high-yield conventional systems as key to saving forests and grasslands from conversion to agriculture of any kind—which would result in large biodiversity losses and carbon fluxes into the atmosphere.

Opportunities to increase organic yields exist, and such systems offer other benefits that must be considered. For example, given their emphasis on maintaining healthy soils, organic systems may offer increased resilience to ecological stressors such as drought, an important factor as agriculture feels the impacts of climate change (see Box 9-3).[74] Furthermore, organic farms tend to be smaller and multifunctional and have higher productivity in terms of overall output of multiple crops per acre compared to larger, industrialized systems.[75] Not surprisingly, there is real interest in the metrics to be used to conceptualize and assess the future sustainability of agricultural systems, conventional or organic.

Box 9-3   Climate Change and Food

The nation's farm sector likely noted that the 2014 *National Climate Assessment* opens as follows:

> Climate change, once considered an issue for a distant future, has moved firmly into the present. Corn producers in Iowa, oyster growers in Washington State, and maple syrup producers in Vermont are all observing climate-related changes that are outside of recent experience.[1]

Among its findings, the assessment lays out specific implications of climate change for the U.S. food system:

- **Climate disruptions to agricultural production,** ranging from more frequent heavy rains to longer and more serious droughts.
- **Declines in crop and livestock production** due to weeds, diseases, insect pests, and other climate change–induced stresses.
- **Loss and degradation of critical agricultural soil and water assets** due to increasing extremes in precipitation.

Add to this picture climate-induced stresses on the world's oceans, the primary source of food for at least one billion people,[2] and implications are clear. As the assessment warns, climate change will "alter the stability of food supplies and create new food security challenges for the United States as the world seeks to feed nine billion people by 2050."[3]

---

1. Jerry Hatfield et al., "Agriculture," in *Climate Change Impacts in the United States: The Third National Climate Assessment*, ed. Jerry Melillo, Terese Richmond, and Gary Yohe (U.S. Global Change Research Program, 2014), 1. See also doi:10.7930/ J02Z13FR.
2. Ibid., 49.
3. Ibid., 151.

Bolstering Local and Regional Food Systems

Many consumers are looking more locally as a way to lessen the ecological impacts of their food. The definition of local varies, and is generally marked by a set distance between farm production and consumption. Local food largely is sold to consumers via farmers' markets, farm stands, and Community Supported Agriculture (CSA) shares, with an expanding share going to restaurants, institutions like universities, food service providers, and supermarkets. Buying food locally, even when its ecological advantages aren't clear, also can restore transparency in the food system and the relationships that people once had to agriculture by "knowing their farmer." Finally, local food is seen as a mechanism for economic development, with a documented ability to increase employment and income in communities.

However, focusing on local is limiting in terms of scale, price, and variety. Perhaps more useful is the notion of a *regional* food system that includes local and is nested within national and global systems.[76] While Congress has defined a local or regional food product as one that is sold no more than 400 miles from its origin or within the state of production,[77] Clancy and Ruhf argue that the optimal regional system would be "self-reliant" insofar as it leverages a geographic area's productive, economic, and social resources to meet as much of its food needs as possible in a sustainable way.[78] At the regional level, more opportunities exist to aggregate food from multiple farms for sale at lower prices through traditional venues like supermarkets. Larger volumes of food shipped can lead to efficiency increases in transportation, reducing per-unit GHG emissions, and to lower per-unit costs for processing (e.g., freezing and canning), although obtaining such gains would depend on rebuilding much of the regional processing infrastructure that has disappeared in recent decades of industry consolidation. Moreover, from an agronomic perspective, regional systems inherently include multiple climates and growing zones, enabling greater diversity and resilience of production than a strictly localized system.

Perhaps most relevant to this discussion is what local and regional foods are *not*. While consumers understandably look to nearby sources as a solution to the ills brought about by the globalized, industrialized paradigm, the mere fact that a product is local conveys only information about the locus and scale of the supply chain. Local and regional are *not* inherently more ecologically benign, fair, or equitable, just as "global" need not connote "exploitative" and "destructive." Increasing overall food system sustainability and resilience will require nesting systems at different scales—local, regional, national, and global—and identifying the goals such a nested system should achieve.[79]

The Future of Food

In March 2001, the chronologically senior contributor to this chapter participated in a forum at Iowa State University, *Extreme Demands/ Extraordinary Products*, at which his role was to speak about the broadening range of non–farm sector interests, including environmental and consumer health advocacy groups, seeking to influence agriculture and food policy. The forum attracted dozens of Iowa farmers, many who expressed a similar lament: "We produce reliable, nutritious, and inexpensive food. What *more* do they want from us?"

Given the distance, however defined, between most Americans and the origins of their food, what "they" wanted was more of a voice about it. More than a decade later, even more Americans, few who ever farmed for a living, express clear concerns about where their food comes from, the conditions under which it is produced, and the impacts of food production on their health and environment. While this attentive public is on average whiter, older, more affluent, and more educated—similar to the foundation of mainstream environmentalism—it is becoming broader and more diverse. After all, Walmart, not Whole Foods, is the largest retail source for organic produce.[80] McDonald's now requires its egg suppliers to provide hens with larger enclosures and its pork suppliers to phase out "gestation crates" for pregnant sows,[81] actions the iconic American fast-food chain is taking to please its mass customer base, not "elitist" animal rights activists. Consumer concerns, however expressed, also induced major dairy producers to keep their milk free of artificial growth hormones despite Food and Drug Administration rulings of no health risk from such stimulants, in turn leading Monsanto to sell off its dairy hormone business.[82] More Americans than ever are purchasing some of their food from an ever-increasing number and range of local sources, many created and run by a new generation of activist/ entrepreneurs. College students, led by the Real Food Challenge, are working to make their schools' food more local, community based, ecologically sustainable, fairly traded, and humane—whatever those terms mean in actual implementation. Inner-city farm-to-school and urban agricultural initiatives multiply, particularly among racial and ethnic populations seeking alternatives to a food system many see as complicit in high community rates of obesity and related health problems.

In short, more Americans, for diverse reasons, care about how their food is produced. At one level, Frances Moore Lappé and many like her have had profound effects on the dominant food system, with consequent impacts on the relationship between food production and the environment. However, as Earl Butz would have foreseen, the basic demands on that food system remain: we still want what we want, when we want it, at a price we're willing to pay. While our demands are for food that is more local, more organic, more humane, and more fairly traded, we also want it to be plentiful, diverse, and inexpensive. Moreover, demands on the food system will get more complicated with the expected need to feed an estimated 9 billion people by 2050 amidst the effects of climate change. "One way or another," as agricultural economist Parke Wilde bluntly puts it, "there will be a reckoning between human food needs and the natural environment."[83] As such, the future of food is too important to be left to farmers alone.

Suggested Websites

Farm Policy News (FarmPolicy.com) Possibly the best nonsubscriber source for the latest news on food and agriculture policy issues.

Food Day (www.foodday.org) National organizer of Food Day, held each October to promote "healthy, affordable, and sustainable food."

Real Food Challenge (www.realfoodchallenge.org) A national organization helping college students to transform university food services and, by extension, the broader food system.

U.S. EPA National Agriculture Center (www.epa.gov/oecaagct/index .html) The EPA's source for information, guidelines, and regulations pertaining to agriculture.

Notes

1. Wendell Berry, "The Pleasures of Eating," *What Are People For?* (New York: North Point Press, 1990), 145–52.
2. William H. Blair, "Butz Says He'll Speak for All Farmers," *New York Times*, November 18, 1971.
3. "A Special Tribute to Earl Butz," *Farm Futures*, February 4, 2008, farmfutures.com/story-a-special-tribute-to-earl-butz-17-28780.
4. USDA, *Food Expenditures*, Table 7, www.ers.usda.gov/data-products/food-expenditures .aspx#.U3UFT17rVa.
5. Frances Moore Lappé, *Diet for a Small Planet*, 20th anniversary ed. (New York: Ballantine Books, 1991), 66–88.
6. Bruce Gardner, *American Agriculture in the Twentieth Century: How It Flourished and What It Cost* (Cambridge, MA: Harvard University Press, 2002).
7. Eric Schlosser, *Fast Food Nation: The Dark Side of the All-American Meal* (New York: HarperCollins, 2002); Marion Nestle, *Food Politics: How the Food Industry Influences Nutrition and Health* (Berkeley: University of California Press, 2002); Michael Pollan, *The Omnivore's Dilemma: A Natural History of Four Meals* (New York: Penguin, 2006).
8. USDA, *Farms and Farm Acreage*, www.nass.usda.gov/index.asp; USDA, *2012 Census of Agriculture*, www.agcensus.usda.gov/Publications/2012/Preliminary_Report/Full_ Report.pdf.
9. USDA, *2012 Census of Agriculture*, www.agcensus.usda.gov/Publications/2012/Full_ Report/Volume_1,_Chapter_1_US/st99_1_002_002.pdf.
10. Robert Hoppe and James McDonald, "Classifying U.S. Farms to Reflect Today's Agriculture," USDA, www.ers.usda.gov/amber-waves/2013-may/the-revised-ers -farm-typology-classifying-us-farms-to-reflect-todays-agriculture.aspx.
11. Purdue University, 2002, as cited in EPA, *Farm Demographics*, www.epa.gov/oecaagct/ ag101/demographics.html
12. USDA, *U.S. Corn Acreage and Yield*, www.ers.usda.gov/media/521667/corndatatable .htm; *Background on Corn*, www.ers.usda.gov/topics/crops/corn/background.aspx# .U3Tpr17rVa8.
13. Pollan, *Omnivore's Dilemma*, 63.
14. American Meat Institute, *The U.S. Meat Industry at a Glance*, www.meatami.com/ ht/d/sp/i/47465/pid/47465; USDA, *Livestock and Meat Domestic Data*, www.ers.usda .gov/data-products/livestock-meat-domestic-data.aspx#.U3Yb817rVa8.

15. USDA, *Dairy: Overview*, www.ers.usda.gov/topics/animal-products/dairy/back ground.aspx#.UzmFzNyE4dI; *Milk: Production per Cow by Year*, www.nass.usda.gov/ Charts_and_Maps/Milk_Production_and_Milk_Cows/cowrates.asp.

16. James McDonald and William McBride, "The Transformation of U.S. Livestock Agriculture: Scale, Efficiency, and Risks," USDA, 2009, www.ers.usda.gov/publications/ eib-economic-information-bulletin/eib43.aspx#.U3tToV7rVa8.

17. Stuart Melvin et al., "Industry Structure and Trends in Iowa," *Iowa Concentrated Animal Feeding Operations Air Quality Study* (University of Iowa, 2003), www.public -health.uiowa.edu/ehsrc/CAFOstudy/CAFO_finalChap_2.pdf.

18. USDA, *Hogs & Pork*, http://www.ers.usda.gov/topics/animal-products/hogs-pork.aspx.

19. USDA, *2012 Census of Agriculture*, www.agcensus.usda.gov/Publications/2012/Full_ Report/Volume_1,_Chapter_1_US/st99_1_055_055.pdf.

20. The amount of energy needed to heat or cool one pound of water by one degree Fahrenheit. Jayson Beckman et al., "Agriculture's Supply and Demand for Energy and Energy Products," USDA, 2013, www.ers.usda.gov/media/1104145/eib112.pdf.

21. Patrick Westhoff, *The Economics of Food: How Feeding and Fueling the Planet Affects Food Prices* (Upper Saddle River, NJ: Pearson, 2010).

22. USDA, *U.S. Agricultural Trade*, www.ers.usda.gov/topics/international-markets-trade/ us-agricultural-trade.aspx#.UzrIU9yE4dI.

23. USDA, *Import Share of Consumption*, www.ers.usda.gov/topics/international-markets -trade/us-agricultural-trade/import-share-of-consumption.aspx#.UzrL8tyE4dJ.

24. Quoted in James McWilliams, *Just Food: Where Localvores Get It Wrong and How We Can Truly Eat Responsibly* (Boston: Little Brown, 2009), 7.

25. World Bank, *Agricultural Land as Percent of Land Area*, data.worldbank.org/indicator/ AG.LND.AGRI.ZS?order=wbapi_data_value_2011+wbapi_data_value+wbapi_data_ value-last&sort=asc.

26. USDA, *Natural Resources Inventory, 2007*, www.nrcs.usda.gov/wps/portal/nrcs/detail full/national/technical/nra/nri/?cid=nrcs143_013656.

27. Parke Wilde, *Food Policy in the United States: An Introduction* (New York: Routledge, 2013), 46.

28. Christopher Bosso, *Environment, Inc.: From Grassroots to Beltway* (Lawrence: University Press of Kansas, 2005), 27–33.

29. Chensheng Lu et al., "Sub-lethal Exposure to Neonicotinoids Impaired Honey Bees Winterization before Proceeding to Colony Collapse Disorder," *Bulletin of Insectology* 67, no. 1 (2014): 125–30.

30. Michael Wines, "Wells Dry, Fertile Plains Turn to Dust," *New York Times*, May 19, 2013.

31. Marc Reisner, *Cadillac Desert: The American West and Its Disappearing Water*, 2nd ed. (New York: Penguin, 1993).

32. Robert Paarlberg, *Food Politics: What Everyone Needs to Know* (New York: Oxford University Press, 2010), Chapter 6.

33. USDA, *Fertilizer Use and Price*, www.ers.usda.gov/data-products/fertilizer-use-and -price.aspx.

34. USDA, *Pesticide Use and Markets*, www.ers.usda.gov/topics/farm-practices-management/ chemical-inputs/pesticide-use-markets.aspx.

35. USDA, *Agricultural Chemical Use Program*, www.nass.usda.gov/Surveys/Guide_to_ NASS_Surveys/Chemical_Use/.

36. Rachel Carson, *Silent Spring* (Boston: Houghton Mifflin, 1962); Christopher Bosso, *Pesticides and Politics: The Life Cycle of a Public Issue* (Pittsburgh, PA: University of Pittsburgh Press, 1987).

37. Union of Concerned Scientists, *The Rise of Superweeds—and What to Do About It*, 2013, www.ucsusa.org/assets/documents/food_and_agriculture/rise-of-superweeds.pdf.

38. Charles Benbrook, "Impacts of Genetically Engineered Crops on Pesticide Use in the U.S.—The First Sixteen Years," *Environmental Sciences Europe* 24, no. 1 (2012): 1–13.

39. Jan Willem Erisman et al., "How a Century of Ammonia Synthesis Changed the World," *Nature Geoscience* 1 (2008): 636–39.

40. Stephen Preston et al., "Factors Affecting Stream Nutrient Loads: A Synthesis of Regional SPARROW Model Results for the Continental United States," *Journal of the American Water Resources Association* 47, no. 5 (2011): 891–915.

41. Ellen Hanak et al., *Managing California's Water: From Conflict to Reconciliation* (Public Policy Institute of California, 2011).

42. Liang Dong and David Nedwell, "Sources of Nitrogen Used for Denitrification and Nitrous Oxide Formation in Sediments of the Hypernutrified Colne, the Nitrified Humber, and the Oligotrophic Conwy Estuaries, United Kingdom," *Limnology and Oceanography* 51, no. 1 (2006): 545–57.

43. Lex Bouwman et al., "Exploring Global Changes in Nitrogen and Phosphorus Cycles in Agriculture Induced by Livestock Production over the 1900–2050 Period," *Proceedings of the National Academy of Sciences* 110, no. 52 (December 24, 2013): 20882–87.

44. Robert Kellogg et al., "Environmental Indicators of Pesticide Leaching and Runoff from Farm Fields," USDA, 2000, www.nrcs.usda.gov/wps/portal/nrcs/detail/national/technical/?cid=nrcs143_014053.

45. Johns Hopkins Center for a Livable Future, *Industrial Food Animal Production in America: Examining the Impact of the Pew Commission's Priority Recommendations*, 2013, www.jhsph.edu/research/centers-and-institutes/johns-hopkins-center-for-a-livable-future/research/clf_publications/pub_rep_desc/pew_report.html.

46. Jeff Benedict, *Poisoned: The True Story of the Deadly E. coli Outbreak That Changed the Way Americans Eat* (Buena Vista, VA: Inspire Books, 2011).

47. Based on 2009 totals. EPA, *Greenhouse Gas Inventory Report*, as reported in Wilde, *Food Policy in the United States*, 48.

48. Christopher Weber and H. Scott Matthews, "Food-Miles and the Relative Climate Impacts of Food Choices in the United States," *Environmental Science & Technology* 42 (2008): 3508–13.

49. United Nations Food and Agriculture Organization, *Emissions—Agriculture, 1990–2011 Average*, faostat3.fao.org/faostat-gateway/go/to/browse/G1/*/E.

50. Weber and Matthews, "Food-Miles and the Relative Climate Impacts," 2008.

51. ETC Group, *Who Owns Nature? Corporate Power and the Final Frontier in the Commodification of Life*, 2008, www.etcgroup.org/content/who-owns-nature.

52. "GM Crops: A Story in Numbers," *Nature* 497 (2013): 22–23.

53. Megan Stubbs, *Environmental Regulation and Agriculture*, Congressional Research Service, U.S. Congress, CRS Report R41622 (2013): 1.

54. Ibid., 6–7.

55. Christopher Klyza and David Sousa, *American Environmental Policy, 1990–2006: Beyond Gridlock* (Cambridge, MA: MIT Press, 2008).

56. David Wilcove, *The Condor's Shadow: The Loss and Recovery of Wildlife in America* (New York: Anchor Books, 1999).

57. Felicity Berringer, "Federal Protection of Gray Wolves May Be Lifted, Agency Says," *New York Times*, June 7, 2013.

58. Jacqueline Vaughn Switzer, *Green Backlash: The History and Politics of Environmental Opposition in the U.S.* (Boulder, CO: Lynne Rienner, 1997).

59. Teresa Clemer, "Agriculture and the Clean Air Act," in *Food, Agriculture, and Environmental Law*, ed. Mary Jane Angelo (Washington, DC: Environmental Law Institute, 2013), 163–84.

60. EPA, *Modification to the 112(b)1: Hazardous Air Pollutants*, www.epa.gov/ttn/atw/pollutants/atwsmod.html.
61. Sierra Club, letter to EPA Commissioner Lisa Jackson, March 30, 2009, www.earthworksaction.org/files/publications/H2SLetterToEPA.pdf.
62. *Waterkeeper Alliance v. EPA*, 399 F.3d 486 (2nd Cir. 2005); Ryan A. Mohr, "*Waterkeeper Alliance v EPA:* A Demonstration in Regulating the Regulators," *Great Plains Natural Resources Journal* 10 (2006): 17–41.
63. EPA, *Are There CAFOs in Region 7?* www.epa.gov/region7/water/cafo/are_cafos_in_r7.htm.
64. Stubbs, *Environmental Regulation and Agriculture*, 43–44.
65. Charles Duhigg, "Debating How Much Weed Killer Is Safe in Your Drinking Water," *New York Times*, August 22, 2009.
66. USDA, *2012 Census of Agriculture*, Table 1, www.agcensus.usda.gov/; *National Resources Inventory: Soil Erosion on Cropland*, www.nrcs.usda.gov/wps/portal/nrcs/main/national/technical/nra/nri/results/.
67. Jorge Delgado et al., "A Decade of Advances in Cover Crops," *Journal of Soil and Water Conservation* 62, no. 5 (2011): 110A–20A.
68. Christina Tonitto et al., "Replacing Bare Fallows with Cover Crops in Fertilizer-Intensive Cropping Systems: A Meta-Analysis of Crop Yield and N Dynamics," *Agriculture, Ecosystems & Environment*, 112, no. 1 (2006): 58–72.
69. Gunnar Torstensson et al., "Nutrient Use Efficiencies and Leaching of Organic and Conventional Cropping Systems in Sweden," *Agronomy Journal* 98, no. 3 (2006): 603.
70. Robert Buman et al., "Profit, Yield, and Soil Quality Effects of Tillage Systems in Corn-Soybean Rotations," *Journal of Soil and Water Conservation* 59, no. 6 (2004): 260–71.
71. USDA, *Crop Production Practices*.
72. Hanna Tuomisto et al., "Does Organic Farming Reduce Environmental Impacts? A Meta-analysis," *Journal of Environmental Management* 112 (2012): 309–20.
73. Verena Seufert et al., "Comparing the Yields of Organic and Conventional Agriculture," *Nature* 485, no. 7397 (2012): 229–32.
74. Rodale Institute, *The Farming Systems Trial: Celebrating 30 Years*, 2011, rodaleinstitute.org/our-work/farming-systems-trial/farming-systems-trial-30-year-report/.
75. Ivette Perfecto and John Vandermeer, "The Agroecological Matrix as Alternative to the Land-Sparing/Agriculture Intensification Model," *Proceedings of the National Academy of Sciences* 107, no. 13 (2010): 5786–91.
76. Brian Donahue et al., *A New England Food Vision*, Food Solutions New England, 2014, www.foodsolutionsne.org/new-england-food-vision.
77. Stephen Martinez et al., *Local Food Systems: Concepts, Impacts, and Issues*, Economic Research Service, USDA, May 2010, www.ers.usda.gov/publications/err-economic-research-report/err97.aspx.
78. Kate Clancy and Kathy Ruhf, "Is Local Enough? Some Arguments for Regional Food Systems," *Choices: The Magazine of Farm, Food, and Resource Issues*, 25, no. 1 (2010).
79. Committee on Twenty-First Century Systems Agriculture, *Toward Sustainable Agricultural Systems in the 21st Century* (Washington, DC: National Research Council, 2010).
80. Elizabeth Harris and Stephanie Strom, "Walmart to Sell Organic Food, Undercutting Big Brands," *New York Times*, April 10, 2014.
81. Mark Bittman, "OMG: McDonald's Does the Right Thing," *New York Times*, February 13, 2012.
82. Andrew Martin and Andrew Pollack, "Monsanto Looks to Sell Dairy Hormone Business," *New York Times*, August 7, 2008.
83. Wilde, *Food Policy in the United States*, 36.

10

Applying Market Principles
to Environmental Policy

Sheila M. Olmstead

Each day, you make decisions that require trade-offs. Should you walk to work or drive? Walking takes more time; driving costs money for gasoline and parking. You might also consider the benefits of exercise if you walk, or the costs to the environment of the emissions if you drive. In considering this question, you need to determine how to allocate important scarce resources—your time and money—to achieve a particular goal.

Economics is the study of the allocation of scarce resources, and economists typically apply two simple concepts, efficiency and cost-effectiveness, for systematically making decisions. Let's take a concrete environmental policy example. The Snake River in the Pacific Northwest provides water for drinking, agricultural irrigation, transportation, industrial production, and hydroelectricity generation. It also supports rapidly dwindling populations of endangered salmon species. If there is not enough water to provide each of these services and to satisfy everyone, we must trade off one good thing for another.

Some scientific evidence indicates that removing hydroelectric dams on the upper Snake River may assist in the recovery of salmon populations. Salmon declines may also be caused by too little water in the river, which might be addressed by reducing agricultural or urban water withdrawals. Each of these measures could be implemented at some cost. Benefit-cost analysis would compare the benefits of each measure (the expected increase in salmon populations) to its costs. An *efficient* policy choice would maximize net benefits; we would choose the policy that offered the greatest difference between benefits and costs.

What if the Endangered Species Act requires that a specific level of salmon recovery be achieved? In this case, the benefits of salmon recovery may never be monetized. But economics can still play a role in choosing policies to achieve salmon recovery. Cost-effectiveness analysis would compare the costs of each potential policy intervention that could achieve the mandated salmon recovery goal. Decision makers would then choose the least costly or most *cost-effective* policy option.

This discussion is highly simplified. Explaining the causes of Snake River salmon decline and forecasting the impact of policy changes on salmon populations are complex scientific tasks, and different experts have different models that produce different results.[1] The trade-offs can also be multidimensional. Removing dams may sound like a great environmental idea, but hydroelectric power is an important source of clean energy in the Pacific Northwest. Would the dams' hydroelectricity be replaced by coal- or gas-fired power plants? What would be the impacts of the increased emissions of local and global air pollutants? In this chapter, we discuss some simple economic tools for examining such trade-offs. The basic intuition we develop to assess these issues functions well even in complex settings.

Economic Concepts and Environmental Policy

Economic Efficiency and Benefit-Cost Analysis of Environmental Policy

Many countries regulate emissions of sulfur dioxide (SO_2), an air pollutant that can damage human health and also causes acid rain, which harms forest and aquatic ecosystems. In the United States, power plants are a major source of SO_2 emissions, regulated under the Clean Air Act (CAA). As evidence accumulated in the 1980s regarding the damages from acid rain in the northeastern United States, Congress considered updating the CAA so that it would cover many old power plants not regulated by the original legislation. This process culminated in the 1990 CAA Amendments, which set a new goal for SO_2 emissions reductions from older power plants. Assume that it is 1989, and you have been asked to tell the U.S. Congress, from an economic perspective, how much SO_2 emissions should be reduced.

First, consider the costs of reducing SO_2 emissions. Economic costs are *opportunity costs*—what we must give up by abating each ton of emissions rather than spending that money on other important things. Emissions abatement can be achieved by removing SO_2 emissions from power plant smokestack gases using a "scrubber," which requires an up-front investment, as well as labor and materials for routine operation. Power plants can also change the fuels they use to generate electricity, switching from high-sulfur to more expensive low-sulfur coal or from coal to natural gas. Spending this money on pollution control leaves less to spend to improve a plant's operations or increase output. These costs are passed on by the firm to its employees (in the form of reduced wages), stockholders (in terms of lower share prices), consumers (in the form of higher prices), and other stakeholders.

If required to reduce emissions, firms will accomplish the cheapest abatement first, and resort to more and more expensive options as the amount of required abatement increases. The cost of abating each ton of pollution tends to rise slowly at first, as we abate the first tons of SO_2 emissions, and then more quickly. This typical pattern of costs is represented by the lower, convex curve in Figure 10-1, labeled total costs, or $C(Q)$.

The value of reducing emissions declines as we abate more and more tons of SO_2. At high levels of SO_2 emissions (low abatement), this pollutant causes acid rain as well as respiratory and cardiovascular ailments in populated areas. But as the air gets cleaner, low SO_2 concentrations cause fewer problems. Thus, while the total benefits of reducing SO_2 may always increase as we reduce emissions, the benefit of each additional ton of abatement will go down. This typical pattern of benefits is represented by the upper, concave curve in Figure 10-1, labeled total benefits, or $B(Q)$.[2]

Figure 10-1   Comparing the Total Benefits and Costs of Pollution Abatement

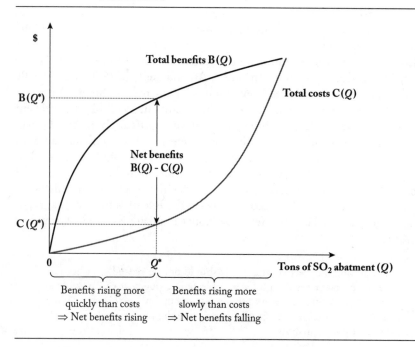

Economic efficiency requires that we find the policy that will give us the greatest net benefits—the biggest difference between total benefits and total costs. In Figure 10-1, the efficient amount of SO_2 emissions abatement is marked as Q^*, where the vertical distance between the benefit and cost curves is biggest. Why would it be inefficient to abate more or less than Q^* tons of SO_2 emissions? To the right of Q^*, the total benefits of reducing pollution are still positive and still rising. But costs are rising faster than benefits. So for every dollar in benefit we gain by eliminating a ton of emissions, we incur greater costs. To the left of Q^*, the benefits of each ton of abatement are rising more quickly than costs, so if we move to the left, we will also reduce the policy's net benefits.

Note that we have emphasized the costs and benefits of reducing each individual ton of pollution. Where total benefits increase quickly, at low levels of abatement, the benefit of an additional ton is very high. Where the total benefits curve flattens out, the benefit of an additional ton is low. This concept of the decreasing "benefit of an additional ton" defines the economic concept of *marginal benefit*. On the cost side, where total costs are almost flat, at low levels of abatement, the cost of adding an additional ton is very low. As total costs get very steep, the cost of abating an additional ton is high. This concept of the increasing "cost of an additional ton" defines the concept of *marginal cost*. The efficient quantity of pollution abatement is the number of tons at which the marginal benefit of abating an additional ton is exactly equal to the marginal cost.[3]

What we have just done is a benefit-cost analysis of a potential SO_2 emissions reduction policy. If you had completed the analysis to advise Congress, the information amassed on benefits, costs, and the efficient quantity of pollution to abate would illuminate the trade-offs involved in improving air quality. When Congress passed the CAA Amendments of 1990, it eventually required 10 million tons of SO_2 emissions abatement, roughly a 50 percent reduction in power plant emissions of this pollutant. Was this the efficient level of pollution control? Subsequent analysis (particularly of the human health benefits of avoided SO_2 emissions) suggests that the efficient amount of SO_2 abatement would have been higher than the 10-million-ton goal.[4] But economic efficiency is one of many criteria considered in the making of environmental policy, some others of which are detailed elsewhere in this book. An excellent summary of how economists see the role of benefit-cost analysis in public decision making is offered by Nobel Laureate Kenneth Arrow and coauthors:

> Although formal benefit-cost analysis should not be viewed as either necessary or sufficient for designing sensible public policy, it can provide an exceptionally useful framework for consistently organizing disparate information, and in this way, it can greatly improve the process and, hence, the outcome of policy analysis.[5]

There are many critiques of benefit-cost analysis.[6] A common critique is that basing environmental policy decisions on whether benefits outweigh costs ignores important political and ethical considerations. As is clear from the preceding quotation, most economists reject the idea that policy should be designed using strict benefit-cost tests. Even when citizens and their governments design policy based on concerns other than efficiency, however, collecting information about benefits and costs can be extremely useful. Some critics of benefit-cost analysis object to placing a dollar value on environmental goods and services, suggesting that these "priceless" resources are devalued when treated in monetary terms.[7] But benefit-cost analysis simply makes explicit the trade-offs represented by a policy choice—it does not create the trade-offs themselves. When environmental policy is made, we establish how much we are willing to spend to protect endangered species or avoid the human health impacts of pollution exposure. Whether we estimate the value of such things in advance and use these numbers to guide policy, or set policy first based on other criteria and then back out our implied values for such things, we have still made the same trade-off. No economic argument can suggest whether explicit or implicit consideration of benefits and costs is *ethically* preferable. But the choice does not affect the outcome that a trade-off has been made. Used as one of many inputs to the consideration of policy choices, benefit-cost analysis is a powerful and illuminating tool.

The Measurement of Environmental Benefits and Costs

Thus far, we have discussed benefits and costs abstractly. In an actual economic analysis, benefits and costs would be measured, so that the horizontal and vertical axes of Figure 10-1 would take on specific numerical units. Quantifying the costs of environmental policies can require rough approximations. For example, one study has estimated the costs of protecting California condors, designated an endangered species following the near extinction of these enormous birds and their later reintroduction into the wild from a captive breeding program.[8] Figure 10-2 describes the costs of each potential step that policymakers might take to protect the condor population; when the number of condors saved per year is graphed against the cost of each potential step taken to save them, a marginal cost curve results that is upward sloping like those we discussed for pollution abatement.

Economists measure the benefits of an environmental policy as the sum of individuals' willingness to pay for the changes it may induce. This notion is clearly anthropocentric—the changes induced by an environmental policy are economically beneficial only to the extent that human beings value them. This does not suggest that improvements in ecosystem function or other "nonhuman" effects of a policy have no value. Many people value open space, endangered species preservation, and biodiversity and have shown through their memberships in environmental advocacy groups, votes in local referenda, and lobbying activities on global environmental issues that they are willing to sacrifice much for these causes. The economic value of an environmental amenity (like clean air, or water, or open space) comprises the value that people experience from using it, and the so-called nonuse value. Nonuse value captures the value people have for simply knowing that an endangered species (like the grizzly bear) or a pristine area (like the Arctic National Wildlife Refuge) exists, even if they never plan to see or use such resources. To carry out a benefit-cost analysis, however, it is not enough to know that people have some value for a policy's goal; we must measure that value to compare it to the policy's costs.

An in-depth discussion of environmental benefit estimation methods is beyond the scope of this chapter.[9] But we can sketch out the basic intuition behind the major approaches. Some benefits of environmental policies can be measured straightforwardly through their impacts on actual markets. For example, if we are considering a policy to reduce water pollution that may increase commercial fish populations, estimates of the increased market value of the total catch would be included in an estimate of the policy's total benefits.

Figure 10-2   Marginal Costs of Protecting the California Condor

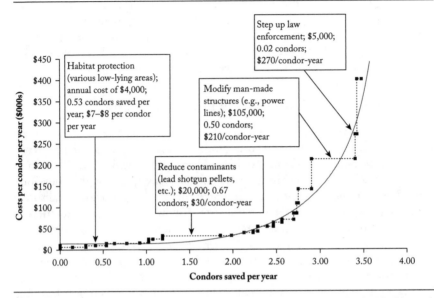

Source: From *Markets and the Environment*, by Nathaniel O. Keohane and Sheila M. Olmstead. Published by Island Press. Copyright © 2007 by the authors.

For most environmental goods and services, however, measuring benefits is much trickier. The values that people have for using environmental amenities can often be measured indirectly through their behavior in markets. For example, many people spend money on wilderness vacations. While they are not purchasing wilderness, per se, when they do this, economists can estimate the recreational value of wilderness sites from travelers' expenditures. Travel-cost models are a class of statistical methods that economists use for this purpose.

Another method, the hedonic housing price model, is based on the idea that what people are willing to pay for a home reflects, in part, the environmental attributes of its neighborhood. Economists use statistical techniques to estimate what portion of a home's price is determined by environmental attributes, such as the surrounding air quality, controlling for other price determinants, like the home's physical characteristics, school district quality, and proximity to jobs and transportation. To estimate the value of human health impacts of an environmental policy, economists primarily use hedonic wage studies. These models estimate people's willingness to pay for small decreases in risks to life and health by examining the differences in wages for jobs with different levels of risk. As in the hedonic housing price model, statistical methods must be used to control for the many other determinants of wages (for example, how skilled or educated a worker must be to take a particular job).

Travel-cost and hedonic models are *revealed preference* models—they estimate how people value a particular aspect of an environmental amenity from their actual behavior, revealed in markets. But if we were to stop with values expressed in markets, the benefits we could estimate for things like wilderness areas and species preservation would be incomplete. Nonuse value leaves no footprint in any market. Thus a *stated preference* approach must be used to quantify nonuse values. Economists design carefully structured surveys to ask people how much they are willing to pay for a specific improvement in environmental quality or a natural resource amenity, and they sum across individuals to assess a society's willingness to pay.

The Environmental Protection Agency's (EPA's) 1985 benefit-cost analysis of reducing the lead content of gasoline offers an example of what each side of such an analysis might include. The analysis quantified the main benefits from phasing out leaded gas: reduced human health damages from lead exposure (retardation of children's cognitive and physiological development and exacerbation of high blood pressure in adult males), reduction in other local air pollutants from vehicle emissions (since leaded gas destroyed catalytic converters, designed to reduce emissions), and lower costs of engine maintenance and related increases in fuel economy. The costs were primarily installation of new refinery equipment and production of alternative fuel additives. The study found that the lead phasedown policy had projected annual net benefits of $7 billion (in 1983 dollars), even though only a portion of benefits were actually monetized. The health benefits of the regulation that the EPA estimated included the avoided costs of medical care and of remedial education for affected children. Americans, if surveyed, would likely have had significant willingness to pay to avoid the lasting health and cognitive impacts of childhood lead exposure, but these benefits were never monetized. Even with these gaps, acknowledged by the study's authors, this analysis helped to "sell" the regulation; a few years earlier, the EPA had decided on a much weaker rule, citing potential costs to refineries.[10]

The fact that the EPA did not monetize some benefits of the U.S. lead phasedown brings us to an important point. In some cases, existing estimation methods may be sufficient to evaluate the benefits of an environmental policy but are too complex and expensive to implement. In the lead case, this was immaterial. The benefits of the policy exceeded the costs by a large margin, even excluding those (presumably large) unmonetized benefits, so the eventual policy decision was not affected by this choice. In other cases, when benefits are hard to monetize, doing so may matter for the ultimate policy outcome.

In some cases, economic tools simply prove insufficient to estimate the benefits (or avoided damages) from environmental policy. For example, climate science suggests that sudden, catastrophic events (like the reversal of thermohaline circulations or sudden collapse of the Greenland or West Antarctic ice sheets) are possible outcomes of the current warming trend. The probabilities of such disastrous events may be very small. Combined with the fact that important climate change impacts may occur in the distant future, this makes estimating the benefits of current climate change policy a challenging and controversial task.[11] Some analysts have attempted, incorrectly, to estimate the benefits of avoiding the elimination of vital ecosystem services, such as pollination and nutrient cycling, using economic benefit estimation tools.[12] Used correctly, these tools measure our collective willingness to pay for small changes in the status quo. The elimination of Earth's vital ecosystem services would cause dramatic shifts in human and market activity of all kinds. While the benefit estimation techniques we have discussed are well suited to assessing the net effect of specific policies, like reducing air pollutant concentrations, or setting aside land to preserve open space, they are inadequate to the task of measuring the value of drastic changes in global ecosystems— efforts to use them for this purpose have resulted in, as one economist quipped, a "serious underestimate of infinity."[13] Estimation of the benefits from environmental policy is the subject of a great deal of economic research, and much progress has been made. But, in some situations, the limits of these tools remain a significant challenge to comprehensive benefit-cost analysis.

Cost-Effective Environmental Policy

Economists' goal of maximizing net benefits is one of many competing goals in the policy process. Even when an environmental standard is inefficient (too stringent, or not stringent enough), economic analysis can still help to select the particular policy instruments used to achieve that goal. Earlier we defined the concept of cost-effectiveness as choosing the policy that can achieve a given environmental standard at least cost. Let's return to our SO_2 example to see how this works in practice.

Imagine that you are a policy analyst at the EPA, given the job of figuring out how U.S. power plants will meet the 10-million-ton reduction in SO_2 emissions required under the 1990 CAA Amendments. One important issue to consider is how much the policy will cost. All else equal, you would like to attain the new standard as cheaply as possible. We can reduce this problem to a simple case to demonstrate how an economist would answer this question. Assume that the entire 10-million-ton reduction will be achieved by two power plants, firms A and B. Each has a set of SO_2 abatement technologies, and the sequence of technologies for each firm and their associated costs determine the marginal cost curves in Figure 10-3, labeled MC_A and MC_B. Notice that abatement increases from left to right for firm A, and from right to left for firm B. At any point along the horizontal axis, the sum of the two firms' emissions reductions will always equal 10 million tons, as the CAA Amendments require.

Let's begin with one simple solution that seems like a fair approach: divide the total required reduction in half and ask each firm to abate 5 million tons of SO_2. This allocation of pollution control is represented by the leftmost dotted vertical line in Figure 10-3 and is often referred to as a "uniform pollution control standard," because the abatement requirement is uniform across firms. Is this the cheapest way to reduce pollution by 10 million tons? Suppose we require firm A to reduce one extra ton and require firm B to reduce one ton less? We would still achieve a 10-million-ton reduction, but that last ton would cost less than it did before. Firm B's cost curve lies above

A's at the uniform standard, so when we shift responsibility for abating that ton from B to A, we reduce the total cost of achieving the new standard. How long can we move to the right along the horizontal axis and continue to lower total costs? Until the marginal costs of abatement for the two firms are exactly equal: where the two curves intersect, when firm A abates 6 million tons and B abates 4 million tons.

The cost savings from allocating abatement in this way rather than using the uniform standard is equivalent to the difference in costs between firm A and firm B for the last million tons of abatement. On Figure 10-3, that is equal to the area between the two firms' marginal cost curves (the cost to firm B minus the cost to firm A), bounded by the dotted lines marking the uniform standard and the cost-effective allocation. Working in two dimensions, we cannot easily demonstrate how this works for more firms. But the rule of thumb for a cost-effective environmental policy instrument is the same for a large number of firms as it is in this simple example: a pollution control policy minimizes costs if the marginal abatement costs of all firms reducing pollution under the policy are equal.

You may have noticed that in order to identify the cost-effective pollution control allocation in this simple case, we needed a lot of information about each firm's abatement costs—we used their marginal cost curves to accomplish the task. As an EPA policy analyst, it is unlikely that you would

Figure 10-3   Cost-Effective Pollution Abatement by Two Firms

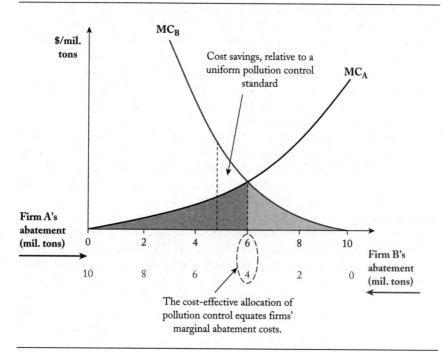

The cost-effective allocation of pollution control equates firms' marginal abatement costs.

have this information, and even less likely if we move from two power plants to the thousands eventually covered by the CAA Amendments of 1990. In a competitive market, the structure of firms' costs is proprietary information that they will not likely share with regulators. So how can a cost-effective pollution control policy be designed?

One class of environmental policy instruments, often called "market-based" or "incentive-based" approaches, does not require regulators to have specific information about individual firms' marginal abatement costs in order to attain a particular pollution control standard at least cost. In the case of the SO_2 emissions reduction required by the CAA Amendments of 1990, regulators chose one of these approaches, a system of tradable pollution permits, to achieve this goal.

A market for tradable pollution permits works quite simply. Return to the world of two firms, and assume that you have advised the EPA administrator to allocate responsibility for 5 million tons of SO_2 emissions abatement to each of the two firms. You add, however, the provision that the firms should be able to trade their allocations, so long as the aggregate reduction of 10 million tons is achieved. If we begin at the (5 million, 5 million) allocation in Figure 10-3, we can imagine the incentives for the two firms under this trading policy.

The last ton abated by firm B costs much more than the last ton abated by A if they each stick to their 5-million-ton abatement requirements. Firm B would be willing to pay A to increase its own abatement, so that B could abate fewer tons of SO_2. In fact, B would pay any price that lies below its own marginal abatement cost. Firm A would be willing to make such a deal, so long as B paid more than A's own marginal abatement cost. So the vertical distance between the two cost curves at (5 million, 5 million) represents the potential gain from trading for that last ton of abatement. The same is true of the next ton, and the next, all the way to the point at which B is abating 4 million tons and A is abating 6 million. Notice that the firms will trade permits until exactly the point at which the total costs of reducing 10 million tons of SO_2 are minimized.[14] The bigger the differences in abatement costs across regulated firms, the larger the potential cost savings from trading.

How much of a difference did this make in the SO_2 emissions abatement regulation we have been discussing? While it operated, the U.S. SO_2 trading program produced cost savings of about $1.8 billion annually, compared with the most likely alternative policy considered during deliberations over the 1990 CAA Amendments (which would have required each firm to install the same technology to reduce emissions).[15] In fact, the Environmental Defense Fund, an environmental advocacy organization, agreed to endorse and help write the legislation proposed by the George H. W. Bush administration to amend the CAA if the administration would increase the required emissions reduction (from 8 million tons, which it was proposing) to the eventual 10 million tons of SO_2, based on the potential cost savings of the tradable permit approach. In this case, the tradable permit policy was not only cost-effective, but it allowed political actors to take a step closer to the efficient level of abatement, with significant benefits for human and ecosystem health.[16]

Principles of Market-Based Environmental Policy

You may have noticed that the notion that firms A and B are inherently doing something wrong when they produce SO_2 emissions along with electricity has been conspicuously lacking from our discussion. In economic terms, pollution is the result of a simple set of incentives facing firms and consumers that is "stacked against" environmental protection. The consumption and production decisions that result can be changed if we alter the relevant incentives. The social problem of pollution results from what economists call market failure. The three types of market failure most relevant to environmental policy are externalities, public goods, and the "tragedy of the commons."[17]

Let's consider externalities first. If you have driven a car, checked e-mail, or turned on a light today, you have contributed to the problem of global climate change. With near unanimity, the scientific community agrees that the accumulation of carbon dioxide (CO_2) and other heat-trapping gases in Earth's upper atmosphere has increased global mean surface temperatures by about 1 degree Fahrenheit since the start of the twentieth century, with consequences including sea level rise, regional changes in precipitation, increased frequency of extreme weather events, species migration and extinction, and spatial shifts in the prevalence of disease. Ask an economist, however, and he or she will suggest that the roots of the problem are not only in the complex dynamics of Earth's atmosphere, but also in the incentives facing individuals and firms when they choose to consume and produce energy. Each such decision imposes a small cost in terms of its contribution to future atmospheric carbon concentrations. However, the individuals making these decisions do not bear these costs. Your electricity bill does include the cost of producing electricity and moving it from the plant to your home, but (in most countries) it does not include the cost of the carbon emissions from electricity production. Carbon emissions are an *externality*—their costs are external to the transaction between the buyer and the seller of electricity. The market for energy is incomplete, since its price does not reflect the full cost of its provision.[18]

You also may have noticed that bringing nations together to negotiate a solution to the problem of global climate change seems to be difficult. Clean air and a stable global climate are *public goods*: everyone benefits from their provision, whether or not they have contributed, and we can all enjoy these goods without interfering with the ability of others to enjoy them. Other public goods include national defense, weather forecasting, and public parks. If you have ever listened to public radio or watched public television without contributing money to these institutions, then you have been a free rider. Free riding is a rational response to the incentives created by a public good: many beneficiaries will pay nothing for its provision, and those who do pay will generally pay less than what, in their heart of hearts, they would be willing to pay. Markets for public goods are incomplete. Left to their own devices, markets will underprovide these valuable goods and services.

The third category of market failure most relevant to environmental policy is the tragedy of the commons.[19] A group of individuals sharing access to a common resource (a pasture for grazing cattle, a fishery, or a busy highway) will tend to overexploit it. The "tragedy" is that, if individuals could self-regulate and reduce their collective use of the resource, the productivity of the resource would increase to everyone's benefit. But the actions of single individuals are not enough to make a difference. Individuals restricting their own use only bear the costs of this activity, with no benefits. The resulting spiral of overexploitation can destroy the resource entirely. A prominent example of the tragedy of the commons is the collapse of many deep-sea fisheries over the past few decades. But climate change is also an example of this type of market failure. The global upper atmosphere is a resource shared by everyone and owned by no one. The incentive for individual citizens to reduce carbon emissions (their exploitation of this resource) is small; thus the resource is overexploited.

When markets fail in these three ways and environmental damages result, government intervention may be required to fix the situation. Governments can correct externalities, provide public goods, and avert the tragedy of the commons. From an economic perspective, market principles should be used to correct these market failures.

Using Market Principles to Solve Environmental Problems

Like the global damages from carbon emissions, the local and regional damages from SO_2 emissions (for example, human health problems and acid rain) are external to power plants' production decisions and their consumers' decisions about how much energy to use. The tradable permit program described earlier is an excellent example of using market principles to correct market failures. The government distributed permits to power plants and allowed them to trade. Plants made these trades by deciding how to minimize the costs of producing power—for each ton of SO_2 that they produced before the regulation was passed, they now faced a choice. Either a plant could continue to emit that ton, and use one of its permits, or it could spend money to abate that ton, freeing up a permit to sell to another power plant (and earning the permit price as a reward). The result was an active market for SO_2 emissions permits. In June 2008 alone, 250,000 tons of emissions were traded in this market, at an end-of-month price of $325 per ton. By putting a price on pollution, the government internalized its cost, represented by the price of a permit to emit one ton of SO_2, a cost that firms took into account when they decided how much electricity to produce.

Unfortunately, regulatory and judicial actions in 2008 to 2010 effectively dismantled the U.S. SO_2 allowance market, one of the most significant experiments with a market-based approach to pollution control.[20] Since the late 1990s, scientific evidence regarding the health effects of fine particulate matter associated with SO_2 emissions had suggested that further reductions would be required under the CAA. The initial approach of the EPA during the George W. Bush administration was to tighten the SO_2 emissions cap, requiring Midwestern states contributing to violations of CAA fine particulate standards on the East Coast to surrender three permits for every one ton of SO_2 emissions. A legal challenge by states and electric utilities resulted in a 2008 federal court decision vacating this new approach, on the grounds that the EPA could not modify the existing interstate SO_2 market to meet stricter standards in the absence of legislation from Congress. After further revisions and an additional court challenge under the Obama administration, the SO_2 market was replaced by state-level and source-level emissions constraints by 2012. When governments create environmental markets, even well-functioning markets that dramatically reduce the costs of pollution control, they can also dismantle them.

Another way to use market principles to reduce pollution is to impose a tax. Rather than imposing a cap on the quantity of pollution, and allowing regulated firms to trade emissions permits to establish a market price for pollution, a tax imposes a specific price on pollution and allows firms to decide how much to pollute in response. A tax has an effect on firms' decisions that is essentially identical to the effect of the permit price created by a cap-and-trade policy; polluters decide, for each ton of emissions, whether to abate that ton (incurring the resulting abatement costs) or to pay the tax and continue to emit that ton.

Taxes on air and water pollution are quite common, though existing environmental taxes tend to be lower than efficient levels.[21] British Columbia's carbon tax, established in 2008, may be an exception; the current tax of about $27.50 per ton is in the range of current economic estimates of the marginal damages from carbon emissions.[22] Australia's carbon tax was levied at a similar level beginning in 2012 but repealed in July 2014, after an election in which debate over the carbon tax played an important role. Developing countries such as China, Malaysia, and Colombia have also experimented with environmental taxes.

Some important differences exist between taxes and tradable permits. First, a cap-and-trade system pins down a total quantity of allowable pollution. The trade among firms that results establishes the permit price. Before any trading has taken place, we know exactly how much pollution the policy is going to allow, but we are uncertain how much it will cost society to achieve that goal. In setting a tax, regulators pin down the price of pollution instead, creating some degree of certainty about how much a regulation may cost. As under the permit policy, firms make private choices about how much pollution to emit, comparing their abatement costs to the tax. But the total quantity of pollution that will result is uncertain. To be certain about how much pollution will result after the tax is imposed, regulators need to have good information about the cost of reducing pollution in the regulated industry. Both the total quantity of allowable pollution and the total cost of pollution reduction are important pieces of information to consider in designing environmental policy. Each of the two primary market-based approaches to internalizing the cost of pollution, taxes and permits, offers certainty over one, but not both, of these important variables.[23]

228 Sheila M. Olmstead

Taxes and tradable permits can also differ in their costs to regulated firms. Under a pollution tax, a firm must pay the tax for every ton of pollution it emits. Under a permit system, permits are typically given to firms for free, at least initially. So a permit system only requires firms to pay for pollution in excess of their permit allocations. For this reason, complying with a tax can be more expensive for firms than a permit system.[24] The political opposition that results may be one reason that there are few significant environmental taxes in the United States. Taxes may be preferable to tradable permits along many dimensions as a policy to address climate change, but serious discussion of a global carbon tax is lacking.[25] If taxes and tradable permits are fundamentally equivalent pollution regulations from an economic perspective, what about those extra compliance costs? Taxes create revenues for the government agency that collects them, exactly equal to the aggregate tax bill for all firms, whereas tradable permits distributed for free do not. The net impact of this difference between the two policies depends on how tax revenues are spent. From the standpoint of efficiency, the best thing to do with environmental tax revenues may be to use them to reduce other taxes in the economy that tend to distort consumers' and firms' decisions—taxes on income, sales, and capital gains, for example.[26] Society may benefit to a smaller degree if governments use tax revenues to provide additional goods and services.

Taxes on pollution may also be imposed indirectly. For example, many countries tax gasoline. In the United States, the revenues from most state gasoline taxes are used to maintain and expand transportation infrastructure; U.S. gas taxes are not explicit pollution control policies. However, economists have estimated the optimal U.S. gasoline tax, taking into account the most significant externalities: emissions of local pollutants (particulate matter and nitrous oxides), CO_2 emissions (which contribute to global climate change), traffic congestion, and the costs of accidents not borne by drivers.[27] In their estimation, the efficient tax would be $0.83 per gallon. A more recent study suggests potential regional heterogeneity in the optimal gas tax; California's efficient tax may be about $1.37 per gallon (including oil security externalities, as well as the others).[28] However, most of these externalities depend on the number of miles driven, not the amount of gasoline consumed (only a proxy for miles driven); taxing miles driven rather than gasoline would be better from an economic perspective. This highlights the important fact that the choice of what to tax may be as important as the level of a tax.

Notice that as we have discussed the virtues of market-based approaches to environmental policy, all of the options we have mentioned require some role for government intervention, setting a tax, for example, or enforcing a cap on pollution. This is a critical point. Market-based approaches should not be conflated with voluntary (nonregulatory) environmental policies, which would not be expected to have a strong impact on environmental quality.

Market-Based Environmental Policy Instruments in Practice

Using Markets to Reduce Air Pollution

Market-based approaches have reduced air pollutants other than SO_2. In the 1980s, the EPA implemented a lead-trading policy to enforce a regulation reducing the allowable lead content of U.S. gasoline by 90 percent. Earlier in this chapter, we discussed the benefit-cost analysis of this policy, which suggested that the benefits of eliminating lead in gasoline exceeded its costs. The policy the EPA chose to implement the lead phasedown had something to do with this; it lowered costs relative to a more prescriptive approach. Refiners producing gasoline with a lower lead content than was required earned credits that could be traded and banked. In each year of the program, more than 60 percent of the lead added to gasoline was associated with traded lead credits.[29] This policy successfully met its environmental goal, and the EPA estimated cost savings from the lead trading program of approximately $250 million per year until the phasedown was completed in 1987.[30]

The Kyoto Protocol, the 1997 international climate change treaty ratified by 191 countries and the European Union, included emissions trading as a mechanism for achieving national emissions reduction targets. Among industrialized countries that took on emissions reduction targets under the Kyoto Protocol, the countries of the EU opted to use an emissions trading system, established in 2005, to meet their emissions reduction targets. The protocol sets a cap on CO_2 emissions for the EU as a whole, allocated by the EU to member countries. Member countries then divide emissions allotments among the following industries: electric power generation; refineries; iron and steel; cement, glass, and ceramics; and pulp and paper.

The EU ETS is the world's largest emissions trading system, covering almost twelve thousand facilities in twenty-seven countries in 2014 (as well as intra-EU airline flights), and accounting for about 45 percent of EU CO_2 emissions.[31] The Kyoto Protocol's emissions caps did not begin to bind until 2008, so the pilot phase of the EU ETS (2005–2007) was designed to set up the institutional and operating structures necessary for trading. The cap in the EU system in this pilot phase was a small reduction (a few percentage points) below expected emissions in the absence of the policy, though in retrospect permits in the pilot phase were overallocated.[32] A more stringent cap was introduced in 2008. Determining the impact of the EU ETS on emissions in the pilot phase is difficult, in part because the binding of caps beginning in 2008 coincided with a global economic recession (resulting in falling CO_2 emissions). However, several studies suggest that the ETS has decreased emissions independent of reductions from the recession, by 2–5 percent below "business as usual" in the pilot phase, and about 8 percent in 2008–2009.[33] Going forward, the aggregate emissions target under the EU ETS in phase 3 (2013–2020) will decline by almost 2 percent per year. No studies have estimated the cost savings from this approach, relative to counterfactual policies that might have achieved the same level of aggregate emissions reduction.

The United States did not ratify the Kyoto Protocol, though the Obama administration has set a national goal of reducing carbon emissions by 17 percent over 2005 levels by 2020 largely through prescriptive regulations (discussed further in Chapters 7 and 12).[34] However, support for action on climate change has led some states to enact market-based policies to reduce greenhouse gas (GHG) emissions. California's Global Warming Solutions Act of 2006 (AB 32) seeks to reduce GHG emissions to 1990 levels by 2020, with a cap-and-trade policy as its centerpiece; the program's first allowance auction took place in November 2012, and the cap began to bind in January 2013. In 2015, California's market covers 85 percent of GHG emissions (from power plants, industrial sources, natural gas, and the transportation sector). It is too early to measure the impact of California's cap-and-trade system on GHG emissions, and on abatement costs relative to alternative approaches. Another U.S. market-based initiative is the Regional Greenhouse Gas Initiative (RGGI), a cap-and-trade system among electricity generators in nine northeastern states. The RGGI began in 2009, but the combination of reduced electricity demand due to the economic recession of 2008–2009 and lower natural gas prices (due to increased U.S. supplies of shale gas) resulted in the RGGI emissions cap being nonbinding in early years.[35] A new, more stringent 2014 cap, scheduled to decline by 2.5 percent per year from 2015 to 2020, may bode well for the RGGI's future.

Individual Tradable Quotas for Fishing

Thus far, we have talked about cap-and-trade policies as if they applied only to pollution problems. But a common application is to fisheries management, to avert the tragedy of the commons. The world's largest market for tradable individual fishing quotas (IFQs), created in 1986, is in New Zealand.[36] By 2004, it covered seventy different fish species, and the government of New Zealand had divided coastal waters into "species-regions," generating 275 separate markets that covered more than 85 percent of the commercial catch in the area extending two hundred miles from New Zealand's coast. In the United States, Pacific halibut and sablefish off the coast of Alaska, mid-Atlantic surf clams and ocean quahogs, South Atlantic wreckfish, and red snapper in the Gulf of Mexico are all regulated using IFQ markets. Iceland manages stocks of twenty fish and shellfish species using IFQ markets, in a system established in 1990.

A market for fishing quotas works similarly to a market for pollution permits. The government establishes a total allowable catch (TAC), distributing shares to individual fishers. Fishers can trade their assigned quotas, which represent a percentage of the TAC for a particular species-region. An analysis of catch statistics from 11,315 global fisheries between 1950 and 2003 provides the first large-scale empirical evidence for the effectiveness of these approaches in halting, and even reversing, the global trend toward fisheries collapse. The authors empirically estimate the relative advantage of IFQ fisheries over non-IFQ fisheries in terms of a lower probability of collapse, and estimate that, had all non-IFQ global fisheries switched to management through tradable quotas in 1970, the percentage of collapsed global fisheries by 2003 could have been reduced from more than 25 percent to about 9 percent.[37]

Waste Management Policies

Market-based approaches have also been used to manage solid waste. Some waste products have high recycling value. If you live in a community with curbside recycling, you may have seen low-income residents of the community picking aluminum cans out of recycling bins at the curb; they do this because it is much less costly to produce aluminum from scrap metal than from virgin ore, and as a result, those cans are quite valuable. But most household waste ends up as trash, disposed of legally in landfills or incinerators or illegally dumped. The marginal cost of public garbage collection and disposal for an American household has been estimated at $1.03 per trash bag, but until recently, the marginal cost of disposal borne by households was approximately zero.[38] An increasingly common waste management policy is the "pay-as-you-throw" system, a volume-based waste disposal charge often assessed as a requirement for the purchase of official garbage bags, stickers to attach to bags of specific volume, periodic disposal charges for official city trash cans of particular sizes, and (rarely) charges based on the measured weight of curbside trash. These systems function like an environmental tax, internalizing the costs of disposing of household waste. In 2006, more than seven thousand U.S. communities had some form of pay-as-you-throw disposal.[39] A comprehensive study of a pay-as-you-throw policy was performed in Charlottesville, Virginia, which imposed a charge of 80 cents per trash bag.[40] This tax was estimated to have reduced the number of bags households threw out by about 37 percent. However, the effect was offset by two factors that have proven to be common problems with such programs. First, the reduction in the total weight of trash thrown away was much smaller (about a 14 percent reduction), since consumers compacted their trash in order to reduce the number of bags they used. Second, illegal disposal increased. As noted earlier in the discussion of the gasoline tax, Charlottesville's experience suggests that the decision of *what* to tax may be as important as (or more important than) how high the tax should be. A more recent study of two hundred towns in New Hampshire (31 percent of which had adopted pay-as-you-throw policies) suggests that the introduction of such policies reduces municipal solid waste generation very significantly, with an additional marginal effect of increasing the disposal cost per bag.[41]

Habitat and Land Management Policies

Tradable development rights (TDRs) have been applied to solve problems as diverse as deforestation in the Brazilian Amazon and the development of former farmland in the Maryland suburbs of Washington, DC.[42]

About 140 U.S. communities have implemented TDRs, with many other potential programs in the pipeline.[43] The program in Calvert County, Maryland, preserved an estimated thirteen thousand acres of farmland between 1978 and 2005. In Brazil since 1998, TDRs have been used to slow the conversion of ecologically valuable lands to agriculture; each parcel of private property that is developed must be offset by preserving a forested parcel elsewhere (within the same ecosystem and with land of greater or equal ecological value). Simulations of the Brazilian policy for the state of Minas Gerais suggest that TDRs lower the cost to landowners of protecting a unit of forested land. Landowners can develop the most profitable land and preserve less profitable land. But this highlights two of the chief problems with TDRs. First, how can land developers prove (and regulators ensure) that a preserved parcel is really additional—that it would not have remained in forest without the developer's efforts? Second, how can we measure the ecological equivalence of two land parcels? In the case of carbon emissions, each ton of emissions has essentially the same impact on our ultimate concern—atmospheric carbon concentrations—no matter where it is emitted. The same cannot be said of land preservation.

A related policy, wetlands mitigation banking, holds similar promise and faces similar challenges. Wetlands are classic public goods. They provide a rich set of ecosystem services, for which there are no markets, and from which everyone benefits, regardless of who pays for their preservation. Wetlands have been depleted rapidly in the United States and other parts of the world by conversion to agricultural and urban use. The externalities to wetlands conversion, such as increased flood risk; loss of habitat for birds, fish, and mammals; and reduced groundwater recharge are taken into account only when governments intervene to require it.

Since the early 1990s, the United States has experimented with mitigation banking, a policy under which land developers compensate for any lost wetlands by preserving, expanding, or creating wetlands elsewhere.[44] Wetlands banks serve as central brokers, allowing developers to purchase credits, and fulfilling credits through the physical process of wetlands preservation, creation, and management. In 2005, there were 405 approved U.S. wetland banks in operation. We can think of mitigation banking as a market-based approach in two different ways. First, it is a tax on land development, internalizing some of the externalities of wetlands depletion. Second, given that the U.S. federal government has purported to enforce a "no net loss" policy with regard to the national stock of wetlands since 1989, we can think of mitigation banking as a cap-and-trade policy in which the cap on acres of wetlands lost is zero.

As in the case of TDRs, wetlands mitigation banking reduces the costs of preserving wetlands acreage but faces significant challenges. A wetland in a particular location provides a specific portfolio of biophysical services. For example, coastal wetlands support shellfish nurseries and may reduce damages from storm-related flooding. Inland wetlands may filter contaminants and provide islands of habitat for migratory bird species in overland flight. If development pressures in coastal cities create incentives for landowners to develop wetlands in these locations, and pay for wetlands creation inland, the net effect of these kinds of trades must be considered. This is a significant change from the simple ton-for-ton trading that occurs for some air pollutants.

This section offered a handful of examples of the many applications of market principles to environmental policy.[45] We emphasized the strong arguments in favor of taxes, tradable permits, and other market-based approaches, especially given that these policies can achieve environmental policy goals at less cost than more prescriptive approaches. But they are not appropriate solutions to all environmental problems. The issues we raised in our discussion of market-based land management policies arise in other contexts, as well. Market-based policies can be designed for situations in which the location of pollution emissions or natural resource amenities matters for the benefits of pollution control or resource management. But they are not workable in extreme cases. For example, the impacts of a toxic waste dump are highly localized. Economists would not advise setting a national limit on toxic waste disposal, and allowing firms to trade disposal permits, letting the waste end up where it may. Environmental problems at this end of the spectrum—the opposite end from a problem like carbon emissions, which can be reduced anywhere with essentially the same net effect—may be better addressed through prescriptive approaches.

Conclusions

Economics offers a powerful pair of tools—efficiency and cost-effectiveness—to consider environmental policy trade-offs. Efficiency has to do with the setting of environmental policy goals: how much pollution should we reduce, or how many acres of wetlands should be preserved? An efficient pollution control policy equalizes the monetized benefits and costs of the last ton of pollution eliminated. The process used to determine whether an environmental policy is efficient is benefit-cost analysis. If a strict benefit-cost test were applied to the decision of how much SO_2 pollution to eliminate from power plant smokestacks in the 1990s, additional reductions would have been required. Benefit-cost analysis would also have suggested that lead be eliminated from U.S. gasoline sooner than it was. In other cases, applying the rule of efficiency suggests that environmental standards should be weakened.

However, efficiency is not the only potential input to good environmental policy. The treatment of benefit-cost analysis in the major U.S. environmental statutes is a good indication of our ambivalence toward analyzing environmental trade-offs in this systematic way; the statutes alternately "forbid, inhibit, tolerate, allow, invite, or require the use of economic analysis in environmental decision making."[46] For example, the CAA forbids the consideration of costs in setting the National Ambient Air Quality Standards, and the U.S. Safe Drinking Water Act requires benefit-cost analysis of all new drinking water contaminant standards. Environmental regulatory agencies are not economic agencies. While laying out the trade-offs involved in setting environmental standards is critically important from an economic perspective, political, social, and ethical concerns may hold more influence than benefit-cost analysis in this process.

Even when environmental standards are inefficient, however, policy-makers can choose policies to achieve those standards at least cost. The billions of dollars saved by policies like SO_2 trading, paired with their proven environmental effectiveness, have made market-based approaches like tradable permits and taxes appealing policy instruments for solving environmental problems. Ironically, as the theoretical and empirical evidence of their cost savings and environmental effectiveness have stacked up, U.S. political support for these policies not only eroded during the recent economic recession but has been thoroughly demonized, and especially so by Republicans in Congress,[47] in direct conflict with their unwavering support for markets in most other contexts. This may make it much harder in the future to implement market-based policies, unnecessarily raising the cost of environmental regulation to firms and consumers. Market-based environmental policy approaches are not appropriate for all situations. But where market incentives create environmental problems, market principles should be harnessed to solve them.

Suggested Websites

EPA National Center for Environmental Economics (yosemite.epa.gov/ee/epa/eed.nsf/webpages/homepage) Provides access to research reports, regulatory impact analyses, and other EPA publications.

OMB Office of Information and Regulatory Affairs (www.whitehouse.gov/OMB/inforeg) Provides a variety of information on the Office of Management and Budget's regulatory oversight mission, including pending regulations, the status of regulatory reviews, and prompt letters that encourage federal agencies to consider regulations that appear to have benefits greater than costs.

Center for Effective Government (www.foreffectivegov.org) Follows budgets and regulatory policies.

Resources for the Future (www.rff.org) Nonprofit research organization devoted to environmental and resource economics and policy.

Notes

1. For competing scientific opinions about Snake River salmon decline, see Charles C. Mann and Mark L. Plummer, "Can Science Rescue Salmon?" *Science* 298 (2000): 716–19, with letters and responses. See also David L. Halsing and Michael R. Moore, "Cost-Effective Management Alternatives for Snake River Chinook Salmon: A Biological-Economic Synthesis," *Conservation Biology* 22, no. 2 (2000): 338–50.
2. In reality, each ton of emissions is not equivalent. SO_2 emissions in urban areas or those upwind of critical ecosystems may cause relatively greater harm. In addition,

costs and benefits may not follow the smooth, continuous functions we depict in Figure 10-1. The simple curves help us to develop intuition that carries through even in more complex situations.

3. Since marginal benefits and costs represent the rate at which benefits and costs change when we add an additional ton of emissions reduction, they are also measured by the slope of the total benefit and cost curves; notice that net benefits are largest in Figure 10-1 (at Q^*) when the slopes of B(Q) and C(Q) are equal.

4. Dallas Burtraw et al., "The Costs and Benefits of Reducing Air Pollutants Related to Acid Rain," *Contemporary Economic Policy* 16 (1998): 379–400.

5. Kenneth J. Arrow et al., "Is There a Role for Benefit-Cost Analysis in Environmental, Health, and Safety Regulation?" *Science* (April 12, 1996): 221–22.

6. Stephen Kelman, "Cost-Benefit Analysis: An Ethical Critique," with replies, *AEI Journal on Government and Social Regulation* (January/February 1981): 33–40.

7. Frank Ackerman and Lisa Heinzerling, *Priceless: On Knowing the Price of Everything and the Value of Nothing* (New York: New Press, 2004).

8. This discussion is based on Nathaniel O. Keohane, Benjamin Van Roy, and Richard J. Zeckhauser, "Managing the Quality of a Resource with Stock and Flow Controls," *Journal of Public Economics* 91 (2007): 541–69.

9. See A. Myrick Freeman III, *The Measurement of Environmental and Resource Values*, 2nd ed. (Washington, DC: Resources for the Future, 2003).

10. Albert L. Nichols, "Lead in Gasoline," in *Economic Analyses at EPA: Assessing Regulatory Impact*, ed. Richard D. Morgenstern (Washington, DC: Resources for the Future, 1997), 49–86.

11. See Martin L. Weitzman, "A Review of the Stern Review on the Economics of Climate Change," *Journal of Economic Literature* 45, no. 3 (2007): 703–24.

12. Robert Costanza et al., "The Value of the World's Ecosystem Services and Natural Capital," *Nature* 387 (1997): 253–60.

13. Michael Toman, "Why Not to Calculate the Value of the World's Ecosystem Services and Natural Capital," *Ecological Economics* 25 (1998): 57–60.

14. We emphasize the cost-effectiveness of market-based approaches to environmental policy in the short run, a critical concept and one that is relatively easy to develop at an intuitive level. However, the greatest potential cost savings from these types of environmental policies may be achieved in the long run. Because they require firms to pay to pollute, market-based policies provide strong incentives for regulated firms to invest in technologies that reduce pollution abatement costs over time, either developing these technologies themselves or adopting cheaper pollution control technologies developed elsewhere.

15. Nathaniel O. Keohane, "Cost Savings from Allowance Trading in the 1990 Clean Air Act," in *Moving to Markets in Environmental Regulation: Lessons from Twenty Years of Experience*, ed. Charles E. Kolstad and Jody Freeman (New York: Oxford University Press, 2007).

16. The definitive overview of the SO_2 permit trading program is found in A. Denny Ellerman et al., *Markets for Clean Air: The U.S. Acid Rain Program* (New York: Cambridge University Press, 2000).

17. These concepts are described in much greater detail in Nathaniel O. Keohane and Sheila M. Olmstead, *Markets and the Environment* (Washington, DC: Island Press, 2007), Chapter 5.

18. Pollution is a negative externality, but externalities can also be positive. For example, a child vaccinated against measles benefits because she is unlikely to contract that disease. But a vaccinated child in turn benefits her family, neighbors, and schoolmates, since she is less likely to expose them to disease.

19. Garrett Hardin, "The Tragedy of the Commons," *Science* 162 (1968): 1243–48.

20. Richard Schmalensee and Robert N. Stavins, "The SO$_2$ Allowance Trading System: The Ironic History of a Grand Policy Experiment," *Journal of Economic Perspectives* 27 (2013): 103–22.

21. Robert N. Stavins, "Experience with Market-Based Environmental Policy Instruments," in *Handbook of Environmental Economics*, vol. I, ed. Karl-Göran Mäler and Jeffrey Vincent (Amsterdam: Elsevier Science, 2003), 355–435.

22. Interagency Working Group on Social Cost of Carbon, United States Government, *Technical Support Document: Technical Update of the Social Cost of Carbon for Regulatory Impact Analysis under Executive Order 12866*, May 2013.

23. This difference between the two approaches—taxes and permits—can cause one approach to be more efficient than the other; see Martin L. Weitzman, "Prices v. Quantities," *Review of Economic Studies* 41 (1974): 477–91.

24. This distinction disappears if permits are auctioned rather than given away. But auctioned permit systems are rare. Even the biggest existing tradable permit systems, including the U.S. SO$_2$ trading program and the European Union Emissions Trading System (EU ETS), auction only a very small percentage of permits.

25. The EU tried to implement a carbon tax in the early 1990s but failed to achieve unanimous approval of its (then) fifteen member states; the ETS faced much less opposition. Some European countries, including Norway, implemented carbon taxes prior to the establishment of the ETS. On the potential advantages of a carbon tax over permits, see William D. Nordhaus, "To Tax or Not to Tax: Alternative Approaches to Slowing Global Warming," *Review of Environmental Economics and Policy* 1, no. 1 (2007): 26–44.

26. This is actually more complicated, since environmental taxes can exacerbate the distortions introduced by other taxes. For a straightforward discussion of this and other comparisons between taxes and permits, see Lawrence H. Goulder and Ian W. H. Parry, "Instrument Choice in Environmental Policy," *Review of Environmental Economics and Policy* 2, no. 2 (2007): 152–74.

27. Ian Parry and Kenneth Small, "Does Britain or the United States Have the Right Gasoline Tax?" *American Economic Review* 95 (2005): 1276–89.

28. C.-Y. Cynthia Lin and Lea Prince, "The Optimal Gas Tax for California," Working Paper, University of California, Davis (2014).

29. Robert W. Hahn and G. L. Hester, "Marketable Permits: Lessons for Theory and Practice," *Ecology Law Quarterly* 16 (1989): 361–406.

30. EPA, Office of Policy Analysis, *Costs and Benefits of Reducing Lead in Gasoline, Final Regulatory Impact Analysis* (Washington, DC: EPA, 1985).

31. See A. Denny Ellerman and Barbara K. Buchner, "The European Union Emissions Trading Scheme: Origins, Allocation, and Early Results," *Review of Environmental Economics and Policy* 1, no. 1 (2007): 66–87; A. Denny Ellerman and Paul L. Joskow, *The European Union's Emissions Trading System in Perspective* (Washington, DC: Pew Center on Global Climate Change, 2008); Frank J. Convery and Luke Redmond, "Market and Price Developments in the European Union Emissions Trading Scheme," *Review of Environmental Economics and Policy* 1, no. 1 (2007): 88–111; European Commission, *The EU Emissions Trading System (EU ETS)*, http://ec.europa.eu/clima/policies/ets/index_en.htm.

32. A. Denny Ellerman, Barbara Buchner, and Carlo Carraro, *Allocation in the European Emissions Trading Scheme: Rights, Rents and Fairness* (Cambridge, UK: Cambridge University Press, 2007).

33. Christian Egenhofer, Monica Alessi, Anton Georgiev, and Noriko Fujiwara, *The EU Emissions Trading System and Climate Policy towards 2050: Real Incentives to Reduce Emissions and Drive Innovation?* CEPS Special Report (Brussels: Center for European Policy Studies, 2011).

34. In June 2009, the U.S. federal government appeared to be taking significant steps toward setting up an economy-wide cap-and-trade system to reduce CO_2 emissions, with the passage in the House of Representatives of the American Clean Energy and Security Act, also known as the Waxman-Markey bill. In July 2010, the U.S. Senate abandoned its effort to draft companion legislation (see Chapter 5).

35. While small effects of the RGGI on emissions have been estimated, the effects of the (low) carbon price from the cap-and-trade system cannot be separated from the effects of the RGGI's other components. In addition, some or all of those declines may have been offset by increased emissions in surrounding states. See Brian C. Murray, Peter T. Maniloff, and Evan M. Murray, "Why Have Greenhouse Emissions in RGGI States Declined? An Econometric Attribution to Economic, Energy Market and Policy Factors," Division of Economics and Business Working Paper 2014-04 (Golden: Colorado School of Mines, April 2014).

36. See Suzanne Iudicello, Michael Weber, and Robert Wieland, *Fish, Markets and Fishermen: The Economics of Overfishing* (Washington, DC: Island Press, 1999). For assessments of New Zealand's policy, see John H. Annala, "New Zealand's ITQ System: Have the First Eight Years Been a Success or a Failure?" *Reviews in Fish Biology and Fisheries* 6 (1996): 43–62; Richard G. Newell, James N. Sanchirico, and Suzi Kerr, "Fishing Quota Markets," *Journal of Environmental Economics and Management* 49, no. 3 (2005): 437–62.

37. Christopher Costello, Stephen D. Gaines, and John Lynham, "Can Catch Shares Prevent Fisheries Collapse?" *Science* 321 (2008): 1678–81.

38. See Robert Repetto et al., *Green Fees: How a Tax Shift Can Work for the Environment and the Economy* (Washington, DC: World Resources Institute, 1992).

39. Skumatz Economic Research Associates, Inc., "Pay as You Throw (PAYT) in the U.S.: 2006 Update and Analyses," Final report to the EPA Office of Solid Waste, December 30, 2006, Superior, CO. See www.epa.gov/osw/conserve/tools/payt/pdf/sera06.pdf.

40. Don Fullerton and Thomas C. Kinnaman, "Household Responses to Pricing Garbage by the Bag," *American Economic Review* 86, no. 4 (1996): 971–84.

41. Ju-Chin Huang, John M. Halstead, and Shanna B. Saunders, "Managing Municipal Solid Waste with Unit-Based Pricing: Policy Effects and Responsiveness to Pricing," *Land Economics* 87, no. 4 (2011): 645–60.

42. On Brazil, see Kenneth M. Chomitz, "Transferable Development Rights and Forest Protection: An Exploratory Analysis," *International Regional Science Review* 27, no. 3 (2004): 348–73. On Calvert County, Maryland, see Virginia McConnell, Margaret Walls, and Elizabeth Kopits, "Zoning, Transferable Development Rights and the Density of Development," *Journal of Urban Economics* 59 (2006): 440–57.

43. Virginia McConnell and Margaret Walls, "U.S. Experience with Transferable Development Rights," *Review of Environmental Economics and Policy* 3, no. 2 (2009): 288–303.

44. National Research Council, *Compensating for Wetland Losses under the Clean Water Act* (Washington, DC: National Academies Press, 2001); and David Salvesen, Lindell L. Marsh, and Douglas R. Porter, eds., *Mitigation Banking: Theory and Practice* (Washington, DC: Island Press, 1996).

45. For surveys of these approaches, see Stavins, "Experience with Market-Based Environmental Policy Instruments"; Thomas Sterner and Jessica Coria, *Policy Instruments for Environmental and Natural Resource Management*, 2nd ed. (Washington, DC: Resources for the Future, 2011); and Theodore Panayotou, *Instruments of Change: Motivating and Financing Sustainable Development* (London: Earthscan, 1998).

46. Richard D. Morgenstern, "Decision Making at EPA: Economics, Incentives and Efficiency," draft conference paper in *EPA at Thirty: Evaluating and Improving the Environmental Protection Agency* (Durham, NC: Duke University Press, 2000), 36–38.

47. Richard Schmalensee and Robert N. Stavins, "The SO_2 Allowance Trading System: The Ironic History of a Grand Policy Experiment," *Journal of Economic Perspectives* 27 (2013): 103–22.

11

Toward Sustainable Production
Finding Workable Strategies for Government and Industry

Daniel Press and Daniel A. Mazmanian

The greening of industry emerged as an important topic among business, environmental, and government leaders in the mid-1980s. It has since evolved through several transitional stages benefiting from the experience of especially leading firms, of different public policy drivers, and of a far greater appreciation in society of the significant changes required to truly place us on the path to a more sustainable world. Today, standard corporate messaging espouses some or many aspects of environmental sustainability. Major firms employ sustainability officers at senior levels, devote high-level website space to their corporate environmental responsibilities, and garner accolades from state or federal environmental agencies. Each year, more firms earn some form of sustainability certification for their products, whether these are from organic farms, sustainable fisheries and forests, or renewables.

The contemporary regulatory focus has thus become sustainable production, which reaches well beyond the attention to waste reduction and pollution prevention of the previous decades. Every indication is that this will be a transformation more than a transition in public policy and business practices by the time it is complete. This new focus raises a strategic question for the United States: which business and industry practices are most in need of change, and how can these be brought about? We also face tactical choices. Is policy intervention best applied at the stage of waste management, air and water pollution control, or energy usage? Can the most change be realized in production methods, product design, or the end products themselves? Will the strongest drive for change come at the stage of consumption and usage of products? Perhaps most importantly, what information will tell us whether greening is truly occurring versus greenwashing?

Equally debated is the best position for society to adopt in order to promote the most comprehensive and cost-effective transformation.[1] Four broad approaches to this question illustrate the differences of opinion about the best way to achieve sustainable production. The first and most traditional approach, reaching back to the 1970s and 1980s, involves government imposing on business- and industry-prescribed environmental protection technologies and methods of emissions reduction. A second, more flexible approach that emerged in the 1980s and 1990s allows businesses to select their own cost-effective strategies for reducing emissions, under the watchful eye of government. A third approach, introduced out of recognition of the enormity of the challenge of transforming business and industry, uses market-based incentives that provide bottom-line rewards for environmentally friendly business behavior, leaving change to the natural workings of the marketplace. The fourth approach relies largely on volunteerism, wherein businesses commit to environmental and sustainability goals that match or exceed those required in exchange for relief from the prescribed technology and command-and-control regulations that would otherwise be imposed. This is more of a hybrid of the prior approaches, attempting to find a viable balance between the overly restrictive regulatory approach and the free market.

The range and extent of research on these approaches has expanded appreciably, and heated debate has ensued about which approach or which mix of approaches to utilize. Some experts focus their attention mainly on the shortcomings of the nation's long-standing environmental pollution policies—variously referred to as "command-and-control," "top-down," and "deterrence-based" policies for air, water, land use, noise, and endangered species protection—and the need to appreciably loosen the strictures of these policies. Others focus on the growing importance of the corporate responsibility and quality management movements within and across industries that emerged in the 1990s—domestically and internationally—and how this shift is moving many businesses toward a greener path. Most recently, attention has turned to the need for firms, individually and working within their business and industry sectors, to contribute to society's environmental goals that extend beyond their business or industry, such as reducing greenhouse gas emissions that contribute to global climate change.[2] All reformers want to know how best to accelerate their preferred strategy through various flexible governmental and voluntary policies, particularly in light of the unrelenting challenges to the environment posed by modern technological society and ever-expanding global population and the growing recognition of the serious challenges posed by climate change that will be with us for decades to come.

In assessing the contending positions and approaches, it is reasonable to assume that, all else being equal, business and industry owners, managers, and workers would prefer to live and work in a cleaner, more environmentally sustainable world. Yet seldom is all else equal. The market economy in which businesses operate has a long history of freely using natural resources and nature's goods, such as clean air, water, and soil as well as food and fodder, and shielding both producers and consumers from the environmental pollution and resource degradation associated with the extraction of these goods, their use in production, and their consumption. This is the very same market economy, after all, that nurtures consumer tastes and expectations, ultimately their demands, for ever more goods and services, resulting in the extraordinary material consumption of today's American lifestyle.[3] Consequently, and despite a few very laudable exceptions,[4] sustainable production can be understood not as a private business matter or a minor marketplace imperfection so much as a serious "public" problem, in need of a public policy solution. Because significant costs can be associated with the transformation to a green economy, we cannot expect businesses to automatically or enthusiastically assume these costs.[5] Indeed, it is typically in a firm's best interest to minimize if not avoid the additional costs of transformation to the extent that such investments do not demonstrably improve its near-term market position. This is precisely why the first generation of environmental laws, starting in the 1970s in the United States, was compulsory for all business, creating the "command-and-control" regulatory regime of the first environmental epoch. As this chapter shows, a good deal of progress resulted but at great expense; arguably, many unnecessary costs were incurred by business and government, costs that might be avoided under a different approach. During the early 2000s, it seemed that the challenge was no longer about persuading an individual enterprise or even a business or industrial sector, but about how to move toward a sustainable economy. However, a combination of corporate greenwashing and fierce resistance to climate change policies during and since the Great Recession of 2007–2009 calls into question not just how society can achieve a more sustainable economic system, but also industry's basic commitment to greening.

The Dilemma of Collective Action for Environmental Protection

How to bring about significant changes that are in the best interest of all society can be understood as one of a category of problems known as "collective action problems" or "collective action dilemmas."[6] These occur when individuals would be better off if they cooperated in pursuit of a common goal, but for one reason or another each chooses a less optimal course of action—one that typically satisfies some other highly important goal. The challenge to policymakers when facing collective action problems is to devise an approach that anticipates and counteracts the normal (in the language of game theory, the "rational") tendency of actors to forgo the better *joint* gain for a nearer-term assured and secure, but lesser, *individual* gain.

The collective action dilemma in the case of sustainable production has been portrayed by Matthew Potoski and Aseem Prakash as a two-dimensional game-theoretic problem, which we have adapted in Figure 11-1. The vertical and horizontal labels show the options available to each player, and the four cells represent the payoff (or benefits) and risk (or costs) to each of the actors based on the combinations of each option. For example, should they decide to cooperate to maximize the gains to each (Cell B)? Or should they not cooperate in order to avoid the possibility of being taken advantage of by the other or incurring some other cost (Cell C), such as the loss of public confidence and trust on the part of government and market share and profitability on the part of business?

Although simplified, the game situation approximates closely the real world of the relations between business and society. Consequently, if left to its own devices, business would choose to have little or no governmental requirement placed on it to protect the environment. This would be only reasonable (rational) for a business trying to maximize its profits in a market economy. This

Figure 11-1   Green Industry as a Collective Action Dilemma

		Firm's choice	
		Evasion	Self-policing
		Cell A	**Cell B**
	Flexible regulation	Government as potential "sucker"	Win-win: superior outcomes for government and industry
		Cell C	**Cell D**
	Deterrence (through command-and-control)	Suboptimal for both government and business but a typical outcome	Green industry initiatives of the 1980s to today, with industry as potential "sucker"

(Government's choice shown along the vertical axis.)

Source: Based on Matthew Potoski and Aseem Prakash, "The Regulation Dilemma: Cooperation and Conflict in Environmental Governance," *Public Administration Review* 64 (March/April 2004): 137–48.

option is represented by the "evasion" position on the horizontal dimension, on the "Firm's choice" axis. However, if compelled by law to provide environmental protection and safeguards, and possibly go even further to transform itself into a green company, business would prefer an approach that allowed for self-policing and regulatory flexibility. It would find this superior to being heavily regulated by a command-and-control government bureaucracy.

Government, in turn, has the choice of opting for a policy of "deterrence," which experience has shown to be workable based on the command-and-control regulatory approach taken to environmental protection since 1970. The downside, as experience has also shown, is that this approach has required the growth and support of a large government bureaucracy to carry out the oversight and regulation of businesses, the suppression of the creative energy on the part of firms that could be used to develop their own green business strategies, and ultimately the less-than-promised and far less-than-imaginable transformation of industry than could have occurred. Conversely, government could choose to be more flexible and lenient on industry, relying instead on a modest amount of monitoring combined with market forces, consumer demands, and new technology to ensure greater protection of the environment. There is risk in this approach for the government. It embraces the promise of an eventually large payoff, but as market forces and modest oversight combine to bring about the desired green transformation of business in the short term, some, if not most, businesses will not change their behavior or will do so insufficiently or slowly, absent stringent regulation. In the language of game theory, this raises the dual problems of "free riding" (not paying one's share of the costs) and "shirking" (paying less than one's share of the costs).

This is the dilemma: As the logic of game theory suggests and a fair amount of experience affirms, under flexible regulatory systems that rely on market forces to bring about changed behavior, market forces are insufficient, and many businesses do not change or do so only minimally. When firms know that they are unlikely to be detected or penalized even when caught, they too often opt for evasion over committing the capital required to transform. The result is that government (and thus the public) ends up being betrayed, realizing even less movement toward the green transformation than under a command-and-control approach: government finds itself in the position of the "sucker," which is the worst possible outcome in a collective action game.

Armed with the insights of game theory, we find it logical that, left to its own resources and absent compulsion, business will choose evasion over greening. Government, in turn, will choose command-and-control over flexibility, not because it is optimal but to avoid the risk of ending up the sucker. Thus game theory tells us that most of the activity surrounding environmental protection can be expected to take place in the lower-left cell of Figure 11-1, Cell C, the zone in which government regulates with a heavy hand to prevent business from evading environmental protection laws and regulations. This is precisely where the action took place throughout the first environmental epoch, which began in the 1970s.[7] A second epoch began in the 1980s and continues today, characterized by recognition of the collective action dilemma and efforts to extricate government and business from its grasp. The challenge is how to combine flexible regulatory strategies with market forces to move the central theater of action out of the lower-left Cell C to the upper-right Cell B.

A number of pilot and experimental programs by government and business have been initiated and are reviewed in this chapter. The experience underscores how difficult it has been to dislodge the players from their long-standing positions. This should come as no surprise in light of the dilemma they face and the amount of time they have spent living and working under the command-and-control approach. The crux of the matter remains that, by and large, government is usually loath to relinquish its reliance on deterrence, and most businesses can be expected to evade when circumstances allow.

Yet the need for society to find a win-win solution—a more optimal mix of flexibility and self-policing—continues and has motivated the continuing search for the needed policy breakthrough. A growing body of research on strategies that appear to work is guiding these efforts among self-motivated businesses, at least on an experimental basis.[8] Thus devising a new hybrid public policy approach seems feasible, at least in principle, within a game-theoretic framework. Of course, the direction of public policy is set by the politics of policymaking, not simply the logic of policy analysis, so this too will be considered in our final assessment.

What follows is an overview of the efforts made since 1970 to address the problems of environmental pollution and the degradation of our natural resources base by greening the practices of business and industry. This overview moves through the strict command-and-control environmental policy epoch, located schematically in Cell C, and then turns to the market-oriented and flexible regulatory strategies that reflected a significant change in the understanding of the problem. In actuality, the debate and center of activity has moved only part way, with innovative action taking place "under the shadow of regulation" (in Cell D).

We examine several impressive examples of corporate self-regulation and voluntary green approaches of individual firms, often in conjunction with government, as illustrative of how change has occurred and how it can occur. These accomplishments need to be juxtaposed against political efforts to slow down, if not derail, the greening of America's economy. The chapter ends with an assessment of how we can best accomplish the much needed green transformation of America's business and industry as we look to a future with ever increasing threats to our environment and natural resources at home and around the world, the need for revitalization of the nation's economy, and the desire to maintain the quality of life most Americans strive for and have come to expect.

The Accomplishments of
Command-and-Control since 1970

Although the needed green transformation of the economy and society per se is actively being discussed and dominates the policy debate today, in large measure in response to concerns about climate change and energy pricing, command-and-control regulation remains the most widespread policy approach in practice. In a number of important respects, the approach has worked and continues to work to clean up the environment, in some instances quite admirably.[9] Moreover, evidence indicates that the nation's strict environmental regulations have spurred innovation in businesses, which ultimately provides them a source of competitive advantage in the market economy.[10] Also, one can point to the creation of jobs in the pollution control technology sector as a source of the economic growth and employment that has resulted from the traditional form of environmental regulation.[11]

Since the 1970s, government rules and regulations have spurred reductions throughout the nation in air, water, and soil contamination; these reductions are noted at numerous points throughout this book (see especially Chapter 1). Nationwide, air emissions trends from all industrial sources (including electricity-generating power plants) show that air emissions reached a peak in the early to mid-1970s, declined sharply, and then plateaued by the mid-1980s after which, year after year, they diminished decisively. Official records for all environmental data are often unavailable for the same years (here we present ranges for the closest years); however, all of these figures should be viewed as rough approximations. Although the U.S. Environmental Protection Agency (EPA) officially reports impressive emissions reductions in its annual inventories, the agency admits, when pressed, that "estimates for the non-utility manufacturing sector are some of the most unreliable data we have in the national emission inventory."[12]

Between 1990 and 2008, sulfur oxides emissions declined consistently (by as much as 54 percent), very likely as a consequence of the 1990 Clean Air Act's Acid Rain Program. Lead and volatile organic compounds also declined, by 60 percent and 43 percent, respectively. Other air pollutants exhibit some worrisome trends. Carbon monoxide from industrial fuel combustion fluctuated over the years, probably as a function of economic conditions, but factories burning fuel emitted about as much carbon monoxide in 2013 as they did in the early 1990s. Industrial nitrogen oxides decreased overall during the same time period, thanks to much cleaner fuel combustion. However, in recent years NOx emissions have increased in some industries, including pulp and paper, petroleum refining, oil and gas production, and the merchant marine. Emissions of particulate matter 2.5 microns or smaller (referred to as "$PM_{2.5}$"), widely considered to be some of the most threatening to public health, have persistently increased since the early 2000s. One in eight Americans currently lives in a county out of attainment with the $PM_{2.5}$ standard.[13] Even more worrisome, at least a third of Americans live in areas with unacceptable ozone levels.[14] Water quality is even harder to assess reliably but has also improved somewhat, thanks largely to the thousands of municipal wastewater treatment plants built with financing from the federal government since 1970.[15] Today, almost every American can expect drinkable water as a matter of course, with regular monitoring for quality and reasonably rapid responses to contamination threats. It is less clear, however, how industry's overall contribution to water quality protection has changed over the years, because such data are not routinely collected or centrally distributed.

Energy consumption also presents some progress. Manufacturing firms slowly reduced their annual primary energy consumption between the 1970s and 2000s, going from a high of 24.7 quads (quadrillion British thermal units, or BTUs) in 1973 to 18.8 quads in 2010.[16] This roughly 24 percent overall (or total) decrease in primary energy consumption from 1973 to 2010 occurred while manufacturing output more than doubled during the same time period.[17] Looking at more recent trends, total energy consumption in the manufacturing sector fell by 17 percent between 2002 and 2010, while manufacturing output fell by only 3 percent, signaling that factories reduced their energy intensity (the amount of energy it takes to manufacture a product).[18] In one high-energy sector, iron and steel, energy intensity decreased between 1998 and 2006, whether measured as the energy it took to produce a ton of steel or the energy it took to produce a dollar of value added.[19] This was probably a result of the industry's greater reliance on cleaner electric arc furnaces than the old basic oxygen furnaces, which consume enormous quantities of coal.

A great deal of money has been spent to accomplish these results, in terms of total dollars and as a percentage of the gross national product, and with them the costs borne by industry have increased. This is reflected in the increasing level of expenditures by industry. In 1973, U.S. industries spent about $4.8 billion on pollution abatement, split almost equally between capital and operating costs. By 1994, American manufacturing was spending $10 billion on capital costs, but these costs dropped to just under $6 billion by 2005 (both in 2005 dollars). Operating costs dropped in the same decade, from $24.7 billion to $20.7 billion.[20] Chemical, coal, and petroleum companies spent the most in capital and operating costs, about $12 billion among them. Perhaps most significantly, today's operating costs represent steadily smaller proportions of industry's total economic output—this finding suggests either that new pollution abatement equipment can run more efficiently (and thus at less cost) or that industry is cutting corners.[21] Both explanations may be true.

Is the news about industrial pollution good, bad, or uncertain? Undeniably, the country's air would have been far worse if industry had not been installing abatement equipment since 1970. Moreover, it is remarkable that, thus far, air pollution seems to rise at a smaller rate than economic growth. The bad news is that, globally, industry is consuming as much or more energy and raw materials, which in turn creates serious pollution and resource degradation, and is burdening U.S. and other nations' air, land, and water with larger pollutant loads each year. Thus, even if the rate of increase is small, the overall burden grows, which is not the right direction for protecting public and environmental health.

Regulatory Experiments in Industrial Greening

Command-and-control approaches have clearly resulted in better environmental practices in business and industry and a significant curbing of traditional patterns of environmental pollution, but they ultimately fall short of the fundamental transformation needed in business and industry. The best end-of-pipe pollution management has not sufficiently reduced the overall pollution load generated by an economy that is ever expanding to satisfy the needs of a global population projected to grow by 50 percent over the next fifty years.

Therefore, attention has begun to shift from pollution reduction to pollution prevention, and to doing so by devising incentive-based, self-regulatory, and voluntary policy approaches (see Chapter 10). Building on the successes and limitations of command-and-control regulation, U.S. industry and government moved on a limited basis toward an industrial greening approach (see Figure 11-1, Cell D). Characterized by industry self-policing and government deterrence, this approach has achieved some successes but is clearly suboptimal—from economic and environmental perspectives—to the relationship that could exist if the situation in Cell B were the case (across-the-board cooperation by both business and industry).

A first phase in the movement toward greening has used market incentives, self-reporting, and environmental management systems to improve corporate environmental performance. More recently, bolder experiments in self-regulation have advanced industry closer to the cooperative zone.

Phase I: Market Incentives,
Self-Reporting, and Environmental Management Systems

As indicated in Chapter 10, incentive-based approaches to environmental policy, such as emissions taxes, tradable permit systems, and deposit-refund programs, can be both effective at preventing pollution and more economically efficient. The EPA and many states have experimented with a wide range of market incentives, mostly since the 1980s, many of which have demonstrated promising results.[22] Experimentation with these "efficiency-based regulatory reforms" characterizes the second epoch of the environmental movement.[23] Two of the most well-known experiments with market incentives include the Acid Rain Program of the 1990 Clean Air Act and the tradable permits program in the Los Angeles basin, known as the Regional Clean Air Incentives Market (RECLAIM). By most accounts, the Acid Rain Program made good on economists' predictions: emissions decreased, and industry spent less money overall.[24] The Los Angeles program has also worked reasonably well in reducing emissions overall and in keeping down pollution control costs. However, it has been faulted for failing to effectively address the serious pollution "hot spots" existing within the overall region.[25] Another significant second-epoch regulatory experiment consisted of self-reporting, auditing, and disclosure requirements, beginning in 1986 with the Superfund Amendments and Reauthorization Act. This legislation created the Toxics Release Inventory (TRI), the first major federal environmental program that moved away from the traditional command-and-control approach (characterized by heavy fines, specified emissions levels, and mandatory pollution abatement technologies) toward a "softer, gentler" self-reporting and cooperative framework. The TRI requires companies that have ten or more employees, and that use significant amounts of any one of the hundreds of listed chemicals, to report their annual releases and transfers of these chemicals to the EPA, which then makes these data available to the public through an annual report, the TRI *Public Data Release.*

The TRI requires companies to report their activities but does not require that they change their behavior. To view such policies as "all study and no action," however, would be to miss their contribution to what David Morell calls "regulation by embarrassment."[26] Indeed, environmental groups such as Communities for a Better Environment, INFORM (a national nonprofit that produces short films designed to educate the public about the effects of human activity on the environment and human health), and Greenpeace have seized on TRI data to publicize particularly heavy polluters. Some organizations make TRI data easily available over the Internet, allowing communities to view local toxic releases in map form.[27] Moreover, many state environmental agencies are basing their rulemaking on the TRI reports for industries in their states. Some industries have called for an end to the TRI reporting process because of these new regulatory uses.

In 2012, U.S. industry generated about 1.8 million tons of toxic waste—or about 11.5 pounds per American—a little over a third of which was released to air, land, and water treated or untreated.[28] Making year-to-year comparisons in toxic releases is difficult, because the EPA has expanded the kinds of facilities required to report releases as well as added to the list of chemicals to report. But if we limit ourselves to the three hundred or so core chemicals from the original reporting industries, total on- and off-site releases decreased 67 percent from 1989 to 2012.[29] Unfortunately, not all parts of the country enjoyed the same toxic release reductions. As the authors of *Coming Clean*, a new comprehensive study of the TRI, point out, there is substantial variation in releases across regions, industrial sectors, and individual firms themselves.[30] Although the EPA and industry applaud declines in toxic releases with every new TRI report, critics of the program have raised serious doubts about the validity of TRI data. For example, the Environmental Integrity Project (EIP) challenged the TRI results in a 2004 report titled "Who's Counting? The Systematic Underreporting of Toxic Air Emissions." The EIP compared TRI reports for refineries and chemical facilities in Texas with actual smokestack emissions, in some cases using infrared scanners aboard aerial surveys. The EIP and the Texas Commission on Environmental Quality found that, for ten of the most common hydrocarbons, the EPA's reports underestimated actual emissions by 25 percent to 440 percent, raising serious concerns about outdated or inaccurate estimation methods that never actually measure releases themselves.[31] It's very unlikely that TRI releases continue their decades-old decline primarily because industries simply move offshore—there were about as many facilities reporting releases to the TRI in 2013 (21,513) as in 1999 (23,424).[32] The TRI only reports on a subset of the nation's dangerous wastes. Hazardous wastes—as defined by the Resource Conservation and Recovery Act (RCRA) and its amendments—comprise a much larger set. Some of these wastes are not nearly as dangerous as those on the TRI list (e.g., oily water), but many are quite toxic. All are required by law to receive some kind of treatment before disposal. In stark contrast to the TRI reports, RCRA waste totals have barely changed since the late 1990s, fluctuating from thirty million to forty million tons per year, depending largely on the state of the national economy.[33] If the TRI faithfully represented American pollution prevention trends, why wouldn't these trends mirror the RCRA totals?

The TRI is the most widely known and used database of self-reported information, but it is not unique. Thousands of companies around the world implement corporate environmental reports (CERs) every year and submit annual documents similar to their financial reports. These include "management policies and systems; input/output inventor[ies] of environmental impacts; financial implications of environmental actions; relationships with stakeholders; and the [company's] sustainable development agenda."[34] Despite the appealing logic of self-reporting and auditing, it is exceedingly difficult to tell what such information achieves. Firms may be reluctant to accurately disclose potential problems with their facilities, fearing that regulators or third-party organizations (such as environmental litigants) may seize on the data to impose fines, facility changes in equipment and operation, or both.[35]

The relatively small amount of research done on self-reporting suggests that, at best, CER systems improve company data collection and internal management, while possibly rendering environmental issues more transparent to government and the public.[36] More critical research shows that self-audits overwhelmingly reveal inventory and reporting violations (for example, of hazardous materials) rather than the much more serious unlawful emissions releases that the EPA discovers during its standard enforcement procedures.[37] The third innovation of industrial greening actually modifies company management philosophies and practices. To implement green strategies, firms have adopted environmental management systems (EMSs) that include corporate environmental pledges, internal training programs, environmental education programs, and the use of cradle-to-grave systems of management control such as full-cost accounting and total quality management.[38] Environmental management systems vary enormously, but the basic idea is to (1) track a firm's environmental footprint, (2) assign management responsibility for company-wide environmental performance, (3) establish environmental improvement goals, and (4) establish a means to assess whether a company is meeting its environmental targets.

Given their interest in avoiding environmental protection costs, why do firms adopt environmental management systems? After all, they are costly— in terms of both money and staff time—and they open private firms to external scrutiny that may not be welcome. Prakash and Potoski report that annual third-party audits for ISO 14001 certification (an international environmental management system discussed later in this chapter) can cost a small firm from $25,000 to $100,000 and much, much more for larger firms.[39] Based on a survey of over two hundred U.S. manufacturing plants, Richard Florida and Derek Davison identify the three most important reasons given for adopting such systems: management "commitment to environmental improvement . . . corporate goals and objectives . . . and business performance." Compliance with state and federal regulations and improved community relations were other frequently cited reasons.[40] Firms that go green can also be rewarded by the financial markets. Some investment brokers offer socially responsible environmental investment portfolios, although they are only a small (but growing) part of the investments market. By the mid-1990s, about forty mutual funds were managing $3 billion of green investments.[41] In 2012, the Forum for Sustainable and Responsible Investment reported that socially responsible investment portfolios—those that select companies through a wide range of social screens, include shareholder advocacy, or invest in communities—had reached $3.31 trillion in assets, or a little over 11 percent of the total investment assets under U.S. management. Moreover, socially responsible investment (SRI) assets performed better during the recent financial crisis. From 1995 to 2012, SRI assets grew at a compound annual rate of 11 percent, about 1.2 percent faster than all professionally managed U.S. investments.[42] Managers of green mutual funds are constantly updating their social ratings of industries worthy of investment. Indeed, a number of studies now suggest a strong correlation between profitability and greening, although researchers are quick to point out that just how a company's profits are tied to its investments in pollution prevention or abatement is not clear.[43] Do environmental management systems make a difference? Because of the difficulty linking management changes to verifiable, objective environmental outcomes—and because EMSs are all so different[44]—the jury is still out on that question.[45] Some researchers conclude that such systems are effective when they have strong support from top management, who in turn rely on the systems to greatly improve company environmental awareness and to better track the flow of raw materials, energy, labor, quality, and costs throughout the firm's operations.[46] And adopters of environmental management systems report that they recycle more; release fewer air, water, and waste emissions; and use less electricity than do nonadopters, but such findings are not based on third-party audits.[47]

Phase II: Self-Regulation

More recently, greening includes businesses and industries coming together in voluntary self-regulatory associations, at home and around the world. Some of these efforts are "invited" by regulators, whereas others are initiated and implemented by corporate leaders themselves or, in a few cases, by nongovernmental organizations. The primary attractions of self-regulating voluntary associations are that they reduce the compliance costs that can come with the avoidance of command-and-control regulation; they signal a company's green intent to consumers and those up- and downstream in the production chain (green branding); and they help companies to establish greater rapport with regulators and policymakers.[48] From a public policy perspective, voluntary self-regulation also reduces the cost to government that comes with regulating many thousands of firms throughout the nation, and it fills a void where, for whatever reason, regulations do not exist.

Nonetheless, critics raise several objections to self-regulation. It may be nothing more than "greenwashing" by firms wishing to improve their public image without fundamentally changing their production practices, although some companies address this charge by subjecting their environmental practices to third-party audits and then reporting the results using widely accepted indicators.[49] By its very nature, adopting changes internal to a firm, the exact effect of self-regulation may be exceedingly difficult to assess; regulators and the public, in effect, must trust that firms are honest when reporting on their voluntary activities. Also, cleaner manufacturing often requires management, labor, equipment, or process changes, usually up front, before potential savings can be realized. As a result, these initial costs of self-regulation can seriously discourage participation. Finally, it can be argued that voluntary environmental management may lead to lower productivity if new practices are cleaner but less efficient than old ones.[50]

Since the mid-1980s, the EPA has launched more than fifty voluntary programs, emanating mostly from its office specific to air regulations, followed by its office for toxics and pollution prevention, and its waste, water, policy, and research offices.[51] Performance Track was the most comprehensive of the EPA's voluntary program initiatives before President Barack Obama's first EPA administrator, Lisa P. Jackson, scrapped the program just weeks after assuming her duties. Begun in 2000, it encouraged companies to adopt management practices that would lead to emissions reductions beyond those legally required.[52] Participants had to commit to measurable improvements in environmental performance, implement an environmental management system, and demonstrate their compliance. In turn, the EPA could grant regulatory flexibility or a reduction in other reporting requirements. According to a survey of program participants, the primary reason for participation was the resulting positive rapport with the EPA and public recognition for their environmental care and responsibility accruing to those enrolled in the program. Since the program's inception in 2000, membership grew at 12 percent a year and by mid-2008 was approaching 550 companies.[53]

So why did the new EPA administrator cancel a program launched under the Bill Clinton administration? A deteriorating reputation may explain her decision. The EPA's own independent inspector general, Nikki Tinsley, issued a very critical report in 2007, faulting the program for not connecting clear goals to measurable activities and also for including members whose environmental performance was not necessarily above average.[54] Shortly thereafter, at the end of 2008, three *Philadelphia Inquirer* reporters, John Sullivan, John Shiffman, and Tom Avril, published a very critical four-part series on the EPA titled "Smoke and Mirrors: The Subversion of the EPA."[55] Their third story, "Green Club an EPA Charade," argued that too many Performance Track members continued to violate their permit limits while receiving less scrutiny by virtue of their "club" membership.[56] Doing away with the Performance Track also signaled a shift from the George W. Bush era focus on voluntary initiatives, which, in turn, was seen by environmentalists as a justification for lax regulatory enforcement and rule development.[57] After its demise, many Performance Track members formed a new "Stewardship Action Council," ostensibly to continue publicizing their excellent environmental programs and performance. While the SAC comprises several large environmental organizations, it arguably asks even less of its members than did the Performance Track.[58]

In a thoroughgoing postmortem of Performance Track, Cary Coglianese and Jennifer Nash made the environmental performance comparisons that EPA was never willing or able to carry out. Combining case studies of five sets of matching industry pairs, including Performance Track facilities and nonenrolled facilities, plus a large-scale survey, Coglianese and Nash could not distinguish between firms that were in the program and those that were not. Participating facilities did not outperform similar facilities in their industrial sectors; rather, Performance Track facilities simply appeared to be the ones most aggressively seeking government recognition and community engagement. While laudable qualities, Coglianese and Nash found no evidence that such characteristics resulted in better environmental performance.[59]

The EPA is not alone in its efforts to promote green management. In 1996, the International Organization for Standardization (ISO) released its ISO 14001 environmental management standards. A company registering for ISO 14001 certification must (1) develop an environmental management system, (2) demonstrate compliance with all local environmental laws, and (3) demonstrate a commitment to continuous improvement.[60] By 2013, over 300,000 firms had been ISO 14001 certified worldwide, but the North American countries—with 8,917 certified firms—lagged dramatically behind Europe (with 119,107 firms).[61]

Increasingly, large manufacturers require that their suppliers become ISO 14001 certified as well.[62] Ford Motor Company led the way in the mid-1990s but was soon followed by all the major automakers.[63] Prakash and Potoski analyzed ISO 14001 certified firms in the United States, asking whether their air emissions were significantly lower than those of noncertified firms, and indeed they were. Their explanation is that, on the spectrum of voluntary measures, ISO 14001 represents a "weak sword," because it requires only third-party audits. A "strong sword" system (what the EPA's Performance Track program was supposed to be) requires third-party monitoring, public disclosure of audit information, and sanctions by program sponsors.[64]

Ultimately, we will know whether greening or greenwashing occurs only with high-quality data. Currently, one of the most widespread forms of corporate environmental and social responsibility activity involves information. Increasingly, companies disclose some aspect of their activity (e.g., reporting carbon dioxide emissions to the Carbon Disclosure Project[65]) or promise to clean up their supply chain. To boost their credibility, firms employ third parties, like the Forest Trust,[66] to verify their claims. Third-party certifiers are only as good as their reputation, and their work raises the question of who will guard the guardians. Our ability to verify certified claims is next to nil, especially when emissions are not directly measured or the verifiers themselves do not disclose their own contracts or data.[67]

Win-Win as a Business Proposition

Overall, the national effort, under the Clean Air Act, to reduce the air pollution emitted by business and industry, particularly in major urban areas across the United States, has been reasonably successful. Significantly helping this effort, since 1970, there has been a dramatic reduction of emissions per automobile on the road today. Many of our most polluted waterways have been cleaned up over this time period as well.

Balanced against this record, automobiles burning gasoline are approaching hard limits in their per-mile emissions, while U.S. ridership (officially measured as "vehicle miles traveled") has reached nearly three *trillion* miles per year, about two hundred billion miles more than in 2000.[68] And there is little evidence indicating that the emissions reduction and cleanup was accomplished in the most cost-effective manner. Possibly more important in looking forward, more than three decades of experience did not result in any visible commitment by a majority of businesses in the United States to a comprehensive, green transition.

As a result, we cannot be certain about the continuation of abating large-scale pollution, or that the aggregate of emissions from American industry will remain below previous levels. That is, businesses have made little commitment to moving beyond the long-standing command-and-control regulatory approach to a life cycle environmental analysis of their products. We are even less likely to see widespread closed-system toxics management in manufacturing or product use, or sustained attention to more global and growing problems such as greenhouse gas emissions, destruction of natural habitats, or depletion of ocean resources. Equally important, no national policy goals or mandated regulations exist in the United States to move industry in this direction.

An instructive lesson from the voluntary programs established since 1991 is that when businesses form an alliance within their sector, either voluntarily or under the pressure of government policy, significant reductions can be realized, especially in high-profile sectors, like the chemical industry. Yet this very example suggests that chemicals may be the proverbial exception to the rule, since the change in that industry was due to the extraordinary public pressure brought to bear in the early 1990s as a result of the few colossal environmental disasters experienced in the United States and abroad and the fact that the industry is fairly well concentrated. Thus cooperation was brought about among a relatively few number of actors. In effect, the conditions for moving into a win-win game position for both government and the chemical industry existed, in that flexible regulation and volunteerism could be achieved, and the action moved into Cell B of Figure 11-1. Today, few other such examples can be found within major business and industrial sectors.[69] How might this situation be changed? After a thorough review of the pilots and experiments in flexible regulation, self-regulation, and voluntary approaches since the mid-1990s, Marc Eisner has woven together the best components from each into a promising synthesis.[70] His approach is designed to overcome the natural (that is, rational) reticence of business and industry, and move the greening agenda beyond Cell D, into Cell B. He focuses on bridging the gap between business and government, on "harnessing the market and industrial associations to achieve superior results by creating a system of government supervised self-regulation."[71] The central propositions of his policy synthesis are as follows:

- Market rewards should be the primary motivator (placing emphasis on the "carrot") while retaining in reserve the traditional regulatory "stick."
- Reliance should be placed on trade and business associations; these sectoral and quasi-governmental organizations can serve as the central implementers of greening policy (they are "quasi" in that they are nonprofit organizations, although they would be imbued with governing authority).

- Emphasis should be placed on disclosure and "sunshine" provisions over government-prescribed techniques of emissions reduction and on-site government inspection.
- Sectoral associations would serve as intermediary entities, both to implement policy and to assure the government that policy would be carried out as intended.

The proposal does not require significant new public laws or the creation of new government bureaucracy because they can be woven together from existing programs and authority.

The critical virtue of this approach is that, if adopted as the overall framework for greening, it would mitigate, on the one hand, the businesses' fear of an overbearing regulatory regime and government's fear of becoming a "sucker"—and on the other hand the concern of other businesses evading their responsibilities to go green. In short, we have in Eisner's proposal a game-theoretic and pragmatically attractive approach to moving government and business into Cell B. As we mentioned at the outset, policy is set by the politics of policymaking and not simply by the logic of policy analysis, as attractive as it may be, and to which we now turn.

Another instructive lesson comes from those who are reengineering to compete in the twenty-first-century worldwide economy and doing so in ways that are beginning to anticipate when green production will be the norm, not the exception, in the economic marketplace. Box 11-1 illustrates how some firms are implementing this strategy.[72]

Box 11-1   Three Industries, Three
Companies, One Industrial-Ecological Strategy

In an era of global trade dominated by Chinese manufacturing, it's easy to wonder how American manufacturers can remain in business, much less whether they will pursue greening strategies. On the one hand, companies in the Global South enjoy access to large pools of low-wage workers and structure their manufacturing at very high outputs. On the other hand, many American facilities are old, employ a mature and higher-paid workforce, face very high cultural and legal expectations of environmental and health considerations, and enjoy few protections from the United States' open trade access policies. Combined, these factors reasonably suggest that the downward spiral in American manufacturing of the past several decades should end in complete collapse.

But there is a new and promising *industrial-ecological* manufacturing paradigm imaginable for mature industrial nations like the United States that takes advantage of very short supply and distribution chains. The idea is simple. Raw materials and energy have become so expensive that recycling often appears more attractive than making commodities

---

(like steel, paper, aluminum, glass, and plastic containers) from virgin materials. In most heavy industries, recycled raw materials require far less energy than do new inputs to turn them back into usable products. The United States also produces enormous amounts of high-quality recyclables every year, some of which find their way to reprocessors overseas.

Asian exporters put a high value on recyclables, too. They send full container ships to U.S. ports but have relatively little to fill them with for the return voyage, so scrap metals, paper, and plastics fit the bill nicely. While it may seem sensible to ship recyclables to any country willing or able to reprocess them, the fuel demand for transporting, say, a load of scrap metal, from the American Midwest to an inland Chinese mill, *and back to the United States,* is enormous.

Increasingly, American firms find ways to capitalize on their local or regional advantages: very highly productive labor, sophisticated automation, a weak dollar (which makes U.S. exports possible), steady supplies of recyclables, and nearby markets for finished products. Three midwestern companies provide very good examples of how manufacturers can be green and competitive.

- **SSAB, Iowa, Inc., Davenport, Iowa** This relatively new (1996) steel mill on the banks of the Mississippi uses exclusively old steel from scrap yards, brokers, and pipe makers within a couple hours of the plant. SSAB bought 1.4 million tons of scrap steel in 2007 (for $250–$500 per ton, depending on the quality). Using an electric arc furnace, the plant's five hundred highly paid (but nonunion) employees produced about 1.2 million tons of high-strength steel plate and coil, worth nearly $1 billion. In recent years, SSAB's heavy plate steel became bulldozer buckets and other parts of heavy equipment manufactured in the many Caterpillar and John Deere facilities located nearby. Interestingly, 20 percent of SSAB's sales now go to makers of wind turbines, most of which also are manufactured and sold regionally.
- **Jupiter Aluminum Corporation, Hammond, Indiana** Nearly every American driver knows what his or her license plates look and feel like. Most people don't know that one company in the gritty, northern Indiana town of Hammond makes almost all of the aluminum used for license plates in the United States. Jupiter Aluminum produces the aluminum for license plates as well as gutters and downspouts entirely from recycled aluminum. Most recently, the company produced about 150 million tons of aluminum coil, drawing on 160 million tons of

(Continued)

Box 11-1   *(Continued)*

scrap that it purchases for about $1 per pound from scores of sellers in the Midwest. Jupiter's 268 employees shipped about $250 million worth of aluminum products in recent years, making their workforce tremendously productive (in terms of dollars of product per worker).

- **Corenso North America, Wisconsin Rapids, Wisconsin** Situated close to the banks of the Wisconsin River, Corenso produces the corrugated cardboard cores (tubes) on which many other companies wind their papers, sheet metals, fabrics, and ribbons. Employing about 170 union workers, Corenso uses exclusively scrap cardboard from the upper Midwest to make the cardboard strips the company then winds and glues into tubular cores. In recent years, Corenso bought over 45,000 tons of scrap cardboard for $100–$125 per ton, relying on three to five regional scrap brokers and distributors as well as cardboard drop-off locations for local residents. Corenso turns that scrap into some 35,000 tons of coreboard valued at about $18 million.

Each of these facilities faces strong command-and-control regulations requiring them to keep air emissions and wastewater low. But they all went much further than this regulatory "floor." Under pressure by a very tough Iowa Department of Natural Resources, SSAB steel meets some of the most stringent particulate matter requirements faced by any steel mill anywhere in the world. Jupiter Aluminum installed an "oxyfuel"–fired furnace, allowing it to burn natural gas in a pure oxygen environment, thereby eliminating all of its nitrogen oxide emissions. And Corenso's reliance on recycling means that the company can repulp scrap cardboard with no chemicals, thereby releasing almost no waste to the city sewage treatment plant or to the Wisconsin River.

Mixed Signals from Industry and Washington

Despite the effort by the Obama administration to update and make more efficient environmental regulations and procedures, and the good image nurtured by corporate public relations officers, many industry lobbyists still work assiduously at blocking or rolling back environmental mandates.[73] With respect to the former, in response to Obama's executive order to all federal agencies to undertake a thorough review of their practices and procedures (see Chapter 4), in the summer of 2011, the EPA developed a plan focused on four goals: introducing greater electronic reporting, improving agency transparency, working with affected parties to develop innovative compliance approaches, and developing integrated problem-solving and systems approaches to replace its segmented activities and disparate activities that had grown by accretion over four decades.[74] Some three dozen initiatives were launched between 2011 and 2014, in areas from technical updating of water quality standards, to introducing electronic industry reporting, to integrated research and compliance procedures, half or more of which have been completed.[75]

While working with the EPA on the retrospective review on one hand, on the other hand industry political action committees are keeping up a steady stream of campaign contributions to anti-environmentalist legislators, just as they have done for years.[76] If anything, industry opposition to new or strengthened environmental initiatives intensified during President Obama's second term. For example, the EPA's Clean Air Scientific Advisory Committee recommended lowering the ozone standard from 75 to 60 parts per billion. What should have been fairly routine revisions to air quality standards were met with staunch opposition; for example, the American Petroleum Institute asserted that the new rule would pose "massive and disruptive" challenges to states and factories.[77] And as one of the arguably most important environmental issues of our time, climate change should be an area most benefiting from the greening of industry. Despite some first movers, the top American industrial emitters put on a full court press to block the Obama administration's implementation of curbs on power plant carbon dioxide emissions in 2014 and to urge approval of the Keystone XL pipeline from the tar sand fields of Canada.

Reaching beyond Win-Win

We assume that devising ways to improve protection of the environment will need to build on the several generations of existing law and public policy, and any thought of disregarding these and starting anew is unrealistic. For this reason, the synthetic approach conceived by Eisner, designed to harness the core self-interested impulses of business and government on behalf of protection of the natural environment, is appealing. To be successful, these policies require business to improve the production of material goods and services while reducing to a minimum the adverse impacts on the natural environment. Indeed, this is not only the win-win of game theory but also the "double bottom-line" aspiration of industrial ecology today. As a blueprint for politically realistic, near-term policy goals, we believe Eisner provides an ambitious though realizable approach to environmental protection and the greening of industry.

Not even the best policy ideas succeed in the real world, of course. With this in mind, should the Eisner approach fail and it become necessary to look for more ambitious though over-the-horizon approaches, they do exist. We can suggest two options in particular to underscore the point. These are the "theory of economic dynamics of environmental law" articulated by David Driesen,[78] and steady-state, or "true cost economics," long advocated by Herman Daly.[79] In a recent treatise on law and the environment, Driesen argues that dramatic greening is unlikely until the priority given to efficiency and benefit-cost thinking in neoclassic microeconomic behavior is replaced by the goal of encouraging "dynamic technology change" and adaptation, in a world of growing natural resource scarcity.

A second and similarly ambitious and transformative approach consists of efforts to refocus attention at the macroeconomic level away from the exclusive attention on production of material goods and human services to balancing production with the costs to natural assets and the environment, a movement led by Daly and a small but growing number of "ecological economists" around the world.

In the effort to deal with climate change, many new policy ideas are being introduced that will address the range of environmental and resources issues raised throughout the first and second environmental epochs and that have been addressed piecemeal by the EPA and the federal policy it reflects. Today, these issues are being tackled with new vigor and in a more comprehensive manner and, in many ways, not simply as public policy that government imposes on business and industry, but from myriad business concerns. These concerns motivate business and industry to think more in the longer term and strategically. On the one hand, both will anticipate enormous market opportunities at home and abroad. On the other hand, they will feel strong government pressure as the world begins to feel the unprecedented and challenging effects of climate change.

Market opportunities or challenges like the meltdown in the financial services sector in 2008 may shape industrial greening as much as or more than new policy programs. The relatively low energy prices that American companies enjoyed throughout the 1990s and early 2000s have disappeared and are not likely to return soon. And for the first time in perhaps a generation, many large companies view green tech as the next high-growth frontier for the United States. Despite a sputtering economic recovery, the second decade of the 2000s saw venture capitalists pouring money into solar power, battery and fuel cell technology, biofuels research, and other clean energy research and development.[80] How rapidly and extensively green industry will grow may depend not only on energy and materials prices but also on whether state and federal policymakers connect environmental policy to trade, development, labor, and tax policies.

Suggested Websites

Independent Analysis of
Corporate Environmental and Social Performance

The Forest Trust (www.tft-forests.org) A third-party group focused on products and supply chains to bring about sustainable development, especially in land-based forest and extractive industries.

Global Reporting Initiative (www.globalreporting.org) An independent nongovernmental organization charged with developing and disseminating globally applicable sustainability reporting guidelines.

Greening of Industry Network (www.greeningofindustry.org) An independent network of professionals focused on aligning industrial development strategies with sustainable development practices.

Six Sigma (www.isixsigma.com) Promoting in business the adoption, advancement, and integration of Six Sigma, a management and auditing methodology to identify errors or defects in manufacturing and service.

Business Sustainability Councils

World Business Council for Sustainable Development (www.wbcsd.ch) A global green industry clearinghouse.

World Resources Institute (www.wri.org) Global environmental clearinghouse with programs tying industry to development.

Leading Business and Environment Journals

Business Strategy and the Environment (http://onlinelibrary.wiley.com/journal/10.1002/%28ISSN%291099-0836) Publishes scholarship on business responses to improving environmental performance.

Corporate Social Responsibility and Environmental Management (http://onlinelibrary.wiley.com/journal/10.1002/%28ISSN%291535-3966) A journal specializing in research relating to the development of tools and techniques for improving corporate performance and accountability on social and environmental dimensions.

Environmental Quality Management (http://onlinelibrary.wiley.com/journal/10.1002/%28ISSN%291520-6483) An applied and practice-oriented journal demonstrating how to improve environmental performance and exceed new voluntary standards such as ISO 14000.

The Green Business Letter (www.greenbiz.com) A monthly newsletter providing information for businesses and universities wishing to integrate environmental thinking throughout their organizations in profitable ways.

U.S. Environmental Protection Agency Sites

Energy Star (www.energystar.gov) A good site for learning about energy efficiency programs and efficient equipment, lighting, and buildings.

Partnership Programs Home (www.epa.gov/partners) A clearinghouse for the EPA's voluntary pollution prevention and management programs.

Toxics Release Inventory (www.epa.gov/triexplorer) The nation's list of toxic chemical releases from manufacturing, power generation, and mining facilities.

Notes

1. Robert B. Gibson, ed., *Voluntary Initiatives: The New Politics of Corporate Greening* (Peterborough, ON: Broadview Press, 1999).
2. Charles A. Jones and David L. Levy, "Business Strategies and Climate Change," in *Changing Climates in North American Politics*, ed. Henrik Selin and Stacy VanDeveer (Cambridge, MA: MIT Press 2010), 219–40.
3. Thomas Princen, Michael Maniates, and Ken Conca, eds., *Confronting Consumption* (Cambridge, MA: MIT Press, 2002).
4. Richard Kashmanian, Cheryl Keenan, and Richard Wells, "Corporate Environmental Leadership: Drivers, Characteristics, and Examples," *Environmental Quality Management* 19, no. 4 (Summer 2010): 1–20.
5. Tobias Hahn, Frank Figge, Jonatan Pinkse, and Lutz Preuss, "Trade-Offs in Corporate Sustainability: You Can't Have Your Cake and Eat It," *Business Strategy and the Environment* 19 (2010): 217–29.
6. Huib Pellikaan and Robert J. van der Veen, *Environmental Dilemmas and Policy Design* (New York: Cambridge University Press, 2002); Nives Dolak and Elinor Ostrom, eds., *The Commons in the New Millennium: Challenges and Adaptation* (Cambridge, MA: MIT Press, 2003).
7. Daniel A. Mazmanian and Michael E. Kraft, "The Three Epochs of the Environmental Movement," in *Toward Sustainable Communities: Transition and Transformations in Environmental Policy*, 2nd ed., ed. Daniel A. Mazmanian and Michael E. Kraft (Cambridge, MA: MIT Press, 2009).
8. Daniel C. Esty and Andrew S. Winston, *Green to Gold: How Smart Companies Use Environmental Strategy to Innovate, Create Value, and Build Competitive Advantage* (New Haven, CT: Yale University Press 2006); Matthew Potoski and Aseem Prakash, eds., *Voluntary Programs: A Club Theory Perspective* (Cambridge, MA: MIT Press, 2009).
9. U.S. Environmental Protection Agency, *Planning, Budget, and Results* (Washington, DC: U.S. EPA, 2014), http://www2.epa.gov/planandbudget.
10. Michael E. Porter and Claas van der Linde, "Green and Competitive: Ending the Stalemate," *Harvard Business Review* 73 (September/October 1995): 120–34; Esty and Winston, *Green to Gold*.
11. Doris Fuchs and Daniel A. Mazmanian, "The Greening of Industry: Needs of the Field," *Business Strategy and Environment* 7 (1998): 193–203; Daniel Press, "Industry, Environmental Policy, and Environmental Outcomes," *Annual Review of Environment and Resources* 32 (2007): 1.1–1.28.
12. Roy Huntley, Environmental Engineer, Emission Factor and Inventory Group, EPA, personal communication, August 26, 2004.
13. U.S. EPA, Clearinghouse for Inventories & Emissions Factors, *National Emissions Inventory (NEI) Air Pollutant Emissions Trends Data, 1970–2013*, www.epa.gov/ttn/chief/trends/index.html; U.S. EPA, *Summary Nonattainment Area Population Exposure Report*, www.epa.gov/airquality/greenbook/popexp.html.
14. U.S. EPA, *Summary Nonattainment Area Population Exposure Report*, www.epa.gov/airquality/greenbook/popexp.html.
15. Cary Coglianese and Jennifer Nash, eds., *Regulating from the Inside: Can Environmental Management Systems Achieve Policy Goals?* (Washington, DC: Resources for the Future, 2001).
16. Energy Information Administration, *Manufacturing Energy Consumption Survey (MECS)* (Washington, DC: U.S. Department of Energy, 2014), www.eia.gov/consumption/manufacturing/reports/2010/decrease_use.cfm?src=%E2%80%B9%20Consumption%20

%20%20%20%20%20Manufacturing%20Energy%20Consumption%20Survey%20
%28MECS%29-f2.

17. U.S. Census Bureau, *Annual Survey of Manufactures*, http://www.census.gov/
manufacturing/asm.

18. Energy Information Administration, *Manufacturing Energy Consumption Survey (MECS)*
(Washington, DC: U.S. Department of Energy, 2014), www.eia.gov/consumption/
manufacturing/reports/2010/decrease_use.cfm?src=%E2%80%B9%20Consumption%20
%20%20%20%20%20Manufacturing%20Energy%20Consumption%20Survey%20
%28MECS%29-f2.

19. Energy Information Administration, *Steel Industry Brief* (Washington, DC: U.S.
Department of Energy, 2002), www.eia.gov/consumption/manufacturing/briefs/steel/
index.cfm.

20. U.S. Department of Commerce, *Pollution Abatement Costs and Expenditures*,
MA-200(80)-1 and MA-200(05) (Washington, DC: U.S. Department of Commerce,
Bureau of the Census, 1980, 1985, 1993, 1994, 2005).

21. U.S. EPA, National Center for Environmental Economics, *Pollution Abatement Costs
and Expenditures: 2005 Survey*, http://yosemite.epa.gov/ee/epa/eed.nsf/webpages/
pace2005.html#whyimportant.

22. Walter A. Rosenbaum, *Environmental Politics and Policy*, 6th ed. (Washington, DC:
CQ Press, 2005), 163.

23. Mazmanian and Kraft, "The Three Epochs of the Environmental Movement."

24. U.S. EPA, *The EPA Acid Rain Program 2009 Progress Report*, August 2010, http://
www.epa.gov/airmarkets/progress/ARP09.html.

25. Daniel A. Mazmanian, "Los Angeles's Clean Air Saga: Spanning Three Decades," in
Toward Sustainable Communities, 2nd ed. (Cambridge, MA: MIT Press, 2009), Chapter 4.

26. David Morell, STC Environmental, personal communication, 1995.

27. For an example, see the Right-to-Know Network (www.rtknet.org) or GoodGuide's
website (www.scorecard.org).

28. U.S. EPA, *2012 Toxics Release Inventory Public Data Release*, www.epa.gov/triexplorer.

29. Ibid.

30. Michael E. Kraft, Mark Stephan, and Troy D. Abel, *Coming Clean: Information Disclosure and Environmental Performance* (Cambridge, MA: MIT Press, 2011).

31. Environmental Integrity Project and Galveston-Houston Association for Smog Prevention, "Who's Counting? The Systematic Underreporting of Toxic Air Emissions," June
22, 2004, http://environmentalintegrity.org/pdf/publications/TRIFINALJune_22.pdf.

32. U.S. EPA, *TRI Basic Data Files: Calendar Years 1987–2012*, www2.epa.gov/toxics
-release-inventory-tri-program/tri-basic-data-files-calendar-years-1987-2012.

33. Solid Waste and Emergency Response, "The National Biennial RCRA Hazardous
Waste Report." EPA530-R-10-014A (Washington, DC: U.S. EPA, 1997, 1999, 2001,
2003, 2005, 2007, 2009, 2011).

34. David Annandale, Angus Morrison-Saunders, and George Bouma, "The Impact of
Voluntary Environmental Protection Instruments on Company Environmental Performance," *Business Strategy and the Environment* 13 (2004): 1–12.

35. Alexander Pfaff and Chris William Sanchirico, "Big Field, Small Potatoes: An
Empirical Assessment of EPA's Self-Audit Policy," *Journal of Policy Analysis and Management* 23 (Summer 2004): 415–32.

36. Annandale et al., "The Impact of Voluntary Environmental Protection Instruments."

37. Pfaff and Sanchirico, "Big Field, Small Potatoes."

38. John T. Willig, ed., *Environmental TQM*, 2nd ed. (New York: McGraw-Hill, 1994);
Coglianese and Nash, *Regulating from the Inside;* Marc Allen Eisner, "Corporate

Environmentalism, Regulatory Reform, and Industry Self-Regulation: Toward Genuine Regulatory Reinvention in the United States," *Governance: An International Journal of Policy, Administration, and Institutions* 17 (April 2004): 145–67.

39. Aseem Prakash and Matthew Potoski, *The Voluntary Environmentalists: Green Clubs, ISO 14001, and Voluntary Environmental Regulations* (Cambridge, UK: Cambridge University Press, 2006), 92.

40. Richard Florida and Derek Davison, "Why Do Firms Adopt Advanced Environmental Practices (and Do They Make a Difference)?" in Cary Coglianese and Jennifer Nash, eds., *Regulating from the Inside: Can Environmental Management Systems Achieve Policy Goals?* (Washington, DC: Resources for the Future, 2001), 87.

41. Ricardo Sandoval, "How Green Are the Green Funds?" *Amicus Journal* 17 (Spring 1995): 29–33. One widely respected eco-rating of Fortune 500 companies is provided by the Investor Responsibility Research Center in Washington, DC, http://www.irrcinstitute.org.

42. Social Investment Forum, *2012 Report on Socially Responsible Investing Trends in the United States*, http://ussif.org.

43. David Austin, "The Green and the Gold: How a Firm's Clean Quotient Affects Its Value," *Resources* 132 (Summer 1998): 15–17.

44. Dagmara Nawrocka and Thomas Parker, "Finding the Connection: Environmental Management Systems and Environmental Performance," *Journal of Cleaner Production* 17 (2009): 601–07.

45. Press, "Industry, Environmental Policy, and Environmental Outcomes."

46. Annandale et al., "The Impact of Voluntary Environmental Protection Instruments"; Bruce Smart, ed., *Beyond Compliance: A New Industry View of the Environment* (Washington, DC: World Resources Institute, 1992).

47. Florida and Davison, "Why Do Firms Adopt Advanced Environmental Practices?"

48. Potoski and Prakash, *Voluntary Programs.*

49. Jan Mazurek, "Third-Party Auditing of Environmental Management Systems," in Robert Durant, Daniel Fiorino, and Rosemary O'Leary, eds., *Environmental Governance Reconsidered* (Cambridge, MA: MIT Press, 2004), Chapter 13; Eisner, "Corporate Environmentalism." For a study of selective environmental disclosure, see Eun-Hee Kim and Thomas P. Lyon, "Strategic Environmental Disclosure: Evidence from the DOE's Voluntary Greenhouse Gas Registry," *Journal of Environmental Economics and Management* 61 (2011): 311–26.

50. Natalie Stoeckl, "The Private Costs and Benefits of Environmental Self-Regulation: Which Firms Have Most to Gain?" *Business Strategy and the Environment* 13 (2004): 135–55.

51. Daniel J. Fiorino, *The New Environmental Regulation* (Cambridge: MIT Press, 2006); Daniel J. Fiorino, "Green Clubs: A New Tool for Government," in Matthew Potoski and Aseem Prakash, *Voluntary Programs: A Club Theory Perspective* (Cambridge, MA: MIT Press, 2009), Chapter 7.

52. Cary Coglianese and Jennifer Nash, *Beyond Compliance: Business Decision Making and the U.S. EPA's Performance Track Program* (Regulatory Policy Program, Kennedy School of Government, Harvard University, 2006).

53. Cary Coglianese and Jennifer Nash, "Government Clubs: Theory and Evidence from Environmental Programs," in Matthew Potoski and Assem Prakash, *Voluntary Programs A Club Theory Perspective* (Cambridge, MA: MIT Press, 2009), Chapter 8.

54. Office of Inspector General, "Performance Track Could Improve Program Design and Management to Ensure Value," 2007-P-00013 (Washington, DC: U.S. EPA, 2007).

55. The "Smoke and Mirrors" stories ran in the *Philadelphia Inquirer* on December 7, 8, 9, and 10, 2008: http://www.philly.com/philly/news/special_packages/inquirer/36110664 .html.

56. John Sullivan and John Shiffman, "Green Club an EPA Charade: The EPA Touts the Perk-Filled Program, but Has Recruited Some Firms with Dismal Environmental Records," *The Philadelphia Inquirer*, December 9, 2008.

57. Robin Bravender, "EPA: Voluntary Programs under Scrutiny as Regulatory Obligations Rise," *EE News*, February 5, 2010.

58. See the Stewardship Action Council at www.stewardshipaction.org.

59. Cary Coglianese and Jennifer Nash, "Performance Track's Postmortem: Lessons from the Rise and Fall of EPA's 'Flagship' Voluntary Program," *Harvard Environmental Law Review* 38, no. 1 (2014).

60. Information on ISO 14001 is available at www.iso.org/iso/home/standards/management -standards/iso14000.htm.

61. International Organization for Standardization (ISO), *The ISO Survey, 2012*, www .iso.org/iso/home/standards/certification/iso-survey.htm?certificate=ISO%20 14001&countrycode=#standardpick.

62. Toshi H. Arimura, Nicole Darnall, and Hajime Katayama, "Is ISO 14001 a Gateway to More Advanced Voluntary Action? The Case of Green Supply Chain Management," *Journal of Environmental Economics and Management* 61 (2011): 170–82.

63. Eisner, "Corporate Environmentalism," 150.

64. Prakash and Potoski, *The Voluntary Environmentalists*.

65. The Carbon Disclosure Project, www.cdp.net/en-US/Pages/HomePage.aspx.

66. The Forest Trust: "Delivering Responsible Products," www.tft-forests.org/.

67. Fred Pearce, "Monitoring Corporate Behavior: Greening or Merely Greenwash?" *Yale Environment 360*, January 27, 2014, http://e360.yale.edu/feature/monitoring_corporate_ behavior_greening_or_merely_greenwash/2732/.

68. U.S. Federal Highway Transportation Administration, "Quick Find: Vehicle Miles of Travel," www.fhwa.dot.gov/policyinformation/quickfinddata/qftravel.cfm.

69. Tobias Hahn et al., "Trade-Offs in Corporate Sustainability."

70. Eisner, "Corporate Environmentalism." See also Marc Allen Eisner, *Governing the Environment: The Transformation of Environmental Regulation* (Boulder, CO: Lynne Rienner, 2007).

71. Eisner, "Corporate Environmentalism," 145.

72. For many more examples of innovative industrial greening, see Esty and Winston, *Green to Gold*; Aseem Prakash, *Greening the Firm: The Politics of Corporate Environmentalism* (Cambridge, UK: Cambridge University Press, 2000); Roy Lewicki, Barbara Gray, and Michael Elliott, eds., *Making Sense of Intractable Environmental Conflicts: Concepts and Cases* (Washington, DC: Island Press, 2003); and Andrew Hoffman, *Carbon Strategies: How Leading Companies Are Reducing Their Climate Change Footprint* (Ann Arbor: University of Michigan Press, 2007).

73. Marc S. Reisch, "Twenty Years after Bhopal: Smokescreen or True Reform? Has the Chemical Industry Changed Enough to Make Another Massive Accident Unlikely?" *Chemical and Engineering News*, June 7, 2004, 19–23.

74. Environmental Protection Agency, "Improving Our Regulations: A Preliminary Plan for Periodic Retrospective Review of Existing Regulations," May 24, 2011.

75. Environmental Protection Agency, "History of Our Retrospective Review Plan," http://www.epa.gov/regdarrt/retrospective/history.html.

76. Larry Makinson and Joshua Goldstein, *The Cash Constituents of Congress* (Washington, DC: Center for Responsive Politics, 1994).

77. Amanda Peterka, "Oil Industry Warns against 'Massive and Disruptive' Tightening of Ozone Standard," *EE News PM*, May 27, 2014.
78. David M. Driesen, *The Economic Dynamics of Environmental Law* (Cambridge, MA: MIT Press, 2003).
79. Herman Daly, *Beyond Growth: The Economics of Sustainable Development* (Boston: Beacon Press, 1996). For a discussion of true cost economics, see Brendan Themes, "True Cost Economics: The Current Economic Model Has Failed Us," *Utne Reader*, August 26, 2004, www.utne.com/webwatch/2004_163/news/11366-1.html.
80. Tiffany Hsu, "Venture Capital Sweeps into Clean-Tech Industry," *Los Angeles Times*, May 2, 2011; Charles Fleming, "Tesla Motors Picks Nevada for Planned $5-Billion Factory Site," *Los Angeles Times*, August 4, 2014.

12

Taking Sustainable Cities Seriously
What Cities Are Doing
Kent E. Portney

I f the "sustainability epoch" of environmental policy described by Daniel Mazmanian and Michael Kraft seems completely foreign to national policymakers in Washington, DC, it has nonetheless taken hold in much of the world's cities, including many in the United States.[1] This chapter takes a close look at what cities in the United States are doing in order to try to become more sustainable. The focus here is on local public policies and programs that are designed to make progress toward protecting and improving cities' biophysical environments while still seeking to grow economically. Over the last twenty years or more, many U.S. cities have made significant commitments to achieving these goals. They have enacted and implemented many different types of programs and policies, and have sought to do this with an eye toward becoming more livable and sustainable places.

Of course, cities vary in how seriously they pursue these goals, and they vary in what kinds of programs and policies they create. After briefly discussing the idea and origins of city sustainability, this chapter will review the wide array of local policies and programs that major U.S. cities have adopted and implemented in the pursuit of sustainability, providing examples from a range of cities that have made significant commitments. The chapter ends with a look at some of the challenges that cities face as they try to do more, and some suggestions for strategies to facilitate these efforts.

The Idea of Sustainability in Cities

Over the more than twenty years since U.S. cities started developing sustainability programs, experience and research have painted a fairly clear picture of what cities can do if they wish to try to become more sustainable places. The concept of sustainability has been around much longer than this, and although the term seems somewhat vague and ambiguous, it has taken on significant specific meanings. One aspect of sustainability that seems to be constant across nearly all definitions is the fact that the environment is at the core of what it means to be, or become, more sustainable. Today, as will be elaborated below, cities' efforts to try to become more sustainable have included policies and programs on mass transit and transit-oriented development, smart growth, energy efficiency, housing densification, water conservation and protection, climate protection (climate mitigation and adaptation), carbon footprint reduction, urban agriculture and food systems, and many others. Although early research argued that such sustainability programs were only in the realm of wealthy places, very well-educated places, or cities on the West Coast, subsequent analysis has firmly established that communities of all sorts have successfully pursued sustainability policies.

City Sustainability Policies and Programs

What can a city do to try to become more sustainable? In fact, based on the efforts of cities all around the United States, cities can do a lot. What have cities done as a matter of local public policy in order to try to become more sustainable? By 2011, at least forty-five of the fifty-five largest cities in the United States had created significant sustainability programs, and only five seem to have made no effort to explicitly try to become more sustainable as a matter of public policy.[2] Sustainability programs take many different forms and include many different programmatic elements. In Seattle, the heart of the program is found in the city's comprehensive plan "Toward a Sustainable Seattle." In New York City, sustainability represents the core of its PlaNYC. In Philadelphia, the program is encapsulated in its Greenworks Philadelphia program. In Denver, the sustainability program got its start in the Greenprint Denver program. After more than twenty years of experience, cities have tended to settle on several dozen specific types of programs and policies. Of course, not all cities are the same. Some take a much more comprehensive approach to their policies than others. After reviewing an array of sustainability policies and programs, variations across the fifty-five largest U.S. cities will become evident.

The content of cities' sustainability efforts spans a wide range of programs and environmental results. The policies and programs include general statements of sustainability policy as reflected in city comprehensive plans, planning documents, and resolutions of chief executives and legislative bodies. They also include specific programs designed to address climate protection (climate change mitigation and adaptation), energy efficiency, smart growth, and reduction of metropolitan sprawl including transit-oriented housing and housing densification, protection of environmentally sensitive lands, and many other initiatives. Looking at thirty-eight categories of these programs focuses on programs and policies including household and industrial recycling, hazardous waste recycling, brownfield redevelopment, hazardous waste site remediation, tax incentives for environmentally friendly development, alternatively fueled city vehicles, car pool lanes, operation of public transportation, eco-industrial projects, the use of zoning to protect environmentally vulnerable land, air emissions (greenhouse gas) reduction and climate mitigation and adaptation, bicycle ridership, asbestos and lead abatement, green building, urban infill and transit-oriented housing development, energy efficiency, renewable energy for city and general residential customers, water conservation and water quality protection, recycling wastewater and reduction in stormwater runoff, creating a citywide comprehensive sustainability plan, having a single city agency responsible for managing sustainability, green city purchasing, and a sustainability indicators or performance management program.

Table 12-1 shows the results of an assessment designed to determine how many different program elements each of the largest U.S. cities had adopted and implemented as of July 2012. This assessment is based on a comprehensive effort to examine cities' policies and programs from materials available on each city's respective website, from independent surveys of city officials, and from talking to selected city administrators. In order to be counted, there must be tangible evidence that a city's program has actually been implemented in some way. A program that exists only on paper would not be counted in this assessment. The evidence to support the assessments is found in the context of city sustainability and comprehensive plans, and the programs that are operated by a variety of different city departments.

The results show that three cities have adopted and implemented thirty-five of the thirty-eight different policies and programs—Portland, Oregon, San Francisco, California, and Seattle, Washington. Denver, Colorado, has adopted thirty-three programs; Oakland, California, Charlotte, North Carolina, and Albuquerque, New Mexico, have adopted thirty-two; and six cities have adopted thirty-one each. At the lower end, Virginia Beach, Virginia, and Detroit, Michigan, have adopted seventeen; Santa Ana, California, and Pittsburgh, Pennsylvania, have adopted sixteen each; and Wichita, Kansas, has adopted only seven. The exact content of these efforts may well vary considerably. Although Portland, San Francisco, and Seattle reside at the top of the list, the character of any one particular type of program could very well differ. All three cities have energy efficiency programs, yet they differ in how they have gone about trying to achieve greater efficiency. These latter differences are not captured in the sustainability scores presented in Table 12-1.

It should also be noted that this chapter focuses on cities' policies and programs—the programs that they have adopted and implemented in their efforts to try to become more sustainable. It is perhaps natural to want to know what these programs have achieved—what their results are. Yet assessing the "outcomes" of these programs is no small task, and indeed, there are no comprehensive data available to allow such assessments to be conducted. As cities push forward with their programs, our understanding of the efficacy of these programs will improve. At this moment in time, it is not possible to know with any degree of accuracy whether these programs have improved the quality of the air, the water, and the environment broadly.

City Sustainability Programs: A Closer Look

One way to get a sense of the character of cities' sustainability programs is to look at them as individual cases, and to describe in detail what they are doing. This chapter provides at least a glimpse into what a number of U.S. cities are doing in their efforts to try to become more sustainable. We will first look at the four large cities—New York City, Los Angeles, Chicago, and Philadelphia. These cities are very similar in terms of the numbers of specific

Table 12-1 2012 Sustainability Scores for the Fifty-Five Largest U.S. Cities

(Cities profiled in this chapter are in **bold**.)

City	Sustainability Score	City	Sustainability Score
Portland	35	Louisville	26
San Francisco	35	Miami	26
Seattle	35	Raleigh	26
Denver	33	San Antonio	26
Albuquerque	32	Baltimore	25
Charlotte	32	El Paso	25
Oakland	32	Cleveland	24
Chicago	31	Milwaukee	24
Columbus	31	Atlanta	23
Minneapolis	31	Jacksonville	23
Philadelphia	31	Honolulu	22
Phoenix	31	Houston	22
Sacramento	31	Long Beach	22
New York City	30	Mesa	22
San Diego	30	Arlington, TX	20
San Jose	30	Memphis	20
Austin	29	Tampa	20
Dallas	29	Tulsa	20
Fort Worth	29	Colorado Springs	19
Nashville	29	Omaha	19
Tucson	29	St. Louis	19
Washington, D.C.	29	Oklahoma City	18
Boston	28	Detroit	17
Kansas City	28	Virginia Beach	17
Los Angeles	28	Pittsburgh	16
Indianapolis	27	Santa Ana	16
Fresno	26	Wichita	7
Las Vegas	26		

Source: Drawn from Kent E. Portney, *Taking Sustainable Cities Seriously: Economic Development, the Environment, and Quality of Life in American Cities*, 2nd ed. (Cambridge, MA: MIT Press, 2013), 23–24, updated. The sustainability score in the table refers to the number of sustainability programs enacted and implemented out of a maximum of thirty-eight.

programs they have implemented, having adopted and implemented between twenty-eight and thirty-one of the programs. After discussing these four cities, our attention will turn to a group of five cities with populations of between 450,000 and 800,000 people according to the 2010 U.S. Census. This group represents the cities that are the most aggressive in trying to become more sustainable. All of these cities have adopted between twenty-nine and thirty-five of the programs, with Seattle, San Francisco, and Portland at the top of the list of the largest U.S. cities. Finally, we will take a look at two smaller cities within this group—Denver and Austin—chosen to illustrate how much even smaller cities can accomplish.

Sustainability in Four Large Cities

Although four of the five largest cities in the United States, New York City, Los Angeles, Chicago, and Philadelphia, came to the pursuit of sustainability somewhat later than many other cities, they nonetheless have gotten very serious about enacting and implementing programs. Because of their population sizes, and perhaps their geographic sizes as well, these four cities face a somewhat more formidable set of challenges than other cities, and that is perhaps why these cities did not stand out as early adopters of sustainability programs and policies.

New York City. New York City's sustainability effort is summarized in its PlaNYC 2030, a comprehensive plan first released in 2007 covering ten different sustainability-related policy areas and involving at least twenty-five major city departments and agencies.[3] This plan contains 132 specific program initiatives with over four hundred "milestones" or goals to be achieved between 2013 and 2030, and addresses the city's housing and neighborhoods, parks and public spaces, brownfield redevelopment, waterways and water resources, transportation, energy, air quality and climate action, solid waste, and "crosscutting" issues including public health, food, natural systems, green building, waterfront development, economic development, and public engagement. The 2011 plan update provided a comprehensive implementation plan and assessment, showing each milestone or goal, its timeline, what has been accomplished, who is responsible for accomplishing it, where the funding is supposed to come from, and what progress has been made to date. It also presents the city's sustainability indicators report, with annual assessment of accomplishments in twenty-nine broad indicators. The explicit inclusion and treatment of public health as part of its sustainability plan stands out, since very few other cities make this connection.[4]

So what does PlaNYC prescribe for programs and goals on the environment? It addresses climate protection, energy, air quality, water, hazardous and solid waste, and many other areas. The city's climate plan contains thirteen different action areas with their associated milestones, including conducting and releasing an annual inventory of greenhouse gas emissions, assessing opportunities to further reduce greenhouse gas emissions by 80 percent by 2050, regularly assessing climate change projections, partnering with the Federal Emergency Management Agency to update flood insurance rate maps, developing tools to measure the city's current and future climate exposure, updating regulations to increase the resilience of buildings, working with insurance industry to develop strategies to encourage the use of flood protection in buildings, protecting New York City's critical infrastructure, identifying and evaluating citywide coastal protective measures, mitigating the urban heat island effect, enhancing the city's understanding of the impacts of climate change on public health, integrating climate change projections into emergency management and preparedness, and working with communities to increase their climate resilience.[5]

PlaNYC is designed to be used, in part, as an implementation tool by specifying performance metrics or measures, along with goals and milestones for each action area. Even so, some of the action areas and milestones do not seem terribly well tailored to serve this purpose, particularly when the milestone is just a restatement of the action area. Ostensibly, all of the programs and projects outlined in the plan, along with those associated with the "crosscutting areas" such as the city's GreeNYC, a public information and education initiative, make up New York City's sustainability initiative. Of course, as with most plans, the challenge is in implementation. PlaNYC and its updates provide assessments of progress on each milestone, although unlike many other sustainability plans, there are no clear-cut interventions prescribed when milestones are not met. Presumably, the designation of funding sources, while typically not very specific, does provide some sense that internal funding decisions may well be tied to these action areas, milestones, and goals. And, of course, there is always a question as to whether any of the specific programs, when implemented, will have their intended results on the environment. For example, although there are no serious assessments available, Brian Paul argued that the NYC approach to transit-oriented development would actually increase the city's greenhouse gas emissions by putting many more motor vehicles on the streets.[6]

Los Angeles. Although Los Angeles had developed elements of a sustainability plan earlier, the sustainability policy became official with the 2007 issuance by then Mayor Antonio Villaraigosa's Executive Directive 10, instructing all city departments to create sustainability plans. The city Department of Environmental Affairs had primary responsibility for managing and coordinating these plans. Much of this sustainability effort focused on the environment. Programs such as the "Mayor's Green Agenda" and green infrastructure, air quality and climate change, green building, energy, solid and hazardous waste, brownfield redevelopment, water, and urban habitats initiatives were all placed under the auspices of the Environmental Affairs Office. Los Angeles has not worked from a single comprehensive sustainability plan; instead, it defined specific programs, which, taken together, make up its initiative. With the election of Eric Garcetti as mayor in 2013, as in other cities, only time will tell whether these initiatives continue, get stronger, or take a back seat to others. It is already clear that sustainability is not particularly important to Garcetti as reflected in the elimination of the Department of Environmental Affairs, with its functions distributed to numerous other agencies, and his message of "back to basics," which apparently do not place a high priority on sustainability.

Over the last decade, one of the key components of the Los Angeles sustainability program has been the city's Green LA climate change initiative.

The program is complemented by a Clean Air Action Plan, which calls for the city to reduce its greenhouse gas emissions 35 percent below 1990 levels by 2030, and to increase the city's use of renewable energy to 40 percent by 2020. The plan includes about fifty specific initiatives designed to produce the targeted carbon reduction levels, such as increased use of energy-efficient lighting, extensive plans for green building, and the hallmark creation of an extensive wind turbine farm. In 2009, Los Angeles completed the construction of the Pine Tree Wind Power Project, consisting of eighty municipally owned wind turbines producing about 120 megawatts of electricity to serve about 56,000 households in the city. The Los Angeles Department of Water and Power operates this facility, along with numerous other energy efficiency and alternative energy programs, and claims to be on track to generate 20 percent of the city's energy from renewable courses by 2020.

The Los Angeles sustainability program also includes efforts to convert the city's fleet vehicles to alternative fuels, a bicycle ridership program, a significant brownfield redevelopment effort, extensive tree and native planting efforts, and many others. Two specific initiatives deserve special mention. The first, a major initiative on water conservation, is important because of the limited supplies available to the city. The second, a commitment to public transit, focuses its attention on the city's relatively new subway system. Operated by Los Angeles County Metropolitan Transportation Authority (Metro), the regional transit authority, the subway system is much smaller than those in other major cities including New York, Boston, Philadelphia, Washington, DC, and San Francisco. About 150,000 people ride the subway daily, with estimated ridership per mile of track making it the ninth busiest subway in the United States. The system has received extensive criticism, primarily for its cost and, because the population of Los Angeles is so widely dispersed, for "not going anywhere" that people want to go. Yet one of the purposes of the system was to influence the patterns of new development, encouraging more transit-oriented development and nudging people back toward the "downtown" of the city. Whether and to what extent this has started to happen is still unclear.

Chicago. By the time Mayor Richard M. Daley declared that Chicago would become the greenest city in America, he had already made a commitment to improving the biophysical environment of the city. Particularly over the last five or so years of his twenty-two-year tenure as mayor, Daley's administration made significant commitments to sustainability. Although making substantial changes to the way the people operate in a city is fraught with challenges and obstacles, the city created a Department of Environment, headed by a commissioner, with four offices each headed by a deputy commissioner. These offices, Energy and Sustainable Business, Permitting and Enforcement, Natural Resources and Water Quality, and Urban Management and Brownfield Redevelopment, combine a number of traditional city functions, such as permitting, with a broader environmental mandate. Additionally, the city's department of Planning and Development has a division of Sustainable Development with responsibility for applying sustainable design to all of the city's economic and housing development projects. Together, these make up the heart of the administrative apparatus responsible for sustainability.

Unlike New York City or Philadelphia, Chicago does not have a unified, comprehensive sustainability plan. "Greening" efforts are defined fairly piecemeal, with many different departments developing a part of the overall effort. For example, the Sustainable Development division works with a guide for encouraging, and sometimes requiring, green urban design in new construction. This plan, *Adding Green to Urban Design*, is probably the closest thing to a full sustainability plan in the city.[7] The primary purpose of this document was to provide all city departments, the city council, and the city Plan Commission with some guidance to what constitutes sustainable development when it comes time to review and approve specific development projects. The guide provides a rationale for why each considered project needs to take into consideration a wide array of environmental impacts on the land, the air, the water, and ultimately the quality of life in the city. Presumably, the intent behind this effort was to encourage disapproval of projects that don't meet the implied standards of what constitutes sustainable development.

But certainly not all of the programs and policies that make up Chicago's sustainability activities are contained in this, or any other, single document. For example, the Sustainable Development division also has responsibility for the Eat Local, Live Healthy program, outlined in a separate document.[8] This program seeks to coordinate Chicago's sustainable food system in order to support local and regional agriculture while improving human nutrition and health. Another program not represented in any comprehensive plan is the Department of Aviation's Sustainable Airport Initiatives, designed to encourage the airports in the city to adopt a variety of practices that are consistent with sustainability in construction, renovation, and daily operations.[9] The city's Department of Transportation has responsibility for traffic management, including a bicycle ridership program, but the mass transit system is managed by the Chicago Transit Authority, an independent agency. Climate action has been tackled by a task force appointed by the mayor and operating as a nonprofit organization called the Chicago Climate Action Plan. This group, which works with the Chicago Department of the Environment and Sustainability and many other city agencies, has responsibility for the city's greenhouse gas inventory, and for the plan to reduce the city's carbon footprint.[10]

Philadelphia. Although there were rumblings of interest in sustainability during the latter part of the term of former Mayor John F. Street, it wasn't until the beginning of Mayor Michael Nutter's administration in 2008 that the city seemingly started to get interested in sustainability issues. Nutter campaigned, in part, on a platform of engaging the city in a major sustainability effort and, upon taking office, created the Mayor's Office of Sustainability, now a permanent part of the city's administrative structure.

With emphasis on energy, environment, equity, economy, and engagement, the city has developed these "five *E*s" of sustainability as the foundation of its comprehensive plan. It has outlined three target areas for energy:

to lower city government energy use by 30 percent between 2008 and 2015; to reduce citywide building energy consumption by 10 percent over this same period of time; and to retrofit 15 percent of the city's housing stock with insulation, air sealing, and cool roofs. Three environmental target areas include reducing greenhouse gas emissions by 20 percent, improving overall air quality to attain federal standards, and diversion of 70 percent of solid waste from landfills. Four equity targets are to manage stormwater to meet federal standards, to provide parks and recreation resources within ten minutes for 75 percent of residents, to bring local food within ten minutes of 75 percent of residents, and to increase tree coverage toward 30 percent in all neighborhoods by 2025. Three economy targets focus on reducing vehicle miles traveled by 10 percent, increasing the state of repair of the city's resilient infrastructure, and doubling the number of low- and high-skill green jobs. The single engagement target is to engage residents in the definition, planning, and evaluation of the results of the initiatives used to support achievement of the targets' goals.

Philadelphia's Local Action Plan for Climate Change is a significant part of the responsibility of Greenworks Philadelphia. Unlike many other cities, Philadelphia conceives of climate action as an explicit part of sustainability. Its greenhouse gas emission reduction goals are embedded in its environmental targets.[11] Its greenhouse gas inventory, efforts to reduce emissions, and progress toward achieving those reductions are reported in the Greenworks Philadelphia annual report.[12] Additionally, the city has worked closely with its regional transit authority, the Southeastern Pennsylvania Transit Authority (SEPTA), to coordinate their emissions reduction strategies.

Although the Greenworks Philadelphia progress report itemizes dozens of specific activities, projects, and programs designed to achieve results in the fifteen targets, including the installation of biodiesel fueling stations for city vehicles, the installation of porous pavement on city streets, and partnerships with local businesses, including the Philadelphia Eagles professional football team to make its stadium energy independent, three specific efforts at implementing its programs deserve additional discussion here. First, as one of Greenworks Philadelphia's Equity targets, the Mayor's Office of Sustainability worked with the U.S. Forest Service to launch a local carbon offset market. This simple idea makes a personal carbon footprint calculator available to residents, and provides an opportunity for residents to purchase carbon offsets where the funds go to the Fairmount Park Conservancy to support its extensive tree planting program.[13] Second, in order to implement its energy conservation and climate action programs, the city developed numerous initiatives to help building owners retrofit their facilities. Although many cities have created similar programs, Philadelphia has explicitly made this an Equity target with the intent of making sure that the benefits of energy savings are broadly distributed across neighborhoods within the city. And third, the city took the unusual step of creating an Office of Watersheds within the Water Department to explicitly manage its water resources and wastewater with an eye toward protecting the seven watershed areas that service the city. Although all cities are serviced by watersheds, and all cities have administrative agencies responsible for managing water and wastewater, Philadelphia is perhaps the first to explicitly organize and manage these functions with this attention to watersheds. This, of course, requires a high degree of collaboration and cooperation with other municipal water agencies.[14]

Five Cities That Seem to Take Sustainability Seriously

The next set of five selected cities profiled here provides a glimpse into the actual workings of cities' sustainability initiatives. Although their programs differ, they share the fact that sustainability plays a prominent role in the cities' activities. The operational definition of sustainability varies across the cities, but all five cities seem to understand sustainability as a multidimensional concept, involving many different functional departments and activities, engaging at some level other levels of government, and requiring a relatively high level of internal coordination. All five cities have populations of nearly half a million people or more. Two of the cities, Austin and San Francisco, are fairly large, with populations of around three-quarters of a million. San Francisco, Seattle, and Portland are cities whose populations are part of much larger metropolitan areas, while Austin makes up substantial portions of its metropolitan area. All of these cities experienced population growth over the twenty-year period starting in 1990, with San Francisco (already one of the more densely populated major cities in the United States) experiencing the slowest growth.

These five cities have perhaps the most extensive commitments to sustainability policies and programs of any of the largest cities in the United States. With San Francisco, Seattle, and Portland at the very top of the ranking of the fifty-five largest cities, Denver is close behind. If American cities have made significant strides in taking sustainability seriously, it is cities in this population range that deserve the lion's share of the credit. A look at some of the central policies and programs in these cities gives an idea of the depth and breadth of their commitment.

San Francisco. The sustainability initiative in San Francisco is notable for the remarkable breadth of the city's conception of sustainability and perhaps for the lack of early success in moving sustainability issues onto the public agenda. It is also one of the few cities that incorporates a serious equity dimension in the broad view of sustainability, going well beyond the equity concerns that may be reflected in an indicators project. Overall, San Francisco is at the very top of the list of cities in terms of the numbers of programs and policies, with an Index score of 35.

Sustainability in San Francisco received a major initial push in 1996 with the release of its Sustainability Plan.[15] This plan created the blueprint for a wide array of programs, policies, and resolutions across numerous substantive areas, including air quality, biodiversity, energy, climate change and ozone depletion, food and agriculture, hazardous materials, human health, parks, open spaces and streetscapes, solid waste, transportation, water and wastewater, the economy and economic development, environmental justice, and several other areas.

The sustainability initiative, particularly the indicators project, was the product of the operation of a nonprofit organization called Sustainable City, which sought not only to develop the indicators but also to serve as an advocacy voice to help place sustainability on the city's public agenda. Largely as a result of the work of this organization, the city government's involvement has been through the city's Commission on the Environment, consisting of seven members all appointed by the mayor, which is charged with setting policy and advising all other city agencies and the Board of Supervisors. The commission works primarily with the city's Department of the Environment (often referred to as SFEnvironment), which is the central agency with any responsibility for developing and implementing the sustainability plan itself. The Department of the Environment is one of a handful of departments in the city that reports directly to the city's professional chief administrator.

Finding programmatic manifestations of the sustainability program in the city's administrative agencies is somewhat more challenging than in most other cities profiled here. The Commission on the Environment and the Department of the Environment are fairly active in identifying specific and narrowly targeted issues to confront and to seek approval from the Board of Supervisors, and the department has focused much of its attention on ordinances that require, and pilot projects that achieve, greater resource efficiency in city buildings. The standard operating mode for the commission is to present specific issue resolutions to the Board of Supervisors for its ratification. Over the last several years, the board has approved resolutions on such issues as discouraging the purchase of nonrecycled beverage bottles; the intentional release of balloons into the air; encouraging the use of alternatively fueled public transit vehicles; pesticide reduction; and numerous other issues.[16]

One of the more unusual programs of the Environment Department is the city's biodiesel initiative. Spearheaded by the Environment Commission and the Biodiesel Access Task Force, established in 2006, the city embarked on a major effort to promote the refining and use of biodiesel fuels, made up of about 20 percent refined cooking oils collected from around the city. Policies called for city vehicles to maximize their use of such fuels because of lower greenhouse gas emissions than pure diesel fuel. The policy was designed to make biodiesel as available generally as possible, and called for creation of a full infrastructure and permit process to refine, distribute, store, and sell such fuels.[17] Accompanying then Mayor Gavin Newsom's announcement that all 1,500 diesel vehicles had been prepared to run on diesel fuel, he also announced plans to build a refining facility to produce up to ten million gallons of fuel a year, a plan that came into conflict with its environmental justice policy.[18]

Sustainability in San Francisco seems to incorporate environmental justice or equity at a higher level than the vast majority of other cities. Although equity is often described as one of the key "*Es*" in sustainability, most cities are very slow or very reticent to operationalize this concept at the policy level. San Francisco's sustainability effort focuses on environmental justice with respect to five environment outcomes: air quality, energy, land use, food security, and

health. Essentially, when the city formulates, adopts, and especially implements its policies in these areas, there is elevated cognition that officials need
to be particularly sensitive to the distributional aspects of these policies. In
one area, land use, there is reason to believe that a decision to decommission
a fossil fuel–burning electricity-generating facility at Bayview–Hunters Point
was motivated, at least in part, by concerns over the disproportionate effects
local minority residents experienced from the air emissions.[19] Even so, the
policies on equity ended up being confronted by its policy to build the biodiesel refinery when Hunters Point was designated as the site for this facility.

Seattle. The city that stands at the top of virtually every list of sustainable cities, particularly those cities that have developed major indicators
projects, is Seattle. The sustainability efforts in Seattle are found in both the
nonprofit and governmental sectors, but the city's initiative is primarily associated with the activities of a single organization. "Sustainable Seattle," the
name of this initiative, was founded in 1990 and began its operations in
1991. The Sustainable Seattle initiative was conceived of as an operation
defined as a nonprofit organization (it currently operates under a 501(c)(3)
tax status designation), and its origins are significantly more "grassroots" than
are the sustainability initiatives in most other cities. The organization, which
is governed by a board of directors and has a small staff, describes itself as a
"volunteer-based civic network and forum . . . with a focus on the metropolitan city/county area" of Seattle. The articulation of this organization's
mission has changed over time, from an effort to "protect and improve [the
Seattle] area's long-term health and vitality by applying sustainability to the
links between economic prosperity, environmental vitality, and social equity"
in 2000 to an effort "to balance concerns for social equity, ecological health,
and economic vitality to create livable communities today while ensuring a
healthy and fulfilling legacy for our children's children" in 2014.[20] Out of the
mission has grown some six specific goals that include influencing individual
and collective local actions that are thought to move the city toward greater
sustainability; preparing and publishing sustainable community indicators;
providing extensive information about sustainability to residents and local
leaders; putting issues of sustainability on the "agendas" in people's homes,
neighborhoods, places of employment, and schools, and in civic life generally; providing an open forum for "cross-community dialog" on issues of
sustainability; and serving as a general resource center.

Perhaps the key defining characteristic of Sustainable Seattle, the characteristic that gave this initiative national notoriety and attention, is its Sustainable Indicators Project.[21] This project's notoriety grew not only out of the
resulting indicators themselves, but also out of the processes that were used to
produce them. Consistent with Sustainable Seattle's goal of providing a cross-
community forum for discussion of sustainability issues, the Indicators Project sought to derive its indicators through a fairly participatory process.

As impressive as the Sustainable Seattle organization and its Indicators
Project have been, they tell only part of the sustainable city story in Seattle.
The organization certainly articulates a goal of influencing local collective

actions, but the organization does not itself have any sort of legal authority for adopting or implementing policies that promote sustainable growth. The organization can use (and has used) its sustainability indicators as a political weapon by, for example, reporting the nonattainment of specific environmental goals, but it cannot directly establish public programs that will ensure that the goals are met or that progress is made toward meeting the goals. In other words, Sustainable Seattle can measure progress toward achieving greater sustainability or the lack thereof, but it cannot directly change the city's policies and programs that affect this progress. Yet what makes the Seattle experience most impressive is the way that the city's leaders, particularly the city's administrative agencies, have begun to internalize the goals of sustainability.

In 1994, the city adopted its "Comprehensive Plan," called "Toward a Sustainable Seattle," that provides a statement of a "20-year policy plan that articulates a vision of how Seattle will grow in ways that sustain its citizens' values." This comprehensive plan represents a sustainability effort that is about as well-developed and coordinated as found in any U.S. city. The plan outlines policies that affect land use, transportation, housing, capital facilities, utilities, economic development, neighborhood development and planning, human development, and cultural resources in a fairly integrated way.

The Sustainable Seattle "model" or "approach" is one that prescribes the creation of a grassroots nonprofit organization that begins its initiative independent of city government or city agencies. The basic idea seems to be that once the organization takes hold, once it embarks on an indicators project and shows that it has the support of significant segments of the local population, then it can appeal to city policymakers—the mayor and city councilors—and city agency administrators to make the case that sustainability should be on the city's agenda. To local advocates of sustainability, this model or approach seems to make perfect sense. Yet to at least one observer of the Seattle experience, the inability of the nonprofit organization to directly affect sustainability itself constitutes a major shortcoming. Because the nonprofit organization possesses no legal authority for affecting public policy, and typically does not actually operate any pollution reduction programs directly, the impact of the organization on sustainability is indirect at best. This constitutes a major problem according to Jeb Brugmann, who discounts the role that this organization may have played in helping to affect the local political agenda.[22] Yet nothing in the mandatory strategic planning process in Seattle ensured that sustainability would become the cornerstone of the effort. Indeed, without the efforts of the Sustainable Seattle organization, it is entirely possible that sustainability would have played no more than a minor part in the city's planning.

Portland. Although Portland, Oregon, is not often identified as a prototypical sustainable city, there is little question that upon examination it possesses one of the most impressive sustainability initiatives of any major city. Portland was one of the earliest cities to become involved in explicit efforts to become more sustainable, enacting in 1993 a policy on global warming that called for the reduction of the city's carbon dioxide emissions by 20 percent from 1990 to 2010. In 1994, the city adopted a set of ten sustainable city principles that reflected a long-term commitment of the city government to pursue a variety of specific policies. Portland's sustainability initiative is perhaps most like that found in Seattle where sustainability goals are an integral part of the city's Comprehensive Plan. The role of sustainability in the city oozes out of every ounce of the city's government operations, and affects the way the government is organized and functions. The city established a single agency with central programmatic and coordinating functions, the Office of Sustainable Development, an expanded version of the office previously called the Office of Energy, and now called the Bureau of Planning and Sustainability. In conjunction with the Sustainable Portland Commission, an organization of volunteers appointed by the mayor, this office operates or coordinates programs on business conservation, residential conservation, global warming, solid waste and recycling, and sustainable development. Much of the clean water operations and services falls to the Bureau of Water and the Bureau of Environmental Services.

Perhaps the most important part of Portland's sustainability effort can be found in its comprehensive plan, the *Portland Plan*. Like the Comprehensive Plan found in Seattle, sustainability represents a high priority that permeates Portland's plan. Although the environment and energy constitute two of the twelve main elements in the plan, sustainability goals are threaded throughout the plan. The plan specifies for each element, including energy and the environment, a set of goals along with the policies, programs, and actions that are necessary to achieve those goals. In 1996, for example, the plan called for the city to "promote a sustainable energy future by increasing energy efficiency in all sectors of the city by ten percent by the year 2000," goals that were apparently achieved. The goals are accompanied by specification of numerous specific objectives, along with two-year and long-term action plans for implementing and accomplishing these goals and objectives. For example, a two-year action plan for a goal of increasing waste reduction and recycling specified that the city had to "set up recycling programs for an additional 500 multifamily buildings and 20 downtown commercial buildings." Frequently, the plan specifies which agencies are responsible for accomplishing the goals, and identifies any changes in policies or ordinances that may be required to achieve them. Although the Portland Plan presents a comprehensive view of its sustainability goals, the city also works under a separate climate action plan.[23]

Denver. Denver has a fairly lengthy history of efforts to become more sustainable. Substantial support for the goal of sustainability was clearly expressed in the city's 2000 comprehensive plan, which called for specific attention to "environmental sustainability," and its strategic transit-oriented development plan.[24] The city's sustainability efforts became formalized in 2007 when then Mayor John Hickenlooper signed an executive order creating the Greenprint Denver city office, and charged it with administering a full array of sustainability programs including green building, the city's alternative fuel replacement vehicle program, waste management and recycling, water conservation, environmental health, and other areas.[25] Hickenlooper also created the

Mayor's Greenprint Council, an oversight committee composed of representatives from various city agencies, experts from the University of Colorado in Denver, and others. Near the very top of the rankings reported in Table 12-1, by 2012, Denver had embarked on efforts to adopt and implement thirty-three of the thirty-eight policies and programs, putting it squarely in fourth place among the largest U.S. cities.

Greenprint Denver works under an "action agenda" with efforts to increase city forest and tree coverage (including implementing the former mayor's challenge to plant a million trees), reduce wastes, increase reliance on renewable energy, increase green affordable housing, implement the city's green building program, expand the city's green motor fleet, promote and expand mass transit, improve the quality of, and conserve, water supplies, promote green industry economic development, operate a bicycle ridership program, develop an urban agriculture and sustainable food system, implement an energy efficiency and water conservation program for low-income residents, and implement the city's climate action plan. It also operates a small business energy efficiency program.

Greenprint Denver and the Mayor's Greenprint Council have had primary responsibility for the city's climate action plan. Denver was an early signatory to the U.S. Conference of Mayors' Climate Protection Agreement. As a result, the city prepared and issued its action plan, including its greenhouse gas inventory based on 1990 and 2005 data, in 2007, along with a one-year progress report.[26] The action plan articulated a goal of reducing per capita greenhouse gas emissions by 10 percent from 1990 levels by 2012, and made ten specific programmatic recommendations for meeting this and subsequent targeted reductions. No climate action progress reports have been issued since 2007, and by 2014, the climate action plan had morphed into a "climate adaptation" plan.[27]

Although the vast majority of programs and policies related to sustainability fall in the realm of responsibility of Greenprint Denver, many other agencies have programmatic responsibilities as well. Much of the city's sustainability effort is summarized in its comprehensive plan, and the Community Planning and Development Department and the Denver Planning Board have had major coordinating responsibilities for these. For example, in 2006, Denver announced a major initiative on transit-oriented development in order to facilitate creation of urban villages, and this initiative involved other city agencies, county government, and the regional transit authority.[28] The city created a 2008 strategic plan for multimodal transportation to address the serious and growing problem of roadway congestion and reliance on personal motor vehicle for transportation.

One of Denver's most important sustainability-related accomplishments is associated with the Stapleton Development Plan. When Denver's Stapleton Airport was replaced in 1995, the city was left with a huge parcel of land available for redevelopment. Working with a number of regional partners, nonprofit groups, and governmental agencies, the city decided to embark on a $1 billion–plus effort to add well over ten thousand housing units, and to do it in a sustainable way with green building and transit-oriented planning, consistent with its "Green Book" sustainable development principles articulated by the Stapleton Foundation. By 2004, this redevelopment project became a full-fledged sustainability initiative.[29] With the development located well west of the downtown area of the city, light rail transit is intended to link residents with the city and with the new Denver International Airport, easing the need for reliance on personal motor vehicles.

Austin. In conjunction with the surrounding Travis, Williamson, and Hays Counties that constitute the greater Austin metropolitan area, Austin has created an important sustainability initiative. It is important not just for its programmatic and policy elements, but also because of its accomplishments in a state that does not make the pursuit of sustainability easy.[30] Austin's sustainability programs, including its Climate Protection Program, are primarily administered by its Sustainability Office.[31] The foundation of Austin's sustainability policies is found in its comprehensive plan, first called *Austin Tomorrow*, and updated as *ImagineAustin* in 2012.[32] This document provides guidance into the policies, programs, and priorities expressed by city leaders, and includes sections outlining the city's desire to ensure the protection of the natural environment and open spaces, to engage in transit-oriented development and to combat sprawl, and to manage its natural resources consistent with these goals. There are numerous elements to Austin's overall sustainability effort, and some of these are highlighted here.

Austin has had two sustainability indicators initiatives, one based in the larger multicounty metropolitan area, and one for the city itself. The first is associated with what was originally the "Sustainability Indicators Project of Hays, Travis, and Williamson Counties," and expanded subsequently to include Bastrop, Burnet, and Caldwell Counties, the counties that constitute the metropolitan area for Austin (Austin is in Travis County).[33] This indicators project, first developed in 1997, now focuses on a comprehensive array of some forty indicators and over 120 measures in nine major categories—demographics, public safety, education and children, social equity, engagement, economy, environment, health, and land use and mobility.[34]

Additionally, as the City of Austin moved more explicitly into sustainability efforts, it operated its own indicators project. Called "Sustainable Community," this project started in 1999 and became part of a citywide initiative to manage city government by results, and to provide comprehensive reporting on government performance. The city's sustainability performance indicators covered public safety (fire and medical services, police, and the courts); youth, family, and neighborhood vitality (including health services, housing, libraries, and parks and recreation); sustainability (traffic and road maintenance, air quality, recycling and waste diversion, drinking water quality, lake and stream quality and water conservation, energy conservation, and inspections and site plan/subdivision review); and affordability.[35] These indicators were used as measures of the performance of local government, and until 2004, results were reported annually in the City of Austin "Community Scorecard." After 2004, the performance indicators became folded into the performance management of each department.[36]

Another major component of Austin's sustainability effort is associated with its publicly owned electric utility, known as Austin Energy, and the recommendations of the Sustainable Energy Task Force. The sustainability efforts on energy use stem from the city council's resolution that 5 percent of the city's electricity should come from renewable sources by the year 2005. The utility operates a program that allows customers to elect the "Green-Choice" option where they receive electricity generated from renewable sources (wind, solar, and biogas, especially methane, from closed landfills) at a fixed rate guaranteed for ten years, while traditional customers' rates are not guaranteed and fluctuate with the market price of fossil fuels. The utility owns and operates a wind turbine farm in West Texas that has generated 439 megawatts of electricity, and purchases electricity from numerous other wind, solar, and biogas sources to provide additional renewable sources to power up to twenty thousand homes and businesses. Austin Energy also operates extensive building energy conservation programs, and created rebate programs for installation of solar facilities on homes and commercial buildings.[37] In 2014, the Austin City Council passed a resolution approving a goal of zero carbon emissions from power plants by 2030, a far more ambitious goal than generating 35 percent of its electricity from renewable sources by 2020. Subsequently, the Austin Energy utility company made clear its opposition to this goal, claiming that electricity rates would skyrocket as a result.

Additionally, the city has developed and made a substantial investment in a "green building program" to provide technical information and guidance to developers concerning how to build more environmentally and energy-efficient construction. The green building program, first established in 1991, has residential, municipal, and commercial components and includes an effort to encourage developers to engage in smart development. The Austin conception of green building, as noted in the program description, is that it "is based on a market-pull mechanism whereby the Green Building Program promotes green building practices, rates buildings that feature these practices, thus creating more demand from the public because these buildings are perceived as more attractive products for people to buy."[38]

Austin also engages in "transit-oriented development" land use planning to minimize reliance on private transportation, the development of a "sustainable purchases protocol" for the municipal government that sets standards for city purchases of goods and services that are environmentally friendly, and a public private partnership with the regional chamber of commerce, called Greater Austin@Work, designed to foster economic development and job growth in sectors that produce fewer environmental impacts.[39]

Taking Sustainable Cities' Policies and Programs Seriously: A Summary and Thoughts for the Future

City sustainability policies span a wide array of specific programs designed to try to improve and protect the quality of the biophysical environment. These policies do this by addressing the quality of the air and by seeking to reduce greenhouse gas emissions, by trying to improve and protect access to high-quality drinking water, by managing wastewater and stormwater runoff, by managing how environmentally vulnerable or sensitive land is used, and many other goals. By looking at the efforts in these nine U.S. cities, it is clear that there is substantial variation in the extent to which cities seem to take the goal of sustainability seriously. Some cities, notably Portland, Seattle, San Francisco, and Denver, stand out as having the greatest commitment in their policies and programs. But all of the cities profiled here have accomplished impressive policy changes in pursuit of their sustainability goals. The exact content of their sustainability policies and programs varies, perhaps having been tailored to the specific conditions these cities face. Yet they all seem to have found ways of defining these policies in such a way as to promote sustainability and to protect and improve the quality of the environment in ways never entertained years ago.

As these and other cities face increasing needs to create and improve their sustainability programs, they will discover that the challenge only gets more difficult. With two to three decades of experience, cities now face the challenge of developing a deeper understanding of what their policies and programs have accomplished. Have cities' climate protection programs really decreased their carbon and other greenhouse gas emissions? Have their energy conservation programs reduced and altered the form of energy consumption? Has the quality of drinking water improved? These are the kinds of questions that cities and researchers need to focus on in the future.

Despite the idea that they will be able to share their experiences and find "best practices" they can use as models, new environmental challenges will undoubtedly make their work more daunting. Problems surrounding climate change—rising sea levels and increased storm surges from more intense weather events in coastal communities, drought and water shortages, and rising carbon dioxide emissions—promise to be long-term challenges. At the same time, many cities will find their efforts to pursue sustainability met with political resistance from those who neither understand the magnitude of the environmental problem nor appreciate the governmental actions required to address them. Yet cities will likely continue to provide an important location for the pursuit of sustainability.

Suggested Websites

Partnership for Sustainable Communities (www.sustainablecommunities .gov) A collaborative effort on the part of the U.S. Environmental Protection Agency, the U.S. Department of Housing and Urban Development, and the U.S. Department of Transportation providing information and support to cities and towns.

ICLEI Local Governments for Sustainability USA (www.icleiusa.org) The chapter of the international organization that was originally formed to help cities implement local Agenda 21 programs. It provides information and technical assistance to cities and towns that elect to become members.

STAR Communities (www.starcommunities.org/about) A Washington, DC–based nonprofit organization that provides its member cities and towns with "Sustainability Tools for Assessing and Rating Communities."

Our Green Cities (ourgreencities.com) Website/blog offers news and updates on progress in cities around the United States, and provides summaries of and access to research on local sustainability policies and programs.

Smart Growth America (www.smartgrowthamerica.org) Advocates for a wide range of local "smart growth" policies and programs, and provides support and advice to communities to promote sustainability leadership and coalition building.

U.S. Conference of Mayors Climate Protection Program (www.usmayors.org/climateprotection/revised) Provides mayors who enroll in the program with guidance, technical assistance, and "best practices" information focused on efforts to reduce carbon emissions.

International City County Management Association Center for Sustainable Communities (icma.org/en/results/sustainable_communities/home) Provides its members with extensive information about "best practices," and facilitates communications across cities.

Clinton Foundation Climate Change (www.clintonfoundation.org/our-work/by-topic/climate-change) An international effort providing technical assistance and resources to major cities around the world in order to help them reduce their air pollution and carbon emissions.

Notes

1. See Daniel A. Mazmanian and Michael E. Kraft, "The Three Epochs of the Environmental Movement," in *Toward Sustainable Communities: Transition and Transformations in Environmental Policy*, ed. Daniel A. Mazmanian and Michael E. Kraft (Cambridge, MA: MIT Press, 2009), 3–32.

2. Kent E. Portney, *Taking Sustainable Cities Seriously: Economic Development, the Environment, and Quality of Life in American Cities*, 2nd ed. (Cambridge, MA: MIT Press, 2013), 23–24.

3. PlaNYC 2030 (2011).

4. Jason Corburn, *Toward the Healthy City: People, Places, and the Politics of Urban Planning* (Cambridge, MA: MIT Press, 2009).

5. City of New York, *PlaNYC: A Greener, Greater New York* (Update April 2011), 196–97. See http://s-media.nyc.gov/agencies/planyc2030/pdf/planyc_2011_planyc_full_report .pdf.

6. Brian Paul, "How 'Transit-Oriented Development' Will Put More New Yorkers in Cars," *Gotham Gazette*, April 21, 2010, www.gothamgazette.com/article/Transportation/20100421/16/3247.

7. City of Chicago, *Adding Green to Urban Design: A City for Us and Future Generations*, www.cityofchicago.org/content/dam/city/depts/zlup/Sustainable_Development/Publications/Green_Urban_Design/GUD_booklet.pdf.

8. City of Chicago, *Eat Local, Live Healthy*, www.cityofchicago.org/content/dam/city/depts/zlup/Sustainable_Development/Publications/Eat_Local_Live_Healthy_Brochure/Eat_Local_Live_Healthy.pdf.

9. Chicago Department of Aviation, *Sustainable Airport Manual*, www.airportsgoinggreen
   .org/Content/Documents/CDA%20SAM%20-%20v2%200%20-%20November%20
   15%202010%20-%20FINAL.pdf.

10. City of Chicago, *Climate Action Plan*, www.chicagoclimateaction.org/filebin/pdf/
    finalreport/CCAPREPORTFINALv2.pdf.

11. City of Philadelphia, *Greenworks Philadelphia*, www.phila.gov/green/greenworks/pdf/
    Greenworks_OnlinePDF_FINAL.pdf.

12. City of Philadelphia, *Greenworks Philadelphia 2010 Progress Report*, www.phila.gov/
    green/PDFs/Greenworks_PrgrssRprt_2010.pdf.

13. See "Erase Your Trace," *Ms. Philly Organic*, August 24, 2009, http://msphillyorganic
    .wordpress.com/2009/08/24/erase-your-trace/.

14. See Philadelphia Water Department, Office of Watersheds, "What's on Tap," http://
    phillywatersheds.org.

15. See Sustainable City, "Biodiversity," *Sustainability Plan for San Francisco*, available at
    www.sustainable-city.org/Plan/Biodiver/intro.htm; and Sustainable City, "Energy,
    Climate Change, and Ozone Depletion," *Sustainability Plan for San Francisco*, available
    at www.sustainable-city.org/Plan/Energy/intro.htm.

16. San Francisco Environment Commission, Meeting Minutes and Agendas, https://
    sites.google.com/a/sfenvironment.org/commission/environment-commission.

17. San Francisco Environment Commission, Biodiesel Access Task Force, https://sites
    .google.com/a/sfenvironment.org/commission/biodiesel-access-task-force.

18. Mike Chino, "San Francisco Announces 10 Million Gallon Biodiesel Plant," *Inhabitat*,
    September 9, 2008, http://inhabitat.com/san-francisco-announces-10-million-gallon
    -biodiesel-plant/; Katie Worth, "San Francisco Falling Short on Use of Biodiesel for
    Public Vehicle," *San Francisco Examiner*, January 3, 2011, www.sfexaminer.com/local/
    transportation/2011/01/san-francisco-falling-short-use-biodiesel-public-vehicles.

19. San Francisco Commission of the Environment, *Bayview Hunters Point Community
    Diesel Pollution Reduction Project* (Final Report, February 2009), www.sfenvironment
    .org/sites/default/files/fliers/files/sfe_ej_bvhp_diesel_pollution_reduction_project_
    report.pdf.

20. Sustainable Seattle, "Who We Are," www.sustainableseattle.org/whoweare.

21. Alan Atkisson, "Developing Indicators of Sustainable Community: Lessons from
    Sustainable Seattle," *Environmental Impact Assessment Review* 16 (1996): 337–50.

22. Jeb Brugmann, "Is There a Method in Our Measurement? The Use of Indicators in
    Local Sustainable Development Planning," *Local Environment* 2, no. 1 (February
    1997): 59–72; Jeb Brugmann, "Sustainability Indicators Revisited: Getting from
    Political Objectives to Performance Outcomes—A Response to Graham Pinfield,"
    Local Environment 2, no. 3 (1997): 299–302.

23. City of Portland Bureau of Planning and Sustainability, *City of Portland and Mult-
    nomah County Climate Action Plan 2009*, www.portlandoregon.gov/bps/article/268612.

24. See "Denver Plan 2000," p. 26, www.denvergov.org/Portals/646/documents/planning/
    comprehensiveplan2000/CompPlan2000.pdf; and "Moving People: Denver's Strate-
    gic Transportation Plan," 2008, www.denvergov.org/Portals/688/documents/Denver
    STP_8-5x11.pdf.

25. See City of Denver, "Executive Order 123 as amended 2010," www.greenprintdenver
    .org/about/executive-order-123/.

26. Mayor's Greenprint Denver Advisory Council, *City of Denver Climate Action Plan*
    (October 2007), www.denvergov.org/Portals/771/documents/Climate/DenverClimate
    ActionPlan_2005_Original.pdf.

27. Denver Environmental Health, *City and County of Denver Climate Adaptation Plan* (2014), www.denvergov.org/LinkClick.aspx?fileticket=URNoYf2IgAI%3d&tabid=44 4803&mid=514160.

28. Transit-Oriented Denver, *Transit-Oriented Development Strategic Plan 2014*, www .denvergov.org/Portals/193/documents/DLP/TOD_Plan/TOD_Strategic_Plan_ FINAL.pdf

29. Forest City Stapleton, Inc., *Stapleton Sustainability Master Plan* (2004), www.staple tondenver.com/sites/default/files/resources/Stapleton_Sustainability_Plan.pdf.

30. Steven A. Moore, *Alternative Routes to the Sustainable City: Austin, Curitiba, and Frankfurt* (New York: Lexington Books, 2007).

31. "City of Austin Sustainability Achievements in Municipal Buildings and Sites," www.aus tintexas.gov/sites/default/files/Public_Works/Capital_Improvement/2013-08-27_ Sustainability_ReportFINAL.pdf; Lucia Athens, *Building an Emerald City: A Guide to Creating Green Building* Policies (Washington, DC: Island Press, 2010).

32. "ImagineAustin Comprehensive Plan," www.austintexas.gov/sites/default/files/ Planning/ImagineAustin/webiacpreduced.pdf.

33. Central Texas Sustainability Indicators Project, "2012 Data Report," www.soa.utexas .edu/files/csd/CTSIP%202012%20Report%201-16.pdf.

34. Central Texas Sustainability Indicators Project, "2009 Data Report," http://www .canatx.org/CAN-Research/Reports/2010/ar2009.pdf.

35. City of Austin, *Report on Performance Information for Fiscal Year Ended September 30, 2004*, www.ci.austin.tx.us/budget/03-04/downloads/performance2004.pdf.

36. City of Austin, *Performance Measures*, www.ci.austin.tx.us/budget/eperf/index.cfm.

37. "Austin Energy: More Than Electricity," www.austinenergy.com; City of Austin Office of Sustainability, www.austintexas.gov/department/sustainability.

38. City of Austin, *Performance Measures.*

39. "Austin Energy: More Than Electricity."

Part IV

Global Issues and Controversies

13

Global Climate Change Governance
The Long Road to Paris
Henrik Selin and Stacy D. VanDeveer

Climate change issues and policy debates are visible worldwide. In the Arctic, indigenous peoples struggle to sustain their economic and cultural lives, polar bears fight to stay alive, and rapidly melting sea ice opens up new sea-lanes between North America, Europe, and Asia for oil tankers, cargo vessels, and warships. In coastal areas and low-lying islands around the world, people worry about the consequences of sea level rise and intensifying storm surges. Farmers in already dry areas from California to Cameroon grow more anxious about severe droughts and extreme weather events. The list of climate change–related concerns is long—and it is growing. In response, people participate in climate change governance in churches, schools, campuses, boardrooms, and public offices from city governments to the United Nations (UN), where UN Secretary-General Ban Ki-moon declared climate change "the defining issue of our time."[1] Despite strong political statements and the looming dangers associated with changing the climate system, international institutions and the states that drive decision making have moved very slowly over the last twenty-plus years, failing to reverse global greenhouse gas (GHG) emissions.

Climate change politics focus on both mitigation and adaptation issues. Mitigation efforts center on ways to reduce GHG emissions. Many current mitigation policies focus on switching to less carbon-intensive energy sources (including wind, solar, and hydro power); improving energy efficiency for vehicles, buildings, and appliances; and supporting the development and deployment of technologies that help reduce GHG emissions. Adaptation efforts seek to improve the ability of human societies (broadly) and local communities (more specifically) to adjust to a changing climate (for example, to alter agricultural practices in response to seasonal and precipitation changes, or to prepare urban areas in coastal areas for rising sea levels and severe weather occurrences). Complicating climate change policymaking is the fact that both mitigation and adaptation issues are fraught with difficult moral and ethical challenges, as some countries contribute much more to the causes of climate change than others even as many people and societies struggle to adapt to dangerous climatic changes that they largely did not cause.

This chapter explores climate change governance across global, regional, national, and local levels. As countries struggle to formulate meaningful mitigation and adaptation policies, more aggressive action from intergovernmental forums to small communities and individuals is necessary to meet the challenges posed by climate change causes and impacts. The next section discusses the history of climate change science and the Intergovernmental Panel on Climate Change (IPCC). This is followed by an outline of the global political framework on climate change that has developed in conjunction with the IPCC assessments, the 1992 UN Framework Convention on Climate Change (UNFCCC), the 1997 Kyoto Protocol, and the 2009 Copenhagen Accord. Next, three important aspects of climate change politics are addressed: (1) European Union (EU) leadership and policy responses, (2) North American climate change policymaking, and (3) challenges facing the developing world and the BRICS (Brazil, Russia, India, China, and South Africa). The chapter ends with a few remarks about the future of global climate change governance.

Science, GHG Emissions, and the IPCC

Energy from the sun reaches Earth in the form of visible light, penetrating the atmosphere. Some of this energy is absorbed by clouds and Earth's atmosphere, while some is radiated back into space by clouds and the Earth's surface in the form of long-wave infrared radiation. Naturally occurring gases in the lower atmosphere trap some of this outgoing infrared radiation in the form of heat, in what has been termed the greenhouse effect. GHGs have been present in the atmosphere for much of Earth's 4.5 billion–year history; without them, the planet would have average surface temperatures of approximately -20°C (0°Fahrenheit). The amount of solar energy that remains trapped in the atmosphere by GHGs has important long-term effects on the climate.[2]

Researchers working across academic disciplines and fields for over 150 years have contributed to our current—and still developing—understanding of the global climate system.[3] British researcher John Tyndall, as early as 1859, formulated a theory of how carbon dioxide (CO_2) and other gases in the atmosphere keep Earth from freezing, arguing that Earth's temperature is maintained at a higher level with CO_2 than without CO_2. In 1896, Swedish scientist Svante Arrhenius explored what could happen to the climate system if atmospheric CO_2 concentrations increased, but he did not predict actual, significant changes. In 1938, however, British engineer Guy Stewart Callendar proposed that human CO_2 emissions were changing the climate. Furthermore, Gilbert Plass, an American scientist, in 1956 calculated that adding CO_2 to the atmosphere would have significant heat-trapping effects, contributing to a warming climate.

Science advanced when Charles David Keeling at the Mauna Loa Observatory in Hawaii began measuring actual CO_2 concentrations in open air in 1960. Before industrialization, atmospheric CO_2 concentrations were approximately 280 parts per million by volume (ppmv). Ice core data show that historical concentrations were relatively stable for several hundreds of thousands of years prior to the industrial revolution. Atmospheric CO_2 concentrations exceeded 400 ppmv in 2014 (far above historical levels), and they are growing at a rate of about 2 to 4 ppmv per year. While other GHGs besides CO_2 add to the warming trend, other emissions (mostly sulfate aerosols) have a cooling effect in that they repel incoming sunlight. This cooling effect is estimated to roughly cancel out the warming effect of the GHGs in addition to CO_2, but this warming-cooling balance may change in the future with increases and decreases in specific emissions.[4]

Current global climate changes are different from earlier alterations between warmer and cooler eras in that critical changes are driven by human behavior. Human activities influence both the amount of incoming energy absorbed by the Earth's surface (through land use changes including deforestation) and the amount of energy trapped by GHGs (largely by releasing CO_2 into the atmosphere through the burning of fossil fuels in manufacturing and transport but also GHGs from agricultural production). Since the beginning of the industrial revolution in the early nineteenth century, human activities have dramatically altered the composition of GHGs in the lower atmosphere by adding to the volume of naturally occurring gases (for example, CO_2 and methane) as well as by releasing human-made GHGs (for example, hydrofluorocarbons, or HFCs). Between 1990 and 2011, global GHG emissions increased by 37.2 percent, but with enormous differences in historical and current national and per capita GHG emissions (see Table 13-1).

The 2011 data in Table 13-1 are of GHG emissions as measured in CO_2 equivalents, where the global warming potential of other GHGs is converted into that of CO_2.[5] Many GHGs, including methane and HFCs, trap much more energy in the atmosphere than does the same amount of CO_2. Thus, relatively small quantities of some highly potent GHGs contribute significantly to warming. The data also include land use changes. Approximately 10 percent of global anthropogenic CO_2 emissions stem from land use changes (mainly deforestation).[6] Including such emissions can have a major impact on the reporting of national GHG emissions—in extreme cases over a 100 percent difference. A country such as Indonesia where deforestation is problematic gets a higher number than if land use changes are excluded, but a country with more sustainable forest practices and areas of reforestation like Costa Rica gets lower numbers when land use changes are included, as these biological resources act as CO_2 "sinks" (see also below).

In 2011, China, the United States, and the EU-27 were responsible for 45 percent of global GHG emissions. Middle Eastern countries, lead by Kuwait at 62.92 metric tons, top the per capita emissions list (the global average was 6.59 metric tons). Many European countries have per capita emissions similar to China's (7.63)—less than half those of the United States (19.69) and one quarter of Canada's (24.67). These differences result from multiple factors, including environmental policy, the profile of the national economy, country size and population density, public transportation infrastructure, trade patterns, consumption habits, and varying access to renewable energy. For example, Sweden's electric power consumption per capita was just above that of the United States and over four times higher than China's.[7] But Sweden's GHG per capita emissions were merely 3.94 metric tons largely due to ample availability of, and investments in, renewable energy, the use of nuclear power, and adopting a set of policy measures including a carbon tax and emissions trading through the EU. Many developing countries emit less than 3 metric tons per person.

Table 13-1   Top Nine Global Emitters of GHG Emissions (CO_2 Equivalent), Including Land Use Change and Forestry in 2011

Country/Region	Percentage Change in Emissions 1990–2011	Percentage Share of Global Emissions	Metric Tons CO_2 Equivalent per Capita (Global Ranking of States and EU-27)
1. China	+236.7	22.3	7.63 (69)
2. United States	+7.7	13.4	19.69 (16)
3. EU-27	−17.6	9.3	8.47 (62)
4. India	+127.7	7.5	1.93 (155)
5. Russian Federation	−29.2	4.8	15.50 (24)
6. Indonesia	+90.7	4.5	8.42 (63)
7. Brazil	−18.4	3.1	7.21 (73)
8. Japan	+4.2	2.5	9.16 (55)
9. Canada	+42.0	1.8	24.67 (9)

Source: World Resources Institute, *The Climate Analysis Indicator Tool* (CAIT 2.0) online database (http://cait2.wri.org).

Note: Different emissions reports will vary, depending on their inclusion/exclusion of land use changes, whether CO_2 emissions or all GHGs (or carbon equivalents) are used, or as a result of slightly different estimation techniques.

Today, most scientists agree that changes to Earth's climate system pose significant ecological, humanitarian, and economic risks. Through the IPCC—established in 1988 by the World Meteorological Organization and the UN Environment Programme—thousands of climate change scientists and experts from around the world work together, tasked with assessing, summarizing, and publishing the latest peer-reviewed data and analysis. The IPCC was created to inform policymaking, but not to formulate policy. Most IPCC work is divided into three Working Groups (WGs). WG I studies the physical science basis of the climate system and climate change. WG II focuses on the vulnerability of socioeconomic and natural systems to climate change, negative and positive consequences of climate change, and adaptation options. WG III examines mitigating options through limiting or preventing GHG emissions and enhancing activities that remove them from the atmosphere.

The IPCC has produced five sets of assessments with WG I reports released in 1990, 1995, 2001, 2007, and 2013–2014.[8] The first of these reports stated that, although much data indicated that human activity affected the variability of the climate system, the authors could not reach consensus. Signaling a higher degree of consensus, the 1995 report stated that the "balance of evidence" suggested "a discernable human influence on the climate." The subsequent three reports were critical in building a much higher degree of confidence within the scientific community. The 2013 report states that human influence is clear as the warming of the climate system (atmosphere and ocean) is "unequivocal" with atmospheric concentrations of CO_2, methane, and nitrous oxide having increased to levels unprecedented in at least the last eight hundred thousand years. Additional GHG emissions will cause further warming and changes in all components of the climate system.

The 2014 WG II report outlines a litany of impacts of climate change including precipitation patterns and amounts, ice loss, sea levels, ocean acidification, and the frequency and intensity of extreme weather events. Such changes already impact ecological systems and human health and societies, raising the risk of conflict. WG III reports include emissions scenarios that project possible GHG emissions levels decades into the future, based on a different set of assumptions about future levels of economic growth and choices made by governments and citizens that affect the generation of GHG emissions. Scenarios are designed to help decision makers and planners think about how climate change may impact societies and how quickly various mitigation strategies could change future emissions. They also inform thinking about projects such as building new sewage treatment systems in a coastal area, new power plants, or the design of new water policies in drought-stricken regions. Together with reports by WG I and WG II, they make it clear that all countries face adaptation challenges, even if these vary tremendously across societies and regions.

IPCC reports are widely reviewed and cited by people in international organizations, local governments, large and small firms, environmental advocacy groups, scholars, scientific researchers, and many more. However, the IPCC has also come under criticism, with some claims in the reports later turning out to be based on inconclusive or incorrect information. While this leads some critics of climate change science and policy to question the integrity of the IPCC process, the vast majority of climate change scientists support the IPCC reports and their main conclusions.

International Law and Climate Change Negotiations

International law on climate change is shaped by a complex mix of evolving scientific consensus and the material interests and values of state, nongovernmental, and private sector actors. Over two decades of global negotiations have left many frustrated and disappointed with the results and dispirited about the prospects of addressing the problem.[9] Along with a growing number of policy responses at every level of the public, private, and civil society spheres, two major multilateral treaties exist: the 1992 UNFCCC and the 1997 Kyoto Protocol. The UNFCCC was negotiated between publication of the first IPCC report and the 1992 UN Conference on

Environment and Development in Rio de Janeiro, where it was adopted. It entered into force in 1994, and by 2014, 195 countries and the EU were parties to the treaty. As a framework convention, the UNFCCC sets out a broad strategy for countries to work jointly to address climate change.

Like other framework conventions, the UNFCCC defines the issue at hand, sets up an administrative secretariat to oversee treaty activities, and lays out a legal and political framework under which states cooperate over time. The UNFCCC contains shared commitments by states to continue to research climate change, to periodically report their findings and relevant domestic implementation activities, and to meet regularly to discuss common mitigation and adaptation issues at Conferences of the Parties (COPs). Usually, framework conventions do not include detailed regulatory commitments, leaving those issues to be addressed in subsequent protocols. Similar approaches using the framework convention–protocol model have been applied to issues such as protection of the stratospheric ozone layer, acid rain and related transboundary air pollution problems, and biodiversity loss.

The UNFCCC sets the long-term objective of "stabilization of greenhouse gas concentrations in the atmosphere at a level that would prevent dangerous anthropogenic interference with the climate system" (Article 2). The UNFCCC establishes that the world's countries have "common but differentiated responsibilities" in addressing climate change (Article 3). This principle refers to the notion that all countries share an obligation to act, but industrialized countries and countries with economies in transition (that is, former communist countries) listed in Annex I have a particular responsibility to take the lead because of their relative wealth and contribution to the problem through historical emissions. This Annex currently lists forty countries and the EU. Annex I countries agreed to reduce their anthropogenic emissions to 1990 levels, but no clear deadline was set for this target (Article 4). The UNFCCC did not assign developing countries any GHG reduction commitments.

Responding to mounting scientific evidence about human-induced climate change in the mid-1990s, much of it presented in the second IPCC report, and to growing concern about negative economic and social effects of climate change among environmental advocates and policymakers, the UNFCCC parties negotiated the Kyoto Protocol between 1995 and 1997. The final stage of the protocol negotiations was contentious on a number of issues. In particular, U.S. and European negotiators differed on both the targets for emissions cuts that should be included in the agreement and the policy mechanisms that should be allowed or recommended for parties to reach their GHG reduction targets. Only as a result of last-minute compromises by a number of participants, brokered in part by an intervention by then U.S. Vice President Al Gore, did the parties agree on a final text.

The Kyoto Protocol initially regulated six GHGs: CO_2, methane, nitrous oxide, perfluorocarbons, HFCs, and sulfur hexafluoride. UNFCCC Annex I countries committed to collectively reduce their GHG emissions by

5.2 percent below 1990 levels by 2008–2012. Toward this goal, thirty-nine states had individual targets.[10] Some agreed to cut their emissions, while others merely consented to slow their emissions growth. For example, the EU-15 took on a collective target of an 8 percent reduction while the United States and Canada committed to cuts of 7 percent and 6 percent, respectively. In contrast, Iceland committed to limit its emissions at 10 percent above 1990 levels. Russia and post-communist countries in Central and Eastern Europe agreed to cuts from 1990 levels, but many of these cuts were easily achieved by the economic restructuring that followed the end of their communist political and economic systems.

The Kyoto Protocol outlined five ways for countries with reduction commitments to meet their targets. States could (1) develop any kind of national policies that lower domestic GHG emissions; (2) calculate benefits from domestic carbon sinks (including forests and benefits from reforestation) that soak up more carbon than they emit, and count these toward national emission targets; (3) participate in transnational emissions trading schemes with other Annex I parties (that is, Annex I countries can create markets in which actors can buy and sell emissions permits); (4) develop Joint Implementation (JI) programs with other Annex I parties and get credit for lowering GHG emissions in those countries; and (5) design a partnership venture with a non–Annex I country through what is known as the Clean Development Mechanism (CDM) and get credit for lowering GHG emissions in the partner country. The latter three options were intended to provide flexibility and reduce mitigation costs by allowing parties to cut emissions wherever and however it was most efficient, including in other countries.

Almost all the UNFCCC parties eventually ratified the Kyoto Protocol, which entered into force in 2005, but it still engendered substantial controversy and criticism. Developing countries, lacking individual GHG reduction requirements, strongly supported it and the principle of common but differentiated responsibility. Among industrialized countries, a stark transatlantic difference emerged.[11] The EU took an early leadership role in defense of the Kyoto Protocol, succeeding in reducing GHG emissions beyond its target (see also EU section below). In contrast, the United States refused to ratify the Kyoto Protocol (also trying to convince other countries to do the same). Canada ratified the Kyoto Protocol in 2002, but announced in 2011 that it officially withdrew from the agreement, after failing to implement it or curb emissions. Both U.S. and Canadian GHG emissions have increased significantly since 1990 (see below). Australia, Japan, New Zealand, and Russia all became parties, but displayed varying levels of support.

In Bali in 2007, the UNFCCC parties launched a process to negotiate a follow-up agreement to the Kyoto Protocol, to be considered at the 2009 COP in Copenhagen.[12] However, national leaders were unable to agree to a legally binding agreement. Instead, they settled on a Copenhagen Accord, under which countries adopt their own voluntary and widely divergent GHG targets for 2020. By 2014, 113 countries and the EU had agreed to the Copenhagen Accord, which sets the goal that average global temperature increases should remain below 2 degrees Celsius (related to the UNFCCC goal to prevent dangerous anthropogenic interference with the climate system). Scientists linking atmospheric GHG levels with temperatures believe that this requires stabilizing atmospheric GHG concentrations around 450 ppmv before bringing them down close to preindustrial levels. In addition, the Copenhagen Accord notes that industrialized countries will try to mobilize $30 billion from 2010 to 2020, with the goal of reaching $100 billion a year by 2020, to support mitigation and adaptation projects in developing countries. Numerous analyses, however, make clear that the voluntary GHG reduction targets under the Copenhagen Accord fall well short of those needed to remain below 2 degrees Celsius of warming, and the pledged financial assistance is not on track to meet stated goals.

After Copenhagen, parties at the 2010 COP in Cancun created the Green Climate Fund to support mitigation and adaptation projects in developing countries alongside other bodies including the Global Environment Facility and the World Bank. They also raised the profile of adaptation issues in the UNFCCC negotiations through the creation of a Cancun Adaptation Framework. At the 2011 COP in Durban, the parties adopted the Durban Platform for Enhanced Action, launching a new round of negotiations to develop "a protocol, another legal instrument or an agreed outcome with legal force," to be concluded in 2015. The 2012 COP in Doha formulated a second Kyoto commitment period wherein Annex I countries agreed to reduce their overall GHG emissions by at least 18 percent (collectively) below 1990 levels by 2020. However, some Annex I countries—Canada, Japan, New Zealand, Russia, and the United States—refused to take on a second, formal round of Kyoto targets for 2020. Parties also added nitrogen trifluoride (NF3) to the list of regulated GHGs, bringing the total to seven GHGs, and extended the CDM and JI mechanisms. The 2013 COP in Warsaw saw some progress on how to address forest issues through the Reducing Emissions from Deforestation and Forest Degradation (REDD+) program. The 2014 COP in Lima attempted to lay the foundation for a broad global agreement in Paris in 2015, as both industrialized and developing countries for the first time seek to move forward with a system of GHG reduction pledges for the post-2020 period.[13]

Within the continuing UNFCCC negotiations, governments and advocacy groups express substantial disagreements over many central issues:

- Targets and timetables: Which collective GHG reduction targets are both aggressive enough to make a real difference to atmospheric GHG concentrations consistent with the 2 degrees Celsius goal and politically, economically, and technically feasible? By which dates should the different targets be met?
- National commitments: Should all or only some countries take on national GHG emissions reduction commitments? Should these commitments be mandatory or voluntary (or some combination of both)?
- Forest issues: Should issues of deforestation and forest management under the REDD+ program and other initiatives be directly linked to

climate change efforts? If so, how should related goals and commitments be formulated, how stringent should they be, and to which countries should they apply?

- Adaptation: How should mechanisms associated with the growing need to adapt to environmental, social, and economic impacts of climate change be designed, and which countries should be eligible for various kinds of support?
- Capacity building and technology transfer: Which are the best ways to promote and support capacity building and technology transfer related to climate change mitigation and adaptation around the world?
- Financing: Which is the most appropriate way to utilize the Green Climate Fund and other funding sources in support of climate change mitigation and adaptation, and should there be a move toward more mandatory funding obligations? What mix of public and private funding?

A few specific examples of these general nodes of debate include the Alliance of Small Island States wanting swift and strong action from all major emitters. The larger group of developing countries stresses the principle of common but differentiated responsibilities, arguing that industrialized countries should continue to lead. They, in turn, want mandatory targets for at least the major developing country emitters, such as the BRICS. The EU and many developing countries stress the importance of a legally binding agreement, while countries including China and the United States see advantages of more voluntary mechanisms. Donor and recipient countries continue to debate how to generate resources for the Green Climate Fund and other mechanisms including REDD+, as capacity building, technology transfer, and adaptation needs grow.

EU Leadership and Policy Responses

Since the 1990s, the EU, representing the majority of the world's industrial countries, has emerged (comparatively) as a global leader in climate change politics and policymaking.[14] Even as the EU grew from fifteen members in the mid-1990s to twenty-eight members during a series of enlargements, EU bodies such as the European Commission (the administrative bureaucracy), the Council of the European Union (comprising member state government officials), and the European Parliament (representatives elected by member state citizens) have worked together and collaborated with civil society and private sector actors to enact and implement a set of pan-European climate change and energy-related goals and policies. With the population of EU-28 over five hundred million, meaning roughly one in fourteen humans live in the EU, and member states that total twenty-six of the forty UNFCCC Annex I countries, the EU remains a major contributor to climate change and a major player in global climate change politics and policymaking.[15]

The desire to meet the Kyoto target served as an important impetus for EU policymakers to develop a growing number of joint policies and initiatives. The EU-15 collective Kyoto target (8 percent below 1990 GHG emission levels by 2012) was divided among member states under a 1998 burden-sharing agreement. Intended to facilitate intra-EU decision making and implementation, each member state took on a differentiated target.[16] Several member states, including Luxembourg (−28 percent), Denmark (−21 percent), Germany (−21 percent), and the United Kingdom (−12.5 percent), took on relatively far-reaching commitments, while less wealthy member states such as Portugal (+27 percent), Greece (+25 percent), and Spain (+15 percent) could increase their GHG emissions in the period up to 2012, as part of these countries' efforts to expand industrial production and accelerate economic growth.

In 2007, EU political leaders endorsed the so-called 20-20-20 by 2020 goals contained in a major climate and energy package of policies enacted in 2009. These policies, all with a 2020 deadline, refer to a 20 percent reduction in GHGs below 1990 levels, 20 percent of the total energy consumption coming from renewable sources, and a 20 percent reduction in primary energy use compared with projected trends. This suite of policies also uses a burden-sharing approach, setting differentiated national targets for GHG emission reductions from sources not covered by the EU's Emissions Trading System (ETS) and for the expansion of renewable energy use. An EU 20 percent GHG reduction goal by 2020 was submitted as the EU goal under the Copenhagen Accord and included in the Kyoto Protocol's second commitment period. In 2014, with an eye toward the 2015 Paris COP, EU member states raised EU goals to a 40 percent GHG reduction together with 27 percent goals for renewable energy generation and improved energy savings, all to be achieved by 2030.

Receiving much attention as the world's first international GHG trading system, the ETS served as a main EU policy instrument for meeting Kyoto targets, and it remains central for the 2020 and 2030 policy goals. Ironically, the EU was opposed to GHG emissions trading during the Kyoto negotiations—an issue championed by the United States, which drew on its domestic experience with emissions trading for sulfur dioxide and nitrogen oxide. The EU attempted to enact a carbon tax in the late 1990s, but this effort failed when member states could not agree on a common tax. In the face of this policy failure and the need to meet its Kyoto target, EU officials developed the ETS.[17] The ETS launched with a first phase (2005 and 2007) slowly, a second trading period (2008 to 2012), and a third starting in 2013. The scheme has been significantly amended and expanded since 2005, and now includes all twenty-eight EU members as well as Iceland, Lichtenstein, and Norway.

Currently, the ETS sets a regional cap for three GHGs—carbon dioxide, nitrous oxide, and perfluorocarbons—from over eleven thousand major point sources in power generation and manufacturing and aviation, collectively covering 45 percent of all EU GHGs.[18] The cap is designed to shrink annually so that emissions from covered sectors in 2020 will be 21 percent lower than in 2005. Every year the EU allots emissions allowances to each participating country, which in turn allocate these to domestic firms. Allowances are increasingly auctioned off, rather than distributed for free, across different economic sectors. Firms can also use some emission credits generated under the Kyoto Protocol to meet their obligations. Those without enough allowances to cover their emissions by the end of each year are fined.

To date, EU climate change and energy policies have produced mixed outcomes.[19] Official EU data show that the EU-15 GHG cut collective emissions by 12.2 percent from 1990 to the 2008–2012 period, thus exceeding their Kyoto Protocol target. However, a few member states missed their specific burden-sharing targets. The EU is largely on track to surpass its 2020 GHG reduction goal—EU-27 emissions were 18 percent below 1990 levels in 2012. On the other two 2020 targets, the EU seems likely to meet its renewable energy goal, but member states are making less progress toward their energy efficiency targets. Transportation and agriculture emissions also remain high. In addition, recent efforts by EU bodies, some member states, and advocacy groups to further tighten the ETS and strengthen other requirements have been met by substantial resistance from some member states and private sector groups.[20]

North American and U.S. Climate Change Policy and Politics

In contrast to the EU, North American federal governments have been slow to act, and they have produced a much less regionally integrated response despite sharing a common market under the North American Free Trade Agreement (NAFTA).[21] The United States and Canada since the late 1990s have been viewed as laggards among the Annex I countries, at times hostile to global climate change cooperation. Both countries' GHG emissions (excluding land use changes) are higher than in 1990—U.S. emissions by 9.3 percent and Canadian emissions by 25.2 percent in 2011. If land use changes are included, U.S. emissions increased by 7.7 percent while Canadian emissions increased by a whopping 42.0 percent during the same time period.[22] In recent years, U.S. national emissions have dropped considerably as a result of an ongoing switch from coal to natural gas, state-level GHG reduction policies, and reduced energy demand related to the economic recession and slow recovery. Canada has seen a much smaller national drop despite GHG reductions in some provinces, as oil production from tar sands and associated land conversion in Alberta and Saskatchewan increased sharply. In Mexico (a non–Annex I country), GHG emissions increased by 71.8 percent without land use changes and 66.8 percent with land use changes between 1990 and 2011.

U.S. skepticism of global climate change policy dates back to the Kyoto Protocol. A few months before it was signed by Bill Clinton's administration, the Senate passed by 95-0 a "Sense of the Senate" resolution that opposed the draft treaty "because of the disparity of treatment between Annex I Parties and Developing Countries and the level of required emission reductions . . . could result in serious harm to the United States economy, including significant job loss, trade disadvantages, increased energy and consumer costs, or any combination thereof."[23] The Senate thereby rejected the principle of common but differentiated responsibilities embedded in the UNFCCC, despite having ratified the UNFCCC only a few years earlier. President George W. Bush made U.S. rejection of the Kyoto Protocol official U.S. policy. The Canadian federal government, led by Prime Minister Jean Chrétien, ratified the Kyoto Protocol in 2002, but failed to enact any serious implementation policies. The subsequent Stephen Harper administration took the very rare step of formally withdrawing Canada from the protocol in 2011, and it has made no concerted attempt to enact policies that reduce Canadian GHG emissions.

At the 2009 Copenhagen summit, neither the Barack Obama administration (lacking Senate support) nor the Harper administration supported the EU vision (preferred also by many smaller developing countries) of a legally binding agreement mandating national GHG reductions. The United States and Canada submitted identical targets under the Copenhagen Accord: a 17 percent reduction below 2005 levels by 2020. Mexico stated a goal to reduce GHG emissions by 30 percent compared to a business as usual scenario by 2020. During the formulation of the Durban Platform, the United States and Canada stressed that all major GHG emitters including China be included in any agreement, and that voluntary programs should be part of the international policy mix. Given the dysfunctional state of the U.S. Congress and the dim prospects for Senate approval of any international climate change agreement, the Obama administration, with Canadian support, continued to seek some sort of nonbinding agreement in Paris.[24] This approach of voluntary commitments was encapsulated in the 2014 joint U.S.-China climate change deal, where the United States agreed "to make best efforts" to cut national GHG emissions by 28 percent from 2005 levels by 2025.[25]

Alongside international cooperation, North American climate change politics have evolved significantly at national and, especially, subnational levels since the 1990s. President George W. Bush opposed mandatory national GHG reductions throughout his presidency (2001–2009), despite having expressed support for CO_2 regulations during his first presidential campaign.[26] U.S. federal policy under the Bush administration focused instead on voluntary programs and the funding of scientific research and technological development. Yet, the 2007 Energy Independence and Security Act raised the national Corporate Average Fuel Economy (CAFE) standards for vehicles— the first increase in over thirty years. The Obama administration (2009–) expressed early support for regulating GHG emissions, pushed for increases in U.S. international climate change funding, and appointed a large number of climate change scientists and policy advocates to government. Yet Obama's first term saw little regulatory action during beyond raising CAFE standards through 2025, as the U.S. Congress failed to agree on climate change mitigation or adaptation legislation. Because the president dedicated so little time to climate change and gave no major speeches about it, one assessment characterized the first term as "some walk" and "no talk."[27]

During its second term, the Obama administration launched more ambitious regulatory proposals declaring that it will act, where it can, even if Congress will not. These regulatory actions are based on a 2007 U.S. Supreme Court ruling that CO_2 can be classified as a pollutant under the Clean Air Act. An endangerment finding issued by the Environmental Protection Agency (EPA) in 2009 stated that the current and projected atmospheric concentrations of the six GHGs first covered by the Kyoto Protocol threaten the public health and welfare of current and future generations. Based on this, in 2014, EPA issued a regulatory plan containing a series of measures. Chief among these were the proposal to cut national CO_2 emissions from large power plants by 30 percent below 2005 levels by 2030. The plan also supports expanded investments in renewable energy production and measures to improve energy efficiency. The proposals seek to give states wide latitude in choosing how to achieve federally mandated goals. In addition, the plan stresses the need to prepare the United States for impacts of climate change and the need for international cooperation. Beyond policies that explicitly address GHG emissions, the EPA has developed a set of measures to reduce air pollutants such as ozone, particulates, and methane. These regulations are likely to have substantial co-benefits in terms of improving human health conditions and climate change mitigation.

As U.S. federal policy changes toward more aggressive action, Canada's Harper government generally has elected not to institute any meaningful federal GHG policy. Mexico, which early on engaged in modest voluntary initiatives, has recently taken more ambitious steps. Legislation enacted in 2012 passed Mexico's Copenhagen Accord commitment into law. This was followed in 2013 by a legal commitment to cut GHGs by 50 percent from 2000 levels by 2050, in part supported by a modest carbon tax, and the goal of generating 35 percent of energy from renewable sources by 2024.[28] The 2012 and 2013 legislation gave Mexico the distinction of having the most comprehensive federal climate change law in North America, and it established Mexico as a Latin American leader in climate change policymaking and prodded other South and Central American states to move forward.[29]

In response to the slow development of federal-level climate change policy over the past two decades, an important and diverse set of subnational responses have developed in both the United States and Canada (see Chapter 2), as an array of cities, states, and provinces exercise impressive leadership around climate change and related energy policy areas.[30] There are also significant subnational differences in GHG emissions and trends. Table 13-2 illustrates the extreme variance among GHG emission trends and per capita emissions among U.S. states. These differences stem from a host of factors, including differential economic and population growth rates, differing energy and environmental policies, diverging transportation needs, substantial variance in the sources of energy used, and large differences in state and local climate change policies. Illustrating the global importance of U.S. emissions, U.S. states emit as many GHGs as large and small countries, notably impacting global emissions. In 2011, Texas, the U.S. state with highest total emissions, emitted 10 percent more than all of Canada, 13 percent more than Mexico, and 45 percent more than the United Kingdom (excluding land use changes). California emitted a little less than France and more than Turkey, while a small state like Massachusetts emitted about as much as Portugal and New Zealand.

Table 13-2   Select U.S. State Emitters of GHG Emissions (CO_2 Equivalent), Excluding Land Use Change and Forestry

State	Percentage Change in Total Emissions 1990–2011 (national ranking)	Percentage Change in per Capita Emissions 1990–2011 (national ranking)	Per Capita Emissions Metric Tons CO_2 Equivalent in 2011 (national ranking)	Percentage of Total U.S Emissions in 2011 (national ranking)
ID	+50.8 (1)	−3.6 (13)	18.02 (30)	0.4 (44)
NE	+48.5 (2)	+27.5 (2)	45.10 (7)	1.3 (31)
AZ	+47.4 (3)	−16.0 (34)	16.03 (33)	1.6 (26)
ND	+39.8 (5)	+30.2 (1)	101.12 (2)	1.1 (37)
WY	+18.1 (21)	−5.5 (20)	150.01 (1)	1.3 (28)
NV	+16.6 (22)	−47.7 (50)	14.31 (39)	0.6 (42)
TX	+14.3 (26)	−23.9 (45)	30.86 (16)	12.1 (1)
CA	+2.0 (35)	−18.9 (37)	11.39 (47)	6.5 (2)
NY	−16.4 (48)	−22.8 (40)	10.02 (50)	3.0 (9)
MA	−16.4 (49)	−23.8 (42)	11.46 (46)	1.2 (34)
DE	−25.9 (50)	−45.4 (49)	15.54 (35)	0.2 (48)

Source: World Resources Institute, *The Climate Analysis Indicator Tool* (CAIT 2.0) online database (http://cait2.wri.org).

Many U.S. states have taken policy actions such as establishing renewable portfolio standards requiring electricity providers to obtain a minimum percentage of their power from renewable sources, formulating ethanol mandates and incentives, pushing to close some coal-fired power plants, setting vehicle emissions standards, adopting green building standards, mandating the sale of more efficient appliances and electronic equipment, and changing land use and development policies to curb emissions. In fact, several U.S. states, through their respective attorneys general, were a driving force behind the 2007 Supreme Court decision declaring CO_2 a pollutant, as they called for greater action by Congress and the federal government. California, building on its tradition of air pollution and energy leadership, has enacted a suit of climate change policies aiming to increase energy efficiency across the state; reduce GHG emissions from power plants, homes, business, and transportation; and dramatically expand renewable energy generation. In fact, California's set of climate policies is comparable to that of the EU. Among Canadian provinces, British Columbia distinguished itself (in Canada, and globally) by implementing a relatively comprehensive carbon tax to curb emissions.[31]

States and provinces also enact collaborative standards and policies. Originally proposed in 2003 and formally launched in 2009, the Regional Greenhouse Gas Initiative (RGGI) creates a cap-and-trade scheme across nine states: Maryland, Maine, Vermont, New Hampshire, Massachusetts, Rhode Island, Connecticut, New York, and Delaware (New Jersey was an original member, but left in 2011). The RGGI was designed to stabilize CO_2 emissions from the region's major power plants between 2009 and 2015 and to achieve a 10 percent reduction by 2019. By 2013, emissions were already far below the cap, prompting states to cut the 2014 emissions cap by 45 percent and plan for it to decline through 2020. Emissions in the RGGI states averaged 178 million tons annually, between 2000 and 2006. The 2014 cap is ninety-one million tons (48 percent below the 2000–2006 average), with scheduled declines though 2020 to fifty-six million tons (68 percent below the 2000–2006 average).[32] In the process, auctioning emission permits has produced over $700 million for energy efficiency and other public benefits investments, saving consumers an estimated $2 billion. Under the Western Climate Initiative, British Columbia, California, Ontario, Quebec, and Manitoba work to harmonize GHG mitigation efforts involving emissions trading. California's cap-and-trade program was launched in 2013 and became linked with Quebec's GHG reduction efforts in 2014. California climate change and renewable energy collaboration with Mexico expands subnational efforts into the third NAFTA member. The Obama administration EPA proposals, if implemented, are designed to further incentivize state action and collaboration.

In addition, small and large municipalities all over North America are taking action, both individually and through networks including the International Council for Local Environmental Initiatives and its Cities for Climate Protection program, the U.S. Conference of Mayors' Climate Protection Agreement, the Federation of Canadian Municipalities' Partners for Climate Protection program, and the C40 group.[33] Although many municipal climate change programs are modest, cities such as New York City, Toronto, and Portland have achieved noteworthy results. North American municipalities are also increasingly developing new GHG reduction and energy efficiency programs that rely in part on innovative private financing. Additionally, a growing number of North American firms are voluntarily reducing GHG emissions and investing in low carbon technology, but it is important to note that a significant number of firms are still taking only limited (if any) action.[34]

Even as important political and technical precedents for future climate change actions are being set all over the United States and Canada, there continues to be significant public and private sector resistance against mandatory action and controls. A few states, provinces, and municipalities have also decided to delay or even to roll back enacted climate change policies due to combinations of local political opposition and tougher economic times during the economic downturn starting in the late 2000s. In the U.S. Congress, particularly in the House, opposition has also included many attempts to limit the EPA's regulatory authority and efforts to restrict executive branch agencies from developing emissions reduction or adaptation policies (see Chapter 5). The new EPA rules issued in mid-2014 are also under intense scrutiny as opponents are taking political and legal action to delay or block their implementation.

The energy futures of all three North American countries are deeply linked. On the one hand, opportunities exist for much more cross-border renewable energy development and trade between both Canada and the United States and the United States and Mexico. On the other hand, the expansion of tar sands extraction in Alberta is related to the controversy over whether to build the Keystone XL pipeline system connecting Canadian oilfields with U.S. refineries and ports in the Gulf of Mexico—an issue on which the Obama administration has long been reluctant to make a final decision. Other related controversies fester, around whether to expand U.S. oil, gas, and coal exports; how many new areas to open for additional fossil fuel extraction; and what, if any, subsidies to offer to renewable energy investments and production. These and many other future energy decisions and investments in North America—and other countries around the world—will have a direct impact on future efforts to curb GHG emissions.

The Developing World and the BRICS

As the international community struggles to address climate change under the UNFCCC and a multitude of associated programs and initiatives, many developing countries face myriad mitigation and adaptation problems, alongside multitude other critical sustainable development issues (see Chapter 14). The situation of relatively vulnerable countries to climatic changes gives rise to important procedural and distributive social justice issues, from a global equity perspective.[35] Procedural justice refers to the ability to fully partake in collective decision-making processes focusing on mitigation and adaptation issues, including under the UNFCCC. Distributive justice concerns how climate change impacts or how mitigation policies affect societies and people differently, having greatly varying domestic capacities to deal with these challenges.

For many developing countries, procedural justice issues relate to how international climate change policy is formulated and how these countries' domestic interests are represented and taken into account. Many governments of smaller developing countries face multiple problems engaging actively in multilateral environmental negotiations and assessments.[36] These problems include having fewer human, economic, technical, and scientific resources (compared with leading industrialized countries) with which to prepare for international negotiations or implement resulting agreements. The significant capacity differences between wealthier industrialized countries and poorer developing countries risk skewing international assessments, debates, and decision making in favor of the perspectives and interests of more powerful countries, often interested in minimizing their own mitigation costs.

On distributive justice issues, the UNFCCC recognizes that some countries are "particularly vulnerable" to adverse effects of climate change (Preamble). This includes "low-lying and other small island countries, countries with low-lying coastal, arid and semi-arid areas or areas liable to floods, drought and desertification, and developing countries with fragile mountainous ecosystems." For example, countries in South Asia with vast and densely populated low-lying coastal areas, including Bangladesh and India, will experience many of the first impacts of sea level rise and increased storm intensity. Changes in seasons and precipitation present a more acute threat to millions of poor, small-scale farmers in Africa and other tropical countries than they do to those in rich countries. Similar issues can be extended to indigenous populations, including those in the Arctic, who are often among the most vulnerable in any society.[37]

The developing world often tries to speak with one voice on climate change through the Group of 77 (G-77).[38] This includes their strong interest in the principle of common but differentiated responsibilities as key for assigning GHG reduction requirements as well as prioritizing economic development partly based upon the continued use of fossil fuels. The ability of the very diverse group of G-77 members to present a unified front has always been inconsistent, becoming more difficult in recent times. One major change over the last two decades of international politics is the rapid economic growth and increasingly assertive positions of major developing countries, often exemplified by the BRICS. This creates challenges both for G-77 unity and for efforts to stitch together a global agreement. Despite increasing debates about whether rapidly industrializing countries like China and India are well suited to represent the "Global South"—or even belong in such a category—Indian and Chinese officials remain extremely attached to many of the ideas, values, and principles associated with developing country identity in global politics.[39]

As the list of major global emitters above makes clear (see Table 13-1), the BRICS are joining the ranks of top emitters. Major industrializing countries are under increased pressure to accept GHG restrictions from a diverse set of groups. For example, low-lying islands fear Chinese emissions as much as those originating from Europe and North America, industrialized countries want a level economic playing field for their firms on international markets, and environmental organizations push for emission cuts as a central sustainable development issue. In China, as air pollution and public health issues are rapidly becoming more salient domestically, the government is stepping up mitigation actions. This includes investing heavily in greener technologies, expanding wind and solar power generation capacities, and launching pilot cap-and-trade programs.[40] Several non–Annex I countries have pledged to reduce their emissions (usually from business-as-usual expectations), including China, Brazil, and Mexico, while China and South Korea have announced plans to establish GHG emissions trading systems.[41] Indian Prime Minister Narendra Modi has expressed more support for renewable energy generation and GHG reductions. While BRICS officials all agree that developing countries should pledge substantial reductions, consistent with the principle of common but differential responsibilities, they are likely to find it much more difficult to agree on what they (and other developing countries) should be expected to do beyond 2020.

While industrialized countries and countries with economies in transition may continue to set national GHG reduction targets in absolute terms, some analysts and policymakers argue that at least some developing countries might be better served by a system based on per capita income or per capita emissions, or targets focusing on reducing CO_2 emissions per unit of gross domestic product, or by some percentage compared to business-as-usual estimates of future emissions growth—options used by Brazil, China, India, Indonesia, Mexico, South Africa, and others under the Copenhagen Accord. Such a system may also better allow for strengthening commitments over time and gradual expanding of international cooperation.[42] A diversity of goals and metrics may be politically necessary, but may also prove difficult to monitor and assess collectively. Furthermore, national GHG emissions under many of these pledges are predicted to continue to grow in the short and medium terms.

Finally, developing countries pay close attention to developments with the Green Climate Fund in the years to come, as an important indication of the level of commitment shown by the international community. They generally argue in global climate change negotiations that fulfillment of their national GHG reduction targets is dependent on the delivery of adequate financial and technological assistance from donor countries. For example, Mexico stated this explicitly in its voluntary commitment under the Copenhagen Accord. While the 2014 COP in Lima brought increased pledges from several industrialized countries including the United States (where congressional approval may prove difficult), developing countries have cause to be skeptical about pledges until funds are delivered.

Last Tango in Paris?

Climate change policy is developing across global, regional, national, and local governance levels, but it remains unclear if these initiatives collectively can meet mitigation and adaptation needs in time to avert catastrophe. The world's industrialized and developing countries do not face the same challenges, but climate change threatens all. While some opponents of climate change action believe that short-term mitigation costs are too high, a growing number of analysts and policymakers argue that early action is less costly for societies than is coping with severe climatic changes in the future (see also Chapter 10).[43] As global GHG emissions continue to rise, the challenge of finding ways to significantly reduce these—by upwards of 80–90 percent by 2050 as often stated—while simultaneously tackling poverty and promoting sustainable economic and social development cannot be overstated (see Chapters 14, 15, and 16). Even if the global climate change negotiations were to produce a broader and stronger agreement, climate change politics and policymaking will continue to evolve for decades to come.

Because of frustration with the UNFCCC process and the intransigence of many states, some look to the plethora of governance experiences outside and under global institutions.[44] Analysts catalogue the myriad ways that actors at every level of social organization are experimenting with new policies and institutions to address mitigation and adaptation needs. Some such arrangements allow private sectors to set rules and launch initiatives to reduce GHG emissions, or to work collaboratively with public and civil society actors to achieve common goals in the absence of government mandates. Such research makes it clear that innovation around climate and energy collaboration is nearly infinite, but questions remain about whether this huge variety of non–state governance can meet the climate change challenge without much more significant state action in both the Global North and the Global South.

Formulating global climate change action through the UNFCCC and its associated mechanisms is increasingly criticized for not being flexible enough to promote the scale of change needed to significantly cut GHG emissions within desirable time frames.[45] The failure to reach a meaningful agreement in Copenhagen in 2009 leaves much riding on the 2015 Paris meeting. This could be seen as the last dance for the UNFCCC process—a failure to gain necessary momentum in Paris for 2020 and beyond would provide much ammunition for those who believe that the global multilateral process is inherently gridlocked and that we need to find alternative approaches.[46] Debates also continue about the relative merits of internationally mandated GHG reductions (providing a clear legal obligation for countries to act) versus more voluntary approaches (offering greater flexibility and more palatable for many countries, but producing only modest national commitments in the short and medium terms).[47]

Constructive signals from the political leaders of China and the United States, the world's two largest emitters, in their 2014 bilateral announcement pointed to the emergence of a (long overdue) more serious approach to GHG reductions, positively influencing the 2014 COP in Lima. Importantly, this was the first time China publicly stated an intention of curbing the upward trajectory of national CO_2 emissions around 2030. Yet, without much more substantial cuts by all large- and medium-sized national emitters, it is impossible to meet the 2 degrees Celsius target. Countries traditionally classified as developing currently account for approximately 60 percent of global annual GHG emissions, and their relative contribution will continue to grow. At the same time, the vast majority of the world's poorest people live in these countries, facing growing climate-related adaptation problems, as differences among developing countries become more pronounced. Failure to mitigate makes adaptation challenges more urgent, costly, and difficult for all countries, hitting weaker and poorer ones much more harshly.

The scientific debate about the reality of human-induced climate change is settled, but significant disagreements remain among countries and public and private sector actors about allocation of costs and responsibilities for cutting GHG emissions and switching to cleaner technology. International politics and national and local governments are central to addressing major climate change mitigation and adaptation challenges, but large and small firms are also critical players in their roles as investors, polluters, innovators, experts, manufacturers, lobbyists, and employers.[48] Major economic and social changes—such as the drive for low-carbon lifestyles—create both business constraints and opportunities. Collective action is required, but individual actions by consumers and citizens are needed, as well. If the challenges posed by climate change are to be met, we must all take responsibility for our impact on the global climate system, using and expanding our influence over our own behavior and in our local communities, workplaces, and governments.

Suggested Websites

Center for Climate and Energy Solutions (www.c2es.org) Offers information about international and U.S. climate change policymaking and private sector action.

Climate Ark (www.climateark.org) A portal, search engine, and news feed covering climate change issues.

Dot Earth (http://dotearth.blogs.nytimes.com) Blog run by *New York Times* reporter Andrew C. Revkin; focuses on climate change science and policy issues.

European Union (http://ec.europa.eu/clima) Provides information about European perspectives and policy initiatives to address climate change.

Intergovernmental Panel on Climate Change (www.ipcc.ch) Panel of international experts conducting periodical assessments of scientific and socioeconomic information about climate change.

Real Climate (www.realclimate.org) Provides commentaries on climate change science news by scientists working in different fields.

UN Framework Convention on Climate Change (http://unfccc.int) Website operated by the UNFCCC Secretariat; contains information about meetings and other activities organized under the UNFCCC.

U.S. Environmental Protection Agency (www.epa.gov/climatechange) Provides information about climate change science, U.S. policy, and what people can do to lower their personal GHG emissions.

Notes

1. Robert O'Neill, "Ban Ki-moon Delivers Call to Action on Global Challenges," Harvard Kennedy School, October 22, 2008, www.hks.harvard.edu/news-events/news/articles/ban-ki-moon-forum-oct.
2. Kerry Emanuel, *What We Know about Climate Change*, 2nd ed. (Cambridge, MA: Boston Review/MIT Press, 2012).

3. Spencer R. Weart, *The Discovery of Global Warming*, 2nd ed. (Cambridge, MA: Harvard University Press, 2008).

4. For discussions about the latest developments in climate change science, see Real Climate (www.realclimate.org).

5. For a chart of different global warming potentials, see https://unfccc.int/ghg_data/items/3825.php.

6. IPCC, *Climate Change 2013: The Physical Science Basis*, http://www.ipcc.ch/report/ar5/wg1/.

7. See http://data.worldbank.org/indicator/EG.USE.ELEC.KH.PC?order=wbapi_data_value_2011+wbapi_data_value+wbapi_data_value-last&sort=desc.

8. The IPCC reports and other data are available on the IPCC website (www.ipcc.ch).

9. Christian Downie, *The Politics of Climate Change Negotiations* (Northampton, MA: Edward Elgar, 2014); Harro van Asselt, *The Fragmentation of Climate Change Governance* (Northampton, MA: Edward Elgar, 2014); and Thomas Hale, David Held, and Kevin Young, *Gridlock: Why Climate Change Cooperation Is Failing When We Need It Most* (London: Polity, 2013).

10. These were Australia, Austria, Belarus, Belgium, Bulgaria, Canada, Croatia, Czech Republic, Denmark, Estonia, Finland, France, Germany, Greece, Hungary, Iceland, Ireland, Italy, Japan, Latvia, Lichtenstein, Lithuania, Luxembourg, Monaco, Netherlands, New Zealand, Norway, Poland, Portugal, Romania, Russian Federation, Slovakia, Slovenia, Spain, Sweden, Switzerland, Ukraine, United Kingdom, and the United States.

11. Miranda A. Schreurs, Henrik Selin, and Stacy D. VanDeveer, eds., *Transatlantic Environment and Energy Politics: Comparative and International Perspectives* (Aldershot, UK: Ashgate, 2009).

12. Raymond Clemoncon, "The Bali Roadmap," *Journal of Environment and Development* 17, no. 1 (2008).

13. Detailed reports about all COPs, for the UNFCCC and many other international environmental negotiations, can be found in the *Earth Negotiations Bulletin*, available at www.iisd.ca/enbvol/enb-background.htm.

14. Andrew Jordan et al., eds., *Climate Change Policy in the European Union: Confronting Dilemmas of Mitigation and Adaptation?* (Cambridge, UK: Cambridge University Press, 2010).

15. The fourteen Annex I countries that are not EU members are Australia, Belarus, Canada, Iceland, Japan, Lichtenstein, Monaco, New Zealand, Norway, Russia, Switzerland, Turkey, Ukraine, and the United States.

16. Henrik Selin and Stacy D. VanDeveer, *European Union Environmental Governance* (New York: Routledge, 2015).

17. Jon Birger Skjærseth and Jørgen Wettestad, *EU Emissions Trading: Initiating, Decision-Making and Implementation* (Aldershot, UK: Ashgate, 2008).

18. European Commission, *The EU Emissions Trading System (EU ETS)* (Brussels: European Commission, 2013); Selin and VanDeveer, *European Union Environmental Governance*, 2015.

19. European Environment Agency, *Trends and Projections in Europe 2013: Tracking Progress Towards Europe's Climate and Energy Targets until 2020* (Copenhagen: European Environment Agency, 2013).

20. Jorgen Wettestad, "Rescuing EU Emissions Trading: Mission Impossible?" *Global Environmental Politics* 14, no. 2 (2014): 64–81.

21. Henrik Selin and Stacy D. VanDeveer, eds., *Changing Climates in North American Politics: Institutions, Policy Making and Multilevel Governance* (Cambridge, MA: MIT Press, 2009).

22. http://cait2.wri.org/wri.
23. U.S. Senate, "Byrd-Hagel Resolution," www.nationalcenter.org/KyotoSenate.html.
24. Coral Davenport, "Obama Pursuing Climate Accord in Lieu of Treaty," *New York Times*, August 27, 2014.
25. White House, Office of the Press Secretary, "U.S.-China Joint Announcement on Climate Change," November 12, 2014, http://www.whitehouse.gov/the-press -office/2014/11/11/us-china-joint-announcement-climate-change.
26. Miranda A. Schreurs, Henrik Selin, and Stacy D. VanDeveer, "Conflict and Coopera-tion in Transatlantic Climate Politics: Different Stories at Different Levels," in *Trans-atlantic Environment and Energy Politics: Comparative and International Perspectives*, ed. M. A. Schreurs, H. Selin, and S. D. VanDeveer (Aldershot, UK: Ashgate, 2009), 165–85.
27. Graciela Kincaid and J. Timmons Roberts, "No Talk, Some Walk: Obama Adminis-tration First-Term Rhetoric on Climate Change and U.S. International Climate Budget Commitments," *Global Environmental Politics* 13, no. 4 (2013): 41–60.
28. "Mexico Unveils National Climate Change Strategy," *SustainableBusiness.com*, June 11, 2013, http://www.sustainablebusiness.com/index.cfm/go/news.display/id/24967.
29. Lisa Friedman, "Latin Americans Forge Ahead on CO_2 Reduction Plans," *ClimateWire*, June 9, 2014.
30. For a comprehensive list of U.S. state and regional actions, see the Center for Climate and Energy Solutions at www.c2es.org/us-states-regions. On Canada, see David Suzuki Foundation, *All Over the Map 2012* (Vancouver, BC: David Suzuki Founda-tion, 2012), www.davidsuzuki.org/publications/downloads/2012/All%20Over%20 the%20Map%202012.pdf.
31. Stewart Elgie and Jessica McClay, "BC's Carbon Tax Is Working Well after Four Years (Attention Ottawa)," *Canadian Public Policy* 39, no. 2 (2013): 11–22.
32. RGGI website: www.rggi.org.
33. Christopher Gore and Pamela Robinson, "Local Government Responses to Climate Change: Our Last, Best Hope?" in *Changing Climates in North American Politics: Insti-tutions, Policy Making and Multilevel Governance*, ed. Henrik Selin and Stacy D. VanDeveer (Cambridge, MA: MIT Press, 2009).
34. Charles A. Jones and David L. Levy, "Business Strategies and Climate Change," in *Chang-ing Climates in North American Politics: Institutions, Policy Making and Multilevel Gover-nance*, ed. Henrik Selin and Stacy D. VanDeveer (Cambridge, MA: MIT Press, 2009).
35. W. Neil Adger, Jouni Paavola, and Saleemul Huq, "Toward Justice in Adaptation to Climate Change," in *Fairness in Adaptation to Climate Change*, ed. W. Neil Adger, Jouni Paavola, Saleemul Huq, and M. J. Mace (Cambridge, MA: MIT Press, 2006).
36. Pamela S. Chasek, "NGOs and State Capacity in International Environmental Nego-tiations: The Experience of the Earth Negotiations Bulletin," *Review of European Community and International Environmental Law* 10, no. 2 (2001): 168–76; Ambuj Sagar and Stacy D. VanDeveer, "Capacity Development for the Environment: Broad-ening the Scope," *Global Environmental Politics* 5, no. 3 (2005): 14–22.
37. Arctic Climate Impact Assessment, *Impacts of a Warming Arctic: Arctic Climate Impact Assessment* (Cambridge, UK: Cambridge University Press, 2004).
38. Adil Najam, "The View from the South: Developing Countries in Global Environ-mental Negotiations," in *The Global Environment*, 4th ed., ed. Regina Axelrod and Stacy D. VanDeveer (Washington, DC: CQ Press, 2015).
39. Shangrila Joshi, "Understanding India's Representation of North-South Climate Politics," *Global Environmental Politics* 13, no. 2 (2013): 128–47; Philip Stalley, "Prin-ciples Strategy: The Role of Equity Norms in China's Climate Change Diplomacy," *Global Environmental Politics* 13, no. 1 (2013): 1–8.

40. Joanna I. Lewis and Kelly Sims Gallagher, "Energy and Environment in China: National and Global Challenges," in *The Global Environment*, 4th ed., ed. Regina Axelrod and Stacy D. VanDeveer (Washington, DC: CQ Press, 2015); and Joanna I. Lewis, *Green Innovation in China* (New York: Columbia University Press, 2013).
41. David Held, Charles Roger, and Eva-Maria Nag, *Climate Governance in the Developing World* (Malden, MA: Polity, 2013).
42. Joseph E. Aldy and Robert N. Stavins, "Climate Policy Architecture for the Post-Kyoto World," *Environment* 50, no. 3 (2008): 6–17.
43. Nicholas Stern, *The Economics of Climate Change: The Stern Review* (Cambridge, UK: Cambridge University Press, 2005).
44. Harriett Bulkely et al., *Transnational Climate Change Governance* (Cambridge, UK: Cambridge University Press, 2014); Jennifer Green, *Rethinking Private Authority* (Princeton, NJ: Princeton University Press, 2014); Matthew Hoffmann, *Climate Governance at the Crossroads* (Oxford, UK: Oxford University Press, 2011).
45. Robert O. Keohane and David G. Victor, "The Regime Complex for Climate Change," *Perspectives on Politics* 9, no. 1 (2011): 7–23.
46. Thomas Hale, David Held, and Kevin Young, *Gridlock: Why Global Cooperation Is Failing When We Need It Most* (Cambridge: Polity, 2013).
47. Matthew J. Hoffmann, *Experimenting with a Global Response after Kyoto* (Oxford, UK: Oxford University Press, 2011).
48. Jones and Levy, "Business Strategies and Climate Change."

14

Environment, Population, and the Developing World

Richard J. Tobin

Environmental problems occasionally make life in the United States unpleasant, but most Americans tolerate this situation in exchange for the comforts associated with a developed economy. Most Europeans, Japanese, and Australians share similar lifestyles, so it is not surprising that they typically also take modern amenities for granted.

When lifestyles are viewed from a global perspective, however, much changes. Consider, for example, what life is like in much of the world. The U.S. gross national income (GNI) per capita was $53,670 per year, or more than $1,000 per week, in 2013. In contrast, weekly incomes are less than 5 percent of this amount in almost thirty-five countries, even when adjusted for differences in prices and purchasing power. In several African countries, real per capita incomes are about one-hundredth of those in the United States. Much of the world's population lives on less than $2 a day. In south Asia and sub-Saharan Africa, much of the population is below this level.[1]

Low incomes are not the only problem facing many of the world's inhabitants. In some developing countries, women, often illiterate and with no formal education, marry as young as age thirteen. In Chad, Bangladesh, and Niger, more than a quarter of girls are married by the age of fifteen. In south Asia, over 40 percent of all females are married before their eighteenth birthday.[2] Many of these marriages are with much older men with less education than their teenage brides. During their childbearing years, women in many developing countries will typically deliver as many as five or six babies, most without skilled birth attendants. This absence is not without consequences. The likelihood that a woman will die due to complications associated with pregnancy, childbirth, or an unsafe abortion is many times higher in poor countries than in Western Europe or the United States. In Chad, as an illustration, one of every fifteen women dies in childbirth (compared to about 1 of 1,800 in the United States).

Many of the world's children are also at risk. Only seven of one thousand American children die before the age of five; in some Asian and African countries, the infant mortality rate exceeds 150 per 1,000 children. *Every week*, about 130,000 children under age five die in developing countries from diseases that rarely kill Americans. Malaria, diarrhea, and acute respiratory infections cause more than half of these deaths, most of which can be easily and cheaply cured or prevented. In sub-Saharan Africa, more than one of ten children dies before age five.[3]

Of the children from these poor countries who do survive their earliest years, millions will suffer brain damage because their pregnant mothers had no iodine in their diets; others will lose their sight and die because they lack vitamin A. Many will face a life of poverty, never to taste clean water, use a toothbrush, enter a classroom, learn to read or write, visit a doctor, have access to even the cheapest medicines, or eat nutritious food regularly. To the extent that shelter is available, it is rudimentary, rarely with electricity or proper sanitary facilities. Hundreds of millions in the developing world will also become victims of floods, droughts, famine, desertification, land degradation, waterborne diseases, infestation of pests and rodents, and noxious levels of pollution because their surroundings have been abused or poorly managed.

Many countries, especially in the Middle East and North Africa, suffer from shortages of water, and the water that is available is often from nonrenewable sources. Most sewage in developing countries is discharged without any treatment, and pesticides and human wastes often contaminate well water. According to the Millennium Ecosystem Assessment, about half the urban population in Asia, Africa, and Latin America suffers from one or more diseases associated with inadequate water and sanitation.[4]

As children in developing countries grow older, many will find that their governments cannot provide the resources to ensure them a reasonable standard of living or even a seat in a classroom. Yet all around them are countries with living standards well beyond their comprehension. The average American uses more than twenty times more electricity and consumes about 60 percent more calories per day—far in excess of minimum daily requirements—than does the typical Indian. An Indian mother might wonder why Americans consume a disproportionate share of the world's resources when she has malnourished children she cannot clothe or educate.[5]

In short, life in much of the world provides an array of problems different from those encountered in developed nations. Residents of poor countries must cope with widespread poverty, scarce opportunities for employment, and a lack of development. Yet both developed and developing nations often undergo environmental degradation. Those without property, for example, may be tempted to denude tropical forests for land to farm. Concurrently, pressures for development often force people to overexploit their natural and environmental resources.

These issues lead to the key question addressed in this chapter: Can the poorest countries, with the overwhelming majority of the world's population, improve their lot through sustainable development? Sustainable development meets the essential needs of the present generation for food, clothing, shelter, jobs, and health without "compromising the ability of future generations to meet their own needs."[6] Achieving this goal will require increased development without irreparable damage to the environment.

Whose responsibility is it to achieve sustainable development? One view is that richer nations have a moral obligation to assist less fortunate ones. If the former do not meet this obligation, not only will hundreds of millions of people in developing countries suffer, but the consequences will be felt in the developed countries as well. Others argue that poorer nations must accept responsibility for their own fate because outside efforts to help them only worsen the problem and lead to an unhealthy dependence. Advocates of this position insist that it is wrong to provide food to famine-stricken nations because they have exceeded their environment's carrying capacity.[7]

The richer nations, whichever position they take, cannot avoid affecting what happens in the developing world. It is thus useful to consider how events in rich nations influence the quest for sustainable development. At least two related factors affect this quest. The first is a country's population; the second is a country's capacity to support its population.

Population Growth: Cure or Culprit?

Population growth is one of the more contentious elements in the journey toward sustainable development. Depending on one's perspective, the world is either vastly overpopulated or capable of supporting as many as thirty times its current population (about 7.2 billion in mid-2014 and increasing at an annual rate of about 82 million per year).[8] Many developing nations are growing faster than the developed nations (Table 14-1), and more than 80 percent of the world's population lives outside the developed regions. If current growth rates continue, the proportion of those in developing countries will increase even more. Between 2014 and 2050, more than 97 percent of the world's population increase, estimated to be about 2.4 billion people, will occur in the latter regions, exactly where the environment can least afford such a surge. Many of the new inhabitants will live in countries that are experiencing little, if any, economic growth.

Africa is particularly prone to high rates of population growth, with some countries facing increases of 3 percent or more per year. This may not seem to be a large percentage until we realize that such rates will double the countries' populations in about twenty-four years. Fertility rates measure the number of children an average woman has during her lifetime. Twenty-three of the twenty-four countries with fertility rates at five or above in 2013 were in sub-Saharan Africa. By comparison, the birthrate in the United States was thirteen per thousand, and its fertility rate was 1.9.

Although many countries have altered their attitudes about population growth, many have also realized the immensity of the task. The theory of demographic transition suggests that societies go through three stages. In the first stage, in premodern societies, birth and death rates are high, and populations remain stable or increase at low rates. In the second stage, death rates decline and populations grow rapidly because of vaccines, better health care, and more nutritious foods. As countries begin to reap the benefits of development, they enter the third stage. Infant mortality declines, but so does the desire or need to have large families. Population growth slows considerably.

Table 14-1   Estimated Populations and Projected Growth Rates

Region or Country	Estimated Population (millions)			Rate of Annual Natural Increase (%)	Number of Years to Double Population
	Mid-2014	2030	2050		
World total	7,238	8,444	9,683	1.2	60
More developed countries	1,249	1,292	1,309	0.1	720
Less developed countries	5,989	7,152	8,375	1.4	51
United States[a]	318	354	395	0.4	180
Canada	36	42	48	0.4	180
Mexico	120	137	151	1.4	51
China	1,364	1,400	1,312	0.5	144
India	1,296	1,510	1,657	1.5	48
Japan	127	117	97	−0.2	—
Sub-Saharan Africa	920	1,360	2,081	2.6	28
Angola	22	36	61	3.2	23
Chad	13	22	37	3.3	22
Democratic Republic of Congo	71	115	193	3.0	24
Niger	18	34	68	3.9	18
Uganda	39	63	104	3.4	21

Source: Population Reference Bureau, *2014 World Population Data Sheet* (Washington, DC: Population Reference Bureau, 2014), www.prb.org.

a. Although rates of natural increase in the United States are modest, immigration accounts for much of the projected increase in the U.S. population.

This model explains events in many developed countries. As standards of living increased, birthrates declined. The model's weakness is that it assumes economic growth; in the absence of such growth, many nations are caught in a demographic trap. They get stuck in the second stage. This is the predicament of many countries today. In some African countries, the situation is even worse. Their populations are growing faster than their economies, and living standards are declining. These declines create a cruel paradox. Larger populations produce increased demands for food, shelter, education, and health care; stagnant economies make it impossible to provide them.

The opportunity to lower death rates can also make it difficult to slow population growth. As of 2013, in nine African countries, the average life expectancy at birth was fifty years or less, compared with seventy-nine years in the United States and eighty-three years in Japan. If these Africans had access to the medicines, vitamins, clean water, and nutritious foods readily available elsewhere, then death rates would drop substantially. Life expectancies in these countries could be extended by twenty years or more.

There are several reasons to expect death rates to decline. Development agencies have attempted to reduce infant mortality by immunizing children against potentially fatal illnesses and by providing inexpensive cures for diarrhea, malaria, and other illnesses. These efforts have met with enormous success, and more progress is anticipated. Reduced mortality rates among children should also reduce fertility rates. Nonetheless, the change will be gradual, and millions of children will be born in the meantime. Most of the first-time mothers of the next twenty years have already been born.

The best known population programs have been in India and China. India's family planning program started in the early 1950s as a low-key effort that achieved only modest success. The program changed from being voluntary to being compulsory in the mid-1970s. The minimum age for marriage was increased, and India's states were encouraged to select their own methods to reduce growth.

Through a variety of approaches, India has been able to cut its fertility rate significantly, but cultural and religious resistance may stifle further gains.[9] India currently adds about nineteen million inhabitants each year. If such growth continues, India could become the world's most populous country before 2025.

Whether India does so depends on what happens in China. To reduce its growth rate, the Chinese government discourages early marriages. It also adopted a one-child-per-family policy in 1979. Until the policy was relaxed in late 2013 to allow families to have two children if one of the parents is an only child, the government gave one-child families monthly subsidies, educational benefits for their child, preferences for housing and health care, and higher pensions at retirement. Families that had previously agreed to have only one child but then had another were deprived of these benefits and penalized financially. The most controversial elements of China's population policy involved the government's monitoring of women's menstrual cycles, forced sterilizations and late-term abortions, and female infanticide in rural areas.[10]

China's initial efforts lowered annual rates of population growth considerably. Total fertility rates declined from 5.8 in 1970 to 1.6 in 2014. As a result of its one-child policy, Chinese officials claimed that nearly four hundred million births had been averted.[11]

For many years, the U.S. government viewed rapidly growing populations as a threat to economic development. The United States backed its rhetoric with money; it was the largest donor to international population programs. The U.S. position changed dramatically during the Ronald Reagan administration. Due to its opposition to abortion, the administration said the United States would no longer contribute to the United Nations Population Fund (UNFPA) because it subsidized some of China's population programs. None of the fund's resources are used to provide abortions, but the U.S. ban on contributions nonetheless continued during George H. W. Bush's administration.

Within a day of taking office, President Bill Clinton announced his intention to alter these policies, to provide financial support to the UNFPA, and to finance international population programs that rely on abortions. Just as Clinton had acted quickly, so too did George W. Bush. Within two days of becoming president in 2001, he reinstated Reagan's policy banning the use of federal funds by international organizations to support or advocate abortions. The cycle continued with President Barack Obama. He reversed the Bush rules and urged Congress to restore funding for the UNFPA.[12]

Concerns about abortion are not the only reason many people have qualms about efforts to affect population increases. Their view is that large populations are a problem only when they are not used productively to enhance development. The solution to the lack of such development is not government intervention, they argue, but rather individual initiatives and the spread of capitalist, free-market economies. Advocates of this position also believe that larger populations can be advantageous because they enhance political power, contribute to economic development, encourage technological innovation, and stimulate agricultural production.[13] Other critics of population control programs also ask if it is appropriate for developed countries to impose their preferences on others.

Another much-debated issue involves the increased access to abortions, and who chooses to have them. The consequences of efforts to affect population growth are not always gender neutral. In parts of Asia, male children are prized as sources of future financial security, whereas females are viewed as liabilities. In years past, the sex of newborns was known only at birth, and in most countries, newborn males slightly outnumber newborn females. With the advent of ultrasound, however, the sex of a fetus is easily ascertained months before a child is born. This knowledge can be the basis of a decision to abort female fetuses, notably in parts of China and India.[14] Other practices also seem to disadvantage females. In China, the infant mortality rate is more than 30 percent higher for females than it is for males.

In sum, the appropriateness of different population sizes is debatable. There is no clear answer about whether growth by itself is good or bad. The important issue is a country's and the world's carrying capacity. Can it ensure a reasonable and sustainable standard of living? Can it do so in the future when the world's population will be substantially larger?

Providing Food and Fuel for Growing Populations

Sustainable development requires that environmental resources not be overtaxed so that they are available for future generations. When populations exceed sustainable yields of their forests, aquifers, and croplands, however, these resources are gradually destroyed.[15] The eventual result is an irreversible collapse of biological and environmental support systems. Is there any evidence that these systems are now being strained or will be in the near future?

The first place to look is in the area of food production. Nations can grow their own food, import it, or, as most nations do, rely on both options. The Earth is richly endowed with agricultural potential and production. Millions of acres of arable land remain to be cultivated, and farmers now produce enough food to satisfy the daily caloric and protein needs of a world population exceeding twelve billion.[16] These data suggest the ready availability of food as well as a potential for even higher levels of production. This good news must be balanced with the realization that hundreds of millions of people barely have enough food to survive.

As with economic development, the amount of food available in a country must increase at least as fast as the rate of population growth; otherwise, per capita consumption will decline. If existing levels of caloric intake are already inadequate, then food production (and imports) must increase faster than population growth to meet minimum caloric needs. Assisted by the expanded use of irrigation, pesticides, and fertilizers, many developing countries, particularly in Asia, have dramatically increased their food production. Asia's three largest countries—China, India, and Indonesia—are no longer heavily dependent on imported food.

Other countries can point to increased agricultural production, but many of these increases do not keep pace with population growth. The consequence is that average caloric consumption declines or imports of food (or both) must increase dramatically. With frequent spikes in food and fuel prices, many countries find themselves without sufficient resources to import enough food to ensure that even minimal levels of nutrition can be maintained. As an illustration, the Food and Agriculture Organization (FAO) identified thirty-four countries in 2008 that were expected to lack the resources to respond to critical problems of food security. Two years later, the FAO identified twenty-two countries, all but five in sub-Saharan Africa, that face a "protracted crisis" in food security. On average, nearly 40 percent of their populations are undernourished; their daily intake of calories is less than the minimum dietary energy required. More recently, the FAO estimated that more than 840 million people suffered from chronic hunger between 2011 and 2013 and thus did not regularly consume enough food to conduct an active life.[17]

Among the consequences of insufficient food are stunted growth, weakened resistance to illness and disease, and impaired learning abilities and capacity for physical labor.[18] Agricultural production can be increased, but many countries suffer a shortage of land suitable for cultivation. Other countries have reached or exceeded the sustainable limits of production. Their populations are overexploiting the environment's carrying capacity. Farmers in India, Pakistan, Bangladesh, and West Africa may already be farming virtually all the land suitable for agriculture, and the amount of arable land per capita is declining in many developing countries. The World Bank estimates that production has declined substantially in approximately one-sixth of the agricultural land in these countries. Likewise, the FAO estimates that nearly a quarter of the world's population depends on land whose productivity and ecosystem functions are declining.[19] If these trends continue, millions of acres of barren land will be added to the millions that are already beyond redemption.

Shortages of land suitable for farming are not the only barrier to increased agricultural production. With more people to feed, more water must be devoted to agriculture. To feed the world's population in 2050, one estimate suggests that the amount of water devoted to agriculture will have to double between 2000 and 2050.[20] Doing so will be a challenge. All the water that will ever exist is already in existence, and much of this water is already overused, misused, or wasted in much of the world, including the United States, one of the world's largest users of water on a per capita basis. Some countries are already desperately short of water, as frequent droughts in Africa unfortunately confirm. Other countries, notably Yemen and several countries in North Africa and the Middle East, are only a few years away from depleting what little water they do have. Farmers in developing countries must also address the prospect that climate change will reduce their yields by as much as 10 to 20 percent by 2050.

Many developing countries rely on fish as their major source of protein. Unfortunately, the condition of many of the world's fisheries is perilous. Recent estimates suggest that 70 percent of all the world's fish populations are unsustainably exploited while many other populations are depleted or over-harvested. Over four hundred oxygen-starved "dead zones" have been identified in the world's oceans and coastal areas. These zones, which can barely sustain marine life, have doubled in number every ten years since the 1960s. Further evidence of a collapsing ecosystem came in mid-2011 when an international panel of marine scientists concluded that the world's oceans are at "high risk of entering a phase of extinction of marine species unprecedented in human history." The experts also concluded that the speed and rate of degeneration in the oceans is far faster than anyone has predicted and that many of the negative impacts previously identified are more ominous than the worst predictions.[21]

It is important to appreciate as well that the nature of diets changes as nations urbanize. Irrespective of differences in prices and incomes, according to the International Food Policy Research Institute, "urban dwellers consume more wheat and less rice and demand more meat, milk products, and fish than their rural counterparts." This preference leads to increased requirements for grain to feed animals, the need for more space for forage, greater demands for water, and increased pollution from animal waste. Changes in the composition of diets can be anticipated in many countries. In fact, in virtually every low-income country, urbanization is increasing faster than overall population growth (in many instances, three to four times faster).

China provides an example. The World Bank estimates that China's urban population increased to nearly 700 million in 2012 from only 300 million in 1990. This means that more than half of all Chinese now live in urban areas. Government officials want to increase this proportion even further. In what has been called "one of the most ambitious human migration plans in history," China intends to relocate as many as 260 million people from rural to urban areas by 2020.[22] The purpose of the relocation is to stimulate economic development through increased construction and consumption.

Increased urbanization is not without its consequences. On a per capita basis, China's urban residents consumed more than four times as much beef and five times as much milk and dairy products in 2010 than did the country's rural residents.[23]

Increased demand for food also has environmental consequences. More grain must be produced to feed the livestock and poultry. In a typical year, as much as 35 to 40 percent of the world's grain production is used for animal feed, but the conversion from feed to meat is not a neat one. As many as ten pounds of grain and about 1,900 gallons of water are required to produce one pound of beef. Production of beef is especially problematic for the environment. In a report completed for the National Academy of Sciences in 2014, researchers concluded that beef production requires twenty-eight, eleven, and five times more land, irrigation water, and greenhouse emissions, respectively, than the average of the other livestock categories.[24] Ruminant livestock need grazing land, which is already in short supply in many areas. Throughout the world, about twice as much land is devoted to animal grazing as is used for crops. If a land's carrying capacity is breached due to excessive exploitation, then the alternative is to use feedlot production, which requires even higher levels of grain and concentrates waste products in small areas.

Relying on Domestic Production

Imports offer a possible solution to deficiencies in domestic production, but here, too, many developing countries encounter problems. To finance imports, countries need foreign exchange, usually acquired through their own exports or from loans. Few developing countries have industrial products or professional services to export, so they must rely on minerals, natural resources (such as timber or petroleum), or cash crops (such as tea, sugar, coffee, cocoa, and rubber).

Prices for many of these commodities fluctuate widely. To illustrate, commodity prices for cocoa, coffee, and cotton were lower in 2013 than in 1970.[25] To cope with declining prices for export crops, farmers often intensify production, which implies increased reliance on fertilizers and pesticides, or expand the area under cultivation to increase production. Unfortunately, these seemingly rational reactions can depress prices as supply eventually outpaces demand. As the area used for export crops expands, production for domestic consumption may decline. In contrast, high prices are good for farmers but reduce affordability for cash-strapped consumers.

Opportunities exist to increase exports, but economic policies in the developed world can discourage expanded activity in developing countries. Every year, farmers in Japan, Europe, and the United States receive hundreds of billions of dollars in subsidies and other price-related supports from their governments.

In 2012, the European Union provided over $110 billion for agricultural support for its farmers, including Queen Elizabeth of the United Kingdom. In some years, 40 percent or more of its annual budget is devoted to farm subsidies. So large are these supports, the president of the World Bank once noted, that the average European cow received a subsidy of about $2.50 per day, or more than the average daily income of about three billion people.[26] Japanese cows were more privileged. They received a daily subsidy of about $7.50, or more than 1,800 times as much foreign aid as Japan provided to sub-Saharan Africa each day.

Subsidies often lead to overproduction and surpluses, which discourage imports from developing countries, remove incentives to expand production, encourage the use of environmentally fragile land, and can increase prices to consumers in countries that provide the subsidies. Rice, sugar, cotton, wheat, and peanuts are easily and less expensively grown in many developing countries, but the U.S. government subsidizes its farmers to grow these crops or imposes tariffs on their importation.

Developing countries are increasingly irritated with trade and agricultural policies that they consider to be discriminatory. In response to a complaint from Brazil, the World Trade Organization (WTO) agreed that European subsidies for sugar exports violate international trade rules. This decision followed another WTO decision in which it ruled that U.S. price supports for cotton resulted in excess production and exports as well as low international prices, thus causing "serious prejudice" to Brazil. African producers of cotton have also called for an end to government support for the production of cotton in developed countries, especially the United States, the world's largest exporter of cotton. Without access to export markets, developing countries are denied their best opportunity for development, which, historically, has provided the best cure for poverty and rapid population growth.

The Debt Conundrum

Developing countries could once depend on loans from private banks or foreign governments to help finance imports, but many low- and middle-income countries are burdened with considerable debts. A common measure of a nation's indebtedness is its *debt service*, which represents the total payments for interest and principal as a percentage of the country's exports of goods and services. These exports provide the foreign currencies that allow countries to repay their debts denominated in foreign currencies and to import food, medicines, petroleum, and machinery. When debt service increases, more export earnings are required to repay loans, and less money is available for development. Many developing nations, especially in Africa and Latin America, have encountered this problem.

The largest bilateral donors, including the United States, as well as the World Bank, the International Monetary Fund, the African Development Fund, and the Inter-American Development Bank have agreed to cancel the debt of the world's most indebted countries, most of which are in Africa. In exchange for this debt relief, these so-called highly indebted poor countries (HIPCs) are required to adopt reforms designed to encourage sustainable economic growth and to complete poverty reduction strategies that provide the poor with a better quality of life.

Initial reviews of the debt relief initiative have been positive. By the end of 2012, debt repayments had been reduced in thirty-six countries, nearly all in sub-Saharan Africa, by nearly $75 billion; their average debt service payments had also dropped as a result. Despite these improvements, considerable uncertainty remains. Several of the HIPCs have not been repaying the debt they owe, and the debt relief has not eliminated the risk of future "debt distress" among many of the beneficiaries. Likewise, adopting reforms does not guarantee their implementation. As the World Bank noted, in the quest to meet the initiative's eligibility requirements, HIPCs have faced internal conflict, problems with governance, and difficulties in formulating their own strategies for poverty reduction.[27]

The Destruction of Tropical Forests

The rain forests of Africa, Asia, and South America are treasure chests of incomparable biological diversity. These forests provide irreplaceable habitats for as much as 80 percent of the world's species of plants and animals. Viable forests also stabilize soils; reduce the impact and incidence of floods; and regulate local climates, watersheds, and river systems.[28] In addition, increasing concern about global warming underscores the global importance of tropical forests. Through photosynthesis, trees and other plants remove carbon dioxide from the atmosphere and convert it into oxygen. More than one-quarter of the prescription drugs used in the United States have their origins in tropical plants.

At the beginning of the twentieth century, tropical forests covered approximately 10 percent of the Earth's surface, or about 5.8 million square miles. The deforestation of recent decades has diminished this area by about one-third. If current rates of deforestation continue unabated, only a few areas of forest will remain untouched. Humans will have destroyed a natural palliative for global warming and condemned half or more of all species to extinction.

Causes

Solutions to the problem of tropical deforestation depend on the root cause.[29] One view blames poverty and the pressures associated with growing populations and shifting cultivators. Landless peasants, so the argument goes, invade tropical forests and denude them for fuel wood, for grazing, or to grow crops with which to survive. Tropical soils are typically thin, are relatively infertile, and lack sufficient nutrients, so frequent clearing of new areas is necessary. Such areas are ill suited for sustained agricultural production.

Another explanation for deforestation places primary blame on commercial logging intended to satisfy demands for tropical hardwoods in developed countries. Whether strapped for foreign exchange, required to repay loans, or subjected to domestic pressure to develop their economies, governments in the developing world frequently regard tropical forests as sources of ready income. Exports of wood now produce billions of dollars in annual revenues for developing countries, and some countries impose few limits in their rush to the bank.

Recognizing the causes and consequences of deforestation is not enough to bring about a solution. Commercial logging can be highly profitable to those who own logging concessions, and few governments in developing countries have the capacity to manage their forests properly. These governments often let logging companies harvest trees in designated areas under prescribed conditions. All too frequently, however, the conditions are inadequate or not well enforced, often due to rampant corruption.

An Alternative View of the Problem

One cause of deforestation is the demand for tropical hardwoods in developed countries, so these countries have been under pressure to reduce that demand. Leaders of developing countries quickly emphasize how ironic it is that developed countries, whose consumption creates the demand for tropical woods, are simultaneously calling for developing countries to reduce logging and shift cultivation. In addition, developing countries point to Europe's destruction of its forests during the industrial revolution and the widespread cutting in the United States in the nineteenth century. Why then should developing countries be held to a different standard than the developed ones? Just as Europeans and Americans decided how and when to extract their resources, developing countries insist that they too should be permitted to determine their own patterns of consumption.

Will tropical forests survive? Solutions abound. What is lacking, however, is a consensus about which of these solutions will best meet the essential needs of the poor, the reasonable objectives of timber-exporting and -importing nations, and the inflexible imperatives of ecological stability.

Fortunately, there is a growing realization that much can be done to stem the loss of tropical forests. Many countries have developed national forest programs that describe the status of their forests as well as strategies to preserve them. Unfortunately, implementation of these plans does not always parallel the good intentions associated with them. Likewise, rather than seeing forests solely as a source of wood or additional agricultural land, many countries are now examining the export potential of forest products other than wood. The expectation is that the sale of these products—such as cork, rattan, oils, resins, and medicinal plants—will provide economic incentives to maintain rather than destroy forests.

Other proposed options to maintain tropical forests include efforts to certify that timber exports are from sustainably managed forests. Importers and potential consumers presumably will avoid timber products without such certification. For such initiatives to be successful, however, exporters have to accept the certification process, and there must be widespread agreement about what is meant by sustainable management. Such agreement is still absent. In addition, no country wants to subject itself to the potentially costly process of internationally accepted certification only to learn that its forestry exports do not meet the requirements for certification or that less expensive timber is available from countries that do not participate in a certification program.

There is no shortage of separate but competing third-party certification programs. One estimate places that number at more than fifty. As one author has suggested, however, different programs may confuse consumers with less rigorously enforced but similarly named competing standards.[30] Indeed, the author suggests that logging companies encourage such confusion through their support of multiple programs. Despite the large number of certification programs, most of the forested areas that are certified—more than 80 percent—are in Europe and North America.

Other approaches to sustainable management impose taxes on timber exports (or imports). The highest taxes are imposed on logging that causes the greatest ecological damage; timber from sustainable operations faces the lowest taxes. Yet another option is to increase reliance on community-based management of forest resources. Rather than allowing logging companies with no long-term interest in a forest to harvest trees, community-based management places responsibility for decisions about logging (and other uses) with the people who live in or adjacent to forests. These people have the strongest incentives to manage forest resources wisely, particularly if they reap the long-term benefits of their management strategies.

Still another promising initiative is Reducing Emissions from Deforestation and Forest Degradation (REDD). This international program involves developed countries' willingness to pay developing countries not to harvest their tropical forests. The goal is to reduce deforestation by half between 2010 and 2020, but sufficient financing for REDD is uncertain, especially in light of the world's recurring financial problems.

Conflicting Signals from the Developed Nations

Improvements in the policies of many developing countries are surely necessary if sustainable development is to be achieved. As already noted, however, developed countries sometimes cause or contribute to environmental problems in the developing countries.

Patterns of consumption provide an example. Although the United States and other developed nations can boast about their own comparatively low rates of population growth, developing nations reply that patterns of consumption, not population increases, are the real culprits. This view suggests that negative impacts on the environment are a function of a country's population growth, its consumption, and the technologies, such as automobiles, that enable this consumption.[31]

Applying this formula places major responsibility for environmental problems on rich nations, despite their relatively small numbers of global inhabitants. The inhabitants of these nations consume far more of the Earth's resources than their numbers justify. Consider that the richest one-quarter of the world's nations control about 75 percent of the world's income (and, according to the UN Development Programme, the richest 10 percent of Americans have a combined income greater than two billion of the world's poorest people). In addition, these nations consume a disproportionate share of all meat and fish and most of the world's energy, paper, chemicals, iron, and steel. One estimate suggests that people in the developed world consume, on average, about thirty-two times as many resources as do people in developing countries.[32] Put in other terms, this means that the consumption of a single American is comparable to the consumption of thirty-two Kenyans. The United States leads the world in per capita production of trash and has one of the lowest rates of recycling among developed countries.

Americans represent less than 5 percent of the Earth's inhabitants, yet they use about one-fifth of the world's energy. In 2012, the United States was both the world's largest consumer and its largest importer of petroleum. During a typical day in the United States, Americans consume more petroleum than all the countries in Africa, the Middle East, and Central and South America combined. Much of this petroleum is used to fuel Americans' love for the automobile. There are more motor vehicles than licensed drivers in the United States, and they consume more than 40 percent of the world's gasoline. An average American driver uses about five times more gasoline than the typical European. Part of the explanation is that many European cars, often designed by U.S. manufacturers, are more fuel efficient than are U.S. cars. Despite many Americans' common belief that gasoline prices are too high, the price of gasoline in much of Western Europe is more than two times higher than in the United States.

Americans' extravagance with fossil fuels provides part of the explanation for U.S. production of about one-sixth of the emissions that contribute to global warming. The Intergovernmental Panel on Climate Change believes that a relatively safe level of carbon dioxide emissions is about 2.25 metric tons per person per year.[33] Each metric ton is about 2,205 pounds. With the exception of Australia and a few ministates, no country produces as much carbon dioxide emissions per capita as does the United States. It produced 16.4 metric tons per capita in 2012, seven times higher than what sustainable levels of development would require. In Germany, China, and India, per capita emissions in the same year were 9.7, 7.1, and 1.6 metric tons, respectively.[34] Although China's production of carbon dioxide has increased considerably in recent years, a notable portion is attributable to the production of goods destined for Europe and the United States.

Americans' patterns of food consumption are also of interest. An average American consumes about 3,750 calories per day, among the highest levels in the world. Among young adults, about 25 percent of these calories are from sweetened beverages. Not surprisingly, almost three-quarters of American adults are either obese or overweight. According to the U.S. Centers for Disease Control and Prevention, no American state had a prevalence of adult obesity of more than 15 percent in 1990. By 2000, all states except Colorado exceeded this percentage. By 2012, no state had an obesity prevalence of *less* than 20 percent, and thirteen states had rates exceeding 30 percent.[35] For these reasons, *The Economist* labeled the United States the "fattest country in the Western World." Weight-related illnesses consume as much as one-fifth of the nation's costs for medical care each year and are responsible for the deaths of more Americans each year than are motor vehicle accidents.

Few nations waste as much food as does the United States. Estimates based on research at the University of Arizona suggest that as much as half of all food is wasted in the United States, with undesirable environmental consequences. Energy is required to produce, harvest, transport, market, and prepare food, and all of this energy is wasted when food is wasted, and food rotting in landfills contributes to greenhouse gas emissions. As *The Economist* has noted, if the developed world reduced the food it wasted by half, the challenge of feeding the world's population in 2050 would vanish.[36]

Due to these kinds of inequalities in consumption, continued population growth in rich countries is a greater threat to the global environment than is such growth in the developing world. As the World Wildlife Fund explained in 2012, "If everyone lived like an average resident of the USA, a total of four Earths would be required to regenerate humanity's annual demand on nature." Other experts suggest that if Americans want to maintain their present standard of living and levels of energy consumption, then their ideal population is about 50 million, far less than the mid-2014 U.S. population of about 318 million.[37]

Causes for Optimism?

There is cause for concern about the prospects for sustainable development among developing countries, but the situation is neither entirely bleak nor beyond hope. The rates of deforestation and population growth are slowing in many developing countries. Smallpox, a killer of millions of people every year in the 1950s, has been eradicated (except in laboratories). Polio may soon be the next scourge to be eliminated, and deaths due to AIDS, diarrhea, measles, and respiratory infections such as tuberculosis have dropped significantly.

All members of the United Nations adopted eight Millennium Development Goals (MDG) in 2000 with the intent of achieving them by 2015. The first of these goals was to reduce the proportion of people living in extreme poverty by half between 1990 and 2015. The target was achieved in 2010. In developing regions, according to the United Nations, the proportion of people living on less than $1.25 a day fell from 47 percent in 1990 to 22 percent in 2010. About seven hundred million fewer people lived in conditions of extreme poverty in 2010 than in 1990. Similarly, the mortality rate for children under five dropped by 41 percent—to fifty-one deaths per one thousand live births in 2011 from eighty-seven deaths per one thousand live births in 1990. Over the same time period, 1.9 billion people gained access to a latrine, flush toilet, or other improved sanitation facility.[38] In mid-2014, the world community was on the verge of approving seventeen post-MDG sustainable development goals, to be achieved by 2030.

Equally notable, since 1970, over 150 countries have experienced increases in real per capita incomes, but this progress is not universally shared. In several countries in sub-Saharan Africa (plus Belarus and Ukraine), life expectancies in 2010 were less than what they were in the 1970s. Similarly, more than a dozen countries had lower average real incomes in 2011 than they did in 1970. In short, much remains to be done, but the global community has demonstrated an increasing awareness of the need to address the problems of the developing world.

At the initiative of President George W. Bush, as an illustration, the United States committed $15 billion over five years, beginning in 2004, to fight HIV/AIDS, tuberculosis, and malaria in the developing world. The President's Emergency Plan for AIDS Relief (PEPFAR) was deemed to be so successful and well received that Congress authorized the expenditure of an additional $48 billion in 2008 to continue the program for another five years. Furthermore, private philanthropic support for development has grown more than tenfold over the past decade. As an example, the Bill and Melinda Gates Foundation donated $500 million to the Global Fund to Fight AIDS, Tuberculosis and Malaria in 2006. The William J. Clinton Foundation's HIV/AIDS initiative has been similarly active and has successfully negotiated major reductions in the cost of antiretroviral drugs in many countries.

The international community is also demonstrating attention to the Earth's ecological interconnectedness. This attention manifested itself most noticeably in the UN Conference on Environment and Development in Rio de Janeiro, Brazil, in 1992 and a World Summit on Sustainable Development in Johannesburg, South Africa, in 2002. The 1992 conference led to the creation of the UN Commission on Sustainable Development, which meets annually to review progress in achieving sustainable development. The commission organized Rio+20 in June 2012.

Delegates at the first Rio conference approved Agenda 21, a plan for enhancing global environmental quality. The price tag for the recommended actions is huge. Rich nations could provide the amount needed to meet the goals of Agenda 21 if they donate as little as 0.7 percent (not 7 percent, but seven-tenths of 1 percent) of their GNI to the developing world each year. Only Denmark, Luxembourg, Norway, Sweden, the United Arab Emirates, and the United Kingdom exceeded this target in 2013. The United States typically provides more foreign aid than any other country, about $31.5 billion in 2013, but this aid represented only 0.19 percent of the U.S. GNI in 2012. U.S. development assistance was thus well below the target level of 0.7 percent and among the lowest of the world's major donors. This situation has led some observers to label the United States as a "global Scrooge" based on its seeming unwillingness to share its wealth.

Of the U.S. aid that is provided, much is used to advance U.S. foreign policy objectives rather than to help the poorest countries. In recent years, Iraq and Afghanistan have been the largest recipients of this aid. Much U.S. aid never leaves the United States. American firms are typically hired to implement U.S. foreign aid programs, and "Buy American" provisions often require recipients to purchase U.S. products, even when locally available items are less expensive.

Surveys of Americans' opinions about development assistance present an interesting but mixed picture. More than 80 percent of those surveyed in 2008 agreed that developed countries have "a moral responsibility to work to reduce hunger and severe poverty in poor countries." Despite such support, most Americans also believe that the United States is already doing more than its share to help less fortunate countries. In a survey conducted in late 2010, Americans estimated that the average amount of the annual federal budget devoted to foreign aid is 27 percent. They further indicated that an appropriate amount would be about 13 percent.[39]

The United States is among the largest donors of emergency food aid. Rather than allowing the U.S. Agency for International Development to purchase less expensive food closer to where it is needed, Congress requires that almost all of the food be purchased in the United States. The United States is the only major donor that does not purchase food produced in the region of need. In addition, the law requires that most of the food be shipped on American-flagged vessels, which are among the most expensive to use. As a result of these requirements, U.S. food aid is more expensive than it would otherwise be, and the food often arrives well after it is most needed.[40] Critics of the program also claim that the U.S. food aid destabilizes local markets and competes with farmers close to affected areas who cannot afford to donate their food.

In contrast to Americans' seeming reluctance to share their wealth, other nations have demonstrated an increased willingness to address globally shared environmental problems. The international community now operates a Global Environment Facility, a multibillion-dollar effort to address global warming, loss of biological diversity, pollution of international waters, and depletion of the ozone layer.

Many developing nations recognize their obligations to protect their environments as well as the global commons. At the same time, however, these nations argue that success requires technical and financial assistance from their wealthy colleagues. However desirable sustainable development is as an objective, poor nations cannot afford to address their environmental problems in the absence of cooperation from richer nations. Consumers in rich nations can demonstrate such cooperation by paying higher prices for products that reflect sustainable environmental management. One example of this situation would be Americans' willingness to pay higher prices for forestry products harvested sustainably. In fact, however, Home Depot found that only a third of its customers would be willing to pay a premium of 2 percent for such products.[41]

A further issue of growing importance is resentment in some poor countries toward the environmental sermons from developed countries. Global warming provides one of several examples. As China and India grow, they are under pressure from Europe and the United States to reduce the production of greenhouse gases. As some Indians and Chinese respond, however, why should they slow or alter their path to development to accommodate high standards of living elsewhere? Per capita consumption of petroleum and emissions of carbon dioxide are far lower in India and China than in the United

States. When India released its policy on climate change in 2008, its prime minister declared that fairness dictates that everyone deserves equal per capita emissions, regardless of where they live.[42] India is not willing, he noted, to accept a model of global development in which some countries maintain high carbon emissions while the options available for developing countries are constrained.

Brazil has been subject to international criticism for deforestation of the Amazon, but it has responded to complaints from Europeans by declaring that they should look at a map of Europe to see how much forested land remains there before telling Brazilians what they should do.[43] According to Brazil's government, Europeans have 3 percent of their native flora remaining, compared with nearly 70 percent in Brazil. Indeed, recent successes in reducing deforestation in Brazil earned it the title of the "world leader in tackling climate change" in 2014.[44]

U.S. officials upset Chinese and Indians with remarks indicating that their consumption of food is a primary cause of rapidly rising food prices. Speaking in 2008, President Bush identified a growing middle class in India, which is "demanding better food and nutrition," as a cause of higher prices. The reaction from India was understandably negative. "Why do Americans think they deserve to eat more than Indians?" asked one journalist. An Indian public official characterized the U.S. position as "Guys with gross obesity telling guys just emerging from emaciation to go on a major diet." This characterization may be indicative of a larger concern. The perception that Americans are global environmental culprits is widespread. When people in twenty-four countries were asked in 2008 which country is "hurting the world's environment the most," majorities or pluralities in thirteen countries cited the United States.[45]

Contentious debates and inflammatory rhetoric about blame and responsibility are not productive. The economic, population, and environmental problems of the developing world dwarf those of the developed nations and are not amenable to quick resolution. Nonetheless, immediate action is imperative. Hundreds of millions of people are destroying their biological and environmental support systems at unprecedented rates to meet their daily needs for food, fuel, and fiber. The world will add several billion people in the next few decades, and all of them will have justifiable claims to be fed, clothed, educated, employed, and healthy. To accommodate these expectations, the world may need as much as 50 percent more energy in 2030 than it used in 2010. Most of the increase will come from fossil fuels, especially coal. The nuclear-related problems associated with Japan's tragic earthquake and tsunami in 2011 are likely to reinforce this reliance.

Whether the environment can accommodate these unprecedented but predictable increases in population and consumption depends not only on the poor who live in stagnant economies but also on a much smaller number of rich, overconsuming nations in the developed world. Unless developed nations work together to accommodate and support sustainable development everywhere, the future of billions of poor people will determine Americans' future as well.

As the authors of the Millennium Ecosystem Assessment concluded, the ability of the planet's ecosystems to sustain future generations is no longer assured.[46] Over the past fifty years, the world has experienced unprecedented environmental change in response to ever-increasing demands for food, fuel, fiber, freshwater, and timber. Much of the environmental degradation that has occurred can be reversed, but as these authors warned, "The changes in policy and practice required are substantial and not currently underway."

If these experts are correct, unless the United States acts soon and in collaboration with other nations, Americans will increasingly suffer the adverse consequences of environmental damage caused by the billions of poor people we have chosen to neglect and perhaps even abandon—just as these people will suffer from the environmental damage we inflict on them. In short, there are continuing questions about whether the current economic model that depends on growth and extravagant consumption among a few privileged countries is ecologically sustainable and morally acceptable for everyone.[47]

Suggested Websites

Organisation for Economic Co-operation and Development (OECD) (www.oecd.org/development) Provides extensive information on aid statistics and effectiveness, environment and development, and gender and development.

Population Reference Bureau (www.prb.org) A convenient source for data on global population trends. Its annual World Population Data Sheet includes statistics for most of the world's nations on birthrates, growth rates, per capita income, percentage undernourished, percentage in urban areas, and projected population size for 2025 and 2050.

UN Development Programme (www.undp.org) Provides links to activities and reports on economic development and the environment, including the Millennium Development Goals.

UN Division for Sustainable Development (http://sustainabledevelopment.un.org) Provides useful links to the goals and targets on sustainable development for the post-2015 development agenda.

UN Food and Agriculture Organization (www.fao.org) Focuses on agriculture, forestry, fisheries, and rural development. The FAO works to alleviate poverty and hunger worldwide.

UN Population Fund (www.unfpa.org) Funds population assistance programs, particularly family planning and reproductive health, and reports on population growth and its effects.

World Bank (www.worldbank.org) One of the largest sources of economic assistance to developing nations; also issues reports on poverty and global economic conditions, including progress toward the Millennium Development Goals.

Notes

1. World Bank, "Gross National Income per Capita 2013, Atlas Method and PPP," *World Development Indicators Database*, December 16, 2014, databank.worldbank.org/data/download/GNIPC.pdf. Due to differences in the costs of goods and services among countries, GNI per capita does not provide comparable measures of economic well-being. To address this problem, economists have developed the concept of purchasing power parity (PPP). PPP equalizes the prices of identical goods and services across countries, with the United States as the base economy. For an amusing explanation of PPP, see the "Big Mac Index" of *The Economist*, at www.economist.com/content/big-mac-index, which compares the price of a McDonald's Big Mac hamburger in more than forty countries.
2. UNICEF, *Ending Child Marriage: Progress and Prospects* (New York: UNICEF, 2014), http://data.unicef.org/resources/ending-child-marriage-progress-and-prospects.
3. United Nations, *The Millennium Development Goals Report 2013* (New York: United Nations, 2013), www.un.org/millenniumgoals.
4. Millennium Ecosystem Assessment, *Ecosystems and Human Well-Being: Current State and Trends*, vol. 1 (Washington, DC: Island Press, 2005), www.millenniumassessment.org/en/About.aspx.
5. Readers interested in learning about the daily challenges of poverty in the slums of India are encouraged to read Katherine Boo's prize-winning book, *Behind the Beautiful Forevers: Life, Death and Hope in a Mumbai Undercity* (New York: Random House, 2012).
6. World Commission on Environment and Development, *Our Common Future* (London: Oxford University Press, 1987), 8, 43.
7. John N. Wilford, "A Tough-Minded Ecologist Comes to Defense of Malthus," *New York Times*, June 30, 1987, C3.
8. Population Reference Bureau, *2014 World Population Data Sheet* (Washington, DC: Population Reference Bureau, 2014), www.prb.org. For a discussion of the world's carrying capacity, see Jeroen C. J. M. Van Den Bergh and Piet Rietveld, "Reconsidering the Limits to World Population: Meta-analysis and Meta-prediction," *BioScience* 54 (March 2004): 195–204 and Erle C. Ellis, "Overpopulation Is Not the Problem," *New York Times*, September 13, 2013.
9. O. P. Sharma and Carl Haub, "Change Comes Slowly for Religious Diversity in India," Population Reference Bureau, March 2009, www.prb.org/Articles/2009/indiareligions.aspx.
10. Joseph Kahn, "Harsh Birth Control Steps Fuel Violence in China," *New York Times*, May 22, 2007, A12; Jim Yardley, "China Sticking with One-Child Policy," *New York Times*, March 11, 2008.
11. Leo Lewis, "China Looks to a Boom as It Relaxes One-Child Policy," *The Times* (London), November 16, 2013.
12. Peter Baker, "Obama Reverses Rule on U.S. Abortion Aid," *New York Times*, January 23, 2009.
13. For example, see Julian Simon, *The Ultimate Resource* (Princeton, NJ: Princeton University Press, 1981).
14. Carl Haub and O. P. Sharma, "India's Population Reality," *Population Bulletin* 61, no. 3 (September 2006), http://www.prb.org/pdf06/61.3indiaspopulationreality_eng.pdf; Therese Hesketh and Zhu Wei Xing, "Abnormal Sex Ratios in Human Populations: Causes and Consequences," *Proceedings of the National Academy of Sciences* 103 (2006): 13271–275, www.pnas.org/content/103/36.toc.

15. Lester R. Brown, "Analyzing the Demographic Trap," in *State of the World 1987*, ed. Lester R. Brown (New York: Norton, 1987), 21.

16. Per Pinstrup-Andersen, former director of the International Food Policy Research Institute, believes the world can easily feed twelve billion people. See "Will the World Starve?" *The Economist*, June 10, 1995, 39.

17. FAO, *The State of Food Insecurity in the World* (Rome, Italy: FAO, 2013), http://www.fao.org/docrep/018/i3434e/i3434e.pdf.

18. FAO, *The State of Food and Agriculture 2007* (Rome, Italy: FAO, 2007); FAO, *Crop Prospects and Food Situation: Countries in Crisis Requiring External Assistance* (Rome, Italy: FAO, February 2008), http://www.fao.org/docrep/010/ah881e/ah881e02.htm; FAO, *The State of Food Insecurity in the World* (Rome, Italy: FAO, 2010).

19. World Bank, *World Development Indicators 2007*, http://data.worldbank.org/products/data-books/WDI-2007; FAO, *Land Degradation Assessment in Drylands* (Rome, Italy: FAO, 2008).

20. Colin Chartres and Samyuktha Varma, *Out of Water: From Abundance to Scarcity and How to Solve the World's Water Problems* (Upper Saddle River, NJ: FT Press, 2011), xvii.

21. Tony J. Pitcher and William W. L. Cheung, "Fisheries: Hope or Despair?" *Marine Pollution Bulletin* 74 (September 30, 2013): 508; Robert J. Diaz and Rutger Rosenberg, "Spreading Dead Zones and Consequences for Marine Ecosystems," *Science* 321 (2008): 926–29; International Programme on the State of the Ocean, "Multiple Ocean Stresses Threaten 'Globally Significant' Marine Extinction," June 20, 2011, http://www.stateoftheocean.org/pdfs/1806_IPSOPR.pdf.

22. Bruce Kennedy, "Can China's Ambitious Urbanization Plan Succeed?" *Money Watch*, March 26, 2014, http://www.cbsnews.com/news/can-chinas-new-urbanization-plan-succeed.

23. Zhangyue Zhou, Weiming Tian, Jimin Wang, Hongbo Liu, and Lijuan Cao, "Food Consumption Trends in China," April 2012, www.daff.gov.au/agriculture-food/food/publications/food-consumption-trends-in-china; see also Damien Ma and William Adams, "Appetite for Destruction: Why Feeding China's 1.3 Billion People Could Leave the Rest of the World Hungry," *Foreign Policy*, October 1, 2013.

24. Gidon Eshel et al., "Land, Irrigation Water, Greenhouse Gas, and Reactive Nitrogen Burdens of Meat, Eggs, and Dairy Production in the United States," *Proceedings of the National Academy of Sciences of the United States*, July 21, 2014. Available at 10.1073/pnas.1402183111.

25. In contrast, the cost of petroleum, which most developing countries must import, rose to $98 a barrel in 2013 from only $5 a barrel in 1970.

26. Statement of James D. Wolfensohn, cited in David T. Cook, "Excerpts from a Monitor Breakfast on Poverty and Globalization," *Christian Science Monitor*, June 13, 2003.

27. World Bank, *World Development Indicators 2008*, http://data.worldbank.org/sites/default/files/wdi08.pdf; International Development Association and the International Monetary Fund, "Heavily Indebted Poor Countries (HIPC) Initiative and Multilateral Debt Relief Initiative (MDRI)—Status of Implementation," September 27, 2007.

28. National Academy of Sciences (NAS), *Population Growth and Economic Development: Policy Questions* (Washington, DC: NAS, 1986), 31.

29. For discussions of the causes of deforestation, see Helmut J. Geist and Eric Lambin, "Proximate Causes and Underlying Driving Forces of Tropical Deforestation," *BioScience* 52 (February 2002): 143–50; and Michael Williams, *Deforesting the Earth: From Prehistory to Global Crisis* (Chicago: University of Chicago Press, 2003).

30. Jared Diamond, *Collapse: How Societies Choose to Fail or Succeed* (London: Penguin, 2005).

31. Paul R. Ehrlich and John P. Holdren, "Impact of Population Growth," *Science* 171 (1971): 1212–17.
32. Jared Diamond, "What's Your Consumption Factor?" *New York Times*, January 2, 2008, A19.
33. Commission on Growth and Development, *The Growth Report: Strategies for Sustained Growth and Inclusive Development* (Washington, DC: World Bank, 2008), 85–86, www.growthcommission.org/index.php.
34. PBL Netherlands Environmental Assessment Agency, *Trends in Global CO$_2$ Emissions: 2013 Report* (The Hague: PBL Publishers, 2013), http://edgar.jrc.ec.europa.eu/news_docs/pbl-2013-trends-in-global-co2-emissions-2013-report-1148.pdf.
35. Centers for Disease Control and Prevention, "Overweight and Obesity," http://www.cdc.gov/obesity/data/adult.html.
36. FoodNavigator-USA, "US Wastes Half Its Food," November 26, 2004, foodnavigator-usa.com; "The 9-billion People Question," *The Economist*, May 26, 2011. Dina El Boghdady, "In U.S., Food Is Wasted from Farm to Fork," *Washington Post*, August 22, 2012, A2.
37. World Wildlife Fund, *Living Planet Report 2012: Biodiversity, Biocapacity and Better Choices* (Gland, Switzerland: World Wildlife Fund, 2012), 43; David and Marcia Pimentel, "Land, Water and Energy Versus the Ideal U.S. Population," *NPG Forum* (January 2005), npg.org/forum_series/forum0205.html.
38. United Nations, *The Millennium Development Goals Report 2013* (New York: United Nations, 2013), www.un.org/millenniumgoals.
39. "Confidence in U.S. Foreign Policy Index," *Public Agenda* 6 (Spring 2008): 14 and *Public Agenda* 3 (Fall 2006): 26, publicagenda.org; Council on Foreign Relations, *Public Opinion on Global Issues* (New York: The Council, 2012). University of Maryland, Program on International Policy Attitudes, "American Public Vastly Overestimates Amount of U.S. Foreign Aid," www.worldpublicopinion.org.
40. Ron Nixon, "Typhoon Revives Debate on U.S. Food Aid Methods," *New York Times*, November 22, 2013, A3.
41. "The Long Road to Sustainability," *The Economist*, Special Report, September 25, 2010.
42. Voice of America, "India Rejects Binding Commitment to Cut Greenhouse Gas Emissions," February 7, 2008, www.voanews.com.
43. "Welcome to Our Shrinking Jungle," *The Economist*, June 7, 2008, 49; "Brazilian President Rages at 'Meddlers' Criticizing Amazon Policies," June 5, 2008, www.terradaily.com.
44. "Cutting Down on Cutting Down, *The Economist*, June 7, 2014, 83.
45. Heather Timmons, "Indians Find U.S. at Fault in Food Cost," *New York Times*, May 14, 2008; "Melting Asia," *The Economist*, June 7, 2008, 30; Pew Global Attitudes Project, "Some Positive Signs for U.S. Image," June 12, 2008, 65, www.pewglobal.org.
46. Millennium Ecosystem Assessment, *Ecosystems and Human Well-Being*.
47. UN Development Programme, *Human Development Report 2007/2008*, http://hdr.undp.org/sites/default/files/reports/268/hdr_20072008_en_complete.pdf.

15

China's Quest for a Green Economy

Kelly Sims Gallagher and Joanna I. Lewis

O n October 11, 2003, the first riders stepped onto the Shanghai Maglev Train that runs back and forth between Shanghai's Pudong International Airport and the newer part of Shanghai on the east side of the Huangpu River called Pudong. As riders settled into their seats, they could watch the speed of the train steadily increase on the monitors above the doors as the train began to gently rock back and forth as it hurtled along its track. But before anyone had time to do more than take a photo or two, the train came to a stop at its arrival destination—the whole trip of thirty kilometers took no more than ten minutes.

This magnetic levitation (Maglev) train is the first commercially operated high-speed magnetic levitation train in the world. At a cost of more than $1 billion, this train is a grand experiment with magnetic levitation technology, but also a big step in China's march toward developing a high-speed rail network for the country. The Chinese government realized during the 1980s that with China's huge population there would be a gigantic demand for high-speed passenger transportation. If China could develop a comprehensive high-speed rail system, then it might be able to prevent greater urban sprawl and increased air pollution and greenhouse gas emissions from automobiles and airplanes. It could also prevent the need to increase oil imports since people would take trains rather than cars, buses, and airplanes, all of which rely on gasoline and diesel. High-speed rail lines, such as the Maglev project in Shanghai, are designed to link cities, ease transportation bottlenecks, and create easy ways to transfer from trains to subways in urban centers.

While the Maglev train has not been duplicated elsewhere in China, so-called conventional high-speed train lines are being laid down at a great rate. Chinese spending on rail networks increased nearly fourfold in recent years, from $22.7 billion in 2006 to $88 billion in 2009. The government plan was to construct forty-two high-speed lines by the end of 2012, by far more than any other country.[1] Moving beyond high-speed rail, China invested a total of ¥2 trillion ($301 billion) in plans to save energy and reduce emissions during the Eleventh Five-Year Plan (2006–2010).[2] This level of spending demonstrates the Chinese government's remarkable commitment to building a green economy.

The concept of a "green economy" emerged only recently in China. But, the Chinese government has pursued different versions of sustainable development for many years. Despite China's good intentions to alleviate poverty

and achieve rapid economic growth in an environmentally responsible manner, many of its industrial policies have been and continue to contradict its
environmental goals.

China first signaled its commitment to sustainable development after
the global Earth Summit in Rio in 1992, when China adopted the Agenda
21 agreement. The Chinese government subsequently developed a document
called "China's Agenda 21: White Paper on China's Population, Environment, and Development in the 21st Century," which was intended to serve as
a guiding document for the sustainable development process in China. In this
document, the Chinese government acknowledged the many different pressures and challenges that the country faced in trying to achieve sustainable
development:

> Because China is a developing country, the goals of increasing social pro-
> ductivity, enhancing overall national strength and improving people's qual-
> ity of life cannot be realized without giving primacy to the development of
> the national economy and having all work focused on building the econ-
> omy. China has been undergoing rapid economic growth, despite the weak
> fundamentals of having a very large population, insufficient per capita
> resources and relatively low levels of economic development and science
> and technology capabilities.... Given this situation, the Chinese Govern-
> ment can only consider strategies for development that are sustainable and
> only by coordinating the work of all segments of society can it successfully
> reach its already defined second and third strategic objectives of quadru-
> pling its GNP against that of 1980 by the end the century and increasing
> per capita GNP to the levels of moderately developed countries.[3]

At the time this document was written, the Chinese government was
beginning a massive period of industrialization, and it set the ambitious goals
for economic growth mentioned above. The quotation highlights the tension
between economic growth and environmental protection that remains today.
Critics noted at the time that the Chinese government appeared to be granting primacy to economic growth rather than according environment, social,
and economic issues "equal" consideration.[4]

Since 1992, different concepts or terms related to sustainable development have come into vogue in China. One that was dominant in the late
1990s was the "circular economy," and more recently, there is talk of a "green
economy." The idea of a circular economy originated from the industrial ecology paradigm, which emphasized the need to design industrial systems to
utilize waste streams as inputs, to reuse materials, to maximize efficiency, and
to achieve an integrated closed-loop system. The circular economy concept
was formally approved by the central government in 2002,[5] and the Circular
Economy Promotion Law of the People's Republic of China was promulgated
in 2008.[6] Although various incentives and fines were introduced in the law, a
number of challenges to its implementation arose, including lack of financial
support for implementing circular economy measures and lack of public
awareness and participation.[7]

The latest conceptual version of China's quest to achieve sustainable development is the idea of a "green" economy. While no formal definition is yet enshrined in Chinese law, the Twelfth Five Year Plan (FYP) of China's central government for the period 2011 to 2015 embraces the term and provides a number of new environmental targets.[8] Most notable about the Twelfth Five Year Plan is that for the first time the Chinese government set a target to reduce the carbon dioxide intensity of the economy. Specifically, emissions of carbon dioxide per unit of economic output must decline 17 percent below 2010 levels by 2015. This chapter begins with an overview of the main energy and environmental challenges in China and then reviews the major policies that have thus far been implemented toward the goal of achieving a "green economy." A case study of China's coal consumption serves to illustrate that China's current energy system is still largely reliant on the most greenhouse gas–intensive fuel even though China is at the forefront of cleaner coal technology development. In contrast, a second case study shows China's considerable efforts to transition to renewable energy. The conclusion aims to put China's quest for a green economy into perspective.

Throughout this chapter, we highlight tensions to demonstrate the frequent contradictions between the Chinese government's push for a green economy on the one hand and rapid economic growth on the other. The key to truly achieving a green economy in China will be to reconcile economic growth strategies with policies and mechanisms to reduce the environmental impact of China's rapid growth.

Overview of Energy and Environmental Challenges in China[9]

China's economic development during the past thirty years has been remarkable by nearly all metrics. Since 1978, China has consistently been the most rapidly growing country in the world.[10] Although rapid economic growth has made China the second largest economy in the world, its gross domestic product (GDP) per capita is still below the world average. While GDP per capita in rural China lags that of urban areas, the year 2011 marked the first time in history that more than one-half of China's population lived in urban China.[11] As a result of this steady and rapid economic growth, an estimated two hundred million people have been pulled out of absolute poverty since 1979.[12]

Despite these impressive achievements, the Chinese government continues to face difficult economic development challenges. China's overall economic development statistics reveal that, despite the emergence of modern cities and a growing middle class, China is still largely a developing country.

Part of why China's per capita income is relatively low, of course, is that China's population is enormous—the largest in the world. As of 2014, China's population was 1.4 billion people, and its birthrate was twelve births per one thousand people, exactly the same as the birthrates in France and the United

Kingdom.[13] This low birthrate is attributable to China's one-child policy, which mandated that couples living in urban areas were restricted to one child (see Chapter 14).

Economic growth is not just a crucial part of China's development strategy, but it is also crucial to the political stability of the country. A fundamental target of the Twelfth Five Year Plan articulated by China's leadership is an annual economic growth rate of 7 percent. Many have argued that continued rapid economic growth is critical to the Communist Party's legitimacy. The Communist Party leadership in China "considers rapid economic growth a political imperative because it is the only way to prevent massive unemployment and labor unrest."[14]

Energy is directly tied to economic development, and the relationship between energy use and economic growth matters greatly in China. Although China quadrupled its GDP between 1980 and 2000, it did so while merely doubling the amount of energy it consumed during that period. This allowed China's *energy intensity* (ratio of energy consumption to GDP) and consequently the *emissions intensity* (ratio of carbon dioxide–equivalent emissions to GDP) of its economy to decline sharply, marking a dramatic achievement in energy intensity gains not paralleled in any other country at a similar stage of industrialization. This achievement has important implications not just for China's economic growth trajectory but also for the quantity of China's energy-related pollution. Reducing the total quantity of energy consumed also contributes to the country's energy security. Without this reduction in the energy intensity of the economy, China would have used more than three times the energy than it actually expended during this period.

The beginning of the twenty-first century has brought new challenges to the relationships among energy consumption, emissions, and economic growth in China. Starting in 2002, China's declining energy intensity trend reversed, and energy growth surpassed economic growth for the first time in decades. This trend of increasing intensity continued until 2005. During that period, the reversal had negative implications for energy security and greenhouse gas emissions growth in China. In 2007, China's GHG emissions were up 8 percent from the previous year, making China the largest national emitter in the world for the first time (surpassing U.S. emissions that year by 14 percent).[15] As of 2014, China accounted for 30 percent of global carbon dioxide emissions.[16] Looking ahead, recent projections put China's emissions in 2030 in the range of 400 to 600 percent above 1990 levels. Globally, this means that China will account for almost 50 percent of all new energy-related carbon dioxide emissions between now and 2030.[17] China's long-term energy security is dependent not only on having sufficient supplies of energy to sustain its incredible rate of economic growth but also on being able to manage the growth in energy demand without causing intolerable environmental damage.

China's increase in energy-related pollution in the past few years has been driven primarily by industrial energy use, fueled by an increased percentage of coal in the overall energy mix. Industry consumes about 70 percent of

China's energy, and China's industrial base supplies much of the world. As a result, China's current environmental challenges are fueled in part by the global demand for its products. For example, China in 2010 produced about 44 percent of the world's steel and 66 percent of aluminum.[18] The centerpiece of the Eleventh Five Year Plan was to promote the service industries—the so-called tertiary sector—because of their higher value added to the economy and the energy and environmental benefits associated with a weaker reliance on heavy manufacturing. The goal was to move the economy away from heavy industry and toward the service-based industries. In so doing, energy use should decline, and environmental quality should improve. The recent resurgence in heavy industry in China, responsible for the rapid emissions growth in the past few years, illustrates the challenge of facilitating this transition. In the Twelfth Five Year Plan, the government more explicitly identifies a new set of high-value strategic industries such as biotechnology and information technology, and also identifies energy saving, environmental protection, and new energy technologies as essential to the future of the Chinese economy (see Table 15-1).[19]

China's rapidly growing economy, population, and energy consumption are all threatening its future environmental sustainability. China faces many environmental challenges, including water scarcity—exacerbated by water pollution—and the release of toxic substances in the environment. Coal is at the heart of most of China's environmental woes, with major implications for human health. Most of China's air pollution emissions come from the industrial and electricity sectors. In recent years, air pollution became so severe that many Chinese people in Beijing and elsewhere now wear face masks when they go outdoors. One study estimated that people living in more polluted northern China live five years fewer than those who live in southern China.[20]

Particulate matter from coal is a foremost air pollutant. Concentrations of PM10 (particles the size of 10 microns or less that are capable of penetrating deep into the lungs) in China's cities are extremely high and hit the extremely dangerous level of 512 on February 25, 2014, in Beijing, 140 in Chongqing, and 100 in Shanghai. These numbers can be compared with a recommended World Health Organization limit of 25. PM10 can increase the number and severity of asthma attacks, cause or aggravate bronchitis and other lung diseases, and reduce the body's ability to fight infections. Certain people are especially vulnerable to PM10's adverse health effects; they include children, the elderly, exercising adults, and those suffering from asthma or bronchitis.[21] In 2013, only three out of seventy-four Chinese cities fully complied with state pollution standards according to China's Ministry of Environmental Protection.[22] In addition, each year, more than four thousand miners die in China's coal mines, mostly in accidents.[23]

Sulfur dioxide emissions from coal combustion, a major source of acid deposition, rose 27 percent between 2001 and 2005. Acid rain affects southeastern China especially, and Hebei Province is most severely affected, with acid rain accounting for more than 20 percent of crop losses. Hunan and Shandong Provinces also experience heavy losses from acid rain. Eighty

Table 15-1   China's Old and New Strategic Industries

The old pillar industries	*The new strategic and emerging industries*
National defense	Energy saving and environmental protection
Telecom	Next-generation information technology
Electricity	Biotechnology
Oil	High-end manufacturing (e.g., aeronautics, high-speed rail)
Coal	New energy (nuclear, solar, wind, biomass)
Airlines	New materials (special and high-performance composites)
Marine shipping	Clean energy vehicles (PHEVs[a] and electric cars)

Sources: Central People's Government of the People's Republic of China, *Guowuyuan tongguo jiakuai peiyu he fazhan zhanluexing xinxing chanye de jueding* ["Decision on Speeding Up the Cultivation and Development of Emerging Strategic Industries"], September 8, 2010, http://www.gov.cn/ldhd/2010-09/08/content_1698604.htm; and HSBC, *China's Next 5-Year Plan: What It Means for Equity Markets* (Hong Kong and Shanghai: HSBC Global Research, October 6, 2010).

a. PHEVs are plug-in hybrid electric vehicles.

percent of China's total losses are estimated to be from damage to vegetables.[24] The economic costs of China's air pollution are very high. According to a recent report from China's government and the World Bank, conservative estimates of illness and premature death associated with ambient air pollution in China cost 6.5 percent of China's GDP per year.[25]

In December 2012, the first ever comprehensive air pollution prevention and control plan was issued by the Chinese government, the "'Twelfth Five-Year Plan' on Air Pollution Prevention and Control in Key Regions." Covering the regions with the highest air pollution levels in the country, the plan set binding targets for sulfur dioxide, nitrogen oxides, PM10, and PM2.5 reductions.[26] Even while the provisions of this plan were being implemented, a new set of even more stringent regulations was announced in response to growing concern over air pollution levels. In 2013, the Chinese government initiated a potentially significant policy response to the air pollution crisis though several quite aggressive policy measures. This included placing new caps on total national coal consumption (65 percent of total primary energy consumption by 2017), the ban of new coal-fired power plants in three regions, an increase in the target for the percentage of non–fossil energy in primary energy consumption to 13 percent by 2017, and an increase in the target for nuclear energy to fifty gigawatts (GW) by 2017. These measures are in addition to the existing laws already in place to promote environmental protection and low-carbon energy sources.

China has an extensive range of environmental laws, including six overarching environmental laws, nine natural resources laws, twenty-eight environmental administrative regulations, twenty-seven environmental standards, and more than nine hundred local environmental rules.[27] The key challenge with environmental laws and regulations in China is in their implementation. Many environmental regulations are top-down in nature, meaning they come from the central government, but their implementation must take place at the local level, where the environmental challenges occur. The relatively weak central government authority that oversees environmental regulation in China has not been very successful at encouraging implementation at the local level. The enforcement of environmental regulations is generally less of a priority for local officials than ensuring that economic growth targets are met. In March 2009, the State Environmental Protection Administration (SEPA) was upgraded to the Ministry of Environmental Protection (MEP), although it remains to be seen whether this increases the leverage of the environmental mandate or helps with the challenge of implementation of current laws and regulations. China has some very stringent environmental regulations in place, but many of the standards and targets are not being met. Many foreigners assume that because China is a centrally planned economy, the government can easily implement any policy that it wishes to enforce; but the reality is that because of China's vast population, huge number of enterprises and factories, and limited environmental governance capacities, many environmental policies are inadequately enforced.

Overview of the Chinese Government's Policies to Achieve a Green Economy

China has begun to implement national policies and programs to address its increasing greenhouse gas emissions and reliance on fossil fuels. The previously discussed energy intensity increases from 2002 to 2005 encouraged Beijing to launch a variety of energy efficiency programs, including a nationwide energy intensity target. Promoting energy efficiency and renewable energy, as well as its climate change mitigation, has become a fundamental part of China's national development strategy. Many of China's environmental policies derive from targets set by the central government during its five-year planning process. In the Five Year Plans, the government sets targets, and then either assigns responsibility for meeting the targets to provinces and municipalities or implements national-level policies. In Table 15-2, some of the most important targets are provided.

Energy Efficiency Programs

A suite of energy efficiency and industrial restructuring programs has driven China's energy intensity down for the last four years. One of the core elements of China's Eleventh Five Year Plan period, spanning 2006 to 2010, was to lower national energy intensity by 20 percent. China's Top-1000 Energy-Consuming Enterprises Program has helped to cut energy use among China's biggest energy-consuming enterprises (representing 33 percent of its overall energy consumption, 47 percent of its industrial energy consumption, and 43 percent of its carbon dioxide emissions).[28] The Ten

Key Projects program provides financial support to companies that implement energy-efficient technology. In addition, many inefficient power and industrial plants have been targeted for closure. While China built a reported 89.7 gigawatts of new power-plant capacity in 2009, it also shut down 26.2 gigawatts of small, inefficient fossil fuel power stations. Thus, one-third of China's new power plant growth in that year was offset by old plant closures—a significant share of the nation's annual capacity additions. It is very unusual, if not unprecedented elsewhere in the world, to shut down such a large number of power plants in the name of efficiency.

The government also strengthened local accountability for meeting targets by intensifying oversight and inspection. China's 2007 Energy Conservation Law requires local governments to collect and report energy statistics and requires companies to measure and record energy use. In addition, each province and provincial-level city is required to help meet China's goal to cut energy intensity by 20 percent (with targets ranging from 12 to 30 percent). Governors and mayors are held accountable to their targets, and experts from Beijing conduct annual site visits of facilities in each province to assess their progress. The Ten Key Projects program requires selected enterprises to undergo comprehensive energy audits, and offers financial rewards based on actual energy saved. The audits follow detailed government monitoring guidelines and must be independently validated. There have also been increases in staffing and funding in key government agencies that monitor energy statistics and implement energy efficiency programs. In 2008 alone, China reportedly allocated RMB 14.8 billion (renminbi—the official currency of the People's Republic of China) or ($2.2 billion) of treasury bonds and central budget, as well as RMB 27 billion ($3.9 billion) of governmental fiscal support this year to energy-saving projects and emission cuts.[29]

While industrial energy consumption in China is increasing, it has been offset considerably by energy efficiency improvements. Recent surges in energy consumption by heavy industry in China have caused the government to implement measures to discourage growth in energy-intensive industries compared with sectors that are less energy intensive. Beginning in November 2006, the Ministry of Finance increased export taxes on energy-intensive industries. Simultaneously, import tariffs on twenty-six energy and resource products, including coal, petroleum, aluminum, and other mineral resources, were reduced. Whereas the increased export tariffs were meant to discourage relocation of energy-intensive industries to China for export markets, the reduced import tariffs were meant to promote the utilization of energy-intensive products produced elsewhere.

Implemented in response to the increasing energy intensity trends experienced during the first half of the decade, China's energy intensity target and the supporting policies described above seemed to be a successful means of reversing the trend. While the country likely fell just short of meeting its Eleventh FYP energy intensity target of 20 percent (the government reported a 19.1 percent decline was achieved), there is no doubt that much was learned though efforts to improve efficiency nationwide. Many

Table 15-2   Key Energy and Environmental Targets from China's Five-Year Plans

	11th FYP (2006–2010) Target	11th FYP Actual	12th FYP (2011–2015)	13th FYP (planned target)
Indicators				
Energy Intensity (% reduction in 5 years)	20%	19.1%	16%	TBA
Carbon Intensity (% reduction in 5 years	None		17%	40%–45% relative to 2005 levels
Non–Fossil Energy (% primary energy)	10%	9.6%	11.4%	15%
Annual Growth Rates				
Primary Energy Consumption	4%	6.3%	3.75%–5% (estimated)	
Electricity Energy Consumption		11%	8.5% (estimated)	5.5% (estimated)
Electricity Generating Capacity	8.4%	13.2%	8.5% (estimated)	5.6% (estimated)
GDP	7.5%	10.6%	7%	

Source: Adapted from Figure 1 of "Delivering Low Carbon Growth: A Guide to China's 12th Five Year Plan" by Allison Hannon, Ying Liu, Jim Walker, and Changhua Wu, The Climate Group, 2011.

changes were made to enforcement of national targets at the local level, including the incorporation of compliance with energy intensity targets into the evaluation for local officials. The Twelfth FYP builds directly on the Eleventh FYP energy intensity target and its associated programs, setting a new target to reduce energy intensity by an additional 16 percent by 2015.[30] While this may seem less ambitious than the 20 percent reduction targeted in the Eleventh FYP, it probably represents a much more substantial challenge. It is likely the largest and least efficient enterprises have already undertaken efficiency improvements, leaving smaller, more efficient plants to be targeted in this second round. [31]

Carbon Policies

While estimates have been made of the potential carbon emissions savings that could accompany the 20 percent energy intensity reduction target,[32] China never put forth any targets that explicitly quantified its carbon emissions until late 2009. In November of that year, the Chinese leadership announced its intention to implement a domestic carbon intensity target of a 40 to 45 percent reduction below 2005 levels by 2020.[33] This target came within hours of President Barack Obama's announcement that the United States would reduce its carbon emissions "in the range of 17 percent" from 2005 levels by 2020, and that the president himself would attend the United Nations international climate change negotiations in Copenhagen.[34]

This first-ever carbon target for China will require an important change in the country's data collection and transparency practices. The government has announced that the national-level target will be allocated across each province, municipality, and economic sector and enforced with new monitoring rules.[35] Measuring and enforcing these targets will require a periodic national inventory of greenhouse gas emissions and a significantly improved statistical monitoring and assessment system to ensure greenhouse gas emissions goals are met, and Beijing has indicated that these systems are in the works.[36] China agreed in Copenhagen and again in Cancun to publically report its emissions every two years, which would be a marked improvement in transparency. The United States established mandatory reporting of greenhouse gas emissions for large sources of emissions (such as a factory or power plant) in 2009.

There is no question that China's announcement of its first carbon target represents a monumental change in China's approach to global climate change. It is also important to recognize, however, that even with this target in place, growth in absolute emissions is likely to continue to increase rapidly. A meaningful reduction of emissions by a carbon intensity target—that is, a ratio of carbon emissions and GDP—hinges on future economic growth rates and the evolving structure of the Chinese economy, as well as on the types of energy resources utilized and the deployment rates of various technologies, among other factors. Carbon intensity, like energy intensity, has declined substantially over the past two decades. Between 1997 and 2011, China reduced its carbon intensity by 5 percent, but its absolute carbon dioxide emissions grew 38 percent.[37] These trends have sparked much debate over whether this domestic policy target is sufficient based on China's role in the global climate challenge.

China is still experimenting with policies that will reduce its greenhouse gas emissions. In October 2011, the Chinese government announced seven provinces and municipalities selected to pilot a cap-and-trade program for carbon dioxide: Guangdong, Hubei, Beijing, Tianjin, Shanghai, Chongqing, and Shenzhen, and most of these are now up and running.[38] As of May 2014, carbon credits worth ¥100 million ($16 million) had been traded. China is also preparing to pilot a system of carbon taxes.[39] The main method of greenhouse gas reduction in China so far is indirect: reducing carbon intensity through a combination of promoting low-carbon energy sources and energy efficiency measures. Every improvement in energy efficiency has the effect of avoiding emission of greenhouse gases. Still, if implemented effectively, a carbon intensity target will not only accelerate the energy efficiency improvements already taking place in response to the energy intensity target but will also further promote the development of low-carbon energy sources like nuclear, hydropower, and renewables.

Renewable Energy

China's promotion of renewable energy was kick-started with the passage of the Renewable Energy Law of the People's Republic of China that became effective on January 1, 2006.[40] The Renewable Energy Law created a framework for regulating renewable energy and was hailed at the time as a breakthrough in the development of renewable energy in China. It created four mechanisms to promote the growth of China's renewable energy supply: (1) a national renewable energy target, (2) a mandatory connection and purchase policy, (3) a feed-in tariff system, and (4) a cost-sharing mechanism, including a special fund for renewable energy development.[41] Several additional regulations were issued to implement the goals established in the Renewable Energy Law, including pricing measures that established a surcharge on electricity rates to help pay for the cost of renewable electricity, plus revenue allocation measures to help equalize the costs of generating renewable electricity among provinces.

In addition to the Renewable Energy Law, the 2007 "Medium and Long-Term Development Plan for Renewable Energy in China," produced by China's National Development and Reform Commission (NDRC), put forth several renewable energy targets, including a nationwide goal to raise the share of renewable energy in total primary energy consumption to 15 percent by 2010 (later revised to refer to all non–fossil sources, including nuclear power). In addition to this ambitious target, the government established a number of very specific but complementary policies to boost renewable energy generation.

Power companies have mandatory renewable energy targets for both their generation portfolios and annual electricity production that they must meet. In December 2009, amendments to the Renewable Energy Law were passed, further strengthening the process through which renewable electricity projects are connected to the grid and dispatched efficiently.[42] They also addressed some of the issues related to interprovincial equity in bearing the cost of renewable energy development.

Industrial Policy for Clean Energy Industries

China's policies to promote renewable energy have always included mandates and incentives to support the development of domestic technologies and industries. China invested more in clean energy than any other country in the world in 2009 and 2010 and was ranked first in Ernst & Young's renewable energy "country attractiveness" index, which examines the domestic environment for investment in renewables in 2010.[43] While some elements of these industrial policies—like requirements for using locally manufactured materials—are unduly protectionist, others are far less controversial, and far more effective. Beijing identified several renewable energy industries as strategic national priorities for science and technology investment in the Twelfth Five Year Plan (2011–2015) and established a constant and increasing stream of government support for research, development, and demonstration. In this way, it made renewable energy promotion a primary target of industrial policy. Specific industrial policies used to support the wind and solar power industries in China are discussed in more detail below.

Coal: China's Dominant Energy Source

China is the largest producer and consumer of coal in the world—it consumed 47 percent of the world's coal in 2012. Until recently, China was self-sufficient in coal supply, but it gradually began importing coal during the 1990s. Around 2009, China became a net importer of coal for the first time, and as of 2011, it became the largest coal importer in the world. Most of its coal imports are high quality or precisely blended coals.[44] Because of China's large consumption of coal, it has become the largest overall emitter of greenhouse gases in the world, though not the largest on a per capita basis or in terms of cumulative historical emissions.

Most of China's energy system relies on coal; it is used for electricity generation, industrial use, residential and commercial boilers, and even some railways. As of 2010, primary coal use was 50 percent for electric power generation and 44 percent for industrial use, with the remainder in residential use. Going forward, China's electricity consumption of coal is projected by the U.S. Energy Information Administration to increase while industrial consumption will decline.[45] China's energy infrastructure is presently locked into coal consumption, and this presents a gigantic challenge to its ability to green its economy. It is unlikely that investors and the government are willing to prematurely retire existing and long-lived infrastructure given the cost, and so far, higher-priced lower-carbon options are typically not chosen for new projects. Thus, China continues to lock itself into a high-carbon future with each new coal-fired power plant or factory that is built. The two technological options that mitigate carbon dioxide emissions from coal are efficiency and carbon capture and storage (CCS). It is important to note that China is rapidly moving to more efficient coal technologies, and beginning to support research and demonstration projects in CCS as well. While China is investing in carbon capture and storage research, development, and demonstration, by mid-2014, it had yet to begin any commercial-scale carbon sequestration projects.

Coal is China's main energy resource endowment, although the nation is consuming coal so quickly that at current rates of consumption its current coal reserves of 114,500 million tons are only projected to last thirty-five years.[46] The hard truth is that coal will continue to dominate China's energy mix for decades to come.[47] Coal use in its current form is environmentally unacceptable, but it is virtually inevitable that China will use its economically recoverable coal reserve because of its desire for energy security and the relatively low cost of production.

By far, the majority of electricity in China is derived from coal, as illustrated in Figure 15-1, where fossil electricity is predominantly coal-fired power. Hydroelectric is the second largest source of electricity (17 percent), and nuclear and renewables both account for tiny fractions of total electricity generation (2 percent and less than 1 percent, respectively), notwithstanding their rapid growth in recent years. Natural gas is not commonly used for power generation owing to its high price and lack of availability due to limited domestic resources. In 2009, coal accounted for 81 percent of electricity generation in China.

The Chinese government has made a major effort to improve coal use efficiency, as well as to reduce the emissions of nitrogen oxides and sulfur dioxide from coal combustion, but, as discussed above regarding air pollution policies, its emissions reduction policies are still a long way from being as stringent as U.S. policies currently are under the Clean Air Act. In improving the efficiency of coal use, the government has shut down thousands of small and inefficient coal-fired electricity plants and replaced them with large, higher-efficiency ones. Indeed, China leads the world in the construction of the most efficient kind of coal-fired power plant: ultrasupercritical coal plants. It has also installed more coal gasification technology than any other country. Coal gasification is not only very efficient, but it also offers the option of capturing relatively economically the carbon dioxide after the coal is gasified. Once the carbon dioxide is captured, it can be sequestered in underground geologic formations or depleted oil and gas reservoirs. Although there are no commercially operating plants that capture and sequester carbon dioxide in China now, the government is supporting a number of smaller-scale demonstration plants. It is also building a large-scale integrated gasification combined cycle (IGCC) plant called the GreenGen plant near Tianjin that will eventually separate and then capture carbon dioxide in a later phase. Indeed, since the 1980s, through the Ministry of Science and Technology and the Chinese Academy of Sciences, great effort has been placed by the Chinese government on conducting research and development on advanced and cleaner coal technologies.[48] China has become one of the world leaders in coal gasification technology, and this is evidenced by the fact that Chinese firms began licensing their own coal gasification technology to the United States in the late 2000s.[49]

Another major policy change was to deregulate coal prices, which used to be tightly controlled by the government. This deregulation began in 1993, and was gradually expanded throughout the 1990s. Now, the government allows coal prices to be determined mainly by the market, within a band set by the government. In fact, coal prices have risen considerably in recent years, which should have the effect of encouraging greater conservation on the part of users. The government still regulates electricity prices, however, and since most electricity is generated from coal, electricity generators have increasingly complained of not being able to raise their prices in line with rising coal prices.[50] Without higher electricity prices, electricity consumers will have little incentive to reduce consumption.

China's current heavy reliance on coal presents the largest challenge to its quest for a green economy. The good news is that China is aggressively exploring and developing alternatives to coal, especially nuclear and wind power. China's efforts to promote renewable energy are analyzed in the next section.

Figure 15-1   China's Electricity Generation Mix (1980–2011)

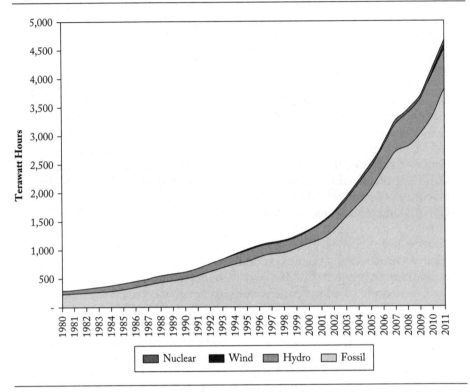

Source: China Energy Group, Lawrence Berkeley National Laboratory, *China Energy Databook Version 8.0* (CD-ROM), (2013), Table 2A.4.1.

Wind and Solar: China's Rapidly Emerging Industries

China is playing an increasingly significant role in the manufacturing of renewable energy and other advanced energy technologies. The manufacturing scale it brings to these industries, as well as its comparatively low-cost inputs to the manufacturing process, may contribute to cost reductions in these technologies. For some technologies, such as wind power, the Chinese market is directly supporting their deployment by using the technologies within China. For others, such as solar photovoltaics (PV), the market is almost entirely outside of China.

Wind Power

At the end of 2013, China was by far the largest wind power market in the world, in terms of annual installations that year, with 91.4 GW of installed capacity. By comparison, the next largest installer of wind power, the United States, had a reported 60.1 GW at the end of 2013.

Wind power technology has been particularly successful in China due to excellent wind resources and rapid technological improvements in China's domestic wind industry. According to recent studies, China has an estimated 2,380 GW of exploitable onshore wind resources, and 200 GW offshore.[51] Wind power still represents a small contribution to total electric power generation capacity in China, representing about 3 percent of total installed power capacity, and around 2 percent of total electricity production, although new wind power installations represented about 12 percent of total electric power–generating capacity additions in 2013.

China's best wind resources are concentrated in the northern and western parts of the country where there is less electricity demand. This increasingly requires transmission to be built to bring the power to provinces that need it. However, the northern and western provinces, such as Gansu and Inner Mongolia, are less developed, and poor electric grids cannot manage the fluctuations in electricity production inherent in wind power.[52] As a result, some problems with power delivery due to grid challenges have been reported.

China's 2007 Medium and Long-Term Development Plan for Renewable Energy first announced the government's strategy for developing large-scale wind power bases, and the first target for *offshore* wind power (1 GW by 2020). Wind energy is the clear leader of the non–hydro renewables in China, and was first targeted for aggressive development in the mid-1990s. But it was not until the domestic wind industry got off the ground in the 2000s that wind power deployment became a major focus of government efforts. As a result, the wind power target set in the 2007 plan for 5 GW of grid-connected wind power by 2010 was exceeded by about 35 GW. In 2009, the 2020 target for 30 GW was revised upwards to 100 GW, although many believe that even that target will be far exceeded. Also in 2009, the Chinese government introduced a feed-in tariff for wind power, establishing premium prices for wind-generated electricity over a twenty-year operational period.

While China has experimented with feed-in tariffs (guaranteed subsidies to producers of renewable energy for a certain period of time) for wind power over the years with various levels of success, a July 2009 central government announcement set four feed-in tariff levels across the country, varying by region based on wind resource class. Setting a higher tariff in low–wind resource regions encourages wind power development there despite less opportunity for electricity production.

China has taken several steps to directly encourage local wind turbine manufacturing, including policies that encourage joint ventures and technology transfers in large wind turbine technology, policies that mandate locally made wind turbines, differential customs duties favoring domestic rather than overseas turbine assembly, and public research and development support. Beginning in about 2003, all wind farms in China were encouraged to use locally produced wind turbine technology. The Ministry of Science and Technology (MOST) is now supporting the development of megawatt-size wind turbines, including technologies for variable-pitch rotors and variable-speed generators, as part of the "863 Wind Program" under the Eleventh Five Year Plan (2006–2010). In

April 2008, the Chinese Ministry of Finance issued a new regulation stating that the tax revenue for the key components and raw materials for large turbines (2.5 megawatts [MW] and above) will be returned to the state to channel the money back into the technology innovation and capacity building in the wind industry. Also that year, the Ministry of Finance announced funding support for the commercialization of wind power generation equipment. For all "domestic brand" wind turbines (with over 51 percent Chinese investment), the first fifty wind turbines over 1 MW produced will be rewarded with RMB 600/kW (€60) from the government. The rule specifies that the wind turbines must be tested and certified by China General Certification (CGC) and must have entered the market, been put into operation, and be connected to the grid.[53]

Solar Power

The last decade has seen a dramatic increase in the deployment of large-scale PV electric generation capacity globally.[54] Until the late 1990s, the majority of PV being installed globally was off-grid, but by 2007 approximately 80 percent of PV systems installed worldwide were grid-connected. The global PV market began growing rapidly in 1997 and has been increasing exponentially since 2003. From 2003 to 2009, the average annual growth rate for the industry was 45 percent, driven primarily by grid-connected solar PV deployment in industrialized countries. China's largest solar PV manufacturing companies together had almost one quarter of global market share in 2009.[55] The global economic downturn was a difficult time for the solar industry, however, with many firms losing markets as solar expansion programs slowed globally. Even Chinese solar manufacturers, which had risen before the crisis to have the highest levels of production globally, decreased production dramatically during 2011–2012 as many companies were forced to consolidate or went through bankruptcies.

One outcome of China's green stimulus programs was the support for a domestic solar industry. While a leading solar technology manufacturer, China's own domestic deployment had long lagged that of other countries. Unlike the wind turbine industry, which was primarily developed in China for domestic use, the solar industry was almost entirely an export market. At the end of 2010, China had installed just 0.6 GW of solar PV domestically, but from 2011 to 2013, China's domestic solar market saw an enormous expansion.[56] In 2013, 12–14 GW of solar PV were installed in China— more than any other country in the world has ever installed in a single year.[57] This also exceeded the existing target to install 10 GW of solar PV by 2015 two years ahead of schedule. (As recently as 2009, the national target for solar PV installations by 2020 was just 1.6 GW.) China's solar target for 2020 is larger than the total installed capacity of all solar power in use globally in 2010.

Chinese government policy support for solar PV goes back to the Sixth Five-Year Plan, and has appeared in every plan since. China's Agenda 21 white paper, released in Rio in 1992, promoted China's commitment to renewable energy as a key component of its sustainable development strategy. Most of China's early policy support for solar was for off-grid, decentralized applications. For example, China's Brightness Program, implemented in 1996, was the first major program to promote rural electrification through off-grid solar, targeting twenty million people through 2010.[58] Support for large-scale solar manufacturing industries and for solar deployment is a much more recent phenomenon in China.

In March 2009, the Ministry of Finance released two documents, which together provided the framework for China's "Solar-Powered Rooftops Plan."[59] This program encouraged the use of building-integrated PV by establishing a subsidy of RMB 20/Wp, which is estimated to cover about 50 to 60 percent of the total cost of the system. Projects were to be at least 50 kW in size, and meet minimum efficiency requirements. In October 2009, 111 projects (out of about six hundred applications from thirty provinces) were approved, totaling 91 MW of PV capacity and a cost of about RMB 1.27 billion.[60]

The Ministry of Finance, Ministry of Science and Technology, and National Energy Administration announced the "Golden Sun Demonstration Program" on July 21, 2009. The program established a subsidy for grid-connected solar PV equal to 50 percent of the investment cost, and for off-grid PV of 70 percent of the investment cost. Overall the program targeted over 600 MW of PV to be installed across the country by 2012, with a minimum of 20 MW in each province. In total, 314 projects and 630 MW of capacity were approved in November 2009. The anticipated total construction costs of the program are RMB 20 billion.[61] In July 2011, the first national feed-in tariff policy for solar photovoltaics was announced, providing a subsidy to encourage the deployment of solar energy within China. It sets an on-grid solar power price of RMB 1.15/kWh (about $0.18/kWh).[62] Funding is provided by the Renewable Energy Development Fund (collected as a surcharge on ratepayers).

China's Role in International Climate Policy

With China rapidly emerging as a new global power, its role in the international climate negotiations is dramatically changing. When the first global treaty on climate change, the United Nations Framework Convention on Climate Change (UNFCCC) was negotiated prior to its adoption in 1992, China was still very much a developing country. It aligned itself with the Group of 77 (G-77) and did not take a leadership role in those negotiations. Now that China is a large economy and the largest greenhouse gas emitter in the world (Figure 15-2), it has no choice but to be a central figure in the international negotiations.

While China still wants to be (and still is) aligned with the G-77, its interests are very different from than they were in the late 1980s, and today, China has little in common with most other developing countries. Together with other major emerging economies, it formed a new coalition called BASIC: Brazil, South Africa, India, and China. But even in this coalition, China's interests diverge substantially from those of the other members.

Figure 15-2   Carbon Dioxide Emissions Trends in Selected Countries

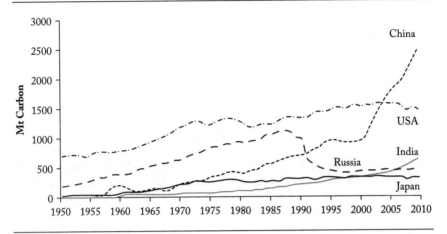

Source: China Energy Group, Lawrence Berkeley National Laboratory, *China Energy Databook Version 8.0* (CD-ROM), (2013), Figure 9B.17.

Brazil's emissions mostly come from deforestation, India's per capita emissions are far lower than China's, and South Africa has a much smaller economy than China does.

By 2011, China's negotiating position at the UNFCCC meeting in Durban, South Africa, saw two potentially significant changes to long-held elements of China's negotiating position. The first was a potential shift in China's willingness to adopt legally binding commitments as part of a future climate change agreement, as reflected in China's support of the Durban Platform in which UNFCCC parties agreed "to launch a process to develop a protocol, another legal instrument or an agreed outcome with legal force under the Convention applicable to all Parties," with a target of 2015.[63] The second was a new openness toward discussing absolute greenhouse gas emissions targets, rather than just intensity targets. These changes are very likely a result of the programs that have been implemented domestically in the wake of China's carbon intensity target and since the Copenhagen negotiations to both measure and monitor domestic emissions and to implement domestic carbon trading programs.

As a major economy, China is now included in the Major Economies Forum (MEF), which has emerged as another negotiation forum. The two largest emitters today, of course, are China and the United States, which together account for almost half of global emissions. Many observers have noted that the bilateral relationship between these two countries may be the most important of any in the global climate negotiations. In the midst of preparations for Copenhagen, 2009 also saw the launch of several new clean energy agreements between the two countries that have allowed for a broad expansion of the bilateral channels for discussing energy and climate issues. In 2013, the Obama administration worked with the incoming administration of Xi Jinping to sign several new agreements building on the robust package of bilateral cooperation signed back in 2009, including the establishment of a high-level Climate Change Working Group. The two countries' interests are increasingly converging, as was reflected in the November 11, 2014, joint climate change announcement. The United States and China surprised much of the world by jointly announcing new climate change targets following the APEC meetings in Beijing. President Obama announced a new target to cut net greenhouse gas emissions 26–28 percent below 2005 levels by 2025, and President Xi Jinping announced targets to peak CO_2 emissions around 2030, with the intention to try to peak early, and to increase the non–fossil fuel share of all energy to around 20 percent by 2030.[64] While it is too early to assess the impact that these targets may have, it is widely expected that this joint announcement will positively influence the UN climate negotiations as counties aim to reach a global deal in Paris in December 2015.

Conclusions

The Chinese government has made significant and detailed efforts to transition the country's economy toward a more sustainable path. Despite all of these efforts, China's current economic structure, which still relies on heavy manufacturing and energy-intensive infrastructure, and its dependence on coal for the majority of its current energy supply, makes it extremely difficult to switch to a green economy. Nevertheless, renewable energy sources such as solar and wind are receiving considerable policy support and subsidies, and the government is investing in high-efficiency coal technologies as well as methods to capture carbon dioxide from coal. These are excellent steps in the right direction, but they are still not enough.

This chapter has highlighted examples of contradictions between the Chinese government's push for a green economy on the one hand, and rapid economic growth on the other. The decisions that Chinese policymakers make in the next few years will have important implications for the future of China's energy system, and for the future of the global climate system. China's quest for a green economy will require a continued commitment to pursue the development of clean technologies, energy efficiency and conservation, and environmental protection programs, but will also require major nationwide changes to the country's economic structure.

Suggested Websites

China Dialogue (www.chinadialogue.net) Online resource that provides news coverage and analysis on environmental issues, both in English and in Chinese.

China Energy Group at Lawrence Berkeley National Laboratory (china.lbl.gov) Works collaboratively with energy researchers, suppliers, regulators, and consumers to better understand the dynamics of energy use in China. Website includes an extensive list of group publications on energy efficiency and carbon mitigation.

China Environment Forum at the Woodrow Wilson International Center for Scholars (www.wilsoncenter.org/program/china-environment -forum) Encourages dialogue among U.S. and Chinese scholars, policymakers, businesses, and nongovernmental organizations on environmental and energy challenges in China. Publishes the China Environment Series and research briefs addressing a variety of environmental topics in China.

ChinaFAQs (www.chinafaqs.org) A network for China energy and climate information coordinated by the World Resources Institute. Includes fact sheets and expert blog posts on timely topics.

Clean Air Initiative for Asian Cities (http://cleanairinitiative.org/ portal/countrynetworks/china) Promotes better air quality and livable cities in Asia with over two hundred member organizations and eight country networks, including China.

Global Environmental Institute (www.geichina.org) A Chinese nonprofit, nongovernmental organization that was established in Beijing, China, in 2004. Their mission is to design and implement market-based models for solving environmental problems in order to achieve development that is economically, ecologically, and socially sustainable.

Natural Resources Defense Council (http://switchboard.nrdc.org/ blogs/issues/greening_china) Environmental advocacy group that runs clean energy and legal training projects in China.

Probe International (http://journal.probeinternational.org) Environmental group that closely follows China's dam projects and broader water-related issues.

Professional Association for China's Environment (PACE) (https:// groups.yahoo.com/neo/groups/PACELISTSERVER/info) A global network of professionals who are committed to improving the quality of life of people and the environment in China. Produces a weekly email newsletter called "Environmental China" providing a comprehensive update of news concerning China's environment.

The U.S. Embassy in Beijing (Beijing Air iPhone app and Twitter feed) (http://iphone.bjair.info and https://twitter.com/#!/beijingair) Provides daily measurements of Beijing's air quality.

World Wildlife Fund (www.wwfchina.org) Online resource for the international group's conservation and environmental education projects in China.

Notes

1. Keith Bradsher, "China Sees Growth Engine in a Web of Fast Trains," *New York Times*, February 12, 2010.
2. Yiyu Liu and Zhou Siy, "China Pushes to Develop Green Economy," *China Daily*, November 23, 2010.
3. State Planning Commission, "China's Agenda 21—White Paper on China's Population, Environment, and Development in the 21st Century," 1994, www.acca21.org.cn/ english/index.html [Chinese], www.acca21.org.cn/ca21pa.html [English].
4. Ian Bradbury and Richard Kirkby, "China's Agenda 21: A Critique," *Applied Geography* 16, no. 2 (April 1996): 97–107.

5. Zhengwei Yuan, Jun Bi, and Yuichi Moriguichi, "The Circular Economy: A New Development Strategy in China," *Journal of Industrial Ecology* 10, no. 2 (February 8, 2008): 4–8.

6. Order of the President of the People's Republic of China, "Circular Economy Promotion Law of the People's Republic of China," August 2008, www.fdi.gov.cn/pub/FDI_EN/Laws/GeneralLawsandRegulations/BasicLaws/P020080919377641716849.pdf [Chinese], http://www.fdi.gov.cn/1800000121_39_597_0_7.html [English].

7. Yong Geng, Zhu Yong, Qinghua Zhu, Brent Doberstein, and Tsuyoshi Fujita, "Implementing China's Circular Economy Concept at the Regional Level: A Review of Progress in Dalian, China," *Waste Management* 29, no. 2 (February 2009): 996–1002.

8. "China's Twelfth Five Year Plan (2011–2015)—The Full English Version," translated by the Delegation of the European Union in China, May 11, 2011, http://cbi.typepad.com/china_direct/2011/05/chinas-twelfth-five-new-plan-the-full-english-version.html.

9. This section draws from Joanna I. Lewis and Kelly Sims Gallagher, "Energy and Environment in China: Achievements and Enduring Challenges," in *The Global Environment: Institutions, Law, and Policy*, 3rd ed., ed. Regina S. Axelrod, Stacey D. VanDeveer, and David Leonard Downie (Washington, DC: CQ Press, 2010).

10. Barry Naughton, *The Chinese Economy: Transitions and Growth* (Cambridge, MA: MIT Press, 2007).

11. *Zhongguo chengshi renkou shouci chaoguo nongcun renhou* ["China's Urban Population Exceeded Rural Population for the First Time"], *BBC Chinese News*, January 17, 2012, http://www.bbc.co.uk/zhongwen/simp/chinese_news/2012/01/120117_china_urban.shtml.

12. "World Bank Says China Is Poverty Reduction Model," *Xinhua*, February 25, 2003, www.china.org.cn/english/2003/Feb/56694.htm.

13. U.S. Central Intelligence Agency (CIA), "The World Factbook: Birth Rate" (2014 estimate), https://www.cia.gov/library/publications/the-world-factbook/fields/2054.html#13.

14. Susan Shirk, *China: Fragile Superpower* (New York: Oxford University Press, 2007), 54.

15. Netherlands Environmental Assessment Agency (MNP), "China Contributing Two Thirds to Increase in CO_2 Emissions," *Press Release*, December 6, 2008, www.pbl.nl/en/news/pressreleases/2008/20080613ChinacontributingtwothirdstoincreaseinCO2emissions.html.

16. Netherlands Environmental Assessment Agency, *Trends in Global CO_2 Emissions: 2013 Report* (The Hague: PBL Publishers, 2013), http://edgar.jrc.ec.europa.eu/news_docs/pbl-2013-trends-in-global-co2-emissions-2013-report-1148.pdf.

17. The 2011 International Energy Outlook's reference case estimates China's carbon dioxide emissions in 2030 will be 463 percent above 1990 levels, while the high–oil price and low–oil price cases estimate 567 percent and 396 percent above 1990 levels, respectively. Energy Information Administration, *International Energy Outlook 2011* (Washington, DC: U.S. Department of Energy, 2009). Newer reports can be found at the Energy Information Administration.

18. World Steel Association, "Statistics," 2012, www.worldsteel.org; International Aluminum Institute, "Statistics," 2012, www.world-aluminum.org.

19. "China's Twelfth Five-Year Plan."

20. Yuyu Chen, Avraham Ebenstein, Michael Greenstone, and Hongbin Li, "Evidence on the Impact of Sustained Exposure to Air Pollution on Life Expectancy from China's Huai River Policy," *PNAS* 110, no. 32 (2013), http://www.pnas.org/content/110/32/12936.abstract.

21. California Air Resources Board, "Air Pollution—Particulate Matter," *Research Report* (Sacramento: California Air Resources Board, May 2003).

22. "China Says Polluting Industry Still Growing Too Fast, Heavy Smog Alert for Beijing," *Reuters*, March 25, 2014.

23. David Biallo, "Can Coal and Clean Air Co-exist in China?" *Scientific American*, August 4, 2008, www.sciam.com/article.cfm?id=can-coal-and-clean-air-coexist-china.

24. World Bank and China State Environmental Protection Administration, *Cost of Pollution in China: Economic Estimates of Physical Damages* (Washington, DC: World Bank and China State Environmental Protection Administration, 2007).

25. World Bank and Development Research Center of the State Council, the People's Republic of China, *China 2030: Building a Modern, Harmonious, and Creative Society* (Washington, DC: World Bank, 2013), www.worldbank.org/content/dam/Worldbank/document/China-2030-complete.pdf.

26. Clean Air Alliance of China, issued by the Ministry of Environmental Protection, National Development and Reform Commission, and Ministry of Finance, "'Twelfth Five-Year Plan' on Air Pollution Prevention and Control in Key Regions: English Translation," *China Clean Air Policy Briefings* 1 (April 2013), www.epa.gov/ogc/china/air%20pollution.pdf.

27. Liu Xielin, "Building an Environmentally Friendly Society through Innovation: Challenges and Choices," *Background Paper* (Beijing: China Council for International Cooperation on Environment and Development, 2007).

28. Lynn Price and Xuejun Wang, *Constraining Energy Consumption of China's Largest Industrial Enterprises through Top-1000 Energy-Consuming Enterprise Program* (Berkeley, CA: Lawrence Berkeley National Laboratory, 2007).

29. "China's Energy Consumption per Unit of GDP Down 3.46 Percent in First 3 Quarters," *Xinhua News*, December 13, 2008, http://news.xinhuanet.com/english/2008-12/13/content_10497268.htm.

30. "Key Targets of China's 12th Five-Year Plan," *Xinhua*, March 5, 2011, http://news.xinhuanet.com/english2010/china/2011-03/05/c_13762230.htm.

31. Joanna Lewis, *Energy and Climate Goals of China's 12th Five-Year Plan* (Washington, DC: Pew Center on Global Climate Change, March 2011), www.pewclimate.org/docUploads/energy-climate-goals-china-twelfth-five-year-plan.pdf.

32. Jiang Lin et al., *Taking Out One Billion Tons of CO_2: The Magic of China's 11th Five Year Plan?* (Berkeley, CA: Lawrence Berkeley National Laboratory, 2007).

33. "China State Council Executive Will Study the Decision to Control Greenhouse Gas Emissions Targets," translated from Chinese (Beijing: Central People's Government of the People's Republic of China, 2009), www.gov.cn/ldhd/2009-11/26/content_1474016.htm.

34. "President to Attend Copenhagen Climate Talks: Administration Announces U.S. Emission Target for Copenhagen" (Washington, DC: White House Press Office, November 25, 2009).

35. Implementation of China's national carbon intensity target across all sectors and regions of the country is being supported by government-funded analysis led by China's leading academic and research institutions.

36. "Premier Wen Delivers Gov't Work Report," *China.org.cn*, March 5, 2011, china.org.cn/china/NPC_CPPCC_2011/2011-03/05/content_22060564.htm.

37. Data calculated from the Energy Information Administration's International Energy Statistics, available at www.eia.gov/countries/data.cfm.

38. National Development and Reform Commission, *Guojiafazhangaigewei bangongting guanyu kaizhan tan paifangquan jiaoyi shi dian gongzuo de tongzhi* ["NDRC Notice on Pilot Trading Programs for the Development of Carbon Emissions Rights"], Notice 2601 (2011).

39. Coco Liu, "China Finds It's Hard to Trade Global Warming Pollution," *Scientific American*, May 23, 2014, www.scientificamerican.com/article/china-finds-its-hard -to-trade-global-warming-pollution/.

40. National People's Congress, *The Renewable Energy Law of the People's Republic of China*, 2005, www.china.org.cn.

41. Sara Schuman, *Improving China's Existing Renewable Energy Legal Framework: Lessons from the International and Domestic Experience*, White Paper (Natural Resources Defense Council, October 2010), 12–13; National People's Congress Standing Committee, *China Renewable Energy Law Decision*, 2009, www.npc.gov.cn/huiyi/cwh/1112/2009 -12/26/content_1533217.htm.

42. National People's Congress Standing Committee, *China Renewable Energy Law Decision*, 2009.

43. Ernst & Young, "Renewable Energy Country Attractiveness Indices: Country Focus—China," http://www.ey.com/GL/en/Industries/Power—Utilities/RECAI— China.

44. Keith Bradsher, "A Green Solution or the Dark Side to Cleaner Coal?" *New York Times*, June 14, 2011.

45. U.S. Energy Information Administration, "International Energy Outlook 2013," July 2013, available at http://www.eia.gov/pressroom/presentations/sieminski_07252013 .pdf.

46. British Petroleum Statistical Review of World Energy 2011, http://www.bp.com/ content/dam/bp-country/de_de/PDFs/brochures/statistical_review_of_world_ energy_full_report_2011.pdf.

47. Hengwei Liu and Kelly Sims Gallagher, "Catalyzing Strategic Transformation to a Low Carbon Economy: A CCS Roadmap for China," *Energy Policy* 38 (2010): 59–74.

48. Lifeng Zhao and Kelly Sims Gallagher, "Research, Development, Demonstration, and Early Deployment Policies for Advanced Coal Technologies in China," *Energy Policy* 35 (2007): 6467–77.

49. Kelly Sims Gallagher, "Key Opportunities for U.S.-China Cooperation on Coal and CCS," Discussion Paper, John E. Thornton China Center at Brookings, December 2009, http://www.brookings.edu/~/media/Files/rc/papers/2010/0108_us_china_coal_ gallagher/0108_us_china_coal_gallagher.pdf.

50. IEA/OECD 2009, "Cleaner Coal in China" (Paris: OECD), http://www.iea.org/ publications/freepublications/publication/coal_china2009.pdf.

51. Until recently, the Chinese Meteorological Association (CMA) estimated that the total wind resources onshore were just 250 gigawatts. Recent estimates for onshore resources assume a fifty-meter hub height and only include areas technically and geographically feasible for wind development. Offshore resources are measured at depths between five and twenty-five meters. Rong Zhu, "Study on Wind Resources Potential for Large Scale Development of Wind Power," PowerPoint Presentation (Chinese Metrological Association, National Climate Center, April 13, 2010).

52. Sarah Wang, "The Answer to China's Future Energy Demands May Be Blowing in the Wind," *Scientific American*, September 10, 2009.

53. Joanna I. Lewis, "Building a National Wind Turbine Industry: Experiences from China, India and South Korea," *International Journal of Technology and Globalisation* 5, no. 3/4 (2011): 281–305.

54. Joanna Lewis, *The Chinese Solar Photovoltaic Industry: Structure, Policy Support and Learning Achievements*, Working Paper (Prepared for the Center for Resource Solutions and the Regulatory Assistance Project, India Program, June 8, 2011).

55. International Trade Group of Dewey and LeBeouf LLP, *China's Promotion of the Renewable Electric Power Equipment Industry* (Prepared for the National Foreign Trade Council, March 2010).

56. Jennifer Duggan, "China Sets New World Record for Solar Installations," *The Guardian*, January 30, 2014, www.theguardian.com/environment/chinas-choice/2014/jan/30/china-record-solar-energy.

57. Due to year-end project data still being verified, the estimate is currently somewhere between 12 and 14 GW. The largest amount of solar PV ever installed by a county in a single year is 8 GW.

58. National Renewable Energy Laboratory, *Renewable Energy in China: Brightness Rural Electrification Program* (Washington, DC: U.S. Department of Energy, Office of Energy Efficiency and Renewable Energy, 2004), www.nrel.gov/docs/fy04osti/35790.pdf.

59. Lou Schwartz, "China Takes Steps to Rebalance Its Solar Industry," *Renewable Energy World*, April 13, 2009, www.renewableenergyworld.com/rea/news/article/2009/04/shining-a-light-on-the-domestic-market-china-takes-steps-to-rebalance-its-solar-industry.

60. Dewey and LeBeouf LLP, *China's Promotion of the Renewable Electric Power Equipment Industry*.

61. Ibid.

62. NDRC Pricing Department, "NDRC Notice on Improving Solar PV Electricity Pricing Policy (No. 1594)," in Chinese, *National Development and Reform Commission*.

63. UNFCCC, *Establishment of an Ad Hoc Working Group on the "Durban Platform for Enhanced Action" Draft Decision* (CP.17), 2011.

64. White House, "Fact Sheet: U.S.-China Joint Announcement on Climate Change and Clean Energy Cooperation," http://www.whitehouse.gov/the-press-office/2014/11/11/fact-sheet-us-china-joint-announcement-climate-change-and-clean-energy-c.

Part V

Conclusion

16

Conclusion
Future Environmental Challenges and Solutions
Norman J. Vig and Michael E. Kraft

Climate change, once considered an issue for a distant future, has moved firmly into the present.

—National Climate Assessment, May 2014

There is no Planet B

—Sign at People's Climate March,
New York City, September 21, 2014

W hen the first edition of this book was published a quarter-century ago (1990), the future of environmental policy appeared optimistic.[1] The pathbreaking legislation of the "environmental decade" of the 1970s had survived the onslaught of the Reagan administration, and a "second generation" of laws had been enacted in the 1980s to deal with a wider range of problems such as hazardous chemicals and toxic waste from diverse sources (Chapter 1 and Appendix 1). Institutions such as the Environmental Protection Agency (EPA) and the Council on Environmental Quality were recovering from budget and personnel cuts. President George H. W. Bush had adopted the mantle of Theodore Roosevelt and had proposed amendments to strengthen the Clean Air Act. The outlook for new, more efficient approaches to environmental regulation such as Bush's cap-and-trade plan for acid rain looked good. Bipartisan support for environmental policy remained strong in Congress.

It also appeared that the United States was ready to resume a leading role in international environmental diplomacy. President Reagan had signed the Montreal Protocol on Substances That Deplete the Ozone Layer, and Bush endorsed creation of the United Nations Intergovernmental Panel on Climate Change (IPCC) and launched preparations for what became the Earth Summit in 1992. As the Soviet Union collapsed and the Cold War ended, a new era of global environmental cooperation appeared feasible. "Third generation" issues such as climate change, protection of rainforests and biodiversity, and elimination of trade in hazardous substances such as chlorofluorocarbons (CFCs) and highly toxic pesticides could now be addressed. The recently minted concept of "sustainable development" provided a new guiding principle for global change.[2]

Finally, the American public appeared squarely behind stronger governmental action to protect the environment. The organized environmental movement had grown by leaps and bounds in the 1980s, especially after the worst nuclear power accident in history at Chernobyl in Ukraine in 1986 and the huge Exxon Valdez oil spill off the coast of Alaska in 1989. More than 80 percent of the public agreed that the environment should be protected "regardless of cost."[3] According to one pollster, "Protection of the environment, in fact, has become . . . a basic American value—with no consequential voting bloc opposed to it."[4] We concluded that "the political climate seems more propitious for environmental reform than at any time since 1970."

It is far more difficult to be optimistic today. After passage of the Clean Air Act Amendments in 1990, consensus on environmental policy largely disappeared in Congress (Chapter 5). The environmental movement stalled also as public attention shifted to other priorities. The Republican and Democratic Parties began to diverge sharply on environmental issues, leading to a far more conservative approach to environmental protection by the time George W. Bush was elected in 2000. As described in Chapter 4 and elsewhere in this volume, the Bush administration rejected both national and international initiatives on climate change and attempted to weaken other environmental legislation. The attacks of 9/11 in 2001, the wars in Afghanistan and Iraq, and the Great Recession of 2007–2009 further displaced environmental issues from the national political agenda.

Despite these setbacks, there are hopeful signs that the nation is moving forward again on many environmental fronts. President Barack Obama has carried out a positive environmental agenda and has moved unilaterally to address climate change for the first time (Chapter 4). The EPA and other federal departments and agencies are implementing new regulations that strengthen environmental protection and accelerate the development of clean energy sources (Chapters 7 and 8). State and local governments have also adopted a broad range of innovative policies that promote sustainable development (Chapters 2 and 12). Many private corporations and businesses as well continue to make substantial progress toward greater energy efficiency, reduction in use of materials and waste, and other measures of sustainability (Chapter 11). The chances for stronger international cooperation on climate change—through new bilateral and multilateral agreements to limit carbon emissions—are more promising again (Chapter 13). Finally, a new grassroots movement among young people engaged in what Geoffrey Wandesforde-Smith called "the politics of moral outrage" may again enervate the American environmental movement.[5]

In the following sections, we discuss some of the major environmental challenges of the future that are raised in this volume. We also discuss the potential for alternative approaches to environmental regulation that might both improve the effectiveness of federal policies and help to build greater consensus over the role of government. Finally, we assess the state of environmental governance today and highlight new needs for the future.

Major Issues

Most of the environmental problems discussed in earlier editions of this book are still with us—including those relating to management of public lands, control of hazardous and toxic wastes, and protection of biological diversity, endangered species, and threatened ecosystems. We focus here on three areas that have received the most attention in the recent years: climate change, energy production, and air and water pollution.

Climate Change: Dire Warnings and First Steps

What appeared in 1990 as an abstract and distant threat has now become a reality for most Americans. Extreme weather events such as record temperatures, droughts, hurricanes, torrential rains, floods, and wildfires have now become commonplace. In 2014, California was suffering through one of the worst droughts in history, hundreds of wildfires had burned large swaths of forestland in the western states, and much of the Midwest and Northeast had been through one of the severest winters and wettest springs in memory. Although individual events such as these cannot be linked to global warming with certainty, the National Climate Assessment, prepared by a panel of more than three hundred scientists and experts and released in May 2014, declared that "climate change, once considered an issue for a distant future, has moved firmly into the present. . . . Summers are longer and hotter, and extended periods of unusual heat last longer than any living American has ever experienced. . . . Winters are generally shorter and warmer. Rain comes in heavier downpours. People are seeing changes in the length and severity of seasonal allergies, the plant varieties that thrive in their gardens, and the kinds of birds they see in any particular month in their neighborhoods."[6]

The leading international body responsible for tracking climate change—the IPCC—has published five comprehensive reports since 1990, each more urgent than the last. The fifth assessment report, released in four installments in late 2013 and 2014, contained the most dire warnings yet about current climate trends and future risks throughout the world.[7] The scientific report concluded that it is "extremely likely" (a greater than 95 percent chance) that human activities are "the dominant cause" of the observed global warming since the 1950s. It further documented global changes already occurring, from rapidly melting sea and land ice and rising sea levels, to intense heat waves and heavy rains, to strains on food production and water supplies, to deterioration of coral reefs and threats to fish and other wildlife.[8] The final draft report recognized progress in limiting carbon emissions in some countries, but stated that these gains are being overwhelmed by growing emissions in rapidly developing countries such as China and India.[9] The report thus called for much greater commitments to both policies to mitigate emissions growth and major investments to allow social and economic adaptation to climate changes that are inevitable in the coming decades. Unless new technologies are put in place by 2030, the report argued, it will probably be too late to avoid catastrophic damage to human life on the planet.[10] "Continued emission of greenhouse gases will cause further warming and long-lasting changes in all components of the climate system, increasing the likelihood of severe, pervasive and irreversible impacts for people and ecosystems," the report stated.[11]

The new realities are thus that climate change is already occurring, and that almost all of the growth in global greenhouse gas (GHG) emissions is now being driven by population increases and economic development in "emerging" nations such as China, India, Brazil, and Indonesia (see Chapters 13–15). The world's population is expected to grow by over 2 billion (to nearly 9.7 billion) by 2050, with almost all of the increase in developing countries; growth is expected to continue through the end of the century. As happened previously in the United States and Europe, *per capita* consumption of food, energy, and goods of all kinds is also rising rapidly in these countries as hundreds of millions of people are lifted out of poverty and pursue a middle-class lifestyle. Fossil fuel use—especially coal for electricity generation—is thus contributing enormous amounts of additional carbon dioxide to the atmosphere. Other GHGs, such as methane from cattle grazing and agricultural production, are also rising (see Chapter 9). Indeed, the EPA reports that "globally, the agricultural sector is the primary source" of methane emissions.[12]

China surpassed the United States as the largest source of GHGs in 2006 and now accounts for more than 22 percent of net global emissions, compared to 13.4 percent by the United States and 9.3 percent by the European Union (see Table 13-1).[13] However, U.S. *per capita* consumption of energy and emission of GHGs is still far higher than in China and the European Union, and varies greatly among states and regions (Table 13-1). It is unrealistic to expect other nations—especially those with lower *per capita* incomes—to curtail their emissions unless we do much more to control ours.

In this context, it is critically important that President Obama has taken the first major steps toward reducing U.S. carbon emissions, especially by imposing GHG limits on power plants and other sectors of industry for the first time, by sharply raising auto mileage standards, and by accelerating the development of renewable energy such as wind and solar power (Chapters 4, 7, and 8). In November 2014, Obama also announced a landmark agreement with China, by which China agreed for the first time to cap its carbon emissions by 2030 and the United States pledged to further reduce its CO_2 emissions to 26–28 percent below 2005 levels by 2025 (see Chapters 13 and 15).[14] Although this goal may be achievable if all of the Obama administration policies are fully implemented, further measures are likely to be necessary in the years ahead.[15]

A more comprehensive U.S. approach would entail putting a price on carbon through taxation of fossil fuels or establishment of a national cap-and-trade system that would gradually reduce the number of emission allowances within and across sectors. These and other approaches will be discussed later in this chapter. It would also probably require either a crash program to phase out coal-fired power plants or rapid deployment of carbon capture and storage (CCS) technologies to recover carbon from coal emissions and pump it deeply into the earth.[16] Other approaches such as energy production from biomass with carbon capture and storage could permanently remove carbon from the atmosphere. These and other carbon removal and mitigation technologies are still in an early stage of development, and require more research and testing.[17] The shift toward natural gas as an alternative "bridge" fuel will also have to be carefully monitored and regulated to prevent methane leaks from offsetting climate gains from use of the lower carbon fuels (see next section).

Given the gridlock in Congress, much of the progress toward climate change mitigation and adaptation will also have to come from political actors outside Washington. Nearly thirty states already have climate change policies such as renewable energy portfolio standards (see Chapter 2). More than one thousand mayors have also signed the U.S. Conference of Mayors' Climate Protection Agreement, which among other things calls for an 80 percent reduction in carbon emissions from their cities by 2050.[18]

At least ten states have already reduced their carbon emissions from power plants by at least 30 percent compared to 2005 levels; indeed, Maine, Massachusetts, New Hampshire, and New York have cut theirs by more than 40 percent.[19] These states are among nine northeastern states that are members of the Regional Greenhouse Gas Initiative (RGGI), which began implementing a cap-and-trade system in 2008 that is projected to reduce carbon dioxide emissions from power plants in the region as a whole by 45 percent by 2020, as compared to 2005 levels.[20] California is also a model for the nation, with its broader cap-and-trade system that will pump billions of dollars into climate change mitigation by 2020. In addition, California has cooperative agreements with Oregon, Washington, British Columbia, and other Canadian provinces to maximize carbon reduction (Chapter 13).[21]

President Obama's proposed regulation for reducing carbon emissions from coal-fired power plants by 30 percent by 2030 looks modest in comparison with these gains. But the highest emissions now come from coal- and oil-dependent states that have opposed regulation of greenhouse gases, and their cooperation will also be needed to attain the national standard. With this in mind, the president's plan would allow states to meet their emission reduction obligations in a variety of ways—for example, by investing in efficient natural gas plants, by reducing electricity demand, by offsetting carbon emissions with renewable energy or nuclear power, or by establishing cap-and-trade systems or joining those already operating in other states (see below for further discussion of market-based approaches).[22] Nevertheless, strong opposition to the new rules is already apparent in many states.[23]

Businesses will also have to get much more involved. Risky Business, a group co-chaired by former New York mayor Michael Bloomberg, former Bush administration Treasury secretary Hank Paulson, and retired hedge fund manager Tom Steyer, issued a report in June 2014 that attempts to quantify the potential risks to coastal property, agricultural production, and other economic activity in different regions of the country if current policies are not changed.[24] Paulson, a Republican, compared the risks of a "climate bubble" to those of the credit bubble that triggered the financial crisis of

2008, and called on businesses to integrate climate planning into their operations and to change their practices to both reduce risks and build resiliency.[25] In fact, a growing number of business leaders and corporations now "see global warming as a force that contributes to lower gross domestic products, higher food and commodity costs, broken supply chains and increased financial risk."[26]

Colleges and universities, religious groups, and other nonprofit organizations have also become increasingly involved in the politics of climate change. One avenue is through pressure on institutional shareholders such as universities and pension funds to divest stock holdings in corporations such as coal and oil companies that deny climate science or oppose efforts to limit carbon emissions (see Chapter 3). More than 180 institutions, including the Rockefeller Brothers Fund, have pledged in recent years to sell assets tied to fossil fuel companies.[27] Many energy investments, especially those in coal companies, may be "stranded" and lose value as the nation moves toward cleaner fuels.[28] Another approach would require companies to disclose much more information about their climate impacts and the risks they face from climate change. Most large companies now have professional environmental staffs and publish information on their "green" activities (Chapter 11). However, according to former Treasury secretary Robert Rubin, "investors should demand that companies disclose their exposure to climate risks, including the impact that climate change could have on their businesses and assets, the value of their assets that could be stranded by climate change, and the costs they may someday incur to address their carbon emissions."[29] The Securities and Exchange Commission does not yet mandate such disclosures in financial reports.

Finally, it is likely that a new global environmental agreement on climate change will be adopted at the Paris climate change conference in December 2015 (Chapter 13). The preparatory meetings held in Lima, Peru, in December 2014 laid the basis for a new international regime after 2020 in which nearly all nations (including developing countries) will agree to declare their greenhouse gas emission intentions for the first time.[30] Under the "Lima Accord," each country will set its own emission goals ("Intended Nationally Determined Contributions"), but these targets will not be legally binding, and the results will be difficult to monitor and verify.[31] Nevertheless, it is hoped that even a relatively weak voluntary agreement of this kind will put political pressure on governments to cut their emissions.[32] The United States should work with China and other large emitting countries to strengthen implementation measures in the final Paris agreement.

Energy Supply: Critical Choices

However serious the potential threats of climate change, we also need an adequate and reliable supply of energy through the transition to lower-carbon fuels. As explained in Chapter 8, all types of energy production—including renewable sources such as wind and solar—involve environmental as well as economic trade-offs. For example, solar installations require a great deal of land, and solar collection towers that concentrate the sun's rays to heat electricity-generating boilers also require a lot of water and kill a large number of birds and other wildlife.[33] Other carbon-free modes of production, such as nuclear power, present long-term problems of waste storage and ultimate disposal. Ethanol, the production of which now accounts for 40 percent of all corn produced in the United States, may require as much energy to create as it provides for end use (see Chapter 9). Even natural gas, which releases only about half as much carbon dioxide when burned as coal, requires other forms of energy to produce and results in methane leaks and other problems that could offset the benefits of lower carbon emissions.[34]

President Obama has followed a "balanced approach," in the sense that his "all-of-the-above" energy strategy has encouraged rapid development of oil and gas production as well as renewable sources.[35] Energy production from renewable sources such as wind and solar doubled during his first term and is expected to double again before he leaves office. In some states, renewables are rapidly replacing coal: for example, in Iowa, "wind energy grew to account for nearly 25 percent of the state's electricity generation from 2006 to 2012, while coal's share fell by 12 percent over the same period."[36] Meanwhile, oil and gas production are at the highest levels in more than twenty years and could make the United States the world's largest producer of both as early as 2015. Increased production in the United States and Canada, together with falling demand in Europe and Asia, led to a sharp decline in oil and gasoline prices in the second half of 2014.[37] While a boon to consumers, lower fuel prices will encourage people to buy less fuel-efficient cars and to drive more, thus potentially undermining carbon reduction goals.

Much of the recent controversy over energy policy has revolved around two issues that symbolize the differences between environmentalists and fossil fuel industries: oil and gas "fracking" and the Keystone XL pipeline (Chapter 8). Fracking has resulted in a massive increase in natural gas production that is largely responsible for an approximately 10 percent decline in U.S. GHG emissions since 2005, as well as for the revival of manufacturing industry in many parts of the country.[38] It has also reduced U.S. dependence on oil imports from the Middle East and elsewhere as domestic production exceeded imports in 2013 for the first time since 1995.[39] Energy "independence" is a goal shared by both parties and has broad public support. However, fracking has become controversial in many states due to its potential environmental effects, including increased air and water pollution, congestion, and seismic activity.[40] So far fracking is regulated, if at all, by state and local governments with widely varying policies (Chapter 2). But pressures are mounting for states to either tighten regulation or allow towns and counties greater authority to restrict drilling, and in late 2014, New York State banned fracking entirely.[41] The EPA is also working on new rules to regulate fracking processes and to control methane emissions across the country.

The Keystone XL pipeline that would carry crude oil from the tar sands of Alberta, Canada, to refineries on the Gulf Coast has become a central organizing issue for the environmental movement and a matter of bitter partisan dispute (see Chapter 3). The 1,700 mile pipeline, first proposed in 2006, has been strongly supported by Republicans and some Democrats in Congress who claim that it would create thousands of new jobs and provide the United States a more secure oil supply than oil imports from the Middle East. Many unions also support the project, as does the general public according to recent polls (Chapter 8). However, environmentalists and many Democrats see the pipeline as a disaster in the making that will result in far more greenhouse gas emissions, devastate pristine forestlands and native communities in Canada, and pose enormous risks of pollution along the pipeline route.[42] They also question whether the pipeline would create many permanent new jobs or add to U.S. energy security, since the oil or its refined products could be re-exported to countries anywhere in the world.

The Canadian tar sands oil creates 17 percent more carbon pollution than domestic U.S. oil, according to the State Department. It also contains much higher levels of sulfur, nitrogen, and toxic substances such as lead. On the other hand, increasing transport of the oil by railroad rather than pipeline also poses major environmental and health risks.[43]

Under pressure from environmentalists, President Obama repeatedly postponed a decision on the pipeline through 2014. The Keystone pipeline thus became a flashpoint in the 2014 midterm elections. Virtually all Republican candidates endorsed the project, as did many Democratic candidates for the Senate. Despite support from fourteen Democrats and all Republicans, the Senate narrowly defeated a bill requiring construction of the pipeline shortly after the election.[44] The new Republican-controlled Senate finally passed a similar bill in January 2015 by a 62-36 vote and the House followed suit, but President Obama was expected to veto the legislation. However, even if the pipeline is eventually approved, it is not clear when it might be built. The drastic fall in crude oil prices in the second half of 2014 could make the project uneconomical in the near future.[45]

The Keystone pipeline is only one among many issues surrounding international commerce in fossil fuels. One of the most important concerns, heretofore little discussed, is U.S. coal exports. As demand for coal declines in this country due to increased use of natural gas and new GHG regulations, coal exports to other countries are expected to rise and, according to some calculations, could cancel out much of the gain from domestic cutbacks in carbon emissions.[46] The exported coal will simply shift the problem to other countries and may result in even higher emissions from less efficient coal plants (a problem known as "emissions leakage"). The same can be said for potential oil and gas exports as the United States becomes the world's largest producer. To President Obama's credit, he has pledged to halt U.S. government support for construction of new coal-fired plants elsewhere in the world, but the administration has so far not taken a position on increased coal exports.[47]

Air and Water Pollution

Our current focus on energy and climate change should not blind us to more traditional environmental problems such as air and water pollution. These forms of pollution are regulated by the EPA under statutes largely written in the 1970s and, in some cases, revised in the 1980s and 1990s (see Chapters 5 and 7). As pointed out in Chapter 1, air quality has improved greatly over the decades, with aggregate emissions of the six primary or "criteria" pollutants controlled by the Clean Air Act falling by two-thirds between 1980 and 2012—despite the fact that our economy more than doubled in size during that period. Emissions of other pollutants such as hazardous chemicals and toxic metals have also declined markedly (Chapter 11). Nevertheless, air quality varies greatly in different localities and among different population groups, with many urban areas still suffering high concentrations of ozone, particulates, and chemicals that can cause severe health effects and even death.

Among the most controversial policies of the George W. Bush administration were efforts to weaken the Clean Air Act (CAA) by exempting power plants from the "New Source Review" (NSR) requirements of the law. Power plants that existed when the CAA was written in 1970 (that is, all of the older coal-fired plants) were not required to meet emission standards for basic air pollutants unless they underwent more than routine maintenance and repair or significantly increased their output—in which case they would be considered "new sources" and would have to undergo NSR, which could force them to install currently available pollution control equipment. The Clinton administration had filed lawsuits against dozens of electric utility companies for failing to upgrade their facilities as they expanded, but the Bush administration declined to pursue these suits and instead issued a new rule allowing the utilities to undertake huge expansion projects—costing up to 20 percent of the entire plant's replacement value—without triggering NSR requirements. This loophole effectively guaranteed that hundreds of older power plants would remain exempt from pollution standards, thereby strengthening incentives to keep them in operation.[48] Although the federal courts eventually struck down the rule in 2007, it slowed progress toward controlling the largest sources of conventional air pollutants as well as GHGs during the Bush years (Chapter 7).

Two other rules required by the CAA—the Interstate Rule to limit emissions from power plants that pollute neighboring states in the eastern half of the country, and the Mercury Rule to regulate mercury and other toxic air emissions—were proposed by the Bush administration, but both were also found inadequate by the courts. Under Obama, the EPA issued a new Mercury and Air Toxics Standard (MATS) in 2011, which would further tighten emission standards for mercury, lead, asbestos, and other toxic air pollutants.[49] These regulations affect major industries such as cement manufacturing and oil refineries as well as power plants. The EPA also issued a new Cross-State Air Pollution Rule in 2011 to replace the Bush Interstate

Rule that would require power plants in twenty-seven eastern states to limit downwind emissions of pollutants such as sulfur dioxide, nitrogen oxides, and particulates to other states.[50]

Urban air quality has improved greatly, as pointed out in Chapter 1, but about 45 percent of Americans still live in counties that have at least one major type of air pollution that exceeds EPA standards—in most cases excess ozone levels caused by exhaust emissions from cars, trucks, and buses, as well as factories and power plants. The new fuel economy and tailpipe gas emission standards established by the Obama administration should help to reduce these impacts in the future. The regulations limiting carbon emissions from new and existing power plants will also further cut emissions of all of the other air pollutants. In announcing the "Clean Power Plan" in June 2014, for example, the EPA stated that it would have major "co-benefits" by reducing emissions of conventional pollutants by more than 25 percent which would avoid up to 6,600 premature deaths and 150,000 asthma attacks in children.[51] Finally, in November 2014, the EPA also issued its long-delayed ozone rule, which would cut allowable levels of ambient ozone from the current standard of 75 parts per billion (set in the Bush administration) to 65–70 parts per billion by 2025. Although somewhat less stringent than originally proposed in 2011, these threshold limits will further improve urban air quality if they are met.[52]

The environmental laws enacted in the 1970s were mainly intended to address pollution from heavy industries, power plants, motor vehicles, and municipal waste treatment plants. But as Chapter 9 makes clear, agriculture and food production have also become major sources of both air and water pollution and account for many of the health hazards we face. What is now industrial-scale farm production uses enormous quantities of fossil fuel energy, chemicals for fertilizer and pesticides, and surface water and groundwater for irrigation. It is also the nation's largest source of water pollution from field crop runoff and drainage and from Concentrated Animal Feeding Operations (CAFOs). Except for some of the largest feedlots, which require permits for manure storage, agricultural operations are considered "indirect sources" under the Clean Water Act and are not regulated by the EPA. The EPA issues guidelines for maximum allowable levels of water pollutants in rivers and other water bodies, but it is largely up to state and local governments to devise and implement plans to achieve them.

As a result, progress in controlling water pollution has been slow and uneven at best, and more than half of the nation's lakes and rivers are still considered "impaired" for uses such as fishing and swimming. Groundwater and drinking water supplies are also contaminated by agricultural runoff, especially by nitrogen and phosphorous fertilizers. For example, toxic algae blooms in Lake Erie caused by such runoff forced Toledo and other Ohio cities to shut off tap water supplies for several days in August 2014.[53] Residues of agricultural pesticides are also found in many rural wells and public water systems, causing unknown health effects. Some of the chemicals used are neurotoxins that are suspected of causing birth defects and other developmental problems in children.[54]

Alternative Policy Approaches

Traditional "command and control" regulation has been generally success-ful in improving environmental quality since the 1960s (Chapters 1 and 11). Using this form of regulation, the EPA sets national standards for acceptable air or water quality, drinking water safety, or pesticide use, and then requires regulated industries to install specific types of pollution control equipment or limit their use and discharge of dangerous wastes. Under the Clean Air Act, states must develop state implementation plans (SIPs) that meet EPA stan-dards; otherwise, the EPA will impose its own plan and regulate the industries directly. As indicated above, the Clean Water Act gives states more latitude in deciding how to meet the national standards and in issuing discharge permits, but the EPA can also step in and regulate major sources if a state fails to do so. Similarly, as pointed out in Chapter 7, state and local governments are largely in charge of implementing drinking water standards. We thus have a system of "environmental federalism," even when the EPA has ultimate legal oversight authority.[55] The results have been uneven but generally positive, with some states choosing to move well ahead of federal requirements and others lagging behind (see Chapter 2).

Nevertheless, critics of the EPA have long argued that its "one size fits all" regulations are economically inefficient and often inappropriate for spe-cific local circumstances. Legal mandates under these rules have also resulted in endless litigation and have tended to discourage innovation and voluntary improvements that could improve outcomes (though most laws allow states to set higher standards if they choose to). Many environmental policy scholars have thus advocated new forms of "smart regulation" that utilize more flexible, less intrusive, and more cost-effective methods for reducing pollution and addressing other environmental problems.[56] Many economists, especially, have advocated market-based regimes that maximize economic efficiency and cost-effectiveness, as explained in Chapter 10. We briefly assess some of the most important of these alternative policy approaches.

Cap-and-trade systems set overall limits on the quantity of pollution emissions allowed, and lower the number of allowances or permits available for use over time to meet reduction goals. Affected entities can buy and sell emission allowances, with the price being determined by the trading market (some new allowances are usually auctioned off by the government or trading authority, raising funds for pollution control as well). As the cap is tightened, the price of allowances should go up, encouraging companies to cut their emissions or incur higher costs for allowances. This form of market pricing and trading gives regulated parties freedom to make their own decisions and should result in the most cost-effective way of lowering pollution. The Amer-ican Clean Energy and Security Act of 2009, which passed in the House of Representatives but died in the Senate in 2010, would have established an economy-wide system of this kind to control GHGs.

Despite the act's failure, two large GHG emissions trading systems are operating today in the United States. The RGGI market, now including nine states, began operations in 2008 and the California system in 2013. As a result, some eighty million people, or one-quarter of the American population, are now covered by such systems, which have already contributed to substantial carbon emission reductions, as discussed earlier.[57] The new EPA rules for cutting emissions from coal-fired power plants proposed in June 2014 could also encourage other states to form carbon markets, or to join the California or RGGI systems. We are thus likely to see larger regional trading markets in the coming years. Many other countries and the European Union also have such regimes, and China is reported to be planning the world's largest carbon trading market as early as 2016.[58] The effectiveness of many of these systems remains to be seen, but they now appear to be the most widely utilized means of combating climate change.[59]

Since the failure of the climate change legislation in 2010, many economists, business leaders, and politicians of different political persuasions have endorsed *carbon taxes* as an alternative to cap and trade.[60] In theory, putting a price on carbon or other forms of pollution via taxes or fees could achieve cost-effective outcomes similar to those of emission trading systems (Chapter 10). Taxes are also easier to administer and more transparent, thus conveying clearer signals to consumers. On the other hand, taxes do not guarantee any given level of emissions reduction, and currently face perhaps even greater opposition in Congress, from businesses, and from the general public than cap and trade.[61]

Some of these obstacles might be overcome if these taxes were revenue neutral—that is, part of a larger tax reform in which other taxes such as corporate, income, or payroll taxes were simultaneously reduced to offset the carbon tax.[62] Several carbon tax proposals introduced in the last Congress would rebate all of the taxes collected to the taxpayers or to the general public in the form of a "carbon dividend."[63] This would be similar to Alaska's oil revenue fund, a highly popular policy. At least ten other countries and provinces have carbon taxes, some more successful than others.[64] There is some evidence that those that are revenue neutral and clearly offset by cuts in other visible taxes can gain wide public acceptance.[65]

Voluntary collaboration and self-policing programs are another alternative to traditional regulation. In this approach, regulated parties such as corporations or industrial sectors voluntarily agree to meet higher performance standards than required by law, in return for greater regulatory flexibility (Chapter 11). Most of these programs were created during the Clinton administration as part of its "reinventing government" initiative.[66] Although many of these experiments, such as the Performance Track program, failed to produce measurably better results than traditional regulation and have been discontinued, they did help some sectors of business and industry to improve their environmental management and reporting, and in some cases their operations. But stronger organization and governmental supervision, or effective oversight by independent bodies, appear necessary if a genuine "greening"—defined as a transformation to sustainable production—is to occur. Sectoral organizations such as trade and business associations could become more effective intermediaries if they are given stronger authority to monitor their members and enforce environmental policies. But even without such quasi-governmental devolution, all companies could be given stronger incentives to adopt management practices such as those required for ISO-14001 certification (see Chapter 11).

One key to stronger environmental performance is public *disclosure of information*. The leading example of such information disclosure is the federal Toxics Release Inventory (TRI), which has operated since the late 1980s. Over twenty thousand industrial facilities a year report on their release of some 650 toxic chemicals to the air, water, or land. The information is made available to the public in a variety of ways, including the EPA's own TRI website.

The key assumption in such policies is that an informed public may bring some pressure to bear on poorly performing industrial facilities and their parent companies, what some have called regulation by embarrassment. It is just as likely that companies will seek to avoid such public censure by proactively altering their production processes to reduce chemical releases even if they are not subject to any regulatory requirements to do so. Although the disclosed information is often quite technical and difficult to translate into meaningful risks to the public's health, the program has led to significant decreases in release of toxic chemicals over time, and to improved environmental performance on the part of industry. Such programs may be especially important at a time when even modest reforms of chemical safety policies have faced obstacles in Congress.[67]

The success of some information disclosure programs such as the TRI led the federal government to try much the same approach with GHG releases. The EPA maintains a Greenhouse Gas Reporting Program that collects and releases emissions data from facilities in forty-one different source categories, and is easily accessible by the public. Much like the TRI, the assumption is that facilities will seek to reduce their emissions precisely because the data are available to the public, and thus may embarrass those companies that choose to do little to curtail their emissions. It is too early in the life of the EPA program to know whether it is having such an effect. Nonprofit organizations, of course, can play a very similar role, as demonstrated by the Carbon Disclosure Project. Since 2007, it has ranked companies on their carbon emissions.

We may soon see a new variation of this kind of corporate reporting related to GHG emissions. As discussed in Chapter 3, there are increasing calls for corporate recognition and accounting for financial risks associated with climate change, and companies may be required to disclose those risks much as they do for other kinds of financial risks, such as changes in economic competition or vulnerability to lawsuits. Colleges and universities in particular have been calling for such considerations.

More recently, many states have begun requiring a somewhat comparable reporting of chemicals used in natural gas fracturing, largely in response to public concern over possible contamination of water supplies and other health risks. The reporting systems used to date are not as informative as they might be. Nonetheless, experience with the TRI program suggests that making this kind of information available can be very effective in improving environmental performance, especially if the reporting system is carefully designed to provide the right kind of information in a way that ordinary people can readily understand and use.[68]

Another promising policy approach, *local and regional sustainability planning*, has been used with impressive results in many cities and regions in the United States as well as in other nations. The concept of sustainability or sustainable development came into wide use following the 1987 Brundtland Commission report, and later the Earth Summit of 1992. It also was promoted heavily during the Clinton administration by the President's Council on Sustainable Development (PCSD), which focused on how communities might develop "bold, new approaches to achieve economic, environmental, and equity goals."[69]

As Chapter 12 showed, both large and small cities in the nation have embarked on intriguing programs to pursue economic development in a way that seeks to integrate environmental and equity considerations into the equation. While some of the cities, such as Seattle, Washington, and Portland, Oregon, are well known and often celebrated for their remarkable sustainability achievements and their highly supportive local citizenry, they are by no means the only examples of successful sustainability planning. New efforts to promote sustainability are found in large cities such as New York, Chicago, and Los Angeles; midsized cities such as San Francisco, Austin, and Boston; and smaller cities such as Boulder, Colorado, and Chattanooga, Tennessee. These include often innovative programs to improve air quality, water quality, building efficiency and energy use, local transportation planning, land use, water conservation, and more. Some cities also are moving ahead in planning for adaptation to climate change.

It now seems likely that the most creative and effective actions to put the idea of sustainability into practice will be found not within the federal government, but in such cities, as well as among colleges and universities, and some of the most progressive corporations. Successes at these levels, however, will make it possible eventually to adopt sustainability programs at the national and international levels as well.

Two other critical needs are a committed investment in *scientific research and development* and improvement of *public education in science*. As evident throughout the book, little progress is possible on environmental challenges without strong scientific evidence to document the problems the nation faces and to identify potential solutions. The role of science is particularly important today when public trust in science and scientists appears to be in decline and where political ideology often trumps scientific findings.[70] The United States historically has been highly supportive of investment in scientific research and technology development, and both Democratic and Republican administrations have given such research a high priority. Yet in recent years, budgetary constraints as well as rising partisanship over environmental and energy issues provide less assurance that such investment will continue.

While many different kinds of research in the natural and social sciences and engineering are needed, we hope the federal government and other organizations that invest in science follow the advice of the National Science Foundation in supporting interdisciplinary environmental research. As the Advisory Committee for Environmental Research and Education observed in 2009, the world "is at a crossroads," and human beings are stressing both natural and social systems beyond their capacity. The problems we face are complex, and our knowledge is both limited and fragmented. Solving such problems requires an unprecedented integration of knowledge from many disciplines as well as discovery of new ways to encourage the use of knowledge in decision making and to build public understanding of the problems.[71]

Environmental Governance for the Future

As the example of climate change makes clear, both the nation and the world need to rethink the nature of environmental governance for the twenty-first century. The governmental institutions and decision-making processes that have served us well in the past may not be as suitable for the future. The problems we face are no longer so simple, and their causes are not as amenable to governmental intervention, as was the case in the 1970s. Moreover, as we argue just above, the tools on which governments have relied, such as command-and-control regulation, need to be drawn from a more diverse public policy repertoire. It would include, for example, carefully designed market incentives such as carbon taxes, information disclosure, public education, inclusive collaborative decision making, and comprehensive local and regional planning rooted in long-term sustainability goals.[72] These new tools are not likely to replace regulation as the bedrock of environmental policy, but they may supplement it in a way that achieves better environmental results at lower cost while also reducing the burdens on business.

What new forms of governance might best allow us to address the complex and multifaceted third generation of environmental problems such as climate change, the loss of biological diversity, and the impact of global population growth and economic development on the natural systems that sustain life? What kinds of institutional reforms would allow governments to respond to such problems more quickly and more effectively than they have in the past? What policy approaches will work best under varying circumstances? There are no definitive answers to any of these questions. Yet political scientists and other scholars increasingly have sought to tackle precisely these kinds of inquiries, and they will continue to command attention over the next few decades. Over time, knowledge of how various forms of governance, institutional arrangements, and public policy tools produce different results should be of great value as we seek to improve governing capacity.[73]

One message in this emerging body of work is that we need to reexamine old assumptions about government and public policy as well as the prevailing set of political values that we have embraced, particularly as they relate to individual autonomy and the limitations we place on governmental authority.[74] None of that will be easy to do in the face of determined opposition by those forces in society that fear the consequences. At a minimum, however, we need to ask about what public policies and institutional arrangements work and which do not, and what alternatives we have to replace those that fall short. We also need to search for innovative ways to build a stronger societal capacity to identify and act on environmental problems before they reach crisis proportions.[75]

Given the transboundary character of environmental problems such as climate change (and also some forms of air and water pollution), one certainty is that we will see more multilevel governance, in which the problems are addressed locally and regionally as well as nationally and internationally, at the same time. As Chapters 2 and 13 make evident, state and local governments necessarily have acted independently of the federal government when it has been unable to establish sufficient political consensus to move forward with appropriate public policy. Consistent with such independence, under the new EPA regulations governing coal-fired power plants, the federal government will work closely with the states as each state is given considerable flexibility in how it chooses to reduce GHG emissions.

Actions like these remind us of the continuing importance of the federal structure of U.S. government in which states retain a great deal of autonomy in deciding how to deal with the environmental and energy challenges they face. Much the same can be said about cities, where, as Chapter 12 demonstrates, many have chosen explicit goals and policies to help them move toward sustainability or sustainable development, often with little if any federal guidance or assistance.[76] At the same time, these actions hint at the kind of multilevel governance system that is now evolving.[77]

One thing is clear. With the continuation of divided government and the likelihood of congressional gridlock following the 2014 elections, much of the pressure for policy reform will have to come from a more engaged public. Traditional lobbying and electoral tactics have not been effective in making climate change and related environmental issues a salient voting issue for most Americans. There is thus a strong argument for mobilizing younger, less partisan voters through a new social movement to make climate change a dominant *personal and moral issue* in future elections, as explained in Chapter 3. That is what happened around Earth Day in 1970, and it occurred again in the 1980s in response to the threat of nuclear weapons, nuclear power plant accidents, and other environmental disasters. In September 2014, more than three hundred thousand people took part in the "People's Climate March" in New York City, and similar climate demonstrations were held in more than 150 other countries.[78] Recent poll data also suggest that the public is considerably less divided over government action to combat climate change than are party leaders.[79] There is thus hope that the next quarter century will see greater progress than the last one.

Notes

1. Norman J. Vig and Michael E. Kraft, "Conclusion: Toward a New Environmental Agenda," in *Environmental Policy in the 1990s*, ed. Norman J. Vig and Michael E. Kraft (Washington, DC: CQ Press, 1990), 369–89.

2. World Commission on Environment and Development, *Our Common Future* (Oxford, UK: Oxford University Press, 1987).

3. Robert Cameron Mitchell, "Public Opinion and the Green Lobby: Poised for the 1990s?" in Norman J. Vig and Michael E. Kraft, *Environmental Policy in the 1990s* (Washington, DC: CQ Press, 1984), 86–87.

4. Vig and Kraft, *Environmental Policy in the 1990s*, 381.

5. Geoffrey Wandesforde-Smith, "Moral Outrage and the Progress of Environmental Policy: What Do We Tell the Next Generation about How to Care for the Earth?" in Norman J. Vig and Michael E. Kraft, *Environmental Policy in the 1990s* (Washington, DC: CQ Press, 1990), 325–47.

6. Justin Gillis, "U.S. Climate Has Already Changed, Study Finds, Citing Heat and Floods," *New York Times*, May 6, 2014. See also Editorial, "Climate Disruptions," *New York Times*, May 7, 2014. The quotations are from the report itself, *Climate Change Impacts in the United States: The Third National Climate Assessment*, available at www .globalchange.gov. The website contains interactive maps to study regional impacts.

7. This and previous IPPC reports are available at www.ipcc.ch.

8. Justin Gillis, "Climate Panel Cites Near Certainty on Warming," *New York Times*, August 20, 2013; Gillis, "U.N. Climate Panel Seeks Ceiling on Global Carbon Emissions," *New York Times*, September 28, 2013; Gillis, "By 2047, Coldest Years May Be Warmer Than Hottest in Past, Scientists Say," *New York Times*, October 10, 2013; Gillis, "Panel Says Global Warming Carries Risk of Deep Changes," *New York Times*, December 3, 2013," Gillis, "Panel's Warning on Climate Risk: Worst Is Yet to Come," *New York Times*, March 30, 2014.

9. Justin Gillis, "U.N. Draft Report Lists Unchecked Emissions' Risks," *New York Times*, August 27, 2014.

10. Justin Gillis, "U.N. Climate Panel Warns Speedier Action Is Needed to Avert Disaster," *New York Times*, April 13, 2014; and Gillis, "Climate Efforts Falling Short, U.N. Panel Says," *New York Times*, April 14, 2014. For a critical view of the assessment report, see Matt Ridley, "Climate Forecast: Muting the Alarm," *Wall Street Journal*, March 27, 2014.

11. Quoted in Justin Gillis, "U.N. Panel Warns of Dire Effects from Lack of Action over Global Warming," *New York Times*, November 2, 2014.

12. Robert Pear, "In Final Spending Bill, Salty Foods and Belching Cows Are Winners," *New York Times*, December 14, 2014.

13. It should be noted that the percentages in Table 13-1 are for net carbon dioxide equivalents, including offsetting land use and forestry changes. If CO_2 emissions alone are compared, China accounted for 27.6 percent of the global total and the United States for about 14.5 percent in 2013, according to the Global Carbon Project. See Justin Gillis, "Global Rise Reported in 2013 Greenhouse Gas Emissions," *New York Times*, September 22, 2014. See Figure 15-2.

14. Mark Landler, "U.S. and China Reach Deal on Climate Change in Secret Talks," *New York Times*, November 11, 2014. China has since announced limits on coal use by 2020; see Edward Wong, "In Step to Lower Carbon Emissions, China Will Place a Limit on Coal Use in 2020," *New York Times*, November 20, 2014.

15. See Henry Fountain and John Schwartz, "Climate Accord Relies on Environmental Policies Now in Place," *New York Times*, November 12, 2014.

16. Henry Fountain, "Corralling Carbon Before It Belches from Stack," *New York Times*, July 22, 2014.

17. Henry Fountain, "Climate Aids in Study Face Big Obstacles," *New York Times*, January 17, 2014.

18. Ari Phillips, "Mayors Sign Climate Protection Agreement, Endorse Innovative Climate Solutions," Climate Progress, June 22, www.thinkprogress.org/climate/2014/06/22/3451702.

19. Justin Gillis and Michael Wines, "In Some States, Emissions Cuts Defy Skeptics," New York Times, June 7, 2014. Some of these reductions are due to factors other than carbon regulation, as noted in Chapter 10.

20. Center for Climate and Energy Solutions, Regional Greenhouse Gas Initiative (RGGI), www.c2es.org/us-states-regions/regional-climate-initiatives/rggi.

21. Jennifer Medina, "In California, Climate Issues Moved to Fore by Governor," New York Times, May 20, 2014; Tom Hayden, "Brown's March to an Alternative Energy Future," Sacramento Bee, June 1, 2014. Quebec is also part of the California cap-and-trade system.

22. Coral Davenport, "Unveiling New Carbon Plan, E.P.A. Focuses on Flexibility," New York Times, June 2, 2014; Davenport and Peter Baker, "Taking Page from Health Care Act, Obama Climate Plan Relies on States," New York Times, June 3, 2014.

23. Tom Hamburger, "Fossil-Fuel Lobbyists, Bolstered by GOP Wins, Work to Curb Environmental Rules," Washington Post, December 7, 2014; and Eric Lipton, "Energy Firms in Secretive Alliance with Attorneys General," New York Times, December 6, 2014.

24. The full report is available at www.riskybusiness.org.

25. Henry F. Paulson Jr., "The Coming Climate Crash," New York Times, June 22, 2014. See also Robert E. Rubin, "How Ignoring Climate Change Could Sink the U.S. Economy," Washington Post, July 24, 2014.

26. Coral Davenport, "Industry Awakens to Threat of Climate Change," New York Times, January 23, 2014, and Burt Helm, "The Climate Bottom Line," New York Times, February 1, 2015.

27. John Schwartz, "Heirs to an Oil Fortune Join the Divestment Drive," New York Times, September 22, 2014. Yale University is considering taking similar action; see Geraldine Fabrikant, "Yale Fund Takes Aim at Climate Change," New York Times, September 7, 2014.

28. Richard Martin, "Falling Stock," and Reed McManus, "Financial Statement," Sierra Magazine, September/October 2014, 38–45.

29. Rubin, "How Ignoring Climate Change Could Sink the U.S. Economy."

30. Coral Davenport, "A Climate Accord Based on Global Peer Pressure," New York Times, December 14, 2014.

31. Edward Wong, "At Climate Meeting, China Balks at Verifying Cuts in Carbon Emissions," New York Times, December 9, 2014; Neela Banerjee, "Climate Negotiators in Peru 'Did the Bare Minimum,' One Critic Says," Los Angeles Times, December 14, 2014.

32. Coral Davenport, "Deal on Carbon Emissions by Obama and Xi Jinping Raises Hopes for Upcoming Paris Climate Talks," New York Times, November 12, 2014; and Eric Voeten, "How the Lima Accord May Nudge Countries to Do Better on Climate Change (But Won't Solve the Problem)," Washington Post, December 14, 2014.

33. See Dan Frosh, "A Struggle to Balance Wind Energy with Wildlife," New York Times, December 16, 2013; and Ellen Knickmeyer and John Locher, "Emerging Solar Plants Scorch Birds in Mid-Air," Associated Press, August 18, 2014.

34. Michael Wines, "Emissions of Methane Exceed Estimates," New York Times, November 26, 2013; Coral Davenport, "White House Unveils Plans to Cut Methane Emissions," New York Times, March 28, 2014.

35. White House, Blueprint for a Secure Energy Future, March 30, 2011; and www.whitehouse.gov/energy/securing-american-energy#energy-menu.

36. Martin, "Falling Stock," 42.
37. Clifford Krauss, "Free Fall in Oil Price Underscores Shift Away from OPEC," *New York Times*, November 28, 2014; Krauss, "Oil Falls to 5-Year Low, and Companies Start to Retrench," *New York Times*, December 9, 2014.
38. See Nelson D. Schwartz, "An Energy Boom Lifts the Heartland," *New York Times*, September 8, 2014.
39. Clifford Krauss and Eric Lipton, "U.S. Inches toward Goal of Energy Independence," *New York Times*, March 23, 2012; Elisabeth Rosenthal, "Report Predicts U.S. as No. 1 Oil Producer in a Few Years," *New York Times*, November 14, 2014; and Sean Cockerham, "Fracking Boom in U.S. at Core of Energy Revolution," *Sacramento Bee*, November 28, 2013.
40. See Daniel Jacobson, "Fracking Undercuts Climate Change, Water Advances," *Sacramento Bee*, December 17, 2014. Oklahoma now has more earthquakes than California.
41. Thomas Kaplan, "Citing Health Risks, Governor Will Ban Fracking in New York," *New York Times*, December 18, 2014.
42. Sarah Wheaton, "Keystone XL Pipeline Fight Lifts Environmental Movement," *New York Times*, January 24, 2014. On damages from other oil pipeline spills, see Dan Frosch, "Amid Pipeline Debate, Two Costly Cleanups Forever Change Towns," *New York Times*, August 11, 2013.
43. Coral Davenport, "Report Finds Higher Risks If Oil Line Is Not Built," *New York Times*, June 7, 2014.
44. Ashley Parker and Coral Davenport, "Senate Defeats Bill on Keystone XL Pipeline in Narrow Vote," *New York Times*, November 18, 2014.
45. "Coral Davenport, "Senate Approves Keystone XL Pipeline Bill, Testing Obama," *New York Times*, January 29, 2015; and Ian Austen, "Low Oil Prices Upend Economics in Canada," *New York Times*, February 3, 2015."
46. Dina Cappiello, "Not in My Backyard: US Sending Dirty Coal Abroad," *Associated Press*, July 27, 2014; Andrew C. Revkin, "U.S. Coal Exports Eroding Domestic Greenhouse Gains," *New York Times*, July 28, 2014.
47. Dina Cappiello, "5 Things to Know about Coal Trade, Global Warming," *Associated Press*, July 27, 2014. The United States accounted for about 9 percent of the global coal export market in 2012, but construction of three new terminals in the Pacific Northwest could double exports.
48. See Christopher McGrory Klyza and David J. Sousa, *American Environmental Policy: Beyond Gridlock*, updated and expanded ed. (Cambridge, MA: MIT Press, 2013), 123–35.
49. John M. Broder, "E.P.A. Sets Poison Standards for Power Plants," *New York Times*, December 22, 2011. The new rule is scheduled to come into force in 2015, but the Supreme Court has agreed to hear a case challenging it.
50. This rule was overturned by the District of Columbia Court of Appeals, but was reinstated by the U.S. Supreme Court in April 2014. See Coral Davenport, "Eastern States Press Midwest to Improve Air," *New York Times*, December 9, 2013; Adam Liptak, "Justices Hear Case on Cross-State Pollution Rules," *New York Times*, December 11, 2013; and Davenport, "Justices Back Rule Limiting Coal Pollution," *New York Times*, April 30, 2014.
51. EPA Press Release, June 2, 2014.
52. Coral Davenport, "E.P.A. Ozone Rules Divide Industry and Environmentalists," *New York Times*, November 26, 2014. Environmentalists and many scientists had argued for a lower standard of 60 parts per billion.
53. Michael Wines, "Behind Toledo's Water Crisis, a Long-Troubled Lake Erie," *New York Times*, August 4, 2014.

54. For example, studies at the University of California–Davis and elsewhere have found that pregnant women exposed to agricultural pesticides have a higher risk of having children with autism. See Edward Ortiz, "UC Davis Study Finds Link between Pesticides, Autism," *Sacramento Bee*, June 23, 2014.

55. Denise Scheberle, "Environmental Federalism and the Role of State and Local Governments," in *The Oxford Handbook of U.S. Environmental Policy*, ed. Sheldon Kamieniecki and Michael E. Kraft (New York: Oxford University Press, 2013), 394–412.

56. See, for example, Robert F. Durant, Daniel J. Fiorino, and Rosemary O'Leary, eds., *Environmental Governance Reconsidered* (Cambridge, MA: MIT Press, 2004); Daniel J. Fiorino, *The New Environmental Regulation* (Cambridge, MA: MIT Press, 2006); and Neil Gunningham and Peter Grabowsky, *Smart Regulation: Designing Environmental Policy* (Oxford, UK: Oxford University Press, 1998).

57. See Justin Gillis, "In Price Tag on Carbon, Plans to Save the Planet," *New York Times*, May 30, 2014, for an excellent summary. The California system will apply to all significant GHG sources, including motor fuels, when it is fully implemented in 2015. The RGGI only covers CO_2 emissions from power plants; see www.rggi.org for recent plans and projections.

58. "China Plans a Market for Carbon Permits," *Reuters*, August 31, 2014.

59. According to a recent World Bank Report, about sixty countries, states, and provinces are considering such systems. See Dirk Forrister and Paul Bledsoe, "Pollution Economics," *New York Times*, August 10, 2013; and Robert N. Stavins, "The Only Feasible Way of Cutting Emissions," *New York Times*, June 2, 2014.

60. See Adele Morris, "Want a Pro-growth Pro-environment Plan? Economists Agree: Tax Carbon," at www.brookings.edu/blogs/up-front/posts/2013/02/07-carbon-tax-morris.

61. Republicans introduced at least six bills and resolutions in the House of Representatives during 2013–2014 to prohibit any carbon taxes. See also Shi-Ling Hsu, *The Case For a Carbon Tax* (Washington, DC: Island Press, 2011), especially Chapter 7.

62. For detailed analysis, see Adele C. Morris and Aparna Mathur, *A Carbon Tax in Broader U.S. Fiscal Reform: Design and Distributional Issues*, Center for Energy and Climate Solutions, May 2014, www.c2es.org/federal/policy-solutions/carbon-tax.

63. See, for example, James K. Boyce, "The Carbon Dividend," *New York Times*, July 20, 2014. Many climate activists such as James Hansen and Bill McKibben support such taxes, provided they are high enough.

64. Center for Climate and Energy Solutions, "Options and Considerations for a Federal Carbon Tax," www.c2es.org/publications/options-considerations-federal-carbon-tax.

65. Australia repealed its carbon tax in 2014, but others, such as that of British Columbia, are more popular. See Brendon Steele, "A Tale of Two Taxes," Minneapolis *Star Tribune*, July 28, 2014; Michelle Innis, "Australia Scraps Tax on Carbon," *New York Times*, July 17, 2014.

66. Daniel J. Fiorino, *The New Environmental Regulation* (Cambridge, MA: MIT Press, 2006), Chapter 5.

67. See Michael E. Kraft, Mark Stephan, and Troy D. Abel, *Coming Clean: Information Disclosure and Environmental Performance* (Cambridge, MA: MIT Press, 2011). On the continuing challenge of reforming such laws, particularly the Toxic Substances Control Act, see Frederic J. Frommer, "Bill to Overhaul How Chemicals Are Regulated Faces Uphill Battle in Senate," *Associated Press*, September 13, 2014.

68. Michael E. Kraft, "Using Information Disclosure to Achieve Policy Goals: How Experience with the Toxics Release Inventory Can Inform Action on Natural Gas Fracturing," *Issues in Energy and Environmental Policy*, no. 6 (March 2014).

69. The quotation is taken from the archives of the PCSD, at http://clinton4.nara.gov/PCSD/. For a fuller history of sustainability concepts and actions, see Daniel A.

Mazmanian and Michael E. Kraft, eds., *Toward Sustainable Communities: Transition and Transformations in Environmental Policy*, 2nd ed. (Cambridge, MA: MIT Press, 2009); and Kent E. Portney, *Taking Sustainable Cities Seriously: Economic Development, the Environment, and Quality of Life in American Cities*, 2nd ed. (Cambridge, MA: MIT Press, 2013).

70. See, for example, Aaron M. McCright, Katherine Dentzman, Meghan Charters, and Thomas Dietz, "The Influence of Political Ideology on Trust in Science," *Environmental Research Letters* 8 (2013), open access, available at http://iopscience.iop .org/1748-9326/8/4/044029; and "Symposium on Climate Change Skepticism and Denial," *American Behavioral Scientist* 57, no. 6 (June 2013).

71. See Advisory Committee for Environmental Research and Education, *Transitions and Tipping Points in Complex Environmental Systems* (Washington, DC: National Science Foundation, 2009); and Michael E. Kraft and Sheldon Kamieniecki, "Research on U.S. Environmental Policy in the New Century," in Sheldon Kamieniecki and Michael E. Kraft, eds., *The Oxford Handbook of U.S. Environmental Policy* (New York: Oxford University Press, 2013).

72. See Daniel A. Mazmanian and Michael E. Kraft, eds., *Toward Sustainable Communities: Transition and Transformations in Environmental Policy*, 2nd ed. (Cambridge, MA: MIT Press, 2009); Klyza and Sousa, *American Environmental Policy*; and Marc Allen Eisner, *Governing the Environment: The Transformation of Environmental Regulation* (Boulder, CO: Lynne Rienner).

73. See Kraft and Kamieniecki, "Research on U.S. Environmental Policy in the New Century."

74. See, for example, William Ophuls, *Plato's Revenge: Politics in the Age of Ecology* (Cambridge, MA: MIT Press, 2011).

75. See Walter A. Rosenbaum, "Capacity for Governance: Innovation and the Challenge of the Third Era"; Daniel A. Mazmanian and Laurie Kaye Nijaki, "Sustainable Development and Governance"; and Kate O'Neill, "Global Environmental Policy Making," in Sheldon Kamieniecki and Michael E. Kraft, eds., *The Oxford Handbook of U.S. Environmental Policy* (New York: Oxford University Press, 2013).

76. See also Kent E. Portney, *Taking Sustainable Cities Seriously: Economic Development, the Environment, and Quality of Life in American Cities*, 2nd ed. (Cambridge, MA: MIT Press, 2013).

77. For example, see Michele M. Betsill and Barry G. Rabe, "Climate Change and Multilevel Governance: The Evolving State and Local Roles," in Daniel A. Mazmanian and Michael E. Kraft, eds., *Toward Sustainable Communities: Transition and Transformations in Environmental Policy*, 2nd ed. (Cambridge, MA: MIT Press, 2009); and Daniel C. Esty, "Bottom-Up Climate Fix," *New York Times*, September 22, 2014.

78. Lisa W. Foderaro, "At March, Clarion Call for Action on Climate," *New York Times*, September 22, 2014.

79. Coral Davenport and Marjorie Connelly, "Most in G.O.P. Say They Back Climate Action," *New York Times*, January 31, 2015.

Appendix 1 Major Federal Laws on the Environment, 1969–2014

Legislation	Implementing Agency	Key Provisions
		Nixon Administration
National Environmental Policy Act of 1969, PL 91–190	All federal agencies	Declared a national policy to "encourage productive and enjoyable harmony between man and his environment"; required environmental impact statements; created Council on Environmental Quality.
Resources Recovery Act of 1970, PL 91–512	Health, Education, and Welfare Department (later Environmental Protection Agency)	Set up a program of demonstration and construction grants for innovative solid waste management systems; provided state and local agencies with technical and financial assistance in developing resource recovery and waste disposal systems.
Clean Air Act Amendments of 1970, PL 91–604	Environmental Protection Agency (EPA)	Required administrator to set national primary and secondary air quality standards and certain emissions limits; required states to develop implementation plans by specific dates; required reductions in automobile emissions.
Federal Water Pollution Control Act (Clean Water Act) Amendments of 1972, PL 92–500	EPA	Set national water quality goals; established pollutant discharge permit system; increased federal grants to states to construct waste treatment plants.
Federal Environmental Pesticide Control Act of 1972 (amended the Federal Insecticide, Fungicide, and Rodenticide Act [FIFRA] of 1947), PL 92–516	EPA	Required registration of all pesticides in U.S. commerce; allowed administrator to cancel or suspend registration under specified circumstances.
Marine Mammal Protection Act of 1972, PL 92–532	EPA	Regulated dumping of waste materials into the oceans and coastal waters.

(Continued on next page)

Appendix 1 Major Federal Laws on the Environment, 1969–2014 (Continued)

Legislation	Implementing Agency	Key Provisions
Coastal Zone Management Act of 1972, PL 92–583	Office of Coastal Zone Management, Commerce Department	Authorized federal grants to the states to develop coastal zone management plans under federal guidelines.
Endangered Species Act of 1973, PL 93–205	Fish and Wildlife Service, Interior Department	Broadened federal authority to protect all "threatened" as well as "endangered" species; authorized grant program to assist state programs; required coordination among all federal agencies.
		Ford Administration
Safe Drinking Water Act of 1974, PL 93–523	EPA	Authorized federal government to set standards to safeguard the quality of public drinking water supplies and to regulate state programs for protecting underground water sources.
Toxic Substances Control Act of 1976, PL 94–469	EPA	Authorized premarket testing of chemical substances; allowed the EPA to ban or regulate the manufacture, sale, or use of any chemical presenting an "unreasonable risk of injury to health or environment"; prohibited most uses of PCBs.
Federal Land Policy and Management Act of 1976, PL 94–579	Bureau of Land Management, Interior Department	Gave Bureau of Land Management authority to manage public lands for long-term benefits; officially ended policy of conveying public lands into private ownership.
Resource Conservation and Recovery Act of 1976, PL 94–580	EPA	Required the EPA to set regulations for hazardous waste treatment, storage, transportation, and disposal; provided assistance for state hazardous waste programs under federal guidelines.
National Forest Management Act of 1976, PL 94–588	U.S. Forest Service, Agriculture Department	Gave statutory permanence to national forestlands and set new standards for their management; restricted timber harvesting to protect soil and watersheds; limited clear-cutting.

Surface Mining Control and Reclamation Act of 1977, PL 95–87	Interior Department	Established environmental controls over strip mining; limited mining on farmland, alluvial valleys, and slopes; required restoration of land to original contours.
Clean Air Act Amendments of 1977, PL 95–95	EPA	Amended and extended Clean Air Act; postponed deadlines for compliance with auto emissions and air quality standards; set new standards for "prevention of significant deterioration" in clean air areas.
Clean Water Act Amendments of 1977, PL 95–217	EPA	Extended deadlines for industry and cities to meet treatment standards; set national standards for industrial pretreatment of wastes; increased funding for sewage treatment construction grants, and gave states flexibility in determining spending priorities.
Public Utility Regulatory Policies Act of 1978, PL 95–617	Energy Department, states	Provided for Energy Department and Federal Energy Regulatory Commission regulation of electric and natural gas utilities and crude oil transportation systems in order to promote energy conservation and efficiency; allowed small cogeneration and renewable energy projects to sell power to utilities.
Alaska National Interest Lands Conservation Act of 1980, PL 96–487	Interior Department, Agriculture Department	Protected 102 million acres of Alaskan land as national wilderness, wildlife refuges, and parks.
Comprehensive Environmental Response, Compensation, and Liability Act of 1980 (CERCLA), PL 96–510	EPA	Authorized federal government to respond to hazardous waste emergencies and to clean up chemical dump sites; created $1.6 billion "Superfund"; established liability for cleanup costs.

Nuclear Waste Policy Act of 1982, PL 97–425; Nuclear Waste Policy Amendments Act of 1987, PL 100–203	Energy Department	Established a national plan for the permanent disposal of high-level nuclear waste; authorized the Energy Department to site, obtain a license for, construct, and operate geologic repositories for spent fuel from commercial nuclear power plants. Amendments in 1987 specified Yucca Mountain, Nevada, as the sole national site to be studied.

(Continued on next page)

Appendix 1 Major Federal Laws on the Environment, 1969–2014 *(Continued)*

Legislation	Implementing Agency	Key Provisions
Resource Conservation and Recovery Act Amendments of 1984, PL 98–616	EPA	Revised and strengthened EPA procedures for regulating hazardous waste facilities; authorized grants to states for solid and hazardous waste management; prohibited land disposal of certain hazardous liquid wastes; required states to consider recycling in comprehensive solid waste plans.
Food Security Act of 1985 (also called the farm bill), PL 99–198 Renewed in 1990, 1996, 2002, 2008, and 2014	Agriculture Department	Limited federal program benefits for producers of commodities on highly erodible land or converted wetlands; established a conservation reserve program; authorized Agriculture Department technical assistance for subsurface water quality preservation; revised and extended the Soil and Water Conservation Act (1977) programs through the year 2008. The 1996 renewal of the farm bill authorized $56 billion over seven years for a variety of farm and forestry programs. These include an Environmental Quality Incentives Program to provide assistance and incentive payments to farmers, especially those facing serious threats to soil, water, grazing lands, wetlands, and wildlife habitat. Spending was increased substantially in 2002.
Safe Drinking Water Act of 1986, PL 99–339	EPA	Reauthorized the Safe Drinking Water Act of 1974 and revised EPA safe drinking water programs, including grants to states for drinking water standards enforcement and groundwater protection programs; accelerated EPA schedule for setting standards for maximum contaminant levels of eighty-three toxic pollutants.
Superfund Amendments and Reauthorization Act of 1986 (SARA), PL 99–499	EPA	Provided $8.5 billion through 1991 to clean up the nation's most dangerous abandoned chemical waste dumps; set strict standards and timetables for cleaning up such sites; required that industry provide local communities with information on hazardous chemicals used or emitted.

Clean Water Act Amendments of 1987, PL 100–4	EPA	Amended the Federal Water Pollution Control Act of 1972; extended and revised EPA water pollution control programs, including grants to states for construction of wastewater treatment facilities and implementation of mandated nonpoint-source pollution management plans; expanded EPA enforcement authority; established a national estuary program.
Global Climate Protection Act of 1987, PL 100–204	State Department	Authorized the State Department to develop an approach to the problems of global climate change; created an intergovernmental task force to develop U.S. strategy for dealing with the threat posed by global warming.
Ocean Dumping Ban Act of 1988, PL 100–688	EPA	Amended the Marine Protection, Research, and Sanctuaries Act of 1972 to end all ocean disposal of sewage sludge and industrial waste by December 31, 1991; revised EPA regulation of ocean dumping by establishing dumping fees, permit requirements, and civil penalties for violations.

George H. W. Bush Administration

Oil Pollution Act of 1990, PL 101–380	Transportation Department, Commerce Department	Sharply increased liability limits for oil spill cleanup costs and damages; required double hulls on oil tankers and barges by 2015; required federal government to direct cleanups of major spills; required increased contingency planning and preparedness for spills; preserved states' rights to adopt more stringent liability laws and to create state oil spill compensation funds.
Pollution Prevention Act of 1990, PL 101–508	EPA	Established Office of Pollution Prevention in the EPA to coordinate agency efforts at source reduction; created voluntary program to improve lighting efficiency; stated waste minimization was to be primary means of hazardous waste management; mandated source reduction and recycling report to accompany annual toxics release inventory under SARA in order to promote voluntary industry reduction of hazardous waste.

(Continued on next page)

Appendix 1 Major Federal Laws on the Environment, 1969–2014 *(Continued)*

Legislation	Implementing Agency	Key Provisions
Clean Air Act Amendments of 1990, PL 101–549	EPA	Amended the Clean Air Act of 1970 by setting new requirements and deadlines of three to twenty years for major urban areas to meet federal clean air standards; imposed new, stricter emissions standards for motor vehicles and mandated cleaner fuels; required reduction in emission of sulfur dioxide and nitrogen oxides by power plants to limit acid deposition and created a market system of emissions allowances; required regulation to set emissions limits for all major sources of toxic or hazardous air pollutants and listed 189 chemicals to be regulated; prohibited the use of chlorofluorocarbons (CFCs) by the year 2000 and set phase-out of other ozone-depleting chemicals.
Intermodal Surface Transportation Efficiency Act of 1991 (ISTEA, also called the highway bill), PL 102–240	Transportation Department	Authorized $151 billion over six years for transportation, including $31 billion for mass transit; required statewide and metropolitan long-term transportation planning; authorized states and communities to use transportation funds for public transit that reduces air pollution and energy use consistent with Clean Air Act of 1990; required community planners to analyze land use and energy implications of transportation projects they review.
Energy Policy Act of 1992, PL 102–486	Energy Department	Comprehensive energy act designed to reduce U.S. dependency on imported oil. Mandated restructuring of the electric utility industry to promote competition; encouraged energy conservation and efficiency; promoted renewable energy and alternative fuels for cars; eased licensing requirements for nuclear power plants; authorized extensive energy research and development.
The Omnibus Water Act of 1992, PL 102–575	Interior Department	Authorized completion of major water projects in the West; revised the Central Valley Project in California to allow transfer of water rights to urban areas and to encourage conservation through a tiered pricing system that allocates water more flexibly and efficiently; mandated extensive wildlife and environmental protection, mitigation, and restoration programs.

Food Quality Protection Act of 1996, PL 104–170	EPA	A major revision of FIFRA that adopted a new approach to regulating pesticides used on food, fiber, and other crops by requiring EPA to consider the diversity of ways in which people are exposed to such chemicals. Created a uniform "reasonable risk" health standard for both raw and processed foods that replaced the requirements of the 1958 Delaney Clause of the Food, Drug, and Cosmetic Act that barred the sale of processed food containing even trace amounts of chemicals found to cause cancer; required the EPA to take extra steps to protect children by establishing an additional tenfold margin of safety in setting acceptable risk standards.
Safe Drinking Water Act Amendments of 1996, PL 104–182	EPA	Granted local water systems greater flexibility to focus on the most serious public health risks; authorized $7.6 billion through 2003 for state-administered loan and grant funds to help localities with the cost of compliance; created a "right-to-know" provision requiring large water systems to provide their customers with annual reports on the safety of local water supplies, including information on contaminants found in drinking water and their health effects. Small water systems are eligible for waivers from costly regulations.
Transportation Equity Act for the 21st Century (also called ISTEA II or TEA 21), PL 105–178	Transportation Department	Authorized a six-year, $218 billion program that increased spending by 40 percent to improve the nation's highways and mass transit systems; provided $41 billion for mass transit programs, with over $29 billion coming from the Highway Trust Fund; provided $592 million for research and development on new highway technologies, including transportation-related environmental issues; provided $148 million for a scenic byways program and $270 million for building and maintaining trails; continued support for improvement of bicycle paths.

(Continued on next page)

Appendix 1 Major Federal Laws on the Environment, 1969–2014 *(Continued)*

Legislation	Implementing Agency	Key Provisions
		George W. Bush Administration
The Small Business Liability Relief and Brownfields Revitalization Act of 2002, PL 107–118	EPA	Amended CERCLA (Superfund) to provide liability protection for prospective purchasers of brownfields and small business owners who contributed to waste sites; authorized increased funding for state and local programs that assess and clean up such abandoned or underused industrial or commercial sites.
The Healthy Forests Restoration Act of 2003, PL 108–148	Agriculture Department, Interior Department	Intended to reduce the risks of forest fires on federal lands by authorizing the cutting of timber in selected areas managed by the Forest Service and the Bureau of Land Management. Sought to protect communities, watersheds, and certain other lands from the effects of catastrophic wildfires. Directed the Secretary of Agriculture and the Secretary of the Interior to plan and conduct hazardous fuel reduction programs on federal lands within their jurisdictions.
The Energy Policy Act of 2005, PL 109–58	Energy Department	Intended to increase the supply of energy resources and improve the efficiency of energy use through provision of tax incentives and loan guarantees for various kinds of energy production, particularly oil, natural gas, and nuclear power. Also called for expanded energy research and development, expedited building for new energy facilities, improved energy efficiency standards for federal office buildings, and modernization of the nation's electricity grid.
Energy Independence and Security Act of 2007, PL 110–140	Energy Department, Transportation Department	Set a national automobile fuel-economy standard of 35 miles per gallon by 2020, the first significant change in the Corporate Average Fuel Economy (CAFE) standards since 1975. Also sought to increase the supply of alternative fuel sources by setting a renewable fuel standard that requires fuel producers to use at least thirty-six billion gallons of biofuels by 2022; twenty-one billion gallons of that amount are to come from sources other than corn-based ethanol. Included provisions to improve energy efficiency in lighting and appliances, and for federal agency efficiency and renewable energy use.

Obama Administration

The American Recovery and Reinvestment Act of 2009, PL 111–5	Energy Department, Transportation Department, Treasury Department	Although not a stand-alone environmental or energy policy, the economic stimulus bill contained about $80 billion in spending, tax incentives, and loan guarantees to promote energy efficiency, renewable energy sources, fuel-efficient cars, mass transit, and clean coal, including $3.4 billion for research on capturing and storing carbon dioxide from coal-fired power plants, $2 billon for research on advanced car batteries, $17 billion in grants and loans to modernize the nation's electric grid and increase its capacity to transmit power from renewable sources, and nearly $18 billion for mass transit, Amtrak, and high-speed rail.
Omnibus Public Lands Management Act of 2009, PL 111–11	Interior Department, Agriculture Department	Consolidated 164 separate public lands measures that protect two million acres of wilderness in nine states; establish new national trails, national parks, and a new national monument; provide legal status for the twenty-six-million-acre National Landscape Conservation System that contains areas of archaeological and cultural significance; and protect 1,100 miles of eighty-six new wild and scenic rivers in eight states. Together the measures constitute the most significant expansion of federal land conservation programs in fifteen years.

Note: As of late 2014, no other major laws had been approved by Congress and signed by President Obama other than the two 2009 statutes listed here. As always, for an update on legislative developments, consult *CQ Weekly* or other professional news sources, or Congressional Quarterly's annual *Almanac*, which summarizes key legislation enacted by Congress and describes the major issues and leading policy actors.

Appendix 2 Budgets of Selected Environmental and Natural
Resource Agencies, 1980–2015 (in billions of nominal
and constant dollars)

Agency	1980	1990	2000	2010	2015 (Est.)
Environmental Protection Agency (EPA) Operating Budget[a]	1.269	1.901	2.465	3.889	3.782
(Constant 2013 dollars)	2.992	3.153	3.128	3.776	3.438
Interior Department Total Budget	4.592	6.669	8.363	12.843	12.763
(Constant 2013 dollars)	10.839	11.060	10.613	12.469	11.603
Selected Natural Resource Agencies					
Bureau of Land Management	0.919	1.226	1.616	1.074	1.344
(Constant 2013 dollars)	2.167	2.034	2.051	1.043	1.222
Fish and Wildlife Service	0.435	1.133	1.498	1.588	2.818
(Constant 2013 dollars)	1.027	1.879	1.901	1.542	2.562
National Park Service	0.531	1.275	2.071	2.289	3.647
(Constant 2013 dollars)	1.253	2.115	2.628	2.222	3.315
Forest Service	2.250	3.473	3.728	5.297	5.366
(Constant 2013 dollars)	5.306	5.760	4.731	5.143	4.878

Source: Office of Management and Budget, *Budget of the United States Government,* fiscal years 1982, 1992, 2002, 2009, 2012, 2015 (Washington, DC: Government Printing Office, 1981, 1991, 2001, 2008, 2011, 2014), and agency websites.

Note: The upper figure for each agency represents budget authority in nominal dollars, that is, the real amount for the year in which the budget was authorized. The lower figure represents budget authority in constant 2013 dollars to permit comparisons over time. These adjustments use the implicit price deflator for federal nondefense expenditures as calculated by the Bureau of Economic Analysis, Department of Commerce.

a. The EPA operating budget, which supplies funds for most of the agency's research, regulation, and enforcement programs, is the most meaningful figure. The other two major elements of the total EPA budget historically have been Superfund allocations and sewage treatment construction or water infrastructure grants (which are now called state and tribal assistance grants). We subtract both of these items from the total EPA budget to calculate the agency's operating budget. The EPA and the White House define the agency's operating budget differently. They do not exclude all of these amounts and arrive at a different figure. The president's proposed fiscal 2015 budget called for a total EPA budget of $7.774 billion.

For consistency, all figures in the table are taken from the president's proposed budget for the respective years, and all represent final budget authority.

Appendix 3   Employees in Selected Federal Agencies and Departments, 1980, 1990, 2000, and 2010

Agency/Department	Personnel[a]			
	1980	1990	2000	2010
Environmental Protection Agency	12,891	16,513	17,416	17,417
Bureau of Land Management	9,655	8,753	9,328	12,741
Fish and Wildlife Service	7,672	7,124	7,011	9,252
National Park Service	13,934	17,781	18,418	22,211
Office of Surface Mining Reclamation and Enforcement	1,014	1,145	622	521
Forest Service	40,606	40,991	33,426	35,639
Army Corps of Engineers (civil functions)	32,757	28,272	22,624	23,608
U.S. Geological Survey	14,416	10,451	9,417	8,600
Natural Resources Conservation Service (formerly Soil Conservation Service)	15,856	15,482	9,628	11,446

Source: U.S. Senate Committee on Governmental Affairs, "Organization of Federal Executive Departments and Agencies," January 1, 1980, and January 1, 1990; and Office of Management and Budget, *Budget of the United States Government,* fiscal years 1982, 1992, 2002, and 2012 (Washington, DC: Government Printing Office, 1981, 1991, 2001, and 2011), and agency websites.

a. Personnel totals represent full-time equivalent employment, reflecting both permanent and temporary employees. Data for 2000 are based on the fiscal 2002 proposed budget submitted to Congress by the Bush administration in early 2001, and data for 2010 are taken from agency sources as well as the administration's proposed fiscal 2012 budget submitted to Congress in early 2011. Because of organizational changes within departments and agencies, the data presented here are not necessarily an accurate record of agency personnel growth or decline over time. The information is presented chiefly to provide an indicator of approximate agency size during different time periods.

Appendix 4   Federal Spending on Natural Resources and the
Environment, Selected Fiscal Years, 1980–2015
(in billions of nominal and constant dollars)

Budget Item	1980	1990	2000	2010	2015 (Est.)
Water resources	4.085	4.332	4.800	6.813	5.323
(Constant 2013 dollars)	9.634	7.184	6.091	6.608	4.839
Conservation and land management	1.572	4.362	6.604	11.933	12.568
(Constant 2013 dollars)	3.708	7.234	8.381	11.574	11.425
Recreational resources	1.373	1.804	2.719	3.809	4.192
(Constant 2013 dollars)	3.238	2.992	3.451	3.694	3.811
Pollution control and abatement	4.672	5.545	7.483	10.473	7.895
(Constant 2013 dollars)	11.019	9.196	9.496	10.158	7.177
Other natural resources	1.395	2.077	3.397	6.629	7.246
(Constant 2013 dollars)	3.290	3.444	4.311	6.430	6.587
Total	13.097	18.121	25.003	39.657	37.224
(Constant 2013 dollars)	30.889	30.051	31.730	38.465	33.840

Source: Office of Management and Budget, *Historical Tables, Budget of the United States Government Fiscal Year 2015* (Washington, DC: Government Printing Office, 2014).

Note: The upper figure for each budget category represents budget authority in nominal dollars, that is, the real budget for the given year. Figures for 1980 are provided to indicate pre–Reagan administration spending bases. The lower figure for each category represents budget authority in constant 2013 dollars. These adjustments are made using the implicit price deflator for federal nondefense spending as calculated by the Bureau of Economic Analysis, Department of Commerce. The natural resources and environment function in the federal budget reported in this table does not include environmental cleanup programs within the Departments of Defense and Energy, which are substantial. The president's proposed 2015 budget shows a small increase in spending over the next few years, with a total for all categories listed of $41.844 billion for 2019. Future presidents may request different levels of spending, and Congress may appropriate a higher or lower amount than these estimates indicate.

Index

SAGE was founded in 1965 by Sara Miller McCune to support the dissemination of usable knowledge by publishing innovative and high-quality research and teaching content. Today, we publish more than 750 journals, including those of more than 300 learned societies, more than 800 new books per year, and a growing range of library products including archives, data, case studies, reports, conference highlights, and video. SAGE remains majority-owned by our founder, and after Sara's lifetime will become owned by a charitable trust that secures our continued independence.

Los Angeles | London | Washington DC | New Delhi | Singapore | Boston